Springer Advanced Texts in
Life Sciences

with contributions by

**T. B. Bolton**
Department of Pharmacology
University of Oxford
South Parks Road
Oxford OX1 3QT, England

**M. R. Fedde**
Department of Physiological Sciences
Kansas State University
Manhattan, Kansas 66506

**P. Griminger**
Department of Nutrition
Cook College, Rutgers University
Thompson Hall, Lipman Drive
New Brunswick, New Jersey 08903

**R. L. Hazelwood**
Department of Biology
University of Houston
Cullen Boulevard
Houston, Texas 77004

**M. R. Kare**
Monell Chemical Senses Center
University of Pennsylvania
3500 Market Street
Philadelphia, Pennsylvania 19104

**D. C. Meyer**
Waisman Center on
Mental Retardation and Health Development
University of Wisconsin
Madison, Wisconsin 54306

**W. J. Mueller**
Department of Poultry Science
Pennsylvania State University
University Park, Pennsylvania 16802

**H. Opel**
Department of Avian Physiology
United States Department of Agriculture
Box 65
Beltsville, Maryland 20705

**R. K. Ringer**
Department of Poultry Science
College of Agriculture
Michigan State University
114 Anthony Hall
East Lansing, Michigan 48823

**J. G. Rogers, Jr.**
Monell Chemical Senses Center
University of Pennsylvania
3500 Market Street
Philadelphia, Pennsylvania 19104

**P. D. Sturkie**
Department of Environmental Physiology
Cook College, Rutgers University
Thompson Hall, Lipman Drive
New Brunswick, New Jersey 08903

**G. C. Whittow**
Department of Physiology
School of Medicine
University of Hawaii
2538 The Mall, Room 407
Honolulu, Hawaii 96822

# AVIAN PHYSIOLOGY

THIRD EDITION

P. D. Sturkie, editor

Springer-Verlag
New York Heidelberg Berlin
1976

Library of Congress Cataloging in Publication Data

Sturkie, Paul D.
   Avian physiology.

   (Advanced texts in life sciences)
   Includes bibliographies and index.
   1. Birds—Physiology. I. Title.
QL698.S82   1976        598.2'1        75-9954

Printed in the United States of America

ISBN 0-387-07305-1   Springer-Verlag   New York

ISBN 3-540-07305-1   Springer-Verlag   Berlin Heidelberg

To my wife, Betty

# Preface to the Third Edition

Since the publication of the first and second editions, there has been a considerable increase of research activity in avian physiology in a number of areas, including endocrinology and reproduction, heart and circulation, respiration, temperature regulation, and to a lesser extent in some other areas.

There appeared in 1972–1974 a four volume treatise entitled "Avian Biology," including material on physiology, and earlier a three volume presentation on the biology of the domestic fowl that also involves a great deal on the physiology and biochemistry of certain organ systems.

However, "Avian Physiology" remains a one-volume contribution that gives a balanced account of most of the principal organs and systems of Aves in a classical manner. The type size in this edition is smaller and the page size larger, so actually more material is covered in considerably fewer pages than in previous editions. The aim of this and previous editions has been to serve as a textbook and a source of reference for the experimental physiologist and to provide pertinent material for courses in comparative physiology, zoology, ecology, and ornithology.

The third edition contains two new chapters by P. Griminger on lipid and protein metabolism, which emphasize the differences in the metabolic products and pathways of birds and mammals. New contributors include R. M. Fedde and T. B. Bolton, who have completely revised and expanded the chapters on respiration and the nervous system, respectively, and J. G. Rogers, Jr., W. J. Mueller, H. Opel, and D. C. Meyer, who have made contributions to Chapters 2, 16, 17, and 19, respectively.

R. L. Hazelwood has revised his chapter on carbohydrate metabolism and has written a separate one on the pancreas. R. K. Ringer has revised the material on the thyroid and has contributed the chapter on adrenals. New material on temperature regulation and energy metabolism, particularly on wild species, has been added by C. G. Whittow.

The sections on the blood, heart, and circulation have been revised by the Editor under three chapters. The chapter on the chemical constituents of blood in the earlier editions has been omitted and such data are presented elsewhere. The editor has also contributed the chapters on digestion and absorption (Chapters 9 and 10), kidneys and urine (Chapter 14), hypophysis (Chapter 15), and the greater part of chapters on reproduction in the female (Chapter 16) and the male (Chapter 17).

*July 1975*                                        P.D.S.

# Preface to
# the Second Edition

Since the publication of the first edition in 1954 there has been a considerable increase in research activity in avian endocrinology and reproduction and a modest increase in research in other areas. Much work, however, remains to be done on such systems as respiration, muscle, nerve, and digestion.

New features of the second edition include a chapter on the nervous system by Dr. Jasper ten Cate, Professor of Comparative Physiology, University of Amsterdam, Holland, and contributions from other authors active in various fields. An expanded chapter on chemical constituents has been written, mainly by Dr. D. J. Bell, Head of Biochemistry Section, Poultry Research Center, Edinburgh, Scotland. The section on coagulation of blood was written by Dr. Paul Griminger, Associate Professor of Nutrition, Rutgers University.

Expanded chapters on temperature regulation and on energy metabolism have been contributed by Dr. G. C. Whittow, formerly physiologist at the Hannah Dairy Research Institute, and now Associate Professor of Physiology, Rutgers University.

The chapter on carbohydrate metabolism was completely revised by Dr. R. L. Hazelwood, Associate Professor of Physiology, University of Houston.

The chapter on sense organs was revised by Dr. M. R. Kare, Professor of Physiology, North Carolina State College. Chapter 19, "Thyroids," has been considerably expanded by Dr. Robert K. Ringer, Professor of Avian Physiology, Michigan State University.

Chapter 15, "Reproduction in the Female," has also been expanded. That part of it relating to calcium metabolism and egg laying was contributed by Dr. T. G. Taylor, Reader in Physiological Chemistry, University of Reading, England, and Dr. D. A. Stringer, Unilever Research Laboratory, Bedford, England.

Most of the chapters that I revised have also been enlarged. The revision has resulted in a substantial increase in the size of the book.

The authors are indebted to various investigators, journals, and books for many of the illustrations used. Individual acknowledgment is made in the legends.

*May 1965*                         P.D.S.

# Preface to
# the First Edition

Physiology may be divided into three main categories: cellular, comparative, and special—i.e., the physiology of special groups of organisms. The physiology of special groups has received the most attention. In the animal field, interest has centered largely on mammalian physiology, with particular emphasis on human physiology and its relationship to medicine. By comparison, the physiology of birds has been neglected. Knowledge in certain areas of avian physiology is limited, fragmentary, and often confused, and little or no new research is being conducted. Much of the physiological research on the bird has been conducted from the comparative viewpoint, which is concerned more with broad functional relationships between groups of animals than with details of a special group. In some areas, however, these fundamental functions have not been definitely established. Even in certain fields, such as endocrinology, where there is considerably more research activity on the bird, there are wide gaps in our knowledge.

This book is the first one in any language devoted to the specialized physiology of birds. It deals mainly with the chicken, the duck, and the pigeon, because most of the research has been conducted on these species and they represent species of economic importance to man.

Inasmuch as physiology provides a rational basis for much of animal husbandry and veterinary medicine, this book should be of especial interest to teachers, students, and research workers in poultry science and husbandry and in veterinary medicine. More knowledge and research in avian physiology, particularly on the domestic species, should have important applications to the poultry industry, which is rapidly expanding in this country. Although few poultry departments at present offer course work on the physiology of birds, it is hoped that this book may be instrumental in increasing the number of institutions offering such work and in stimulating more research. It may serve, also, as a source of reference for the experimental physiologist and should provide pertinent physiological material for courses in comparative physiology, ecology, and ornithology.

The bibliography is extensive but not exhaustive. An attempt was made to select the most important and more recent references, with minor considerations given to priority. The references are cited at the end of each chapter.

The writer is indebted to investigators, journals, and books for many of the illustrations used. Separate acknowledgment is made in the legends to the authors and books or journals from which illustrations came. The original drawings and modifications of illustrations of others were prepared by my wife, to whom I am grateful.

Special thanks are extended to colleagues who read one or more chapters and made helpful suggestions. These are Drs. H. H. Dukes, J. A. Dye, F. B. Hutt, R. M. Fraps, C. S. Shaffner, A. V. Nalbandov, T. C. Byerly, J. H. Leathem. J. B. Allison, W. C. Russell, and H. J. Metzger.

*July 1953*                                         P.D.S.

# Contents

# 1

# Nervous System

## T. B. Bolton

2 **INTRODUCTION**

### General Structure of Nervous Tissue

The nervous system consists of the nerve cells proper, the neurons, and of supportive and nutritive cells, the neuroglia. Each neuron consists of a cell body, the perikaryon, containing the nucleus; a single axon that carries excitation away from the perikaryon; and one or more branching dendrites that carry excitation to the perikaryon and axon. The perikarya of neurons lie in the brain, spinal cord, dorsal root ganglia, and ganglia of cranial nerves or in the ganglia of the autonomic nervous system.

Perikaryon. The perikaryon consists of nucleus and cytoplasm. The nucleus contains a large nucleolus and aggregations of chromatin. The cytoplasm contains a number of structures, including small elongated mitochondria, which supply energy for cellular processes, and a basophilic material termed Nissle bodies, which consist of aggregations of endoplasmic reticulum with attached ribosomes. Free ribosomes are also found. Ribosomes are the sites of protein synthesis. The neurofibrils, seen by light microscopy, are bundles of neurofilaments that extend into the axon and dendrites. A series of microtubules is also found. These seem to be associated with the transport of vesicles, containing the enzymes responsible for the synthesis of transmitter substance, from the Golgi region down the axon. Vesicles may be moved down axons by means of the cross-bridges that link them to the microtubules (Smith, 1971). In this way the enzymes that synthesize transmitter reach the nerve terminal. In sympathetic nerves, transmitter is synthesized to some extent during axonal transport and particularly in the nerve terminal. The synthesizing enzymes, however, are produced in the ribsomes of the perikaryon.

Axon. The axons of avian myelinated nerves (like those of mammals) are surrounded by a myelin sheath formed by the spiral growth of the Schwann cell about the axon. Conduction in myelinated nerves is saltatory. In unmyelinated nerves, several axons are embedded in the Schwann cell, which in this case does not form a myelin sheath, and conduction of excitation is continuous, not saltatory. The axon contains neurofilaments, microtubules, some mitochondria, and the vesicles alluded to above. There are few or no ribosomes, although smooth endoplasmic reticulum occurs. The terminal part of the axon is modified where it is apposed to the membrane of another nerve cell (in the CNS and autonomic ganglia), a muscle, or a gland cell. Synapses with other nerve cells may be with the perikaryon (axosomatic), with the dendrites (axodendritic), or with another axon (axoaxonal).

Transport of materials down the axon of sympathetic nerves, involves at least two processes: a slow (1 mm/day) transport and a rapid (120 mm/day) transport. The latter is associated with the movement of the vesicles and their contained synthetic enzymes. The former may be caused by the slow outgrowth of axoplasm and perhaps microtubules and the associated movement of soluble enzymes (Banks and Mayor, 1972). The cytoplasm of nerve cells is in continuous movement, which no doubt contributes to the movement of substances between the perikaryon and its axon and dendrites. The contribution of perikaryal glycoproteins to axonal and synaptic proteins has been studied in the pigeon visual system by Marko and Cuénod (1973), whose paper should be consulted for further references.

Axons, either myelinated or unmyelinated, when bound together by connective tissue, form an important part of the peripheral nerves. White matter in the central nervous system (CNS) is formed by myelinated axons (in conjunction with neuroglial cells), whereas unmyelinated axons, together with dendrites and perikarya (and supportive cells), form the gray matter.

Dendrites. Within the CNS dendrites extend from the perikaryon and branch extensively. They contain the same cytoplasmic organelles as the perikaryon. Dendritic thorns project from their surface. These have a narrow neck and a dilated terminal bulb. They may contain a parallel array of flattened cisternae, known as the spine apparatus. Microtubules and neurofilaments do not extend into the spines.

The dendrites of afferent nerves are extremely long and are an important constituent of the peripheral nerves. Dendrites within the CNS are unmyelinated and are synaptically apposed to other nerve cell membranes. Dendrites outside the CNS may be myelinated or unmyelinated. They arise in intero- and exteroreceptors in various parts of the body and carry sensory impulses from the periphery to the central nervous system.

### Synapse

Because each neuron is completely surrounded by its cell membrane, excitation must pass from one neurone to another across a gap between adjacent neuronal membranes. The membranes at this point show structural modifications and physiologic specialization. Generally this specialization takes the form of the release of some chemical substance, the transmitter, from one neuron (termed the presynaptic neuron) into the narrow cleft, the synaptic gap, between apposed neurons. The postsynaptic membrane exhibits chemosensitivity and responds to the released transmitter in a characteristic way. The ability of one neuron to release transmitter and that of the other neuron to respond to it determines the direction of the excitation's passage across the synapse and the designation of one membrane as "presynaptic" and the other as "postsynaptic." In the periphery, where neuron apposes skeletal muscle, specialized regions of the membrane, such as the "endplate," have sometimes developed. In smooth muscle, cardiac muscle, and gland cells, these specializations are absent or less developed.

Synapses determine the direction taken by excitation through the nervous system, for neurons conduct excitation in either direction with equal facility. Because more than one transmitter may reach a given postsynaptic membrane (although it is generally believed that an individual neuron can release only one transmitter) synapses are sites where the activity of several neurons can interact in producing the final response; i.e., synapses are the sites of the integrative function of the nervous system. Not all synapses involve transmitter release and associated chemosensitivity; some, such as those in the ciliary ganglion of the bird, show electrical coupling (ephaptic transmission).

**Humoral transmission.** Loewi (1921) found that stimulation of the vagus nerve caused a liberation of acetylcholine in the heart. Later, Brown (1937) showed that acetylcholine is the essential transmitter, not only in the parasympathetic nerves but also in those innervating skeletal muscles. It was shown that during the stimulation of the nerve acetylcholine acts on a specialized region of the muscle fiber membrane, the endplate, which is much more sensitive to acetylcholine than is the rest of the membrane (Dale, 1937).

It is now known that acetylcholine is the transmitter released from preganglionic fibers in the autonomic ganglia (both sympathetic and parasympathetic), by postganglionic parasympathetic fibers, and at somatic nerve endings. Noradrenaline and adrenaline (DeSantis *et al.,* 1975) are released at postganglionic sympathetic nerve endings. Acetylcholine, noradrenaline, adrenaline, and a number of other substances, such as γ-aminobutyric acid (GABA), glycine, and dopamine, have been suggested as acting as transmitters at synapses within the CNS. The evidence for their transmitter roles in the bird is reviewed on p. 21.

## Propagation of Excitation in Neurons

The axons of motor nerves and the dendrites of sensory nerves are very long and may conduct excitation over a meter or more. Neurons, and also muscle cells, concentrate potassium within themselves and exclude sodium. The tendency for potassium to leave the cell down its concentration gradient is matched by the concentrating ability of the sodium pump which also pumps potassium. Because the cell membrane is permeable to potassium, a diffusion potential arises from the unequal concentrations of potassium at either side. It is this diffusion potential that is largely responsible for the increased negativity of the interior of the neuron compared to the extracellular space. This negative potential is called the "membrane potential."

During excitation there is a momentary reversal of the potential. This event is termed the "action potential" and its nature has been analyzed in considerable detail. (See other textbooks on nervous system for details.)

An action potential set up in a neuron is conducted to every part of that neuron. The direction in which it normally travels in the neuron depends on the synaptic relationships with other neurons or with muscle, gland, or sensory cells. Propagation of an action potential in a particular axon or dendrite occurs with a characteristic speed that is inversely proportional to the diameter of the fiber and is faster if the fiber is myelinated.

## Function of the Nervous System

In simple animals, behavior is restricted to stereotyped responses to stimuli, but in higher animals the response to a given stimulus varies depending on a variety of interacting factors in the environment and on the memory of past events.

**Reflex arc.** The simplest form of response to a stimulus involves a reflec arc. This consists of three essential parts:

1. The *afferent limb* of the reflex arc consists of receptors in some part of the body and the afferent nerves that supply them.
2. The *center* occurs within the CNS, sometimes in the spinal cord (as in the case of the knee-jerk reflex), and sometimes in the brain (for example, in the blink reflex). Within the CNS the

4

afferent, sensory nerve may excite the efferent neuron directly by a synaptic connection of one of its collaterals with the cell body of the motor neuron. In this case the reflex arc is termed "monosynaptic." In other cases, one or more interneurons may intervene between sensory and motor neurons, and in such a case the reflex arc is termed "polysynaptic."
3. The *efferent limb* of the reflex arc consists of the motor neuron and the effector organ, which may be muscle or gland. The motor neuron arises from a cell body in the gray matter of the spinal cord, in the case of spinal nerves, or from a cranial nerve nucleus within the brain, in the case of the cranial nerves.

Reflex arcs have characteristic properties that may best be studied in spinal animals (see p. 11). The most important aspects of impulse conduction in the reflex arc are:

1. *Forward conduction.* Conduction through a reflex arc is possible in one direction only, because the synapses transmit the excitatory process undirectionally from one axon to the next dendrite.
2. *Facilitation.* If a stimulus is repeated frequently, but not rapidly enough to produce fatigue, the reflex becomes increasingly easy to elicit and the reaction time becomes shorter.
3. *Fatigue.* When the stimuli follow each other rapidly, fatigue may readily be produced.
4. *Summation.* Repetition of a subliminal and therefore ineffective stimulus may produce a reflex response. If two or more subliminal stimuli are given at sufficiently short intervals, their effect is summated so that together they produce an excitation.
5. *Synaptic delay or resistance.* The time between the stimulation and the reflex responses—(the reaction time)—is much longer than it would be if the pathways were continuous nerve fibers only. The synaptic delay has been calculated to be about 0.002 sec per synapse in mammals.
6. *Inhibition.* If two different reflexes are initiated simultaneously, the one more important for the life of the animal inhibits, i.e., suppresses, the less important one.
7. *Afterdischarge.* The contraction of muscle, or other action produced reflexively, does not cease immediately after cessation of the stimulus but continues for a short while (afterdischarge).
8. *Rebound.* If, during the reflex contraction of a muscle the stimulation is suddenly interrupted, after a short pause the muscle exhibits a rebound.

Reflexes can be classified as follows. (1) *The exteroceptive reflex* is provoked by irritation of the cutaneous receptors (the sense organs of the skin for perception of pain, touch, cold, and warmth), the chemoreceptors involved in taste and smell, and the distance receptors, used in vision and hearing. (2) *The interoceptive reflexes* are evoked by irritation of (a) the visceroceptors, the sense organs in the various parts of the intestine, and (b) the proprioceptors, the sense organs that are stimulated by actions of the body itself. These are in the muscle spindles and tendons and also in the organs of equilibrium.

**Feedback control.** When an animal performs some movement, there is usually one or more receptor type that responds to some effect of the movement. These receptors give rise to impulses in afferent nerves which inform the CNS of the degree of movement; i.e., there is "feedback." The CNS can then modify the movement so that it can more efficiently perform some function. This modification involves the comparison of the pattern of receptor impulses, be they from stretch receptors in the muscles and tendons or visual impressions from the retina, with a preferred or desired pattern.

The essential parts of a feedback control system are shown in Figure 1–1. Their function may be illustrated by taking the example of a bird in flight wishing to alight at a particular point on the branch of a tree. As the bird approaches the tree its eyes inform it of its distance from the landing point and of the elevation and the direction of this point. Its proprioceptors inform it of the position and movements of its limbs in space, and its inner ear (and also eyes) inform it of the position and acceleration of its body. These various sensory organs are the *transducers* that produce the feedback informing the CNS of the actual output of the *controlled system,* which in this case is its body in flight related to the landing point. The CNS acts as an *error detector* in comparing these feedback signals with those patterns it knows from experience result from a successful landing at a desired point. A disturbance, such as a sudden gust of wind, may tip the body out of the vertical position and shift the position of the branch. An *error signal* arises that causes the CNS to alter the beating of the wings and the position of the tail and feet to correct equilibrium, and so also the position of the body with respect to the branch. The muscle system, then, is the *controller.* Even in the absence of such a sudden gust of wind, smaller corrections are necessary and are continuously made. The primary input to the system is the *control*

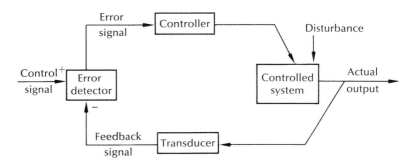

Essential parts of a feedback control system. The arrows indicate the direction of flow of information. The + and − signs indicate that control and feedback signals can be thought of as being summated algebraically by the error detector, the output of which is a function of the resultant sum. [Based on a figure from J. Houk and E. H. Henneman. (1968). In "Medical Physiology" (12th ed.) (V. B. Mountcastle, Ed.) St. Louis: C. V. Mosby Co. Reproduced with permission.]

*signal,* which dictates the desired output, a correct alighting on the branch.

## PERIPHERAL NERVOUS SYSTEM

The peripheral nervous system includes those parts of the nervous system other than the brain and spinal cord. Some details of sensory organs and muscle are included. The general arrangement of the peripheral nervous system does not differ in its basic organization from the mammal's, and this is not the place to include any great detail of gross anatomy, although some differences will be noted. The autonomic nervous system is dealt with separately.

### Spinal and Cranial Nerves

The paired spinal nerves leave the spinal cord and pass anterior to the corresponding vertebrae. For example, the first pair of cervical spinal nerves passes between the skull and the atlas. The number of pairs of cervical spinal nerves varies among species, there being, for example, 15 in domestic fowl (Jungherr, 1969), 14 in the pigeon (Huber, 1936), and 12 in the budgerigar (Evans, 1969). In the fowl there are seven (or more) pairs of thoracic nerves and 14 pairs of lumbosacral nerves.

Each spinal nerve arises by a dorsal sensory and a ventral motor root from the spinal cord. The dorsal root carries a ganglion in which are found the perikarya of afferent nerves.

After fusion of the dorsal and ventral roots, the nerve leaves the spinal canal; each spinal nerve divides into a dorsal branch, which supplies the dorsal muscles, and a ventral branch, supplying the ventral spinal muscles and muscles of the body wall. Both branches give rise to cutaneous nerves, the detailed arrangement of which in the fowl has been described and systematized by Yasuda (1964). Generally the ventral branch of a spinal nerve connects to the corresponding segmental autonomic ganglion in the cervical, thoracic, and lumbosacral regions (Hsieh, 1951).

In the regions of the wings and hind limbs, the spinal nerves branch and anastomose to form the brachial and lumbosacral plexuses, respectively. Different segmental nerves are probably involved in the formation of these plexuses in the various species. In the fowl (*Gallus gallus*) the brachial plexus is formed by the ventral roots of the last two to four cervical nerves and by the first and sometimes the second thoracic nerve. The plexus gives rise to the nerves supplying the wing and adjacent regions. These are the dorsal, short, and lateral thoracic nerves and the cranial pectoral, axillary, radial, median, and ulnar nerves. The muscles that these innervate are given by Bennett (1974). Yasuda (1960) has detailed the innervation of the muscles of the thoracic limb of the fowl.

The lumbosacral plexus arises from the first to the eighth lumbosacral nerves in the fowl. It gives rise to femoral, obturator, and sciatic (ischiadic) nerves. Yasuda (1961) describes the innervation of the muscles of the fowl hind limb.

The gross anatomy of the cranial nerves of the bird has been studied in the domestic fowl (e.g., Watanabe, 1960, 1964; Watanabe and Yasuda, 1968, 1970; Watanabe *et al.,* 1967). In general, the details are surprisingly similar to the mammalian arrangement. There are 12 pairs of nerves. There is no nervus terminalis or vomeronasal organ (organ of Jacobson) (Watanabe and Yasuda, 1968). The oculomotor nerve (third) supplies the palpebral muscles in addition to the extrinsic muscles of the

6 eye (see Bennett, 1974), whereas the abducent nerve (sixth) also supplies the muscles of the nictitating membrane (Watanabe *et al.,* 1967). The trigeminal (fifth), facial (seventh), acoustic (eighth), glossopharyngeal (ninth), and vagus (tenth) nerves bear sensory ganglia. Four pairs of ganglia are associated with the autonomic nervous system in the head. Barnikol (1954) has studied the trigeminal nerve distribution in several avian species and Pearson (1972) reviews in detail the available work on the cranial nerves in birds.

**Conduction in peripheral nerves.** In pigeons, the relative proportions of the various fiber types in the trigeminal, trochlear, sciatic, and the twenty-second to twenty-fourth spinal roots have been studied by Graf (1956). By comparison with mammals, small fiber types are well represented, whereas coarser fibers are relatively scarce.

Carpenter and Bergland (1957) measured the impulse velocity in the sciatic nerves of chick embryos, young chicks, and adult chickens. There was an increase in the velocity of conduction of the fastest component during development from 0.5 m/sec to 50 m/sec concomitant with the deposition of myelin. Brown *et al.* (1972) studied fiber size and conduction velocity in the chicken vagus. There were 10,000 myelinated fibers, the largest being 6–7 $\mu$m, and 87% being less than 3 $\mu$m, in diameter. There were about 5000 unmyelinated fibers. The compound action potential in the cervical vagus showed two main peaks, with conduction velocities of 0.8–1.2 m/msec and 2.2–32.4 m/msec, probably corresponding to conduction in unmyelinated and myelinated fibers, respectively.

**Sensory organs.** Aside from the organs of special senses, the bird possesses an array of sensory organs similar to those found in the mammal. These include proprioceptors, which include both muscle spindles and tendon organs, and cutaneous receptors of various types. Information pertaining to the various aspects has been reviewed by Bowman and Marshall (1971), Pearson (1972), Bennett (1974), and Schwartzkopff (1974).

Cutaneous receptors take the form of free nerve endings or encapsulated organs. Merckel's disks occur in the skin and buccal cavity. Structures resembling Krause's end bulbs have also been described. Herbst's lamellar corpuscles appear to be analogous to the Vater–Pacinian corpuscles of mammals. They occur in the skin of the bill, tongue, and palate. Dorward (1970a) has studied the impulse pattern in nerves supplying sensory organs on the upper surface of the duck's wing. Receptors are classified into four types:

1. Rapidly adapting, low-mechanical-threshold down feather units with large receptive fields.
2. Medium- to high-threshold touch receptors with localized receptive fields and varying rates of adaptation.
3. High-threshold, slowly adapting pressure or nociceptive receptors with diffuse receptive fields.
4. Vibration-sensitive receptors responding to frequencies up to 1000 cps. These are identified with Herbst's corpuscles.

Thermoreceptors and vibration-sensitive and vibration-insensitive mechanoreceptors in the duck's bill and tongue (Gregory, 1973; Leitner and Roumy, 1974a,b) and vibration-sensitive Pacinian corpuscles in the hind limb interosseous tissue (Skoglund, 1960; Dorward and McIntyre, 1971) have also been studied. Pearson (1972) and Bennett (1974) review the literature on cutaneous receptors.

Muscle spindles lie parallel to extrafusal muscle fibers and consist of three types of intrafusal fiber: small-diameter fibers with nuclear chains, large-diameter fibers with nuclear bag, and fibers of intermediate type. Large-diameter intrafusal fibers are innervated by larger diameter nerve fibers, small intrafusal fibers by small nerves. Both have a basketlike arrangement of nerve fibers in the neighborhood of the nuclei. Two types of motor endings are found (de Anda and Rebollo, 1967; Bennett, 1974). Physiologically these spindles behave as if they are "in parallel" with the extrafusal fibers, and they receive a separate, high-threshold efferent supply (Dorward, 1970b). Tendon organs discharge as if they are arranged in series with the muscle (Dorward, 1970b).

Visceral sensory organs are located especially in the heart, lungs, and bronchi but are also found in other tissues within the body. Their discharge is associated with the control of circulation and respiration. The literature on morphology has been collected by Bennett (1974). King and Molony (1971) deal extensively with the innervation of the respiratory system. The role of such receptors in the regulation of respiration is reviewed by Jukes (1971) and by Lasiewski (1972) and in Chapter 6 of this book. Similarly, the effects of baroreceptors on the circulation are covered in Chapters 4 and 5 and by Jones and Johansen (1972).

**Innervation of skeletal muscle.** Two types of muscle fibers have been identified in the bird. *Fibrillenstruktur* fibers have an orderly structure of fibrils and straight Z disks running across the fiber. They have regular T systems and sarcoplasmic reticulum which form triads. They are generally adapted for quick, brief, intermittent contractions and consist predominantly (but not exclusively) of white fibers; i.e., their myoglobin content is low. They are usually but not invariably innervated by one, or not more than a few, axon branches by *en plaque* terminals (Page, 1969; Bowman and Marshall, 1971). The pigeon iris muscle is an exception to these generalizations (Pilar and Vaughan, 1969; Hess, 1970).

*Felderstruktur* fibers are multi-innervated tonic fibers with *en grappe* nerve terminals. They often respond to acetylcholine with a nonpropagated, graded depolarization and contracture. Some are capable of propagated responses and generate action potentials, but the response to nerve stimulation is more usually a graded junction potential and a tonic contracture. (Pilar and Vaughan, 1969; Hess, 1970; Bowman and Marshall, 1971).

The nictitating membrane in the bird, unlike that of mammals, is operated by two striated muscles, the quadratus nictitantis and the pyramidalis nictitantis, supplied by the abducent nerve. The muscle fibers are of the *Fibrillenstruktur* type (Mayr, 1968).

The iris in the bird is also composed of striated *Fibrillenstruktur* fibers but these receive *en grappe* endings. Responses to stimulation of the ciliary nerve that supplies the iris are blocked by curare but not by atropine (Pilar and Vaughan, 1969; Hess, 1970; Bowman and Marshall, 1971).

## Autonomic Nerves and Ganglia; Innervation of Internal Organs

The autonomic nervous system includes those efferent nerves that innervate structures other than skeletal muscle. It is conventionally divided into sympathetic and parasympathetic systems, although to some extent this division is artificial, as pointed out by Bennett (1974). The sympathetic system includes all such efferent fibers leaving the spinal cord via the ventral roots in the cervical, thoracic, and lumbar regions and entering the segmental (paravertebral) and prevertebral ganglia, where they synapse. This distinguishes such fibers from parasympathetic fibers, which leave in the cranial nerves and sacral nerves and synapse in scattered small ganglia in or on the innervated organ. An exception to this rule is the discrete ciliary ganglion receiving preganglionic fibers from the oculomotor nerve, which supplies postganglionic (and postsynaptic) fibers to the iris. In the bird this is again exceptional, because the iris is composed of striated muscle. In the mammal, and possibly also in the bird, some sympathetic fibers innervating the internal sex organs are exceptional in that they synapse in scattered ganglia close to the organs (Sjöstrand, 1965).

In the fowl two autonomic nerve trunks bearing segmental ganglia extend along the vertebral column from the base of the skull to the level of the sixth coccygeal vertebra, where the trunks fuse. There is no ganglion impar at this point. There are usually 37 ganglion pairs (14 cervical, 7 thoracic, 13 lumbosacral, 3 coccygeal), the most anterior pair being the anterior cervical ganglia. Variations in the number of ganglia (35–38) are common. The anterior cervical ganglion (or the sympathetic fibers issuing from it) is connected to all the cranial nerves except the optic and the acoustic. It is also connected by a branch to the medulla oblongata. In the cervical region, the ventral ramus of each spinal nerve passes through a notch in the corresponding segmental sympathetic ganglion. At this point there is an exchange of nerve fibers between the spinal nerve and the ganglion. However, the anterior cervical ganglion and the last two cervical ganglia are connected to the spinal nerves by communicating branches. This is also the case in the posterior lumbosacral and coccygeal regions; in the thoracic and anterior lumbosacral regions, however, the segmental sympathetic ganglion is fused to the corresponding dorsal root ganglion of the spinal nerve (Hsieh, 1951).

Sympathetic nerves may synapse in the paravertebral ganglion of the vertebral segment where they leave the spinal cord. The postsynaptic fiber may then join somatic efferent fibers and be distributed via the peripheral nerves to blood vessels. On other occasions fibers do not synapse in the paravertebral ganglion but pass beyond to synapse in another paravertebral or often in an unpaired prevertebral ganglion.

The parasympathetic fibers in the head region are generally stated to leave in cranial nerves 3, 7, 9, and 10 (see Figure 1–4, below). However, it is possible that other cranial nerves carry autonomic nerve fibers, although this has not been subjected to careful experimental test. Certainly, anastomoses between cranial nerves, parasympathetic nerves, and sympathetic nerves are numerous in this region. Bennett (1974) outlines these.

Four pairs of autonomic ganglia are associated with the efferent autonomic nerves to the head. These are the ciliary, ethmoidal, sphenopalatine, and submandibular ganglia. There are no otic ganglia. The details of the anastomoses between these ganglia and the cranial nerves are given by Hsieh (1951). Bolton (1971a) and Bennett (1974) summarize the available information.

The sacral autonomic fibers are conventionally designated parasympathetic. They anastomose with

8 sympathetic fibers to form the hypogastric plexus, which contributes to the posterior mesenteric and pelvic plexuses. These supply the posterior viscera. Sympathetic and parasympathetic nerves to the heart are discussed in Chapters 4 and 5.

In the chicken the greater splanchnic nerves arise from the second to fifth thoracic ganglia and form the coeliac plexus. The lesser splanchnic nerves arise from the fifth to the seventh thoracic and first and second lumbosacral ganglia. They form the aortic plexus. Nerves from the sixth to the twelfth lumbosacral ganglia form the hypogastric plexus, the posterior mesenteric plexus, the pelvic plexus, and the cloacal plexus. Several plexuses designated by appropriate names are found in the region of the heart, the stomachs, the coeliac artery, the liver, the spleen, the adrenals, the kidney, etc. Considerable details of these can be found in Bennett (1974).

The nerve of Remak is a ganglionated trunk arising from the anterior mesenteric, pancreaticoduodenal, aortic, posterior mesenteric, and hypogastric plexuses. This nerve supplies the jejunum, ileum, and large intestine (Hsieh, 1951).

**Alimentary tract—actions of drugs.** The tongue, pharynx, and upper esophagus are innervated by the glossopharyngeal nerve. Its fibers anastomose with those of the vagus, which supplies the crop, proventriculus, gizzard, and small intestine. The large intestine and rectum are generally considered to be supplied by parasympathetic fibers from the sacral region. Although anatomical studies (see Bolton, 1971a,b; Bennett, 1974) suggest that sympathetic nerves innervate all parts of the alimentary tract, physiological studies have not revealed effects of sympathetic nerve stimulation in the esophagus and crop. However, inhibitory effects of vagal nerve stimulation have been observed (Sato et al., 1970).

Electrical stimulation of nerves supplying the alimentary canal may elicit contractions sensitive to the blocking action of atropine and these presumably are caused by cholinergic parasympathetic fibers, which supply all parts and arise in the glossopharyngeal, vagus, and sacral nerves. Frequently such contractions are blocked or reduced by ganglion blocking agents, indicating that it is the preganglionic fibers of such nerves that are being stimulated. On other occasions, the response is resistant to such agents, suggesting that it is the postganglionic fibers that are being excited. Because parasympathetic ganglia occur close to or on the innervated organ, such ganglion stimulating agents as nicotine produce contractions of some organs. They

do this presumably by stimulating the postsynaptic membrane of the postganglionic neurons. Contractions produced by transmural stimulation generally excite postganglionic nerve fibers.

Sympathetic fibers are generally considered to be adrenergic, although cholinergic sympathetic fibers have been identified in some organs of mammals. Stimulation of perivascular nerves generally produces relaxation in the gut, and the actions of various blocking agents indicates that this is mediated by the release of a catecholamine, probably noradrenaline. Transmural stimulation may also produce relaxation by exciting these nerves. In all cases, because the synapse is in para- or prevertebral ganglia, the relaxation responses are insensitive to ganglionic blocking agents. Sympathetic nerves are excitatory to some parts of the alimentary tract, however, e.g., gizzard, lower esophagus, proventriculus. Where contractions occur they are mediated by $\alpha$ receptors and contractile responses to perivascular nerve stimulation are blocked by phenoxybenzamine. Relaxant or inhibitory effects of sympathetic nerves often require a combination of $\alpha$- and $\beta$-receptor blockades to abolish them.

The above picture is complicated by the existence of inhibitory responses to transmural nerve stimulation that do not have the characteristics of being adrenergically mediated. This type of response may also be obtained by stimulating discrete nerves, such as vagal branches, supplying an organ. Such nerve fibers are designated "nonadrenergic, inhibitory nerves." Their origin at the CNS is sometimes obscure but they appear often to be carried in the vagus nerve. Such responses are usually reduced by ganglion blocking agents but are resistant to adrenergic neuron blocking agents or $\alpha$- and $\beta$-receptor blockers (see also Chapters 4 and 5).

Sometimes, noncholinergic, nonadrenergic contractions of intestinal muscle occur. Generally these follow transmural stimulation. These, as Bennett (1974) suggests, may be rebound contractions following nonadrenergic inhibition. The following papers should be consulted for details: Bowman and Everett (1964), Everett (1966, 1968), Ohashi and Ohga (1967), Bennett (1969), and Sato et al. (1970).

The distribution of adrenergic nerves to the alimentary tract has been studied histochemically. Catecholamine-containing cells have been found in Auerbach's plexus in the gizzard (Bennett et al., 1973). A review of the literature can be found in Bennett (1974).

A number of transmitter substances and drugs has been shown to cause changes in spontaneous activity, contraction, or relaxation of alimentary smooth muscle of the bird. Acetylcholine contracts all parts, an action potentiated by physostigmine and blocked by atropine. Larger concentrations of histamine also contract and mepyramine blocks this effect. Low concentrations of histamine relax, apparently by releasing catecholamine. This action is potentiated by low concentrations of mepyramine and blocked by $\alpha$ and $\beta$ blockers, such as pronethalol or phentolamine. Both $\alpha$ and $\beta$ blockers are generally required to block relaxation produced by adrenaline in intestinal smooth muscle (Everett and Mann, 1967; Everett, 1968).

**Heart and cardiovascular system — actions of drugs.** There is general agreement that both the atria and the ventricles of the bird heart receive adrenergic and cholinergic nerve fibers. Akester *et al.* (1969) and Bennett and Malmfors (1970) (see also Chapters 4 and 5) were able to demonstrate an especially dense innervation of the sinoatrial and atrioventricular nodes. Gossrau (1968) studied the distribution of acetylcholinesterase-positive fibers (presumably cholinergic neurons) in pigeon, chaffinch, and canary hearts. Histochemical studies have been supported by physiological experiments on isolated strips of ventricular muscle from fowl and pigeon (Bolton and Raper, 1966; Bolton, 1967). Avian ventricular strips were more sensitive to the action of acetylcholine than those from guinea pigs and rats, which depressed the force of contraction. This effect was antagonized by atropine. Field stimulation of avian ventricular strips produced evidence of the activation of both adrenergic and cholinergic nerve fibers (see also Chapter 5). Postganglionic fibers were stimulated because ganglion blocking agents were without effect. In the presence of atropine, field stimulation increased the force of contraction, an effect that was blocked by $\beta$-adrenoreceptor blocking agents, such as propranolol, or by adrenergic neurone blocking agents, such as guanethidine. This indicated that adrenergic transmitter was released by electric stimulation, presumably from sympathetic nerve endings, and produced a positive inotropic effect by acting on $\beta$ receptors on myocardial cells. If similar experiments were done in which the adrenergic nerves were first blocked by guanethidine, then field stimulation of avian, but not of rat or guinea pig ventricular strips, produced a negative inotropic effect blocked by atropine (Chapter 5).

The results indicate an appreciable cholinergic innervation of the avian ventricle not present in rat and guinea pig. The greater functional effect of cholinergic nerves to the avian ventricle was confirmed by Kissling *et al.* (1972), who also identified cholinergic fibers histochemically and claimed to have identified acetylcholine released by transmural stimulation.

Section of the vagus nerves produces an increase in heart rate in most birds and bradycardia follows the stimulation of the peripheral end of either vagus in the chicken and duck (see also Chapter 5). The chronic pulmonary alterations that follow vagotomy have been studied by Burger and Fedde (1964); further information can be found in Bolton (1971b) and in Chapter 5.

Although both $\alpha$ and $\beta$ receptors are present on both arterial and venous smooth muscle of the chicken, large concentrations of conventional $\alpha$-receptor blocking agents are required to reverse the adrenaline pressor response to a depressor response. Nevertheless, isoproterenol may produce a depressor response and occasionally a mild vasodilation when injected intraarterially to the vascular bed of skeletal muscle (Bolton and Bowman, 1969). Isoproterenol and even small doses of adrenaline similarly injected in the cat have produced appreciable vasodilation (Bowman, 1959). Cocaine potentiates the actions of directly acting sympathomimetic amines on vascular muscle and on the blood pressure, but not on cardiac muscle (Bolton and Bowman, 1969). Reserpine pretreatment reduces the pressor response to tyramine and its effect on vascular muscle. The pressor response to tyramine is reduced by pretreatment with reserpine but can be restored by infusions of dopamine, noradrenaline, or adrenaline (Bolton, 1967).

The anterior mesenteric artery is peculiar in possessing a longitudinal muscle layer that is contracted by cholinergic nerves and relaxed by adrenergic nerves acting on $\beta$ receptors (see Chapter 4).

**Other tissues.** The autonomic innervation has been extensively reviewed by Burnstock (1969) and by Bennett (1974). Space precludes a consideration of all tissues here. The innervation of the avian respiratory tract has been studied in some detail (King and Molony, 1971). The lung (Cook and King, 1970; Bennett, 1971; McLelland *et al.*, 1972), bronchi (Akester and Mann, 1969), trachea (Walsh and McLelland, 1974), and air sacs (Groth, 1972) have received attention.

The distribution of adrenergic nerves throughout the chicken has been investigated histochemically by Bennett (1971) and by Bennett and Malmfors (1970). The carotid body was intensely fluorescent. Vinblastin (Bennett *et al.*, 1973b) and 6-hydroxydopamine (Bennett *et al.*, 1970; Bennett *et al.* 1973a) deplete the fowl's sympathetic nerves of catecholamine. The latter drug loads the vesicles

10 before degeneration begins, whereas vinblastin blocks the transport of adrenergic transmitter.

**Transmission through autonomic ganglia.** Electrophysiologic studies of ganglionic transmission in the bird have been made only in the ciliary ganglion. In the embryo, transmission through the ciliary ganglion is wholly chemical; in the young chick, however, a high proportion of the postganglionic cell bodies becomes capable of direct electrical excitation by the preganglionic nerve endings (ephaptic transmission). Electrical records from the postganglionic neuron therefore come to show two components by 4 weeks of age, only the second of which is blocked by curare (Martin and Pilar 1963a, b; 1964a). Ephatic transmission seems to arise because of the development of myelin lamellae that ensheathe the pre- and postsynaptic parts of the neuron (Hess et al., 1969).

Ephaptic transmission is restricted to postgan-glionic neurons that innervate the iris and ciliary body. Here transmission is nicotinic. Another group of postganglionic cells can be identified that innervates the choroid. These cells are chemically excited by the presynaptic nerve. Transmission to the choroid cells is muscarinic, being blocked by atropine. Cells of both groups receive endings of only a single presynaptic neuron (Marwitt et al., 1971). After section of the presynaptic nerve, the presynaptic neurons innervating the two groups of cells selectively reinnervate their respective groups (Landmesser and Pilar, 1970, 1972). Transmitter release in the ciliary ganglion is quantal and shows "posttetanic potentiation" (Martin and Pilar, 1964b,c). Chemical transmission through other avian autonomic ganglia has received little attention.

Ganglion stimulants, such as nicotine or DMPP, can contract many parts of the alimentary tract. Sometimes they produce biphasic responses or simply relaxation. These actions are explained by stimulation of the postsynaptic membrane of cholinergic or nonadrenergic inhibitory neurons. These actions are blocked by such ganglion blocking agents as hexamethonium, pempidine, or mecamylamine (Everett, 1968). Ganglion blocking agents often reduce the alimentary tract smooth muscle contractions elicited by stimulating parasympathetic nerves. Nonadrenergic, vagal, inhibitory responses are also blocked (Bowman and Everett, 1964; Everett, 1966, 1968; Sato et al., 1970).

## SPINAL CORD

The gross anatomy of the avian spinal cord presents some interesting features. The cervical, thoracic, and lumbosacral regions correspond to these parts of the vertebral column; compared with the mammal, the cervical and lumbosacral regions are relatively long and the thoracic region short. The cord is enlarged in those regions from which the brachial and lumbosacral plexuses arise to supply the limbs. It also exhibits a collection of glycogen-containing cells that expands the dorsal septum in the lumbosacral region (Figure 1−2). The function of this large dilation, called the lumbosacral or rhomboid sinus (or glycogen body), is unknown. Peripherally in many species there is a column termed the accessory lobe of Lachi, which contains gray matter.

Histologically, the avian cord shows very similar general arrangement to the mammal. An X-shaped core of gray matter is surrounded by white fiber tracts. The relative sizes of the dorsal and ventral horns vary considerably, depending on the lev-

1−2 Lumbosacral part of the spinal cord of a flamingo *(Phoenicopterus)* showing the three nerve plexuses and the rhomboid sinus. (After Imhof, 1905.)

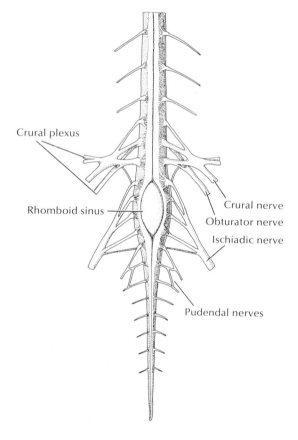

Crural plexus

Rhomboid sinus

Crural nerve

Obturator nerve

Ischiadic nerve

Pudendal nerves

el of the cord sectioned. Sensory fibers enter via the dorsal root and pass into the dorsal horn, where some synapse. Cell bodies in this region have led to the designation of a dorsal magnocellular column. Motor fibers arise in the ventral horn from large multipolar cells. This horn is divided into medial and lateral portions. More details can be found in Ariëns-Kappers et al. (1936) and in Pearson (1972). Interesting features are the presence of paragriseal cells (lying outside the gray matter of the spinal cord) in two situations: first as scattered paragriseal cells in the white matter lateral and ventral to the ventral horn, and second as discrete peripheral paragriseal cells that lie in a group forming a column just under the pia at the junction of lateral and ventral funiculi. These form the accessory lobe of Lachi alluded to above. Some motor fibers are thought by many authors to leave via the dorsal root, although the ventral root is seemingly exclusively composed of motor fibers (see Ariëns-Kappers et al., 1936). Levi-Montalcini (1950) maintains that preganglionic visceral efferent neurons originate from perikarya in a medial column (of Terni) close to the central spinal canal.

Little is known about the arrangement of ascending tracts in the spinal cord. Incoming dorsal root sensory impulses pass via monosynaptic and polysynaptic pathways to the dorsal funiculus of the same side. Here they are carried forward in tracts corresponding to the cuneate and gracilis columns of mammals to small cuneate and gracilis nuclei in the medulla (Karten, 1963). Fibers entering progressively rostrad are placed laterally to those entering behind. Friedlander (quoted by Ariëns-Kappers et al., 1936) showed that following hemisection of the lumbar cord, contralateral degeneration occurred at the lumbar level in the spinomesencephalic tract situated in the ventral funiculus. Ipsilateral degeneration occurred in the more posterior cord in the ventral funiculus close to the ventral fissure and in the peripheral, dorsolateral funiculus. Ascending ipsilateral degeneration was also found in these two locations, as was contralateral degeneration in the spinomesencephalic tract. The peripheral dorsolateral funicular degeneration corresponds to the position of the spinocerebellar tract (Whitlock, 1952). The degeneration in the ventral funiculus corresponds to tracts identified by Ariëns-Kappers et al. as forerunners of the mammalian spinothalamic tracts for tactile, pain, and thermal sensibilities. Karten (1963) has confirmed that the ventral and lateral funiculi contain ascending fibers that pass to the medulla, midbrain, tectum, and thalamus of the same side (Karten and Revzin, 1966). An important electrophysiological study was carried out by Oscarsson et al. (1963). By electrical recordings from fascicules of the spinal cord while stimulating muscle, skin, and mixed leg and wing nerves in the duck, they found that dorsal funicular tracts were activated only ipsilaterally by mono- and polysynaptic pathways. Ventral tracts were monosynaptically activated only by contralateral pathways but were polysynaptically activated both ipsi- and contralaterally. Their results confirm that dorsal tracts are uncrossed, whereas ventral and lateral tracts are crossed. Low-threshold muscle afferents from the leg activated contralateral tracts, the discharge of which was inhibited by high-threshold skin and muscle afferent stimulation. Low-threshold muscle afferents from the wings were uncrossed and not so inhibited.

A number of descending tracts have been identified and reviewed by Ariëns-Kappers et al. (1936). A cerebellospinal tract occurs medial to the spinocerebellar. Tectospinal tracts occur in the lateral funiculus and also in the ventral funiculus, where it is accompanied by a vestibulospinal tract. Rubrospinal tracts may also be found as well as descending fibers adjacent to the ventral fissure mentioned above. A system comparable to the pyramidal tracts of mammals is absent. Modern verification of these results of older work is lacking.

**Functional capability of spinal cord.** Many investigations of the functions of the spinal cord and other parts of the central nervous system have been made by transecting the nervous axis at different levels or by the removal of some part of it. Separation of a lower part of the central nervous system from a higher part causes a loss of certain functions because of the interruption of the pathways between the higher and lower centers. After transection of the thoracic or lumbar cord, birds and other animals may survive for months or even years, and the reactions in the spinal cord can be studied without interfering influences from higher centers of the central nervous system.

An animal with a transected spinal cord is called a *spinal animal.* It shows loss of motility and sensation on both sides in the areas of the body supplied by the nerves below the transection for the initial period of what is called *spinal shock,* during which all reflexes are absent. After a certain time typical protective spinal reflexes appear; later other reflexes of the limbs and of the trunk may take place. After complete transection of the thoracic cord, pigeons lay passively with their legs drawn up toward the body. When starting an attempt at flight they beat their wings violently (ten Cate, 1960).

As early as 1858 Schiff drew attention to the

12   great reflex capacity of spinal birds. After transection of the spinal cord at the level of the thoracic segments it is possible, by passively bending and stretching one foot of the bird, to produce antagonistic stretching and bending reflexes of the opposite foot. Later, when reflex activity has further increased, lifting the pigeon causes rapid rhythmical motions of both feet, similar to the alternating movements of the hind legs of transected dogs, first described by Freusberg (1874). Various reflex movements of the tail may be provoked in a spinal animal. If a pigeon with head and body extended vertically is suddenly raised upward to the horizontal position, there is a fanlike spreading of the main tail feathers. If the pigeon is pushed back to its original position, there is only a brief upward flick of the tail. These reflexes normally serve to maintain the bird's balance.

No true locomotor movements of the hind limbs have been elicited in the spinal bird. Tarchanoff (1895) described a kind of walking movement in decapitated ducks, but this was observed only immediately after decapitation and was of very short duration. The walking movements of the legs were accompanied by violent beating of the wings, but these movements certainly did not have the character of normal walking movements.

A spinal bird is usually unable to walk because it can no longer maintain the upright posture in the absence of the control of the higher centers. When such a bird (pigeon) was fixed in a small four-wheeled carriage in a normal position and in such a way that its extended legs could reach the ground, a true walking movement in the hind limbs could be evoked by applying painful stimuli to the hind part of the body and the pigeon could move over relatively great distances. The lumbosacral cord of birds therefore shows a high degree of autonomy in the coordination of walking movements. The higher centers initiate and regulate these movements (ten Cate, 1960).

The reflex movements of the wings are generally identical and simultaneous. A weak stimulus causes only a slight movement of the irritated wing: a somewhat stronger one causes identical, simultaneous, and well-coordinated movements of both wings, which are rhythmically fanned and raised as in normal flight. Unlike the leg reflexes, the reflex movements of the wings in spinal birds are very monotonous (ten Cate, 1936; ten Cate et al., 1937).

After unilateral transection of the dorsal roots of the wings, Trendelenburg (1910) found that the position in which the wings were held was identical on the two sides, even when the pigeon was suspended with its head downward. Artificially induced abnormal positions of the wings were corrected only in the normal innervated wing. The capacity for flight and even for performing turns was retained. If a spinal pigeon is held by the tail, it beats both wings normally. After complete transection of the dorsal roots that innervate the wings, flying capacity is lost.

After unilateral denervation of one wing, the loss of centripetal afferent stimuli from the one side is amply replaced by those of the other side. Such pigeons can therefore fly well and maintain their balance. When the pigeon is forced into a position in which only one wing is normally used, then abnormalities arise if the wing needed for correction is the denervated one. Rhythmic beating of the wings depends on the reflex stimulus exerted on each wingbeat by the preceding one.

Experiments in which the dorsal roots of one leg were divided showed that centripetal stimuli from the normal side could not compensate, as occurred in the wings. The explanation must be found in the differing innervation of the extremities — simultaneous in the former, alternating in the latter (see also the experiments by Oscarssen et al., 1963 mentioned above).

If only one side of the spinal cord is dissected the ipsilateral leg is paralyzed and the tail is twisted toward the intact side. Sensation is only slightly reduced. All these phenomena gradually diminish, and after 1 or 2 weeks the pigeons can both stand and walk. Only a slight weakness of the paralyzed leg remains (ten Cate, 1960).

The famous experiments by Goltz and Evald (1896) with dogs were repeated with pigeons by Sammartino (1933), who extirpated the entire lumbar cord. Sensation and movement in the caudal part of the body were lost. The cloacal sphincter (skeletal muscle) lost its tone completely after the operation, but some time later it was regained (unlike smooth muscle) and the feces once again were voided spontaneously at regular intervals.

**Regeneration in the spinal cord.** It is important to know how far the process of nerve fiber regeneration can take place in the cord following transection. Experiments for determining this on birds have been carried out by Clearwaters (1954). She demonstrated that complete structural restitution after transection of the cord occurred only in chick embryos after 2–5 days of incubation.

ten Cate (1960 and earlier) made microscopical preparations of the spinal cord of adult pigeons to establish the anatomical alterations at the place of transection. A regeneration of the whole spinal cord was not observed, but some growth of nerve fibers in the proximal as well as in the distal part of the cord was found. These abortive attempts at regeneration appear as fine fibers growing in various directions. The failure of the restoration of the connections between the two parts of the cord appears to be caused not so much by a lack of the possibility of nerve fiber regeneration as by the presence of insurmountable obstacles on their way.

Hamburger (1955) reports that in numerous investigations of reflexes and other problems of neurophysiology, involving transection of the central nervous system of adult birds, the regeneration and restoration of functional activity has never been observed.

# BRAIN

## Anatomy of the Brain

Although this chapter does not deal extensively with the neuroanatomy of the brain, some facts are essential for an understanding of avian physiology. In Figures 1–3 and 1–4 are depicted the gross appearences of some avian brains. There is variation between the different avian groups, but a common difference from the mammalian brain is the striking development of the optic tectum. The cerebral hemispheres of birds, instead of being composed very largely of cortex as in the mammal,

consist mainly of striatum, which is subdivided into a number of regions and is a collection of fiber tracts and nuclei (see Figure 1–6a).

**The medulla oblongata.** This connects spinal cord and midbrain and lies beneath the floor of the fourth ventricle and the cerebellum. It contains the nuclei of the cranial nerves, fifth to twelfth inclusive (Figure 1–4), and through it pass the fiber tracts connecting the spinal cord to cerebellum, midbrain, and forebrain. It is connected to the cerebellum by the cerebellar peduncles and contains the physiologically important reticular formation. Within this area are found the centers controlling the cardiovascular system and respiration (see Chapters 4 and 5). Richards (1971) has localized more anterior regions of the brainstem involved in the control of polypnea (see Chapter 6 for further details).

Besides the nuclei of the cranial nerves (which are covered in the sections on motor and sensory pathways of the brain) there are a number of other nuclei in the medulla. Brodal *et al.* (1950) describe the medial and lateral pontine nuclei in the chick. These supply fibers to the cerebellum and receive fibers from the tectum. The inferior olive is probably concerned with proprioception (Sanders, 1929; Ariëns-Kappers *et al.*, 1936; Brodal *et al.*, 1950). The medullary reticular formation is divided into

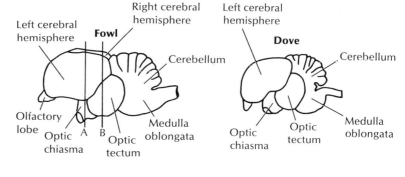

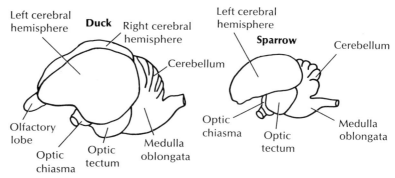

**1–3**

Gross appearances of some avian brains viewed from the left side. Lines A and B represent approximately the level of sections shown in Figure 1–6.

14

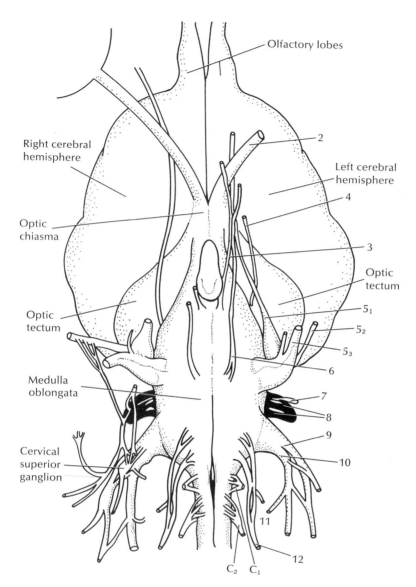

Olfactory lobes

Right cerebral hemisphere

Optic chiasma

Optic tectum

Medulla oblongata

Cervical superior ganglion

Left cerebral hemisphere

Optic tectum

2

4

3

5₁

5₂

5₃

6

7

8

9

10

11

12

C₂  C₁

**1–4**
Ventral view of the brain of a goose *(Anser)* showing the disposition of the cranial nerves. 1–12, cranial nerves; $5_1$, $5_2$, and $5_3$, branches of trigeminal nerve; $C_1 = C_2$, cervical nerves. (After Cords, 1904.)

inferior, middle, and superior reticular nuclei. Fibers from these enter the medical longitudinal fasciculus. Small cuneate and gracilis nuclei have been described. Fibers from these may decussate to form a medial lemniscus reaching the nuclei of the thalamus. However, following lesions in the cuneate and gracilis nuclei, Karten and Revzin (1966) did not observe any degeneration in nucleus rotundus. Further details can be found in Ariëns-Kappers *et al.* (1936), van Tienhoven and Juhász (1962), and Jungherr (1969)

**Cerebellum.** The cerebellum may be divided into anterior, middle, and posterior lobes by the anterior fissure primura and the more posterior fissure secunda. The numbering of the folia, accord-

ing to Larsell (1948) and Senglaub (1963), is shown in sagittal section in Figure 1–5. The histology of the cerebellum is similar to that of other vertebrates. Four central nuclei are recognized. They give rise to efferent tracts to the spinal cord and to the medulla, ending in relation to the vestibular nuclei. Other tracts end in relation to the nuclei of the third, fourth, and sixth cranial nerves; the inferior olive; and nuclei of cranial nerves 5 and 7.

Numerous tracts end in the cerebellum. These include fibers from the spinal cord, vestibular nuclei, pontine nuclei (Brodal *et al.*, 1950), trigeminal nuclei, tectum, and forebrain. The somatotopic representation of the parts of the body on the cerebellum was studied by Whitlock (1952), who recorded the responses elicited in the cerebellum by

1–5 Sagittal section of cerebellum of *Columba palumbus* showing numbering and arrangement of folia. (Reproduced with permission from Senglaub, 1963.)

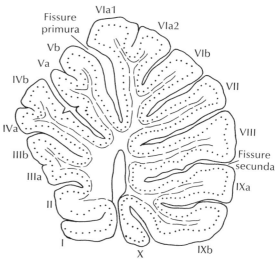

tactile stimuli and by electrical excitation of peripheral nerves. The representation was localized as follows: Face, folia VIa, b, and c; wing, folia IV, V and VIa; leg, folia III, IV, and V; tail, folia III and IV. Whitlock (1952) also studied auditory and visual receiving areas and found these to be identical. These areas were located in folia VIc, VII, and VIII. Tactile stimuli and electrical stimulation of peripheral nerves elicited ipsilateral responses; visual stimuli elicited contralateral responses.

**Midbrain.** This receives the optic nerve and is the origin of cranial nerves 3 and 4. It is a region of considerable complexity involved in the reception of visual impulses and their integration. The main structure is the tectum, which consists of 15 histologically differentiable layers. Medial to this are found several nuclei, in particular the nucleus mesencephalicus lateralis pars dorsalis, which is an auditory relay center (Figure 1–6b). Two important commissures occur, the posterior commissure and the supraoptic decussation, which connect the tectal regions of both sides and other adjacent nuclei.

**Forebrain.** The main divisions are the cerebral hemispheres, the thalamus, and the hypothalamus. Little is said in this chapter about the hypothalamus because this is dealt with in detail in Chapter 15.

The thalamus contains a very large number of distinguishable nuclei and some fiber tracts. The details of these can be found in Jungherr (1969) and in the stereotaxic atlases of van Tienhoven and Juhász (1962, domestic fowl) and Karten and Hodos (1967, pigeon). Pearson (1972) also reviews the anatomy. Of particular importance are the nucleus rotundus, which is a visual relay center; the nucleus ovoidalis, an auditory relay center; and the dorsal thalamic nuclei, which receive medial optic tract fibers.

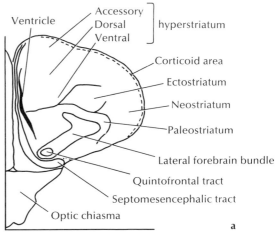

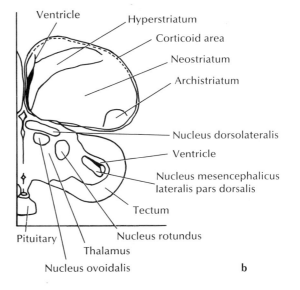

1–6 Transverse hemisections of the domestic fowl brain (a) through cerebral hemisphere at level indicated by line A in Figure 1–3. (b) through midbrain at level indicated by line B in Figure 3–1. (Based on stereotaxic atlas of van Tienhoven and Juhász, 1962. Reproduced with permission.)

16    The hemispheres consist of several distinguishable areas (Figure 1 – 6); namely, hyperstriatum, cortex, archistriatum, ectostriatum, paleostriatum, and neostriatum. The hyperstriatum and ectostriatum appear to be important forebrain areas associated with the visual sense, whereas auditory impulses reach the neostriatum.

### Sensory Pathways

The pathways whereby sensory impulses reach the brain via the spinal cord have already been mentioned. There remain those sensory impulses that are carried by the cranial nerves from the organs of special sense and from the proprioceptors and cutaneous sense organs of the head region.

**Olfactory impulses.** The olfactory bulb shows great diversity of form in the various avian species. *Passer domesticus* (house sparrow) and *Serunus canarius* (canary) have a single bulb representing a fusion of the two paired bulbs occurring in others. The diameter of the olfactory bulbs relative to the hemispheres varies also; in sparrows it is small (6 – 12% of the hemisphere), whereas in water birds, especially, and in the kiwi it may exceed 30% of hemisphere diameter. This variation is part of the anatomical basis for the classification of birds into microsmatic – macrosmatic series (Cobb 1960a,b; Bang, 1971; Pearson 1972).

Histologically, olfactory nerve fibers can be seen to end in relation to the mitral cell layer. Mitral cells give rise to fibers that form lateral and medial olfactory tracts. In microsmatic species (e.g., the sparrow) the former is very reduced. The medial tract runs to the anterior olfactory nucleus. In some species this is connected to the hippocampus (Ariëns-Kappers *et al.*, 1936), the size of which in many species parallels the development of the olfactory lobes (Pearson, 1972). The lateral olfactory tract runs to the prepyriform area and ventral part of the basal nucleus. Jones and Levi-Montalcini (1958) describe a tract arising from this area.

Tucker (1965) was able to record impulses in olfactory nerves in response to odoriferous compounds. Gentle (1975) used an EEG arousal test as an indicator of odor discrimination. Wenzel and Sieck (1972) recorded changes in activity in the olfactory bulb with chronically implanted electrodes in several avian species when these were presented with various odors borne on clean air. Changes in respiratory and heart rate were also observed. Changes in olfactory bulb activity occurred in response to a sudden illumination of the darkened chamber in which the birds were kept.

Various species of birds apparently vary considerably in the extent to which they utilize the olfactory sense to localize food or for other purposes. Some forms, such as vultures and albatross, seem to locate food at considerable distances by means of odors carried on thermal updraughts (Bang, 1960; see also Chapter 2). Michaelsen (1959) and Calvin (1960) have demonstrated odor discrimination in pigeons.

**Visual impulses.** The optic nerve decussates virtually completely, but there is evidence that a few fibers do not cross (Knowlton, 1964). It forms two main roots, medial and lateral, although Ariëns-Kappers *et al.* (1936) also distinguished a basal root and Wingstrand (1951) and Meier (1973) have discovered some fibers passing to the hypothalamus. The basal root is said to terminate in the nucleus ectomammillaris. The medial root, or isthmooptic tract, carries efferent fibers from the nucleus isthmoopticus and other fibers ending in thalamic nuclei, namely the nucleus lateralis anterior and the nucleus dorsolateralis anterior. Karten *et al.* (1973) call these dorsal thalamic nuclei the nucleus opticus principalis thalami. The lateral afferent root (marginal root) ends in the optic tectum, the lateral geniculate nucleus, the nucleus lateralis anterior, the nucleus externus, and the nucleus superficialis synencephali (Cowan *et al.*, 1961).

The dorsal thalamic nuclei, which receive retinal fibers, project to the contralateral hyperstriatal region via the lateral forebrain bundle. This in turn gives fibers to the hyperstriatal region of the opposite side, to the thalamic nuclei from which it receives projections, and to the neostriatum, periectostriatum, and lateral geniculate nucleus and tectum of both sides (Powell and Cowan, 1961; Karten and Nauta, 1968; Karten *et al.*, 1973).

The *tectum* can be distinguished histologically into a large number of laminae. Incoming retinal fibers lie in the stratum opticum; this lies beneath the more superficial stratum zonale. Pale-staining cells separate the stratum opticum from the stratum griseum et fibrosum superficiale, which can be subdivided into ten laminae (Jungherr, 1945; Cowan *et al.*, 1961; Lavail and Cowan, 1971a,b). Beneath this is found the stratum griseum centrale, which contains the cell bodies of efferent neurons. Their axons form the stratum album centrale. The deepest layer, adjacent to the ventricular ependyma, is the stratum fibrosum periventriculare, which receives hypothalamic fibers and fibers from the nucleus mesencephalicus lateralis pars dorsalis and the cerebellum.

The retina and visual field has a topographical representation on the contralateral tectum. This is arranged so that the inferior retinal field is represented anteriorly and dorsally, whereas the anterior retinal field is represented posteriorly and dorsally (Hamdi and Whitteridge, 1954; McGill, 1964; McGill et al., 1966; see also Chapter 2). Holden (1968a,b) studied the potential evoked at different depths in the tectum on stimulation of the optic nerve. Negativity coincided with the optic nerve terminals in the stratum griseum et fibrosum superficiale.

The tectum connects to many parts of the brain. Important efferent fibers go to the nucleus isthmoopticus, which is located medial to the nucleus mesencephalicus lateralis pars dorsalis. McGill (1964), McGill et al. (1966), and Holden and Powell (1972) have shown that there is ordered representation of the retina on the isthmooptic nucleus via the lateral optic tract and tectum. The isthmooptic nucleus projects via the medial optic tract into the contralateral retina. The regions of the isthmooptic nucleus supply centrifugal fibers to those parts of the contralateral retina from which they receive afferent impulses via the tectum. The tectum also projects to nucleus rotundus, which does not appear to receive important afferents from any other source (Karten, 1965, 1969). It projects via the lateral forebrain bundle to the central ectostriatum (Revzin and Karten, 1967) and paleostriatum augmentatum (Powell and Cowan, 1961). The dorsal tectobulbar tract leaves the stratum album centrale, supplies the oculomotor nucleus, decussates, and joins the medial longitudinal fasciculus. The ventral tectobulbar tract contributes fibers to the tegmentum, partially decussates, and continues into the medulla, possibly to the spinal cord; lateral and ventral tectospinal tracts have been described. Important fibers also pass to the opposite tectum.

Visual impulses therefore reach the forebrain by two routes; one, the lateral optic tract, tectum, and nucleus rotundus to the ectostriatum and the other, the medial optic tract to the dorsal thalamic nucleus and hence to the hyperstriatal region. Tectal impulses can feed back to modify retinal input via the isthmooptic nucleus and efferent fibers in the medial optic tract, whereas the hyperstriatum has descending connections to all the important visual centers of the midbrain and thalamus. Visual stimuli have also been observed to produce electrical changes in the archistriatum (Philips, 1966), hyperstriatum, and corticord regions (Bremer et al., 1939; Spooner and Winters, 1965; Adamo and King, 1967; Belekhova, 1968). Discrimination of visual patterns or intensity in pigeons was not impaired by destruction of dorsal thalamic nuclei or

hyperstriatum but was impaired when the lesion involved the nucleus rotundus (Hodos et al., 1973). Lesions of the hyperstriatum or paleostriatum, however, have been found to impair the acquisition and retention of visual patterns (Zeigler, 1963; Hodos and Karten, 1966; Cohen 1967a,b) but not if the lesions are confined to the neostriatum, archistriatum, and corticoid areas (Zeigler, 1963). Lesions of the tectum or nucleus rotundus do impair visual discrimination (Hodos and Karten, 1966; Cohen 1967a). Muscular coordination is unimpaired by destruction of the colliculi (Popa and Popa, 1933), whereas stimulation of the tectum in some parts causes opening of the eyelids (Moruzzi, 1947).

**Auditory impulses.** Auditory impulses are carried in the acoustic branch of the eighth nerve. The basal cochlear fibers enter the brainstem most caudally and dorsally and the middle and apical fibers enter progressively more anteriorly and ventrally. Three pairs of cochlear nuclei are recognized; the nucleus angularis, nucleus magnocellularis, and nucleus laminaris. In the magnocellular nucleus, the fibers from the basal third of the spiral ganglion end most anteriorly and medially, the apical third most caudally and laterally. In the angular nucleus the basal third fibers end most caudally and dorsally and the apical third enter most anteriorly and ventrally. The ventrolateral part of the magnocellular and the ventral part of the angular nucleus are receptive areas for fibers from the macula lagenae. Erulkar (1955) has produced physiological evidence that the laminar nucleus receives cochlear fibers: it is connected to both the ipsi- and the contralateral magnocellular nuclei but apparently not to the angular nuclei (Ariëns-Kappers et al., 1936; Levi-Montalcini, 1949; Boord and Rasmussen, 1963; Boord, 1965, 1968, 1969).

Fibers from the laminar nucleus, the lateral part of nucleus magnocellularis, and the medial part of nucleus angularis pass to the homolateral superior olive and then anteriorly. After they decussate in the trapezoid body, they form the lateral lemniscus. The lateral lemniscus ends only in the nucleus mesencephalicus lateralis pars dorsalis, according to Boord (1968), but possibly also in nucleus semilunaris and nucleus isthmi pars principalis. These are therefore regarded as the auditory projection centers. Some fibers also pass from cochlear centers to the cerebellum. The superior olive gives fibers to the medial longitudinal fasciculus (Levi-Montalcini, 1949; Erulkar, 1955; Boord, 1969).

Responses have been recorded in the nucleus mesencephalicus lateralis pars dorsalis following

18 auditory stimuli (Hamdi and Whitteridge, 1954; Harman and Phillips, 1967; but see Erulkar, 1955). Presumably after relaying in this nucleus, impulses pass to the nucleus ovoidalis of the same side and also to the contralateral side (Karten, 1966, 1967a; Harman and Phillips, 1967; but see Erulkar, 1955). From here they pass to the archistriatum (Phillips, 1966), via the paleostriatum augmentatum (Harman and Phillips, 1967), to end in the capsula occipitalis interna and medial caudal neostriatum (Erulkar, 1955; Harman and Phillips, 1967; Karten, 1967b, 1968). Impulses also reach the frontal neostriatum (Ilytchev, quoted by Schwartzkopff, 1968; Harman and Phillips, 1967) and possibly the hyperstriatal region (Adamo and King, 1967; Spooner and Winters, 1965), ectostriatum, and nucleus basalis (Naumow and Iljitschew, 1964; Schwartzkopff, 1968). Karten (1969) and Boord (1969) have recently reviewed the ascending pathways and both conclude that, in the pigeon at least, these pathways terminate predominantly in the mediocaudal neostriatum (field L of Rose).

Efferent fibers run in the acoustic nerve. They arise in the floor of the medulla, where they decussate and leave in the vestibular root (Boord, 1961). Their activation reduces auditory imput (Desmedt and Delwaide, 1963; Schwartzkopff, 1968).

**Vestibular impulses.** Impulses associated with the sense of balance are carried in the vestibular branch of the eighth nerve. The vestibular nerve is distributed to six main vestibular nuclei; the tangentialis, ventrolateralis (Deiter's nucleus), descendens, dorsomedialis, dorsolateralis, and superioris. Some fibers pass to the cerebellum. The superior and the dorsolateral nuclei also connect to the cerebellum. Their fibers pass to the central nuclei and the cortex after crossing in the lateral cerebellar commissure. Whitlock (1952) localized their termination to folia IV and X, including the auricle. The ventrolateral (Deiter's) nucleus gives both crossed and uncrossed fibers to the medial longitudinal fasciculus. Crossed and uncrossed ascending fibers end in the trochlear and oculomotor nuclei and in the reticular formation. Similar descending fibers reach the dorsal nucleus of the hypoglossal nerve and probably the motor neurons of the ventral horn of the spinal cord via the vestibulospinal tract (Sanders, 1929; Ariëns-Kappers et al. 1936; Levi-Montalcini, 1949).

**Gustatory impulses, proprioceptive impulses, and those associated with cutaneous sensation.** Birds have few taste buds (see Chapter 2). The facial nerve does not seem to carry any taste im-

pulses, these being carried in the glossopharyngeal nerve. The facial nerve does, however, have a small sensory nucleus. The ninth and tenth nerves supply afferent fibers to the large solitary nucleus, which because of its large size is thought to be associated with general visceral afferent input as well as taste. Some fibers run with the solitary nucleus before they terminate in the dorsolateral visceral sensory area of the medulla, and a few fibers from the ninth and tenth nerves terminate in the descending sensory nucleus of the fifth nerve (Ariëns-Kappers et al., 1936; Pearson, 1972).

Proprioceptive impulses from the jaw muscles are carried in the mesencephalic root of the fifth nerve. This has a characteristic mesencephalic termination, the development of which has been recently studied by Rogers and Cowan (1973). Large monopolar cells are scattered in the tectum and innervate muscle spindles, whereas their collaterals synapse on the motor neurons of the trigeminal supplying the jaw muscle. Manni et al. (1965) and Azzena and Palmieri (1967) have studied the physiology of these cells. Ganglion cells associated with the third, fourth, and sixth nerves may represent the proprioceptive input from the extrinsic eye muscle (Rogers, 1957).

Cutaneous impulses arrive mainly at the chief sensory nucleus of the trigeminal nerve but also in a descending root. The former receives impulses from those specialized sensory corpuscles (e.g., corpuscles of Grandry) distributed around the bill or beak. Zeigler and Witkovsky (1968) have studied the electrophysiological responses of the main sensory trigeminal nucleus to touch and pressure stimuli applied in the beak and orbit region of the pigeon. There was a dorsoventral topographic representation of mandibular, maxillary, and ophthalmic regions.

From the chief nucleus arises the quintofrontal tract, which after a partial decussation runs forward to the forebrain. A quintomesencephalic tract runs to the lateral mesencephalic nucleus and to the tectum after decussation (Ariëns-Kappers et al., 1936; Pearson, 1972).

The connections of the chief nucleus with the forebrain and the production of feeding deficits by lesions in this nucleus indicate an important role in feeding (Zeigler and Karten, 1973).

## Motor pathways

Besides the motor outflow from the brain, which leaves by way of descending tracts in the spinal cord, the cranial nerves carry a considerable motor supply to the extrinsic muscles of the eyes, the masticatory muscles, the secretory glands of the head region, the heart, and the alimentary tract.

The third, fourth, and sixth nerves supply the extrinsic muscles of the eye and certain adjacent muscles as already described. The third and fourth nerves arise from nuclei in the midbrain, whereas the sixth nerve arises from two nuclei in the medulla. These nuclei are acted on by vestibular impulses carried in the medial longitudinal fasciculus and by tectal impulses. The impulses are largely responsible, in conjunction with those coming from the cerebellum, for the fixation of the visual field during movement of the body. The nuclei of the nerves to the extrinsic eye muscles also receive proprioceptive impulses from muscle spindles within the muscles (Ariëns-Kappers et al., 1936; Pearson, 1972).

In addition to the chief nucleus of the third nerve (divided into three parts) there is an accessory (Edinger-Westphal) nucleus from which arise the preganglionic fibers supplying the ciliary ganglion and, via postganglionic fibers, the iris and choroid. This accessory nucleus receives tectal fibers, no doubt involved in the pupillary response to light.

From the two motor nuclei of the fifth nerve and the motor nucleus of the seventh nerve arise the neurons supplying the masticatory and other muscles of the head region. The ninth, tenth, eleventh, and twelfth nerves arise from a collection of motor nuclei in the medulla. Besides supplying both smooth and striated muscles, as described previously, the ninth and tenth nerves supply glands associated with the alimentary tract. Physiologically it is likely that neurons of the seventh and ninth nerves operate as a "salivary center" controlling the salivary glands of the head. Similarly, those neurons controlling heart rate and force are located in the dorsal motor nucleus of the vagus (tenth) nerve. More details of the control of salivation, cardiovascular, and respiratory systems and gut motility can be found in the relevant chapters of this book.

In attempts to understand the functioning of the various parts of the avian brain, numerous investigators have ablated various parts or stimulated them electrically. The interpretation of many of the observed responses in terms of specific nuclei or tracts is often difficult: for example, both eye and limb movements may be produced by stimulation of the cerebral hemisphere, tectum, or cerebellum. All these regions are involved in some way in the production or control of muscle movement, but stimulation experiments reveal little about their precise role.

The *cerebellum* seems to be involved in the regulation of muscle tone and the coordination of movement. After removal of the cerebellum the neck and leg muscles are subject to spasm, but the wing muscles are little affected. Head swaying and jerking uneven movements of the head occur when feeding. Damage to the vestibular nuclei on one side leads to a deviation of the eyes, rotation and lateral flexion of the head, and spiral rotation of the neck and trunk toward the side of the lesion. A diminution in tone of the limbs on the damaged side and an increase on the opposite side are produced. Rolling movements are frequently observed (Benjamins and Huizinga, 1927; Groebbels, 1928).

Åkerman (1966) produced threatening or defensive reactions in pigeons by stimulating the diencephalon or anterior hypothalamus. Putkonen (1967) made similar but not identical observations in the fowl; he was also able to produce fear and attacking reactions by stimulating areas of the forebrain. For further references, see Bolton (1971b) and Pearson (1972)

**Vocalization.** Production of song by stimulation of discrete brain areas in the bird has been an active field of recent research. The most effective point is located in the midbrain and spoken of as the torus semicircularis. In fact, most experimenters agree that the lowest threshold points from which song can be evoked by electrical stimulation lie in a nucleus that is found medial and adjacent to the nucleus mesencephalicus lateralis pars dorsalis (known to be an ascending auditory relay nucleus). This vocalization region, called the torus externus or nucleus intercollicularis, has been shown to produce song in the redwinged blackbird (Brown, 1969, 1971; Newman, 1972) and *Cortunix coturnix japonica* (Japanese quail) (Potash, 1970). Spectral analysis has been made of the calls, which were of the annoyance type. Other song regions were found in the hypothalamus, septum, and archistriatum.

# ELECTROENCEPHALOGRAPHY

Some aspects of the electroencephalography of the bird have been explored in recent years, particularly the actions of drugs on the electroencephalogram (EEG). The method involves the recording of a potential by electrodes placed in contact with the surface of the hemisphere in the "Wulst" region (the projection on the dorsal surface of the cerebral hemisphere formed by the underlying hyperstriatal regions), although electrodes have been placed in other positions. The indifferent electrode is usually attached to the comb.

20

Excited

Resting

Alert–resting

Drowsy

Deep

Paradoxical

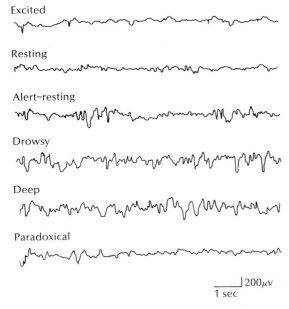

$$\overline{\qquad}|200\mu V$$
1 sec

1–7 EEG patterns during wakefulness and sleep in an adult hen. The EEG's were recorded from the Wulst region. Note that artifacts induced by eye movement were observed in the record taken during the excited state. (Reproduced with permission from Ookawa, 1972.)

A number of states can be distinguished on the basis of the EEG and these correlate well with behavioral changes (Figure 1–7). Most of the work has been done on the domestic fowl. Alert and sleep states are recognized; the former can be subdivided into two stages and the latter into three stages.

1. The alert excited stage is characterized by $20-50\mu V$, $30-60$ Hz waves.
2. The alert unexcited stage shows $50-150\mu V$, $17-24$ Hz waves.
3. Stage 1 sleep (an alert resting stage) is associated with desultory activities such as preening. The trace consists mainly of $50-150\mu V$, $17-24$ Hz waves in which are interspersed bursts of $200-300$ $\mu V$, $3-12$ Hz waves.
4. Stage 2 sleep is the beginning of true sleep. The bird crouches and the head droops. The EEG consists predominantly of $200-400$ $\mu V$, $6-12$ Hz waves with brief periods of slower ($3-4$ Hz) waves.
5. Stage 3 sleep represents sleeping activity in which the head is generally placed under the

wing and both eyes are closed. Most of the EEG activity is $200-400$ $\mu V$, $2-4$ Hz waves but bursts of 50 $\mu V$, $30-60$ Hz activity occur, probably representing paradoxical sleep. At such times twitching has been noticed. Episodes of paradoxical or fast sleep generally last about 6 sec.

To some extent the exact parameters of the wave activity as given above may vary depending on the investigator, the age of the bird, etc. Ookawa (1972b) has recently revised his previous classification of EEG activity in the fowl.

The frequency of EEG activity is reduced and the size increased by a reduction in the visual and auditory stimuli in the bird's environment. While it is asleep, stimuli insufficient to arouse the bird produce a reduction in size and an increase in the frequency of the EEG. Strong stimuli awaken the bird and EEG activity becomes fast and small (Key and Marley, 1962; Ookawa et al., 1962a, b; Ookawa and Gotoh 1965).

Before 2 months of age, the young of the domestic fowl show a slightly atypical EEG. At 1 day old the EEG of the alert excited stage exhibits 25 $\mu V$ and $30-60$ Hz waves whereas the alert unexcited EEG shows 25 $\mu V$ and $17-25$ Hz waves. Stage 3 sleep is characterized by 100 $\mu V$, $1.5-5$ Hz waves with fast sleep ($25\mu V$, $30-60$ Hz waves) bursts. These types of activity persist up to 1 month of age, at which time stage 1 and stage 2 sleep can be distinguished.

The electrical activity of the chick embryo has been reviewed by Corner et al. (1967) and that of the young adult by Corner et al. (1972).

Sugihara and Gotoh (1973) have compared the EEG recorded from a variety of forebrain areas and the optic tectum during arousal, slow wave sleep, and paradoxical sleep. No regular slow waves, such as are seen in the hippocampus of the mammal during arousal and paradoxical sleep, were observed in the hippocampus of chickens, nor did high-voltage fast waves appear in the archistriatum during arousal. Regular $9-13$ Hz waves appeared in the paleostriatum primitivum during slow wave sleep. Monophasic spikes were recorded in the optic tectum during the paradoxical sleep and were therefore associated with rapid eye movements.

## EEG in Abnormal States

**Nutritional deficiencies.** The effects of thiamine deficiency in the pigeon (Tokaji and Gerard, 1939; Swank and Jasper, 1942) and pyridoxine deficiency in the chick (Pomeroy and Welch, 1967) have been studied. Sheff and Tureen (1962) observed erratic bursts of high-voltage waves in encephalomalacic chicks.

**Hypothermia, hyperthermia, and hypoxia.** Hypothermia reduced wave amplitude (Peters *et al.*, 1961), whereas hyperthermia produced a variety of abnormalities before electrical activity disappeared (Peters *et al.* 1964). Hypoxia produced a brief period of higher amplitude activity before quiescence, whereas hypothermic hypoxia produced seizure patterns in the developing chick (Peters *et al.*, 1968; 1969; Peters and Hilgerford, 1971).

**Spontaneous, seizurelike discharges.** Some workers have recorded spontaneous spike discharge from bird brains (Tokaji and Gerard, 1939). In newly hatched chicks various periodic seizure like discharges have been seen. Negative–positive spike discharges, high-voltage rhythmic waves, domic waves, and mixed spike and dome waves were observed (Ookawa and Takagi, 1968).

**Catalepsy or hyposis.** After constraint for a period of minutes, chickens and adult fowls are overtaken by a trancelike state (Gilman *et al.*, 1950). During this cataleptic state the EEG shows 200–400 $\mu$ V, 2–3 Hz waves. Young birds are more easily induced to enter this state. The heart rate is lower and neck muscle electrical activity is decreased (Ookawa, 1972a).

**Spreading depression.** Direct current pulses applied to the exposed surface of the cerebral hemispheres, or even mechanical stimuli, produce an abolition of electrical activity after a latent period of about 90 sec. The effect may also be produced by microinjection of a 25% potassium chloride solution. Using this latter method, Shima *et al.* (1963) found that depression induced in the "Wulst" region of a pigeon spread throughout the hyperstriatum but only spread to the neostriatum on 60–70% of occasions and never to the paleostriatum and tegmentum. Block of the spread of depression probably occurred because of the fiber tracts separating these regions. Ookawa (1973a) records the EEG of the hen during spreading depression and reviews the literature on this subject and on other types of abnormal EEG.

### Effects of Drugs on the EEG

There is a considerable literature on the effects of drugs on the EEG, some of which is reviewed by Bolton (1971b). A number of substances when injected into chicks before the blood–brain barrier has developed, produce a sleeplike state with the appropriate EEG record. These include the catecholamines, noradrenaline, adrenaline, and dopamine; 5-hydroxytryptamine (5HT); and $\gamma$-aminobutyric acid (GABA). Several others produce arousal and excitement with fast, low-amplitude EEG waves. These include acetylcholine if given after atropine, lysergic acid diethylamide (LSD), psilocybin, mesacaline in high doses, amphetamines, and large doses of dopamine.

The actions of strychnine on the EEG have received considerable attention. The drug produces tonic convulsions in the chick (Spooner and Winters, 1966a) and EEG spikes (Garcia-Austt, 1954; Tuge *et al.*, 1960; Katori, 1962). Ookawa (1973b) observed 1–4 mV spikes on intravenous injection of strychnine in curarized adult hens or on its direct application. Such spikes were also recorded by electrodes inserted in the hyperstriatum, neostriatum, and ectostriatum but not from those in the paleostriatum (Ookawa, 1973c). Pentylenetetrazol acted similarly to strychnine in producing spikes (Ookawa, 1973d).

## PUTATIVE TRANSMITTERS

Whereas noradrenaline and acetylcholine are two substances that have been positively identified as transmitters released from peripheral nerve endings in mammals, the transmitters released in the central nervous system have not been positively identified in the fowl, although at a few identified synapses in the mammalian central nervous system the evidence implicating a particular transmitter substance is strong. The evidence that a given substance has a transmitter role must include its presence within the brain and supporting evidence that the enzymes which synthesize and degrade it are also present. However, uptake mechanisms may more commonly replace degrading enzymes as a method of synaptic inactivation. Some variation in the concentration of transmitter can be expected to exist between various parts of the brain on the grounds that a particular type of nerve is likely to be associated with certain fiber tracts or nuclei. This contrasts with a substance involved in a metabolic pathway, which can be expected to have a rather uniform distribution throughout the CNS. A release of the substance is to be expected during nerve activity and the amount released should be greater the more intense is nerve activity. The putative transmitter should have demonstrable pharmacologic activity; in particular, it should be able to mimic

22 the effects at a particular synapse of transmitter released by stimulating an identified nerve (however, access of artificially applied and nerve-released transmitter to the postsynaptic site may differ and this may in some instances mask a similarity of effect.). Substances reducing, enhancing, or modifying the effects of nerve-released transmitter should have similar effects on the response to artificially applied transmitter (access of modifying substance may again mask a basic similarity). In no case of a putative transmitter in the avian CNS have all these criteria been satisfied.

## The Transmitters

**Catecholamines.** The three important catecholamines found in the avian brain are noradrenaline, adrenaline, and dopamine. Although it seems likely that dopamine and noradrenaline may represent two types of nerve, adrenaline and noradrenaline may be interchangeable (Juorio and Vogt, 1970); i.e., they may be released in varying proportions by the same nerve endings and may act on the same receptors (DeSantis *et al.*, 1975).

Dopamine can be formed from the amino acid phenylalanine by the action of a hydroxylase and dopa decarboxylase. Hydroxylation is the rate-limiting step (see Chapter 12). Burack and Badger (1964) reported that these reactions occur in the embryonic primitive streak. Enemar *et al.* (1965) also found dopa decarboxylase activity in the sympathetic chain. Dopamine β-hydroxylase converts dopamine to noradrenaline and has been found in embryonic chick hearts by Ignarro and Shideman (1968). Phenylethanolamine-N-methyltransferase forms adrenaline and has been detected by Pohorecky *et al.* (1968) in hen brain. Monoamine oxidase, which is partly responsible for metabolizing catecholamines, is found in avian brain (e.g., Aprison *et al.*, 1964). It therefore seems that the enzymes responsible for synthesizing and degrading catecholamines are at least present in avian tissues, even if all of them have not yet been definitely demonstrated in avian brain. However, notwithstanding the presence of degrading enzymes, uptake of catecholamines may well be the most important method of synaptic inactivation.

The injection of catecholamines into the young chick (before the blood–brain barrier is mature,) produces quiescence. Typical sleep posture is assumed and the EEG changes to slow, large, wave activity (Zaimis, 1960; Key and Marley, 1962; Marley and Stephenson, 1970; Marley and Nistico, 1972). Dopamine, noradrenaline, and adrenaline have the same action as isoproterenol and several other sympathomimetic amines. The action does not seem to involve typical α and β receptors, for, although weakly antagonized by phenoxybenzamine, a number of other α- and β-blockers are ineffective even though they do have central actions of their own (Dewhurst and Marley, 1965a,b). Large doses of dopamine produce alerting and fast wave EEG's (Spooner and Winters, 1967a).

The levels of catecholamines in the different parts of the pigeon brain were measured by Juorio and Vogt (1967). Highest levels of dopamine occurred in the nucleus basalis, whereas very low levels occurred in the optic lobe, cerebellum, and spinal cord. These regions were also poor in adrenaline and noradrenaline, but the hypothalamus was the region richest in these two amines. The amount of adrenaline relative to noradrenaline was high compared with mammalian brains. Gunne (1962) obtained a value of 17% for the ratio of adrenaline to adrenaline plus noradrenaline. Juorio and Vogt (1970) confirmed this but showed that the ratio was very variable between species and even between breeds of fowl. Callingham and Sharman (1970) found that the amounts of dopamine, adrenaline, and noradrenaline increased with age as did the relative amount of adrenaline.

**5-Hydroxytryptamine.** 5-Hydroxytryptamine (or 5HT) is synthesized from tryptophan by the action of a hydroxylase and a decarboxylase. It is destroyed by an amine oxidase. These enzymes have been detected in pigeon brain (Aprison *et al.*, 1964; Gal and Marshall, 1964). The concentration of 5HT is highest in nucleus basalis and lowest in the cerebellum (Juorio and Vogt, 1967).

The effects of 5HT on the young chick may be sedation or alerting. Some authors observed that 5HT produced sleep (Hehman *et al.*, 1961; Spooner and Winters, 1967b), whereas others have thought that it produces alerting initially and then sedation (Dewhurst and Marley, 1965b). The alerting response is abolished by methysergide.

**Acetylcholine.** The concentration of acetylcholine in the various parts of the pigeon brain have been studied by Aprison and Takahashi (1965). Highest levels were found in the diencephalon–optic lobe, whereas lowest levels were found in the cerebellum. The enzyme synthesizing acetylcholine, choline acetylase, is present in avian brain and its activity is especially high in the optic lobes, with lower levels in the cerebellum and olfactory lobes (Hebb, 1955; Hebb and Ratković, 1962).

Cholinesterase activity is high in avian brain, even in the cerebellum (Aprison *et al.,* 1964).

When acetylcholine is given parenterally to young chicks they collapse and show gasping respiration and profuse salivation. To prevent these effects it is necessary to give atropine. Under these conditions acetylcholine produces alerting (Kramer and Seifter, 1966). Infused into the brain, carbachol (Marley and Seller, 1974a), an acetylcholine analog stable to choline esterase, and muscarine (Marley and Seller, 1972) produced arousal, although Spooner and Winters (1967b) observed that carbachol produced a slow wave EEG. Nicotine produced a sleeplike EEG (Marley and Seller, 1974b) when infused into the brain.

**Other substances.** Prostaglandins have been extracted from chick nervous tissue and have pharmacological effects if injected into young chicks (Horton, 1971). γ-aminobutyric acid (GABA) is present in chicken brain. GABA is formed by the action of glutamic acid decarboxylase, which is present in the chick embryo cerebellum. It is metabolized by GABA transaminase, which is also found (Kuriyama *et al.,* 1968), but uptake is probably the most important method of synaptic inactivation.

GABA, or its precursor glutamic acid, produced a state resembling natural sleep in chicks (Kramer and Seifter, 1966) and altered tectal electrical activity (Scholes and Roberts, 1964).

A number of amino acids, some of which have been suggested as being transmitters in the mammalian CNS, have been detected in hen brain (Frontali, 1964).

Further details of publications pertaining to putative transmitters, and in particular the effects of drugs in modifying their levels, can be found in Bolton (1971b) and Pearson (1972).

### The Blood—Brain Barrier

The popularity of the newly hatched or immature domestic fowl for the study of drug actions lies in the belief that although the chick is behaviorally mature, the ease with which various substances reach the nervous tissue of the brain has not yet declined to the level found in the adult bird. Here, as in adults of other vertebrates, it is found to be relatively difficult to exert effects on the brain following intravenous or systemic administration, so that we speak of a "blood–brain barrier." However, the young of many wild birds when hatched are much less "behaviorally mature" than the domestic chick. For this reason, results obtained on chicks cannot be extrapolated uncritically to other avian species.

The young chick when hatched is almost immediately capable of locomotion and feeding. Providing a sufficient supply of food is available, the chick can grow rapidly and satisfactorily in the absence of parenteral influences. Conditioned responses can be established before it is 10 days old (Marley and Morse, 1966). This behavioral maturity is reflected in the EEG. In the chick, recorded waves are smaller but do not differ much in frequency compared with those recorded from adults engaged in the same activities (Key and Marley, 1962). One minor difference is that it is apparently much harder to define transitional states between the alert and the deeply sleeping condition.

The evidence is that substances reaching the blood enter the brain more rapidly and attain higher concentrations there in the newly hatched chick than in the adult fowl. This applies to such electrolytes as chloride (Waelsch, 1955; Lajtha, 1957) and to various biologically active substances, such as noradrenaline (Spooner *et al.,* 1966; Spooner and Winters, 1966b), 5HT (Hanig and Seifter, 1968; Bulat and Supek, 1968), and GABA (Scholes and Roberts, 1964). After 4 weeks, however, the amounts entering the brain have declined to a level similar to that found in the adult. The behavioral effect of injected noradrenaline in the chick is the same as when it is given directly into the hypothalamus by microinjection and is the opposite to the effect it produces when given to an adult fowl or mammal (Marley and Stephenson, 1970).

### REFERENCES

Adamo, N. J., and R. L. King. (1967). Evoked responses in the chicken telencephalon to auditory, visual and tactile stimuli. *Exp. Neurol., 17,* 498.

Åkerman, B. (1966). Behavioural effects of electrical stimulation in the forebrain of the pigeon. II: Protective behaviour. *Behaviour, 26,* 339.

Akester, A. R., and S. P. Mann. (1969). Ultrastructure and innervation of the tertiary-bronchial unit in the lung of *Gallus domesticus. J. Anat., 105,* 202.

Akester, A. R., B. Akester, and S. P. Mann. (1969). Catecholamines in the avian heart. *J. Anat., 104,* 591.

Aprison, M. H., and R. Takahashi. (1965). Biochemistry of the avian central nervous system: II. 5-hydroxytryptamine, acetylcholine, 3,4, di-hydroxyphenylethylamine and norepinephrine in several discrete areas of the pigeon brain. *J. Neurochem., 12,* 221.

Aprison, M. H., R. Takahashi, and T. L. Folkerth. (1964). Biochemistry of the avian central nervous system: I. 5-Hydroxytryptophan decarboxylase, monoamine oxidase and choline acetylase-acetylcholinesterase systems in several discrete areas of the pigeon brain. *J. Neurochem., 11,* 341.

Ariëns-Kappers, C. U., G. C. Huber, and E. C. Crosby. (1936).

24

"The Comparative Anatomy of the Nervous System of Vertebrates Including Man," Vols. 1 and 2. New York: Macmillan.

Azzena. G. B., and G. Palmieri. (1967). Trigeminal monosynaptic reflex arc. Exp. Neurol., 18, 184.

Bang, B. G. (1960). Anatomical evidence for olfactory function in some species of birds. Nature, 188, 547.

Bang, B. G. (1971). Functional anatomy of the olfactory system in 23 orders of birds. Acta Anat., 79 (Suppl. 58), 1.

Banks, P., and D. Mayor. (1972). Intra-axonal transport in noradrenergic neurons in the sympathetic nervous system. In "Neurotransmitters and Metabolic Regulation," Vol. 36 (R. M. S. Smellie, Ed.). Biochemical Society Symposium, p. 133.

Barnikol, A. (1954). Zur morphologie des Nervus Trigeminus der Vogel unter besonderer Berucksightung der Accipitres, Cathartidae, Striges, and Passerformes. Z. Wiss. Zool., 157, 285.

Belekhova, M. G. (1968). Subcortical-cortical relationships in birds. Neurosci. Trans., 2, 195.

Benjamins, C. E., and E. Huizinga. (1927). Untersuchungen über die funktion des vestibularapparates der Taube. Arch. Ges. Physiol. (Pflügers), 217, 105.

Bennett, T. (1969). Nerve-mediated excitation and inhibition of the smooth muscle cells of the avian gizzard. J. Physiol. (London), 204, 669.

Bennett, T. (1971). The adrenergic innervation of the pulmonary vasculature, the lung and the thoracic aorta and on the presence of aortic bodies in the domestic fowl (Gallus gallus domesticus L.). Z. Zellforsch., 114, 117.

Bennett, T. (1974). The peripheral and autonomic nervous systems. In "Avian Biology," Vol. 4 (D. S. Farner and J. R. King, Eds.). New York: Academic Press, p. 1.

Bennett, T., G. Burnstock, J. L. S. Cobb, and T. Malmfors. (1970). An ultrastructural and histochemical study of the short-term effects of 6-hydroxydopamine on adrenergic nerves in the domestic fowl. Brit. J. Pharmacol., 38, 802.

Bennett, T., and T. Malmfors. (1970). The adrenergic nervous system of the domestic fowl (Gallus domesticus L.). Z. Zellforsch., 106, 22.

Bennett, T., T. Malmfors, and J. L. S. Cobb. (1973a). A fluorescent histochemical study of the degeneration and regeneration of noradrenergic nerves in the chick following treatment with 6-hydroxydopamine. Z. Zellforsch., 142, 103.

Bennett, T., J. L. S. Cobb, and T. Malmfors. (1973b). Fluorescent histochemical and ultrastructural observations on the effects of intravenous injections of vinblastin on noradrenergic nerves. Z. Zellforsch., 141, 517.

Bolton, T. B. (1967). Intramural nerves in the ventricular myocardium of the domestic fowl and other animals. Brit. J. Pharmacol., 31, 253.

Bolton, T. B. (1971a). The structure of the nervous system. In "Physiology and Biochemistry of the Domestic Fowl" (D. J. Bell and B. M. Freeman, Eds.). New York: Academic Press, p. 641.

Bolton, T. B. (1971b) The physiology of the nervous system. In "Physiology and Biochemistry of the Domestic Fowl" (D. J. Bell and B. M. Freeman, Eds.). New York: Academic Press, p. 675.

Bolton, T. B., and W. C. Bowman. (1969). Adrenoreceptors in the cardiovascular system of the domestic fowl. Eur. J. Pharmacol., 5, 121.

Bolton, T. B., and C. Raper. (1966). Innervation of domestic fowl and guinea pig ventricles. J. Pharm. Pharmacol., 18, 192.

Boord, R. L. (1961). The efferent cochlear bundle in the caiman and pigeon. Exp. Neurol., 3, 225.

Boord, R. L. (1965). Efferent projections of cochlear nuclei in the pigeon. Amer. Zool., 5, 669.

Boord, R. L. (1968). Ascending projections of the primary cochlear nuclei and nucleus laminaris in the pigeon. J. Comp. Neurol., 133, 523.

Boord, R. L. (1969). The anatomy of the avian auditory system. Ann. N.Y. Acad. Sci., 167, 186.

Boord, R. L., and G. L. Rasmussen. (1963). Projection of the cochlear and lagenar nerves on the cochlear nuclei of the pigeon. J. Comp. Neurol., 120, 463.

Bowman, W. C. (1959). The effects of isoprenaline on the blood flow through individual skeletal muscles of the cat. J. Pharm. Pharmacol., 11, 143.

Bowman, W. C., and S. D. Everett. (1964). An isolated parasympathetically-innervated oesophagus preparation from the chick. J. Pharm. Pharmacol., 16 (Suppl.) 72T.

Bowman, W. C., and I. G. Marshall. (1971). Muscle. In "Physiology and Biochemistry of the Domestic Fowl" (D. J. Bell and B. M. Freeman, Eds.). New York: Adademic Press, p. 707.

Bremer, F., R. S. Dow, and G. Moruzzi. (1939). Physiological analysis of the general cortex in reptiles and birds. J. Neurophysiol., 2, 473.

Brodal A., K. Kristiansen, and J. Jansen. (1950). Experimental demonstration of a pontine homologue in birds. J. Comp. Neurol., 92, 23.

Brown, G. L. (1937). Transmission at nerve endings by acetylcholine. Physiol. Rev., 17, 485.

Brown, J. L. (1969). The control of avain vocalisation by the central nervous system. In "Bird Vocalisations" (R. A. Hinde, Ed.). Cambridge: Cambridge University Press, p. 79.

Brown, J. L. (1971). An exploration study of vocalisation areas in the brain of the redwinged blackbird (Angelaius phoeniceus). Behaviour, 39, 91.

Brown, C. M., V. Molony, A. S. King, and R. D. Cook. (1972). Fibre size and conduction velocity in the vagus of the domestic fowl (Gallus domesticus) Acta. Anat., 83, 451.

Bulat, M., and Z. Supek. (1968). Passage of 5-hydroxytryptamine through the blood — brain barrier, its metabolism in the brain and elimination of 5-hydroxyindolacetic acid from the brain tissue. J. Neurochem., 15, 383.

Burack, W. R., and A. Badger. (1964). Sequential appearance of dopa decarboxylase, dopamine β-oxidase and norepinephrine N-methyltransferase activities in the embryonic chick. Fed. Proc., 23, 561.

Burger, R. E., and M. R. Fedde. (1964). Physiological and pharmacological factors which influence the incidence of acute pulmonary alterations following vagotomy in the domestic cock. Poultry Sci., 43, 384.

Burnstock, G. (1969). Evolution of the autonomic innervation of visceral and cardiovascular systems. Pharmacol. Rev., 21, 247.

Callingham, B. A., and D. F. Sharman (1970). The concentration of catecholamines in the brain of the domestic fowl (Gallus domesticus). Brit. J. Pharmacol., 40, 1.

Calvin, A. (1960). Olfactory discrimination. Science, 131, 1265.

Carpenter, F. G., and R. M. Bergland. (1957). Excitation and conduction in immature nerve fibres of the developing chick. Am. J. Physiol., 190, 371.

Clearwaters, K. (1954). Regeneration of the spinal cord of the chick. J. Comp. Neurol., 101, 317.

Cobb, S. (1960a). A note on the size of the avian olfactory bulb. Epilepsia, 1, 394.

Cobb, S. (1960b). Observations on the comparative anatomy of the avian brain. Perspect. Biol. Med., 3, 383.

Cohen, D. H. (1967a). Visual intensity discriminiation in pigeons following unilateral and bilateral tectal lesions. J. Comp. Physiol. Psychol., 63, 172.

Cohen, D. H. (1967b). The hyperstriatal region of the avian forebrain. A lesion study of possible functions including its role in cardiac and respiratory conditioning. J. Comp. Neurol., 131, 559.

Cook, R. D., and A. S. King. (1970). Observations on the ultrastructure of the smooth muscle and its innervation in the avian lung. J. Anat., 106, 273.

Cords, E. (1904). Beiträge zur Lehre vom Kopfnervensystem der Vögel. Anat. Hefte., 26, 49.

Corner, M. A., W. L. Bakhuis, and C. van Wingerden. (1972). Sleep and wakefulness during early life in the domestic chicken and their relationship to hatching and embryonic mortality. In "Prenatal Ontogeny of the Central Nervous System and Behaviour" (Gottlieb G., Ed.). Chicago: University of Chicago Press.

Corner, M. A., J. P. Schadé, J. Sedláček, R. Stoeckart, and A. P. C. Bot. (1967). Developmental patterns in the central nervous system of birds. I. Electrical activity in the cerebral hemisphere, optic lobe & cerebellum. *Prog. Brain Res., 26,* 145.

Cowan, W. M., L. Adamson, and T. P. S. Powell, (1961). An experimental study of the avian visual system. *J. Anat., 95,* 545.

Dale, H. H. (1937). The transmission of nervous effects by acetylcholine. *The Harvey Lectures, 32,* 229.

de Anda, G. and M. A. Rebollo. (1967). The neuromuscular spindles in the adult chicken. 1. Morphology. *Acta Anat., 67,* 437.

DeSantis, V. P., W. Längsfeld, R. Lindmar, and K. Löffelholz. (1975). Evidence for noradrenaline and adrenaline as sympathetic transmitters in the chicken *Brit. J. Pharmacol., 55,* 345.

Desmedt, J. E., and P. J. Delwaide. (1963) Neuronal inhibition in a bird. Effect of strychnine and picrotoxin. *Nature, 200,* 585.

Dewhurst, W. G., and E. Marley. (1965a). Methods for quantifying behaviour and cerebral electrical activity and the effect of drugs under controlled conditions. *Brit. J. Pharmacol., 25,* 671.

Dewhurst, W. G., and E. Marley. (1965b). The effects of $\alpha$-methyl derivatives of noradrenaline, phenylethylamine and tryptamine on the central nervous system of the chicken. *Brit. J. Pharmacol., 25,* 682.

Dorward, P. K. (1970a). Response patterns of cutaneous mechanoreceptors in the domestic duck. *Comp. Biochem. Physiol., 35,* 729.

Dorward, P. K. (1970b). Response characteristics of muscle afferents in the domestic duck. *J. Physiol. (London), 211,* 1.

Dorward, P. K., and A. K. McIntyre. (1971). Responses of vibration-sensitive receptors in the interosseous region of the duck's hind limb. *J. Physiol. (London), 219,* 77.

Enemar, A., Falck, and R. Håkanson. (1965). Observations on the appearance of norepinephrine in the sympathetic nervous system of the chick embryo. *Devel. Biol., 11,* 268.

Erulkar, S. D. (1955). Tactile and auditory areas in the brain of the pigeon. *J. Comp. Neurol., 103,* 421.

Evans, H. E. (1969). Anatomy of the budgerigar. In "Diseases of Cage and Aviary Birds" (M. L. Petrack, Ed.). Philadelphia: Lea and Febiger, p. 45.

Everett, S. D. (1966). Pharmacological responses of the isolated oesophagus and crop of the chick. In "Physiology of the Domestic Fowl" (C. Horton-Smith and E. C. Amoroso, Eds.). Edinburgh: Oliver and Boyd, p. 261.

Everett, S. D. (1968). Pharmacological responses of the isolated innervated intestine and rectal caecum of the chick. *Brit. J. Pharmacol., 33,* 342.

Everett, S. D., and S. P. Mann. (1967). Catecholamine release by histamine from the isolated intestine of the chick. *Eur. J. Pharmacol., I,* 310.

Freusberg, A. (1874). Reflex bewegungen beim Hunde. *Arch. Ges. Physiol. (Pflügers), 9,* 358.

Frontali, (1964). Brain glutamic acid decarboxylase and synthesis of $\gamma$-aminobutyric acid in vertebrate and invertebrate species. In "Comparative Neurochemistry" (D. Richter, Ed.), *Proc. 5th Intl. Neurochem. Symp.* Oxford: Pergamon Press, p. 185.

Gal, E. M., and F. D. Marshal. (1964). The hydroxylation of tryptophan by pigeon brain *in vitro. Prog. Brain Res., 8,* 56.

Garcia-Austt, E. (1954). Development of electrical activity in cerebral hemispheres of the chick embryo. *Proc. Soc. Exp. Biol. Med., 86,* 348.

Gentle, M. J. (1974). Using arousal changes in electroencephalogram to measure taste sensitivity in the chicken. *J. Physiol. (London), 244,* 9P.

Gilman, T. T., F. L. Marcuse, and A. U. Moore. (1950). Animal hypnosis: A study in the induction of tonic immobility in chickens. *J. Comp. Physiol. Psychol., 43,* 99.

Goltz, F., and J. R. Evald. (1896). Der Hund mit verkurzten Ruckenmark. *Arch. Ges. Physiol. (Pflugers), 63,* 362.

Gossrau, R. (1968). Über das Reizleitungssystem der Vögel. *Histochemie, 13,* 111.

Graf, W. (1956). Caliber spectra of nerve fibers in the pigeon *(Columba domestica). J. Comp. Neurol., 105,* 355.

Gregory, J. E. (1973). An electrophysiological investigation of the receptor apparatus of the duck's bill. *J. Physiol. (London), 229,* 151.

Groebbels, F. (1928). Die Lage und Bewegungsreflex der Vögel. *Arch. Ges. Physiol. (Pflügers), 218,* 198.

Groth, H. P. (1972). Licht-und fluoreszenzmikroskopische Untersuchungen zur Innervation des Luftsacksystems der Vögel. *Z. Zellforsch., 127,* 87.

Gunne, L. M. (1962). Relative adrenaline content in brain tissue. *Acta Physiol. Scand., 56,* 324.

Hamburger, V. (1955). Regeneration in the central nervous system of reptiles and birds. (W. F. Windle, Ed.). Springfield, Ill.: Charles C. Thomas, Chapter 3.

Hamdi, J. A., and D. Whitteridge. (1954). The representation of the retina on the optic tectum of the pigeon. *Quart. J. Exp. Physiol., 39,* 111.

Hanig, J. P., and J. Seifter. (1968). Amines in the brain of neonate chicks after parenteral injection of biogenic and other amines. *Fed. Proc., 27,* 651.

Harman, A. L., and R. E. Phillips. (1967). Responses in the avian midbrain, thalamus and forebrain evoked by click stimuli. *Exp. Neurol., 18,* 276.

Hebb, C. O. (1955). Choline acetylase in mammalian and avian sensory systems. *Quart. J. Exp. Physiol., 40,* 176.

Hebb, C. O., and D. Ratković. (1964). Choline acetylase in the evolution of the brain in vertebrates. In "Comparative Neurochemistry" (D. Richter, Ed.), *Proc. 5th Intl. Neurochem. Symp.* Oxford: Pergamon Press, p. 347.

Hehman, K. N., A. R. Vonderahe, and J. J. Peters. (1961). Effect of serotonin on the behavior, electrical activity in the brain, seizure threshold in the newly hatched chick. *Neurology, 11,* 1011.

Hess, A. (1970). Vertebrate slow muscle fibres. *Physiol. Rev., 50,* 40.

Hess, A., G. Pilar, and J. N. Weakly. (1969). Correlation between transmission and structure in avian ciliary ganglion synapses. *J. Physiol. (London), 202,* 339.

Hodos, W., and H. J. Karten. (1966). Brightness and pattern discrimination deficits in the pigeon after lesions of nucleus rotundus. *Exp. Brain Res., 2,* 151.

Hodos, W., H. J. Karten, and J. C. Bonbright. (1973). Visual intensity and pattern discrimination after lesions of the thalamofugal visual pathway in pigeons. *J. Comp. Neurol., 148,* 447.

Holden, A. L. (1968a). The field potential profile during activation of the avian optic tectum. *J. Physiol. (London), 194,* 75.

Holden, A. L. (1968b) Types of unitary response and correlation with the field potential profile during activation of the avian optic tectum. *J. Physiol. (London), 194,* 91.

Holden, A. L., and T. P. S. Powell. (1972). The functional organisation of the isthmo-optic nucleus in the pigeon. *J. Physiol. (London), 223,* 419.

Horton, E. W. (1971). Prostaglandins. In "Physiology and Biochemistry of Domestic Fowl," Vol. 1 (D. J. Bell and B. M. Freeman, Eds.). New York: Academic Press, p. 589.

Hsieh, T. M. (1951). The sympathetic and parasympathetic nervous systems of the domestic fowl. Ph.D. thesis, University of Edinburgh, Endinburgh, Scotland.

Huber, J. F. (1936). Nerve roots and nuclear groups in the spinal cord of the pigeon. *J. Comp. Neurol., 65,* 43.

Ignarro, L. J., and F. E. Shideman. (1968). Appearance and concentrations of catecholamines and their biosynthesis in the embryonic and developing chick. *J. Pharmacol. Exp. Ther., 159,* 38.

Imhof, G. (1905). Anatomie und Entwicklungsgeschichte des Lumbalmarkes bei den Vögeln *Archiv. Mikroskop. Anat. Entw. Mech., 65,* 98.

Jones, A. W., and R. Levi-Montalcini. (1958). Patterns of differentiation of the nerve centers and fiber tracts of the avian cerebral hemispheres. *Arch. Ital. Biol., 96,* 231.

Jones, D. R., and K. Johansen. (1972). The blood vascular system of birds. In "Avian Biology," Vol. 2 (D. S. Farner and J. R. King, Eds.). New York: Academic Press, p. 158.

Jukes, M. G. M. (1971). In "Biochemistry and Physiology of the Domestic Fowl," Vol. 1 (D. J. Bell and B. M. Freeman, Eds.) New York Academic Press, p. 171.

Jungherr, E. (1945). Certain nuclear groups of the avian mesencephalon. *J. Comp. Neurol., 82,* 55.

Jungherr, E. (1969). The neuroanatomy of the domestic fowl *(Gallus domesticus). Avian Diseases,* Special Issue, April 1969.

26

Juorio, A. V., and M. Vogt. (1967). Monoamines and their metabolites in the avian brain. *J. Physiol. (London), 189,* 489.

Juorio, A. V., and M. Vogt. (1970). Adrenaline in bird brain. *J. Physiol. (London), 209,* 757.

Karten, H. J. (1963). Ascending pathways from the spinal cord in the pigeon *(Columba livia). Proc. 16th Intl. Cong. Zool., 2,* 23.

Karten, H. J. (1965). Projections of the optic tectum of the pigeon *(Columba livia). Anat. Rec., 151,* 369.

Karten, H. J. (1966). Efferent projections of the nucleus mesencephalicus lateralis, pars dorsalis (MLD) in the pigeon *(Columba livia). Anat. Rec., 154,* 365.

Karten, H. J. (1967a). The organization of the ascending auditory pathway in the pigeon *(Columba livia).* 1. Diencephalic projections of the inferior colliculus (nucleus mesencephalicus lateralis pars dorsalis). *Brain Res., 6,* 409.

Karten, H. J. (1967b). Telencephlic projections of the nucleus ovoidalis in the pigeon *(Columba livia). Anat. Rec., 157,* 268.

Karten, H. J. (1968). The ascending auditory pathway in the pigeon. II. Telencephalic projections of the nucleus ovoidalis thalami. *Brain Res., 11,* 134.

Karten, H. J. (1969). The organization of the avian telencephalon and some speculations on the phylogeny of amniote telencephalon. *Ann. N.Y. Acad. Sci., 167,* 164.

Karten, H. J., and W. Hodos. (1967). "A Stereotaxic Atlas of the Brain of the Pigeon *(Columba livia)."* Baltimore: Johns Hopkins Press.

Karten, H. J., and W. J. M. Nauta. (1968). Organization of retinothalamic projections in the pigeon and owl. *Anat. Rec., 160,* 373.

Karten, H. J., and A. M. Revzin. (1966). The afferent connections of the nucleus rotundus in the pigeon. *Brain Res., 2,* 368.

Karten, H. J., W. Hodos, W. J. H. Nauta, and A. M. Revzin. (1973). Neural connections of the "Visual Wulst" of the avian telencephalon. Experimental studies in the pigeon *(Columba livia)* and owl *(Speotyto cunicularia). J. Comp. Neurol., 150,* 253.

Katori, M. (1962). The development of the spontaneous electrical activity in the brain of a chick embryo and the effects of several drugs on it. *Jap. J. Pharmacol., 12,* 9.

Key, B. J., and E. Marley. (1962). The effect of the sympathomimetic amines on behavior and electrocortical activity of the chicken. *Electroenceph. Clin. Neurophysiol., 14,* 90.

King, A. S., and V. Molony. (1971). The anatomy of respiration In "Physiology and Biochemistry of the Domestic Fowl" (D. J. Bell and B. M. Freeman, Eds.). New York: Academic Press, p. 93.

Kissling, G., K. Reutter, G. Sieber, H. Nguyen-Duong, and R. Jacob. (1972). Negative Inotropic von endogenem Acetylcholin bein Katzen-und Hühnerventrikelmyokard. *Pflügers Arch., 333,* 35.

Knowlton, V. Y. (1964). Abnormal differentiation of embryonic avian brain centres associated with unilateral anophthalmia. *Acta Anat., 58,* 222.

Kramer, S. Z., and J. Seifter. (1966). The effects of GABA and biogenic amines on behavior and brain electrical activity in chicks. *Life Sci., 5,* 527.

Kuriyama, K., B. Sisken, J. Ito, D. G. Simonsen, B. Haber, and E. Roberts. (1968). The γ-aminobutyric acid system in the developing chick embryo cerebellum. *Brain Res., 11,* 412.

Lajtha, A. (1957). The development of the blood–brain barrier *J. Neurochem., 1,* 216.

Landmesser, L., and G. Pilar. (1970). Selective reinnervation of the cell populations in the adult pigeon ciliary ganglion. *J. Physiol. (London), 211,* 203.

Landmesser, L., and G. Pilar. (1972). The onset and development of transmission in the chick ciliary ganglion. *J. Physiol. (London), 222,* 691.

Larsell, O. (1948). The development and subdivision of the cerebellum of birds. *J. Comp. Neurol., 89,* 123.

Lasjewski, R. C. (1972). Respiratory function in birds. In "Avian Biology," Vol. 2. (D. S. Farner and J. R. King, Eds.). New York: Academic Press, p. 288.

Lavail, J. H., and W. M. Cowan. (1971a). The development of the chick optic tectum. I Normal morphology and cytoarchitectronic development. *Brain Res., 28,* 391.

Lavail, J. H., and W. M. Cowan. (1971b). The development of the chick optic tectum. II Autoradiographic studies. *Brain Res., 28,* 421.

Leitner, L. -M., and M. Roumy. (1974a). Mechanosensitive units in the upper bill and in the tongue of the domestic duck. *Pflügers Arch., 346,* 141.

Leitner, L. -M., and M. Roumy. (1974b). Thermosensitive units in tongue and in the skin of the duck's bill. *Pflügers Arch., 346,* 151.

Levi-Montalcini, R. (1949). The development of the acousticovestibular centers in the chick embryo in the absence of the afferent root fibers and of descending fiber tracts. *J. Comp. Neurol., 91,* 209.

Levi-Montalcini, R. (1950). The origin and development of the visceral system in the spinal cord of the chick. *J. Morphol., 86,* 253.

Loewi, O. (1921) Über humorale Übertragbarkeit der Herznervenwirkung. *Arch. Ges. Physiol. (Pflügers), 189,* 239.

Manni, E., G. M. Azzena, and R. Bortolani. (1965). Jaw muscle proprioception and mesencephalic trigeminal cells in birds. *Exp. Neurol., 12,* 320.

Marko, P., and M. Cuénod, (1973). Contribution of the nerve cell body to renewal of axonal and synaptic glycoproteins in the pigeon visual system. *Brain Res., 62,* 419.

Marley, E., and W. H. Morse. (1966). Operant conditioning in the newly hatched chicken. *J. Exp. Anal. Behav., 9,* 95.

Marley, E., and G. Nistico. (1972). Effects of catecholamines and adenosine derivatives given into the brain of fowls. *Brit. J. Pharmacol., 46,* 619.

Marley, E., and T. J. Seller. (1972). Effects of muscarine given into the brain of fowls. *Brit. J. Pharmacol., 44,* 413.

Marley, E., and T. J. Seller. (1974). Effects of cholinomimetic agents given into the brain of fowls. *Brit. J. Pharmacol., 51,* 347.

Marley, E., and T. J. Seller. (1974). Effects of nicotine given into the brain of fowls. *Brit. J. Pharmacol., 51,* 335.

Marley, E., and J. D. Stephenson. (1970). Effects of catecholamines infused into the brain of young chickens. *Brit. J. Pharmacol., 40,* 639.

Martin, A. R., and G. Pilar. (1963a). Dual mode of synaptic transmission in the avian ciliary ganglion. *J. Physiol. (London), 168,* 443.

Martin, A. R., and G. Pilar. (1963b). Transmission through the ciliary ganglion of the chick. *J. Physiol. (London), 168,* 464.

Martin, A. R., and Pilar. (1964a). An analysis of electical coupling at synapses in the avian ciliary ganglion. *J. Physiol. (London), 171,* 454.

Martin, A. R., and G. Pilar. (1964b). Quantal components of the synaptic potential in the ciliary ganglion of the chick. *J. Physiol. (London), 175,* 1.

Martin, A. R., and G. Pilar. (1964c). Presynaptic and postsynaptic events during posttetanic potentiation and facilitation in the avian ciliary ganglion. *J. Physiol. (London), 175,* 17.

Marwitt, R., G. Pilar, and J. N. Weakly. (1971). Characterization of two ganglion cell populations in avian ciliary ganglion. *Brain Res., 25,* 317.

Mayr, R. (1968). Morphologische und physiologische Untersuchungen über den aktiven Bewegungsapparat der Nickhaut des Huhnes. *Gegenbaurs Morphol. Jb., 112,* 113.

McGill, J. J. (1964). Organisation within the central and centrifugal fiber pathways in the avian visual system. *Nature (London), 204,* 395.

McGill, J. J., T. P. S. Powell, and W. M. Cowan. (1966). The retinal representation upon the optic tectum and isthmo-optic nucleus in the pigeon. *J. Anat., 100,* 5.

McLelland, J., R. D. Cook, and A. S. King. (1972). Nerves in the exchange area of the avian lung. *Acta. Anat., 83,* 7.

Meier, R. E. (1973). Autoradiographic evidence for a direct retinohypothalamic projection in the avain brain. *Brain Res., 53* 417.

Michaelsen, W. J. (1959). Procedure for studying olfactory discrimination in pigeons. *Science, 130,* 630.

Moruzzi, G. (1947). Tectal and bulbopontine eyelid reflexes and mechanism of the sleeping attitude of the acute thalamic pigeon. *J. Neurophysiol., 10,* 415.

Naumow, N. P., and W. D. Iljitschew. (1964). Klanganalyse und Grosshirn der Vögel. *Naturwissenchaften, 51,* 644.

Newman, J. D. (1972). Midbrain control of vocalization in red-winged blackbirds *(Agelaius phoeniceus) Brain Res., 48, 227*

Ohashi, H., and A. Ohga. (1967). Transmission of excitation from parasympathetic nerve to smooth muscle. *Nature* (London), *216,* 291.

Ookawa, T. (1972a). Polygraphic recording during adult hen hypnosis. *Poultry Sci., 51,* 853.

Ookawa, T. (1972b). Avian wakefulness and sleep on the basis of recent electroencephalographic observations. *Poultry Sci., 51,* 1565.

Ookawa, T. (1973a). Notes of abnormal electroencephalograms in the telencephalon of the chicken and pigeon. *Poultry Sci., 52,* 182.

Ookawa, T. (1973b). Effect of strychnine on the electroencephalogram recorded from the Wulst of curarized adult chickens. *Poultry Sci., 52,* 1090.

Ookawa, T. (1973c). Effect of intravenously administered strychnine on the EEG recorded from the deep structure of the adult chicken telencephalon. *Poultry Sci., 52,* 806.

Ookawa, T. (1973d). Effect of some convulsant drugs on the electroencephalogram recorded from the Wulst of the adult chicken and pigeon under curarized conditions. *Poultry Sci., 52,* 1704.

Ookawa, T., and J. Gotoh. (1965). Electroencephalogram of the chicken recorded from the skull under various conditions. *J. Comp. Neurol., 124,* 1.

Ookawa, T., and K. Takagi. (1968). Electroencephalograms of free behavioural chicks at various developmental ages. *Jap. J. Physiol., 18,* 87.

Ookawa, T., J. Gotoh, T. Kumazawa, and K. Takagi. (1962). Electroencephalogram of chickens. *Proc. 53rd Meeting Jap. Soc. Vet. Sci., Jap. J. Vet. Sci., 24* (Suppl.), 438.

Oscarsson, O., I. Rosen, and N. Uddenberg. (1963). Organisation of the ascdning tracts in the spinal cord of the duck. *Acta Physiol. Scand., 59,* 143.

Page, S. G. (1969). Structure and some contractile properties of fast and slow muscles of the chicken. *J. Physiol. (London), 205,* 131.

Pearson, R. (1972). "The Avian Brain." New York: Academic Press.

Peters, J. J., and E. J. Hilgeford. (1971). EEG episodes of rhythmic waves and seizure patterns following hypothermic hypoxia in chick embryo. *Electroenceph. Clin. Neurophysiol., 31,* 631.

Peters, J. J., T. P. Bright, and A. R. Vonderahe. (1968). Electroencephalographic studies of survival following hypothermic hypoxia in developing chicks. *J. Exp. Zool., 167,* 179.

Peters, J. J., C. J. Cusick, and A. R. Vonderahe. (1961). Electrical studies of hypothermic effects on the eye, cerebrum and skeletal muscles of the developing chick. *J. Exp. Zool., 148,* 31.

Peters, J. J., A. R. Vonderahe, and E. J. Hilgeford. (1969). Electroencephalographic episodes of 1 to 7 per second rhythmic waves following hypothermic hypoxia in developing chicks. *J. Exp. Zool., 170,* 427.

Peters, J. J., A. R. Vonderahe, and J. J. McDonough. (1964). Electrical changes in brain and eye of the developing chick during hyperthermia. *Am. J. Physiol., 207,* 260.

Phillips, R. D. (1966). Evoked potential study of connections of archistriatum and caudal neostriatum. *J. Comp. Neurol., 127,* 89.

Pilar, G., and P. C. Vaughan. (1969). Electrophysiological investigations of the pigeon iris neuromuscular junctions. *Comp. Biochem. Physiol., 29,* 51.

Pohorecky, L. A., M. J. Zigmond, H. J. Karten, and R. J. Wurtman. (1968). Phenylethanolamine-*N*-methyltransferase activity (PNMT) in mammalian, avian and reptilian brain. *Fed. Proc., 27,* 239.

Pomeroy, L. R., and A. J. Welch. (1967). Computer assisted electroencephalograph analysis of chick pyridoxine deficiency states. Tehcnical Report 36, The University of Texas, Austin, p. 1.

Popa, G., and F. Popa. (1933). Certain functions of the midbrain in pigeons. *Proc. Roy. Soc. (London), B, 113,* 191.

Potash, L. M. (1970). Neuroanatomical regions relevant to production and analysis of vocalisation within the avian torus semicircularis. *Experientia, 26,* 1104.

Powell, T. P. S., and W. M. Cowan. (1961). The thalamic projection upon the telencephalon in the pigeon *(Columba livia). J. Anat., 95,* 78.

Putkonen, P. T. S. (1967). Electrical stimulation of the avian brain. *Ann. Acad. Sci. Fenn. Ser. A.V., 130,* 1.

Revzin, A. M., and H. Karten. (1967). Rostral projections of the optic tectum and the nucleus rotundus in the pigeon. *Brain Res., 3,* 264.

Richards, S. A. (1971). Brain stem control of polypnoea in the chicken and pigeon. *Resp. Physiol., 11,* 315.

Rogers, K. T. (1957). Ocular muscle proprioceptive neurons in the developing chick. *J. Comp. Neurol., 107,* 427.

Rogers, L. A., and W. M. Cowan. (1973). The development of the mesencephalic nucleus of the trigeminal nerve in the chick. *J. Comp. Neurol., 147,* 291.

Sammartino, U. (1933). Sugli animali a midolla spinale accrociato *Arch. Farmacol. Sper., 55,* 219.

Sanders E. B. (1929). A consideration of certain bulbar, midbrain and cerebellarcenters and fiber tracts in birds. *J. Comp. Neurol., 49,* 155.

Sato, H., A. Ohga, and Y. Nakazato. (1970). The excitatory and inhibitory innervation of the stomachs of the domestic fowl. *Jap. J. Pharmacol., 20,* 382.

Scholes, N. W., and E. Roberts. (1964). Pharmacological studies of the optic system of the chick: Effect of $\gamma$-aminobutyric acid and pentobarbital. *Biochem. Pharmacol., 13,* 1319.

Schwartzkopff, J. (1968). In "Hearing Mechanisms in Vertebrates" (A.V.S. de Reuck and J. Knight, Eds.). *CIBA Foundation Symposium.* London: Churchill, p. 41.

Schwartzkopff, J. (1974). Mechanoreception. In "Avian Biology," Vol. 3 (D. S. Farner and J. R. King, Eds.). New York: Academic Press, p. 417.

Senglaub, K. (1963). Das Kleinhirn der Vögel in Beziehung zu phylogenetischer Stellung, Lebensweise and Körpergrosse. *Z. Wiss. Zool. Leipzig, 169,* 1.

Sheff, A. G., and L. L. Tureen. (1962). EEG studies of normal and encephalomalacia chicks. *Proc. Soc. Exp. Biol. Med., 111,* 407.

Shima, I., E. Fifkova, and J. Bureš. (1963). Limits of spreading depression in pigeon striatum. *J. Comp. Neurol., 121,* 485.

Sjöstrand, N. O. (1965). The adrenergic innervation of the vas deferens and the accessory male genital glands. *Acta Physiol. Scand., 65*(Suppl.), 257.

Skoglund, C. R. (1960). Properties of pacinian corpuscles of ulnar and tibial location in cat and fowl. *Acta Physiol. Scand., 50,* 385.

Smith, D. S. (1971). On the significance of cross-bridges between microtubules and synaptic vesicles. *Phil. Trans. Roy. Soc. Lond. Ser. B, 261,* 395.

Spooner, C. E., and W. D. Winters. (1965). Distribution of auditory and visual evoked responses in the central nervous system of the unanaesthetized duck. *Physiologist, 8,* 279.

Spooner, C. E., and W. D. Winters. (1966a). Neuropharmacological profile of the young chick. *Int. J. Neuropharmacol., 5,* 217.

Spooner, C. E., and W. D. Winters. (1966b). Distribution of monoamines and regional uptake of DL-norepinephrine-7-H³ and dopamine-1-H³ in the avian brain. *Pharmacologist, 8,* 189.

Spooner, C. E., and W. D. Winters. (1967a). The influence of centrally active amine induced blood pressure changes on the electroencephalogram and behaviour. *Intl. J. Neuropharmacol., 6,* 109.

Spooner, C. E., and W. D. Winters. (1967b). Evoked responses during spontaneous and monoamine-induced states of wakefulness. *Brain Res., 4,* 189.

Spooner, C. E., W. D. Winters, and A. J. Mandell. (1966). DL-Norepinephrine-7-H³ uptake, water content and thiocyanate

28    space in the brain during maturation. *Fed. Proc., 25*, 451.

Sugihara, K., and J. Gotoh. (1973). Depth electroencephalograms of chickens in wakefulness and sleep. *Jap. J. Physiol., 23*, 371.

Swank, R. L., and H. H. Jasper. (1942). Electroencephalograms of thiamine-deficient pigeons. *Arch. Neurol. Psychiat., 47*, 821.

Tarchanoff J. (1895). Mouvements forcés des canards décapités. *Compt. Rend. Soc. Biol. ,Paris., 47*, 454.

ten Cate, J. (1936). Uni-und-plurisegmentale Reflexen bei Tauben. *Arch. Neerl. Physiol., 21*, 162.

ten Cate, J. (1960). Locomotor movements in the spinal pigeon. *J. Exp. Biol., 37*, 609.

ten Cate, J., J. A. Stommel, and W. G. Walter. (1937). Pflügelreflexe bei Rückenmarkstauben. *Arch Neerl. Physiol., 22*, 332.

Tokaji, E., and R. W. Gerard. (1939). Avitaminosis $B_1$ and pigeon brain potentials. *Proc. Soc. Exp. Biol. Med., 41*, 653.

Trendelenburg, W. (1910). Vergleichende Physiologie des Rückenmarks. *Ergebn. Physiol., 10*, 454.

Tucker, D. (1965). Electrophysiological evidence for olfactory function in birds. *Nature* (London), *207*, 34.

Tuge, H., Y. Kanayama, and C. H. Yueh. (1960). Comparative studies on the development of the EEG. *Jap. J. Physiol., 10*, 211.

van Tienhoven, A., and L. P. Juhász. (1962). The chicken telencephalon, diencephalon and mesencephalon in stereotaxic coordinates. *J. Comp. Neurol., 118*, 185.

Walsh, C., and J. McLelland. (1974). Intraepithelial axons in the avian trachea. *Z. Zellforsh., 147*, 209.

Waelsch, H. (1955). In "Biochemistry of the Developing Nervous System" (H. Waelsch, Ed.). New York: Academic Press, p. 187.

Watanabe, T. (1960). On the peripheral course of the vagus nerve in the fowl. *Jap. J. Vet. Sci., 22*, 145.

Watanabe, T. (1964). Peripheral courses of the hypoglossal, accessory and glossopharyngeal nerves. *Jap. J. Vet. Sci., 26*, 249.

Watanabe, T., and M. Yasuda. (1968). Peripheral course of the olfactory nerve in the fowl. *Jap. J. Vet. Sci., 30*, 275.

Watanabe, T., and M. Yasuda. (1970). Peripheral course of the trigeminal nerve (in the fowl). *Jap. J. Vet. Sci., 32*, 43.

Watanabe, T., G. Isomura, and M. Yasuda. (1967). Distribution of nerves in the oculomotor and ciliary muscles. *Jap. J. Vet. Sci., 29*, 151.

Wenzel, B. M., and M. H. Sieck. (1972). Olfactory perception and bulbar electrical activity in several avian species. *Physiol. Behav., 9*, 287.

Whitlock, D. G. (1952). A neurohistological and neurophysiological study of afferent fiber tracts and receptive areas of the avian cerebellum. *J. Comp. Neurol., 97*, 567.

Wingstrand, K. G. (1951). "The Structure and Development of the Avian Pituitary." Lund, Sweden: C. W. K. Gleerup.

Yasuda, M. (1960). On the nervous supply of the thoracic limb in the fowl. *Jap. J. Vet. Sci., 22*, 89.

Yasuda, M. (1961). On the nervous supply of the hind limb (of the fowl). *Jap. J. Vet. Sci., 23*, 145.

Yasuda, M. (1964). Distribution of cutaneous nerves of the fowl. *Jap. J. Vet. Sci., 5*, 241.

Zaimis, E. (1960). In "Adrenergic Mechanisms" (J. R. Vane, G. E. W. Wolstenholme, and M. O'Connor, Eds.). *CIBA Foundation Symp.* London: Churchill, p. 562.

Zeigler, H. P. (1963). Effects of endbrain lesions upon visual discrimination learning in pigeons. *J. Comp. Neurol., 120*, 161.

Zeigler, H. P., and H. J. Karten. (1973). Brain mechanisms and feeding behaviour in the pigeon *(Columba livia)*. I. Quintofrontal structures. *J. Comp. Neurol., 152*, 59.

Zeigler, H. P., and P. Witkovsky. (1968). The main sensory trigeminal nucleus in the pigeon: A single unit analysis. *J. Comp. Neurol., 134*, 225.

# 2

# Sense Organs

M. R. Kare and
J. G. Rogers, Jr.

## 30    THE EYE AND VISION

The optic lobes in the brain of the bird are unusually large and prominent. The eyes constitute a
much greater volume of the bird's head than do
eyes in mammals. With a few interesting exceptions, the bird is a vision-oriented animal and it has
been used extensively in research on vision. More
detailed reviews on the subject of avian vision can
be found in King-Smith (1971), Pearson (1972),
and Sillman (1973).

The avian eye has structural components similar
to those of the reptile. It also has unique features,
some of which are probably adaptations for flight.
The avian eye, unlike that of mammals, is not
spherical and its exact shape varies with the species
(Figure 2-1). The shape is characterized by a con-
cavity around the cornea. The resultant loss of
strength in the structure is compensated for by a ring
of bony plates, the scleral ossicles.

2–1 Diagram of sections through the eyeball of
a pigeon, which has a flat eye, and of an
owl, which has a tubular eye. [From Atwood,
W. H. (1947). "A Concise Comparative
Anatomy." St. Louis: C. V. Mosby Co.]

**Pigeon eyeball**

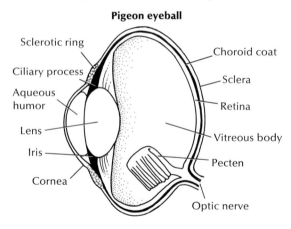

**Owl eyeball**

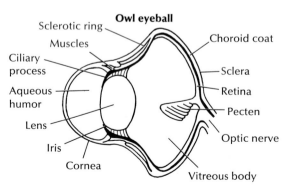

## Structure of the Eye

Birds have upper and lower eyelids, which close
only in sleep. Underneath there is an additional
transparent eyelid, the nictitating membrane, which
is present also in reptiles. This membrane covers
the eye in flight and protects it while allowing the
bird full vision. The eyes are moistened by secretions from the Harderian and lachrymal glands.

The outer layer of the eye, the sclera, contains
cartilage, as it does in reptiles. The sclera is opaque
except at its exposed surface, where it is transparent and unites with other tissues to form the cornea. The cornea is histologically similar to that of
mammals, except that Bowman's membrane is not
always differentiated (Walls, 1942). The size of the
cornea varies with species, being relatively small in
underwater swimmers and large in nocturnal birds.
A ring of bone segments set around the cornea, the
sclerotic ring, serves to offset extra- and intraocular
pressures, and provides a firm origin for the muscles of accommodation.

The two layers of tissue interior to the fibrous
sclera are the choroid membrane and the retina.
The intermediate choroid layer is highly vascular
and nourishes the cells of the retina. The ciliary
body is a thickened, folded anterior part of the
choroid. The ciliary body, in turn, suspends the
lens, which is a biconvex transparent body immediately behind the iris. The lens is chemically similar
to that in mammals and has a comparable refractive
index. The electrophoretic distribution of the soluble proteins from avian lenses has received some
attention as an indicator of phylogenetic relationships on the ordinal level (Cobb *et al.,* 1968). The
iris is a pigmented continuous extension of the
choroid and is pierced by the pupil, which controls
the amount of light striking the lens.

The anterior cavity between the cornea and the
lens is filled with a proteinaceous susbtance, called
the aqueous humor. The interior of the eye, the
posterior cavity, contains a similar but more refractive material, referred to as the vitreous humor. In
chickens the vitreous humor is watery, whereas in
such predaceous birds as the eagle and the owl it is
more gelatinous. These fluids keep the eyeball distended and change the refractive index for the light
passing through the eye. Changes in pressure in
these fluids can cause disturbances in vision.

**Pecten.** The pecten is a highly vascular structure that projects from the retina at the base of the
optic nerve into the vitreous humor. It is pigmented with from three to 30 laminae, folded accordion
fashion. The number of folds and the size of the

**2–2**

Schematic diagram of structure of the vertebrate retina. I, pigment layer; II and III, rod and cone cells extending into outer nuclear layer (III); IV, outer plexiform layer; V to VII, inner nuclear layer; V, horizontal correlation neurons; VI, bipolar cells; VII, amacrine cells (solid black); VIII, inner plexiform layer; IX, ganglion cells; X, axons of ganglion cells entering optic nerve. [After Greef (1950). In "Fulton's Textbook of Physiology" (16th ed.). Philadelphia: W. B. Saunders Co.]

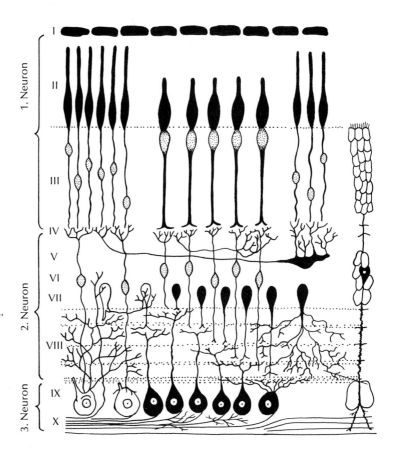

pecten vary greatly with species. The domestic chicken has approximately 18 (Fischlschweiger and O'Rahilly, 1966) and the pigeon has 15–18 laminae (Raviola and Raviola, 1967). Many functions have been suggested for the pecten, and these are reviewed by Wingstrand and Munk (1965). In a series of experiments, Wingstrand and Munk (1965) were able to surgically block the pecten arteries of the pigeon. They noticed a slow and progressive degeneration of the pecten with a concomitant degeneration of the retina. Measurements of oxygen levels revealed a fall from 100 mm Hg near the pecten to about 5 mm Hg near the retina. From this they concluded that the retina is almost completely dependent on the pecten for its oxygen supply. The importance of the pecten in its other suggested functions remains to be conclusively demonstrated. The development and histochemistry of the pecten have been described by O'Rahilly and Meyer (1961).

**Retina.** The innermost layer of the eye is the retina (Figure 2-2). It arises during ontogenesis as a protrusion of each side of the anterior cerebrum. The retina of the bird is essentially like that of all vertebrates in its functional organization (Dowling, 1970). Details of the histology of the avian retina are reported by Polyak (1957) and Morris and Shorey (1967). Light is transmitted through the transparent retina and passes through most of it before forming an image at the pigmented epithelium. The light is absorbed by the pigment molecules of the photoreceptor cells and is transduced into nervous impulses. The vertebrate photoreceptor cell is elongated, polarized, and segmented (Figure 2-3). The *outer segment,* which contains the photosensitive pigment molecules, is elongated and either cylindrical or slightly tapered. The base of the outer segment is sharply constricted and then it widens out to become the inner segment. The *inner segment* is apparently arranged into two zones. The zone nearest the outer segment contains a dense aggregation of mitochondria. The zone proximal to this contains the apparatus necessary for the production of proteins and lipids. Proximal to the inner segment, the cell narrows into a narrow *fiber,* which widens to contain the nucleus. Basally the fiber widens to form the complex synaptic body. Five types of photoreceptors have been identified in the avian eye (Figure 2–3). They are rods, prin-

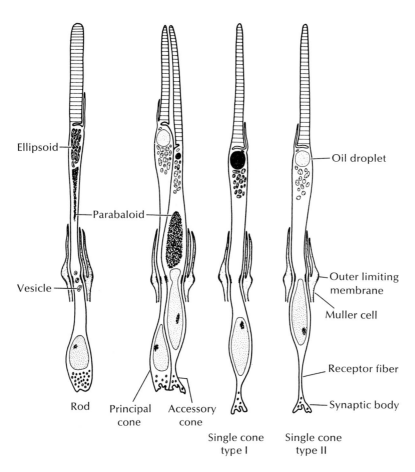

Ellipsoid

Parabaloid

Vesicle

Rod

Principal
cone

Accessory
cone

Single cone
type I

Oil droplet

Outer limiting
membrane

Muller cell

Receptor fiber

Synaptic body

Single cone
type II

2–3
Receptor types in the eye of the
chick. (From Morris and Shorey,
1967.)

cipal and accessory cones (which together form a double cone), and single cones of two types (I and II). The nerve impulse travels from the photoreceptor cells to the bipolar cells. These, in turn, are connected to the ganglion cells, which traverse the inner surface of the retina and eventually converge to form the optic nerve.

The nerve system of the retina consists of small cellular groups, structurally well defined and with more or less distinct functions. Between these groups there are patterns of interconnection. In this the retina differs from such tissues as muscle, which have a more homogeneous pattern. The functional organization of the retina begins with the rod–bipolar cells. Although a number of rod–nerve cells converge on a single rod–bipolar cell, in many instances the individual cone–nerve cells synapse with a single nerve fiber. This provides an exclusive pathway in the optic nerve and suggests the more discriminative function of the cones as opposed to the integrative function of the rods. One ganglion cell may form a synapse with one or more bipolar cells. In the inner nuclear layer of the

retina there is abundance of nerve cells, called amacrine cells, the fibers of which run horizontally across the direction of the bipolar cells to form a synapse with the ganglion cells. The amacrine cells appear to be the principal cell type mediating the complex interactions of motion detection and directional selectivity (Dowling, 1970). A detailed presentation on neural activity in the retina has been made by Granit (1959).

*Areae* are places in the retina of diurnal birds where the cone density is highest, and within which there is usually a depression, forming a pit or fovea (Figure 2–4). Within and near the fovea, where the cones attain their highest density (a million per square millimeter in the larger hawks), is the place of maximum optical resolution.

Diurnal birds of prey and songbirds (Passeriformes) have very deep foveas. Most mammals have only one area of foveas; in some birds there are two (Polyak, 1957). Eagles, hawks, and swallows all have two foveas in each eye: one nasal or central, the other lateral or temporal. The eyes of the hawk and the falcon are so situated that each of the two central

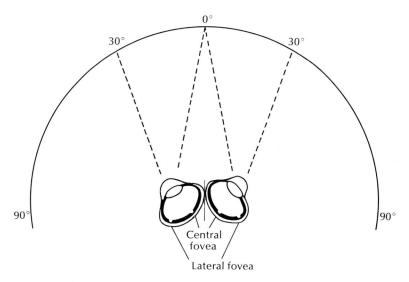

**2–4**
Foveal line of vision in falcon *(Falco tinnunculus)*. The central foveas focus on two different objects simultaneously (monocular vision). The lateral foveas focus on one subject (binocular vision). The four foveas can focus on three different objects at the same time. (After Rochon-Duvigneaud, 1950.)

Central fovea

Lateral fovea

foveas may be directed to one side at separate objects and the temporal foveas directed ahead at one object (Figure 2–4). The eyes of chickens and turkeys have only one central fovea (Rochon-Duvigneaud, 1950).

### Photochemistry

More than a century ago, Schultze (1866) suggested that the rods might be receptors of dim light (scoptopic vision) and the cones receptors of bright light (photopic vision). In all the photoreceptor cells the absorption of light employs a compound of the carotenoid class, conjugated with various proteins. The carotenoids consist of pigments ranging from yellow to red; they are fat soluble when unconjugated, highly unsaturated, and identifiable by their absorption spectra.

In birds the photosensitive portion of the rod cells consists of retinene combined with a protein, opsin. The general term for this carotenoid–protein is rodopsin (visual purple or scotopsin). The wavelength of maximum absorption of rhodopsin is near 500 m$\mu$ (millimicrons) in most vertebrates, e.g., man, 497; chicken, 510.

Photosensitive pigments, referred to as iodopsin (photopsin), have been demonstrated by microspectrophotometric techniques in the cones of several vertebrate classes (mammals, teleost fish, reptiles, and amphibians). The retinas of three bird species (chicken, turkey, and pigeon) have been reported to possess pigments other than rhodopsin. Some workers have considered tham to be photopsin (Sillman, 1969). The pigments studied from these species exhibit absorption maxima from 544 to 562 m$\mu$. The carotenoids from the chicken cone pigment seem to be identical to those from rhodopsin; only the opsin is different (Wald *et al.*, 1954).

### Central Mechanisms

The subcortical visual apparatus in the pigeon is almost entirely decussated (see also Chapter 1). The optic nerve fibers originating in the retina of one eye terminate in the center of the contralateral half of the mesodiencephalon. There is a point-to-point representation of the retina on the optic tectum in the pigeon. The superior retinal quadrants are represented posteriorly and ventrally in the tectum and the anterior quadrants posteriorly and dorsally (McGill *et al.*, 1966; also Chapter 1).

Polyak (1957) commented on the remarkable complexity of the avian visual system. He noted that it involved a variety of subcortical centers directly related to the retinal fibers. The birds' optic lobes are relatively large; they possess an elaborate optic tectum which far exceeds the mammalian homologs, the superior colliculi, and equals the structure of the mammalian striate cortex. This indicates a functional emphasis on the midbrain in the birds' visual septum. An extensive account on the central mechanism of vision has been prepared by Bartley (1959).

### Formation of the Image

Focusing of light on the retina can be explained in terms of basic geometric optics. The image-forming mechanism of the eye has been discussed in detail by Fry (1959).

34

Refraction and accommodation. As light enters the eye it is refracted by the cornea, the aqueous humor, the lens, and the vitreous humor and an inverted image is formed at the retina. The distance between the lens and the point of focus (principal focus) of the image is the focal length of the lens. For a given lens of fixed refractive index the focal length may be varied by varying the curvature of the lens. The refracting power of a lens (diopter) is traditionally expressed as the reciprocal of the focal length in meters. For example, a lens with a focal length of 1 meter has a power of 1 diopter (1D).

The range or distance over which the lens can maintain a focus at the retina is known as the accommodation range. In mammals, birds, and most reptiles, accommodation is effected by changing the curvature of the posteror and anterior surfaces of the lens by means of the ciliary muscles. Contraction of Brücke's muscle compresses the lens, shortening the focal length. The contraction of Crampton's muscle changes the shape of the cornea. In nocturnal birds these muscles are reduced and the focal length is virtually fixed. When the images of distant objects are focused in front of the retina, the condition is called *myopia* or nearsightedness; when the focus is behind or beyond the retina, the condition is called hypermetropia or farsightedness. When the distant image is focused correctly on the retina, the condition is known as emmetropia. Most birds are emmetropic or slightly hypermetropic, except *Apteryx* (wingless kiwi), which is myopic (Walls, 1942; Rochon-Duvigneaud, 1950). Data for the pigeon (Catania, 1964; Galifret, 1968; Millodot and Blough, 1971) suggest that this species has both a myopic and a hypermetropic visual system, depending on where upon the retina the stimulating light falls.

**Visual field; monocular and binocular vision.** The angle or field through which the bird can see without moving its head is called the visual field. This field is determined by the position of the eyes in the head and by the shape of the eye. Birds with flat eyes (pigeons, chickens) have wider visual fields than those with eyes that are globose or elongated and tubular (birds of prey) (Figures 2–1 and 2–4). When the eyes are laterally situated, as in the pigeon, the total visual field is about 300°. In nocturnal raptors, such as *Tyto alba* (barn owl), the eyes of which are frontally located, the total field is less than half that of the pigeon. Owls compensate for their more restricted visual field by frequently turning the head, which can rotate

through greater than 180° The focusing of only one eye on one object at a time is called monocular vision. When both eyes are focused on one object, the result is binocular vision. The movement of the two eyes can be independent but becomes coordinated when binocular vision is involved. Many birds follow a moving object with movement of the entire head and subsequently use monocular or binocular vision. Most birds are capable of binocular vision (penguins are not). The relative portion of the total visual field that is binocular is determined by the shape of the head, the shape of the eye, and the position of the eye in the head. Laterally placed eyes are capable of a smaller binocular field than frontally placed eyes. The binocular field of the homing pigeon is about 24° wide (Walls, 1942), whereas owls and hawks with frontal tubular eyes have a binocular field of from 60° to 70° extending straight ahead. Some birds have the added ability to see objects beneath them while their bills are in the normal vertical position. Depth perception is usually attained through binocularity; but in such birds as pigeons, where there is little overlap of visual fields, the typical back and forth movements of the head while walking, involving successive glances from different positions, may yield information on relative distance.

Thompson (1971) examined the relationship between the behavioral and physiological spectral sensitivites of juvenile herring and lesser black-backed gulls, which show distinctively characteristic color preferences when responding behaviorally to chromatic stimuli. She concluded that the electrophysiologic measures of spectral sensitivity closely resembled those of other diurnal birds. She felt, therefore, that the majority of the color preferences exhibit by these species could not be explained by characteristic retinal sensitivities.

**Visual acuity.** The sensitivity of the eye consists of an ability to respond to weak stimuli or a capacity for continuing to respond to light that is slowly being dimmed. The ability to distinguish details of visual objects as the details are made smaller and brought closer together is known as resolving power. Visual acuity reflects the degree of resolving power.

The acuity or resolving power of the retina depends on the structure of the rods and cones, their spacing and concentration, and the number connected with each fiber of the optic nerve tract. The high resolving power attributed to avian vision is based on the relatively large size of the eye, which permits a relatively large image to be cast on the retina. The bird also has a dense concentration of cone–nerve cells and a high ratio of optic nerve fibers to the visual cells.

The concentration of cones in the fovea of the sparrow averages 400,000 or more per square millimeter. In the hawk, the fovea may contain 1,000,000 cones per square millimeter. Even outside the fovea, the hawk retina has nearly twice the number of cones of the human fovea. In the fovea or fundus of *Motacilla* (wagtails) and *Anthus* (pipit), cone density reaches 120,000 per square millimeter and the density of ganglion cells is about the same, indicating that every visual cell is individually represented in the optic nerve.

Pumphrey (1961) has compared the visual acuity of birds and man and has concluded that visual acuity of birds is not much greater than man's but that the rate of assimilation of detail is higher. The bird's vision is not sharper; instead, it is more rapid. The swiftness of flight makes rapid visual perception essential (Portmann, 1950). Schlaer (1972) has estimated that because of superior visual optics that result in superior retinal images several species of eagles have visual acuities from two to 3.6 times greater than those possible in man. These estimates are far below some of the wilder estimates of the superiority of avian visual acuity.

**Color vision.** All diurnal birds have color or chromatic vision. This attribute is associated with the preponderance of cone cells, whereas the rods are linked with the achromatic vision typical of nocturnal birds. In pigeons, at least, because of the reported similarity in relative size and sensitivity of the retinal color fields, the capacity for color vision seems similar to man (Skinner and Beishon, 1971).

A group of visual pigments, the carotenoid proteins, is identified with the sensitivity of the retina to light and color. The dark-adapted rod-stimulated human eye responds maximally to green light at a wavelength of about 510 m$\mu$. The light-adapted eye responds maximally at 560m$\mu$, or to yellow-green light. The light-adapted eye therefore sees better in light of a longer wavelength than does the dark-adapted eye. This shift or change in response is known as the Purkinje phenomenon (Armington and Thiede, 1956).

Electroretinograms of the chicken eye were found to exhibit components typical of the eyes of other animals. Armington and Thiede (1956) also demonstrated a Purkinje shift in this bird. The eye of the pigeon, subjected to darkness for at least 45 min, becomes dark adapted and responds maximally to light at 534 m$\mu$ and up to 664 m$\mu$. The spectral range for the light-adapted eye is 424–704, with the maximum response to 565m$\mu$.

A comparison of the absorption spectra of visual pigments in the chicken with the retinal spectral sensitivity of pigeons is illustrated in Figure 2–5. These results were obtained microspectrophotometrically by inserting microelectodes into the retina after removal of the lens and cornea. The visual pigments of a number of avian species have been tabulated by Sillman (1973).

The cones of most avian retinas contain brightly colored oil droplets in their inner segments, immediately adjacent to the outer segments. Therefore most light reaching the outer segments has probably passed through a corresponding oil drop. This anatomical arrangement has led to the suggestion that the droplets (orange, yellow, or red) act as intraocular light filters, intensifying similar colors but reducing the discrimination of others (violet and blue) (Walls and Judd, 1933; Portmann, 1950). King-Smith (1969), by correlating absorption spectra measurements of individual oil droplets in both the yellow and red retinal fields of pigeons with hue discrimination data, indicated that all cone cells utilize the same photosensitive pigment. Therefore he feels that, in pigeons at least, color vision is entirely dependent on the presence of the colored oil drops.

A number of reports suggest that certain birds are sensitive to extraspectral frequencies. There are also reports indicating a particular insensitivity to blue. Donner (1953), using a microelectrode technique, reported on the spectral sensitivity of the pigeon. He supported the view that the photochemical substances involved in vision are the same in the avian eye as in other vertebrate eyes. The spectral threshold of *Sturnus vulgaris* (starling) was studied by Adler and Dalland (1959), using an operant conditioning technique. They reported that the dark-adaptation curve of the starling differed considerably from what might be expected of a human being under similar conditions.

Behavioral experiments for color vision in birds began with the work of Hess (1912). He sprinkled grain on a floor and illuminated it with the six colors projected in a spectrum. He reported that the chickens ate the grain illuminated by red, yellow, and green light but not the grain illuminated by the blue and violet light. Later, Honigmann (1921) and others, working with both stained and illuminated rice grains, observed that chickens did eat the blue and violet grains, albeit less avidly than they did the others.

36

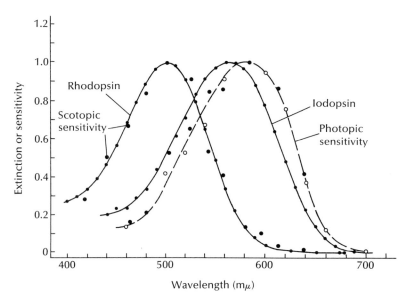

2–5 Absorption spectra of chicken rhodopsin and iodopsin, compared with the spectral sensitivities of dark- and light-adapted pigeons. The latter were measured electrophysiologically and are plotted in terms of the reciprocals of the numbers of incident quanta needed to evoke a constant electrical response. The scotopic data are from Donner (1953), the photopic data from the same source *(barred circles)* and from Granit (1959) *(open circles)*. The scotopic sensitivity agrees well with the absorption spectrum of rhodopsin. The photopic sensitivity is displaced about 20 mμ toward the red from the absorption spectrum of iodopsin, owing in large part to the filtering action of the colored oil globules of the pigeon cones. (From Wald *et al.*, 1954–1955.)

Watson (1915) and Lashley (1916) have shown that the chick's spectral limits are from 700 mμ to 715 mμ at one end of the spectrum and 395 – 405 mμ at the other. The maximum sensitivity of the chick eye is at 560 mμ and that of the adult fowl at 580 mμ (Honigmann, 1921). This shift toward the red end of the spectrum was probably caused by an increase in density of oil droplets with age. Some birds, such as hawks, woodpeckers (Piciformes), and parrots (Psittaciformes), have few or no red oil droplets and probably see blues and violets as man does. Strongly nocturnal birds, such as owls, have only faintly pigmented oil droplets (Portmann, 1950).

**Behavior and vision.** Any discussion of vision in birds should consider specific functions. For example, vision plays a primary role in the securing of food for the hawk, whereas the owl uses hearing to locate prey.

Guhl (1953) studied the effect of limited light on bird behavior. He reported that chicks would start feeding when the light was 1 foot-candle and would begin to peck one another when it was 2 foot-candles. Chickens were observed by Benner (1938) to use shadow to determine depth. They responded to photographs of peas with appropriate shadowing, but failed to respond to pictures that had peas with shadows in all directions. Chicks were reported by Hess (1956) to have a bimodal preference for color, with one peak occurring in the orange region of the spectrum and a second peak in the blue region. Pekin ducklings, in contrast, he found to have a narrower range of preferences, with a single sharp peak within the green and yellow-green region.

Perhaps the most commonly used bird for behavior studies involving vision is the pigeon. Largely with the use of operant conditioning techniques, a number of precise measurements of various psychophysical processes have been made. A general introduction to this research is contained in a review by Blough (1961).

## THE EAR AND HEARING

Hearing does not serve the same purpose in all birds. It is used by owls to locate food, but in many passerine birds its primary functions are in social behavior.

Hearing is generally conceded to be more highly developed in birds and mammals than it is in other classes of animals. The processes of sound reception and transduction to nervous impulses appear to be essentially similar to those of other vertebrate classes but there are substantial differences in structure. For detailed accounts of avian and comparative audition, see reviews by Smith and Takasaka (1971), Pearson (1972), and Schwartzkopff (1973).

## Structure of the Ear

The avian ear has middle ear structures similar to those of lizards and alligators. Unlike these reptiles, however, most birds (except the vultures, some gallinaceous birds, and the Struthioniformes) have specialized auricular features (feathers) that surround and protect the external auditory meatus. These feathers are specially modified so as not to impede the penetration of sound waves. In some groups, these features have combined with part of the external meatus to form an ear funnel which may serve some of the same functions as the pinna of mammals. The external meatus (Figure 2–6) leads from the body surface to the tympanic membrane or eardrum, which is the boundary between the outer and middle ears. The tympanic membrane is cone shaped, being pushed outward by the columella. Because the oval window is situated posterior to the tympanic membrane, the action of the stapes on the oval window is leverlike rather than pistonlike (Gaudin, 1968). The eardrum, columella, and stapes foot plate comprise an efficient impedence-matching device that transforms airborn vibrations of large amplitude and small force into cochlear fluid-borne vibrations of large force and small amplitude (Schwartzkopff, 1973). The middle ear ossicles are situated in an air-filled cavity the pressure of which is equilibrated with that of the oral cavity by the Eustachian tube. The bird's ear is almost inaccessible to bone-conducted sound (Schwartzkopff, 1955) because the inner bone structure is largely surrounded by air spaces. The tympanic cavities of both ears are not truly isolated, so intraear communication of low-frequency vibrations is possible. This situation is most exaggerated in the owl (Payne, 1971). Ceruminous (wax) glands are present only in some species.

Beyond the middle ear lies the inner ear, a fluid-filled complex of tubes and chambers that has become known as the labyrinth. It consists of three functionally distinct structures. (1) The semicircular canals (Figure 2–6), which extend outward from the central bony casing, are concerned with maintaining equilibrium. (2) Closely related to the semicircular canals and probably interconnected with them by nerves are a pair of chambers called the utriculus and sacculus (Figure 2–7). These chambers contain stones or otoliths on slender supporting hairs; the information from these sensory elements concerns the vertical or upright posture. From the standpoint of evolution, these are the oldest parts of the inner ear; they have been found in many vertebrates. (3) A third organ, the cochlea, in the bird is an elongated structure extending from the labyrinth in a direction generally opposite to that of the semicircular canals. Mammals characteristically have a coiled cochlea with from two to four spirals; an interesting exception occurs in the egg-laying monotremes, where the cochlea is similar to that of birds. The avian cochlea differs from the corresponding organ in mammals by being shorter and uncoiled (Figures 2–7 and 2–8). The cochlea of

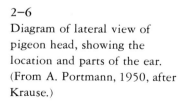

2–6
Diagram of lateral view of pigeon head, showing the location and parts of the ear. (From A. Portmann, 1950, after Krause.)

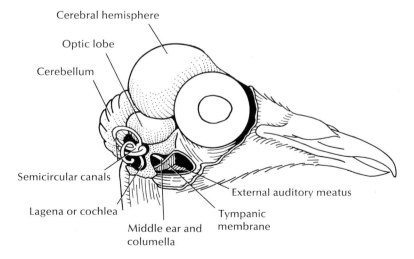

Cerebral hemisphere

Optic lobe

Cerebellum

Semicircular canals

Lagena or cochlea

Middle ear and columella

Tympanic membrane

External auditory meatus

38

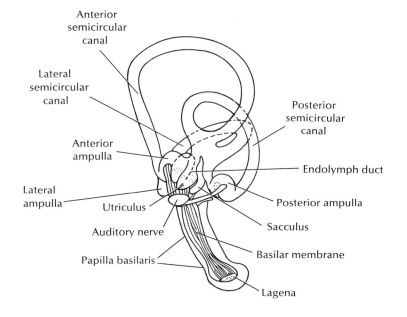

Anterior
semicircular
canal

Lateral
semicircular
canal

Posterior
semicircular
canal

Anterior
ampulla

Endolymph duct

Lateral
ampulla

Posterior ampulla

Utriculus

Sacculus

Auditory nerve

Basilar membrane

Papilla basilaris

Lagena

2-7
Diagram of inner ear of bird.
(From A. Portmann, 1950, after
Satoh.)

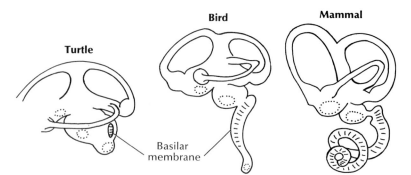

Turtle

Bird

Mammal

Basilar
membrane

2-8
The membranous labyrinths of
a turtle, a bird, and a mammal.
The three canals, at right angles
to one another, are concerned
with the position of the head.
The dotted circles represent
small otolith organs, which serve
in maintaining equilibrium. The
auditory nerve endings are
found in the regions indicated
by cross-hatching; these regions
are concerned with hearing.
(From von Békésy, 1960.)

the chicken consists of a slightly bent tube, about 5 mm long. Within the bony cochlear tube is another tube, the ductus cochlearis (scala media), with an elastic wall, the tegmentum vasculosum, forming a double canal with an elastic partition. This membrane is said to correspond to the membrane of Reissner in mammals.

The basilar membrane is a thin structure the fibers of which run transversely, so that it is stronger and stiffer in the transverse direction than along its length. Together the basilar membrane and the tegmentum vasculosum divide the cochlear cavity into three tubes. The fringelike central tube, the scala media, contains the fluid known as endolymph; the cavities above and below this tube, the scala vestibuli and scala tympani, contain a different fluid, the perilymph. The exact chemical composition of this fluid is still unknown although its physical properties have been investigated

(Money *et al.,* 1971). On the basilar membrane is a complex of structures known as the basilar papilla, which corresponds to the organ of Corti in mammals. The basilar papilla includes a portion of the basilar membrane, hair cells, supporting cells, accessory supporting cells, nerve cells, nerve fibers, and tectorial membrane. In a manner not unlike that found in the retina, cylindrical cells lie in a long narrow row along the length of the basilar membrane. In any one cross-section of the membrane there are 30-50 of these cells. Each one is ciliated at its outer end, with numerous small rod-like hairlets, the roots of which enter the supporting hair cells. The number of these cells in the bird's ear is considerably less than in man. The hairlets are covered over at their outer extremity by the tectorial membrane. The tectorial membrane is stiff with respect to vibrations but lacks resistance to slow static displacements.

Unmyelinated terminal fibers of the auditory nerve enter the cochlea along its length and cross the basilar membrane to enter the basilar papilla, lying in a strip along the floor. They come into contact with the outer portion of the cylindrical hair cells at the roots of the hairlets. At the junction of the hairlets and the hair cells, there is a stiff reticular membrane. At the site of the hair cells the mechnical sound energy is coverted into nervous impulses.

**Mechanism of hearing.** Several different theories have been offered to explain the mechanical aspects of hearing. One is that the number of nerve impulses reaching the brain corresponds exactly to the variations in pressure of the sound waves impinging on the ear. According to this theory, the analysis of the complexities of information carried by the sound is taken over completely by the central nervous processes. A resonance theory proposed by Helmholtz is that a series of separate structures, the arches of Corti, changes dimensions progressively from one end of the cochlea to the other and can probably pick out the constituents of a complex sound and vibrate in sympathy with them. Helmholtz learned, however, that in the bird organ of Corti there are no arches or pillars to interrupt the continuous row of hair cells beneath the tectorial membrane and accordingly changed his suggestions as to the resonating structure. Observing that the basilar mambrane was composed of elastic parallel fibers along its whole length, like the cords of a ve-

netian blind, he concluded that the basilar membrane must resonate in the manner of a reed frequency meter with the component frequencies of the sound. He observed that the variation in length of the basilar fibers would contribute to the frequency discrimination by the cochlea. There are many objections to this theory, including the absence of any clearcut anatomical corroboration. Birds, cats, and rabbits have a basilar membrane made up of two layers of fibers, instead of only one layer as in man (Held, 1926).

von Békésy (1960) has made stroboscopic observations of the actual vibration along the cochlea

2–9 (a) Form of the cochlea and (b) the basilar membrane in the chicken. (c) Positions of maximum stimulation along the cochlear partition of the chicken for various tones. The basilar membrane of the chicken is represented as seen from above and somewhat to the side. The location of the stapedial footplate relative to the double canal is shown by the dotted circle. It can be seen that below 100 cps there can no longer be any mechanical frequency analysis in the chicken, because the cochlear partition vibrates as a whole, and the form of vibration is unaltered because the frequency is lower. (From von Békésy, 1960.)

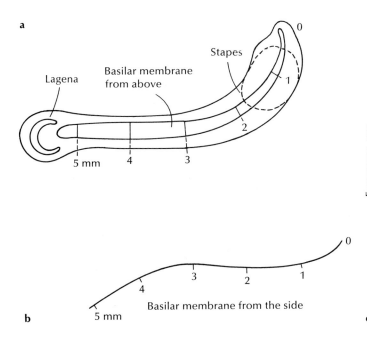

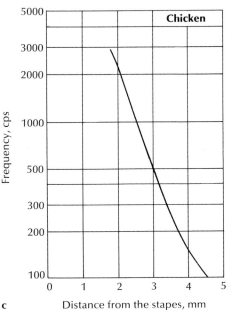

(Figure 2–9) and reports that no structure of the cochlea partition exhibits movements corresponding to a system of resonant elements of the kind seen in a Frahm reed frequency meter.

The most likely mechanism of hearing is that the oscillations of the cochlear fluids displace the hair cells, differentially according to their locations on the basilar papilla, in relation to the tectorial membrane. The cilia are therefore sheared and the mechanical vibrations of the fluid are translated (coded) to the electrical impulses of the nerve.

Electrical potentials recorded from the inner ear are of two types: one is generated by the organ of Corti and is supposed to play a role in stimulating the nerve; the other is produced by the nerve itself and is called the action potential. At low frequencies this electrical activity reproduces the form of the applied sound pressure. This electrical activity is the auditory counterpart of the retinal potentials, as revealed by the electroretinogram, and has become known as cochlear microphonics. The nerve action potentials generated at the level of the organ of Corti travel along the individual fibers of the auditory nerve, to be projected to the cochlear nucleus and from there to several targets in the brainstem. In this function birds and mammals are similar. However, in mammals the brainstem paths arrive in the medial geniculate and thence to the neocortex. In birds the forebrain target is probably the corpus striatum and not the cortex. The peripheral end of the auditory nerve diffuses itself along the path of the bony tube of the cochlea and its ramifications pass though the bony wall that supports the cochlea. These ramifications have become known as the spiral ganglion, because in most higher animals the cochlea is a spiral. There are always two and sometimes three areas from which the responses are projected to the brain. Within each cerebral projection there are specific smaller areas that correspond to specific places along the basilar membrane.

von Békésy has contributed experimental evidence to support a suggestion that different frequencies are represented at different places along the basilar membrane of the cochlea (morphological polarization). It has also been stated that the acoustical neurons in the avian cochlear nucleus are tonotopically arranged according to their sites of innervation by the connecting primary auditory fibers on the basilar membrane (Konishi, 1970). von Békésy has shown that a resonance theory is anatomically unsound; although spatial localization of frequencies along the basilar membrane does occur, it is not produced by a resonator mechanism.

**Equilibrium.** Pumphrey (1961) and Schwartz-kopff (1973) discuss at length the inner ear structures responsible for equilibrium in the bird. The semicircular canals provide continuous stimulation to the somatic musculature and are probably involved in the production of muscular tonus. Impulses arising in the semicircular canals, and their coordination with other stimuli, lead to compensatory body movement.

## Hearing

There are two methods of measuring the distribution of sensitivity to sound in animals. The more difficult is the recording of cochlear potentials of the inner ear. A more convenient method is the use of behavioral tests with trained animals. A reflex movement produced by training can be a very successful index of the auditory capacity of the animal. An example is the pairing of an aversive stimulus, such as electric shock, to a sound that the experimenter wishes to investigate. The sound comes to have a biological value to the animal, and after a number of repetitions the animal responds to the sound alone. Food can be used instead of shock, and some index of the animal's behavior toward the food can be obtained with sound alone after a number of pairings under the appropriate conditions.

Another approach, which might be called an ecological method, is implicit in the work of Payne (1962, 1971) with *Tyto alba* (barn owl). His experiments demonstrated that the owl is capable of locating and striking a mouse in total darkness with a margin of error of less than 1° in both the vertical and horizontal planes. When recorded sounds of rustling leaves were substituted, the owl would strike with the same accuracy, except when frequencies above 8,500 Hz were filtered out of the recorded signal; then the margin of error rose to about 5° in both the vertical and the horizontal planes. When frequencies above 5000 Hz were absent, the owl made no attempt to strike on hearing the sound. In owls the tympanum is exceptionally large, the inner ear is usually long, and there is a modification of the columella. In addition, their ears, unlike those of other birds, are asymmetrical and this aids in the localization of the sounds (Norberg, 1968).

## Hearing Range

The ranges of sound audible to various species of birds are shown in Table 2–1. The hearing range of birds does not extend as high as that of certain mammals, for example the dog, 35,000 Hz; various mice and shrews, up to 30,000 Hz; and whales and

**Table 2-1** *The hearing range of man and several birds*[a]

| Species | Lower limit (Hz) | Highest sensitivity (Hz) | Upper limit (Hz) | Reference |
|---|---|---|---|---|
| *Homo sapiens* (man) | 16 | 1000–3000 | 20,000 | |
| *Melopsittacus undulatus* (budgerigar) | 40 | – | 14,000 | Knecht (1940) |
| *Sturnus vulgaris* (starling) | <100 | 2000 | 15,000 | Granit, (1941) |
| *Loxia curvirostra* (crossbill) | – | – | 20,000 | Knecht (1940) |
| *Passer domesticus* (house sparrow) | – | – | 18,000 | Granit (1941) |
| *Erithacus rubecula* (European robin | – | – | 21,000 | Granit (1941) |
| *Chloris chloris* (greenfinch) | – | – | 20,000 | Granit (1941) |
| *Pyrrhula pyrrhula* (bullfinch) | <100 | 3200 | 20,000–25,000 | Schwartzkopff (1949) |
| *Fringilla coelebs* (chaffinch) | <200 | 3200 | 29,000 | Schwartzkopff (1955) |
| *Pica pica* (magpie) | <100 | 800–1600 | 21,000 | Schwartzkopff (1955) |
| *Corvus sp.* (crow) | <300 | 1000–2000 | <8,000 | Trainer (1946) |
| *Serinus canarius* (canary) | 250 | 2800 | 10,000 | Dooling and Mulligan (1971) |
| *Plectophenax nivalis* (snowbunting) | 400 | – | 7,200 | Schwartzkopff (1973) |
| *Eremophila alpestris* (horned lark) | 350 | – | 7,600 | Schwartzkopff (1973) |
| *Falco sparverius* (sparrow hawk) | <300 | 2000 | <10,000 | Trainer (1946) |
| *Anas platyrhyncos* (mallard) | <300 | 2000–3000 | <8,000 | Trainer (1946) |
| *Aythya valisineria* (canvasback) | 190 | – | 5,200 | Schwartzkopff (1973) |
| *Larus delawarensis* (ring-billed gull) | 100 | 500–800 | 3,000 | Schwartzkopff (1973) |
| *Columba livia* (domestic pigeon) | <300 | 1000–2000 | – | Trainer (1946) |
| | – | – | 12,000 | Wassiljew (1933) |
| | 50 | 1800–2400 | | Wever and Bray (1936) |
| *Phasianius colchicus* (pheasant) | 250 | – | 10,500 | Schwartzkopff (1973) |
| *Asio otus* (long-eared owl) | <100 | 6000 | 18,000 | Schwartzkopff (1955) |
| *Strix aluco* (tawny owl) | <100 | 3000–6000 | 21,000 | Schwartzkopff (1955) |
| *Bubo virginianus* (great horned owl) | 60 | 1000 | <8,000 | Trainer (1946) |
| *Spheniscus dermersus* (penguin) | 4000 | 2000–4000 | 15,000 | Wever *et al.* (1969) |

[a]From Schwartzkopff (1955).

dolphins, up to 100,000 Hz (Prosser and Brown, 1961). The limits of high frequency hearing in birds seem to be related to the transmission characteristics of the middle ear (Saunders, 1972).

The discrimination of frequencies within the range for birds seems to be about equal to that of man. Trained pigeons are able to discriminate between 300 Hz and 365 Hz, 387 Hz and 500 Hz, and 800 Hz and 1000 Hz (Wever and Bray, 1936). Turtledoves and parrots have about equal discrimination (Jellinek, 1926a,b; Knecht, 1940). Quine and Konish (1974) made use of the barn owl's capacity for remembering frequencies that were associated with food reward to study its ability to discriminate between various frequencies. By this method they determined that the barn owl can accurately discriminate frequencies differing by as little as 50 Hz from reference frequencies of 7,000 or 10,000 Hz. Electrical potentials at the lagena show the ear of the pigeon to be less sensitive to loudness than that of the mammal.

*Melopsittacus undulatus* (budgerigars) can differentiate frequencies differing by as little as 0.7% over the frequency range from 1000 to 4000 Hz (Dooling and Saunders, 1973). However, other species, such as the pigeon, have a lesser ability to discriminate (see Schwartzkopff, 1955).

The region of greatest hearing sensitivity in birds is different for different species, but usually falls between 1000 and 6000 Hz. For a particular species the area of best performance usually bears a close relationship to the range of sound frequencies which it produces (Konishi, 1965).

It has commonly been believed that birds exceed man in their ability to hear a wide range of frequencies. However, no evidence in support of this belief has been produced (Konishi, 1970). The remarkable difference between man and most birds lies in the ability of birds to resolve sounds received at short intervals. Young chaffinches can learn details of song that need to be slowed at least tenfold before the human ear can detect them

42 (Thorpe, 1954). *Steatornis caripensis* (oilbird) finds its way by echolocation through the dark caves in which it lives. To do this it must be able to resolve sound pulses separated by silent intervals of as little as 2–3 msec (Griffin, 1953). The speed of resolution of sounds by birds is beyond that of man and most mammals, but none exceeds that of the bat.

**Behavior.** The sight of an agitated chick under a bell jar does not attract the attention of the mother hen. Yet even out of sight, calls of distress from its offspring immediately draw the hen to the place from which the sound emanates (Brückner, 1933). The exposure of a Pekin duckling to a particular sound can lead to subsequent preference for that sound (Klopfer, 1962). However, this imprinting can occur only if the exposure has been during a specific and limited period after hatching, the so-called "critical period." Chicks hear almost nothing above 400 Hz, a frequency that corresponds to the calls of the hen; but the hen responds to the calls (above 300 Hz) of the chick (Collias and Joos, 1953). Schwartzkopff (1955) suggests this may be related to a developmental stage in the middle ear of chicks during which the reception of higher frequencies is impeded. The behavioral and ontogenetic relations in the production and reception of songs and calls by birds has been one of the most fertile areas of avian research (see Hinde, 1969). However, despite the importance of audition to many bird groups and the extensive research in the learning of songs and their production, the details of the physiology of avian audition have received relatively little attention.

The peripheral auditory system of birds exhibits some striking differences compared with that found in most mammals (Manley, 1973; Gaudin, 1968), and the central organization of the auditory pathway is considerably different from the mammalian plan. These great differences in the morphology of the avian system suggest that future detailed study of the auditory system of birds will show that at least some aspects of avian hearing are fundamentally different from mammalian hearing (Dooling and Saunders, 1975).

## THE CHEMICAL SENSES

All birds possess the requisite anatomy for the reception of and response to chemical stimuli from their environment. In air-breathing animals, such as birds, chemoreception is primarily associated with taste buds in the oral cavity and the olfactory epithelium of the olfactory nasal chamber.

The chemical senses are commonly thought to fall into three classes: (1) olfaction (smell), (2) gustation (taste), and (3) the common chemical sense. Olfaction in air-breathing animals is usually thought to be a telereceptor, capable of receiving airborn chemical stimuli in extreme dilution over relatively great distances. Gustation usually requires more intimate contact of higher concentrations of the chemical stimuli with the taste receptors. These receptors are usually in the tastebuds of the oral cavity, although functional taste buds are found outside the oral cavity and on the body surface of some animals (i.e., catfish). The common chemical sense is reserved for nonspecific stimuli, which are often irritating. The divisions between the three chemical senses are often arbitrary, with a single chemical affecting all three senses. In some species, particularly among the less evolved forms, it is difficult if not impossible to distinguish among the three chemoreceptor systems.

### Common Chemical Sense

Moncrieff (1951) suggests that the common chemical sense is probably primitive and that taste and olfaction are later differentiations. The prevalence of the common chemical sense in the lower vertebrates and the diverse, relatively unspecialized nature of the receptors support this interpretation.

Such irritants as ammonia and acids stimulate the free nerve endings of numerous surfaces, such as those in the nasal chambers, mouth, and eyelids of vertebrates. The nasal cavity of birds is innervated by the trigeminal as well as the olfactory nerves (Allison, 1953). Aquatic forms, such as ducks and flamingos, have greater development of the trigeminal nerves than other birds; this may reflect a functional role in feeding, because aquatic birds can be expected to come into contact with chemical irritants more frequently than other birds.

The pigeon and *Perdix perdix* (gray partridge) have been reported to be relatively insensitive to strong ammonia solution (Soudek, 1929). However, systematic studies have not been conducted with chemicals that stimulate the trigeminal nerves in birds.

### Smell

The question of whether birds possess olfactory capabilities has long been debated. The nineteenth century naturalists Audubon and Darwin carried out experiments to test the olfactory ability of vultures. They were preceded and followed by others whose works on smell in birds are as contradictory

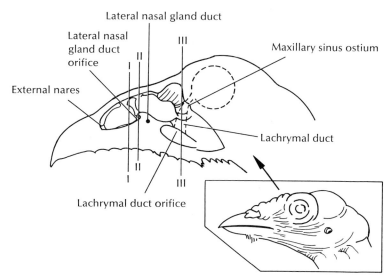

**2-10**
Diagramatic sagittal section of right medial surface of the nasal chambers of a chicken. Not drawn to scale. Olfactory sensory area indicated by diagonal shading, position of eye and lachrymal duct by broken lines. Inserts of partially dissected head of chicken gives an idea of extent of fossa in relation to external landmarks. (From Bang and Bang, 1959.)

as they are numerous. Work over the last two decades has indicated that birds have an olfactory system that is more or less developed depending on the species. Neural events, presumably the result of stimulus–receptor interaction, can be studied electrophysiologically in birds, and some species have been reported to regulate their behavior on the basis of olfactory information. Wenzel (1973) has recently reviewed many of the aspects of avian olfaction.

**The olfactory organ.** Bang (1971) has summarized the functional anatomy of the olfactory system of birds representing 23 orders. The typical avian olfactory system consists of external nares (nostrils); nasal chambers (conchae); internal nares (choane); olfactory nerves, the peripheral terminals of which lie in the olfactory epithelium; and the olfactory bulbs of the brain. There are three nasal chambers, but only the turbinates of the olfactory chamber (posteriosuperior chamber) possess olfactory epithelium (Allison, 1953; Bang, 1971). Birds resemble reptiles in possessing three nasal conchae and in lacking the vomeronasal (Jacobsen's) organ, although the latter has been identified in the very early embryonic life of birds (Matthes, 1934). In pelicans and their allies, two external nares are completely closed and there is a reduction of the size of other parts of the olfactory system. The comparative anatomy of the nose and nasal air streams is discussed by Bang and Bang (1959); see Figures 2–10 and 2–11.

**2-11**
Diagram or map of sections through the anterior part of the respiratory portion of the nasal fossa of a chicken. Cartilage, stippled; bone, solid black; cornified squamous epithelium, solid black line. (From Bang and Bang, 1959.)

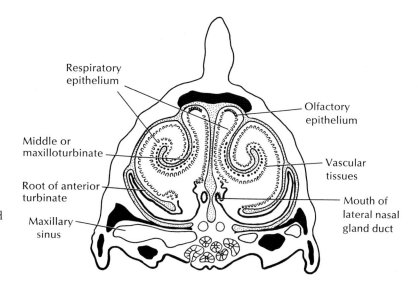

44    The numerous negative reports on olfaction in birds probably have discouraged the use of this animal class in olfactory research and may explain why so little work on the mechanism of olfaction deals with avian species. Much general information on olfactory receptor cells, nerves, and central interpretations can be found in Beidler (1971).

It is difficult to consider the olfactory system of birds collectively because there is so substantial a variation in development between species. The olfactory system is well developed in *Apteryx* (kiwi), vulture, albatross, and petrels; moderately developed in the fowl, pigeon, and most birds of prey; and poorly developed in songbirds (Cobb, 1960; Bang, 1971).

**Olfactory development in various species.** Vultures are carrion eaters and their conspicuous circling behavior in the area of a carcass led to much early speculation that they locate sources of food by olfaction. This has been confirmed for one species, *Cathartes aura* (turkey vulture), and strongly suggested for another, *Sarcoramphus papa* (king vulture) by Stager (1964). By careful release of ethyl mercaptan fumes into the still air of a mountain canyon in the path of migrating turkey vultures, he was able to demonstrate that vultures are led to the general area of food by olfaction. Once in the general area, these birds seem to rely more heavily on vision to lead them to the exact location of a food source.

Grubb (1972, 1974) has presented evidence indicating that several species of the Procellariiformes may use olfaction in navigation and nest location. The most compelling evidence was for *Oceanodroma leucorrhoa* (Leach's storm petrel). He found that this species usually returns to its island nesting location at night by flying upwind, and that severing the olfactory nerves or plugging the nares apparently interferes with the birds' ability to return to the nest. Additionally, nesting material effectively served as a lure for the birds in total darkness and these birds consistently chose the arm of a Y maze that contained their own nesting material.

*Apteryx* (kiwi), one of the flightless birds confined to New Zealand, is nocturnal and feeds largely on earthworms and other hidden food. Its vision is poor, and it is the only bird with nostrils at the tip of the beak; also, unlike any other birds, the kiwi sniffs while foraging. Wenzel (1968, 1972) has demonstrated that kiwi were able to locate at night the one feeding station of three that contained their food.

It has been suggested (Stager, 1967) that *Indica-tor* spp. (African honeyguides) locate beehives, and thus the wax on which they feed, by means of olfaction. He found that a burning beeswax candle would attract these birds. Archer and Glen (1969) report that honeyguides can be trapped successfully in the vicinity of hives which have been abandoned by the bees for as long as 10–12 days when other cues (vision, audition) from bees would no longer be available.

Homing pigeons with bilaterally sectioned olfactory nerves or nares plugged with cotton display an impaired ability to return to the home loft (Papi *et al.,* 1971, 1972, 1973; Benvenuti *et al.,* 1973). Because these experiments indicated no alteration in the homing drive of birds that were directionally trained or sham operated, the conclusions were that olfaction plays an important role in the initial orientation of homing pigeons.

Pigeons and doves have been used most frequently for laboratory studies in birds. The emphasis on this group is unfortunate because their olfactory development is only moderate compared with the species already discussed. Operant conditioning techniques have been successfully used to demonstrate that pigeons have an excellent ability to use olfactory cues to perform key-pecking tasks (Michaelsen, 1959; Henton *et al.,* 1966; Schumake *et al.,* 1970). Earlier behavioral work (Soudek, 1929; Zahn, 1933) indicated that odorants did not influence the palatability of food and fluids.

Gallinaceous birds have been the subjects of very little olfactory research. Tucker (1965) presents electrophysiological evidence that the bobwhite quail can perceive some odors. Although the chicken does possess moderately well-developed olfactory lobes and nerve tracts, observation fails to suggest that it is concerned with the odors of its environment.

The olfactory system in a number of aquatic species, e.g., penguins, geese, and terns (Bang, 1971) has been described as well developed. Neuhaus (1963) has suggested that *Anser anser* (greylag goose) responded to skatol. Walter (1943) was unable to condition gastric juice secretion in domestic ducks in response to olfactory stimuli, although the birds were readily conditioned to visual stimuli.

The reports of olfactory behavior in songbirds, including finches, siskins, robins, tits, and warblers, are predominantly negative.

**Methods of detecting olfaction.** Two general laboratory methods have been used to detect olfactory ability or perception in birds. The neurophysiological methods have involved recording from the olfactory nerve (Tucker, 1965) or directly from the olfactory bulb (Wenzel and Sieck, 1972) during odorant stimulus presentation in an olfactometer. Behavioral methods of the study of olfaction in birds involve two techniques. In the first, birds are asked to discriminate between air and an odor that previous training has made relevant to the test (Michaelsen, 1959; Henton *et al.*, 1966; Shumake *et al.*, 1970). The second technique involves continuous monitoring of the heart rate and/or the respiration rate during intermittent presentation of odorous stimuli (Wenzel, 1968, 1972).

**Summary.** The evidence available on the sense of smell in birds does not permit many generalizations. At one extreme is the kiwi, with anatomical development and sniffing behavior indicating that olfaction is functional in locating food. At the other extreme are the songbirds, for which there is little evidence of a functioning olfactory apparatus.

The failure of birds to react to the odors with which they have been presented in the laboratory raises two questions. The first is that lack of response to the odor in question implies not lack of sensitivity but that the odor has not been carried to the receptor. The lack of sniffing behavior in all birds but the kiwi may require moving air to effect contact between the stimulus and the receptor. The second is that the perfumes or reagent-grade chemical which have been used in the laboratory simply do not correspond to the birds' spectrum of chemical sensitivity.

For most birds, the evidence does not suggest a preeminent role for olfaction among their natural functions. Domesticated birds reveal no concern for odors in their environment. However, the presence of neuroanatomical structures suggests that olfactory information can be transmitted even if it is not generally behaviorally meaningful.

## Taste

The function of taste is to encourage the ingestion of nutrients, to discriminate among foods that are available, and possibly to avoid those that are toxic. The taste system in a particular species can be expectd to complement digestion, metabolism and the dietary requirements of that species.

**Taste receptors.** Avian taste buds were first described by Botezat (1904). Taste receptors in chickens, 30 $\mu$m wide by 70 $\mu$m long, are found at the base of the tongue and the floor of the pharynx, commonly in close association with the salivary glands (Lindenmaier and Kare, 1959). As may be expected, the highly cornified anterior part of the tongue is devoid of taste buds. Avian taste buds, intermediate in shape between those of fish and of mammals, resemble those of reptiles and are innervated by the glossopharyngeal nerve. Taste buds are composed of three types of cells, the respective functions of which are sensory, supporting, and, to a small degree, basal. Engelmann (1957) suggests that taste acuity of the fowl is related to the total number of sensory cells.

Birds have relatively few taste buds compared to other classes. However, the significance of the relationship between numbers of buds and taste behavior has not been explained. The number of taste buds in the domestic fowl is reported to increase with age, whereas the converse has been found in *Pyrrhula pyrrhula* (bullfinch) (Table 2–2).

Little use has been made of birds in neuroanatomical research on taste. The reader is referred to Beidler (1971) for a detailed discussion, based largely on mammalian research, of current knowledge and theories concerning central functions and peripheral mechanisms in taste. A comprehensive review of the sense of taste in birds can be found in Wenzel (1973).

**Methods of study.** The early studies of taste in birds consisted of observing the behavior of birds as they consumed a food or fluid in their natural environment. The preference test is the most common laboratory method used to measure the sensitivity of birds to taste stimuli. Usually the material

*Table 2–2  Number of taste buds in various animals[a]*

| Chicken | 24 | Lindenmaier and Kare (1959) |
|---|---|---|
| Pigeon | 37 | Moore and Elliott (1946) |
| Bullfinch | 46 | Duncan (1960) |
| Starling | 200 | Bath (1906) |
| Duck | 200 | Bath (1906) |
| Parrot | 350 | Bath (1906) |
| Japanese quail | 62 | Warner *et al.* (1967) |
| Snake | 0 | Payne (1945) |
| Kitten | 473 | Elliott (1937) |
| Bat | 800 | Moncrieff (1951) |
| Human | 9,000 | Cole (1941) |
| Pig and goat | 15,000 | Moncrieff (1951) |
| Rabbit | 17,000 | Moncrieff (1951,) |
| Calf | 25,000 | Weber *et al.* (unpublished data, 1961) |
| Catfish | 100,000 | Hyman (1942) |

[a]Modified from Kare and Ficken (1963).

46    to be tested is placed in aqueous solution, and the animal is given a choice between the mixture and distilled water, the two being presented simultaneously (Kare *et al.*, 1957). Duncan (1960), working with the feral pigeon, used a single-stimulus method in which the choices were presented singly at different times, eliminating position bias. Jacobs and Scott (1957) used a three-choice method in testing the taste preferences of chickens. Cafeteria-type tests in which a full array of stimuli are presented simultaneously seem to overwhelm the chicken's discriminatory ability.

Electrophysiological studies of taste in birds have been few in number and have utilized only chickens or pigeons as the experimental animal (Kitchell *et al.*, 1959; Halpern, 1963; Kadono *et al.*, 1966; Landolt, 1970). Such studies usually involve application of substances to the tongue of the subject and measurement of multiunit or single-fiber activity in the glossopharyngeal nerve. The results indicate whether or not the chemical has evoked a peripheral discharge but not whether this chemical has had an appealing or offending taste to the animal. Although there are examples of close correlations between behavioral and electrophysiological response, there are also contradictions (Halpern, 1963). Using these techniques, Kitchell *et al.* (1959) demonstrated the water sense of the bird. Operant techniques, which often have been used successfully in studies on vision (Adler, 1963), have seen limited use in taste research with birds.

Research on taste in birds has been handicapped by the general assumption that they live in the human sensory world. The taste sensations experienced by man cannot be assumed to be the same as for birds. Nevertheless, in order to compare results obtained from birds with data for man or any other species, the classical categories of sweet, sour, bitter,and salty must be used.

**Ability to taste.** *Sweet.* Contrary to the widely held supposition that sugars have a universal appeal, most avian species do not avidly select sugar solutions. Kare and Medway (1959) observed that the fowl on an *ad libitum* diet was indifferent to the common sugars. However, several investigators observed modest preferences for sugar solutions over water. Gentle (1972) reported a preference by Brown Leghorn chickens for 5% sucrose. Japanese and bobwhite quail preferred some concentrations of sucrose and glucose (Brindley, 1965; Harriman and Milner, 1969), and redwinged blackbirds selected pure water over sucrose (Rogers and Maller, 1973). There is unanimity in the literature tht birds reject such synthetic sweeteners as saccharin or dulcin. Although most avian species evidence little or no interest in the common sugars, parrots, budgerigars, and broad-tailed hummingbirds actively select sugar solutions. Collectively, the data suggest that nectar or fruit-eating species are more likely to respond positively to sugars than are insectivorous or graminivorous birds, which respond negatively or not at all.

The discovery that three tropical fruits contain intensely sweet proteins (Cagan, 1973) leads to speculation on the role (if any) of the sweet principles in the plant. It is possible (though not demonstrated) that the sweet taste-active proteins may aid in seed dispersal by birds or other animals. No avian species have yet been tested with any of the sweet proteins.

A number of factors other than taste may be involved, individually or collectively, in the response of a bird to a sugar solution, e.g., osmotic pressure, viscosity, melting point, nutritive value, toxicity, and optical characteristics, among others. However, graded levels of sugar solutions up to a viscous 25% were accepted by chicks equally with water (Kare and Medway, 1959). These authors concluded that no physical or chemical quality could be used to predict reliably how a chick on an adequate diet would respond to the taste of a solution. Visual properties and the surface texture of food have been reported to take precedence over all other qualities in the birds' selection of food (Morris, 1955, Kear, 1960).

*Salt.* The specific appetite for sodium chloride created by a deficiency can be demonstrated with the chicken. The domestic chick delays drinking for extended periods in order to avoid consuming a sodium chloride solution with a concentration exceeding the ability of the chick's kidneys to handle it (Kare and Beily, 1948). In fact, where no alternative is available, many chicks die of thirst rather than consume a toxic 2% salt solution. They accept sodium chloride solutions only up to about 0.9% (0.15$M$; see Pick and Kare, 1962). Various other birds without nasal salt glands that have been studied have similar taste tolerance thresholds (Bartholomew and Cade, 1958; Bartholomew and MacMillan, 1960, 1961; Hamrum, 1953; Willoughby, 1971). Mourning doves freely drink any solution that is hypotonic to their body fluids.

Rensch and Neunzig (1925) investigated sodium choloride thresholds (i.e., the lowest concentration at which solutions are rejected) for 58 species and found that the thresholds ranged from 0.35% in a parrot to 37.5% in the siskin. Unlike the rat, which avidly selects some hypotonic concentrations of sodium chloride, many birds are indifferent up to the concentration at which they reject the salt solutions.

The domestic fowl on a diet very low in sodium or calcium will exhibit a specific appetite and select, in a choice situation, the diet or solution that corrects its deficiency. In calcium-depleted birds, Wood-Gush (personal communication, 1958) observed aggressive exploratory behavior with associated pecking. These birds were able to make the correct selection in two-choice preference tests from some of the presented calcium compound solutions, but not from others.

The common tern, which has a nasal salt gland,

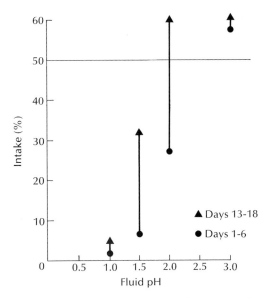

2–12 Daily consumption of HCl solutions for days 1–6 compared with daily consumption for days 13–18, expressed as percent of total fluid intake at four pH levels. (From Fuerst and Kare, 1962.)

**Table 2–3**  *The preference[a] for sodium and chloride metallic solutions at various concentrations over distilled water (chicks)*

|  | Concentration (g/100 ml) | | | | |
|---|---|---|---|---|---|
|  | 0.1 | 0.2 | 0.4 | 0.8 | 1.0 |
| Na acetate | 55[a] | 52 | 56 | 52 | 51 |
| Na sulfate | 54 | 52 | 52 | 53 | 50 |
| Na phosphate (monobasic) | 52 | 53 | 52 | 52 | 54 |
| Na succinate | 49 | 52 | 54 | 50 | 56 |
| Na citrate | 54 | 52 | 54 | 47 | 35 |
| Na phosphate (dibasic) | 51 | 49 | 47 | 44 | 14 |
| Na tungstate | 50 | 46 | 48 | – | – |
| Na bicarbonate | 52 | 43 | 38 | 20 | 14 |
| Na benzoate | 49 | 41 | 23 | 15 | 10 |
| Na bisulfate | 38 | 23 | 35 | 17 | 23 |
| Na pyrophosphate | 46 | 37 | 20 | 3 | 4 |
| Na perborate | 42 | 29 | 10 | 9 | 6 |
| Na carbonate | 42 | 30 | 10 | 4 | 2 |
| Na phosphate (tribasic) | 46 | 20 | 4 | 1 | 2 |
| Na cholate | 4 | 20 | 3 | – | 3 |
| Sodium Cl | 50[a] | 50 | 55 | 50 | 45 |
| Magnesium Cl | 49 | 51 | 51 | 53 | 45 |
| Choline Cl | 51 | 48 | 49 | 50 | 51 |
| Manganese Cl | 49 | 51 | 46 | 16 | – |
| Strontium Cl | 50 | 38 | 44 | 18 | 9 |
| Ammonium Cl | 49 | 46 | 35 | 12 | 6 |
| Barium Cl | 36 | 48 | 41 | – | 15 |
| Calcium Cl | 43 | 45 | 27 | 15 | 5 |
| Zinc Cl | 33 | 24 | 10 | 2 | 2 |
| Cobalt Cl | 26 | 12 | 6 | 5 | 6 |
| Tin Cl | 30 | 7 | 1 | 1 | 2 |
| Copper Cl | 6 | 11 | 3 | 8 | 4 |
| Iron Cl | 2 | 4 | 2 | 3 | 4 |

[a]Preference = (salt solution consumed × 100)/total fluid intake.

has a high threshold for salt that has been associated with the intake of brackish water with its food. However, when given a choice, the herring gull (with salt gland) selects pure water over a saline solution (Harriman and Kare, 1966). The role of the nasal salt gland in the handling of salt is discussed in Chapter 14.

The order of acceptability of ionic series by birds does not appear to fit into the lyotropic or sensitivity series reported for other animals. No physical or chemical theory has been offered to explain the responses to sodium salts and chlorides presented in Table 2–3.

*Sour.* Birds have a wide range of tolerance for acidity and alkalinity in their drinking water (Figure 2–12 and Table 2–3). Fuerst and Kare (1962) reported that over an 18-day period, chicks would tolerate strong mineral acid solutions, i.e., pH 2 (Table 2–4). Organic acids were less acceptable, and the tolerance for the hydrogen ion was not equally equivalent for the hydroxyl ion. The starling and the herring gull also readily accept hydrochloric acid solutions. Gentle (1972) reported a reduction to chick's aversion to acid (sour) solutions by the addition of glucose. Brindley and Prior (1968) report that bobwhites prefer 0.05% HCl.

48    *Table 2–4*    *Percent intake in chickens of acids and bases at different pH levels[a]*

| pH | 1.0 | | 2.0 | | 3.0 | | 4.0 |
|---|---|---|---|---|---|---|---|
| *Acids* | | | | | | | |
| HCl | 4 | 19 | 50 | | 59 | | |
| H₂SO₄ | 15 | 35 | 54 | | 56 | | |
| HNO₃ | 8 | | 62 | | 52 | | |
| Acetic | | | | | 16 | | 53 |
| Lactic | | | | 15 | 61 | | |

| pH | 10.0 | 11.0 | 12.0 | 13.0 |
|---|---|---|---|---|
| *Bases* | | | | |
| NaOH | 45 | 47 | 33 | 2 |
| KOH | | 48 | 36 | 3 |

[a]Tabled values are the mean of replicate lots. The percent intake = (volume of tested fluid/total fluid intake) × 100 (18 daily values were averaged). The position of the numbers is an indication of the pH of the test solution. For example, at pH 1.5 the average daily consumption of HCl was 19% of the total fluid intake. Distilled water was the alternative in every instance.

*Bitter.* Many chemicals are offensive to taste at low concentrations. These include compounds that are bitter to man but quite acceptable to birds, some that are offensive to both man and birds, and a third category of those quite acceptable to man but rejected by some birds.

Sucrose octacetate at a concentration bitter to man is readily accepted by the herring gull and the chicken. Bobwhite quail, which do not respond to sucrose octacetate as very young birds, gradually develop the ability to discriminate this compound (Cane and Vince, 1968). Quinine sulfate, which is used extensively as a standard bitter stimulus for man and rats, is also rejected by many species of birds. Both of these compounds evoked strong neural responses in the chicken. Man's category of what tastes bitter does not always coincide with the bird's reaction.

An interesting compound is dimethyl anthranilate, which is used in flavoring for human food. At dilutions of 1 part to 10,000, it is offensive to starlings, Japanese quail, pigeons, redwinged blackbirds, jungle fowl, herring gulls, and finches. The offensive taste quality of dimethyl anthrnilate has been used to reduce food intake in growing chicks and turkey poults. The concentrations totally unacceptable in a choice situation had to be increased almost tenfold in a no-choice situation to effect a reduced intake over an extended period (Kare and Pick, 1960).

The offensive secretions of many insects serve as a protective device against avian predators. Some of these have a caustic action on the eyes and possess highly offensive tastes (Yang and Kare, 1968).

Taste may serve as an important cue to adverse effects that may occur subsequent to ingestion of certain prey (Rozin and Kalat, 1971; Rogers, 1974). Wilcoxon *et al.,* (1971) found that bobwhites could learn to associate adverse postingestinal effects with particular tastes, but they were more responsive to visual cues. Little is known about the chemistry of offensive tastes in relation to the human senses.

**Nutrition and taste.** The function of taste in nutrition is an enigma. When caloric intake is restricted, a chick selects a sucrose solution to which it is normally indifferent and increases its fluid intake to make up the deficiency (Kare and Ficken, 1963). A similarly correct nutritional choice was not made when the sugar was replaced with an isocaloric solution of fat or protein. In a comparison of the responsiveness of domestic and wild jungle fowl to chemical stimuli in caloric regulation, Kare and Maller (1967) found that the wild strain was much more sensitive than the domestic. Fowl acutely deficient in protein avoid a casein solution and select only water, apparently because casein has an offensive taste to the chicken. In some experimental instances, the bird's preference complements its nutritional needs. However, the preference behavior of laboratory animals is not a reliable guide to the nutritional adequacy of a diet (Kare and Scott, 1962). Feed consumption is also discussed in Chapter 9.

**Temperature and taste.** The domestic fowl is acutely sensitive to the temperature of water. Acceptability decreases as the temperature of the water increases above the ambient. Fowl can discriminate a temperature difference of only 5°F, rejecting the higher temperature. Chickens suffer from acute thirst rather than drink water 10°F above their body temperature.

At the other extreme, the chicken readily accepts water down to freezing temperatures. This pattern of sensitivity to temperature was also observed in electrophysiological studies. A sizable minority of chickens lack this sensitivity, however. Because the response to temperature may take precedence over all chemical stimulants, temperature should be eliminated as a variable in taste studies of the fowl.

**Saliva and taste.** Saliva is involved in the normal phenomena of taste. Birds have been described as having a limited salivary flow. Using a technique that permitted continuous collection, Belman and Kare (1961) observed that the flow of saliva in the chicken was greater than that of man in terms of body weight but less in terms of food consumed.

**Individual variation in taste.** Japanese quail and domestic chickens have been tested individually to measure their reactions to a variety of chemicals, including ferric ammonium and calcium chlorides. Individuals showed markedly different thresholds. The distribution of thresholds was continuous, with reactions among birds to a single concentration of one chemical varying from preference to rejection. Chemical specificity was involved, because an individual that could taste one chloride at either unusually low or only very high concentrations would respond in an average manner to the others. It has been possible to select and breed for taste sensitivity to a specific chemical. This individual variation is not limited to birds (Kare, 1961).

That birds differ in their taste preferences as individuals, strains, or species has obvious ecological advantages. For example, it permits a population to utilize much more of the food in an environment than is possible if all the birds compete for a limited group of foods, and it contributes to an adaptive plasticity of food habits, making the invasion of new habitats and utilization of new foods possible.

Variation in response to taste is further compounded by possible seasonal changes. It is interesting to speculate about whether taste directs or follows the abrupt changes in feeding pattern of birds that are insectivorous for part of the year and graminivorous for the rest. A possible role for taste in the intensive feeding prior to migration is therefore to be considered.

**Summary.** Kare and Beauchamp (1975) in discussing the comparative aspects of the sense of taste in birds and mammals have pointed out that most of the work on the basic mechanism of taste stimulation has been conducted with mammals. This mammalian work has indicated that the initial interaction of a taste stimulus and a receptor cell occurs on the microvilli of the taste receptor cells. Cagan (1971) showed that preparations of bovine taste papillae differentially bound various sugars, indicating the importance of peripheral events in taste discrimination. This idea, however, along with other theories of the biochemical mechanism of taste (see Beidler, 1971) has yet to be tested with any avian species, and the generality of the theories, even across mammalian species, has yet to be unequivocally demonstrated.

Birds have a sense of taste. However, no pattern, whether chemical, physical, nutritional, or physiological, can be correlated consistently with the bird's taste behavior. The behavioral, ecological, and chemical context of a taste stimulant can influence the bird's response. The observed responses, particularly to sweet and bitter, indicate that the bird does not share human taste experiences. However, the supposition that there is a difference in degree between individual birds and an absolute difference between some species appears warranted.

## REFERENCES

Adler, H. E. (1963). Psychophysical limits of celestial navigation hypothesis. *Ergebnisse der Biol., 26,* 235.

Adler, H. E., and J. Dalland. (1959). Spectral thresholds in the starling *(Sturnus vulgaris). J. Comp. Physiol. Psychol., 52,* 438.

Allison, A. C. (1953). The morphology of the olfactory system in the vertebrates *Biol. Rev., 28,* 195.

Archer, A. T., and R. M. Glen. (1969). Observations on the behavior of two species of honey-guides *Indicator variegatus* (Lesson) and *Indicator exilis* (Cassin). *Los Angeles County Mus. Contrib. Sci., 160,* 1.

Armington, J. C., and F. C. Thiede. (1956). Electroretinal demonstration of a Purkinje shift in the chicken eye. *Am. J. Physiol., 186,* 258.

Bang, B. G. (1971). Functional anatomy of the olfactory system in 23 orders of birds. *Acta Anat., 58* (Suppl.), 1.

Bang, B. G., and F. B. Bang. (1959). A comparative study of the vertebrate nasal chamber in relation to upper respiratory infections. *Bull. Johns Hopkins Hosp., 104,* 107.

Bartholomew, G. A., and T. J. Cade. (1958). Effects of sodium chloride on the water consumption of house finches. *Physiol. Zool., 31,* 304.

Bartholomew, G. A., and R. E. MacMillan. (1960). The water re-

50

quirements of mourning doves and their use of sea water and NaCl solutions. *Physiol. Zool., 33,* 171.

Bartholomew, G. A., and R. E. MacMillan. (1961). Water economy of the California quail and its use of sea water. *Auk, 78,* 505.

Bartley, H. S. (1959). Central mechanisms of vision. In "Handbook of Physiology," Sec. 1 (H. W. Magoun, Ed.). Baltimore: Williams and Wilkins, p. 713.

Bath, W. (1906). Die Geschmaksorgane der Vögel und Krokodile. *Arch. Biontol. (Berlin), 1,* 1.

Beidler, L. M. (Ed.). (1971). "Handbook of Sensory Physiology," Vol. 4, Pt. 1. Berlin and New York: Springer-Verlag.

Belman, A. L., and M. R. Kare. (1961). Character of salivary flow in the chicken. *Poultry Sci., 40* 1377.

Benner, J. (1938). Untersuchungen uber die Raumwahrnehmung der Hühner. *Z. Wiss. Zool., 151,* 382.

Benvenuti, S., V. Fiaschi, L. Fiore, and F. Papi. (1973). Homing performances of inexperienced and directionally trained pigeons subjected to olfactory nerve section. *J. Comp. Physiol., 83,* 81.

Blough, D. S. (1961). Experiments in animal psychophysics. *Sci. Am., 205,* 113.

Botezat, E. (1904). Geschmacksorgane und andere nervöse Endapparate im Schnabel der Vögel. *Biol. Centralblatt., 24,* 722.

Brindley, L. D. (1965). Taste discrimination in bobwhite and Japanese quail. *Anim. Behav., 13,* 507.

Brindley, L. D., and S. Prior. (1968). Effects of age on taste discrimination in the bobwhite quail. *Anim. Behav., 16,* 304.

Brückner, G. H. (1933). Untersuchungen zur Tiersoziologie inbesondere zur Auflösung der Familie. *Z. Physiol., 188,* 255.

Cagan, R. H. (1971). Biochemical studies of taste sensation. I. Binding of $^{14}$C-labeled sugars to bovine taste papillae. *Biochem. Biophys. Acta., 252,* 199.

Cagan, R. H. (1973). Chemostimulatory protein: A new type of taste stimulus. *Science, 181,* 32.

Cane, V. R., and M. A. Vince. (1968). Age and learning in quail. *Brit. J. Psychol, 59,* 37.

Catania, A. C. (1964). On the visual acuity of the pigeon. *J. Exp. Anal. Behav., 7,* 361.

Cobb, S. (1960). Observations on the comparative anatomy of the avian brain. *Perspect. Biol. Med., 3,* 383.

Cobb, B. F., and F. Carter, and V. F. Koenig. (1968). The distribution of the soluble protein components in the crystalline lenses of specimens of amphibians, reptiles and birds. *Comp. Biochem. Physiol., 26,* 519.

Cole, E. C. (1941). "Comparative Histology." Philadelphia: Blakiston.

Collias, N., and M. Joos. (1953). The spectrographic analysis of sound signals of the domestic fowl. *Behavior, 5,* 175.

Donner, K. O. (1953). The spectral sensitivity of the pigeon's retinal elements. *J. Physiol., 122,* 524.

Dooling, R. J., and J. A. Mulligan. (1971). Auditory sensitivity and song spectrum of the common canary *(Serinus canarius). J. Acoust. Soc. Am., 50,* 700.

Dooling, R. J. and J. C. Saunders. (1973). Absolute and differential frequency sensitivity in the parakeet *(Melopsittacus undulatus).* Abstract TT9, 86 Meeting of the Acoustical Society of America.

Dooling, R. J. and J. C. Saunders. (1975). Hearing in the parakeet *(Melopsittacus undulatus):* Absolute thresholds, critical ratios, frequency difference limens, and vocalizations. *J. Comp. Physiol. Psychol, 88,* 1.

Dowling, J. E. (1970). Organization of vertebrate retinas. *Invest. Opthalmol., 9,* 655.

Duncan, C. J. (1960). Preference tests and the sense of taste in the feral pigeon. *Anim. Behav., 8,* 54.

Elliott, R. (1937). Total distribution of taste buds on the tongue of the kitten at birth. *J. Comp. Neurol., 66,* 361.

Engelmann, C. (1957). "So Leben Hühner, Tauben, Gänse." Radebeul, East Germany: Neumann Verlag.

Fischlschweiger, W., and R. O'Rahilly. (1966). The ultrastructure of the pecten oculi in the chick. *Acta Anat., 65,* 561.

Fry, G. A. (1959). The image forming mechanism of the eye. In "Handbook of Physiology," Sec. 1, (H. W. Magoun, Ed.). Baltimore: Williams and Wilkins, p. 647.

Fuerst, F. F., and M. R. Kare. (1962). The influence of pH on fluid tolerance and preferences. *Poultry Sci., 41,* 71.

Galifret, Y. (1968). Les diverses aires fonctionelles de la retine du pigeon. *Z. Zeltforsch., 86,* 535.

Gaudin, E. P. (1968). On the middle ear of birds. *Acta Otolaryng.* (Stockholm), *65,* 316.

Gentle, M. J. (1972). Taste preferences in the chicken *(Gallus domesticus L.). Brit. Poultry Sci., 13,* 141.

Granit, O. (1941). Beiträge zur kenntnis des Gehörsinns der Vögel. *Ornis Fenn., 18,* 49.

Granit, R. (1959). Neural activity in the retina. In "Handbook of Physiology," Sect. 1, (H. W. Magoun, Ed.). Baltimore: Williams and Wilkins, p. 693.

Griffin, D. (1953). Acoustic orientation in the oil bird, *Steatornis. Proc. Natl. Acad. Sci., 39,* 884.

Grubb, T. C., Jr. (1972). Smell and foraging in shearwaters and petrels. *Nature* (London), *237,* 404.

Grubb, T. C., Jr. (1974). Olfactory navigation to the nesting burrow in Leach's petrel *(Oceanodroma leucorrhoa). Anim. Behav., 22,* 192.

Guhl, A. M. (1953). The social behavior of the domestic fowl. Tech. Bull. 73, Kansas State College Agr. Exp. Sta., p. 48.

Halpern, B. P. (1963). Gustatory nerve responses in the chicken. *Am. J. Physiol., 203,* 541.

Hamrum, C. L. (1953). Experiments on the senses of taste and smell in the bobwhite quail *(Colinus virginianus virginianus). Am. Midland Naturalist, 49,* 872.

Harriman, A. E., and M. R. Kare. (1966). Aversion to saline solutions in starlings, purple grackles, and herring gulls. *Physiol. Zool., 39,* 123.

Harriman, A. E., and J. S. Milner. (1969). Preference for sucrose solutions by Japanese quail *(Coiurnix coturnix japonica)* in two-bottle drinking tests. *Am. Midland Naturalist, 81,* 575.

Held, H. (1926). Die Cochlea der Sauger und der Vögel, "Handbuch der Normalen und Pathologischen Physiologie" (A. Bethe, Ed.). Berlin: Springer-Verlag, p. 467.

Henton, W. W., J. C. Smith, and D. Tucker. (1966). Odor discrimination in pigeons following section of the olfactory nerves. *J. Comp. Physiol. Psychol., 69,* 317.

Hess, E. H. (1956). Natural preferences of chicks and ducklings for objects of different colors. *Psych. Rep., 2,* 477.

Hess, V. C. (1912). Gesichtssinn. *Handb. Vergl. Physiol., 4,* 555.

Hinde, R. A. (1969). "Bird Vocalizations." Cambridge: Cambridge University Press.

Honigmann, H. (1921). Untersuchungen uber Lichtempfindlichkeit und Adaptierung des Vogelauges. *Arch. Ges. Physiol. (Pflügers), 189,* 1.

Hyman, L. H. (1942). "Comparative Vertebrate Anatomy." Chicago: University of Chicago Press.

Jacobs, H. L., and M. L. Scott. (1957). Factors mediating food and liquid intake in chickens. I. Studies on the preference for sucrose or saccharin solutions. *Poultry Sci., 36,* 8.

Jellinek, A. (1926a). Versuche über das Gehör der Vögel. I: Dressurversuche an Tauben mit akustichen Reizen. *Arch. Ges. Physiol. (Pflügers), 211,* 64. Cited by Wever and Bray, 1936.

Jellinek, A. (1926b). Versuche über das Gehör der Vögel II: Gehörprüfungen an Tauben nach Exstirpation des Mittelohres. *Arch Ges. Physiol. (Pflugers), 211,* 73. Cited by Wever and Bray, 1936.

Kadono, H., T. Okado, and K. Ohno. (1966). Neurophysiological studies of the sense of taste in the chicken. *Res. Bull. Fac. Agri., Gifu Univ., 22,* 149.

Kare, M. R. (1961). "Physiological and Behavioral Aspects of Taste." Chicago: University of Chicago Press, p. 13.

Kare, M. R. and G. K. Beauchamp. (1976). Taste, smell and hearing. In "Duke's Physiology of Domestic Animals," 9th Edition (M. J. Swenson, Ed.). Ithaca, N. Y.: Comstock, Chapter 57.

Kare, M. R., and J. Beily. (1948). The toxicity of sodium chloride and its relation to water intake in baby chicks. *Poultry Sci., 27,* 751.

Kare, M. R., and M. S. Ficken. (1963). Comparative studies on the sense of taste. In "Olfaction and Taste" (Y. Zotterman, Ed.). New York: Pergamon Press.

Kare, M. R., and O. Maller. (1967). Taste and food intake in domesticated and jungle fowl. *J. Nutr.*, 92, 191.

Kare, M. R., and W. Medway. (1959). Discrimination between carbohydrates by the fowl. *Poultry Sci.*, 38, 1119.

Kare, M. R., and H. L. Pick. (1960). The influence of the sense of taste on feed and fluid consumption. *Poultry Sci.*, 39, 697.

Kare, M. R., and M. L. Scott. (1962). Nutritional value and feed acceptability. *Poultry Sci.*, 44, 276.

Kare, M. R., R. Black, and E. G. Allison. (1957). The sense of taste in the fowl. *Poultry Sci.*, 36, 129.

Kear, J. (1960). Food selection in certain finches with special reference to interspecific differences. Ph. D. thesis, Cambridge University, Cambridge.

King-Smith, P. E. (1969). Absorption spectra and function of the colored oil drops in the pigeon retina. *Vision Res.*, 9, 1391.

King-Smith, P. E. (1971). Special senses. In "Physiology and Biochemistry of Fowl" (Bell D. J. and B. M. Freeman, Eds.). New York and London: Academic Press, Chapter 46.

Kitchell, R. L., L. Strom, and Y. Zotterman. (1959). Electrophysiological studies of thermal and taste reception in chickens and pigeons. *Acta Physiol. Scand.*, 46, 133.

Klopfer, P. H. (1962). "Behavioral Aspects of Ecology." Englewood Cliffs, N. J.: Prentice-Hall.

Knecht, S. (1940). Uber den Gehörsinn und die Musikalität der Vögel, *Z. Vergl. Physiol.*, 27, 169.

Konishi, M. (1965). The role of auditory feedback in the control of vocalization in the white-crowned sparrow. *Z. Tierpsychol.*, 22, 770.

Konishi, M. (1970). Comparative neurophysiological studies of hearing and vocalization in song-birds. *Z. Vergl. Physiol.*, 66, 257.

Landolt, J. P. (1970). Neural properties of pigeon lingual chemoreceptors. *Physiol. Behav.*, 5, 1151.

Lashley, K. S. (1916). The colour vision of birds. I: The spectrum of the domestic fowl. *Anim. Behav.*, 6, 1.

Lindenmaier, P., and M. R. Kare. (1959). The taste end-organs of the chicken. *Poultry Sci.*, 38, 545.

Manley, G. A. (1973). A review of some current concepts of the functional evolution of the ear in terrestrial vertebrates. *Evolution*, 26, 608.

Matthes, E. (1934). "Geruchsorgan, Lubosch Handbuch der Vergleichenden Anatomie der Wirbeltiere, Groppert, Kallius, Vol. 11. Urban and Schwarzenbeig.

McGill, J. I., T. P. S. Powell, and W. M. Cowan. (1966). Retinal representation upon the optic tectum and isthmo-optic nucleus in the pigeon. *J. Anat.*, 100, 5.

Michaelsen, W. J. (1959). Procedure for studying olfactory discrimination in pigeons. *Science*, 130, 630.

Millodot, M., and P. Blough. (1971). The refractive state of the pigeon eye. *Vision Res.*, 11, 1019.

Moncrieff, R. W. (1951). "The Chemical Senses." London: Hill, p. 172.

Money, K. E., L. Bonen, J. D. Beatty, L. A. Kuehn, M. Sokoloff, and R. S. Weaver. (1971). Physical properties of fluids and structures of vestibular apparatus of the pigeon. *Am. J. Physiol.*, 220, 140.

Moore, C. A., and R. Elliott. (1946). Numerical and regional distribution of taste buds on the tongue of the bird. *J. Comp. Neurol.*, 84, 119.

Morris, D. (1955). The seed preferences of certain finches under controlled conditions. *Avic. Mag.*, 61, 271.

Morris, V. B., and C. D. Shorey. (1967). An electron microscope study of types of receptor in the chick retina. *J. Comp. Neurol.*, 129, 313.

Neuhaus, W. (1963). On the olfactory sense of birds. In "Olfaction and Taste" (Y. Zotterman, Ed.). New York: Macmillan, p. 111.

Norberg, A. (1968). Physical factors in directional hearing in *Aegolius funereus* (Linné) (Strigiformes) with special reference to the assymmetry of the external ears. *Ark. Zool.*, 20, 181.

O'Rahilly, R., and D. B. Meyer. (1961). The development and histochemistry of the pecten oculi. In "The Structure of the Eye" (G. K. Smelser, Ed.). New York: Academic Press, p. 207.

Papi, F., L. Fiore, V. Fiaschi, and S. Benvenuti. (1971). The influence of of olfactory nerve section on the homing activity of carrier pigeons. *Monit. Zool. Ital. (N.S.)*, 5, 265.

Papi, F., L. Fiore, V. Fiaschi, and S. Benvenuti. (1972). Olfaction and homing in pigeons. *Monit. Zool. Ital. (N.S.)*, 6, 85.

Papi, F., L. Fiore, V. Fiaschi, and S. Benvenuti. (1973). An experiment for testing the hypothesis of olfactory navigation in homing pigeons. *J. Comp. Physiol.*, 83, 93.

Payne, A. (1945). The sense of smell in snakes. *J. Bomb. Nat. Hist. Soc.*, 45, 507.

Payne, R. S. (1962). How the barn owl locates prey by hearing. In "The Living Bird," Vol. 1, Ithaca, N. Y.: Cornell Laboratory of Ornithology, p. 151.

Payne, R. S. (1971). Acoustic location of prey by barn owls (*Tyto alba*). *J. Exp. Biol.*, 54, 535.

Pearson, O. (1972). "The Avian Brain." New York and London: Academic Press.

Pick, H. L., and M. R. Kare. (1962). The effect of artificial cues on the measurement of taste preference in the chicken. *J. Comp. Physiol. Psychol.*, 55, 342.

Polyak, S. (1957). "The Vertebrate Visual System." Chicago: University of Chicago Press.

Portmann, A. (1950). "Traite de Zoologie," Tome XV. *Les Organes des Sens* (P. P. Grassé, Ed.). Paris: Masson & Cie., p. 213.

Prosser, C. L., and F. A. Brown. (1961). "Comparative Animal Physiology." Philadelphia: W. B. Saunders.

Pumphrey, R. J. (1961). "The Sensory Organs: Hearing in Birds," Vol. II (A. J. Marshall, Ed.). New York: Academic Press.

Quine, D. G. and M. Konishi. (1974). Absolute frequency discrimination in the barn owl. *J. Comp. Physiol.*, 93, 347.

Raviola, E., and G. Raviola. (1967). A light and electron microscope study of the pecten of the pigeon eye. *Am. J. Anat.*, 120, 427.

Rensch, B., and R. Neunzig. (1925). Experimentelle Untersuchungen uber den Geschmackssinn der Vogel, II. *J. Ornithol.*, 73, 633.

Rochon-Duvigneaud, A. (1950). Les yeux et la vision. In "Traité de Zoologie," Tome XV (P. P. Grassé, Ed.). Paris: Masson & Co., p. 221.

Rogers, J. G., Jr. (1974). Responses of caged red-winged blackbirds to two types of repellents. *J. Wildl. Manage.*, 38, 418.

Rogers, J. G., and O. Maller. (1973). Effect of salt on the response of birds to sucrose. *Physiol. Psychol.*, 1, 199.

Rozin, P., and J. W. Kalat. (1971). Specific hungers and poison avoidance as adaptive specializations of learning. *Psychol. Rev.*, 78, 459.

Saunders, J. C. (1972). A comparative analysis of middle-ear function in non-mammalian vertebrates. *Acta Oto-Laryngol.*, 73, 353.

Schlaer, R. (1972). An eagle's eye: quality of the retinal image. *Science*, 176, 920.

Schultze, M. (1866). Zur Anatomie und Physiologie der Retina. *Arch. Mikrose. Anat.*, 2, 175.

Schwartzkopff, J. (1949). Über Sitz und Leistung von Gehör und Vibrationssinn bei Vögeln. *Z. Vergl. Physiol.*, 31, 527.

Schwartzkopff, J. (1955). On the hearing of birds. *Auk*, 72, 340.

Schwartzkopff, J. (1973). Mechanoreception. In "Avian Biology," Vol III (S. S. Farner and J. R. King, Eds.). New York and London: Academic Press, Chapter 7.

Shumake, S. A., J. C. Smith, and D. Tucker. (1970). Olfactory intensity difference thresholds in the pigeon. *J. Comp. Physiol. Psychol.*, 67, 64.

Sillman, A. J. (1969). The visual pigments of several species of birds. *Vision Res.*, 9, 1063.

Sillman, A. J. (1973). Avian vision. In "Avian Biology," Vol III (D. S. Farner and J. R. King, Eds.). New York and London: Academic Press, Chapter 5.

Skinner, N. F., and R. J. Beishon. (1971). Similarities in the color vision of pigeons and man. *J. Genet. Psychol.*, 119, 25.

Smith, C. A., and T. Takasaka. (1971). Auditory receptor organs of reptiles, birds, and mammals. *Contrib. Sens. Physiol.*, 5, 129.

Soudek, S. (1929). The sense of smell in the birds. *Intl. Cong. Zool.*, 10, 755.

Stager, K. E. (1964). The role of olfaction in food location by the

52   turkey vulture (Cathartes aura). Los Angeles County Mus.
     Contrib. Sci., 81, 3.

Stager, K. E. (1967). Avian olfaction. Am. Zool., 7, 415.

Thompson, G. (1971). The photoptic spectral sensitivity of gulls
     measured by electroretinographic and pupillometric meth-
     ods. Vision Res., 11, 719.

Thorpe, W. H. (1954). The process of song-learning in the chaffinch
     as studied by means of the sound-spectrograph. Nature
     (London), 173, 465.

Trainer, J. E. (1946). The auditory acuity of certain birds. Unpub-
     lished Ph. D. thesis. Cornell University, Ithaca, N.Y.

Tucker, D. (1965). Electrophysiological evidence for olfactory
     function in birds. Nature (London), 207, 304.

von Békésy, G. (1960). "Experiments in Hearing." New York:
     McGraw-Hill Book Co.

Wald, G., P. K. Brown, and P. H. Smith (1954). Iodopsin. J. Gen.
     Physiol., 38, 623.

Walls, G. L. (1942). "The Vertebrate Eye." Bloomfield Hills, Mich.:
     Cranbrook Institute of Science.

Walls, G. L., and H. D. Judd. (1933). The intraocular colour filters
     of vertebrates. Brit J. Ophthalmol., 17, 641. Cited by Pum-
     phrey, 1961a.

Walter, W. G. (1943). Some experiments on the sense of smell in
     birds studied by the method of conditioned reflexes. Arch.
     Neerl. Physiol. Homme et Animaux, 27, 1.

Warner, R. L., L. Z. McFarland, and W. O. Wilson. (1967). Micro-
     anatomy of the upper digestive tract of the Japanese quail.
     Am. J. Vet. Res., 28, 1537.

Wassiljew, M. Ph. (1933). Über das Tonunterscherdungsvermögen
     der Vögel für hohe Töne. Z. Vergl. Physiol., 19, 424.

Watson, J. B. (1915). Studies on the spectral sensitivity of birds.
     Pap. Dept. Marine Biol. Carnegie Inst. Wash., 7, 87.

Wenzel, B. M. (1968). The olfactory prowess of the Kiwi. Nature
     (London), 220, 1133.

Wenzel, B. M. (1972). Olfactory sensation in the Kiwi and other
     birds. Ann. N.Y. Acad. Sci., 188, 183.

Wenzel, B. M. (1973). Chemoreception. In "Avian Biology," Vol III
     (D. S. Farner and J. R. King, Eds.). New York and London:
     Academic Press, Chapter 6.

Wenzel, B. M., and M. Sieck. (1972). Olfactory perception and
     bulbar electrical activity in several avian species. Physiol.
     Behav., 9, 287.

Wever, E. G., and C. W. Bray. (1936). Hearing in the pigeon as
     studied by electrical responses of the inner ear. J. Comp.
     Psychol., 22, 353.

Wever, E. G., P. N. Herman, J. A. Simmons, and D. R. Hertzler.
     (1969). Hearing in the black-footed penguin, Spheniscus
     demersus, as represented by the cochlear potentials. Proc.
     Natl. Acad. Sci. U.S., 63, 676.

Wilcoxon, H. C., W. B. Dragoin, and P. A. Kral. (1971). Illness-in-
     duced aversions in rat and quail: relative salience of visual
     and gustatory cues. Science, 171, 826.

Willoughby, E. J. (1971). Drinking responses of the red crossbill
     (Loxia curvirostra) to solutions of NaCl, $MgCl_2$ and $CaCl_2$.
     Auk, 84, 828.

Winstrand, K. G., and O. Munk. (1965). The pecten oculi of the
     pigeon with particular regard to its function. Biol. Skr. Dan.
     Videnskab, Selskab, 14, 1.

Yang, R. S. H., and M. R. Kare. (1968). Taste response of a bird to
     constituents of arthropod defense secretions. Ann. Entomol.
     Soc. Am. 61, 781.

Zahn, W. (1933). Über den Geruchssinn einiger Vogel. Z. Vergl.
     Physiol., 19, 785.

# 3

## Blood: Physical Characteristics, Formed Elements, Hemoglobin, and Coagulation

P. D. Sturkie

with P. Griminger

Blood has many functions, among them (1) absorption and transport of nutrients from the alimentary canal to the tissues, (2) transport of the blood gases to and from the tissues, (3) removal of waste products of metabolism, (4) transportation of hormones produced by the endocrine glands, and (5) regulation of the water content of the body tissues. Blood is also important in the regulation and maintenance of body temperature.

Blood contains a fluid portion (the plasma), salts and other chemical constituents, and certain formed elements, the corpuscles. The corpuscles include the erythrocytes (red cells) and leukocytes (white cells).

Certain physical properties of blood are discussed here but such chemical constituents as proteins and lipids are treated in Chapters 12 and 13, carbohydrates in Chapter 11, calcium in Chapters 14 and 15, and other electrolytes in Chapter 14.

## PHYSICAL PROPERTIES OF BLOOD

Viscosity, specific gravity, and osmotic pressure of blood have important physical effects on the circulation and flow of blood and the exchange of fluid between blood and the tissues. Plasma proteins, which exert the greatest effect on plasma osmotic pressure, are discussed in Chapter 12 and the role plasma electrolytes play is discussed in Chapter 14 and elsewhere.

### Viscosity

The viscosity of whole blood is most influenced by the number of cells and, as expected, it is higher in males, because males have more red cells than females (Table 3–1). The viscosity of plasma is also influenced considerably by plasma proteins and is significantly higher in females or estrogenized males, because in each of the latter plasma proteins are higher than in normal males, or capons.

Usami *et al.* (1970) have studied the viscometric behavior of turkey blood over a wide range of hematocrits and shear rates. They have shown that the viscosity of the turkey red cell at high hematocrits is higher than in most mammalian species, which suggests a lower deformability of the nucleated cell.

### Specific Gravity

The specific gravity of blood of various avian species is shown in Table 3–1. Whole blood has a higher specific gravity than plasma because of the erythrocytes. The figure for the plasma of female chickens is significantly lower than for that of males. This is surprising, because the plasma proteins, which supposedly influence specific gravity most, are significantly higher in females. However, female plasma is lipemic and this condition tends to depress specific gravity. The plasma of laying female chickens made hyperlipemic by nicarbazine administration had a lower specific gravity than did the plasma of untreated females (Sturkie and Textor, 1960), demonstrating that plasma specific gravity is not a good measure of plasma protein in birds having lipemic plasma.

### Osmotic Pressure

The colloid osmotic pressure of avian plasma is considerably lower than that of most mammals because plasma albumin, which is relatively lower in birds, has more influence on colloid osmotic pressure than do globulins. Values for colloid osmotic pressure in chickens and doves are 150 and 110 mm $H_2O$, respectively (Albritton, 1952).

## ERYTHROCYTES

The erythrocytes of birds are oval shaped and, unlike those of mammals, are nucleated; they are also larger (Figure 3–1). The sizes of the erythrocytes of some avian species are presented in Table 3–2.

Hartman and Lessler (1963) made measurements on erythrocytes of 124 species in 46 families of wild birds. The range in size extended from 10.7 × 6.1 $\mu$m to 15.8 × 10.2 $\mu$m. The lower forms tended to have the largest erythrocytes; however, in a few families the cells were smaller in the smaller species (passerines and trochilids). Most of the domestic species have sizes intermediate between these ranges. The sizes are much larger than mammalian erythrocytes (5–7 $\mu$m for many species) but smaller than the cells of reptiles (18 × 7 $\mu$m; 23 × 12 $\mu$m).

The extent to which cell size and shape may be influenced by conditions of hydration and dehydration has not been studied.

### Numbers

The number of erythrocytes and corpuscular volume are influenced by age, sex, hormones, hypoxia, and other factors. Erythrocyte numbers for several species are shown in Table 3–3. In most species in which both sex hormones have been

*Table 3−1* *Physical properties of avian blood*

**Viscosity** of blood in relation to water at given temperatures and in centipoise[a]

| Species | Whole blood | Plasma | Temperature (°C) | Reference |
|---|---|---|---|---|
| Chicken, male | 3.67 | 1.42 | 42 | Vogel (1961) |
| capon | 2.47 | 1.28 | 42 | Vogel (1961) |
| female | 3.08 | 1.51 | 42 | Vogel (1961) |
| Duck | 4.0 | 1.5 | 14−20 | Spector (1956) |
| Goose | 4.6 | 1.5 | 14−20 | Spector (1956) |
| Ostrich | 4.5 | — | — | De Villiers (1938) |
| Turkey | — | 1.12[a] | — | Usami *et al.* (1970) |

**Specific gravity**

| Species | Whole blood | Plasma | Serum | Reference |
|---|---|---|---|---|
| Chicken, female | 1.050 | 1.099 | | Sturkie and Textor (1960) |
| female | — | 1.0180 (very lipemic) | | Sturkie and Textor (1960) |
| female | 1.0439 | 1.0177 | | Medway and Kare (1959) |
| male | — | 1.0210 | | Sturkie and Textor (1960) |
| male | 1.054 | — | 1.023 | Sturkie and Textor (1960) |
| Goose, male | 1.061 | 1.020 | | Hunsaker *et al.* (1964) |
| female | 1.052 | 1.022 | | Hunsaker *et al.* (1964) |
| Goose | 1.050 | 1.021 | | Wirth (1931) |
| Duck | 1.056 | 1.020 | | Wirth (1931) |
| Guinea fowl | 1.057 | 1.021 | | Wirth (1931) |
| Ostrich | 1.063 | 1.022 | | DeVilliers (1938) |

[a]Superscript indicates data in centipoise. All other viscosity data measured in relation to water.

studied, there is a difference in numbers and packed cell volume (Table 3−3 and 3−4), with higher levels in males (see Sturkie, 1965). The goose and pheasant appear to be exceptions in which there is little or no difference in hematocrit (Hunsaker *et al.*, 1964; Bond and Gilbert, 1958), although more studies are needed. Gilbert (1963) reported that estrogen administration to adult cocks depressed erythrocyte volumes and presumably numbers, although the latter was not determined; thyroxine administration tended to prevent the estrogen effect.

Estrogen administration to sexually immature *Coturnix* (quail) depressed erythrocyte numbers from 3.2 million to 1.6 million in males and from 3.19 million to 1.44 million in females (Nirmalan and Robinson, 1972) and had a similar effect on hematocrit; androgen, in contrast, increased the number significantly in immature males and females, suggesting a erythropoietic effect. Prolonged androgen administration increased hematocrit in chickens at sea level approximately 45% (Burton

and Smith, 1972) and about the same degree at high altitude (12,500 ft). Domm and Taber (1946) and others have reported that red cell numbers in the castrate male are nearly the same as in the female; when androgen was administered to castrates, the numbers approached the normal male level. Sturkie and Textor (1960), however, found the number in male castrate chickens to be intermediate between those for normal males and females. Female castrates (poulards) have the same number of red cells as normal females, indicating that estrogen has no positive effect on erythropoiesis but that androgen does. Older work by Domm and Taber (1946) indicates that thyroxine has a erythropoietic effect; this tends to counteract the negative effect of estrogen, as later demonstrated by Gilbert (1963) and by Sturkie (1951).

Although Hunsaker (1968) reported that estrogen depressed erythropoiesis in geese, androgen had little or no effect on red cell counts of normal male and females, and castrate male and female geese.

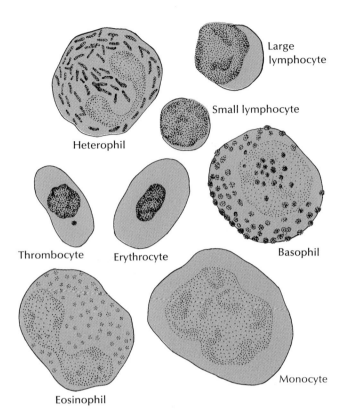

3–1
Drawing of mature blood cells of the bird.

## Corpuscular Volume (Hematocrit)

The corpuscles may be separated from the plasma by centrifugation at speeds of 3000 rpm or higher for 15–60 min. Hunsaker (1969) centrifuged blood of chickens, geese, and turkeys at 3215 × g for 30 min in macrotubes and determined hematocrits and the amount of plasma trapped, with the erythyrocytes and leukocytes making up the packed cell volume. The percentage of trapped plasma averaged from 2.35 in goose blood to 3.21 for chicken blood, with turkey blood intermediate. Cohen (1967) employed a microhematocrit method and centrifugation speeds of 11,650 rpm and 12,800 × g for varying periods up to 9.5 min. Almost complete packing was accomplished after 5 min centrifugation time. Values for several species are shown in Table 3–4.

Factors that affect cell numbers affect hematocrit, but cell size also influences the latter. Changes in cell volume may occur or be induced, without influencing the absolute number of cells, by an increase in plasma water (hemodilution) or a decrease (hemoconcentration). Blood sampling may cause hemodilution (see Sturkie, 1965) and epi-nephrine administration and hypothermia may cause hemoconcentration.

Androgen is erythropoietic in chickens and quails but it does not account solely for the sex differences in red cell numbers because Sturkie and Textor (1960) found the erythrocyte numbers and hematocrits of chicken male castrates to be intermediate between those in normal males and females. Female castrates have the same number of red cells as normal females.

## Anemias

An inherited type of macrocytic–normochromic anemia has been reported in chickens (Washburn and Smyth, 1968) characterized by a reduction of 15% in hematocrit, 14% in hemoglobin, and 23% in erythrocyte numbers.

Different strains of chickens carrying the genetic defect behaved differently in response to a diet low in copper and iron. (Washburn, 1969).

Chickens raised at ambient temperatures of 10°, 21.1°, and 32.2°C had higher hematocrits and hemoglobins than those raised at lower temperature, regardless of dietary regime; those raised at 32.2°C

*Table 3–2   Dimensions of avian erythrocytes*                                     57

| Species | Long diameter ($\mu$m) | Short diameter ($\mu$m) | Thickness ($\mu$m) | Reference |
|---|---|---|---|---|
| Chicken (breed not given) | | | | |
| 3 days old | 12.5 | 7.0 | 3.8 | Groebbels (1932) |
| 25 days old | 13.0 | 7.2 | 3.5 | Groebbels (1932) |
| 70 days old | 13.0 | 6.5 | 3.5 | Groebbels (1932) |
| mature | 12.8 | 6.9 | 3.6 | Groebbels (1932) |
| Chickens, White Leghorn | 10.7 | 6.8 | – | Lucas and Jamroz (1961) |
| Chickens, Brown Leghorn, male | 12.8 | 7.9 | 2.41 | Gilbert (1965) |
| Brown Leghorn, female | 12.2 | 7.4 | 2.53 | Gilbert (1965) |
| Chicken | 10.7 | 7.06 | – | Balasch *et al.* (1973) |
| Duck | 12.8 | 6.6 | – | Groebbels (1932) |
| Turkey, male | 15.5 | 7.5 | – | Groebbels (1932) |
| Turkey, female | 15.5 | 7.0 | – | Groebbels (1932) |
| (sex not given) | 15.0 | 7.2 | – | Usami *et al.* (1970) |
| Pigeon | 12.7 | 7.5 | – | Usami *et al.* (1970) |
| *Numida meleagris* (guinea), male | 11.96 | 5.96 | – | Balasch *et al.* (1973) |
| *Pavo cristatus* (peacock) | 12.55 | 6.97 | – | Balasch *et al.* (1973) |
| *Phasianus colchicus* (pheasant), male | 10.64 | 6.77 | – | Balasch *et al.* (1973) |
| *Alectoris graeca* (rock partridge), male | 11.26 | 6.40 | – | Balasch *et al.* (1973) |
| Falcon | 11 – 18 | 7.3 – 8.7 | – | Hartman and Lessler (1963) |

were more susceptible to deficiencies of iron and copper than were those raised at other temperatures. A significant increase in hematocrit and hemoglobin levels occurred with increasing levels of copper and iron within limits at temperatures of 21.0° and 32.2° (Kubena *et al.,* 1971).

## Hypoxia

Chickens, pigeons, and quail, similarly to mammals, respond to hypoxia by an increase in hematocrit and erythrocyte numbers, which in the acute stages results in a very high hematocrits (60 – 80% in chickens). When such birds become adapted to high altitude (12,500 ft) the increases in hematocrit, hemoglobin, and erythrocyte counts are 27, 36, and 33%, respectively, in male chickens (Burton *et al.,* 1971) Three months after such birds were returned to near sea level, these parameters were not significantly different from birds raised at sea level. Japanese quail, males and females, held at simulated altitude of 20,000 ft and presumably acclimated exhibited increases in hematocrits of 22.1 and 50%,

respectively (Jaeger, 1973). Similar increases in hemoglobin were also reported.

## Formation of Corpuscles

There are two theories on the origin of the blood cells. The proponents of the monophyletic theory of evolution maintain that there is one specific stem cell, developing from the mesenchyme, that gives rise to both of two main types of blood cells, the white and the red. The proponents of the polyphyletic theory believe that erythrocytes and leukocytes have developed from two originally distinct cell types, the erythrocytes from the vascular endothelium of the bone marrow, and the leukocytes from reticular connective tissue cells. Jordan (1939), an adherent of the monophyletic view, regarded the bone marrow as the chief hematopoietic center in birds. Lucas (1959) and Lucas Jamroz and (1961), who reviewed the early literature, stated that most avian hematologists subscribed to the polyphyletic view. Later work by Campbell (1967) suggests a monophyletic origin of blood cells.

*Table 3-3*  *Erythrocyte numbers in birds*

In millions per cubic millimeter

| Species | Age | Sex Male | Female | Sex not given | Reference |
|---|---|---|---|---|---|
| Chicken | Adult | 3.8 | 3.0 | — | Lucas and Jamroz (1961) |
| | Adult | 3.32 | 2.72 | — | Olson (1937) |
| | Adult | 3.26 | 2.72 | — | Lange (Groebbels, 1932) |
| | 3 hr | | | 1.84 | Lange (Sturkie, 1965) |
| | 3 days | | | 2.23 | Lange (Sturkie, 1965) |
| | 12 days | | | 2.65 | Lange (Sturkie, 1965) |
| | 26 days | | | 2.77 | Cook (1937) |
| | 32-47 days | | | 2.83 | Twisselmann (1939) |
| | 50 days | | | 2.34 | Lange (Sturkie, 1965) |
| | 70 days | | | 2.39 | Lange (Sturkie, 1965) |
| | 82 days | | | 2.79 | Cook (1937) |
| Chicken, White Leghorn | 42 days | — | 3.02 | — | Lucas and Jamroz (1961) |
| | 84 days | — | 3.02 | — | Lucas and Jamroz (1961) |
| | Adult | 3.91 | 2.95 | — | Sturkie and Textor (1960) |
| | Adult castrate | 3.50 | — | — | Sturkie and Textor (1960) |
| Turkey (domestic) | Adult | 2.38 | 2.24 | — | Groebbels (1932) |
| Ostrich | Adult | 1.84 (mixed) | | | DeVilliers (1938) |
| Rhenish goose | 8 months | — | — | 3.35 | Kaleta and Bernhardt (1968) |
| | 2 years | — | — | 3.49 | Kaleta and Bernhardt (1968) |
| Italian goose | 5 months | 2.53 (mixed) | | | Sova et al. (1972) |
| Czech goose | 5 months | 2.22 | — | — | Sova et al. (1972) |
| Domestic goose | Adult | — | — | 2.71 | Groebbels (1932) |
| Indian duck, adult, native | 2.92 | 2.42 nonlaying | | — | Surendranathon et al. (1968) |
| Pekin duck, adult | 2.71 | 2.46 | — | — | Halaj (1967) |
| Domestic duck | — | — | 2.00 | — | Groebbels (1932) |
| *Coturnix* (quail) | Young | — | — | 2.86 | Nirmalan and Robinson (1971) |
| | Adult | 4.14 | 3.86 | Not laying | Nirmalan and Robinson (1971) |
| | Adult | — | 3.81 | Laying | Atwal et al. (1964) |
| Bob white (quail) | 5.41 | 4.1 | — | — | Bond and Gilbert (1958) |
| Rock partridge | 2.62 | — | — | — | Balasch et al. (1973) |
| *Numida meleagris* | Adult | 2.82 | — | — | Balasch et al. (1973) |
| *Phasianus colchicus* | Adult | 3.26 | — | — | Balasch et al. (1973) |
| *Pavo cristatus* | Adult | 2.07 (mixed) | | | Balasch et al. (1973) |
| Pigeon | Adult | 4.00 | 3.07 | — | Wastl and Leiner (Sturkie, 1965) |
| | Adult | 3.23 | 3.09 | — | Riddle and Braucher (Sturkie, 1965) |
| Dove | Adult | 3.04 | 2.99 | — | Riddle and Braucher (Sturkie, 1965) |
| Red-tailed hawk | Immature | | | 3.2 | Bond and Gilbert (1958) |
| Great horned owl | Adult | | | 2.2 | Bond and Gilbert (1958) |
| Diving duck | Adult | | | 3.2 | Bond and Gilbert (1958) |
| Dabbling duck | Adult | | | 3.6 | Bond and Gilbert (1958) |
| Red-throated loon | Adult | | | 3.1 | Bond and Gilbert (1958) |
| *Agelaius phoeniceus* (blackbird) | Adult | | | ca. 4.0 | Ronald et al. (1968) |

***Table 3–4*** *Erythrocyte volumes (%) of Aves*

| Species, age, and condition | No sex | Male | Female | Reference |
|---|---|---|---|---|
| Chicken, sexually immature | | 29 | 29 | Newell and Shaffner (Sturkie, 1965) |
|    sexually mature | | 45 | 29 | Newell and Shaffner (Sturkie, 1965) |
|    sexually mature | | 40 | 31 | Lucas and Jamroz (1961) |
|    6 weeks | | | 31 | Lucas and Jamroz (1961) |
|    12 weeks | | | 30 | Lucas and Jamroz (1961) |
|    sexually mature, White Leghorn | | 48 | 31 | Sturkie and Textor (1960) |
|    sexually mature, capon | | 38 | — | Sturkie and Textor (1960) |
|    adult | | 40.8 | 25.5 | Hunsaker (1969) |
| Pilgrim goose, 34 weeks | | 48 | 47 | Hunsaker *et al.* (1964) |
|    50 weeks | | 49 | 36 | Hunsaker *et al.* (1964) |
|    59 weeks | | 42 | 41 | Hunsaker *et al.* (1964) |
| European goose,  32 weeks | 48 | — | — | Kaleta and Bernhardt (1968) |
|    156 weeks | 46 | — | — | Kaleta and Bernhardt (1968) |
| Bronze turkey,  9 months | | 45.1 | 36.4 | Ringer (unpublished) |
|    20 weeks | | 38.5 (mixed) | | Sullivan (1965) |
|    adult | | — | 35.9 | McCartney (Sturkie, 1965) |
|    adult | | 38.5 | 33.5 | Hunsaker (1969) |
| Indian native duck, adult | | 40.7 | 38.1, non-laying | Surendranathan *et al.* (1968) |
| Pekin duck, adult | | 46.7 | 44.2 | Halaj (1967) |
| *Numida meleagris* (guinea)  adult | — | 43 | — | Balasch *et al.* (1973) |
| *Pavo cristatus* (peacock)  adult | | 37 (mixed) | | Balasch *et al.* (1973) |
| *Phasianus colchicus*  adult | | 41.5 | | Balasch *et al.* (1973) |
|   (pheasant)  adult | | 33 | 34 | Bond and Gilbert (1958) |
| *Coturnix* (quail)  adult | — | 53.1 | 48.7, not laying | Nirmalan and Robinson (1971) |
|   adult | — | 42.0 | 37.0 | Atwal *et al.* (1964) |
|   (50 days) | | 46 | — | Ernest *et al.* (1971) |
|   adult | | 45 at sea level | | Jaeger (1974) |
|   adult | | 61 high altitude | | Jaeger (1974) |
| Bobwhite  adult | | 38 | | Bond and Gilbert (1958) |
| *Alectoris g.* (partridge) | | 37 | | Balasch *et al.* (1973) |
| | No sex | | | Bond and Gilbert (1958) |
| Red-tailed hawk, immature | 43 | | | Bond and Gilbert (1958) |
| Great horned owl | 32 | | | Bond and Gilbert (1958) |
| Red-throated loon | 54 | | | Bond and Gilbert (1958) |
| Diving ducks | 37 | | | Bond and Gilbert (1958) |
| Dabbling ducks (mallard) | 43 | | | Bond and Gilbert (1958) |
| Coot | 46 | | | Bond and Gilbert (1958) |
| Redwinged blackbird, adult | 40 | — | — | Ronald *et al.* (1968) |
| Pigeon, adult | — | 58.5 | 56.4 | Kaplan (Sturkie 1965) |
| | 52 | — | — | Bond and Gilbert (1958) |

**Erythrocyte series.** Erythropoiesis in mammalian bone marrow is confined to the extravascular spaces but in birds it occurs in the lumen of the medullary sinuses (Campbell, 1967). The bone marrow of birds, unlike that of mammals, contains large amounts of lymphatic tissue.

The immature erythroid cells of birds are located in the lumen of the medullary sinuses, but only about 2–3% or less of the immature red cells is found in the peripheral circulation according to Lucas and Jamroz (1961). Granulocytes and lymphocytes arise in the extravascular spaces of avian bone marrow and pass through the sinus walls of marrow to enter its circulation (Campbell, 1967).

Based on studies employing light and electron microscopy Campbell (1967) gives the following account. The earliest progenitors of erythroid cells are large, 10–12 $\mu$m in diameter, with large nuclei, large nucleoli, and a basophilic cytoplasm. They are situated within the bone marrow sinuses near the sinus wall. These stem cells are called *hemocytoblasts*. Near these cells are smaller cells, with smaller nuclei and more basophilic cytoplasm, known as *basophil erythroblasts*; these arise from the hemocytoblasts.

More centrally located in the sinuses are smaller cells with nuclear chromatin which is evenly distributed in small masses; these are described as *polychromatophil erythroblasts* and contain hemoglobin. The latter are believed to give rise to mature *erythrocytes,* which are more centrally located in the vascular lumen. Avian erythrocytes (Figure 3–1) are elongated and contain a dense oval nucleus. Nuclear hemoglobin is dispersed among the coarse chromatin particles and is continuous with cytoplasmic hemoglobin at the nuclear pores.

Campbell (1967) presents evidence supporting the view that peripherally located erythroid cells in the sinuses adhere to the sinus wall and do not enter the circulation. The immature avian erythroid cells of the bone marrow therefore resemble those of mammalian bone marrow, except that the avian erythrocyte retains its nucleus, whereas the mammalian normoblast extrudes its nucleus to form the mature mammalian red cell.

Barrett and Scheinberg (1972), who have studied the shape of developing avian red cells in bone marrow tissue culture, have shown that mature avian cells arise from spherical precursor cells that contain hemoglobin and that become flat when conditions favor deoxygenated hemoglobin. The flat cells revert to spherical shape on reoxygenation. The authors suggest that the flat shape increases the survival of the cells because it gives them increased flexibility.

**Control of erythropoiesis.** It is generally agreed that erythropoiesis is under humoral control and that hypoxia, the fundamental erythropietic stimulus, operates through the production of a circulating substance, termed erythropoietin or erythropoiesis stimulating factor (ESF) in mammals. It is a glycoprotein which is formed in he body tissues (kidney) and that acts directly on bone marrow, increasing the production rate of erythroid cells and their conversion to mature erythrocytes.

In mammals, this increased production may cause the release of a large number of immature red cells (reticulocytes) into the circulation but in birds the amount is very small (less than 2%; Lucas and Jamroz, 1961), although some have reported a higher level (6–7%) in avian blood (Nirmalan and Robinson, 1971) and some a level as high as 25–35%. Much of this variation may be attributed to errors in distinguishing these cells. Coates and March (1966) reported that 35% of the differential count in young chickens was reticulocytes; this decreased to 10% at 15 weeks of age or older. Androgen and cortical hormones increase erythropoiesis, whereas estrogens depress it in mammals and birds, as previously pointed out. Androgen stimulates erythropoiesis, increasing ESF in the kidney; this acts to stimulate erythropoiesis in the bone marrow. Estrogen, however, may depress erythropoiesis independently of the kidneys (Mirand and Gordon, 1966). Presumably the mode of action is the same in birds.

Avian erythropoietin, which is stimulated and released following hypoxia and suppressed by induced polycythemia (Rosse and Waldmann, 1966), is different from the mammalian type because the latter does not stimulate erythropoiesis in birds, and the avian type is ineffective in mammals. The erythropoietin of birds differ from mammals in that it is not destroyed by sialidase and does not lose its activity when reacted with antibody to human urinary erythropoietin.

## Life Span of Erythrocytes

The life of red cells may be estimated by marking such cells with radioisotopes, injecting them, and determining the decreasing radioactivity with time or age at death of the marked cells.

The average life span of human erythrocytes is 50–60 days; that of chickens averages 28–35 days (Hevesy and Ottesen, 1945; Brace and Atland, 1956; Rodnan *et al.,* 1957), pigeon cells, 35–45 days; and ducks, 42 days (Rodnan *et al.,* 1957). The figure for Coturnix (quails) is 33–35 days (Nirmalin and Robinson, 1973). The short life span of avian cells is related to the higher avian body temperature and metabolic rates.

In certain mammals, particularly the dog, the spleen is considered a reservoir of erythrocytes that in times of emergency expels the reserve cells into the general circulation. This function was once ascribed to the spleen of chickens by Harman et al. (1932) but later studies of chickens by Sturkie (1943), demonstrated the absence of these reputed functions before and after splenectomy and following hypoxic stress. This is not surprising because the spleen of birds has a thin capsule with few muscle fibers and is capable of contraction to only a slight extent. The organ may store cells, however.

## Resistance of Erythrocytes

Hemolysis is the act of discharging hemoglobin from the corpuscles into the plasma. A number of factors, such as freezing, thawing, and changes in osmotic pressure of the blood, produce hemolysis. Solutions that have the same osmotic pressure as blood and that do not cause hemolysis are isotonic. Solutions with lower osmotic pressures than blood are hypotonic, and those with higher pressures are hypertonic. Hypotonic solutions cause hemolysis and bursting by increasing the water content of the cells; hypertonic solutions cause a shrinking of the corpuscles, because water is lost from the cells. The fragility of the red cells may be measured by their resistance to solutions of known concentrations and osmotic pressures, usually NaCl solutions. Therefore, resistance may be expressed as percent hemolysis to a solution of known concentration. Earlier workers on chicken blood and ostrich blood (see Sturkie, 1965) indicated that blood began to hemolyze in NaCl solutions of 0.40–0.48% and all cells were hemolyzed at 0.27–28% NaCl.

More recent data by March et al. (1966) on chickens also show maximum hemolysis (90–97%) at NaCl solutions of 0.2–0.30% and about 50% hemolysis at 0.4% solution. At 0.5% solution hemolysis dropped to 10% or less. They also reported that the cells of New Hampshire chickens were more resistant than those of White Leghorns and the cells of females were more resistant than those of males; estrogen administered to males increased the resistance to hemolysis but androgen had no significant effect.

Hunter (1953) has studied the permeability of chicken erythrocytes to hypotonic and hypertonic solutions. His results indicate that erythrocytes in chicken, as in man, behave as perfect osmometers in slightly hypotonic and slightly hypertonic solutions. In markedly hypertonic solutions, however,

they shrank less than would be expected if they were behaving as perfect osmometers. The blood of birds contains relatively more potassium and less sodium than does mammalian blood (McManus, 1967).

Physiological saline (Ringer's solution) for birds, formulated by Benzinger and Krebs, takes into account the difference in electrolyte content of bird blood, in grams per liter of solution, as follows:

| NaCl | KCl | CaCl | NaHCO$_3$ | MgSO$_4$ | pH |
|------|------|------|-----------|----------|-----|
| 6.8 | 1.73 | 0.64 | 2.45 | 0.25 | 7.4 |

Details concerning the exchange of Na and K in bird erythrocytes have been reported by Hunter et al. (1956) and by Tosteson and Robertson (1956).

## Sedimentation Rate

**Important factors.** Sedimentation rate of erythrocytes is dependent on two main forces: (1) the force of gravity, causing cells to settle, and (2) the frictional resistance of the surrounding plasma, which holds the cells in suspension. The role played by each of these forces is related to a number of factors, such as cell size and shape, the specific gravity of cells and plasma, and the chemical composition of plasma. The sedimentation rate in human beings may be increased during infections and in diseases associated with tissue injury.

Less is known about the sedimentation rate in birds, because few reports are available, and in most cases the effects of disease, age, and sex have not been ascertained. Mean sedimentation rates ranging from 0.5 to 9 mm/hr, with most values falling between 1.5 and 4, have been reported (see Sturkie, 1965). These values were determined in the usual way, with the sedimentation tube held vertically, and are considerably lower than those reported for man. The vertical position is unsatisfactory for avian blood, because avian blood cells settle very slowly.

It has been demonstrated that the sedimentation rate of human blood can be increased considerably by positioning the tube at 45° (Washburn and Meyers, 1957), and similar results have been obtained with chicken blood (Sturkie and Textor, 1958; Gilbert, 1968), goose blood (Hunsaker et al., 1964), turkey blood (Bierer et al., 1964), and pheasant blood (Dobsinska and Dobsinska, 1972). The results are shown in Table 3–5.

It is apparent that the sedimentation rate is lowest for males, intermediate for capons, and highest for females. Erythrocyte numbers (Sturkie and Tex-

*Table 3–5* *Sedimentation rate in mm/min (tube slanted)*

| | Minutes | | | | |
| --- | --- | --- | --- | --- | --- |
| | 10 | 30 | 60 | 120 | Reference |
| Chicken, adults | | | | | Sturkie and Textor (1958) |
| male | 0.80 | 2.06 | 3.86 | 7.0 | |
| capon | 0.73 | 2.87 | 6.45 | 12.9 | |
| female | 1.35 | 5.30 | 10.5 | 18.05 | |
| Geese | | | | | Hunsaker *et al.* (1964) |
| male, 50 weeks | — | — | — | 10.1 | |
| female, 50 weeks | — | — | — | 21.9 | |
| Pheasant | | | | | |
| mixed sex | — | — | 17.2 | 32.6 | Dobsinska and Dobsinska (1972) |

tor, 1960) were highest in the male, intermediate in the capon, and lowest in the female. The same investigators (1958) showed that the sedimentation rate in the three groups was linear with time from 10 to 120 min and this has been confirmed by Gilbert (1962, 1968).

**Other factors.** Hyperlipemia produced by the drug nicarbazine (Sturkie and Textor, 1960) or by estrogen (Gilbert, 1962) increases the sedimentation rate significantly. Evidence has been presented indicating that the number of cells has the greatest influence on the sedimentation rate and that cell size affects it to a much lesser degree (Sturkie and Textor, 1960; Gilbert, 1968). Differences in specific gravity of plasma and plasma proteins have little effect on the ESR.

It is apparent that the ESR alone has little physiologic or pathologic significance. It must be related to cell number and hematocrit.

The ESR in pheasants was influenced greatly by a *Pseudomonas* infection (experimental). It was doubled following the infection and remained high until 5–8 days afterwards (Dobsinska and Dobsinska, 1972). To what extent the decreased ESR was attributable to decreased hematocrit was not stated, but it has been demonstrated in chickens with certain infections that all changes in the ESR are related to decreased hematocrits (Bierer *et al.* 1963)

## THROMBOCYTES

The thrombocyte or platelet of mammalian blood has its origin from the giant cells, megakaryocytes, of the lungs and bone marrow. The megakaryocyte is lacking in avian bone marrow and the thrombocytes arise from antecedent, mononucleated cells that have a blast stage like others cells (Lucas and Jamroz, 1961). However, Archer (1971) throws some doubt on this view. He stated that although large cells can be found in the bone marrow, they are not comparable to mammalian megakaryocytes; they appear to be multinucleated and may be presumed to be thrombocyte precursors. However, proof is lacking.

The thrombocytes show considerable variation in size, and their shape may vary from oval to round (Figure 3–1). The typical thrombocyte is oval, with a round nucleus in the center of a clear cytoplasm. A constant feature is the one or more brightly red-stained granules present at the poles of the cell when stained with Wright's stain. The chromatin of the nucleus is dense and is clumped into relatively large masses that are distinctly separated by the parachromatin.

Numbers of thrombocytes in avian blood are presented in Table 3–6. The number ranges in most species between 20,000 and 30,000/per cubic millimeter but may be as low as 10,000 in the ostrich and as high as 132,000 in the quail (Nirmalan and Robinson, 1971). The latter number seems inordinately high and should be checked.

When blood is centrifuged the thrombocytes separate out with the leukocytes and are found in the buffy coat. The actual number of thrombocytes appears to be about the same as the total leukocytes (Table 3–6). There is no evidence of a sex difference in thrombocytes. The avian thrombocyte contains extremely high quantities of serotonin (Meyer, 1973).

Evidence from other sources suggests that the thrombocytes are cells belonging to the erythrocyte series. All stages of the erythroblast–thrombocyte

*Table 3-6* Hemoglobin values (g/100 ml, of whole blood of Aves

| Species | Age | Male | Female | No sex | Method | Reference |
|---|---|---|---|---|---|---|
| Chicken | 21 days | — | — | 9.7 | Cyanmethemoglobin | Pilaski (1972) |
| | 46 days | — | — | 9.8 | Cyanmethemoglobin | Pilaski (1972) |
| | 71 days | 11.1 | 11.0 | — | Cyanmethemoglobin | Pilaski (1972) |
| | 126 days | 12.5 | 11.7 | — | Cyanmethemoglobin | Pilaski (1972) |
| | 180 days | 11.3 | 8.9 | — | Cyanmethemoglobin | Pilaski (1972) |
| | 210 days | 11.4 | 8.6 | — | Cyanmethemoglobin | Pilaski (1972) |
| | Adult | — | — | 8.9–9.2 | Cyanmethemoglobin | Wels and Horn (1965) |
| | Adult | — | 9.71 | — | Modified Newcomer | Bankowski (1942) |
| | Adult | — | 8.90 | — | Modified Newcomer | Sturkie (1943) |
| | Adult | — | 8.90 | — | Modified Newcomer | Schultze and Elvehjem (1934) |
| Turkey | Adult | 12.5–14.0 | 13.2 | — | Alkali hematin | Paulsen et al. (1950) |
| White Holland turkey | 28 days | 10.8 | 10.3 | — | Cyanmethemoglobin | Pilaski (1972) |
| | 77 days | 11.1 | 11.5 | — | Cyanmethemoglobin | Pilaski (1972) |
| | 149 days | 12.7 | 12.7 | — | Cyanmethemoglobin | Pilaski (1972) |
| | 217, adult | 15.2 | 13.4 | — | Cyanmethemoglobin | Pilaski (1972) |
| Goose | 56 days | — | — | 11.3 | Cyanmethemoglobin | Hunsaker et al. (1964) |
| | 140 days | — | — | 14.4 | Cyanmethemoglobin | Hunsaker et al. (1964) |
| | Adult | 15.7 | 12.7 | — | Cyanmethemoglobin | Hunsaker et al. (1964) |
| Pekin duck | Adult | 14.2 | 12.7 | — | Sahli | Halaj (1967) |
| Indian native (duck) | Adult | 13.3 | 12.7 | — | Wong (iron) | Balasch et al. (1973) |
| Diving duck | Adult | 15.2 | 13.3 | — | Sahli | Halaj (1967) |
| Diving duck | Adult | — | — | 10.3 | Alkali hematin | Soliman et al. (1966) |
| *Numida meleagris* (guinea) | Adult | 14.9 | — | — | Drabkin | Balasch et al. (1973) |
| *Phasianus colchicus* (pheasant) | Adult | 18.9 | — | — | Drabkin | Balasch et al. (1973) |
| *Pavo cristatus* (peacock) | Adult | Mixed sex | 12.0 | — | Drabkin | Balasch et al. (1973) |
| *Coturnix japonica* | 14 days | Mixed sex | 11.6 | — | Cyanmethemoglobin | Nirmalan and Robinson (1971) |
| | Adult | 15.8 | 14.6 | — | Cyanmethemoglobin | Nirmalan and Robinson (1971) |
| | 22 days | 9.2 | 10.7 | — | Cyanmethemoglobin | Atwal et al. (1964) |
| | 29 days | 12.0 | 11.0 | — | Cyanmethemoglobin | Atwal et al. (1964) |
| | 50 adult | 15.3 | 12.3 | — | Cyanmethemoglobin | Atwal et al. (1964) |
| *Agelaius phoeniceus* (blackbird) | Adult | Mixed | ca. 12.5 | — | Drabkin | Ronald et al. (1968) |

64     series can be detected in smears prepared from the bone marrow.

The role of the thrombocytes in blood coagulation is not clear, and the behavior of avian blood on contact with surfaces other than vascular endothelium is unlike that of mammalian blood. Avian blood-contact tests gave negative results in contrast to positive results on mammalian blood (Archer, 1971). Considerably more work on the origin, fate, and function of avian thrombocytes is needed.

## HEMOGLOBIN

There is every reason to believe that avian hemoglobins contain the four iron-containing heme units characteristic of mammalia; but the protein moieties, the globins, are different and migrate electrophoretically at speeds different from their mammalian counterparts. Avian hemoglobins are easily crystallized and they exhibit variations characteristic of their species; they have been studied in chickens, turkeys, sparrows, owls, ducks, pigeons, crows, geese, cormorants, pheasants, and others (see Klein, 1970; Saha and Ghosh, 1965; Ghosh, 1965; Brown et al., 1970; Bernhardt and Kaleta, 1968; Abercrombie et al., 1969; Brush and Power, 1970; Bell and Sturkie, 1965; Campbell, 1967; Dunlap et al., 1956; Van der Helm and Huisman, 1958).

Most researchers are agreed that all adult avian species so far investigated have at least two main types of hemoglobin, exhibiting slow (I) and fast (II) electrophoretic mobilities. The proportions of these average about 70–80% for type I and 20–30% for the type II. Ghosh (1965), who studied the hemoglobins of 47 species in 13 orders of birds, reported that ten of these species also exhibited a third typed based on migration characteristics.

More than three types of hemoglobin have been demonstrated in embryos (Grinnell and Lee, 1972; Denmark and Washburn, 1969; Fraser et al., 1972). Most of these disappear in adult life, although some may persist in certain strains and species of ducks and sparrows (Bush and Farrar, 1967). After the fifth day of chick embryogenic life there is a marked decrease in the rate of synthesis of embryonic hemoglobin (Grinnell and Lee, 1972).

Aberrant or mutant types of hemoglobin have been reported by Washburn (1968) characterized by a third type (second minor band), migrating at a faster rate thanthe first minor band, and inherited. An aberrant type of hemoglobin was produced experimentally by feeding phenylhydrazine to chickens (Stino and Washburn, 1970).

### Structure

The molecular weights of types I and II hemoglobin average about 68,000–73,000, depending on how estimated. Klein (1970) estimated the mean dry weights of globins I and II of the duck as 34,400 and 39,300, respectively. These values agreed roughly with the corresponding weights of amino acid residues of 32,400 and 35,500 for globulins I and II. The number of amino acid residues per 2 equiv of heme averaged 295 and 319 for globins I and II, respectively, for ducks (Klein 1970); each of these included 18 different amino acids.

Both adult hemoglobins are relatively resistant to alkali and they have almost the same absorption spectra, with maxima at 417 and lesser peaks at 540 and 572 (Gratzer and Allison, 1960). The peak maximum for a number of species of the crow family are within the same range (Dabrowski, 1967).

### Levels of Hemoglobin

The amount of hemoglobin in avian blood, as given in the literature, is highly variable. Recent work has demonstrated that much of this variation may be attributed to the methods of determination. Many of the earlier workers used the Newcomer acid hematin method, but because the erythrocytes of birds are nucleated, the consequent turbidity of the solution following treatment with acid produces readings that usually are too high. A modification of the Newcomer acid hematin method, by which the blood is first hemolyzed with $NH_4OH$, gives more reliable figures because the turbidity of the solution is eliminated or minimized (Schultze and Elvehjem, 1934).

The reliability of six different methods of determining chicken blood hemoglobin was tested by Bankowski (1942), who reported that only two were very reliable and these were a modified Newcomer method and photelometric acid hematin. Wels and Horn (1965) and Pilaski (1972) also reviewed and tested a number of methods. They report that cyanmethemoglobin methods are very reliable and practicable for avian blood and more recent data are based on this method (Table 3–7). Hemoglobin determinations have been made on a number of avian species other than chickens, but in many cases, because of unreliable methods, the values are too high. For example, the figures reported by different investigators for pigeon blood are 10.6, 16.1, 15.2, 13.7, and 15.97 mg per 100 ml.

It is apparent that at sexual maturity there is a

higher level of hemoglobin in males than females. This is correlated with the usual higher number of erythrocytes in the male in most species and the fact that androgen tends to increase red cell numbers (see section on erythrocytes), whereas estrogen tends to decrease numbers (in quail) mainly by depressing erythropoiesis initially (Nirmalan and Robinson, 1972). However, with continued estrogen administration erythropoiesis is not depressed in chickens (Gilbert, 1963). Although estrogen depressed erythrocyte volume in geese, androgen had no significant effect (Hunsaker, 1968). Some have reported levels of hemoglobin lower in laying than in nonlaying chickens but others have reported no difference (see Bell and Sturkie, 1965); however, no attempts have been made to relate these alleged differences to estrogen levels.

Androgen increased the hemoglobin level of chicken castrates to near normal male levels, but estrogen had little effect according to Tanaka and Rosenberg (1955).

Factors that affect erythropoieses and red cell number also affect hemoglobin level, for example, hypoxia and anemia. Exposure to high altitude (hypoxia) increases Hb in chickens (Burton et al., 1971) and quail (Jaeger, 1973), but after chickens are returned to sea level conditions, hematocrit and hemoglobin return to near normal levels.

The mean corpuscular hemoglobin concentration (MCHC) expresses the mean content of hemoglobin in grams per 100 ml of erythrocytes; it is calculated from the packed cell volume (PCV) and the hemoglobin measured in the whole blood. Its primary importance is in the diagnosis of anemic conditions and it reflects the capacity of the bone marrow to produce erythrocytes of normal size, metabolic capacity, and hemoglobin content.

## LEUKOCYTES

### Description of Cell Types

The following description of cell types is that of Olsen (1937) (see Figure 3–1).

**Heterophils.** This type of leukocyte is sometimes designated a polymorphonuclear–pseudo-esinophilic granulocyte, but for the sake of brevity it is usually designated "heterophil." In man and in such other mammals as the dog, these leukocytes possess neutral-staining granules (neutrophils). In rabbits and birds, the granules of these leukocytes are acid in reaction.

The heterophils of the chicken are usually

round and have a diameter of approximately 10 – 15 μm. The characteristic feature of these cells is the presence of many rod- or spindle-shaped acidophilic crystalline bodies in the cytoplasm. In routinely stained smears, these cytoplasmic bodies are frequently distorted, and they may then be variable in shape. In cases of such distortion the color reaction must be used as a criterion for distinguishing them. The bodies are of a distinct and sometimes brilliant red against a background of colorless cytoplasm. The nucleus is polymorphic with varying degrees of lobulation.

**Eosinophils.** Polymorphonuclear eosinophilic granulocytes are of about the same size as the heterophils. The granules are spherical and relatively large. Their color is dull red, as compared to the brilliant red of the heterophil, when stained with Wright's stain. The cytoplasm has a faint yet distinct bluish-gray tint. The nucleus is often bilobed and is of a richer blue than that of the heterophil, giving the impression of a sharper differentiation between chromatin and parachromatin than in the nucleus of the latter.

The question has arisen as to the correctness of distinguishing between the heterophil and the eosinophil in avian blood. Some workers believe that the two cell types represent modified forms of the same group, but others think that the heterophil and eosinophil have different lineages.

**Basophils.** Polymorphonuclear basophilic granulocytes are of about the same size and shape as the heterophils. The nucleus is weakly basophilic in reaction and round or oval in shape; at times it may be lobulated. The cytoplasm is abundant and devoid of color. Deeply basophilic granules abound in the cytoplasm. Electron microscopy reveals that granuler of basophils are variable in size and are fibrillar in nature (Dhingra et al, 1969).

**Lymphocytes.** The lymphocytes constitute the majority of the leukocytes in the blood of the fowl. There is a wide range in the size and shape of these cells. The cytoplasm is usually weakly basophilic. It may consist of a narrow rim bordering one side of the nucleus, as in the small lymphocytes, or it may constitute the major portion of the cell, as in the larger lymphocytes. The nucleus is usually round and may have a small indentation. There is usually a fairly coarse pattern of chromatin. In some instances, however, the chromatin is fine and is not distinctly separated by the parachromatin. Sometimes

Table 3–7 *Number of leukocytes and thrombocytes in bird blood and differential counts*

| Species, age, and sex | Number (×10³/mm³) | | Differential count (%) | | | | | Reference |
|---|---|---|---|---|---|---|---|---|
| | Leuko-cytes | Throm-bocytes | Lympho-cytes | Hetero-phils | Eosino-phils | Baso-phils | Mono-cytes | |
| Chicken, adult male | 19.8 | 25.4 | 59.1 | 27.2 | 1.9 | 1.7 | 10.2 | Olson (1937) |
| nonlaying female | 19.8 | 26.5 | 64.6 | 22.8 | 1.9 | 1.7 | 8.9 | Olson (1937) |
| young, 2–21 weeks, males and females | 29.4 | 32.7 | 66.0 | 20.9 | 1.9 | 3.1 | 8.1 | Olson (1937) |
| Chicken, White Leghorn, 6 weeks to maturity, males and females | | | | | | | | |
| supravital stain | 32.6 | — | 40.9 | 35.6 | 2.7 | 4.3 | 16.5 | Twisselmann (1939) |
| Wright's stain | — | — | 54.0 | 27.8 | 1.5 | 2.7 | 13.7 | Twisselmann (1939) |
| Chicken, average, all ages | 30.4 | — | 73.3 | 15.1 | | 2.7 | 6.3 | Cook (1937) |
| Chicken, 5–10 weeks, males | — | — | 69.5 | 20.4 | 1.3 | 3.3 | 3.7 | Goff et al. (Sturkie, 1965) |
| 6 weeks, female White Leghorn | 28.6 | 30.4 | 81.5 | 10.1 | 1.5 | 2.3 | 4.5 | Lucas and Jamroz (1961) |
| 12 weeks, female White Leghorn | 30.6 | 26.2 | 77.8 | 11.7 | 3.0 | 1.7 | 4.9 | Lucas and Jamroz (1961) |
| adult female White Leghorn | 29.4 | 30.8 | 76.1 | 13.3 | 2.5 | 2.4 | 5.7 | Lucas and Jamroz (1961) |
| adult male White Leghorn | 16.6 | 27.6 | 64.0 | 25.8 | 1.4 | 2.4 | 6.4 | Lucas and Jamroz (1961) |
| adult female farmstock White Leghorn | 28.8 | 37.2 | 71.7 | 23.7 | 1.4 | 2.1 | 1.1 | Lucas and Jamroz (1961) |
| adult female Rhode Island Red | 35.8 | 60.3 | 58.1 | 35.1 | 1.2 | 3.1 | 2.5 | Lucas and Jamroz (1961) |

| | | | | | | | | Reference |
|---|---|---|---|---|---|---|---|---|
| Canada goose, male | — | | 46.0 | 39.0 | 7.0 | 2.0 | 6.0 | Lucas and Jamroz (1961) |
| Crossbred European goose, no sex | | | | | | | | |
| 8 months | 16.8 | — | 38.0 | 44.2 | 5.1 | 3.1 | 10.0 | Kaleta and Bernhardt (1968) |
| 3 years | 18.2 | — | 36.2 | 50.0 | 4.0 | 2.2 | 8.0 | Kaleta and Bernhardt (1968) |
| Czech goose, no sex | 27.0 | — | 48.5 | 34–44 | — | — | — | Sova et al. (1972) |
| Turkey, 20 weeks, mixed sex | 26.8 | — | — | — | — | — | — | Sullivan (1965) |
| no sex | — | — | 50.6 | 43.4 | 0.9 | 3.2 | 1.9 | Johnson and Lange (Sturkie, 1965) |
| Indian native duck, male | 31.5 | 62.6 | 68.0 | 22 | 1.4 | 0.6 | 8.0 | Surendranathanet al. (1968) |
| female | 28.9 | | 26.6 | 2.4 | 0.4 | 8.0 | — | Surendranathanet al. (1968) |
| Pekin duck, male | 24.0 | | 31 | 52 | 9.9 | 3.1 | 3.7 | Halaj (1967) |
| female | 26.0 | | 47 | 32 | 10.2 | 3.3 | 6.9 | Halaj (1967) |
| Duck | 23.4 | 30.7 | 61.7 | 24.3 | 2.1 | 1.5 | 10.8 | Magath and Higgins (Sturkie, 1965) |
| Ringneck, male pheasant | — | — | 34.0 | 48.0 | 1.0 | 10.0 | 8.0 | Lucas and Jamroz (1961) |
| Pigeon (no sex) | 13.0 | — | 65.6 | 23.0 | 2.2 | 2.6 | 6.6 | Shaw (Sturkie, 1965) |
| Ostrich, males and females | 21.0 | 10.5 | 26.8 | 59.1 | 6.3 | 4.7 | 3.0 | DeVilliers (1938) |
| Coturnix (quail), adult male | 19.7 | 117 | 73.6 | 20.8 | 2.5 | 0.4 | 2.7 | Nirmalan and Robinson (1971) |
| adult female | 23.1 | 132 | 71.6 | 21.8 | 4.3 | 0.2 | 2.1 | Nirmalan and Robinson (1971) |
| 10 days | 16.0 | — | 67.0 | 25.0 | 4.0 | 2.0 | 2.0 | Atwal et al. (1964) |
| male adult | 24 | — | 46. | 50.0 | 1.0 | 1.0 | 2.0 | Atwal et al. (1964) |
| female adult | 25 | — | 40.0 | 52.0 | 4.0 | 3.0 | 1.0 | Atwal et al. (1964) |
| Agelaius phoeniceus (blackbird), mixed | — | — | 55.0 | 30.0 | 3.0 | 2.5 | 8.0 | Ronald et al. (1968) |

a few nonspecific azure granules are noted in the cytoplasm.

**Monocytes.** The monocytes in the blood of the fowl are sometimes difficult to identify or to distinguish from large lymphocytes because there are transitional forms between the two. In general, the monocytes are large cells with relatively more cytoplasm than the large lymphocytes. The cytoplasm of these cells has a blue-gray tint. The nucleus is usually irregular in outline. The nuclear pattern in the monocyte is of a more delicate composition than is that in the lymphocyte.

## Counting Methods

Leukocyte counts in the blood of chickens and other avian species have been made by many investigators. There is considerable variation in the numbers of the various cell types. In part, these discrepancies may be attributed to the method of making the count and, in many cases, to the small numbers of birds used (see Lucas and Jamroz, 1961, for details of methods).

Total leukocytes include all of the white cells, and these are counted in a special chamber. The blood is usually diluted 1 : 100 instead of 1 : 200 before it is placed in the counting chamber. Determining the total white cell count is attended with difficulty because the red cells are nucleated. Diluting fluids containing acetic acid that are ordinarily used to dissolve the red cells of mammalian blood are unsatisfactory for bird blood because the stroma of the red cells contract about the nuclei, making it impossible to distinguish these from some of the leukocytes. If a fluid, such as Toisson's solution, which preserves the red and white cells, is used then it is again difficult to distinguish with certainty between the thrombocytes and the small lymphocytes under the powers of magnification that can be used in conjunction with the counting chamber. Natt and Herrick (1952) described a new leukocyte diluent that contained Methyl Violet and that, according to Chubb and Rowell (1959), was the best of the several diluents tried.

For the differential count, a number of stains are available, such as the May-Grunewald, Giemsa, Leishman's, Jenner's, and Wright's. Supravital techniques are more reliable because there are no unidentifiable, degenerated cells present, as occurs with Wright's stain. The monocytes can be unmistakably differentiated, and the staining of the cells is always of the same intensity.

Olson (see Sturkie, 1965) has shown that in differential counts, the error in terms of coefficients of variability are: lymphocytes, 8.6%; heterophils, 27.9%; eosinophils, 58.8%; basophils, 62.6%; and monocytes, 22.2%. The coefficient of variability for total leukocytes was 34.2%, using phloxine as the stain. Because of the great variability in counts, Lucas and Jamroz (1961) have suggested that a large number of determinations on different birds be made.

## Number of Leukocytes

The number of leukocytes changes under various conditions, such as stress, estrogen administration, disease, and certain drugs. Little is known, however, concerning the exact role played by these cell types in combating stresses and diseases, although numbers of lymphocytes and heterophils appear to change most under these conditions. Both of these cell types are believed to be active in phagocytosing or combating infective or foreign material. Topp and Carlson (1972) have demonstrated *in vitro* the phagocytosis of *Staphylococcus* organisms by heterophils.

Numbers of leukocytes for different species of birds are shown in Table 3–7. In most cases, the smears for the differential counts were stained with Wright's stain. Twisselmann (1939) showed that the supravital technique is more reliable, and that the number of lymphocytes is higher and that of heterophils lower with Wright's stain. In most species the percentage of lymphocytes is higher than for any other cell type, comprising 40–70% of the total count, and the heterophils are the second most numerous group. In the ostrich and pheasant the opposite is true, with the heterophils comprising over half of the total count. The significance of this difference is not known.

**Sex and age differences.** Most workers have not found a consistent sex difference in leukocytes. Olson (1937) did report a sex difference in adult chickens, but not in young chickens; Twisselmann (1939) likewise reported no sex difference in the latter. Cook (1937) reported little variation in the count attributable to sex in chickens from 26 to 183 days of age. Lucas and Jamroz (1961), however, reported a significantly higher level of leukocytes in some adult female chickens than males. Slightly higher counts also were observed in *Coturnix* (quail) by Atwal *et al.* (1964) and by Nirmalan and Robinson (1971) and in ducks by Halaj (1967). Some investigators have paid little attention to possible sex differences, nor to whether the females were laying or not.

Estrogen administration definitely increase leukocyte counts in male chickens from 14,600 to 25,700 per cubic millimeter (Meyer, 1973) and in *Coturnix* (Nirmalan and Robinson, 1972). They reported increases from 19,900 to 24,700 following estrogen administration, with a significant increase in heterophils and a decrease in lymphocytes.

Glick (1960) has reported a diurnal variation in the leukocyte count of 3-week-old New Hampshire chicks. The leukocyte numbers were higher from 2 p.m. to 4 p.m.; the relative number of heterophils was lowest and that of lymphocytes highest at this time.

Young chicks and quails show slightly lower counts than adults. According to Burton and Harrison (1969) the blood of the neonate chick is low in leukocytes but relatively high in heterophils and basophils. The picture changes rapidly and by 3 weeks of age, the cell numbers increase and reach essentially the adult level.

**Effects of diet.** Although the work of Cook (1937) suggested that diet might influence the leukocyte count, the data were not conclusive. Work by Goff *et al.* (1953) demonstrates conclusively that a deficiency of riboflavin significantly increases the heterophils and decreases the lymphocytes. Similar results were obtained with vitamin $B_1$ deficiency.

Turkey poults fed a diet deficient in folic acid were anemic and had decreased leukocyte counts, including a decrease in lymphocytes, heterophils, basophils, monocytes, and thrombocytes (Lance and Hogan, 1948). When the diet was deficient in inositol, the total leukocyte count was likewise decreased.

**Effects of environment.** Very little experimental work has been conducted on the effects of changes in environment, exclusive of ration, on leukocyte count. Olson's (1937) studies indicate that more work should be conducted along these lines. He showed that when adult birds were reared in batteries within a building where there was little or no exposure to the elements, their total leukocyte counts were lower than those of chickens reared outside. For the birds raised indoors the leukocyte count was 17,000 and for those raised outside, 23,600. It is known that changes in environment may induce stress, with the consequent release of adrenal corticoids and with changes in leukocyte numbers in mammals and birds. Newcomer (1958) and Besch *et al.* (1967) have shown that physical restraint and the use of ACTH, cortical hormones, and other stressing agents produce a relative increase in number of heterophils in chickens. In mammals such treatments produce a de-

crease in the eosinophils. The mechanism is unknown.

**Effects of hormones, drugs, and other factors.** There is a prominent increase in heterophils and a decrease in lymphocytes following injection of cortical hormones (Siegal, 1968). The sensitivity of the heterophil is such that Wolford and Ringer (1962) have suggested that heterophil counts are a good means of assessing stress in birds.

Cortisone acetate increased the total count from 13,000 to 18,000 cells in chickens $3\frac{1}{2}$ hr after injection. Desoxycorticosterone acetate had a similar effect (Glick, 1961). Growth hormone alone did not influence the differential or the total leukocyte count.

Glick and Sato (1964) reported that ACTH increased heterophils in sham operated and bursectomized chicks and decreased lymphocytes only in bursectomized ones, suggesting that the bursa of Fabricius is involved in lymphocyte formation. Chemical bursectomy, however, did not significantly influence lymphocytes or heterophils (Glick, 1969).

Administration of ACTH to egrets and unilateral adrenalectomy in crows and pigeons produced a decrease in heterophils and an increase in lymphocytes. In myna birds, however, both treatments resulted in an opposite effect (heterophila and lymphopenia; Bhattacharyya and Sarkar, 1968). Bhattacharyya and Sarkar also revealed that certain inhibitors of cortical hormone release caused lymphopenia and heterophilia.

Compound 48/80, which liberates histamine in mammals and birds, decreases considerably the number of basophils in chicken blood and increases the lymphocytes (Hunt and Hunt, 1959).

A detailed study of the effects of x rays on blood cells of the chicken has been conducted by Lucas and Denington (1957). Total body irradiation with dosages from 50 to 300 roentgen units in chicks and hens decreased the total leukocyte count significantly, and the low level persisted for about 12 days after the treatment. There was likewise a decrease in lymphocytes but an increase in heterophils. The number of eosinophils and basophils was also depressed. There was no consistent effect of x rays on the number of monocytes. Usually, by 15 days after the treatment there was some recovery in cell numbers, and younger birds recovered sooner than older ones.

**Leukocytosis and disease.** There is considerable variation in the blood picture of normal birds, and caution should be exercised before changes in

70 the blood picture are attributed to disease. Olson (1965) has reviewed the hematological changes associated with certain diseases. It is known that various disorders in mammals cause an increase in number of leukocytes (leukocytosis). Leukemia of chickens is characterized by an increase in lymphocytes and abnormal cells of the lymphocyte series. Pullorum and typhoid produce leukocytosis and pullet disease (blue comb) increases leukocytes, particularly monocytes (see Sturkie, 1965). Tuberculosis in chickens resulted in leukocytosis with heterophilia and lymphopenia (Von Klimes and Celer, 1960). Administration of antibiotics to turkeys decreased leukocyte count (Sullivan, 1965).

## BLOOD COAGULATION

### Hemostasis

Hemostasis, the arrest of the escape of blood, requires an interplay between the walls of the blood vessels, and certain cellular elements of the blood, with the plasma proteins that are involved in the coagulation of the blood. When an injury occurs, the adjacent vessel walls contract, and a hemostatic plug is formed through blood platelet adhesion and aggregation. Avian blood lacks platelets, and their role in plug formation is assumed by thrombocytes (Grant and Zucker, 1973). In higher animals, a second and final hemostatic plug is then formed through blood coagulation.

The classical theory of blood coagulation developed by Alexander Schmidt and his contemporaries toward the end of the nineteenth century (see Morawitz, 1958) has been the point of departure for modern studies in this field. The decisive step in this theory is the transformation of the soluble protein, fibrinogen, into the insoluble fibrin, followed by polymerization of the fibrin monomers. This step is mediated by the enzymatic activity of thrombin. Thrombin is derived from prothrombin by the proteolytic breakdown of the prothrombin molecule, and the reaction is catalyzed by thromboplastin, calcium ions, and several accessory factors (see Figure 3–2). Thromboplastin may be derived from tissue juices or from blood platelets, and the active elements appear to be phospholipid in character. In the more carefully studied human clotting system, at least seven accessory factors have been designated (factors V and VII through XII; see Table 3–8). They are mainly protein in character and, in electrophoresis, migrate with the plasma globulin fractions. The mode of interaction of these factors is not perfectly understood; for more details and a discussion of the various theories one of the specialized works should be consulted (Biggs and MacFarland, 1962; Bang et al., 1971).

In 1929 Dam, studying the biosynthesis of cholesterol in the hen on a purified diet, observed subcutaneous and intramuscular hemorrhages resembling those of scurvy (McCollum, 1957). This observation later led to the discovery of the role of vitamin K in prothrombin synthesis in the liver. To date there is considerable evidence that vitamin K is involved not only in prothrombin synthesis but also in the synthesis of some of the accessory factors mentioned previously, namely factors VII, IX, and X (Brinkhous, 1959).

Most clotting factors do not exhibit absolute

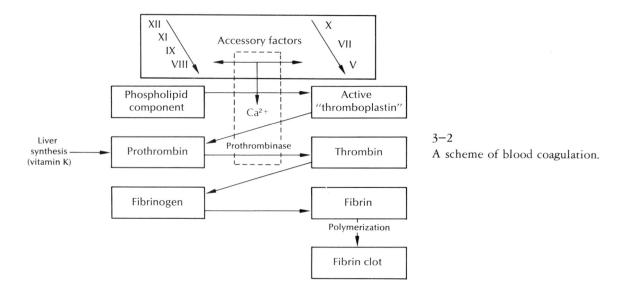

3–2

A scheme of blood coagulation.

**Table 3–8**  *Synonyms for blood coagulation factors*

| Factor | Synonyms |
| --- | --- |
| V | Labile factor, proaccelerin, accelerator globulin |
| VII | Stable factor, proconvertin, serum prothrombin conversion accelerator (SPCA) |
| VIII | Antihemophilic factor A, antihemophilic globulin (AHG), platelet cofactor I, thromboplastinogen A |
| IX | Antihemophilic factor B, plasma thromboplastin component (PTC), platelet cofactor II, Christmas factor (CF) |
| X | Stuart (Prower) factor |
| XI | Antihemophilic factor C, plasma thromboplastin antecedent (PTA) |
| XII | Hageman factor |
| XIII | Fibrin stabilizing factor |

species specificity; there are, nevertheless, pronounced differences between the clotting mechanisms of different classes of animals, and perhaps even between different species of the same class. Although the major factors involved in avian blood coagulation are apparently similar to those observed in mammals, avian plasma lacks the thromboplastin component (factor IX) and the so-called "Hageman factor" (Didisheim et al., 1959). According to Wartelle (1957) these factors are present but in very small amounts. Certain factors shown to exist in chicken blood may very well play a role similar to the above-mentioned factors in avian blood coagulation. Indeed, at least one of these factors seems to be vitamin K dependent (Sørby, 1966), as has been indicated for factor IX in mammals. Compared with mammalian systems, factors V and VII may be low or even absent in chickens, although factor X activity is definitely present (Stopforth, 1970). The coagulation of avian blood appears to be especially dependent on an extrinsic clotting system involving the release of tissue thromboplastin.

## Thromboplastin

A certain degree of species specificity exists for brain tissue thromboplastin, and probably for thromboplastin extracted from other tissues. Therefore, thromboplastic activity for avian prothrombin time determinations should be provided by bird tissue (Griminger, 1965a). Experimentation with ducks and turkeys (Didisheim et al., 1959; Griminger, 1957) has indicated that in assay work it might possibly even be advantageous to use the brain of the same rather than of another avian species.

A dry and relatively stable source of thromboplastic activity can be prepared by repeatedly extracting brain tissue with acetone. The vitamin K nutrition of the donor animal influences the thromboplastic activity of the product. The shorter prothrombin times associated with acetone-extracted brain powder from vitamin K-fed as compared to vitamin K-deficient donors appear to be caused by a vitamin K-dependent plasma clotting factor in the residual blood of the brain (Griminger et al., 1970). Before use in the prothrombin time determination, the brain powder is "activated" in saline. It appears to contain an inhibitor, because discarding the first and using a second extract enhances thromboplastic activity (Shum and Griminger, 1972a).

## Prothrombin Time

Vitamin K, essential for normal blood coagulation, can be supplied both in the food and by intestinal bacterial synthesis; the chicken appears to be particularly dependent on an exogenous source for this vitamin, and growing chickens become severely hypoprothrombinemic after a short time on a vitamin K-deficient diet. This fact has led to the widespread use of this species in vitamin K bioassay work. In this assay, varying amounts of the material to be assayed are fed to groups of vitamin K-deficient chicks, and known amounts of the vitamin are fed to others. A comparison of plasma prothrombin times, usually by the one-stage method of Quick (1966), indicates the amount of vitamin K-active material in the assayed samples. In the determination of prothrombin times blood is drawn and blood calcium is bound chemically to prevent coagulation. This can be accomplished by drawing blood with syringes prefilled with a measured amount of sodium oxalate or sodium citrate solution. Whereas for mammalian samples both solutions appear equally useful, sodium citrate is the anticoagulant of choice for avian blood samples (Shum and Griminger, 1972b). The blood is then centrifuged and calcium and a thromboplastic extract are added to the plasma. The time required for a clot to form is called the prothrombin time.

Prothrombin times of 12 sec or below can be obtained in growing chicks with the one-stage method of Quick (1966) if a carefully prepared chick brain thromboplastin extract is employed. Comparable results can also be obtained with other

72 extracts that promote slower clotting (Griminger, 1962). Prothrombin times even shorter than 12 sec have been observed in our laboratory for adult males, whereas those for adult females tend to be slightly longer. The adult male chicken appears to be relatively resistant to hypoprothrombinemia as a result of a degree of vitamin K deprivation that produces severe intramuscular and subcutaneous hemorrhages in growing chicks and initiates a more moderate hypoprothrombinemia in laying hens.

Whole blood clotting times are much more variable than prothrombin time. From 2 to 10 min appears to be the normal range for nonhypoprothrombinemic birds, although longer clotting times are occasionally recorded (Bigland, 1964). Other coagulation measurements that have been recorded in birds are plasma recalcification time, "Stypven" time, and the thromboplastin generation test (Stopforth, 1970).

A functional clotting system in the chicken embryo can be detected during the second half of the incubation period. Kane and Sizer (1953) found clotting material after 12–13 days of embryonic development but no clotting was demonstrable at 11 days.

### Anticoagulants

Although chickens are more resistant to oral anticoagulants of the coumarin type than are mammals, they succumb to large doses. These anticoagulants reduce plasmatic coagulation factors much in the same way as in a vitamin K deficiency (Losito, 1965). In our laboratory 0.16% dicumarol in the feed given to day-old chicks caused 70% mortality within 2 weeks, and 50% in chicks that were 1 or 2 weeks older at onset of medication. The reaction to lower doses is shown in Table 3–9. The anticoagulant effect of dicumarol and of warfarin, another compound of this type, can be overcome by feeding increased amounts of vitamin K: 800 mg of $K_1$ per kilogram of diet were required to obtain normal prothrombin times in chickens fed 100 mg of warfarin per kilogram of diet (Griminger, 1965b), whereas not more than 1 mg of $K_1$ per kilogram diet is required in the absence of antivitamins or other stress factors. Menadione ($K_3$) is not effective in overcoming high doses of dicumarol-type anticoagulants.

The question has been raised whether the hemorrhages that seem to be the cause of death in hypoprothrombinemia are precipitated by a simultaneous decrease in capillary strength. Increased capillary fragility in hypoprothrombinemia has indeed been demonstrated in the rat (Pastorova, 1957) by the use of the negative-pressure method. In this method, pinpoint hemorrhages are produced by applying negative pressure to a specific area of skin with the aid of a suction cup, varying either the pressure or the application time. Used on the chicken, this method produces bruises in the underlying flesh (vascular faults) that obscure the usual observation of petechiae in the skin (Morissette, 1956). Observations made in our laboratory indicate that in the chicken dicumarol also reduces capillary strength. It is not impossible, however, that the phenomenon in both rat and chicken is an indirect effect of a low level of coagulability on an ever-changing capillary bed rather than a direct effect on capillary fragility.

Blood also contains natural anticoagulants in the form of antithrombin, heparin, and perhaps an antithromboplastin. Heparin is a highly sulfated mucopolysaccharide, probably synthesized by basophilic mast cells throughout the body. It is a useful *in vitro* anticoagulant for studies not concerned with coagulation phenomena. Addition of 0.2 mg of heparin (two drops of a 2 mg/ml solution) prevents the coagulation of 1 ml of blood. On a dry basis, 1 mg heparin contains not less than 120 USP units, one unit being equal to approximately 0.01 mg of heparin sodium. *In vitro,* 500 units/kg body weight, injected intravenously, prevent coagulations. It is possible that heparin acts in conjunction with antithrombin. When a clot is formed, thrombin is also inactivated by the absorptive action of fibrin, thus localizing clot formation.

The shrinking of a blood coagulum, with the simultaneous expression of a serum, is called clot retraction. In chicken blood, clot retraction occurs appreciably slower than in human blood according to Bigland (1960) and is negligible according to Didisheim *et al.* (1959).

*Table 3–9* Response of chicks to the feeding of dicumarol for 1 week

| Dicumarol added (mg/kg diet) | Average prothrombin times[a] (sec) |
| --- | --- |
| 0 | 13.7 |
| 50 | 14.3 |
| 100 | 14.7 |
| 200 | 17.8 |
| 400 | 27.0 |
| 800 | 59.9 |

[a]Averages on the basis of reciprocals of individual plasma prothrombin times.

## Hemorrhagic Syndrome

The so-called "hemorrhagic syndrome" observed in growing chickens is characterized by subcutaneous hemorrhages; anemia and a pale bone marrow have also been observed. The etiology of the syndrome has not been satisfactorily explained. Some of the early field cases of the syndrome were probably results of a deficiency of vitamin K, because new formulations of poultry rations had reduced the amount of the vitamin in practical rations without a compensatory addition of synthetic vitamin K. Another contributory factor in the etiology of the hemorrhagic syndrome may have been the injudicious use of coccidiostatic sulfonamides, such as sulfaquinoxaline. Although sulfonamides may influence intestinal vitamin K synthesis by bacteriostatic action, such synthesis does not play a decisive role in the supply of this vitamin to growing chickens. Because there is also a positive correlation between the sulfonamide dose and the amount of vitamin K necessary to overcome the hypoprothrombinemia induced by the former (Griminger, 1957), it appears that in addition to their bacteriostatic effect sulfonamides can act as vitamin K antagonists. Molds have also been implicated in the hemorrhagic syndrome. Schumaier *et al.* (1961) have been able to produce symptoms typical of this syndrome by providing growing chickens with feed samples contaminated with either of two species of aspergilli. The ingestion of blighted corn heavily infested with a helminthosporium and a fusarium species, in contrast, had no effect on blood clotting time (Washburn and Britton, 1971).

In the so-called fatty liver–hemorrhagic syndrome (FLHS) in laying hens, the characteristic hemorrhages only appear in hens having enlarged livers of a high fat content (Wolford and Murphy, 1972). Although the etiology of the hemorrhages seen in FLHS remains undefined, it is doubtful that it is directly related to a failure of the blood coagulation mechanism.

## REFERENCES

Abercrombie, C., B. R. Maber, and F. Vella. (1969). Studies in the hemoglobin of the great horned owl. *Can. J. Biochem.*, 47, 571.

Albritton, E. C. (1952). "Standard Values of Blood." Philadelphia: W. B. Saunders Co.

Archer, R. K. (1971). Blood coagulation. In "Physiology and Biochemistry of Domestic Fowl," Vol. II (D. J. Bell and B. M. Freeman Eds.). London: Academic Press, Chapter 38.

Atwal, O. S., L. Z. McFarland, and W. O. Wilson. (1964). Hematology of *Coturnix* from birth to maturity. *Poultry Sci.*, 43, 1392.

Balasch, J., L. Palacios, S. Musquera, J. Palomeque, M. Jimenez, and M. Alemany. (1973). Comparative hematological values of several galliformes. *Poultry Sci.*, 52, 1531.

Bang, N. U., F. K. Beller, E. Deutsch, and E. F. Mammen. (1971). "Thrombosis and Bleeding Disorders." New York. Academic Press.

Bankowski, R. A. (1942). Studies of the hemoglobin content of chickens blood and evaluation of methods for its determination. *Am. J. Vet. Res.*, 3, 373.

Barrett, L. A., and S. L. Scheinberg. (1972). The development of Avian red cell shape. *J. Exp. Zool.*, 182, 1.

Bell, D. J., and P. D. Sturkie. (1965). Chemical constituents of blood. In "Avian Physiology" (P. D. Sturkie, Ed.). Ithaca, N.Y.: Cornell University Press

Bernhardt, D., and E. F. Kaleta. (1968). Beitratg zur Hamatologie der Gans II. Elektropherogram Hamoglobin und Gesamtproteinbestimmung. *Arch. Geflugelkunde*, 32, 158.

Besch, E. L., A. H. Smith, R. R. Burton, and S. J. Sluka. (1967). Physiological limitations of animal restraint. *Aerospace Med.*, 38, 1130.

Bhattacharyya, T. K., and A. K. Sarkar. (1968). Avian leucocytic responses induced by stress and corticoid inhibitors. *Indian J. Exp. Biol.*, 6, 26.

Bierer, B. W., T. H. Eleazer, and D. E. Roebuck. (1963). Hematocrit and sedimentation rate values as an acid in poultry disease diagnosis. *J. Am. Vet. Med. Assoc.*, 143, 1096.

Bierer, B. W., T. H. Eleazer, and D. E. Roebuck. (1964). Sedimentation rate, packed cell volume, buffy coat value, and rectal temperature of chickens and turkeys at various ages. *J.A.V.M.A.*, 144, 727.

Biggs, R., and R. G. Macfarlane. (1962). "Human Blood Coagulation." Philadelphia: F. A. Davis Co.

Bigland, C. H. (1960). Studies on avian blood coagulation. Ph.D. thesis, University of Alberta, Edmonton, Canada.

Bigland, C. H. (1964). Blood clotting time of five avian species. *Poultry Sci.*, 43, 1035.

Bond, C. F., and P. W. Gilbert. (1958). Comparative study of blood volume in representative aquatic and nonaquatic birds. *Am. J. Physiol.*, 194, 519.

Brace, K., and P. D. Atland. (1956). Lifespan of the duck and chicken erythrocyte as determined with C14. *Proc. Soc. Exp. Biol. Med.*, 92, 615.

Brinkhous, K. M. (1959). Blood clotting: the plasma procoagulants. *Am. Rev. Physiol.*, 21, 271.

Brown, I. R. F., W. H. Bannister, and C. DeLucca. (1970). A comparison of maltese and sicilian sparrow hemoglobins. *Comp. Biochem. Physiol.*, 34, 557.

Brush, A. H., and D. H. Power. (1970). Electrophoretic studies on hemoglobin of Breevers Blackbird. *Comp. Biochem. Physiol.*, 33, 587.

Burton, R. R., and J. S. Harrison. (1969). The relative differential leucocyte count of the newly hatched chick. *Poultry Sci.*, 48, 451.

Burton, R. R., and A. H. Smith. (1972). The effect of chronic erythrocyte polycythemia and high altitude upon plasma and blood volumes. *Proc. Soc. Exp. Biol. Med.*, 140, 920.

Burton, R. R., R. Sahara, and A. H. Smith. (1971). The hematology of domestic fowl native to high altitude. *Environ. Physiol.*, 1, 155.

Bush, F. M., and W. W. Farrar. (1967). Electrophoretic variation and spectrophotometric content of hemoglobin during differentiation of *Passer domesticus*. *Anat. Rec.*, 157, 222.

Campbell, F., (1967). Fine structure of bone marrow of chicken and pigeon. *J. Morphol.*, 123, 405.

Chubb, L. G., and J. G. Rowell. (1959). Counting blood cells of chickens. *J. Agri. Sci.*, 52, 263.

Coates, V., and B. E. March. (1966). Reticulocyte counts in the chicken. *Poultry Sci.*, 45, 1302.

Cohen, R. R. (1967). Anticoagulation centrifugation time and sample replicate number in the microhematocrit method for avian blood. *Poultry Sci.*, 46, 214.

74

Cook, S. F. (1937). A study of blood picture of poultry and its diagnostic significance. *Poultry Sci., 16,* 291.

Dabrowski, Z. (1967). The absorption spectrum in the ultraviolet light of the hemoglobin of birds of the crow family. *Comp. Biochem. Physiol., 21,* 703.

Denmark, C. R., and K. W. Washburn. (1969). Hemoglobin types in chicks embryos with different adult hemoglolbin genotypes. *Poultry Sci., 48,* 464.

De Villiers, O. T. (1938). Blood of ostrich. *Onderstepoort J. Vet. Sci., 11,* 419.

Dhingra, L. D., W. B. Parrish, and W. G. Venzke. (1969). Electron microscopy of granular leucocytes of chicken. *Am. J. Vet. Res., 30,* 637.

Didisheim, P., K. Hattori, and J. H. Lewis. (1959). Hematologic and coagulation studies in various animal species. *J. Lab. Clin. Med., 53,* 866.

Dobsinska, E., and O. Dobsinska. (1972). Erythrocyte sedimentation rate in pheasant and its practical importance. Paper presented at 5th State Conference on Poultry Physiology at Bratislava, Sept. 1972.

Domm, L. V., and E. Taber. (1946). Endocrine factors controlling erythrocyte concentration in the blood of the domestic fowl. *Physiol. Zool., 19,* 258.

Dunlap, J. S., V. L. Johnson, and D. S. Farner. (1956). Multiple hemoglobins in birds. *Experientia, 12,* 352.

Ernest, R. A., T. H. Coleman, A. W. Kulenkamp, R. K. Ringer, and S. Pangborn. (1971). The packed cell volume and differential leucocyte count of bobwhite quail. *Poultry Sci., 50,* 389.

Fraser, R., B. Horton, D. DuPorque, and A. Chernoff. (1972). The multiple hemoglobins of the chick embryo. *J. Cell Physiol., 60,* 79.

Ghosh, J. (1965). Studies in avian hemoglobins electrophoretic separation of hemoglobins from the chicken. *Science, 122,* 1186.

Gilbert, A. B. (1962). Sedimentation rate of erythrocytes in the domesticated cock. *Poultry Sci., 41,* 784.

Gilbert, A. B. (1963). The effect of estrogen and thyroxine on blood volume of the domestic cock. *J. Endocrinol., 26,* 41.

Gilbert, A. B. (1965). Sex differences in the erythrocyte of the adult domestic fowl. *Vet. Sci., 6,* 114.

Gilbert, A. B. (1968). The relationship between the erythrocyte sedimentation rate and packed cell volume in the domestic fowl. *Brit. Poultry Sci., 9,* 297.

Glick, B. (1960). Leucocyte count variation in young chicks during an 18 hour period. *J. Appl. Physiol., 15,* 965.

Glick, B. (1961). The effect of bovine growth hormone, DCA and cortisone acetate on white cell counts of 2 week old chickens. *Poultry Sci., 40,* 1537.

Glick, B. (1969). Hematology of chemically bursectomized birds. *Avian Dis., 13,* 142.

Glick, B., and K. Sato. (1964). White blood cell counts in bursectomized birds. *Am. J. Physiol., 207,* 1371.

Goff, S., W. C. Russell, and M. W. Taylor. (1953). Hematology of the chick in vitamin deficiencies. I. Riboflavin. *Poultry Sci., 32,* 54.

Grant, R. A., and M. B. Zucker. (1973). Avian thrombocyte aggregation and shape change *in vitro. Am. J. Physiol., 225,* 340.

Gratzer, W., and A. Allison. (1960). Multiple hemoglobins. *Biol. Rev., 35,* 459.

Griminger, P. (1957). On the vitamin K requirements of turkey poults. *Poultry Sci., 36,* 1227.

Griminger, P. (1962). Prothrombin bioassay for vitamin K with different thromboplastin preparations. *Int. J. Vit. Res., 32,* 405.

Griminger, P. (1965a). Blood coagulation. In "Avian Physiology" (2nd ed.) (P. D. Sturkie, Ed.). Ithaca, New York: Cornell University Press.

Griminger, P. (1965b). Vitamin K activity in chickens: phylloquinone and menadione in the presence of stress agents. *J. Nutr., 87,* 337.

Griminger, P., and Y. S. Shum, and P. Budowski. (1970). Effect of dietary vitamin K on avian brain thromboplastin activity. *Poultry Sci., 49,* 1681.

Grinnell, F., and J. O. Lee. (1972). Alterations in the rate of hemoglobin synthesis during chick embryogenesis. *J. Cell Physiol., 79,* 111.

Groebbels, F. (1932). "Der Vogel erster Bond: Atmungswelt und Nahrungswelt." Borntraeger, Berlin: Verlag von Gebruder.

Halaj, M. (1967). A contribution to the study of the blood picture in some kinds and breeds of ducks. *Acta Zootech. Univ. Agri. Nitra (Czechoslovakia), 16,* 91.

Harman, I. W., E. Ogden, and S. F. Cook. (1932). The reservior function of spleen in fowls. *Am. J. Physiol., 11,* 99.

Hartman, F. A., and M. A. Lessler. (1963). Erythrocyte measurements in birds. *Auk, 80,* 467.

Hevesy, G., and J. Ottesen (1945). Life cycle of red corpuscles of the hen. *Nature, 156,* 534.

Hunsaker, W. G. (1968). Blood volume of geese treated with androgen and estrogen. *Poultry Sci., 47,* 371.

Hunsaker, W. G. (1969). Species and sex differences in the percentage of plasma trapped in packed cell volume determinations on avian blood. *Poultry Sci., 48,* 907.

Hunsaker, W. G., J. R. Hunt, and J. Raitken. (1964). I. Physical characteristics of Blood. *Brit. Poultry Sci., 5,* 249.

Hunt, T. E., and E. A. Hunt. (1959). Blood basophils of cockerels before and after intravenous ingestion of compound 48/80. *Anat. Rec., 132,* 19.

Hunter, F. R. (1953). An analysis of the photoelectric method for studying osmotic changes in chicken erythrocytes. *J. Cell. Comp. Physiol., 41,* 387.

Hunter, F. R., D. Chalfin, F. J. Finamore, and M. L. Sweetland. (1956). Sodium and potassium exchange in chicken erythrocytes. *J. Cell. Comp. Physiol., 47,* 37.

Jaeger, J. (1973). A comparison of the effects of chronic hypoxia induced by exposure to carbon monoxide or simulated high altitude in Japanese quail. Ph. D. thesis, Rutgers University, New Jersey.

Jordan, H. E. (1939). The lymphocytes in relation to erythrocyte production. *Anat. Rec., 73,* 227.

Kaleta, E. E., and D. Bernhardt. (1968). Beitrag ur Hematologie der Gans. I. Morphologische Untersuchung des Ganseblutes. *Arch. Geflugelkunde, 32,* 84.

Kane, R. E., and I W. Sizer. (1953). Some studies on the developing blood clotting system of chick embryo. *Anat. Rec., 117,* 614.

Klein, J. R. (1970). Hemoglobin heterogenity in the pekin duck. *Proc. Soc. Exp. Biol. Med., 133,* 665.

Kubena, L. F., J. D. May, F. N. Reece, and J. W. Deaton. (1971). Hematocrit and hemoglobin levels of broilers as influenced by environmental temperature and dietary iron level. *Poultry Sci., 51,* 759.

Lance, B. G., and A. G. Hogan. (1948). Inositol and nicotinic acid in the nutrition of the turkey. *J. Nutri., 36,* 369.

Losito, R. (1965). Investigations into the presence of a competitive inhibitor (preprothrombin) in the plasma of chicks. *Acta Chem. Scand., 19,* 2229.

Lucas, A. M. (1959). A discussion of synonymy in avian and mammalian hematological nomenclature. *Am. J. Vet. Res., 20,* 887.

Lucas, A. M., and E. M. Denington. (1957). Effect on total body x-ray irradiation on the blood of female single comb White Leghorn chickens. *Poultry Sci., 36,* 1290.

Lucas, A. M., and C. Jamroz. (1961). "Atlas of Avian Hematology." U. S. Department of Agriculture Monograph 25.

March, B. E., V. Coates, and J. Biely. (1966). The effects of estrogen and androgen on osmotic fragility and fatty acid composition of erythrocytes in the chicken. *Can. J. Physiol. Pharmacol., 44,* 379.

McCollum, E. V. (1957). "A History of Nutrition." Boston: Houghton Mifflin Co.

McManus, T. J. (1967). Comparative biology of red cells. *Fed. Proc., 26,* 1821.

Medway, W., and M. R. Kare. (1959). Blood and plasma volume hematocrit blood specific gravity and serum protein electrophoresis of the chicken. *Poultry Sci., 38,* 624.

Meyer, D. (1973). Studies on factors regulating blood serotonin levels in the domestic fowl. Ph.D. thesis, Rutgers University, New Jersey.

Mirand, E. A., and A. S. Gordon. (1966). Mechanism of estrogen action on erythropoiesis. *Endocrinology, 78,* 325.

Morawitz, P. (1958). "The Chemistry of Blood Coagulation.",

Springfield, Ill.: Charles C Thomas (Orig. published as "Die Chemie der Blutgerinnung," 1905, Wiesbaden, Germany: J. F. Bergmann).

Morrisette, M. C. (1956). The hematology of broilers in the presence of mild stress, with reference to the hemorrhagic syndrome. Thesis, Oklahoma Agricultural and Mining College, Stillwater.

Natt, M. P., and C. A. Herrick. (1952). A new blood diluent for counting the erythrocytes and leucocytes of the chicken. *Poultry Sci. 31*, 735.

Newcomer, W. S. (1958). Physiologic factors which influence acidophelia induced by stressors in the chicken. *Am. J. Physiol., 194*, 251.

Nirmalan, G. P., and G. A. Robinson. (1971). Hematology of the Japanese quail, *Coturnix japonica*. *Brit. Poultry Sci., 12*, 475.

Nirmalan, G. P., and G. A. Robinson. (1972). Hematology of Japanese quail treated with exogenous stilbestrol diproprionate and testosterone propionate. *Poultry Sci., 51*, 920.

Nirmalan, G. P., and G. A. Robinson. (1973). The survival time of erythrocytes (DF$^{32}$P label) in the Japanese quail. *Poultry Sci., 52*, 355.

Olson, C. (1937). Variation in cells and hemoglobin content in blood of normal domestic chickens. *Cornell Vet., 27*, 235.

Olson, C. (1965). Avian hematology. In "Diseases of Poultry," (H. E. Biester and L. H. Schwarte, Eds.). Ames: Iowa State Press, p 100.

Pastorova, V. E. (1957). Tzmenenie protshnosti kapilljornych sosudov pris K-avitaminose i spetsif tschnost' diestvija vitina K na protschnost' kapilljarov. *Doklady Akad. Nauk SSSR, 113*, 1379.

Paulsen, T. M., A. L. Moxon, and W. O. Wilson. (1950). Blood composition of broad breasted bronze turkeys. *Poultry Sci., 29*, 15.

Pilaski, J. (1972). Vergleichende untersuchungen uber den hamoglobingehalt des huhner und Putenblutes in Abhangigkeit vor alter und geschlecht. *Arch. Geflugelkunde, 36*, 70.

Quick, A. J. (1966). "Hemorrhagic Diseases and Thrombosis." Philadelphia: Lea & Febiger.

Rodnan, G. P., F. G. Ebaugh Jr., and M. R. S. Fox. (1957). Life span of red blood cell volume in the chicken, pigeon, duck as estimated by the use of Na$_2$C, $^{51}$O$_4$ with observations on red cell turnover rate in mammal, bird and reptile blood. *J. Hematol., 12*, 355.

Ronald, K., M. E. Foster, and M. Idyer. (1968). Physical properties of blood of the red-winged blackbird. *Can. J. Zool., 46*, 158.

Rosse, W. F., and T. A. Waldmann. (1966). Factors controlling erythropoiesis in birds. *Blood, 27*, 654.

Saha, A., and J. Ghosh. (1965). Comparative studies of avian hemoglobin. *Comp. Biochem. Physiol., 15*, 217.

Schultze, M. O., and C. A. Elvehjem. (1934). An improved method for the determination of hemoglobin in chicken blood. *J. Biol. Chem., 105*, 253.

Schumaier, G., B. Panda, H. M. DeVolt, N. C. Laffer, and R. D. Creed. (1961). Hemorrhagic lesions in chickens resembling naturally occurring "hemorrhagic syndrome" produced experimentally by mycotoxins. *Poultry Sci., 40*, 1132.

Shum, Y.-S., and P. Griminger. (1972a). Thromboplastic activity of acetone-dehydrated chicken brain powder extracts after repeated extraction and dilution. *Poultry Sci., 51*, 402.

Shum, Y.-S., and P. Griminger. (1972b). Prothrombin time stability of avian and mammalian plasma: effect of anticoagulant. *Lab. Anim. Sci., 22*, 384.

Siegel, H. S. (1968). Blood cells and chemistry of young chickens during daily ACTH & cortisone administration. *Poultry Sci., 47*, 1811.

Soliman, M. K., S. Elamrousi, and A. A.S. Ahmed. (1966). Cytological and biochemical studies on the blood of normal and spirochaete infected chicks. *Zantrabl. Vet. Med. B, 13*, 82.

Sørby, O. (1966). "Studies Related to Coagulation of Chicken Blood." Oslo: Universitetsforlaget.

Sova, Z. D. Trefny, J. Houska, K. Koudela, K. Vranova, Z. Nemec, A. Hrdinova, and K. Kosar. (1972). Hematological findings in 4 goose breeds kept in Czechoslovakia. Presented at

5th State Conference on Poultry Physiology at Bratislava, Sept.

Spector, W. S. (1956). "Handbook of Biologic Data." Philadelphia: W. B. Saunders.

Stino, F. K. R., and K. W. Washburn. (1970). Responses of chickens with different phenotypes to phenylhydrazine induced anemia. *Poultry Sci., 49*, 101.

Stopforth, A. (1970). A study of coagulation mechanisms in domestic chickens. *J. Comp. Pathol., 80*, 525.

Sturkie, P. D. (1943). Reputed reservior function of the spleen of the domestic fowl. *Am. J. Physiol., 138*, 599.

Sturkie, P. D. (1951). Effects of estrogen and thyroxine upon plasma proteins and blood volume in the fowl. *Endocrinology, 49*, 565.

Sturkie, P. D., (1965). In "Avian Physiology" (2nd ed.), (P. D. Sturkie, Ed.). Ithaca, N. Y.: Cornell University Press, Ch. 1 & 2.

Sturkie, P. D., and K. Textor. (1958). Sedimentation rate of erythrocytes in chickens as influenced by method and sex. *Poultry Sci., 37*, 60.

Sturkie, P. D., and K. Textor. (1960). Further studies on sedimentation rate of erythrocytes in chickens. *Poultry Sci., 39*, 444.

Sullivan, T. W. (1965). Hemoglobin, white cell count, packed cell volume and weight gain in turkeys fed certain antibiotics. *Proc. Soc. Exp. Biol. Med., 119*, 731.

Surendranathan, K. P., S. G. Nair, and K. J. Simon. (1968). Hematological constituents of duck. *Indian Vet. J., 45*, 312.

Tanaka, J., and M. M. Rosenberg. (1955). Effect of testosterone and dienestrol diacetate on hemoglobin levels of cockerels and capons. *Poultry Sci., 34*, 1429.

Topp, R. C., and H. C. Carlson. (1972). Studies on avian heterophils III Phagocytic properties. *Avian Dis. 16*, 374.

Tosteson, D. C., and J. S. Robertson. (1956). Potassium transport in duck red cells. *J. Cell. Comp. Physiol., 47*, 147.

Twisselmann, N. M. (1939). A study of the cell content of blood of normal chickens with supravital stains. *Poultry Sci., 18*, 151.

Usami, S., V. Magazinovic, S. Chen, and M. I. Gregersen. (1970). Viscosity of turkey blood: Rheology of nucleated erythrocytes. *Microvasc. Res., 2*, 489.

Van der Helm, H. J., and T. H. J. Huisman. (1958). The two hemoglobin components of the chicken. *Science, 127*, 762.

Vogel, J. (1961). Studies on cardiac output in chicken. Ph.D. thesis, Rutgers University, New Brunswick, N.J.

Von Klimes, B., and V. Celer. (1960). Das Blutbild bei der getlugeltuberkulose. Tierarztliche Wochenschrift. *73 Jahrgang, Heft, 16*, 311.

Wartelle, O. (1957). Mechanisme de la coagulation chez la poule. I: Etude des elements du complexe prothomique et de la thromboplastino formation. *Rev. Hematol., 12*, 351.

Washburn, K. W. (1968). Affects of age of bird and hemoglobin type on the concentration of adult hemoglobin components of the domestic fowl. *Poultry Sci., 47*, 1083.

Washburn, K. W. (1969). Hematological response of different stocks of chickens in iron-copper deficient diet. *Poultry Sci., 48*, 204.

Washburn, K. W., and W. M. Britton. (1971). Effects of diets containing *Helminthosporium maydis* blighted corn on growth rate, feed conversion, mortality and blood clotting time of broilers. *Poultry Sci., 50*, 1161.

Washburn, A. H., and A. J. Meyers. (1957). The sedimentation of erythrocytes at an angle of 45 degrees. *J. Clin. Lab. Med. 49*, 318.

Washburn, K. W., and J. R. Smyth, Jr., (1968). Hematology of an inherited anemia in the domestic fowl. *Poultry Sci., 47*, 1408.

Wels, A., and V. Horn. (1965). Beitrag zur Hamoglobin — Bestimmung in Blut des Geflugels. *Zentbl. Vet. Med., 12A*, 663.

Wirth, D. (1931). "Grundlage einer klinischen Haematologieder Haustiere." Berlin: Urban & Schwarzenberg.

Wolford, J. H., and D. Murphy. (1972). Effect of diet on fatty liver — hemorrhagic syndrome incidence in laying chickens. *Poultry Sci., 51*, 2087.

Wolford, J. H., and R. K. Ringer. (1962). Adrenal weight, adrenal ascorbic acid, adrenal cholesterol and differential leucocyte counts as physiological indicators of stress or agents in laying hens. *Poultry Sci., 41*, 1521.

# 4

## Heart and Circulation: Anatomy, Hemodynamics, Blood Pressure, Blood Flow, and Body Fluids

P. D. Sturkie

# ANATOMY OF THE CIRCULATORY SYSTEM

The heart of most birds is located in the thorax slightly to the left of the median line and is almost parallel to the long axis of the body, except that the apex may be bent to the right. The heart is surrounded by the pericardial sac. The bird heart, like the mammal's, has four chambers, two atria and two ventricles. The right atrium is usually larger than the left. The left ventricle is usually three or more times larger than the right and is considerably thicker. The radii of curvature at the apex are less than at the base and therefore tension and pressure here are less. Avian cardiac muscle has no transverse tubules and the fibers are much smaller than mammalian ones (Sommer and Steere, 1969; Akester, 1971). The atria have openings into the ventricles which are closed by the atrioventricular (AV) valves. The left valve is thin, membranous, and bicuspid, as it is in mammals. The right valve is simply a muscular flap. It originates at the right side of the base of the pulmonary artery, where it is held up by trabecular muscle. Contraction of right ventricle forces the free leaf portion of the valve into the atrioventricular opening, thus closing it. The pulmonary and aortic valves are membranous and tricuspid, as are those of mammals.

The entrance of veins into and exit of arteries from the heart are illustrated in Figures 4–1 and 4–2. The mode of entry of veins into the right atrium exhibits considerable variation. In the chicken the posterior vena cava and right anterior vena cava open together into the sinus venous whose slit-like entrance into the right atrium is demarcated by a pair of sinoatrial valves. In many birds, one or both valves are lacking (Jones and Johansen, 1972).

Size of heart. The size of the heart varies considerably among birds according to body size (Table 4–1). The heart size appears to be relatively greater in small birds, although there is considerable varia-

tion. For more details consult Hartman (1955), who has recorded heart weights of many species, and Brush (1966), who has plotted log heart weights against log body weight in many species. In birds weighing above 100 g the slope of the line (regression) is about 1 and for those weighing less than 100 g the slope is about 0.6. Heart size tends to be greater in birds than mammals of equal weight and this has some obvious advantages and disadvantages (see section on work of heart in Chapter 5).

Environmental factors, such as hypoxia (high altitude), increase heart size (Abati and McGrath, 1973).

Innervation of heart. The atria are innervated by sympathetic and parasympathetic fibers and these influence heart rate considerably. The ventricles, unlike those of most mammals, also receive sympathetic and parasympathetic fibers. Based on pharmacologic data Bolton (1967) reported vagal fibers in the ventricles. Abraham (1969) also reported that atria and ventricles are innervated by parasympathetic fibers, and Hirsch (1970) reported such fibers in the ventricles of owl, penguin, goose, and Columba (pigeon). The presence or absence of vagal fibers influences the results on contractility of ventricle (see section on contractility in Chapter 5).

The distribution of sympathetic fibers to the avian heart has received a great deal of attention by Akester (1971); by Bennett and Malmfors (1970), based on histochemical studies; and by Tummons and Sturkie (1969) and Sturkie and Poorvin (1973). The latter have defintely demonstrated that norepinephrine is the neurotransmitter in chicken hearts. Tummons and Sturkie (1968, 1969) first demonstrated the effects of stimulating the cardioaccelerator nerve of chicken on heart rate (see Chapter 5).

Coronary arteries and veins. Most birds have two main coronary arteries, but some may have three or four (Petren, 1926). The right coronary is located on the ventral surface of the heart and is

*Table 4–1*  *Heart size and body weight*

| Species | Body weight (g) | Heart weight/body weight (%) | References |
|---|---|---|---|
| Goose | 4405 | 0.8 | Sturkie (1965) |
| Duck | 1685 | 0.74 | Sturkie (1965) |
| Chicken | 3120 | 0.44 | Sturkie (1965) |
| Ptarmigan | 258 | 1.05 | Johnson and Lockner (1968) |
| Hummingbird | – | 2.4 | Hartman (1955) |
| *Coturnix* (quail) | 119 | 0.90 | Sturkie (unpublished) |
| Pigeon | 458 | 1.02 | Sturkie (unpublished) |

78 larger than the left one, which originates from the dorsal side of the aorta and courses mainly over the dorsal surface of the heart. The ends and branches of the right and left coronaries anastomose freely, and many are situated deep in the myocardium.

There are four major coronary veins and their branches in chickens are named as follows: great vein, middle vein, left circumflex, and a small cardiac venous complex (Lindsay, 1967). The great coronary vein runs on the left aspect of the heart, and the prominent middle vein courses over the dorsal aspect of the heart. Lindsay (1967) reported no coronary sinus in the chicken, although others have reported such in the chicken and in some other species.

**Blood vessels.** The principal arteries and veins are presented in Figures 4–1 and 4–2. The arterial supply to most organs is similar to that in mammals, except that the arrangement of carotid arteries in birds varies considerably among different species (Glenny, 1940): (1) they may be paired; (2) they may be fused into a median vessel; (3) the

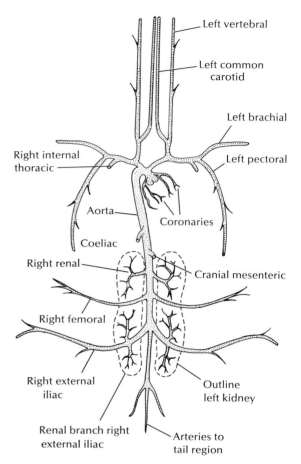

4–2 Principal arteries (ventrodorsal view). The outline of the heart is indicated by the coronary arteries. (After Akester, 1971.)

4–1 Venous system in ventral view. (After Portmann, 1950.)

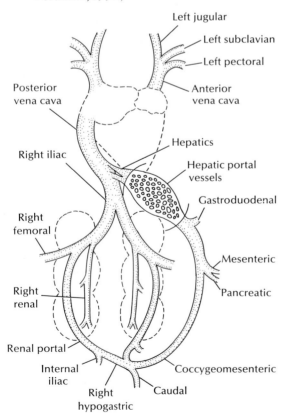

right or left vessels may be unpaired; and (4) the right and left may be paired but with one or the other much smaller. The common carotid gives rise to the vertebral artery in some species and is often referred to as an internal carotid (Figure 4–3). The terminology is conflicting and confusing (Adams, 1958).

The branches of the internal carotids go to the brain. There is no circle of Willis, but there is a direct anastomosis between the two cerebral carotid arteries, immediately caudal to the hypophysis. The types of anastomes involve three arrangements or configurations: (1) an H type, (2) an I type, and (3) an X type (Baumel and Gerchman, 1968). Further details on arteries are treated in a later section on blood flow to individual organs and systems.

Birds, unlike mammals, have a renal portal circulation. This system is treated in detail in the chapters on the digestive tract (Chapter 9) and kid-

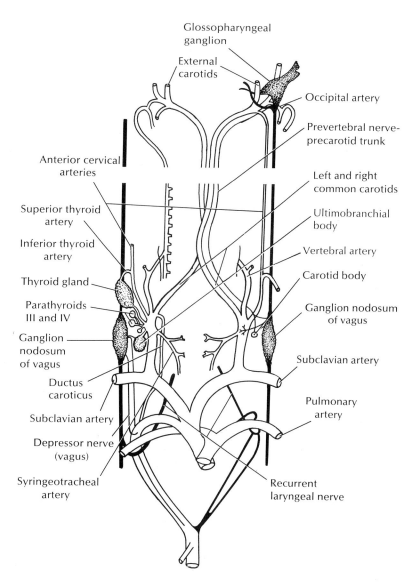

Glossopharyngeal
ganglion

External
carotids

Occipital artery

Prevertebral nerve-
precarotid trunk

Anterior cervical
arteries

Left and right
common carotids

Superior thyroid
artery

Ultimobranchial
body

Inferior thyroid
artery

Vertebral artery

Thyroid gland

Carotid body

Parathyroids
III and IV

Ganglion nodosum
of vagus

Ganglion
nodosum
of vagus

Subclavian artery

Ductus
caroticus

Subclavian artery

Pulmonary
artery

Depressor nerve
(vagus)

Syringeotracheal
artery

Recurrent
laryngeal nerve

**4–3**

Innervation of the carotid
sinus complex and aortic arch
of birds, according to Adams
(1958), based on work by others.

ney (Chapter 14), where it is shown that blood normally flowing to the liver from the coccygeomesenteric and hepatic portal veins may be shunted to the kidney via the renal portal vein, and vice versa. The coccygeomesenteric vein is the intervening link between the renal and hepatic portal systems.

**Innervation of arteries and veins.** Smooth muscle in the veins is innervated with adrenergic fibers (Bennett and Malmfors, 1970; Akester, 1971) and also cholinergic fibers (Akester, 1971) and so are those of arteries. The mesenteric arteries of chickens and turkeys contain longitudinal smooth muscle as well as circular, which is also innervated by adrenergic and cholinergic fibers (Bolton, 1968). The following arteries also receive a dual innerva-

tion according to Akester (1971): renal, coeliac, common carotid, subclavian, and pulmonary, but not femoral, which receives adrenergic fibers only. Practically all veins, including the vena cava, pulmonary, jugular, hepatic, hepatic portal, renal portal vein and valve, and coccygeomesenteric, are dually innervated.

## HEMODYNAMICS

In each cardiac cycle (see Chapter 5) blood is ejected from the left ventricle through the aorta, forced through the arteries and arterioles to capillaries, and goes thence to veins, which carry blood back to the right atrium (systemic circulation). At

80 the same time, blood from the right ventricles is ejected through pulmonary arteries to the lungs, where it is oxygenated and returned to the left atrium via the pulmonary veins (pulmonary circulation).

The heart pumps blood (a non-Newtonian fluid) through blood vessels of varying size, distensibility and resistance. The volume of blood delivered to an organ (flow) is determined by the pressure difference ($\Delta P$) exerted on it between two points and the resistance $(R)$ to flow as follows: $F$ (flow) $= P/R$. It follows therefore that $P = FR$ and $R = P/F$.

Poiseuille's equation describes in more detail the factors involved in resistance to flow:

$$R = \frac{\Delta P}{F} = \frac{8}{\pi} \times \eta \times \frac{L}{r^4}$$

where $r^4$ is the radius of the vessel, $L$ is the length of vessel, $\eta$ is the viscosity of blood, and 8 the factor of integration.

Blood flow or cardiac output and the pressure drop $(P)$ between points are easily measurable, but resistance is more difficult to measure and is usually calculated.

A slight change in radius has a great effect on resistance. Other factors affecting resistance are elasticity coefficient and distensibility, which vary in different blood vessels even of the same radius.

According to the law of LaPlace, tension in vessels varies directly with radius of vessel and transmural pressure; larger vessels with very high blood pressures, such as those of the turkey, are more susceptible to rupture (aortic aneurysm), as has been demonstrated (Speckman and Ringer, 1963).

The static elastic modulus of the thoracic and abdominal aortas of turkeys are 2.26 and 9.55 $\times 10^5$ dynes/$cm^2$, respectively, suggesting a higher content of elastin (more distensible) and lower collagen in thoracic aorta than in the abdominal aorta (Speckman and Ringer, 1964).

Resistance may be calculated in relative units (RU) by dividing cardiac output in liters per minute or other desired units into blood pressure in millimeters Hg. This is a simple way of comparing resistance changes in some species but cannot be used to compare resistances in different species varying widely in cardiac output. In such cases the absolute unit (in dynes-sec/$cm^5$) is used. For example, pressure in millimeters Hg is converted to cgs units where 1 mm Hg P = 1332 dynes/$cm^2$. Blood flow or cardiac output is converted to cubic centimeters per second. For example, the mean blood pressure of a chicken before hyperthermia was 126 mm Hg and cardiac output was 388 ml/min. The peripheral resistance was 31,867 dynes-sec/$cm^5$.

This figure is over 20 times that for average man. Following hyperthermia, blood pressure decreased, cardiac output increased, and resistance decreased to 22,298 dynes (Whittow *et al.*, 1964). Chickens that have become acclimatized to heat, however, exhibit an increase in peripheral resistance, attributable mainly to a greater drop in cardiac output than in blood pressure (Sturkie, 1967). Therefore, peripheral resistance as thus determined is a mathematical expression and does not necessarily reflect differences in constrictor tone of blood vessels.

Peripheral resistance in hypertensive chickens is significantly higher than in hypotensive ones and probably reflects greater vasoconstrictor tone (Sturkie *et al.*, 1962).

RU's in chickens range from 0.88 to 1.43 and in the duck from 0.567 to 0.62 (Sturkie, 1966). In the larger turkey, RU's ranges from 1 to 2 or higher (Speckman and Ringer, 1963).

## BLOOD PRESSURE

The pressure in the heart and aorta reaches its peak on systolic ejection and its minimum during diastole (end diastolic pressure) (see also Chapter 5). The difference between the two pressures is pulse pressure (PP). Mean blood pressure (MBP) is equal to the area under pressure pulse wave × time. In the chicken, MBP = diastolic pressure (DBP) + ³/₈ PP.

### Pressure Pulses

In mammals the pressure pulse increases in amplitude from the aorta to the more peripheral arteries such as femoral and saphenous (McDonald, 1960), and the shape changes from a rectangular to a triangular form; in goose and turkey, however, there is no appreciable change according to Taylor (1964), who suggested a simple "Windkessel" model to characterize the avian systemic circulation. This model represents a lumped-parameter system in which pressure and flow changes occur simultaneously throughout the system. The thoracic aorta of birds (turkey and goose) is relatively distensible, but the arterial branches coming from it have very high wave velocities and act as rigid distributing channels; consequently the pulse forms show little change throughout the aorta (Taylor, 1964).

Langille and Jones (1975), however, have shown that pressure waves along the aorta in the Pekin duck change in both amplitude and contour as they do in mammals. The pressure pulse increase averaged 29% in amplitude.

Pressure and flow oscillations at different sites in the mammalian arterial system are significantly out of phase and these waves are believed to be altered by reflection (Taylor, 1964; Langille and Jones, 1975; and others). Reflection effects are considered to be maximal when the transit time between the heart and the reflecting site in the arterial bed comprises a significant portion of total cardiac cycle as in mammals, but minimal or absent when the transit time is low. Langille and Jones (1975) reported low transit times in the duck, amounting to 5–10% or less of the cardiac cycle. They concluded that the "Windkessel" model does not apply to the avian systemic circulation.

Welkowitz and Fich (1967) have reported that the shape of pulse waves in mammals can be accounted for by the geometric elastic taper of the vessel without regard to reflections from the periphery. The derived pulse wave forms based on their calculations showed close correspondence with actual measurements and this was the case also in chickens (Fich and Welkowitz, 1973), which exhibit no reflected waves.

**Velocity.** The pulse wave velocity in the turkey aorta, based on data of Speckman and Ringer (1966) as calculated by Jones and Johansen (1972), is 4–6 m/sec for the thoracic aorta and 30–35 m/sec in the abdominal aorta; the latter value far exceeds such values in mammalian arteries. Actual determinations of pulse wave velocities in the duck by Langille and Jones (1975) revealed a rate of 4.4 m/sec in the aortic arch to 11.7 m/sec in the abdominal aorta. The total time required for pulse wave to reach the distal end of aorta was about 20 msec, or 5–10% of the cardiac cycle.

## Methods of Determining Blood Pressure

**Direct.** The methods may be classified as direct and indirect. In all of the commonly used direct methods, a cannula or needle is inserted into the artery or vein, and the pressure of the blood is exerted against a tube of liquid (containing an anticoagulant) which is attached to the manometer. Where a mercury manometer is used, the liquid is in contact with the mercury, which rises and falls in the U tube with heartbeat. Because of the inertia of mercury, systolic and diastolic pressures are not recorded accurately. There are other, more sensitive types of manometers, such as strain gages and capacitance manometers, in which the pressure is exerted against a relatively rigid membrane.

**Indirect.** An apparatus which is commonly used clinically for measuring blood pressure is the sphygmomanometer, which consists of a compressing cuff, a manometer, and an air-inflating bulb. The cuff is applied to the upper arm of man and is inflated enough to obliterate the pulse. When the cuff is deflated slowly and when the pulse reappears, the reading of manometer pressure is taken. Indirect methods have been developed for a number of different animals, including the chicken. This method was first developed by Weiss and Sturkie (1951) and was later modified and improved by Sturkie *et al.* (1957). A cuff, 1 inch in diameter for adult chickens and made to fit the lower thigh, is inflated well above the point at which pulse disappears. It is then deflated, and the pressure at the point at which pulse reappears represents systolic pressure. The improved method involves the use of a capacitance pulse pickup, which is small and easily attached to the shank of the bird in an upright position, and a control box. The output from the latter is fed to the input of a suitable amplifier and recorded on a suitable oscillograph.

The appropriate cuff size is most important and must be determined for each age and species of bird, based on size of thigh. If the cuffs are too small or too large, the pressures recorded are too high or too low, respectively.

Changes in heart rate, output of the heart, and elasticity, and resistance of the arteries all influence blood pressure. An increase in heart rate may increase pressure provided the output of the heart is not decreased. It is possible to have a decreased cardiac output with an increased heart rate, resulting in no change in pressure.

## Normal Values

**Development of blood pressure in embryos.** Blood pressure can be recorded in chicks as early as 46 hr of embryonic development in the vitelline arteries and is very low. Then it begins to rise and by the twentieth day measures 36/22 mm Hg, according to Van Mierop and Bertuch (1967; see also Paff *et al.,* 1965).

The most extensive work has been recently reported by Girard (1973). He recorded pressures from the vitelline artery in 3- and 5-day embryos and from the chorioallantoic artery after these ages up to 20 days of age (Table 4–2). The pressures in embryos can be highly variable and are influenced greatly by temperature and hypoxia.

Ventricular pressures have been measured, but such values are also highly variable depending on conditions. Paff *et al.* (1965) reported ventricular pressures in chick embryos as follows:

*Table 4−2*   *Blood pressures and heart rates in chick embryos and young hatched chicks*[a]

| Age (days) | Blood pressure (mm Hg) | | Heart rate (beats/min) |
|---|---|---|---|
| | Systolic | Diastolic | |
| *From chorioallantoic artery* | | | |
| 3 | 0.61 | 0.43 | 138 |
| 5 | 1.19 | 0.83 | 191 |
| 6 | 1.68 | 0.98 | 200 |
| 8 | 3.59 | 1.40 | 213 |
| 10 | 7.43 | 2.76 | 233 |
| 12 | 10.6 | 4.10 | 207 |
| 14 | 11.3 | 4.6 | 200 |
| 16 | 18.9 | 9.4 | 211 |
| 17 | 21.4 | 11.7 | 216 |
| 18 | 26.5 | 16.0 | 207 |
| 19 | 27.8 | 16.5 | 211 |
| 20 | 29.9 | 19.1 | 221 |
| *From carotid artery* | | | |
| 3 hr after hatching | 43.7 | 23.6 | 108 |
| 3 hr + 1 day after hatching | 60.2 | 37.2 | 156 |
| 1 – 2 days after hatching | 61.6 | 35.3 | 116 |
| 3 – 4 weeks after hatching | 114.6 | 72.9 | 345 |
| 5 – 6 weeks after hatching | 130.9 | 95.3 | 376 |

[a]From Girard (1973).

| Age (days) | Systolic (mm $H_2O$) | Diastolic (mm $H_2O$) |
|---|---|---|
| 3 | 29 | 10 |
| 5 | 63 | 17 |
| 6 | 74 | 5.45 |

Van Mierop and Bertuch (1967) reported ventricular pressures in 5-day embryos (chicks) and the diastolic pressures approached zero, indicating, according to them, the operation of an arterial valve mechanism at this stage.

**Values in adult chickens.** Values for normal arterial blood pressures of chickens are shown in Table 4 – 3. The values obtained with the more reliable direct methods indicate that the systolic pressure of the adult unanesthetized male is approximately 190 mm Hg and the diastolic pressure about 150 mm Hg, with a pulse pressure of 40 mm Hg. Systolic pressures for adult females range from about 140 to 160 mm Hg, with a pulse pressure of about 25 mm Hg. This important sex difference in blood pressure of chickens becomes evident at

about 10 – 13 weeks of age (Ringer *et al.,* 1957; Weiss *et al.,* 1957).

**Turkeys.** The values indicate that the blood pressure level in turkeys is much higher than in chickens but it varies between species, sexes, and ages. Values obtained from use of the indirect technique are highly variable, depending on cuff size used (Weiss and Sheahan, 1958; Krista *et al.,* 1963; see Table 4 – 4).

**Others.** Blood pressures on other species, including ducks, pigeons, quails, robins, and sparrows are given in Table 4 – 4. There is no significant sex difference in levels of most of these, unlike the turkey and chicken.

### Effects of Age

Sturkie *et al.* (1953), using a limited number of birds, reported a significant increase in blood pressure in males and females from age 10 – 14 months to age 42 – 54 months. Muller and Carrol (1966) reported a decrease in females during an equivalent period of time but an increase in blood pressure of

*Table 4–3  Blood pressure of chickens*

| Breed | Age | Sex | Blood pressure (mm Hg) | | | Method | Anesthetic | Artery | Reference |
|---|---|---|---|---|---|---|---|---|---|
| | | | Mean | Systolic | Diastolic | | | | |
| | Adult | Male | 196 | — | — | Hg manometer | None | Carotid | Stubel (1910) |
| | Adult | Female | 164 | — | — | Hg manometer | None | Carotid | Stubel (1910) |
| | Adult | Female | 170 | 180 | 160 | Membrane | None | Carotid | Stubel (1910) |
| Mixed | Adult | ? | 108 | 130 | 85 | Hamilton manometer | Barbital, ether | Femoral | Woodbury and Abreu (1944) |
| Mixed | 6–10 weeks | ? | 128 | 125 | 120 | Hamilton manometer | None | Ischiatic | Rodbard and Tolpin (1947) |
| White Leghorn | 7 weeks | Male | — | 151 | 128 | Direct; strain gage | None | Carotid | Ringer et al. (1957) |
| | 7 weeks | Capon | — | 159 | 134 | Direct; strain gage | None | Carotid | Ringer et al. (1957) |
| | 7 weeks | Female | — | 150 | 131 | Direct; strain gage | None | Carotid | Ringer et al. (1957) |
| | 7 weeks | Poulard | — | 136 | 121 | Direct; strain gage | None | Carotid | Ringer et al. (1957?) |
| | 13 weeks | Male | — | 166 | 142 | Direct; strain gage | None | Carotid | Ringer et al. (1957) |
| | 13 weeks | Capon | — | 157 | 135 | Direct; strain gage | None | Carotid | Ringer et al. (1957) |
| | 13 weeks | Female | — | 156 | 131 | Direct; strain gage | None | Carotid | Ringer et al. (1957) |
| | 13 weeks | Poulard | — | 162 | 135 | Direct; strain gage | None | Carotid | Ringer et al. (1957) |
| | 26 weeks Adult | Male | — | 191 | 154 | Direct; strain gage | None | Carotid | Ringer et al. (1957) |
| | 26 weeks Adult | Capon | — | 180 | 149 | Direct; strain gage | None | Carotid | Ringer et al. (1957) |
| | 26 weeks Adult | Female | — | 162 | 133 | Direct; strain gage | None | Carotid | Ringer et al. (1957) |
| | 26 weeks Adult | Poulard | — | 189 | 152 | Direct; strain gage | None | Carotid | Ringer et al. (1957) |
| | 5–7 months | Female | — | 145 | — | Indirect | None | 1-in. cuff on femur | Hollands and Merritt (1973) |
| | | Male | — | 203 | — | Indirect | None | 1-in. cuff on femur | Sturkie (1970a) |
| | 5–7 months Cornell Randon | Female | — | 145 | — | | | | |
| | Cornell Randon | Male | — | 186 | — | Indirect | None | 1-in. cuff on femur | Sturkie (1970a) |

*Table 4–4*  Blood pressure of birds other than the chicken[a]

| Species | Age | Sex | Blood pressure | | | Reference |
|---|---|---|---|---|---|---|
| | | | Mean | Systolic | Diastolic | |
| Turkey, C | – | – | 193 | – | – | Stubel (1910) |
| Turkey, New Jersey Buff, C | 6–7 weeks | Male | – | 197 | 154 | Weiss and Sheahan (1958) |
| | 6–7 weeks | Female | – | 190– | 146 | Weiss and Sheahan (1958) |
| | 8–9 months | Male | – | 226 | 152 | Weiss and Sheahan (1958) |
| | 8–9 months | Female | – | 212 | 157 | Weiss and Sheahan (1958) |
| Turkey, Bronze, C | 8 weeks | Male | | 198 | 164 | Ringer and Rood (1959) |
| | 8 weeks | Female | | 189 | 158 | Ringer and Rood (1959) |
| | 12 weeks | Male | | 219 | 185 | Ringer and Rood (1959) |
| | 12 weeks | Female | | 226 | 185 | Ringer and Rood (1959) |
| | 16 weeks | Male | | 241 | 190 | Ringer and Rood (1959) |
| | 16 weeks | Female | | 248 | 194 | Ringer and Rood (1959) |
| | 22 weeks | Male | | 297 | 222 | Ringer and Rood (1959) |
| | 22 weeks | Female | | 257 | 200 | Ringer and Rood (1959) |
| Turkey, Beltsville, C | 18 months | Male | | 270 | 167 | Ferguson et al. (1969) |
| | 17–21 months | Female | | 223 | 170 | Ferguson et al. (1969) |
| Turkey, Small White | 21 months | Male | | 235 | 141 | Ferguson et al. (1969) |
| | 17–18 months | Female | | 191 | 146 | Ferguson et al. (1969) |
| Pekin duck, C | 4–5 months | Immature male | | 185 | 158 | Ringer et al. (1955) |
| | 4–5 months | Immature female | | 181 | 159 | Ringer et al. (1955) |
| | 12–13 months | Mature male | | 179 | 134 | Ringer et al. (1955) |
| | 12–13 months | Mature female | | 182 | 134 | Ringer et al. (1955) |
| Pekin duck, C | Adult | Male | | 179 | 142 | Sturkie (1966) |
| | Adult | Female | | 168 | 134 | Sturkie (1966) |
| White king, pigeon, C | Adult | Male | | 182 | 136 | Ringer et al. (1955) |
| | Adult | Female | | 178 | 132 | Ringer et al. (1955) |
| Pigeon, B | Adult | – | | 135 | 105 | Woodbury and Hamilton (1937) |
| Starling, C | Adult | – | | 180 | 130 | Woodbury and Hamilton (1937) |
| Robin, V | Adult | | | 118 | 80 | Woodbury and Hamilton (1937) |
| Canary, C | Adult | | | 130 | – | Woodbury and Hamilton (1937) |
| Canary, V | Adult | | | 220 | 154 | Woodbury and Hamilton (1937) |
| Sparrow, C | Adult | | | 180 | 140 | Woodbury and Hamilton (1937) |
| Sparrow, V | Young | | | 108 | – | Woodbury and Hamilton (1937) |
| *Coturnix* (quail), C | Adult | Male | | 158 | 152 | Ringer (1968) |
| | Adult | Female | | 156 | 147 | Ringer (1968) |
| Bobwhite quail, C | Adult | Male | | 149 | 135 | Ringer (1968) |
| | Adult | Female | | 145 | 129 | Ringer (1968) |

males. The reason for the discrepancies is not apparent and further research is indicated.

There is no significant correlation between blood pressure level and plasma cholesterol, or between blood pressure and cholesterol in the thoracic aorta, but there is a significant correlation between systolic blood pressure and cholesterol level in the abdominal aorta (Weiss *et al.*, 1957). A similar relation exists in the turkey (Speckman and Ringer, 1962). Cholesterol content of blood tends to increase with age.

## Effects of Blood Pressure Level on Mortality

High blood pressure in chickens is not associated with higher mortality as it is in man, but low blood pressure is (Sturkie *et al.*, 1956). In more recent studies, Sturkie (1970a,b) reported no association between blood pressure level and mortality, and this was particularly true when total mortality was low.

Hollands and Merritt (1973) have shown higher mortality in some strains with lower than average blood pressure but no relationship in other strains. These results suggested that the differences in viability might be related to general level of mortality and that birds with higher than average blood pressure were better able to withstand greater disease exposure and physical stresses. This premise was tested (Sturkie and Textor, 1961) by exposing healthy birds with high and low blood pressures to physical exertion (walking) and low ambient temperature (hypothermia). The survival time to hypothermia was greater in hypertensive birds and their ability to withstand physical exertion was likewise greater.

In turkeys, higher mortality is associated with hypertension, and an increased incidence of aortic ruptures or aneurysms (Ringer and Rood, 1959; Speckman and Ringer, 1962; Krista *et al.*, 1970); there is little relationship between atherogenesis and blood pressure level in turkeys and chickens, however.

## Heritability of Blood Pressure

Sturkie *et al.* in 1959 reported that heritability of blood pressure in chickens ranged from 25 to 28%, according to the method of calculation. In that study most of the change was in a hypertensive line and no random line was available for comparison. In a later study Sturkie (1970a) selected for high and low blood pressure for seven generations and compared the changes to a random-bred line (Cornell). The results are shown graphically in Figure 4–4. The average realized heritabilities for all 7 years were 34.8 and 28.0% for the hypertensive

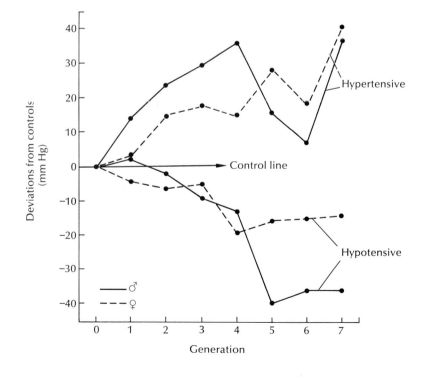

4–4

Effects of selection and breeding on blood pressure differences in hypertensive and hypotensive lines from a control random line. (After Sturkie, 1970a.)

86 and hypotensive males, respectively, compared to 45 and 33% for the females. Hollands and Merritt (1973), who selected chickens for blood pressure in three strains over a 5-year period, reported combined heritabilities of 26–27%. Kirsta *et al.* (1970) reported realized heritabilities in high- and low-blood pressure strains of turkeys of 34 and 23%, respectively.

### Respiratory Influence

When blood pressure is measured directly, waves are often seen in the trace and the frequency of these waves is the same as that of the respiratory movements, although the phase relationship is variable. These waves have been attributed to changes in vasomotor tone, changes in cardiac output, or both. It is generally conceded that these pressure waves reflect changes in cardiac output, which is influenced by the gradient for venous return and by pulmonary vascular volume, which changes during lung inflation in mammals.

Inspiration in mammals with closed chests increases negative pressure in the thorax, venous return, and right heart output, and this is true also in birds that do not have a mammalian-type thorax and diaphragm (see Chapter 6). Aortic blood pressure, however, usually decreases on inspiration in the mammal (Manoach *et al.,* 1971) and increases in birds. If both classes exhibit an increased right heart output on inspiration, differences in the pulmonary vascular volume, and therefore the subsequent return to and output of the left heart, may account for the difference in the change in blood pressure during respiration.

Based on work by Sturkie (1970b) it is concluded that there are minor changes in pulmonary vascular volume in the bird that have little influence on the cardiac output, and the latter is influenced most by changes in intrapulmonic pressure (IPP). Moreover, the outputs of the right and left hearts tend to be synchronous, although there is a phase lag of 58° between them, about half that observed in the rabbit. This can be demonstrated in the bird by unidirectional ventilation, whereby air flow rate and pressure can be kept constant or varied, when respiratory movements are minimized or eliminated by anesthesia or curare. In such instances there are no pressure wave variations. There are waves when positive-pressure breathing is induced by a reciprocating pump but they are opposite in direction to those observed under normal breathing (Durfee and Sturkie, 1963). This suggests an inverse relationship between intrapulmonic pressure and blood pressure and occurs even in animals with vagus and spinal cord transected. This relationship has been examined in detail by Magno and Sturkie (1969), who have studied the effects of changes in intrapulmonic pressure, employing undirectional ventilation (with air flow constant but changes in resistance) on blood pressure and right atrial pressure (RAP) and cardiac output by using electromagnetic flowmeters on the pulmonary artery and aorta. The lung of the bird does not collapse when the chest is opened; it is relatively fixed and moves mainly when the rib cage does.

Figure 4–5 shows that blood pressure and cardiac output are inversely related to IPP and this relationship is linear. A similar relationship exists between IPP and RAP. Blood pressure waves in birds are caused mainly by changes in intrapulmonic pressure.

### Effects of Hypoxia

Durfee and Sturkie (1963); see also Sturkie, (1970b); employing unidirectional artificial respiration, produced hypoxia and a slight degree of hypercapnia in chickens by decreasing the rate of ventilation from 500–350 ml/min to 230–150 ml/min. for 1–8 min (slowly induced asphyxia). The average effects on systolic blood (SB) pressure and heart rate (HR) follow:

| Before asphyxia | After asphyxia | | |
|---|---|---|---|
| | For 1 min | 2 | 8 |
| SB | | | |
| (mm Hg)    191 | 184 | 178 | 151 |
| HR | | | |
| (beats/min)  221 | 228 | 236 | 287 |

The resulting hypotension, which was maintained after vagotomy or spinal cord sectioning, apparently came from the direct effects of low oxygen on the blood vessels, and chemoreceptors were not involved. The effects were reversible by hyperventilation. The increase in heart rate was reflexly induced. These results have been confirmed by Butler (1967), Richards and Sykes (1967), and Ray and Fedde (1969). The increased heart rate could be abolished by vagotomy and beta blockade (Butler, 1967).

Blood pressures in ducks and pigeons exposed to hypoxia, $P_aO_2 < 50$ mm Hg, are only slightly reduced, and heart rate increases only after $P_aO_2$ is reduced to 35 mm Hg or less (Butler, 1970).

Right ventricular hypertrophy has been observed in pigeons, chickens, and ducks exposed to hypoxia

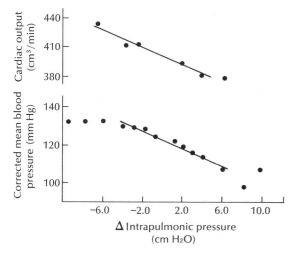

4–5 Effects of changes in intrapulmonic pressure on cardiac output and corrected mean blood pressure. (After Magno and Sturkie, 1970b.)

of high altitude, and chickens exhibit pulmonary hypertension (pressure twice that at sea level) (Burton *et al.,* 1968).

**Hypercapnia and hypoxia.** Breathing high levels of $CO_2$ mixed with low levels of $O_2$ caused a reduction in blood pressure of chickens, according to Richards and Sykes (1967), but hypercapnia alone had little effect. Eiel and Sturkie (unpublished) administered mixtures of 20% $O_2$ and 5% $CO_2$, which had little or no effect; when 10% $CO_2$ and 20% $O_2$ were breathed, however, blood pressure was depressed significantly and heart rate increased reflexily.

**Diving.** The cardiovascular effects of diving reflect changes in heart rate and cardiac output apart from the hypoxia and are treated in the section on cardiovascular adjustments.

## Effects of Drugs and Hormones

**Effects of anesthesia.** Anesthesia may lower blood pressure in birds, as in mammals, depending on the type, the dose, and the time after administration. Sodium pentobarbital (25–30 mg/kg) injected intravenously into adult chickens depresses blood pressure 30 mm Hg within a few minutes after injection (Weiss and Sturkie, 1951). Harvey *et al.* (1954) induced anesthesia in chickens with urethan, 1.4 g/kg body weight; sodium barbital, 180 mg/kg; and sodium phenobarbital, 200 mg/kg, in

each instance administered intraperitoneally. The authors do not report blood pressure levels on unanesthetized birds, but it is apparent from their data that blood pressure levels were depressed, because the basal levels reported by them were quite low.

Dial, a commercial preparation containing urethane, has been used extensively by Durfee (1963) in dosages ranging from 0.50 to 0.75 ml/kg. At the lower level the birds were lightly anesthetized, but this dosage depressed blood pressure significantly.

**Catecholamines.** Most of the drugs and hormones that are pressor and depressor in mammals have the same effect in birds. Some of the pressor substances are epinephrine, benzedrine, ephedrine, and phenylephrine (Thompson and Coon, 1948). A detailed study of the effects of a number of drugs and adrenergic blockers on the blood pressure of chickens was made by Harvey *et al.* (1954). Isopropyl norepinephrine had a depressor effect, and considerable variation occurred in the responses to epinephrine and norepinephrine. The minimal pressor doses of both drugs vary from 0.02 to 1.5 $\mu$g/kg and the maximal doses range from 4 to 10 $\mu$g/kg. In most hens the two sympathomimetics were about equipotent, although occasionally norepinephrine was four times as potent (as a pressor) as epinephrine; however, the latter exhibited greater cardioaccelerator activity. Epinephrine and norepinephrine (1 $\mu$g/kg) increased diastolic pressures 39 and 20 mm Hg, respectively, in anesthetized chickens (Akers and Peiss, 1963). A number of ergot alkaloids (such as ergotamine and ergonovine) were tested, and most of them were consistently pressor at dosages lower than 200 $\mu$g/kg.

Sturkie (unpublished) has shown that norepinephrine (as free base) is effective in increasing blood pressure at dosages of 2–3 $\mu$g/kg. Similar results have been reported by Natoff and Lockett (1957). El-Halawani *et al.* (1973) studied the catecholamine levels in tissues of hypertensive and hypotensive turkeys and found that hypertensive birds had higher levels in the left ventricle and pulmonary aorta than hypotensive ones. They suggested that norepinephrine release was greater in the hypertensive birds, and there was less destruction of catecholamines because of lower monamine oxidase in the tissues.

In chickens, levels of catecholamines in blood or tissues do not appear to be related to blood pressure level. For example, femal chickens have higher levels of catecholamines in blood and tissues but a significantly lower blood pressure (Sturkie and Lin, 1968, and unpublished data).

88

**Serotonin.** Serotin (5-hydroxytryptamine) or angiotonin can be pressor or depressor in the chicken (Harvey et al., 1954). It is normally a depressor, according to Bunag and Walaszek (1962), for they believe it to release histamine, which is depressor. When the tissues of chickens were depleted of histamine by continued administration of 48/80, serotinin and tryptamine were pressor.

Results from my laboratory also demonstrate that serotonin is mainly a depressor in the chicken. Dosages at levels of 0.5 to 10 $\mu$g/kg were effective in depressing blood pressure significantly; the maximum effect (20 mm Hg) was produced within 10 sec and blood pressure level returned to normal within 20–30 sec (Woods, 1971). To determine whether serotinin released histamine, which might have depressed blood pressure, blood samples were taken at the same time as the peak drop in blood pressure occurred and analyzed for histamine with a highly sensitive fluorescent chemical method. There was no evidence of histamine release. The mechanism of the depression effect of serotonin is unexplained; moreover, when the substance is infused into the mesenteric artery of the isolated chickens intestine, it has a pressor effect in both mesenteric arteries and veins (Gross, 1974).

**Histamine.** The depressing effect of histamine has been reported by Natoff and Lockett (1957), Bunag and Walaszek (1962) and El-Ackad (1972). A dose of histamine acid phosphate of 3.23, $\mu$g/kg was required to depress blood pressure 20 mm Hg (Natoff and Lockett, 1957). Histamine (free base) at 5 $\mu$g/kg dropped blood pressure (mean) approximately 40 mm Hg within 15 sec and the level returned to approximately normal within 1–2 min (El-Ackad, 1972). When the blocking agent (trypelennamine) was administered along with the histamine, the latter depressor effect was blocked (El-Ackad, 1972; Meyer et al., unpublished). Similar results were obtained with mepyramine, another blocker. In another series of experiments following histamine administration (5 $\mu$g/kg) systolic blood pressure dropped from 188 mm Hg to 116 mm Hg and diastolic from 135 to 81 mm Hg.

**Reserpine.** Reserpine, when injected intramuscularly in doses of 0.10–0.75 mg/kg, decreased blood pressure in the chicken significantly within 4 hr after the injection (Sturkie et al., 1958). Similar depressing effects have been reported in turkeys by Speckmann and Ringer (1962) and many others since (see Krista et al., 1963). Simpson et al. (1965) reported a slight but significant decrease in systolic blood pressure of turkeys fed reserpine, but reserpine did not reduce the incidence of aortic ruptures.

**Acetylcholine.** Acetylcholine, methacholine, and other parasympathomimetic agents depress blood pressure in birds as they do in mammals. An injection of 0.2 mg of acetylcholine into chicks 6–12 weeks old depresses blood pressure 40–60 mm Hg within 3 sec (Rodbard and Fink, 1948). Intramuscular injections of 5 mg into adult fowls similarly decreases blood pressure and heart rate, but the latter returns to normal shortly thereafter. Methacholine, which has an effect of longer duration than does acetylcholine, produces significant depressor effects at levels as low as 0.15 mg/kg subcutaneously (Durfee, unpublished) and 2 $\mu$g/kg intravenously (Sturkie, unpublished).

**Sex hormones.** The existence of a sex difference in the blood pressure of chickens suggests the influence of sex hormones. It was shown (Sturkie and Ringer, 1955) that the higher blood pressure level of adult males and capons could be depressed by administration of estrogen. Later it was shown that the blood pressure level of the castrate female was about the same as the adult male, and that this level could likewise be depressed to near the level of a normal female by estrogen. The mechanism of estrogen's action is not known but it may have a direct vasodilating effect on the blood vessels by increasing arterial $O_2$ consumption and it may also exert some effect on the medullary centers (Malinow and Moguilevsky, 1961).

**Oxytocin and vasopressin.** Synthetic oxytocin and the oxytocic fraction of posterior pituitary preparations depress blood pressure in the chicken within a few seconds (Chen, 1970). The drop is attributable not to changes in cardiac weakness or in heart rate but to vasodilation. Lloyd and Pickford (1961) found oxytocin always to be depressor in the chicken but not always in mammals.

Vasotocin is a depressor in birds (Sawyer, 1961). The response of the chicken to vasopressin is variable. In some instances a pure pressor response is obtained; in others a transient depressor response occurs, which may or may not be followed by a pressor response.

*Oviposition and blood pressure.* Immediately preceding contraction of the uterus and expulsion of the egg, according to Tanaka and Nakajo (see Chapter 15), there is a release of oxytocin and vasotocin from the posterior pituitary, which these authors believe initiates oviposition. Because both of these hormones have a depressor effect, therefore, blood pressure might be expected to drop just prior to oviposition. Hunsaker and Sturkie (see Sturkie, 1965) recorded blood pressure of unrestrained hens before, during, and after oviposition. Blood pressure level did not change until after the egg was laid; the slight drop was transient and was not believed to be attributable to oxytocin or vasotocin.

**Prostaglandins.** Little work has been conducted on the effects of these on the cardiovascular system of birds. Horton (1971), who reviewed the subject, reported that Pr E (a type of prostaglandin) is an arterial vasodilator, but the pressor action of $F_2$ (another type) is attributable to venoconstriction and increased venous return and cardiac output as in the dog and rat. In the intact anesthetized chicken, the effect of prostaglandin, $F_{2\alpha}$ was depression. Pr $F_{1\alpha}$ and $F_{2\alpha}$ were depressors in chicks anesthetized with ether, chloralose, urethane, or barbitone.

**Pressor substances released by intracranial compression.** Acute compression of the brain causes an increase in both mammals' and birds' blood pressure (Rodbard *et al.*, 1954). The rise in pressure could be blocked or prevented by administration of adrenergic blockers but not by tetraethylammonium, a ganglionic blocker, suggesting the release of a humoral substance akin to norepinephrine.

## Effects of Body Temperature and Ambient Temperature

Sturkie and co-workers observed seasonal changes in blood pressure in chickens, with the pressure tending to drop with the advent of warm weather. Weiss *et al.* (1961) demonstrated conclusively that ambient temperature, and not amount of light, was largely responsible for the seasonal changes observed. Chickens acclimatized to high temperature had a significantly lower blood pressure level than those acclimatized to cold (Sturkie, 1967) and a lower cardiac output.

Chickens exposed to acute heating (40.5°C) and exhibiting hyperthermia experience a decrease in blood pressure, particularly after body temperatures reach 45°C and there is an increase in cardiac output and vasodilation. Above this temperature there is a precipitous drop in blood pressure. Similar results were obtained by Whittow *et al.* (1964), except that the birds were heated in a heating pad and they developed hyperthermia more rapidly; the decline in blood pressure began soon after the start of heating. Hypothermia likewise depresses blood pressure in the chicken and the decrease is proportional to the degree of hypothermia (Rodbard and Tolpin, 1947; Whittow *et al.*, 1965a). Rewarming of the chicken after hypothermia produced an immediate rise in blood pressure and body temperature until normal body temperature was obtained; then, with further heating and hyperthermia, a decrease in pressure was observed.

## Heart Rate and Blood Pressure

A comparison of the heart rates and blood pressures of many avian species suggests that there is little correlation between the two. Even among the same species (chicken or turkey) considerable variation and differences can exist without much change in heart rate (Sturkie *et al.*, 1956). The male chicken has a higher blood pressure and lower heart rate than the female.

## Ventricular and Pulmonary Pressures

Changes in pressure in the heart chambers during the cardiac cycle are discussed in Chapter 5. Bredick (1960) measured the systolic and diastolic intraventricular pressures of chickens (peak pressures) as follows:

| | Pressure (mm Hg) | |
|---|---|---|
| | Systolic | Diastolic |
| Left ventricle | 145 | 0 |
| Right ventricle | 27 | −0.3 to −2.0 |

Respiratory movements caused fluctuations ranging from 2 to 10 mm Hg, averaging 8.8 mm Hg for left ventricular pressures and 3.6 mm Hg for right ventricular pressure.

The right ventricular systolic pressure of 27 mm Hg reported by Bredick is of the same magnitude as that reported for the pulmonary artery of chickens by Rodbard and Katz (1949). Their results follow:

| | Pressure in pulmonary artery | |
|---|---|---|
| | Mean | Range |
| Systolic | 24 | 17−32 |
| Diastolic | 12 | 7−20 |
| Heart rate | 293 | 240−318 |
| Respiratory rate | 49 | 36−60 |

Pressures reported by Burton *et al.* (1968) were lower (systolic, 21.5; diastolic 9.8). Pressure in the turkey pulmonary artery averaged 20 mm Hg (Hamlin and Kondrich, 1969).

Injection of epinephrine had no appreciable effect on pulmonary arterial pressure even though it increased systemic arterial pressure 40–80 mm Hg. The pressures in the pulmonary arteries of most vertebrates are of similar magnitude.

Left ventricular peak systolic pressure in ducks ranged from 160 mm Hg to near 200 mm Hg (Folkow and Yonce, 1967; Jones and Johansen, 1972). These pressures vary with venous return and contractility, which are discussed in Chapter 5. Right atrial pressure ranges from slightly negative on inspiration to slightly positive on expiration (Sturkie, unpublished).

## Control of Blood Pressure and Heart Rate

**Neural.** Very little is known concerning central control of blood pressure and heart rate in Aves, although there is presumptive evidence of medullary centers as in mammals.

There is some evidence that the thalamus influences blood pressure level; it comes from the (crude by modern standards) experiments by Dijk (1932), who reported that stimulation of this area produced changes in blood pressure.

Stimulation of an area in the mesencephalon of ducks near the midline produced a significant increase in blood pressure and a decrease in heart rate, whereas stimulation in the diencephalon produced vasodilation in skeletal muscle (Feigl and Folkow, 1963). Because the latter response could be blocked by atropine, it was attributed to cholinergic fibers.

It appears that the center affecting blood pressure is in the medulla near the center affecting heart rate (see also Chapter 5). Stimulations of the dorsal medulla produced tachycardia and hypertension (Cohen and Schnall, 1970). The need for more work on the location and stimulation of these centers is evident.

*Vasoconstrictors.* Most blood vessels of Aves receive a dual innervation (Akester, 1971; Bolton, 1968). The effects of drugs, hypoxia, and other factors that increase sympathetic discharge and produce vasoconstriction have been discussed, but no studies have been conducted on the effects of directly stimulating such nerves on blood pressure.

*Reflex control of blood pressure.* The carotid sinus of birds is not situated high in the neck, where the external and internal carotids diverge, as it is in mammals (Adams, 1958). It is much lower, just behind the parathyroid glands, near the origin of the common carotid arteries, and rostral to the root of the subclavian arteries (see Figure 4–2). Other studies confirm this. The carotid body is located in the same area (Figure 4–2), and is quite small. The dimensions of the gland are $0.8 \times 0.5$ mm in the chicken and the gland is even smaller in several other species (see Adams, 1958; Murillo-Perrol, 1967). The carotid body receives its blood supply from the carotid artery or a branch of it. It is drained by several veins. The innervation of the body is from the vagus nerve by way of the ganglion nodosum. Apparently the glossopharyngeal nerve does not contribute fibers to the carotid body, at least not in the chicken, although Terni (see Adams, 1958) asserts that the body may receive fibers from the recurrent laryngeal nerve.

Attempts to elicit reflex effects on blood pressure by means of occlusion or stimulation in the region, high in the bird's neck, that corresponds to the sinus area in mammals have been unsuccessful (see Adams; 1958: also Heymans and Neil, 1958). Stimulation of the carotid body or carotid sinus area in the thorax gave variable and unconvincing results (Heymans and Neil, 1958). Durfee (1963) was unable to elicit reflex responses by occluding either the common carotid in the sinus region of the chicken or the brachiocephalic artery; also, significantly reducing blood pressure in one carotid artery had no reflex effect (McGinnis and Ringer, 1966). Moreover, there is no evidence for cephalic receptors as has been postulated; this has been demonstrated by McGinnis and Ringer (1967).

Magno (1973), who isolated and perfused the carotid body of chickens with sodium cyanide, reported no effect on blood pressure or heart rate but produced a respiratory response, indicating respiratory chemoreceptors but no cardiovascular ones.

Jones (1969) reported the presence of mechanoreceptors in the wall of arch of ascending aorta and in pulmonary artery; whether these play a significant role in reflex changes has not been determined.

**Humoral.** Whether or not humoral agents other than catecholamines influence blood pressure and flow in Aves has received little attention. Sturkie and co-workers have conducted extensive studies on the content, production, and release of serotonin and histamine in blood and tissues of avaian species. They reported significantly higher circulating levels of serotonin (Sturkie *et al.*, 1972) and histamine (El-Ackad and Sturkie, 1972) than found in most mammals, but they have not studied the relationship of these levels to blood pressure. These workers showed that most of the circulating serotonin and histamine is carried in the thrombocytes and lymphocytes. The female chicken has a significantly lower blood pressure than males but has higher levels of blood histamine and serotonin.

# BLOOD FLOW, BODY FLUIDS, AND CARDIAC OUTPUT

## Cardiac Output

*Cardiac output* is the amount of blood ejected from the ventricles in a given time and is usually referred to as minute volume. The amount ejected from the right and left ventricles is the same over a period of time but may vary with each heart beat and is influenced by heart rate and stroke volume. The latter is influenced by venous return, and diastolic volume, stretching of heart muscle (Frank-Starling mechanism), and increased force of contraction without change in heart muscle fiber length (see Chapter 5).

### Methods of determining. Cardiac output has been determined by a number of methods, including the direct Fick and various dilution methods (indirect Fick) involving the use of dyes, radioactive substances, and heat or thermodilution. It may also be determined directly by placing electromagnetic flowmeters (probes) on the pulmonary arteries or ascending aorta (For a review of methods, see Kramer *et al.*, 1963; Folkow and Neil, 1971).

With the dye dilution method, a known quantity of dye is injected into a vein or the right heart, where it is mixed; blood from an artery is then sampled. The concentration of dye in the blood passing the sampling point changes with time and forms a concentration curve. By calculating the area under the curve or average concentration $(\overline{C})$ and knowing the concentration of dye injected, cardiac output (CO) can be determined.

$$CO = \frac{A \text{ (amount of dye injected, mg)}}{\overline{C} \cdot \text{time under curve}}$$

or

$$\frac{A}{\int_0^\infty C \, dt} = \frac{A}{\Sigma C \Delta t}$$

**Normal values in birds.** Normal values of 91 chickens, turkeys, and ducks are presented in Table 4–5. The values vary considerably, even within the same species, depending on method, anesthesia, and various other factors. Values in chickens obtained by direct Fick (Piiper *et al.*, 1970) and by isotope dilution (Sapirstein and Hartman, 1959) or thermodilution (Sturkie and Eiel, 1966) appear to be higher than those obtained with dye dilution.

**Factors affecting cardiac output.** The values on turkeys and ducks are highly variable also. Cardiac output changes drastically with demands for blood flow, as illustrated in diving ducks (see later section on cardiovascular effects of diving). There appear to be sex differences in cardiac output, as well as blood pressure, of chickens, with the higher levels in females per kilogram of body weight. However, cardiac output is higher in male ducks (per kilogram body weight) than in females. The sex difference in chickens might be attributable to estrogen in the female. Sturkie and Eiel (1966), however, employing the thermodilution technique of cardiac output, which is not influenced by lipemic plasma, have found that estrogen has no significant effect on cardiac output except to depress blood pressure slightly, which tends to somewhat increase cardiac output.

Boelkins *et al.* (1973) reported that the cardiac output of female chickens was consistently higher when determined by Evans Blue dye (277 ml/kg) than when determined by Indocyanine Green (177 ml/kg). The latter figure agrees closely with those of Vogel and Sturkie (1963a,b).

Oxygen consumption increases cardiac output tremendously, whereas rest, inactivity, and particularly starvation decrease it as indicated in Table 4–5.

*Ambient temperature and acclimatization.* Acute heat increases cardiac output and decreases blood pressure, as it does in mammals (Whittow *et al.*, 1964). Acute cold also increases cardiac output and blood pressure in chickens (Whittow *et al.*, 1965a). Sturkie (1967) demonstrated conclusively that when chickens become acclimated to heat (similar to summer conditions) there is a significant decrease in cardiac output instead of an increase, and the changes (adaptation) occur within 3–4 weeks. Birds were kept at control temperatures (23°–25°C), and at high temperatures (32°C for 12 hr), and 25° C for 12 hr. The differences between treated and controls (treated minus controls) are expressed in percentages, as follows:

*Table 4–5*  Cardiac output, blood pressure, and total peripheral resistance in Aves (means and standard errors)

| Breed | Sex, age, condition | Body weight (kg) | Cardiac output per minute | | Mean blood pressure | Peripheral resistance (units/kg) | Heart rate | Method[a] | Reference |
|---|---|---|---|---|---|---|---|---|---|
| | | | Per bird | Per kg. | | | | | |
| White Leghorn | Male 16 months, starved | 2.39 | 340±18 | 143±7 | 166 | 1.23 | 307 | DD | Sturkie and Vogel (1959) |
| | Female 16 months, starved | 1.79 | 308±17 | 173±7 | 142 | 0.88 | 378 | DD | Sturkie and Vogel (1959) |
| White Leghorn | Male 12–14 months winter | 2.59 | 444±22 | 173±9 | 181 | 1.11 | 303 | DD | Vogel and Sturkie (1963b) |
| | Male 12–14 months summer | 2.95 | 359±11 | 135±7 | 177 | 1.41 | 289 | DD | Vogel and Sturkie (1963b) |
| | Female 18 months winter | 1.95 | 345±15 | 181±12 | 153 | 0.91 | 336 | DD | Vogel and Sturkie (1963b) |
| | Female 18 months summer | 1.96 | 234±7 | 121±5 | 147 | 1.25 | 347 | DD | Vogel and Sturkie (1963b) |
| | Male | 2.2 | — | 190 | 182 | — | 276 | DD | Vogel and Sturkie (1963b) |
| | Mixed female | 1.6 | 218 | — | — | — | — | TD | Sturkie and Eiel (1966) |
| | Female | 1.6 | 430 | 269 | — | — | — | ID | Sapirstein and Hartman (1959) |
| Duck | | | | | | | | | |
| A. platy-rhynchos | Males | 3.3 | — | 286.8 | 161.2 | 0.566 | 175 | DD | Sturkie (1966b) |
| | Females | 3.0 | — | 253.4 | 147.2 | 0.62 | 185 | DD | Sturkie (1966b) |
| A. platyrhynchos | –control | 3.0 | | 482.0 | — | — | — | TD | Folkow et al. (1967) |
| | –diving | 3.0 | | 24.4[b] | — | — | — | TD | Folkow et al. (1967) |
| | –control | 2.1 | 393.9 | 187.5* | — | — | 186.2 | [b] | Jones and Holeton (1972b) |
| | –diving | 2.1 | 25.9 | | — | — | 21.1 | [b] | Jones and Holeton (1972b) |
| A. platyrhynchos Muscovy | | 2.4 | 973 | 405 | — | — | 179.0 | DD | Jones and Holeton (1972a) |
| | | 2.16 | 844 | 390 | — | — | 130 | DD | Jones and Holeton (1972b) |
| Turkey | B. B. Bronze Males | 14.5 | 1615 | 111.3 | 204 | — | 149 | ID | Speckman and Ringer (1963) |
| | — | 14.5 | 1615 | 200.0 | — | — | — | DD | Hamlin and Kondrich (1969) |

[a]DD = dye dilution; TD = thermo dilution; ID = isotope dilution; DF = direct Fick.
[b]Based on flowmeter on one pulmonary artery.

| Weeks exposure | Difference in cardiac output |
|---|---|
| 1 | 8% increase |
| 4 | 23% decrease |

There were slight decreases in blood pressures, which persisted. Exposure to heat first causes vasodilation and increased cardiac output and oxygen consumption. As birds become acclimated to the heat, the demand for oxygen consumption decreases and so does blood flow. Low temperatures and continued exposure to such temperatures had little effect on cardiac output.

*Effects of hypoxia.* Few studies have been conducted on the effects of hypoxia on cardiac output other than hypoxia during diving. Jones and Holeton (1972a) studied changes in oxygen tension from a normal $P_aO_2$ of about 100 mm Hg and at 63, 47, and 38 mm Hg. Cardiac output increased almost linearly over this range, reaching a peak increase of about 50%. The oxygen extraction increased greatly at the lower oxygen tensions with AV oxygen differences of 9.5 mm Hg at a $P_aO_2$ of 38 mm Hg compared to 30 mm Hg at 100 mm Hg.

Artificial ventilation of chickens following administration of succinycholine increased cardiac output; the effect was attributable to the chemical, rather than to ventilation rate (uptake of $O_2$), which was not changed (Piipers *et al.*, 1970).

The chicken is apparently more sensitive to changes in ventilation rate and responds by an increase in cardiac output (Butler, 1967; Sturkie, unpublished). The effects of diving on cardiac output are discussed under cardiovascular adjustments.

### Regional Blood Flow

**Distribution of flow to various organs.** Blood flow to organs is closely related to oxygen extraction and metabolic activity. In cases of decreased oxygen intake (hypoxia) the organ usually compensates by increasing blood flow and also the amount of oxygen extracted. The distribution of blood flow to various organs in the chicken has been studied by Sapirstein and Hartman (1959) and Boelkins *et al.* (1973); the former have employed radioactive Rb and the latter nuclide-labeled microspheres. The latter method has several advantages over the former method. The results are shown in Table 4–6.

***Table 4–6*** *Distribution of total blood flow to organs of laying hens[a] and male chickens[b]*

|  | Weight (g) | Blood flow | | |
|---|---|---|---|---|
|  |  | Percent cardiac output | SH[b] | Per organ (ml/min) |
| Kidney | 15.03 | 9.96 | 15.2 | 38.1 |
| Heart | 5.93 | 5.78 | 4.9 | 16.6 |
| Liver | 47.5 | 7.05 | 6.7 | 28.9 |
| Duodenum | 5.06 | 4.81 | — | 15.9 |
| Colon | 1.52 | 0.40 | — | 1.6 |
| Gut | — | — | 8.6 | — |
| Pancreas | 3.49 | 0.70 | — | 3.0 |
| Gizzard | — | — | 1.6 | — |
| Spleen | 1.95 | 3.37 | 0.47 | 10.3 |
| Femora | 16.80 | 4.08 | — | 12.4 |
| Tibia | 19.66 | 2.62 | — | 8.2 |
| Thyroid | 0.12 | 0.04 | — | 0.25 |
| Parathyroids | 0.015 | 0.06 | — | 0.23 |
| Adrenals | 0.11 | 0.03 | — | 0.08 |
| Shell gland (uterus)[c] | 16.03 | 8.58 | — | 35.4 |
| Isthmus[c] | 6.05 | 1.06 | — | 3.6 |
| Magnum[c] | 27.48 | 5.70 | — | 19.7 |

[a]From Boelkins *et al.* (1973).
[b]From Sapirstein and Hartman (1959).
[c]Blood flow when hard shell egg in uterus for at least 14 hr.

*Table 4–7  Blood flow in veins of intestine of chickens (ml/min)*

White Leghorn males, lightly anesthetized; cranial mesenteric (CM), coccygeomesenteric (COCM), portal (P), and mesenteric artery (MA)

| Blood vessel | Per bird | | Mean per kg | Percent of total blood flow[a] |
|---|---|---|---|---|
| | Mean | SE | | |
| CM | 14.7 | 1.4 | 6.4 | 3.3 |
| COCM | 18.1 | 2.1 | 7.9 | 4.1 |
| P | 32.8 | 2.5 | 14.2 | 7.4 |
| MA | 33 | 3.4 | 14.3 | 7.4 |

[a]Based on estimated cardiac output of 190 ml/kg for White Leghorn males.

Similar studies involving distribution of Rb in ducks (Johansen, 1964) indicates a high blood flow to heart, with moderate flows to gut and kidney. The percentage distribution of total flow in intestinal organs of chickens (shown in Table 4–6) is moderately high in the duodenum and high in the liver. Blood flow in the liver of turkeys in standing positions has been estimated to be 44.2 ml/kg/min (Clarkson and Richards, 1966).

*Blood flow in gut and kidney.* The anatomical arrangement of blood vessels from the intestinal tract and kidney is such that blood can be shunted from the kidney through the intestinal vessels to the liver or vice versa (see also Figure 4–2). Sturkie and Abati (1975) have studied blood flow in various blood vessels (veins) of the intestinal tract as follows: portal vein, cranial mesenteric vein, coccygeomesenteric vein (COCM), and mesenteric artery. The birds were anesthetized, restrained, and surgically opened and electromagnetic probes were placed around the vessels. Flow was then measured under various conditions, such as clamping of certain vessels and observing direction and magnitude of flow in other veins (Table 4–7).

The portal blood flow (P) represents flow from the cranial and coccygeomesenteric veins and liver blood flow, which is roughly 7.4% of total blood flow; this figure compares favorably with the 6.7% figure of Sapirstein and Hartman (1959).

Following deep anesthesia or starvation there is a significant decrease in blood flow of these vessels. Most of the time blood flow from the mesenteric veins is toward the liver; however, under certain rare circumstances it may reverse its direction of flow through the renal portal to the vena cava (see also Akester, 1971, and Chapter 14 on the kidney). Experimentally this is easily demonstrated by clamping the portal vein and then measuring blood flow in the COCM and vena cava.

When the renal portal valve is closed, blood normally flowing from the femoral vein and the renal portal vein may be shunted to the COCM (reversed direction of flow), hepatic portal vein, and liver and thence to the posterior vena cava. Blood flow in the kidney is quite high (Table 4–6) and it probably varies considerably depending on state of opening or closure of renal portal valves (see also Chapter 14). Changes in tone of smooth muscle (resistance) of these blood vessels affect pressure and blood flow. Stimulation studies on the chicken isolated mesenteric artery by Bell (1969) suggests that the longitudinal smooth muscle of this artery does not have a direct vasomotor function but that the circular muscle does.

*Blood flow in reproductive organs.* Hunsaker (1959) reported that when an egg is in the shell gland and calcium is being deposited, blood flow is more than doubled than when no egg is in the gland. During the same time Boelkins *et al.* (1973) (see Table 4–6) reported that blood flow in the shell gland was 8.58% of the total flow, which represents the second highest blood flow of all the organs. The actual flow was 35.4 ml/min per organ or about 2.2 ml/g of tissue. Also the magnum, where the egg albumen is secreted, had a high flow (5.70%) of total flow.

## Cardiovascular Adjustments to Diving, Flight, Starvation, and Restraint

**Starvation.** Complete restriction of food intake for 3 days or more causes a drastic drop in blood pressure, heart rate, and cardiac output of chickens (Vogel and Sturkie, 1963a). Starvation apparently increases vagal tone because atropine administration increases heart rate. A partial restriction of food intake to approximately 70–80% of normal for an extended period reduced blood pressure and heart rate, but not greatly (Hollands et al., 1965).

**Restraint.** Restraining chickens on their back caused an initial increase in heart rate and blood pressure; later (within 2 hr), pressure decreased appreciably, but heart rate and cardiac output actually increased, probably reflexly (Whittow et al., 1965b). The initial increases are no doubt influenced by the release of adrenal and cardiac catecholamines, which are increased with initial excitement. Anesthesia, which lowers heart rate and blood pressure, also decreases blood and cardiac catecholamines (Sturkie et al., 1970). Chronic restraint (50 days or more) produces a type of stress that may depress blood pressure and may ultimately result in death; however, individuals may be trained to withstand certain types of restraint without deleterious cardiovascular effects (Burton and Beljan, 1970).

**Flight.** Flight, even for short periods, increases heart rate considerably. Berger et al. (1970) reported that the heart rates of resting birds in relation to body weight were less in nonflying than in flying birds and the increase in heart rate of small birds in flight (two times resting rate) is less than in larger birds (three to four times resting rate). Oxygen consumption increases during flight about 5–14 times, depending on the species, according to Tucker (1968a), and consequently cardiac output can be expected to increase considerably, although it has not been measured. The demand for oxygen of birds flying at high altitude (6100 m) is estimated to be about eight times that at sea level (Tucker, 1968b), and it has been calculated that the necessary cardiac output must be about 2.8 liters/kg/min, which is unusually high. Jones and Holeton (1972a), who simulated high altitude (in ducks), reported significant increases in cardiac output from a level of 1000 ml/min per bird at a $P_aO_2$ of 95–100 mm Hg (normal oxygen tension) to a level of about 1400 ml/min at $P_aO_2$ of 40–50 mm Hg (hypocapnic hypoxia).

Femoral blood flow in exercising penguins (running, etc.) determined by telemetry increased four times over resting rates (Millard et al., 1972). Mean blood pressure increased from 80 to 125 mm/Hg and heart rate from 90 to 180 beats per minute.

**Diving.** Earlier studies on the cardiovascular adjustments to diving were reviewed by Andersen (1966) and more recently by Jones and Johansen (1972). When diving mammals or birds submerge, there is an immediate apnea, intense bradycardia, and a drop in cardiac output to about one-fifth normal (Folkow et al., 1967) and blood is pooled into the visceral organs. The hypoxia and hypercapnia induced by the dive stimulate vasoconstriction and sympathetic discharge, particularly in the limbs where blood flow virtually ceases, although pressure in the femoral artery is near normal in the early stages of the dive (Folkow et al., 1966); however, there is some evidence that with sustained diving, blood pressure may fall significantly (Andersen, 1966). Butler and Jones (1971) also reported intense vasoconstriction in the femoral or sciatic vessels during the dive in ducks with sciatic flows averaging only 10% of normal flow. After $\alpha$ blockade sciatic flow during the dive fell to only 41% of normal flow, indicating that much of the drop in limb blood during diving resulted from vasoconstriction. $\beta$-Receptor blockade had no effect on any of the measured variables during submersion. Atropine abolishes the reflex bradycardia during diving, indicating that the bradycardia is mediated by vagus nerves (Andersen 1966; Butler and Jones, 1971). Although inhalation of $CO_2$ causes reflex vasoconstriction in ducks, it does not in turkeys (Folkow et al., 1966).

The reflex bradycardia and other adjustments to diving are dependent on a central integration center in the hypothalamic and mesencephalic areas, because stimulation in these areas often mimics the natural reflex responses (Folkow and Rubinstein, 1965; Feigl and Folkow, 1963). The degree of bradycardia in diving varies among the species of wild ducks. *Aythya americana* (redheads) and *Oxyura jamaicensic* (ruddy ducks) exhibit bradycardia most rapidly and more intensively than others; within 5 sec after diving, heart rate has declined an average of 45 beats per minute (Catlett and Johnson, 1974). There is much evidence to show that the reflex bradycardia is induced by apnea, because when ducks with submerged heads are allowed to breathe through a tracheal cannula, no bradycardia occurs (Butler and Jones, 1968).

*Cardiac output.* Following the dive or submergence, cardiac output in the duck decreased from approximately 482 ml/kg/min to 24.4 ml/kg/min (Folkow et al., 1967), based on outputs determined by thermodilution. These predive values are very high.

Jones and Holeton (1972b), employing a more sensitive method, an electromagnetic probe around one pulmonary artery, reported pre- and postdive figures on ducks (Table 4–8). In both cases the cardiac output after the dive was only 5–7% of the predive figure. The heart rate following the dive was approximately 9% of the predive figure.

*Distribution of blood flow in diving.* The distribution of cardiac output following diving has been determined by Johansen (1964), who employed radioactive Rb and studied its distribution in various organs; this represented the blood flow to these organs. He found that blood flow to such organs as skin, skeletal muscle (particularly of legs), gastrointestinal organs, and kidney was severely restricted. The heart, head, thyroid, and adrenals received an increased blood flow.

***Table 4–8*** *Cardiac output and heart rate in diving ducks (average values)*

| | Cardiac output per bird (ml/min)[a] | Heart rate (beat/min) |
|---|---|---|
| *Predive* | 393.9 | 186.2 |
| *Dive* | | |
| 20 sec | 58.4 | 53.3 |
| 60 sec | 37.1 | 26.1 |
| 120 sec | 25.9 | 21.1 |
| *After the dive or recovery* | | |
| 10 sec | 141.4 | 136.7 |
| 60 sec | 136.0 | 142.6 |
| 120 sec | 125.9 | 125.8 |

[a]These values probably represent only half of the total flow because only one pulmonary was measured and the other one probably was not tied.

## Body Fluids

The total water of the body is distributed into intracellular and extracellular compartments. The latter may be partitioned into plasma and interstitial fluids.

**Methods of estimating.** *Body water.* Total body water may be estimated directly by desiccation and indirectly by measuring the dilution of some substance that can come into equilibrium with all water compartments. The volume distribution of an injected substance $X$ equals the amount injected minus the amount excreted, divided by concentration in the diluting fluid. Therefore, $V = q/c$, where $V$ is volume, $q$ is quantity injected minus amount of excreted, and $c$ is concentration in diluting fluid.

Antipyrine is a substance that has been used by a number of investigators in mammals and in chickens by Weiss (1958) and by Medway and Kare (1959) to measure total body water. Extracellular fluid volume is determined also by the dilution principle, employing a substance that is injected and that enters the extracellular but not the intracellular compartment. Thiocyanate ion has been most commonly used; mannitol, inulin, and other substances have also been employed. The interstitial fluid is calculated and is equal to extracellular space minus plasma volume. Intracellular space or fluid is equal to total body water minus extracellular space.

*Blood volume.* Blood volume may be determined directly by bleeding out and measuring the residual volume or indirectly by the dilution principle. The latter may involve labeling red cells by injection with radioactive iron, chromium, or phosphorus, or labeling the plasma with a dye, such as Evans Blue

***Table 4–9*** *Distribution of body fluids in White Leghorn chickens*[a]

| | | Percent of body weight | | | | |
|---|---|---|---|---|---|---|
| | | | | Extracellular water | | |
| Age (weeks) | Weight (g) | Total body water | Intracellular water | Interstitial | Plasma | Total |
| 1 | 55.1 | 72.4 | 11.4 | 52.3 | 8.7 | 61.0 |
| 2 | 108.4 | 71.6 | 21.0 | 42.3 | 7.3 | 50.6 |
| 3 | 175.3 | 70.5 | 24.6 | 39.1 | 6.8 | 45.9 |
| 4 | 241.8 | 68.4 | 24.1 | 38.3 | 6.0 | 44.3 |
| 6 | 372.3 | — | — | 36.8 | 5.9 | 42.7 |
| 8 | 527.3 | 68.7 | 26.6 | 36.1 | 6.1 | 42.2 |
| 16 | 1137.3 | 64.8 | 34.8 | 24.8 | 5.2 | 30.0 |
| 32 | 1759.5 | 57.3 | 31.1 | 21.7 | 4.6 | 26.2 |

[a]Medway and Kare (1959).

**Table 4–10**  *Body water (percent of body weight) in White Leghorn females[a]*

|  | Age (weeks) | | | | | |
|---|---|---|---|---|---|---|
|  | 26 | 30 | 36 | 42 | 55 | 61 |
| Body weight (g) | 1773 | 1996 | 1919 | 2032 | 2054 | 2035 |
| Body water (%) | 66.0 | 61.2 | 56.7 | 53.3 | 52.9 | 53.4 |

[a]Weiss (1958).

(T-1824). A known amount of the dye is injected intravenously and allowed to mix completely with the blood within approximately 2 or 3 min. The rate of disappearance of the dye from the blood of birds is also more rapid than in mammals, averaging about 1% per minute.

$$\text{Blood volume} = \frac{\text{plasma volume} \times 100}{\text{percent plasma}}$$

**Total body water.** The distribution of body fluids of chickens of various ages is shown in Tables 4–9 and 4–10. Total body water is highest in the first 2 weeks of life, and decreases, although not appreciably, until 16 weeks of age. At 32 weeks of age, when the bird has reached full sexual maturity, body water is lowest (57.3% of body weight), according to Medway and Kare (1959). The amount of body water in hens decreased from 26 weeks of age up to 42 weeks of age but did not change appreciably thereafter (Weiss, 1958). This decrease is a reflection of an increase in body fat with aging in the hen, because fat contains less water than does lean tissue.

**Extracellular and intracellular water.** As total body water decreases with age up to sexual maturity, the greatest decrease is in extracellular water

(both interstitial and plasma fractions). At the same time there is an increase in intracellular water, ranging from 11.4% at 1 week of age to above 30% at from 16 to 32 weeks of age. Decreased water consumption and exposure to high and low environmental temperatures produce changes in the compartments of the body waters.

**Blood volume.** Crude blood volume (by bleeding but not washing out the blood vessels) has been determined in the chicken (see Sturkie, 1965). The crude volumes, which average about 4% of body weight, amount to approximately two-thirds of that obtained with the dye technique.

*Normal values.* The dye technique has been used by a number of workers, and in some of the older work the values reported are too high because the mixing time was too long (see Sturkie, 1965). Studies by Sturkie and Newman (1951) and Medway and Kare (1959), employing a mixing time of 3 min, reveal blood volumes ranging from 8.7% of body weight at 1 week of age to 4.6% at sexual maturity (see Tables 4–11 and 4–12). Gilbert (1963), working with adult Brown Leghorn cocks obtained a mean blood volume of 7.8% and a mean plasma volume of 4.65%. Blood volumes for spe-

**Table 4–11**  *Blood volume of female White Leghorn chickens[a]*

| Age (weeks) | Body weight (g) | Mean blood volume (percent of body weight) | Mean plasma volume (percent of body weight) |
|---|---|---|---|
| 1 | 61.8 | 12.0 | 8.7 |
| 2 | 115.0 | 10.4 | 7.3 |
| 3 | 163.3 | 9.7 | 6.8 |
| 4 | 249.9 | 8.7 | 6.0 |
| 6 | 398.7 | 8.3 | 5.9 |
| 8 | 571.6 | 8.4 | 6.1 |
| 16 | 1310.0 | 7.6 | 5.2 |
| 32 | 1789.0 | 6.5 | 4.6 |

[a]Medway and Kare (1959).

*Table 4-12* *Blood volume of avian species other than chicken*

| Species | Body weight (g) | Sex | Total blood volume (ml/100 g) | Plasma volume (ml/100 g) | Reference |
|---|---|---|---|---|---|
| Ducks | | | | | |
|   *A. platyrhynches* | — | — | 10.2 | 6.55 | Portman *et al.* (1952) |
|   mallard and dabbling | 980 | — | 11.3 | 6.4 | Bond and Gilbert (1958) |
| Coot | 550 | — | 9.5 | 5.1 | Bond and Gilbert (1958) |
| Pigeon | 310 | — | 9.2 | 4.4 | Bond and Gilbert (1958) |
| Pheasant | 1190 | Male | 6.7 | 4.5 | Bond and Gilbert (1958) |
| | 1110 | Female | 4.8 | 3.2 | Bond and Gilbert (1958) |
| Red-tailed hawk | 925 | — | 6.2 | 3.5 | Bond and Gilbert (1958) |
| Great horned owl | 1495 | — | 6.4 | 3.4 | Bond and Gilbert (1958) |
| Turkeys, adult, White Holland | — | — | 410[a] | — | McCartney (1952) |
| *Coturnix* | 98 | Male | 7.4 | 4.73 | Nirmalin and Robinson (1972) |
| | 117 | Female | 6.76 | 4.29 | Nirmalin and Robinson (1972) |
| Geese, adult | — | Male | 5.99 | 3.36 | Hunsaker (1968) |
| | | Female | 6.75 | 4.15 | Hunsaker (1968) |
| | | Capon | 5.83 | 3.42 | Hunsaker (1968) |
| | | Poulard | 6.07 | 3.69 | Hunsaker (1968) |

[a]Data in ml/bird.

cies other than the chicken are shown in Table 4-12. The values range from 4.8 to 11.3% of body weight for total blood volume.

*Effects of hormones.* Earlier workers (Sturkie, 1965) reported that estrogen administration increased the crude blood volume, but Sturkie in 1951, using the dye technique, found no change in blood volume following massive doses of estrogen or thyroxine to hens. Estrogen produces hyperlipemia in birds, and consequently a turbidity of the plasma which interferes with the colorimetric determination of dye concentration unless the blood is diluted sufficiently or the fat is extracted.

Sturkie and Eiel (1966) determined the effects of estrogen on blood volume of males and females after extraction of fat from plasma and found no change in blood volume of females but an increase in that of males as was reported by Gilbert (1963), and a decrease in hematocrit. Estrogen also increases blood volume in male and poulard geese significantly; but not in normal females (naturally estrogenized; Hunsaker, 1968). Androgen had little effect on blood volume of male and female geese but increased volume in castrate male and females.

**Hemorrhage and replacement of blood.** Birds are better able to tolerate severe blood loss than are mammals (Kovach *et al.*, 1969). After a loss of 50-70% of total blood volume, blood pressure

and cardiac output drop drastically; within a few hours, however, blood pressures return to about 80% of normal and there is an increased peripheral resistance. As much as 75% of blood volume may be removed from chickens without causing death (Wyse and Nickerson, 1971). Djojosugito *et al.* (1968) studied the effects of hemorrhage in ducks and cats and reported that the greater ability of ducks to replace lost blood was attributable to a very profound reflex vasoconstriction and particularly to a much greater capillary surface area in ducks, which facilitated the increased rate of absorption of tissue fluids.

## REFERENCES

Abati, A., and J. J. McGrath. (1973). Physiological responses to acute hypoxia in altitude acclimatized chicken. *J. Appl. Physiol., 34,* 804.

Abraham, A. (1969). "Microscopic Innervation of the Heart and Blood Vessels in Vertebrates Including Man." Oxford: Pergamon Press.

Adams, W. R. (1958). "Comparative Morphology of the Carotid Body." Springfield, Ill.: Charles C Thomas.

Akers, T. K., and C. N. Peiss. (1963). Comparative study of effect of epinephrine and norepinephrine on cardiovascular system of turtle, alligator, chicken and opossum. *Proc. Soc. Exp. Biol. Med., 112,* 396.

Akester, A. K. (1971). The heart (Chapter 31) and Blood vascular system (Chapter 32). In "Physiology and Biochemistry of the Domestic Fowl," Vol. 2 (D. J. Bell and B. M. Freeman, Eds.). New York: Academic Press.

Andersen, H. T. (1966). Physiological adaptations in diving vertebrates. *Physiol. Rev., 46*, 212.

Baumel, J., and L. Gerchman. (1968). The avian intercarotid anastomosis and its homologue in other vertebrates. *Am. J. Anat., 122*, 1.

Bell, C. (1969). Indirect cholenergic vasomotor control of intestinal blood flow in the domestic chicken. *J. Physiol. (London) 205*, 317.

Bennett, T., and T. Malmfors. (1970). The adrenergic nervous system of the domestic fowl. *Z. Zellforsch. Mikrosk. Anat., 106*, 22.

Berger, M., J. S. Hart, and O. Z. Roy. (1970). Respiration oxygen consumption and heart rate in some birds during rest and flight. *Z. Vergl. Physiol., 66*, 201.

Boelkins, J. N., W. J. Mueller, and K. L. Hall. (1973). Cardiac output distribution in the laying hen during shell formation. *Comp. Biochem. Physiol., 46A*, 735

Bolton, T. B. (1967). Intramural nerves in ventricular myocardium of domestic fowl and other animals. *Brit. J. Pharmacol. Chemother., 31*, 253.

Bolton, T. B. (1968). Studies on the longitudinal muscle of the anterior mesenteric artery of domestic fowl. *J. Physiol. (London) 196*, 273.

Bond, C. F., and P. W. Gilbert. (1958). Comparative study of blood volume in aquatic and nonaquatic birds. *Am. J. Physiol., 194*, 519.

Bredick, H. E. (1960). Intraventricular pressure in chickens. *Am. J. Physiol., 198*, 153.

Brush, A. H. (1966). Avian heart size and cardiovascular performance. *Auk, 83*, 266.

Bunag, R. D., and E. J. Walaszek. (1962). Blockade of depressor responses to serotonin and tryptamine by lysergic acid derivatives in the chicken. *Arch. Int. Pharmacodyn., 135*, 1.

Burton, R. R., and J. R. Beljan. (1970). Animal restraint: Application in space environment. *Aerospace Med., 41*, 1061.

Burton, R. R., E. L. Besch, and A. H. Smith. (1968). Effect of chronic hypoxia on the pulmonary arterial blood pressure of the chicken. *Am. J. Physiol., 214*, 1438.

Butler, P. J. (1967). The effect of progressive hypoxia on the respiratory and cardiovascular systems of chickens. *J. Physiol., 191*:309.

Butler, P. J. (1970). The effect of progressive hypoxia on the respiratory systems of pigeon and duck. *J. Physiol., 210*, 527.

Butler, P. J., and D. R. Jones. (1968). Onset of, and recovery from diving bradycardia in ducks. *J. Physiol. London, 196*, 255.

Butler, P. J., and D. R. Jones. (1971). Variations in heart rate and regional distribution of blood flow on the normal pressor response to diving in ducks. *J. Physiol. London, 214*, 457.

Catlett, R. H., and B. L. Johnson. (1974). Cardiac response to diving in wild ducks. *Comp. Biochem. Physiol., 74A*, 925.

Chen, T. W. (1970). Effects of oxytocin and adrenaline on oviduct motility, blood pressure, heart rate, and respiration rate of domestic hen. *Nanyang Univ. J., 4*, 178.

Clarkson, M. J., and T. G. Richards. (1966). In "Physiology of Domestic Fowl" (C. Horton-Smith, and E. C. Amoroso, Eds). Edinburgh: Oliver & Bodyd, p. 294.

Cohen, D. H., and A. M. Schnall. (1970). Medullary cells of origin of vagal cardioinhibitory fibers in pigeon. II. Electrical stimulation of the dorsal motor nucleus. *J. Comp. Neurol., 140*, 321.

Dijk, J. A. (1932). *Arch. Neerl. Physiol., 17*, 495. Cited from Prosser (1950).

Djojosugito, A. M., B. Folkow, and A. G. B. Kovach. (1968). The mechanisms behind the rapid blood volume restoration after hemorrhage in birds. *Acta Physiol. Scand., 74*, 114.

Durfee, W. K. (1963). Cardiovascular reflex mechanisms in the fowl. Ph.d. thesis Rutgers University, New Brunswick, New Jersey.

Durfee, W. K., and P. D. Sturkie. (1963). Some cardiovascular responses to anoxia in the fowl. *Fed. Proc., 22*, 182.

El-Ackad, T. M. (1972). Histamine in the avian cardiovascular system. Thesis, Rutgers University, New Brunswick, New Jersey.

El-Ackad, T. M., and P. D. Sturkie. (1972). Histamine in blood and tissues of Aves. *Proc. Soc. Exp. Biol. Med., 141*, 448.

El-Halawani, M. E., P. E. Waibel, J. R. Appel, and A. L. Good.

(1973). Catecholamines and monamine oxidase activity in turkeys with high or low blood pressure. *Trans. N. Y. Acad. Sci., 35*, 463.

Feigl, E., and B. Folkow. (1963). Cardiovascular responses in diving and during brain stimulation in ducks. *Acta Physiol. Scand., 57*, 99.

Ferguson, T. M., D. H. Miller, J. W. Bradley, and R. L. Atkinson. (1969). Blood pressure and heart rate of turkeys, 17–21 months of age. *Poultry Sci., 48*, 1478.

Fich, S., and W. Welkowitz. (1973). Perspectives in cardiovascular analysis and assistance. In "Perspectives in Biomedical Engineering" (R. M. Kenedi, Ed.). Baltimore: University Park Press. Proc. of Symposium held at University of Strathclyde, Glasgow, Scotland in 1972.

Folkow, B., N. J. Nilsson, and L. R. Yonce. (1967). Effects of diving on cardiac output in ducks. *Acta Physiol. Scand., 70*, 347.

Folkow, B., and E. H. Rubinstein. (1965). Effect of brain stimulation on diving in ducks. *Hralrad Skrifter NR. Videnck-Akad.* (Oslo), *48*, 30.

Folkow, B., and R. Yonce. (1967). The negative inotropic effect of vagal stimulation on the heart ventricles of the duck. *Acta. Physiol. Scand., 71*, 77.

Folkow, B., K. Fuxe, and R. R. Sonnenschein. (1966). Responses of skeletal musculature and its vasculature during diving in the duck: Peculiarities of adrenergic vasoconstriction innervation. *Acta Physiol. Scand., 67*, 327.

Folkow, B., and E. Neil. (1971). Measurements of pressures, flows and volumes in the cardiovascular system. In "Circulation," London: Oxford University Press. Chapter 7, p. 73.

Gilbert, A. B. (1963). The effect of estrogen thyroxine on blood volume of the domestic cock. *J. Edocrinol., 25*, 41.

Girard. H. (1973). Arterial pressure in chick embryos. *Am. J. Physiol., 224*, 454.

Glenny, F. H. (1940). A systematic study of the main arteries in the region of the heart of aves. *Anat. Rec., 76*, 371.

Gross, K. (1974). Studies on physiology of serotonin in domestic fowl with emphasis on small intestine. Ph.d. thesis, Rutgers University, New Brunswick, New Jersey.

Hamlin, R. L., and R. M. Kondrich. (1969). Hypertension regulation of heart rate and possible mechanisms contributing to aortic rupture in turkeys. *Fed. Am. Soc. Exp. Biol., 28*, 329.

Hartman, F. A. (1955). Heart weight in birds. *Condor, 57*, 221.

Harvey, S. C., E. G. Copen, D. W. Eskelson, S. R. Graff, L. D. Poulsen, and D. L. Rasmussen. (1954). Autonomic pharmacology of the chicken with particular reference to adrenergic blockade. *J. Pharmacol. Exp. Ther., 112*, 8.

Heymans, C., and E. Neil. (1958). "Reflexogenic Areas of the Cardiovascular System." Boston: Little, Brown & Co.

Hirsch, E. F. (1970). "The Innervation of the Vertebrate Heart." Springfield, Ill.: Charles C Thomas.

Hollands, K. G., and E. S. Merritt. (1973). Blood pressure and its genetic variation and co-variation with certain economic traits in egg type chickens. *Poultry Sci., 52*, 1722.

Hollands, K. G., R. S. Gowe, and P. M. Morse. (1965). Effects of food restriction on blood pressure, heart rate and certain organ weights of the chicken. *Brit. Poultry Sci., 6*, 297.

Horton, E. W. (1971). Prostaglandins. In "Physiology and Biochemistry of Domestic Fowl" (D. G. Bell and B. M. Freeman, Eds.), New York: Academic Press, 1971.

Hunsaker, W. G. (1959). Blood flow and calcium transfer through uterus of hen. Ph.D. thesis, Rutgers University, New Brunswick, New Jersey.

Hunsaker, W. G. (1968). Blood volume of geese treated with androgen and estrogen. *Poultry Sci., 47*, 371.

Johansen, K. (1964). Regional distribution of circulating blood during submersion asphyxia in the duck. *Acta Physiol. Scand., 62*, 1.

Johnson, R. E., and F. R. Lockner. (1968). Heart size and altitude in ptarmigan. *Condor, 70*, 185.

Jones, D. R. (1969). Avian afferent vagal activity related to respiratory and cardiac cycles. *Comp. Biochem. Physiol., 28*, 961.

Jones, D. R., and G. F. Holeton. (1972a). Cardiovascular and respiratory responses of ducks to progressive hypocapnic hypoxia. *J. Exp. Biol., 56*, 657.

**100**

Jones, D. R., and G. F. Holeton. (1972b). Cardiac output of ducks during diving. *Comp. Biochem. Physiol., 41A,* 639.

Jones, D. R., and K. Johansen. (1972). The blood vascular system of birds. In "Avian Biology," Vol. 2. (D. S. Farner and J. R. King, Eds.). New York: Academic Press, p. 157.

Kovac, A. G. B., E. Szasz, and N. Pilager. (1969). The mortality of various avian and mammalian species following blood loss. *Acta Physiol. Acad. Sci. Hung., 35,* 109.

Kramer, K., W. Lochner and E. Wetterer. (1963). Methods of measuring blood flow. In "Handbook of Physiology," Section 2, Vol. 2. (W. F. Hamilton & P. Dow, Eds.), American Physiological Society. Chapter 38, p. 1277.

Krista, L. M., R. E. Burger, and P. E. Waibel. (1963). Blood pressure and heart rate in the turkey as measured by indirect methods and their modifications by pharmacological agents. *Poultry Sci., 42,* 646.

Krista, L. M., P. E. Waibel, R. N. Shoffner, and J. H. Souther. (1970). A study of aortic rupture and performance as influenced by selection for hypertension and hypotension in the turkey. *Poultry Sci., 49,* 405.

Langille, B. L. and D. R. Jones. (1975). Central carciovascular dynamics of ducks. *Am. J. Physiol., 228,* 1856.

Lin, Y. C., P. D. Sturkie, and J. Tummons. (1970). Effects of cardiac sympathectomy reserpine and environmental temperatures on catecholamines, in the chicken heart. *Can. J. Physiol. Pharmacol., 48,* 182.

Lindsay, F. E. (1967). The cardiac veins of gallus domesticus. *J. Anat., 101,* 555.

Lloyd, S., and M. Pickford. (1961). The persistence of a depressor response to oxytocin after denervation and blocking agents. *Brit. J. Pharmacol. Chemother., 16,* 129.

McCartney, M. G. (1952). Total blood and corpuscular volume in turkey hens. *Poultry Sci., 31,* 184.

Magno, M. G. (1973). Cardio-respiratory responses to carotid body stimulation with NaCN in the chicken. *Resp. Physiol., 17,* 220.

Magno, M. G., and P. D. Sturkie. (1969). The mechanism of the phase lag of respiratory blood pressure waves in chickens. *Physiologist, 12,* 290 (Abs).

Malinow, M. R., and J. A. Moguilevsky. (1961). Effects of estrogens on atherosclerosis. *Nature (London), 190,* 422.

Manoach, M. A., S. Gitter, I. M. Levinger, and S. Stricker. (1971). On the origin of respiratory waves in the circulation. *Pflugers Arch., 325,* 50.

McDonald, D. A. (1960). "Blood Flow in Arteries." London: Edward Arnold, Ltd.

McGinnis, C. H., and R. K. Ringer. (1966). Carotid sinus reflex in the chicken. *Poultry Sci., 45,* 402.

McGinnis, C. H., and R. K. Ringer. (1967). Arterial occlusion and cephalic baroreceptors in the chicken. *Am. J. Vet. Res., 28,* 1117.

Medway, W., and M. R. Kare. (1959). Thiocyanate space in growing domestic fowl. *Am. J. Physiol., 196,* 873.

Millard, R. W., K. Johansen, and G. Milsom. (1972). Unpublished data; see D. R. Jones and K. Johansen. (1972). In "Blood Vascular System of Birds" (D. S. Farner and J. R. King, Eds.). New York: Academic Press, Chapter 4.

Muller, H. D., and M. E. Caroll. (1966). The relationship of blood pressure, heart rate, and body weight to aging in the domestic fowl. *Poultry Sci., 45,* 1195.

Murillo-Perrol, N. L. (1967). The development of the carotid body in *Gallus domesticus. Acta Anat., 68,* 102.

Natoff, I. L., and M. Lockett. (1957). The assay of histamine, 5-HT, adrenaline and norodrenaline on blood pressure of the fowl. *J. Pharm. Pharmacol., 9,* 467.

Nirmalin, G. P., and G. A. Robinson. (1972). Effect of age, sex and egg laying on the total erythrocyte volume and plasma volume of Japanese quail. *Can. J. Physiol. Pharmacol., 50,* 6.

Paff, G. H., R. J. Boucek, and G. S. Gutten. (1965). Ventricular blood pressures and competency of valves in early embryonic chick heart. *Anat. Res., 151,* 119.

Petren, T. (1926). Die coronararterien des Vogelherzens. *Morph. Jahrb., 56,* 239.

Piiper, J., F. Drees, and P. Scheid. (1970). Gas exchange in the domestic fowl during spontaneous breathing and artificial ventilation. *Resp. Physiol., 9,* 234.

Portmann, A. (1950). Les organes de la circulation sanguine. In "Traite de Zoologie," Vol. 15 (P.P. Grasse, Ed.). Paris: Masson. p. 243.

Portman, O. W., K. P. McConnell, and R. H. Rigdon. (1952). Blood volumes of ducks using human serum albumin labelled with radioiodine. *Proc. Soc. Exp. Biol. Med., 81,* 599.

Rakusan, K., B. Ost-Adal, and M. Wachtlova. (1971). The influence of muscular work on the capillary density in the heart and skeletal muscle of pigeon. *Can. J. Physiol. Pharmacol., 49,* 167.

Ray, P. J., and M. R. Fedde. (1969). Responses to alterations in respiratory $PO_2$ and $PCO_2$ in the chicken. *Resp. Physiol., 6,* 135.

Richards, S. A., and A. H. Sykes. (1967). The effects of hypoxia, hypercapnia, and asphyxia in the domestic fowl. *Comp. Biochem. Physiol., 21,* 691.

Ringer, R. K. (1968). Blood pressure of Japanese and bobwhite quail. *Poultry Sci., 47,* 1602.

Ringer, R. K., and K. Rood. (1959). Hemodynamic changes associated with aging in the bronze turkey. *Poultry Sci., 38,* 395.

Ringer, R. K., P. D. Sturkie, and H. S. Weiss. (1957). Role of gonads in the control of blood pressure in chickens. *Am. J. Physiol., 190,* 54.

Ringer, R. K., H. S. Weiss, and P. D. Sturkie. (1955). Effect of sex and age on blood pressure in the duck and pigeon. *Am. J. Physiol., 183,* 141.

Rodbard, S., and A. Fink. (1948). Effects of body temperature changes on the circulation time in the chicken. *Am. J. Physiol., 152,* 383.

Rodbard, S., and L. N. Katz. (1949). The pulmonary arterial pressure. *Am. Heart J., 38,* 863.

Rodbard, S., and M. Tolpin. (1947). A relationship between body temperature and the blood pressure in the chicken. *Am. J. Physiol., 151,* 509.

Rodbard, S., N. Reyes, G. Mininni, and H. Saiki. (1954). Neurohumoral transmission of the pressor response to intracranial compression. *Am. J. Physiol., 176,* 455.

Sapirstein, L. A., and F. A. Hartman. (1959). Cardiac output and its distribution in the chicken. *Am. J. Physiol., 196,* 751.

Sawyer, W. H. (1961). Neurohypophysial hormones. *Pharmacol. Rev., 13,* 225.

Simpson, C. F., R. H. Harms, and B. L. Damron. (1965). Failure of reserpine to modify the incidence of aortic ruptures induced in turkeys by diethylstilbestrol. *Proc. Soc. Exp. Biol. Med., 120,* 321.

Sommer, J. R., and R. J. Steere. (1969). Transverse tubules in chicken cardiac muscle. *Fed. Am. Soc. Exp. B, 28,* 328.

Speckman, E. W., and R. K. Ringer. (1962). The influence of reserpine on plasma cholestrol, hemodynamics, and arteriosclerotic lesions in Bronze turkeys. *Poultry Sci., 41,* 40.

Speckman, E. W., and R. K. Ringer. (1963). The cardiac output and carotid and tibial blood pressure of the turkey. *Can. J. Biochem. Physiol., 41,* 2337.

Speckman, E. W., and R. K. Ringer. (1964). Static elastic modulus of the turkey aorta. *Can. J. Physiol. Pharmacol., 42,* 553.

Speckman, E. W., and R. K. Ringer. (1966). Volume pressure relationship in the turkey. *Can. J. Physiol. Pharmacol., 44,* 901.

Stubel, H. S. (1910). Beiträge zur kenntnis der physiologie des blutkreislaufes der verschiedenen. *Arch. Ges. Physiol. (Pflügers), 135,* 249.

Sturkie, P. D. (Ed.). (1965). Circulation. In "Avian Physiology," 2nd Ed. Ithaca, N.Y.: Cornell University Press, Chapter 3.

Sturkie, P. D. (1966). Cardiac output in ducks. *Proc. Soc. Exp. Biol. Med., 123,* 487.

Sturkie, P. D. (1967). Cardiovascular effects of acclimatization to heat and cold in chickens. *J. Appl. Physiol., 22,* 13.

Sturkie, P. D. (1970a). Seven generations of selection for high and low blood pressure in chickens. *Poultry Sci., 49,* 953.

Sturkie, P. D. (1970b). Circulation in Aves. *Fed. Proc., 29,* 1674.

Sturkie, P. D., and A. Abati. (1975). Blood flow in mesenteric, hepatic portal, and renal portal veins of chickens. *Pflügers Arch., 359,* 127.

Sturkie, P. D., and J. M. Eiel. (1966). Effects of estrogen on cardiac output, blood volume, and plasma lipids of the cock. *J. Appl. Physiol., 21,* 1927.

Sturkie, P. D. and Yu-chong Lin. (1968). Sex difference in blood norepinephrine of chickens. *Comp. Biochem. Physiol., 24,* 1073.

Sturkie, P. D., and H. N. Newman. (1951). Plasma proteins of chickens as influenced by time of laying, ovulation, number of samples taken, and plasma volume. *Poultry Sci., 30,* 240.

Sturkie, P. D., and D. W. Poorvin. (1973). The avian neurotransmitter. *Proc. Soc. Exp. Biol. Med., 143,* 644.

Sturkie, P. D., W. K. Durfee, and M. Sheahan. (1958). Effects of reserpine on the fowl. *Am. J. Physiol., 194,* 184.

Sturkie, P. D., and R. K. Ringer. (1955). Effects of suppression of pituitary gonadotrophin on blood pressure in the fowl. *Am. J. Physiol., 180,* 53.

Sturkie, P. D., and K. Textor. (1961). Relationship of blood pressure level in chickens to resistance to physical stresses. *Am. J. Physiol., 201,* 1155.

Sturkie, P. D., and J. A. Vogel. (1959). Cardiac output, central blood volume and peripheral resistance in chickens. *Am. J. Physiol., 197,* 1165.

Sturkie, P. D., W. Durfee, and M. Sheahan. (1957). Demonstration of an improved method on taking blood pressure in chickens. *Poultry Sci., 36,* 1160.

Sturkie, P. D., D. Poorvin, and N. Ossario. (1970). Levels of epinephrine, and norepinephrine in blood and tissues of duck, pigeon, turkey and chicken. *Proc. Soc. Exp. Biol. Med., 135,* 267.

Sturkie, P. D., R. K. Ringer, and N. S. Weiss. (1956). Relationship of blood pressure to mortality in chickens. *Proc. Soc. Exp. Biol. Med., 92,* 301.

Sturkie, P. D., J. A. Vogel, and K. Textor. (1962). Cardiovascular differences between high and low blood pressure chickens. *Poultry Sci., 41,* 1619.

Sturkie, P. D., H. S. Weiss, and R. K. Ringer. (1953). The effects of age on blood pressure in the fowl. *Am. J. Physiol., 174,* 405.

Sturkie, P. D., J. J. Woods, and D. Meyer. (1972). Serotonin levels in blood, heart, and spleen of chickens, ducks, and pigeons. *Proc. Soc. Exp. Biol. Med., 139,* 364.

Taylor, M. G. (1964). Wave travel in arteries and the design of the cardiovascular system. In "Pulsatile Blood Flow" (E. O. Attinger, Ed.). New York: McGraw Hill, Chapter 21.

Thompson, R. M., and J. M. Coon. (1948). Effects of adrenolytic agents on response to pressor substances in the domestic fowl. *Fed. Proc., 7,* 259.

Tucker, V. A. (1968a). Respiratory exchange and evaporative water loss in the flying Budgerigar. *J. Exp. Biol., 48, 67.*

Tucker, V. A. (1968b). Respiratory physiology of house sparrows in relation to high altitude flight. *J. Exp. Biol., 48,* 55.

Tummons, J. L. (1970). Nervous control of heart rate in domestic fowl. Ph.D. thesis, Rutgers University, New Brunswick, New Jersey.

Tummons, J. L., and P. D. Sturkie. (1968). Cardio-accelerator nerve stimulation in chickens. *Life Sci., 7,* 377.

Tummons, J. L., and P. D. Sturkie. (1969). Nervous control of heart rate during excitement in the adult Leghorn cock. *Am. J. Physiol., 216,* 1437.

Tummons, J. L., and P. D. Sturkie. (1970). Beta adrenergic and cholinergic stimulants from the cardioaccelerator nerve of the domestic fowl. *Z. Vergl. Physiol., 68,* 268.

Van Mierop, L. H. S., and C. J. Bertuch. (1967). Development of arterial blood pressure in the chick embryo. *Am. J. Physiol., 212,* 43.

Vogel, J. (1961). Studies on cardiac output in the chicken. Ph.D. thesis, Rutgers University, New Brunswick, New Jersey.

Vogel, J. A., and P. D. Sturkie. (1963a). Effects of starvation in the cardiovascular system of chickens. *Proc. Soc. Exp. Biol. Med., 112,* 111.

Vogel, J. A., and P. D. Sturkie. (1963b). Cardiovascular responses on chicken to seasonal and induced temperature changes. *Science, 140,* 1404.

Weiss, H. S. (1958). Application on the fowl of the antipyrine dilu-

tion technique for estimation of body composition. *Poultry Sci., 37,* 484.

Weiss, H. S., and M. Sheahan. (1958). The influence of maturity and sex on blood pressure of turkeys. *Am. J. Vet. Res., 19,* 209.

Weiss, H. S., and P. D. Sturkie (1951). An indirect method for measuring blood pressure in chickens. *Poultry Sci., 30,* 587.

Weiss, H. S., H. Fisher, and P. Griminger. (1961). Seasonal variation in avian blood pressure. *Fed. Proc., 2,*115 (abstr.).

Weiss, H. S., R. K. Ringer, and P. D. Sturkie. (1957). Development of the sex difference in blood pressure of chickens. *Am. J. Physiol., 188,* 383.

Welkowitz, W., and S. Fich. (1967). A non-uniform hybrid model of the aorta. *Trans. N. Y. Acad. Sci.,29,* 316.

Whittow, G. C., P. D. Sturkie, and G. Stein, Jr. (1964). Cardiovascular changes associated with thermal polypnea in the chicken. *Am. J. Physiol., 207,*1349.

Whittow, G. C., P. D. Sturkie, and G. Stein, Jr. (1965a). Cardiovascular effects of hypothermia in the chicken. *Nature (London), 206,* 200.

Whittow, G. C., P. D. Sturkie, and G. Stein, Jr. (1965b). Cardiovascular changes in restrained chickens. *Poultry Sci., 44,* 1452.

Woods, J. J. (1971). Studies on the distribution and action of serotonin in the avian cardiovascular system. Ph.D. thesis, Rutgers University, New Brunswick, New Jersey.

Woodbury, R. A., and B. E. Abreu. (1944). Influence of oxytocin (pitocin) upon heart and blood pressure. *Am. J. Physiol., 142,* 114.

Woodbury, R. A., and W. F. Hamilton. (1937). Blood pressure studies in small animals. *Am. J. Physiol., 119,* 663.

Wooley, P. (1959). The effect of posterior lobe pituitary extracts on blood pressure in several vertebrate species. *J. Exp. Biol., 36,* 453.

Wyse, G. D., and M. Nickerson. (1971). Studies on hemorrhagic hypotension in the domestic fowl. *Can. J. Physiol. Pharmacol.,49,* 919.

# 5

# Heart: Contraction, Conduction, and Electrocardiography

P. D. Sturkie

## THE CARDIAC CYCLE

The sequence of events occurring in a complete heartbeat, a cardiac cycle, includes mechanical contraction of the atria and ventricles (systole) and relaxation of the heart muscle (diastole). This sequence is followed by filling of the ventricles (diastasis). Accompanying these events are changes in volume and pressure in the atria and ventricles.

The contraction phase in mammals is normally the shorter phase and varies little with heart rate, but ventricular relaxation varies greatly and inversely with heart rate. Very little work has been conducted on these events in the avian cardiac cycle, but there is no reason to expect major differences between birds and mammals; the pressure-flow curve of the left ventricle of a duck (Jones and Johansen, 1972) is much like the mammalian one in appearance. The actual pressures reached have been discussed in Chapter 4. Langille and Jones (1975) reported that in the Pekin duck contraction occurred synchronously in the right and left ventricles. At a mean heart rate of 219 beats/min, ventricular systole comprised 44 percent of the cardiac cycle, but the duration of systole in the right ventricular was 30 percent greater than in the left ventricle.

Purton (1971), who recorded atrial and ventricular pressures in chickens, reported no principal differences in the left ventricular pressures curves of birds and mammals, but he revealed significant differences in the atrial pressure waves which he divided into four stages (Figure 5–1). In stage 1 (points 1–2) pressure rises during atrial systole. In stage 2 points (2–3), pressure drops during atrial relaxation and there is a continued flow of blood into ventricules followed by closure of the AV (atrioventricular) valves and ventricular systole. Stage 3 (points 3–4) is atrial filling, in which the pressure shows two peaks; the first may be associated with the bulging of AV valve into atrium and the second represents maximal atrial filling (Purton, 1971). In stage 4, (points 4–1), the AV valves open and atrial pressure falls to its lowest level as blood enters ventricle.

## FACTORS AFFECTING HEART RATE

Small birds and mammals usually have higher heart rates than large ones, but there are exceptions.

Actually most heart rates previously determined (see Table 5–1) have been on birds restrained in different ways and degrees. It is now known that

5–1 Pressure waves in the left atrium of the chicken. See text for explanation. (After Purton, 1971.)

restraint influences heart rate considerably, probably in two ways. The initial excitement attending restraint increases heart rate and sympathetic discharge directly (Cain and Abbott, 1970; Cogger *et al.*, 1974) and continued restraint up to 3 hr causes a progressive decrease in blood pressure and an increase in heart rate (reflexly; Whittow *et al.*, 1965). When birds are allowed to move around (telemetry) or are only partially restrained, heart rates are much lower and probably represent the normal resting rates.

### Normal Heart Rates

The heart rates of several adult species are shown in Table 5–1; those for embryos are given in Table 4–2 (Chapter 4).

**In embryos.** Embryonic chick heart rates have been determined by Girard (1973) (see Table 4–2), by Evans (1972), and by Soliman and Huston (1972), who have described methods of recording embryonic rates directly through the egg shell. These rates have been recorded from day 3 to hatching time and afterwards and range from 138 per minute at 3 days to 221 per minute on the twentieth day (Girard, 1973). The figures found by Soliman and Huston (through the egg shell) range from 218 to 324 per minute during the same periods. Differences in the handling temperature of egg and embryos may have accounted for much of this difference.

**In adults.** It is apparent that adult heart rates vary considerably between and among species. Much of this variation is attributed to variation in tone or restraint of the cardioaccelerator (CA) and cardioinhibitor nerves (vagus) to the heart; the factors influencing the variation are discussed below.

### Neural Control

**Center for heart rate.** There is evidence for a cardioinhibitory center in the medulla (Cohen *et al.*, 1970). The cells involved have their greatest

*Table 5–1*  *Heart rates of birds*

| Species | Age | Sex | Mean heart rate (beats/min) | Reference |
|---|---|---|---|---|
| White Leghorn chicken | 1 day | — | 286 | Ringer *et al.* (1957) |
| | 1 week | — | 474 | Ringer *et al.* (1957) |
| | 7 weeks | Male | 422 | Ringer *et al.* (1957) |
| | 7 weeks | Female | 435 | Ringer *et al.* (1957) |
| | 7 weeks | Capon | 425 | Ringer *et al.* (1957) |
| | 7 weeks | Poulard | 452 | Ringer *et al.* (1957) |
| | 13 weeks | Male | 367 | Ringer *et al.* (1957) |
| | 13 weeks | Female | 391 | Ringer *et al.* (1957) |
| | 22 weeks | Male | 302 | Ringer *et al.* (1957) |
| | 22 weeks | Female | 357 | Ringer *et al.* (1957) |
| | 22 weeks | Capon | 350 | Ringer *et al.* (1957) |
| | 22 weeks | Poulard | 354 | Ringer *et al.* (1957) |
| White Leghorn chicken | | | | |
|   restrained | Adult | Male | 304 | Cain and Abbott (1970) |
|   unrestrained | Adult | Male | 191 | Cain and Abbott (1970) |
| Bronze turkey | 8 weeks | Male | 288 | Ringer and Rood (1959; cited in Chapter 2) |
| | 8 weeks | Female | 283 | Ringer and Rood (1959) |
| | 12 weeks | Male | 234 | Ringer and Rood (1959) |
| | 12 weeks | Female | 230 | Ringer and Rood (1959) |
| | 18 weeks | Male | 198 | Ringer and Rood (1959) |
| | 18 weeks | Female | 212 | Ringer and Rood (1959) |
| | 22 weeks | Male | 198 | Ringer and Rood (1959) |
| | 22 weeks | Female | 232 | Ringer and Rood (1959) |
| | 22 weeks | Adult male | 160 | Ferguson *et al.* (1969) |
| | 22 weeks | Adult female | 219 | Ferguson *et al.* (1969) |
| Pekin duck | 4 months | Male | 194 | Ringer *et al.* (1955) |
| | 4 months | Female | 190 | Ringer *et al.* (1955) |
| | 12–13 months | Male | 189 | Ringer *et al.* (1955) |
| | 12–13 months | Female | 175 | Ringer *et al.* (1955) |
| White king pigeon | Adult | Male | 202 | Ringer *et al.* (1955) |
| | Adult | Female | 208 | Ringer *et al.* (1955) |
| Robin | Adult | | 570 | Woodbury and Hamilton (1937; cited in Chapter 4) |
| | Adult | | 384 | Lewis (1969) |
| Canary | Adult | | 795 | Woodbury and Hamilton (1937; cited in Chapter 4) |
| Blue-winged teal | Adult | | 1000 | Tigerstedt (1921) |
| Blue jay | Adult | | 165 | Owen (1969) |
| Cat bird | Adult | | 307 | Lewis (1967) |
| Brown thrasher | Adult | | 465 | Lewis (1967) |
| Wood thrush | Adult | | 303 | Lewis (1967) |
| | | | 363 | Lewis (1967) |
| *Coturnix* (Japanese quail) | | | | |
|   restrained | Adult | Male | 445 | Cogger *et al.* (1974) |
|   unrestrained (telemetry) | Adult | Male | 368 | Cogger *et al.* (1974) |

numbers in the ventral portion of the nucleus, about 1 mm rostral to the obex. Stimulation in these areas produced bradycardia that could be blocked by atropine. Central stimulation of the vagus gives variable results (Sturkie, unpublished). In some instances it decreased heart rate; in some there was no change and in some it increased, apparently depending on the strength of stimuli and on whether one or both nerves were cut before stimulation. Central stimulation of the cut left vagus with the right one intact decreased heart rate and blood pressure in a duck, but opposite results were obtained when the central end of the right vagus was stimulated with the left vagus intact. The tachycardia persists after section of the left vagus (Johansen and Reite, 1964). This indicates an increase in sympathetic tone or stimulation of the cardioaccelerator center.

**Cardiac nerves.** These are the vagus and cardioaccelerator nerves. Their origin and distribution to the heart are shown in Figure 5–2. The cardiac sympathetic nerve in the chicken arises from the first thoracic ganglion between the first and second ribs, near the most caudal branch of the brachial plexus. It runs as a single discrete nerve parallel to a small vertebral vein and thence with the vena cava to the heart, where it branches and joins with vagal fibers to form a cardiac plexus (Tummons and Sturkie, 1969). According to Ssinelnikow (1928) there are six plexuses; the right and left anterior cardiac plexuses, right and left posterior plexuses, and the anterior and posterior atrial plexuses. The

atria and the sinoatrial and atrioventricular nodes receive the most extensive innervation (Bennett and Malmfors, 1970; Akester, 1971; Bolton, 1967; these references are given in Chapter 4).

The origin and distribution of cardioaccelerator fibers in the pigeon appear to be more complex than in chickens, according to Macdonald and Cohen (1970), who reported that accelerator fibers arise from some of the cervical spinal segments as well as two and sometimes three thoracic segments. The relatively simple anatomical arrangement in the chicken, however, makes the operation of denervation much easier to perform in them; this was first done by Tummons and Sturkie (1968). After bilateral transection of the vagi and sympathetics, electrical stimulation of the peripheral end of right cardioaccelerator nerves (4 V, 40 Hz, 0.2 msec) increased heart rate from 235 to 345 per minute, an increase of 48%; the increase after stimulation of the left nerve was 32%. Stimulation of the right cardioaccelerator (CA) in the pigeon, but not stimulation of the left, consistently increases heart rate (Macdonald and Cohen, 1970).

To assess the degree of control or influence exerted by the intact accelerators and vagi nerves (tone), a series of experiments were conducted involving isolation, transection, and stimulation of nerves, employment of β-adrenergic and cholinergic blockade, various drugs known to deplete cardiac catecholamines, and the effects of various environmental factors.

Earlier work employing adrenergic blockade in ducks and seagulls (Johansen and Reite, 1964) and

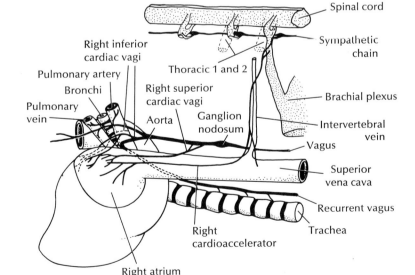

5–2

Diagram of right cardiac nerves. (After Tummons and Sturkie, 1969.)

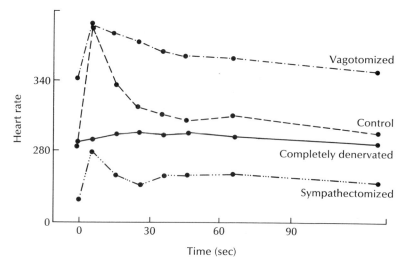

**5–3**

Heart rate response with time to excitement of control, vagotomized, sympathectomized, and completely denervated adult White Leghorn cocks.

pigeons (Cohen and Pitts, 1968) emphasized the important role of accelerators in controlling heart rate. The report here relates to transection and stimulation studies on chickens. The accelerator and vagal nerves were isolated and transected as previously described (Tummons and Sturkie, 1968, 1969); the birds were allowed to recover from surgery, and the stimulation studies were carried out 6 days later. The pertinent results are shown in Figure 5–3. It is clear that sympathectomy alone decreased heart rate about 20% from the basal resting rate (284 per minute). Vagotomy alone increased heart rate about 20% above the resting rate and atropinization gave the same results. When both nerves were cut bilaterally, heart rate was almost the same as the basal resting rate (see Figure 5–3). This figure also illustrates the effect of excitement on relative tones of the vagus and accelerator nerves. Excitement increases heart rate most when the vagi are intact and less so when the vagi are cut. Even after bilateral sympathectomy, excitement increases heart rate some but not above the basal resting rate, indicating a decrease in vagal restraint. After complete denervation, heart rate does not change with excitement and remains near the resting rate level. Similar results have been obtained by complete adrenergic and cholinergic blockade except that basal heart rate is somewhat lower than in the completely denervated birds, presumably because $\beta$ blockade affects circulating catecholamines as well as neuronal ones (Tummons and Sturkie, 1970; Sturkie, 1970).

That the cardiac neurotransmitter in birds is norepinephrine has been found by stimulating the CA nerve in isolated perfused hearts, which causes

the release of norepinephrine in the perfusate (Sturkie and Poorvin, 1973). This is true despite the fact that in the intact chicken, the level of epinephrine in the blood and heart is higher than that of norepinephrine (see also Chapters 12 and 20). The relative degrees of vagal and accelerator nerve tone vary under different conditions and can be assessed by employing $\beta$-adrenergic blockade with propranolol and cholinergic blockade with atropine.

After abolition of vagal tone with atropine (A) or by vagotomy, the heart rate resulting from sympathetic tone (unrestrained by vagus) is evident and is increased. Abolition of sympathetic tone (ST) by propranolol (P) with the vagus intact depresses heart rate below the normal level. Abolition of vagal and sympathetic tone (PA) results in a heart rate about normal. This is also the intrinsic heart rate. In other words, vagal tone (VT) and sympathetic tone operate to about the same degree; therefore the sympathetic nerves increase heart rate to the same degree that the parasympathetic nerves (vagus) decrease heart rate. This technique has been used to determine the effects of age, sex, temperature, drugs, etc., on the degree of vagal and cardioaccelerator tone. This technique is illustrated in Figures 5–4, 5–5, and 5–6.

Thus,

$$ST = \frac{\text{sympathetic rate } (A - PA)}{\text{intrinsic rate } (PA)} \times 100$$

and

$$VT = \frac{\text{parasympathetic rate } (P - PA)}{\text{intrinsic rate } (PA)} \times 100$$

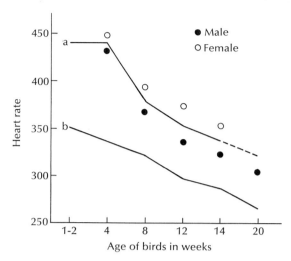

5–4 Normal resting heart rates: (a) of chickens males and females at 2, 4, 8, 12, 16, and 20 weeks of age. (b) Intrinsic heart rates resulting from administration of propranolol and atropine (PA). (After Sturkie and Chillseyzn, 1972.)

*Vagal restraint.* The vagi in mammals and birds exert a tonic effect on heart rate. The degree of tone varies considerably in different species depending on a number of factors. Starvation for extended periods (3 days or more) slows heart rate drastically by increasing vagal tone (Vogel and Sturkie, 1963).

Bilateral vagotomy increases heart rate in chickens (Durfee, 1963; Tummons and Sturkie, 1969) and in ducks (Johansen and Reite, 1964; Butler and Jones, 1968). The degree of increase after vagotomy appears to be greater in those species with slower resting heart rates (duck, pigeons, gulls), indicating a greater degree of vagal tone. The right vagus exerts greater tone normally but vagal control is exerted mostly by only one vagus at a time (right or left) according to experiments based on increasing blockade of the right or the left nerve with cold (Butler and Jones, 1968). Stimulation of the cut peripheral end of the vagus results in bradycardia and cardiac arrest, depending on the strength of the stimulus (Jones and Johansen, 1972).

Injection of cholinergic substances, such as acetylcholine or metacholine (Durfee, 1963), has an effect similar to nerve stimulation and the effect can be blocked with atropine.

**Reflex changes in heart rate.** Durfee (1963) showed that hypoxia and methacholine, which

depress blood pressure, caused a reflex rise in heart rate that could be blocked by atropine or bilateral vagotomy; moreover, norepinephrine-induced increases in blood pressure evoked a reflex decrease in heart rate that could also be blocked by bilateral vagotomy. These results suggest that reflex changes in heart rate (increase or decrease) are mediated via the vagus and that the cardioaccelerator nerve is not involved in such reflexes.

Serotonin, which likewise has a depressor effect in chickens (Woods, 1971), produces a reflex increase in heart rate that can be blocked with atropine but not with propranolol ($\beta$ blockade). Further evidence from Tummons (1970) indicates that the reflex changes in heart rate induced by hypotensive or hypertensive agents are mediated by the vagus nerve and not by the cardioaccelerator nerve. The effects of methacholine and norepinephrine on blood pressure (BP) and heart rate (HR) before and after cardioaccelerator nerve (CA) transection are shown as follows:

| Treatment | Before denervation | | After denervation | |
|---|---|---|---|---|
| | BP | HR | BP | HR |
| Control (no drug) | 204 | 291 | 181 | 242 |
| Methacholine | 113 | 344 | 109 | 276 |
| Norepinephrine | 275 | 220 | 231 | 177 |

The reflex changes in heart rate after CA nerve transection are significant but are apparently not as great as before transection. The increase does not approach or exceed 300 per minute, a value that requires an intact CA nerve (Tummons and Sturkie, 1969).

## Age and Heart Rate

The chicken's heart rate increases greatly from day 1 to 1 week of age and then increases slightly and reaches a maximum at 3–4 weeks of age (Ringer *et al.*, 1957). Thereafter, it declines gradually and reaches the adult level at about 17 weeks of age in White Leghorn chickens. Similar results have been reported by Flick (1967) and by Sturkie and Chillseyzn (1972). The latter investigation also determined the relative influence of sympathetic and parasympathetic control on these heart rate changes. These changes in heart rate are shown in Figure 5–4 before and after complete pharmacologic blockade of accelerator and inhibitor nerves

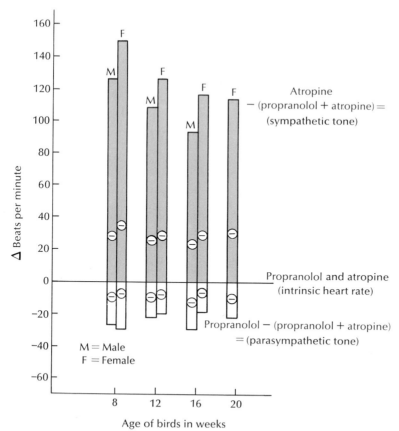

5-5

Differences in heart rate, actual (Δ) and % (Θ), from intrinsic heart rate (free of nervous control) after administration of atropine or propanolol for male (M) and female (F) birds. The use of atropine makes it possible to measure changes in the sympathetic nervous tone; propanolol allows measurement of changes in the parasympathetic nervous tone. Note that although change in sympathetic tone is greatest after 8 weeks and decreases thereafter with age, there are no significant changes in parasympathetic tone with age.

with propranolol (P) and atropine (A) (Figure 5–4, curve b). It is apparent that the latter curve, which represents the intrinsic heart rate, tends to decline with age and parallels the resting heart rate changes. This indicates that factors other than neurogenic ones, such as body temperature, hormones, and metabolic state, are involved. The degree of tone exerted by the accelerator and inhibitor nerves with changes in age is illustrated in Figure 5–5. The differences in A–PA, shown by the bars in the upper part of the figure, represent heart rate changes (freed of parasympathetic or vagal influence) attributable to accelerator nerve influence only. It is evident that these rates decrease with age, indicating a decline in sympathetic tone or influence with age. Moreover, the sex difference in rate also appears to be attributable to the difference in accelerator tone. The difference in P–PA shown in the figure represents parasympathetic tone or influence only, freed of accelerator or sympathetic influence. There are no significant changes here

attributable to age, indicating that parasympathetic tone does not change appreciably with age.

## Effects of Light and Ambient Temperature

Heart rate is lowest at night and increases with exposure to light and exercise (Cain and Abbott 1970) and Sturkie (1963).

Exposure to high or low temperature at first increases heart rate, but after 3 weeks or more exposure to high temperature (Sturkie et al., 1970), when the birds have become acclimatized, heart rates decrease significantly below normal (Figure 5–6). Figure 5–6 shows that there are differences between the heart rates after vagal blockade (atropine, A) of birds at cold, normal, and high temperatures. The birds at high temperature had lower resting rates that increased most after blockade, indicating a higher degree of vagal tone. There were no significant differences after sympa-

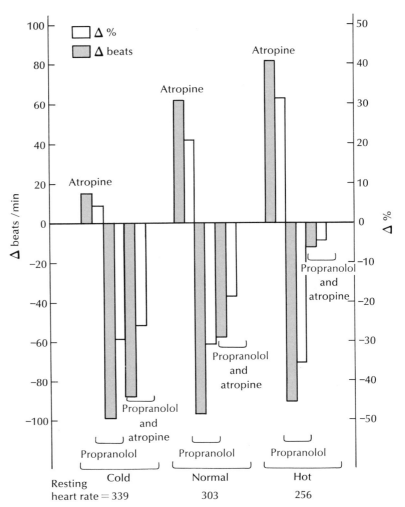

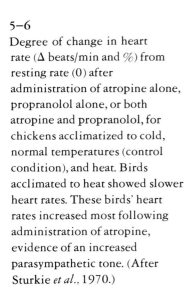

5–6
Degree of change in heart rate (Δ beats/min and %) from resting rate (0) after administration of atropine alone, propranolol alone, or both atropine and propranolol, for chickens acclimatized to cold, normal temperatures (control condition), and heat. Birds acclimated to heat showed slower heart rates. These birds' heart rates increased most following administration of atropine, evidence of an increased parasympathetic tone. (After Sturkie *et al.*, 1970.)

thetic blockade (after propranolol) among those receiving the different temperature treatments.

## Heart Rate and Drugs

The effects of a number of drugs and hormones on blood pressure have been discussed in Chapter 4, and these drugs affect heart rate directly or reflexly. These include acetylcholine, catecholamines, serotonin, histamine, reserpine, oxytocin, vasopressin, estrogen, prostaglandins, and others. The reflex effects of some of these have been discussed under these headings.

Reserpine slows heart rate by decreasing sympathetic tone and increasing vagal tone (Sturkie, 1970). The decrease in sympathetic tone is progressive. This is not surprising because reserpine depletes the catecholamines of the heart and blood appreciably within 4 hr and almost completely 24 hr after treatment (Lin *et al.*, 1970). The effect of reserpine on vagal tone is immediate and is greatest 3–5 hr after administration; 22–24 hr afterwards, however, the vagal effect is dissipated and the sympathetic depressor effect is greatest.

Isoproterenol is a potent $\beta$ stimulator of avian heart rate, as it is of mammalian heart rate (Tummons and Sturkie, 1970). Depletion of catecholamines with reserpine and denervation produces chronotropic supersensitivity to norepinephrine and epinephrine but not to isoproterenol; this is probably attributable to the elimination of intraneuronal binding sites.

Histamine has a positive chronotropic effect that can be blocked or prevented with an $H_1$ recep-

110

tor blocking agent, mepyramine. Beta blockade has little effect on the response (El-Ackad *et al.*, 1974).

## CONTRACTILITY

The contractile force of heart muscle, or the state of inotropy, has been measured in the intact animal and in isolated strips of muscle. In the latter case, the muscle may be allowed to contract under a load with little or no change in muscle length (isometric contraction) or it may shorten or lengthen on contraction (isotonic contraction). In the intact animal contractile force may result from changes in fiber length, with increased end diastolic volume or pressure (Frank–Starling law) and increased or decreased cardiac output or stroke volume. The heart may also exhibit an increased or decreased contractile force and stroke volume with a constant filling pressure or volume (change in contractility).

Contractile force, or contractility, can be measured during isometric contraction by recording the rate of change in ventricular pressure *(dp/dt)* from beginning pressure to peak pressure or during the maximum rate of pressure rise *(dp/dt* max); the shorter the time to reach peak pressure, the greater the contractile force or inotropic effect. There are also other measures of contractility. A number of factors affect contractility, such as epinephrine, norepinephrine, accelerator and vagal nerve stimulation, acetylcholine, histamine, and others.

**Embryos.** Contractility studies on isolated avian embryonic hearts at different stages of development, usually before and after innervation, have been conducted. Lee *et al.* (1960) reported that nicotine had an inotropic effect on noninnervated as well as innervated embryonic heart, and so did acetylcholine on the atropinized heart. Reserpine, which depleted the embryonic hearts of catecholamines, decreased the positive inotropic response to nicotine. Norepinephrine had a positive inotropic effect on embryos at all stages (Michal *et al.*, 1967) but tyramine had no effect until the embryo was at least 14 days old. Its effect may be attributable to a release of catecholamines at this stage.

**Adults.** The effects of acetylcholine or vagal stimulation on the inotropic state of the duck heart are conflicting. Folkow and Yonce (1967), who paced hearts of Pekin ducks electronically and stimulated the vagus, reported a greatly reduced inotropic response (negative). They recorded a drop in ventricular pressure from a normal of about

160 mm Hg to 110 mm Hg and a drop in cardiac output from 1312 ml/min to 950 ml/min. Contrarily, Furnival *et al.* (1973) reported only a slight (3%) reduction in inotropic effect in the same breed of ducks. The latter measured *dp/dt* max before and after vagal stimulation of the paced heart (constant heart rate of 297). The mean figure was 4636 mm Hg/sec before stimulation and 4500 mm Hg/sec afterwards, a change similar to the one they reported in the dog. However, in three other ducks they recorded large increases in the end diastolic pressures in the left ventricle; these were associated with significant decreases in mean aortic pressure and *dp/dt* max. Further vagal stimulation resulted in a great reduction in *dp/dt* from 7046 mm Hg/sec to 4834 mm Hg/sec. At the same time, the end diastolic pressure increased from a level of 11.5 cm $H_2O$ to 18.7 cm $H_2O$. These workers concluded that the repeated subjection of the left ventricle to high end diastolic pressures eventually resulted in failure of the heart muscle and that, under these conditions, further vagal stimulation resulted in the negative inotropic response.

A possible explanation for the results of Folkow and Yonce (1967), according to Furnival *et al.* (1973), could be that the hearts they studied were in failure because of repeated high end diastolic pressures created by infusions of fluid in their experiments to maintain aortic pressures during vagal stimulations. Further studies are indicated.

Histochemical and stimulation studies of avian ventricular muscle strips (see Chapter 1) reveal extensive vagal innervation of ventricles; this could produce a negative inotropic effect when the ventricles are stimulated.

**Contractility in isolated hearts.** Abati (1975) employed isovolumic, isolated avian hearts to study the effects of hypoxia on contractility. The heart volume was kept constant by inserting a balloon of known volume into the left ventricle. Coronary flow was provided by retrograde perfusion. Pressure changes were measured and *dp/dt* max was calculated. The maximum rate of rise in pressure *(dp/dt* max) in the normal hearts of chickens, pigeons and diving ducks were determined as follows:

| | Pressure (mm Hg) | *dp/dt* (mm Hg/sec) |
|---|---|---|
| Chicken | 81.4 | $1049 \pm 45$ |
| Pigeon | 77.3 | $1355 \pm 67$ |
| Duck | 105.0 | $1495 \pm 73$ |

When the isolated hearts of these species were made hypoxic by perfusion with 95% nitrogen and 5% oxygen, contractility was decreased most in chickens, less in pigeons, and least in diving ducks (which in nature are exposed to hypoxia more than are chickens and pigeons and have developed a greater resistance to hypoxia).

Norepinephrine and epinephrine have a positive inotropic effect on avian heart muscle as they do on mammals (Abati, 1975). Histamine, which has been reported to have a positive inotropic effect on some mammalian hearts, has a negative effect in chicken isolated heart muscle strips (El-Ackad et al., 1974).

## WORK OF THE HEART

The work involved in ejecting blood from the heart can be estimated as follows:

$$W = \overline{P}V$$

where $\overline{P}$ is the mean arterial pressure and $V$ is the volume of blood ejected. To be strictly accurate,

$$W = \int P \, dV \text{ over the ejection period.}$$

However, calculations of stroke work using the first formula in mammals closely approximates those calculated from the latter formula.

The power of the heart is its rate of doing work. According to the calculations of Jones and Johansen (1972), the power of the left ventricle of chickens is $(135 \times 1330)$ dynes/cm$^2 \times 200$ ml/min or $35.9 \times 10^6$ ergs/min; the right ventricle has a pressure of 18 instead of 135, giving a value for power of $4.79 \times 10^6$ ergs/min.

The higher the blood pressure (as in turkeys), the higher is the work of the left ventricle in relation to that of the right. The mechanical efficiency of the heart is found as follows:

$$\frac{\text{Mechanical work done}}{\text{Mechanical work done} + \text{maintenance heat (tension energy)}}$$

The tension energy is influenced mainly by $O_2$ consumed. It is much greater than the mechanical work energy because the heart's efficiency is low, ranging from 3 to 15%. The $O_2$ consumption of the chicken heart is estimated to be 7% of the total $O_2$ consumption of the bird (Jones and Johansen, 1972).

The systolic ejection period in birds seems long, occupying 25–33% of the resting cardiac cycle (Johansen and Aakus, 1963). As the heart rate increases, the time spent in ejection increases in relation to diastolic time. It is advantageous to have a high heart rate, with systole occupying a large part of the cycle (Jones and Johansen, 1972). This may also increase contractility.

The relatively larger heart of birds, compared to mammals, has advantages in that it need shorten less in ejection. However, it also has a disadvantage in that it uses more tension energy and is less efficient in accordance with the law of Laplace (see Chapter 4).

## ELECTROPHYSIOLOGY AND ELECTROCARDIOGRAPHY
### Anatomy of Specialized Conducting System

The existence of a specialized conducting system in bird hearts was doubted for a number of years. Later work by Drennan (1927), Davies (1930), Moore (1965), and Yousuf (1965) proves that birds indeed have a specialized conducting system even more than do mammals (see Figure 5–7). This system represents the anatomical pathways by which electrical impulses spread to different parts of the heart; these impulses precede slightly the mechanical contraction which they induce. The system as described by Davies consists of: (1) the sinoatrial node, (2) the atrioventricular node and branches, and (3) the right AV ring of Purkinje fibers. The SA node is located near the entrance of the vena cava to the right atrium.

**The AV node.** The AV node (pigeon) is embedded in connective tissue in the lower and posterior part of the atrial septum, a short distance in front and to the left of the opening of the left superior vena cava (this is a position similar to that of the mammalian node). It is ovoid in shape and its lower and anterior parts narrow into the commencement of the AV bundle. The lower part of the node consists of cells that are larger than the atrial myocardial cells proper and that are frequently multinucleated, the nuclei being rounded in shape and central in position.

**The AV bundle.** Beginning as a narrow rounded bundle continuous with the lower and anterior end of the AV node, the AV bundle soon broadens out and runs forward and to the left in the ventricular septum. It then passes downward, forward, and to the left, to a point slightly below and to the right of the anterior septal attachment of the muscular right AV valve. This site is about one-quarter of the distance from the base to the apex of the ventricular system and is where the bundle divides

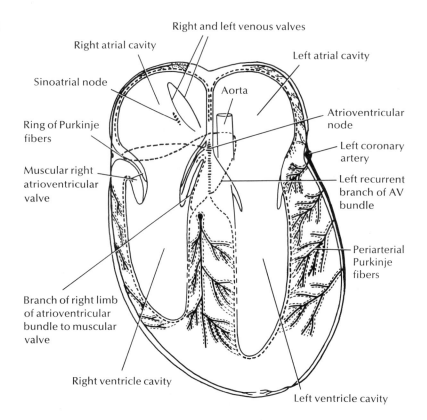

Right and left venous valves

Right atrial cavity

Left atrial cavity

Sinoatrial node

Aorta

Ring of Purkinje
fibers

Atrioventricular
node

Left coronary
artery

Muscular right
atrioventricular
valve

Left recurrent
branch of AV
bundle

Periarterial
Purkinje
fibers

Branch of right limb
of atrioventricular
bundle to muscular
valve

Right ventricle cavity

Left ventricle cavity

5–7
Diagram of the conducting
system in the avian heart
(pigeon). (After Davies, 1930.)

into the right and left limbs. The right limb runs downward and slightly forward. It passes in front of and close to the main septal artery, but no muscle fibers appear to pass directly from the right limb to the collection of Purkinje fibers around the artery. The limb then reaches the subendocardial connective tissue on the right side of the septum, where it spreads out and becomes continuous with the subendocardial network of Purkinje fibers. The cells of the limbs are like those of the bundle.

The right limb also gives off a branch that runs up and around the right AV valve. This suggests, according to Davies (1930), that the right valve actively contracts early in the ventricular systole, so that no reflux of blood occurs before its closure. The left limb branches at the point where the right one branches and passes posteriorly and to the left. It gives rise to another branch, the recurrent branch, which runs upward, forward, and to the left in the ventricular system. Finally, the left limb passes backward in the connective tissue on the left side of the root of the aorta and ends by joining the aortic end of the bundle of Purkinje fibers, which pass from the AV node around the right AV orifice, behind the root of the aorta.

The conducting system is poorly supplied with nerves and appears to be independent of the nervous system. Whereas Davies (1930) reported di-

rect tracts of specialized conducting tissue between the SA and AV nodes of chickens, Moore (1965) did not find such tissue in the chicken and neither did Yousuf (1965) find it in *Passer* (sparrow). The connection between the SA and AV nodes, according to Yousuf, is made by ordinary muscle fibers of the interatrial septum.

## Action Potentials and the Spread of Electrical Excitation

**In embryos.** Action potentials in embryonic hearts have been studied by a number of workers, including Lieberman and Paes de Carvalho (1965), Pappano (1972), Krespi and Sleator (1966), and Sperelakis and Shigenobu (1972).

The electrophysiology of the embryonic heart is similar to that of the adult (Lieberman and Paes de Carvalho, 1965). The P–R interval, for example, is established early in embryonic life (3–4 days) before the AV node is formed. Therefore, conduction delay is caused by tissue or cells other than the AV node, and these investigators found the delay was localized in a narrow band of tissue extending along the AV ring. These authors also suggested that the adult AV node may be a remnant of the embryonic AV ring.

Membrane potentials in embryonic chick atria change with age from 6 to 18 days, particularly the rate of rise ($V_{max}$) of action potentials (Poppano, 1972). Reduction in sodium (Na$^+$) had no effect on resting membrane potentials but diminished overshoot and $V_{max}$. The atrial action potentials therefore underwent a transformation in their sodium electrode properties and in their susceptibility to blockade by tetrodotoxin, which was relatively ineffective in 6-day embryos but effective at 12 and 18 days. The embryonic atrial cells of all ages depended on Na$^+$ because the rate of rise in conductance varied in direct proportion to Na. Embryonic ventricular cells react similarly to tetrodotoxin and Na (Ishima, 1968). Sodium ion is preferable, but not necessary, in early stages for generating the action potential. Further studies on ventricular embryonic action potentials by Sperelakis and Shigenobu (1972) demonstrated that the greatest changes in electrophysiological properties occur between day 2 and day 8. The ratio of permeabilities of sodium to potassium (Na/K) is high in young embryos (0.2) and decreases to about 0.05 in later stage embryos.

**In adults.** The electrical excitation wave precedes mechanical contraction slightly and spreads from the SA node through the other branches of the conducting system. The paths and speed of conduction of this wave may be determined by placing electrodes at different areas of the heart and determining the change in potential at the electrodes (method of relative negativity).

Lewis (1915), Mangold (1919), and Kisch (1949, and 1951) used this method on the bird heart. Lewis and Mangold used bipolar leads. Lewis placed the exploring electrode on the heart and the other on the chest wall; Mangold placed both eletrodes on the heart. Kisch used unipolar leads (chest, direct, and endocavity) for the most part. Mangold and Lewis reported that the impulse started in the region of the SA node and spread to the left side of the right atrium, thence to the left atrium, and then to the septum.

The order of depolarization in the different areas of the ventricles (chicken) according to the three investigators is as follows:

| Region of heart | Kisch (1951) | Lewis (1915) | Mangold (1919) |
|---|---|---|---|
| Apex of right ventricle | 1 | 1 | 1 |
| Base of left ventricle | 3 | 3 | 2 |
| Base of right ventricle | 2 | 4 | 3 |
| Apex of left ventricle | 4 | 2 | 4 |

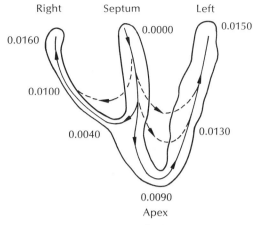

5–8 Diagram of the spread of an impulse or excitation wave in the ventricles of the bird heart. Coronal section: time in seconds. (After Lewis, 1915.)

The time required for the impulse to spread from the region of the septum to other parts of the ventricle's surface, according to Lewis (1915), is shown in Figure 5–8. From the distribution of surface potentials and studies of electrocardiograms, Lewis concluded that the impulse spreads (see Figure 5–8) downward through the septum, then upward through the septum, and later upward through the free walls, almost in line with the latter rather than at right angles to them. The very rapid spread of the impulse downward (electrical axis, +90°; see Figure 5–9) correponds to the small upright R wave of the electrocardiogram. The depolarization wave then shifts abruptly upward (electrical axis approximately −90°), and its duration is relatively long (Figure 5–8). This produces the S wave of the electrocardiogram (Lewis, 1915).

Neither Mangold nor Lewis determined which of the endocardial and epicardial surfaces was activated first. Kisch (1951) made such studies on the hearts of chickens, pigeons, ducks, and seagulls. He showed that the epicardial surfaces of the ventricles were activated or depolarized before the endocardial surfaces. Depolarization on the surface of the right ventricles of the chicken heart begins about 0.02–0.03 sec earlier than it does inside the right ventricle, but on the left ventricle it starts about 0.01 sec earlier than on the inside. Depolarization in the interior of the left and right ventricles occurs at approximately the same time. Leads taken directly from the interior of the ventricle produce electrograms (EG's) with the configuration of waves in the opposite direction; these are similar to the normal ECG's of man and dog, in which the endo-

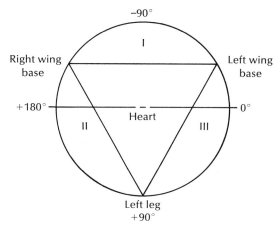

5–9  Limb leads for the ECG of the bird, with heart in center.

cardial surfaces are depolarized before the epicardial surfaces.

Moore (1965) has studied the activation and spread of action potentials in the turkey heart and the sequence according to him is somewhat different from that found by Kisch, Mangold, and Lewis. According to him the apical third of the right ventricle is activated first, and it spreads to the upper basilar part and thence on to the pulmonary conus region, which is the last part activated. The left ventricle is first activated in the anterior septal one-third and middle regions, and the basilar regions later.

## The Electrocardiogram

The electrocardiogram (ECG) is a record of the electrical activity (depolarization and repolarization) of the heart picked up from electrodes attached to parts of the body other than the heart itself (leads). For details concerning the essentials and methods of taking and recording electrocardiograms, textbooks on the subject should be consulted.

**Recording methods.** *Leads.* Leads taken directly from the heart produce records termed electrograms (EG's). Records from any two electrodes constitute a bipolar lead. The standard bipolar limb leads for man are: lead I, right arm and left arm; lead II, right arm and left leg; and lead III, left arm and left leg. The limb leads for the bird heart are the same as for man, except that the electrodes (usually needles) are attached to, or inserted in, the bases of the wings, and in legs. The three limb leads form roughly an equilateral triangle with the heart

located near the center (Figure 5–9). This is more nearly true for the bird heart than for man.

The conventional chest leads, CR, CL, and CF, have also been recorded in birds (Sturkie, unpublished; Kisch, 1951; Douglas, 1960). The exploring electrodes are placed on the right arm (CR), left arm (CL) (of man, and the corresponding wings of birds), and left leg or foot (CF); the chest electrode is the indifferent electrode.

It is impossible to record the true potential at any one point with bipolar leads because of the influence of the other electrode. Wilson devised a method of unipolar leads so that one of the electrodes was zero (see Lamb, 1957). The positive exploring electrode therefore records only the potential received at the point desired. Such electrodes placed on the right arm (VR), left arm (VL), and left leg or foot (VF) constitute the V leads. Because one lead is zero, the potential recorded in V leads is only half that of bipolar leads. Goldberger has augmented (amplified) the potential of unipolar leads by removing the negative electrode from VL when the positive electrode is on the left arm; this can be done in a like manner on the other extremities. Such leads are designated as aVR, aVL, and aVF, or augmented unipolar leads. Even with the augmentation, the amplitude obtained is only about 86% of that measured by bipolar leads (Lamb, 1957).

*Chart speed and wave designations.* The standard speed for the paper of the electrocardiogram for human beings is 25 mm/sec. The vertical lines 1 mm apart on the paper represent units of time (0.04 sec) at standard speeds. The horizontal lines, also 1 mm apart, represent amplitude or voltage. For work with humans, the instrument is usually standardized at 1 mV. When 1 mV is impressed on the instrument, it causes a deflection of 10 mm. As the heart rate of the chicken is considerably faster than that of man, the standard chart speed in most cases is not fast enough to record all waves faithfully. Usually, if the heart rate is 300 per minute or more, the P(depolarization of atrial muscle) and T (repolarization of the ventricles) waves may be fused together, and the P wave is not always discernible (particularly in leads II and III). However, the P wave of the chicken may not be discernible even when the chart speed is increased to 50 or 75 mm/sec or faster (Sturkie, 1948, 1949; Kisch, 1951) and when the frequency response of the instrument is increased to 500 Hz, which is more than adequate (Sturkie, unpublished; see Figure 5–10). It appears that the P and T waves are fused because the atria begin depolarizing before the ventricles are completely repolarized.

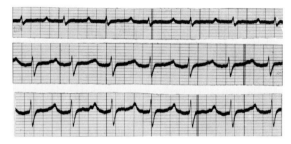

5–10 Electrocardiogram of female chicken taken on a high-frequency instrument (500 cps) showing the limb leads (I, II, and III from top downward). Standardization, 1 mV = 1.5 cm. Chart speed, 75 mm/sec. Note that P and T waves are fused; compare with Figure 5–11, where they are not.

## Characteristics of the Normal Bird Electrocardiogram

The normal ECG of man shows P, Q, R, S, and T waves in the limb leads. The bird ECG exhibits P, S, and T waves and usually a small abortive R wave in some leads, but no Q wave. The P wave, as in man (Figure 5–11) represents the depolarization of atrial muscle and slightly precedes atrial contraction. There is no recognizable wave of atrial repolarization. R and S waves represent the depolarization of ventricular muscle, which signals the onset of ventricular systole. The T wave represents repolarization of the ventricles.

**Results from different leads.** The P wave, when observed, is usually upright (positive) in all leads in the chicken, duck, and pigeon (Sturkie, 1948, 1949; Kisch 1951), although Douglas (1960), based on studies of a small number of birds, claims that the P wave is usually biphasic in leads I and II, and Kisch (1951) has reported negative P III in the sea gull. The ECG of the turkey is essentially like that of chicken (Krista et al., 1970). The P wave is observed most frequently in lead I in the chicken, even though its amplitude is less there than in leads II or III, because the T wave in lead I is usually flat or isoelectric. P and T may be fused in leads II and III. T is positive in leads II and III. A small upright R is usually (Sturkie, 1949, and unpublished) or always (Kisch, 1951) present in lead II of the chicken and pigeon, respectively, but it is of lower amplitude or absent in lead III. Occasionally the R wave is prominent in leads II and III of the duck (Kisch, 1951). The P wave is small and positive in lead I and in lead aVF but small and negative in lead V-10 (Szabuniewicz, 1967).

*Limb leads.* Lead I is the most variable of the limb leads. The amplitude of all the complexes except the P wave is usually low. With respect to the configuration of R, S, and T in lead I, the three main types are described as follows (Sturkie, 1948, 1949):

a. Relatively prominent S or no R or a small R. The T is usually isoelectric or slightly positive.
b. A relatively prominent R and no S or a small S. T is isoelectric or slightly negative.
c. R's and S's of about equal prominence. Type b is the most prevalent (see also Szabuniewicz, 1967).

The electrocardiogram of the chicken, showing limb leads, chest leads, and augmented unipolar leads, is reproduced in Figure 5–11. In leads CR

5–11 Electrocardiograms of male chicken showing limb leads (I, II, III), augmented unipolar leads (aVR, aVL, and aVF), V lead, and chest leads (CR, CL, and CF). Standardization, 1 mV=1.5 cm. Chart speed, 50 mm/sec. Record taken on a high-frequency instrument. P, RS, and T waves clearly observed. (Sturkie, unpublished.)

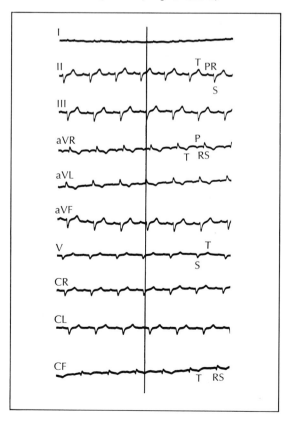

*Table 5–2*  *Intervals or durations and amplitudes of chicken electrocardiograms*

| | Intervals or durations (sec) | | | Amplitude (mV) | | | |
|---|---|---|---|---|---|---|---|
| | Female heart rates (Sturkie, 1949; with Hunsaker, 1957) | | Rakalska (1964) | Szabuniewicz (1967) | | Sturkie and Hunsaker (1957) Sturkie (unpublished) | |
| | 260 to 280 | 300 to 341 | | Lead I | Lead aVF | Lead II | Lead III |
| P | 0.0307 Male[a] 0.0421 – 0.0374 | | 0.027 | 0.109 | 0.095 | 0.57 Male | 0.48 Male |
| R | | | | 0.160 | 0.090 | 0.083 Female 0.265 Male | 0.030 Female 0.182 Male |
| S | 0.0234 | 0.0234 | 0.0235 | 0.146 | 0.320 | 0.247 Female 0.795 Male | 0.250 Female 0.772 Male |
| RS | — | — | — | | | 0.247 Female 0.530 Male | 0.250 Female 0.590 Male |
| T | 0.1048 | 0.0925 | — | 0.074 | 0.120 | — 0.255 Male | — 0.268 Male |
| P–S | 0.0849 | 0.0723 | 0.066 | — | — | — | — |
| S–T | 0.1281 | 0.1164 | 0.105 | — | — | — | — |

[a] Sturkie (unpublished).

and CL, the configurations of the waves are similar to those in leads II and III. In lead CF the P wave is usually biphasic and the amplitude of all waves is low.

*Augmented unipolar leads.* In leads aVR and aVL the QRS complex is inverted when compared to lead II or lead III. The P wave is inverted in lead aVR and biphasic in lead aVL. The configuration of the waves in lead aVF is similar to those in leads II and III.

Lead $V_{10}$, used with lead aVF to determine the electrical axis (z axis) in the dorsoventral position, is similar to lead aVR in the configuration of most waves, with P and T waves inverted. It is a unipolar lead and is obtained by placing the indifferent electrode over the third dorsal thoracic vertebrae (Szabuniewcz, 1967).

*Unipolar leads.* Unipolar leads (VR, VL, and VF, not augmented) have been recorded in chickens and pigeons by Douglas (1960), Kisch (1951), Szabuniewicz (1967), and Sturkie (unpublished). In leads VR and VL of chickens and pigeons there is a prominent R, no S, and an inverted T, but in the duck these leads show an S, a QS, or a small R and a prominent S. In lead VF of all birds studied by Kisch, there was a QS or a small R and prominent S.

**Intervals.** The duration in seconds of the various waves of the avian ECG cannot always be deter-mined because of the fusion of P and T waves, par-ticularly in females (see later section on sex differ-ences); therefore the work that has been reported is on selected ECG's where P and T waves, are clearly discernible (Sturkie, 1949; Kisch, 1951). Durations of P, S, and T waves and the time from the beginning of P to the start of S (P–S interval) and from the beginning of S to the end of T (ST interval) have been determined for leads II and III in the chicken. The R wave in leads II and III is usually small or absent; when it is present, its starting point is diffi-cult to locate. For this reason the P–S instead of the P–R interval is determined. In many cases there is no ST segment. T usually begins where S ends, and that point is used as the starting point for T. ST represents the interval from the beginning of S to the end of T, or the time required for depolari-zation and repolarization of the ventricles.

The P–S interval is the time required for the impulse, beginning in the right atrium, to reach the ventricles. The wave intervals (durations) are shown in Table 5–2 for the chicken.

In general, as heart rate increases, the intervals for all complexes except S decrease; this has also been demonstrated by Kisch (1951) in the chicken, pigeon, duck, and seagull with direct leads. The intervals determined with direct leads on the chick-en by Kisch (1951) are in close agreement with those determined with limb leads by Sturkie (1949), except for that of the ventricular complex. The duration of this interval is 0.037 sec according

*Table 5–3* *Electrical axes (frontal plane) of chicken hearts (female) in*
*relation to type of ECG in lead I*

| Type of ECG in I | Number of birds | ECG's | | RS axes (°) | |
|---|---|---|---|---|---|
| | | Number | % | Range | Average |
| S present | 15 | 17 | 25.8 | −91 to −120 | −102.11 |
| R present | 30 | 46 | 74.2 | −26 to −103[b] | − 74.04 |
| Unknown | 2 | 3 | | +10 to + 30 | |

| Direction of T wave in I | Number of birds | ECG's | | T axes (°) | |
|---|---|---|---|---|---|
| | | Number | % | Range | Average |
| Positive | 34 | 43 | 70.49 | +68 to + 89 | + 81.8 |
| Negative | 10 | 12 | 19.67 | +95 to +115 | +100.3 |
| Isoelectric | 6 | 6 | 9.83 | +88 to + 91 | + 89.6 |

[a]From Sturkie (1949).
[b]Only one ECG above −90°.

to Kisch and 0.024 sec according to Sturkie. The intervals determined by Rakalska (1964) on lead I and aVF leads agree in general with those of Sturkie for S and P–R but not for the P waves.

**Amplitude.** The amplitude of all waves of the bird ECG is relatively low and is considerably less than that of the human ECG. In lead I it is so low that accurate measurements with the usual standardization are difficult or impossible. An estimate of average amplitude in lead I can be deduced from the differences in mean amplitude for the various waves in leads II and III, in accordance with Einthoven's law, which states that the amplitude of a given wave in leads I and III should equal that in lead II. This is true provided the three leads are run simultaneously or, if they are not, provided there is no appreciable change in heart rate and amplitude. For example, the amplitude in millivolts of S in lead I and S in lead III (added algebraically) should equal that in S II, as it does. Where S in lead I is the main ventricular wave (type a, lead I), S II is greater than that of S III. When R is predominant in lead I (type b), then the amplitude of S II is less than that of S III. If S II and S III are equal, then R or S waves are absent in lead I. The amplitudes of most of the waves are shown in Table 5–2 for leads II and III and also for leads I and aVF.

**Electrical axis.** The electrical axis represents the mean or average electromotive force (magnitude of depolarization and repolarization) acting in an average direction during the period of electrical activity of the heart. It is a vector quantity in that it has direction and magnitude. Axes for any of the

waves may be determined by measuring the amplitude of complexes in any two of the limb leads and plotting these values. Leads I and II are usually used for human ECG's and leads II and III for the chicken, for in the latter the amplitude for all waves in lead I is too low for accurate measurement.

*Orthogonal lead system.* The previous lead systems have dealt with ECG's taken only in the frontal plane ($Y$ axis). Leads may also be taken in the horizontal ($X$ axis) and sagittal planes ($Z$ axis). These orthogonal lead systems are involved in obtaining electrical axes or vectors in three different planes. Each orthogonal lead system or plane is perpendicular to each of the others and these should intersect in the same plane in the heart. Szabuniewicz (1967) used the following orthogonal leads in the chicken: frontal *(Y)* plane, leads I (limb) and aVF *(Y)*; horizontal plane *(X)*, I and $V_{10}$ (unipolar lead attached at the base of the third dorsal vertebrae); sagittal or $Z$ plane, $V_{10}$ and aVF. Mean spatial vectors involving these leads have been determined in turkeys by Krista *et al.* (1970).

Electrical axes for chicken ECG's taken in the frontal plane are shown in Table 5–3. An RS axis of −90° (see Figure 5–9) means that the mean electromotive force is directed upward and parallel to the long axis of the body. Seventy-four percent of the chickens studied had RS axes averaging −74.04° and 26% had RS axes averaging −102.11° (between 11 and 12 o'clock). The normal RS axis in the human electrocardiogram ranges from 0 to +90°.

The electrical axes for T are grouped according to the direction of T in lead I (Table 5–3). The

118

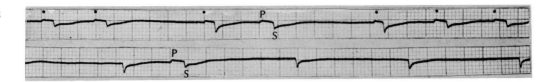

5-12 Partial (upper tracing) and complete sinoatrial (SA) block (lower) with slow heart rate (100 per minute) and mild sinus arrhythmia.

more nearly the electrical axis parallels a given lead line, the higher the amplitude of the waves; when the axis runs almost perpendicular to the lead line (as in lead I of the chicken), the amplitude is low. This can be demonstrated experimentally by rotating the heart on its anterioposterior axis to the left or right (Sturkie, 1948).

*Electrical axes in three planes.* Employing orthogonal leads I, aVF, and $V_{10}$, Szabuniewicz (1967) recorded ECG's taken in three planes for each of the waves in lead I and aVF (Y axis); leads I and $V_{10}$ (X axis); and aVF and $V_{10}$ (Z axis), as follows:

|  | QRS | P | T |
|---|---|---|---|
| Frontal plane *(Y)* | −77.1° | +43° | +59° |
| Sagittal plane *(Z)* | −55.4° | +130° | +132° |
| Horizontal plane *(X)* | +72.4° | −43° | −50° |

Krista *et al.* (1970) reported differences in the spatial vectors of hypertensive and hypotensive turkeys.

**Sex differences in the ECG.** There is a sex difference in the ECG of chickens characterized by a greater tendency toward fusion of P and T waves in leads II and III in females and by the greater amplitude of all waves in the male ECG. The mean amplitude of the RS complex in lead II is 0.530 mV for males and 0.247 mV for females (Sturkie and Hunsaker, 1957). The female sex hormone, estrogen, plays a role in this difference. Administration of estrogen to males over a 2- or 3-week period depresses the amplitude of all waves approximately 35%. It is known that certain organs of the body are good conductors and others poor conductors of cardioelectric force. If the heart of the bird is exposed by removing the sternum, sternal ribs, coracoids, clavicle, and the tissues attached thereto, the amplitude of all waves in the limb leads is increased anywhere from twofold to threefold (Sturkie, 1948). This suggests that the sternum and pectoral muscles influence the spread of cardioelectropotentials. Douglas (1960) has suggested that the air sacs of avian species likewise influence the spread.

## Abnormal Electrocardiograms

Heart disorders as revealed by the electrocardiogram appear to cause few deaths in chickens during the first year of life. Serial ECG's were made on 72 adult female White Leghorns from 5 months (maturity) to 18 months of age (Sturkie, 1949). Although 37% of the birds died during this period, only 5% of these exhibited heart abnormalities that might have caused death.

**Mineral deficiencies.** Acute potassium deficiency in growing chicks produces a high percentage of abnormal ECG's (70%) and 100% mortality within 2–4 weeks (Sturkie, 1950, 1952). Most of these ECG disorders are concerned with the rhythm and conduction of the heartbeat. They include partial and complete atrioventricular block, partial and complete sinoatrial block, sinus arrhythmia and marked sinus slowing, and premature nodal and ventricular systoles. Some examples are shown in Figures 5–12, 5–13, and 5–14.

Pathologic lesions in the AV node or bundle or in the SA node may cause AV and SA block. Gross lesions have not been observed in the hearts of potassium-deficient chickens, and it appears that the blocks result from a functional rather than a pathologic disturbance in conduction. In such cases

5-13 Nodal rhythm and AV dissociation in the chicken, produced by potassium deficiency in the diet.

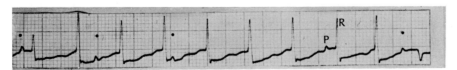

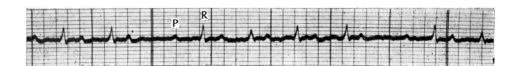

it may be abolished by administration of atropine, a cholinergic blocker. In potassium-deficient chicks, the ECG's of which exhibited AV block and premature systoles, atropine and also diethylaminoethanol were effective in reverting the ECG's to normal. The requirement of potassium for the bird heart may be higher than for mammals, because the blood of birds contains more potassium than that of mammals.

**Excess potassium and cadmium.** Diving ducks, on emerging from the dive, exhibit changes in the ECG characterized by elevated and peaked T waves; Anderson (1964) has attributed these to a hyperpotassemia, which he demonstrated.

Cadmium is known to produce infarction and hypertrophy of the heart. After 15 daily injections of cadmium sulfate to chickens (Sturkie, 1973) the injections were discontinued and ECG's were run for 13–40 days thereafter. Deviations in the ECG's consisted mainly of T-wave changes. Normally the ECG exhibits an upright T in leads II, III, and aVF and inverted T's or RS complexes in leads aVR and aVL (see Figure 5–15). The changes in comparison with normal ECG's are as follows, where + is an upright T wave and − is a negative one.

|     | Normal | Abnormal |
|-----|--------|----------|
| II  | +      | −        |
| III | +      | −        |
| aVR | −      | +        |
| aVL | −      | +        |
| aVF | +      | −        |

Other abnormalities included AV block. Some of the abnormalities persisted for as long as 40 days. The changes are characteristic of varying degrees of myocardial infarction.

**Isoproterenol necrosis.** Repeated and excessive dosages of isoproterenol (McGrath, 1972) produces myocardial infarction and enlarged hearts in rats and *Coturnix* (quails). Electrocardiograms run on quails (Sturkie, unpublished) revealed ECG changes almost identical to those reported for cadmium excess. These changes in T waves were progressive, and the first sign of myocardial damage was evident in the ECG.

5–14 An example of partial atrioventricular (AV) block and prolonged AV conduction in the electrocardiogram of a chicken (lead I). Every fifth ventricular beat (R wave) is blocked. The P–R interval following the dropped beat is shortened, and the interval increases on most successive beats (Wenckebath's phenomenon). (From Sturkie *et al.*, 1954.)

**Vitamin deficiencies.** Acute thiamine deficiency in pigeons results in sinus arrhythmia, bradycardia, and AV block, but chronic deficiency of the vitamin rarely produces heart abnormalities (Swank and Bessey, 1941). Deficiencies of niacin, riboflavin, and vitamins A and D have no effect on the ECG of the chicken (Sturkie, unpublished).

Further studies by Sturkie *et al.* (1954) show that deficiencies in the diet of vitamin E alone, of E and B complex vitamins, or of B complex vitamins (mainly thiamine) produce abnormal ECG's. The principal abnormalities of the vitamin E-deficient birds included right axis deviation, premature ventricular systoles, sinus arrhythmia, and elevated S–T segments. Right axis deviation was rare in thiamine-deficient birds, and the most prominent ab-

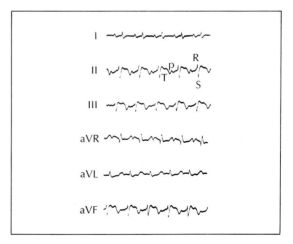

5–15 Electrocardiogram of chickens administered cadmium sulfate. The leads are indicated. Note that T wave is inverted in II, III, and AVF instead of upright (compare with Figure 5–11).

120 normalities observed were premature ventricular systoles and sinus arrhythmia.

**Diseases and ECG's.** Round heart disease is a condition first reported in chickens and later in turkeys, where it causes many heart abnormalities and death (see Hunsaker *et al.*, 1971). The disease occurs in turkeys during the first few weeks of life. The heart is extremely enlarged, particularly the right ventricle, giving the heart apex a rounded rather than a pointed appearance.

The characteristic change in the ECG is one indicating a marked shift in the electrical axis to the right such that the mean RS axis in the frontal plane averages $+70°$ compared to $-85°$ for the normal turkey. This represents a tremendous shift in the axes. Such shift produces significant changes in the configuration of most of the waves, particularly RS complexes and T waves. The RS wave is elevated or the original S wave has become an R wave, evidence of an axis shift. The T wave is usually depressed or inverted in some of the leads. Sturkie (unpublished) also found right axis deviation in turkeys suffering from round heart disease and also some evidence of myocardial infarction not unlike that previously reported and produced by cadmium and isoproterenol.

Experimentally produced *Escherichia coli* infection in chickens causes myocarditis and changes in ECG characterized by a decrease in the R wave and an increase in the S wave in leads I and aVF and by changes in the electrical axes (Gross, 1966).

# REFERENCES

Abati, A. (1975). A comparison of the effect of anoxia on left ventricular function in the isolated perfused heart of the chicken (a non-flying bird), the pigeon ( a flying bird), and the duck (a diving bird). Ph.D. thesis, Rutgers University, New Brunswick, New Jersey.

Andersen, H. T. (1965). Hyperpotassemia and electrocardiographic changes in the duck during prolonged diving. *Acta Physiol. Scand., 63,* 292.

Butler, P. J., and D. R. Jones. (1968). Onset of, and recovery from diving bradycardia in ducks. *J. Physiol. (London), 196,* 255.

Cain, J. R., and U. K. Abbott. (1970). A system for diurnal heart rate measurement in chickens. *Poultry Sci., 49,* 1085.

Cogger, E. A., R. E. Otis, and R. K. Ringer. (1974). Heart rates in restrained and freely moving Japanese quail via radiotelemetry. *Poultry Sci., 53,* 430.

Cohen, D. N., and L. H. Pitts. (1968). Vagal and sympathetic components of conditioned cardio-acceleration in pigeons. *Brain Res., 9,* 15.

Cohen, D. N., A. M. Schnall, R. L. Macdonald, and L. H. Pitts. (1970). Medullary cells of origin of vagal cardioinhibitory fibers in the pigeon. Anatomical studies of peripheral vagus nerve and the dorsal motor nucleus. *J. Comp. Neurol., 140,* 299.

Davies, F. (1930). The conducting system of birds heart. *J. Anat., 64,* 9.

Douglas, S. D. (1960). Correlation between surface electrocardiogram and air sac morphology in the White Leghorn rooster. *Am. J. Physiol., 199,* 355.

Drennan, M. R. (1927). The auriculo-ventricular bundle in the birds heart. *Brit. Med. J., 1,* 132.

Durfee, W. K. (1963). Cardiovascular reflex mechanisms in the fowl. Ph.D. thesis, Rutgers University, New Brunswick, New Jersey.

El-Ackad, T., M. J. Meyer, and P. D. Sturkie. (1974). Inotropic and chronotropic actions of histamine in avian heart. *Fed. Proc., 33,* 585.

Evans, J. H. (1972). A method of recording heart rate of chicken embryo. *Physiol. Behav. 9,* 131.

Ferguson, T. M., D. H. Miller, J. W. Bradley, and R. L. Atkinson. (1969). Blood pressure and heart rate of turkeys, 17–21 months of age. *Poultry Sci., 48,* 1478.

Flick, D. F. (1967). Effects of age and diet on heart rate of the developing cockerel. *Poultry Sci., 46,* 890.

Folkow, B., and L. R. Yonce. (1967). The negative inotropic effect of vagal stimulation on the heart ventricles of the duck. *Acta Physiol. Scand., 71,* 77.

Furnival, C. M., R. J. Linden, and H. M. Snow. (1973). The inotropic effect on the heart of stimulating the vagus in the dog, duck, and toad. *J. Physiol. (London) 230,* 155.

Girard, H. (1973). Arterial pressure in chick embryos. *Am. J. Physiol., 224,* 454.

Gross, W. B. (1966). Electrocardiographic changes of *Escherichia coli* infected birds *Am. J. Vet. Res., 27,* 1427.

Hunsaker, W. K., A. Robertson, and S. E. Magwood. (1971). The effect of round heart disease on the electrocardiogram of turkey poults. *Poultry Sci., 50,* 1712.

Ishima, Y. (1968). The effect of tetrodotoxin and sodium substitution on the action of the embryonic chicken heart. *Proc. Jap. Acad., 44,* 170.

Johansen, K., and T. Aakhus. (1963). Central cardiovascular responses to submersion asphyxia in the duck. *Am. J. Physiol., 205,* 1167.

Johansen, K., and O. B. Reite. (1964). Cardiovascular responses to vagal stimulation and cardioaccelerator nerve blockade in birds. *Comp. Biochem. Physiol. 12,* 474.

Jones, D. R., and K. Johansen. (1972). The blood vascular system of birds. In "Avian Biology," Vol. 2 (D. S. Farner and J. R. King, Eds.). New York: Academic Press, p. 157.

Kisch, B. (1949). Electrocardiographic studies in sea-gulls. *Exp. Med. Surg., 7,* 345.

Kisch, B. (1951). The electrocardiogram of birds (chicken, duck, pigeon). *Exp. Med. Surg., 9,* 103.

Krespi, V., and W. W. Sleator, Jr. (1966). A study of the ontogeny of action potentials in chick embryo hearts. *Life Sci., 5,* 1441.

Krista, L. M., E. F. Jankus, B. E. Waibel, J. H. Souther, R. N. Shoffner, and G. J. Quarfoth. (1970). Comparison of electrocardiogram of hypertensive and hypotensive male turkeys. *Poultry Sci., 49,* 700.

Lamb, L. E. (1957). "Fundamentals of Electrocardiography and Vectorcardiography." Springfield, Ill.: Charles C. Thomas.

Langille, B. L. and D. R. Jones. (1975). Central cardiovascular dynamics of ducks. *Am. J. Physiol., 228,* 1856.

Lee, W. C., L. P. McCarty, W. W. Zodrow, and F. E. Shideman. (1960). Cardiostimulant action of certain ganglionic stimulants on embryonic chick heart. *J. Pharmacol. Exp. Ther., 130,* 30.

Lewis, A. R. (1967). Resting heart rate and respiratory rates of small birds. *Auk, 84,* 131.

Lewis, T. (1915). The spread of the excitatory process in the vertebrate heart. V: The bird's heart. *Phil. Trans. Roy. Soc. London, 207,* 298.

Lieberman, M., and A. Paes de Carvalho. (1965). The spread of excitation in the embryonic chick heart. *J. Gen. Physiol., 49,* 365.

Lin, Y. C., P. D. Sturkie, and J. Tummons. (1970). Effects of cardiac sympathectomy, reserpine and environmental temperatures on catecholamines, in the chicken heart. *Can. J. Physiol. Pharmacol., 48,* 182.

Macdonald, R. L., and D. H. Cohen. (1970). Cells of origin of sympathetic pre-and post-ganglionic cardio-accelerator fibers in the pigeon. *J. Comp. Neurol., 140,* 343.

McGrath, J. J. (1972). Experimental cardiac necrosis in the Japanese quail. *Proc. Soc. Exp. Biol. Med., 139*, 1334.

Mangold, E. (1919). Electrographische Untersuchungen des Erregungsverlaufes im Vogelherzen. *Arch. Ges. Physiol (Pflügers), 175*, 327.

Michal, F., F. Emmett, and R. H. Thorp. (1967). A study of drug action on the developing avian cardiac muscle. *Comp. Biochem. Physiol., 22*, 563.

Moore, E. N. (1965). Experimental electrophysiological studies on Avian hearts. *Ann. N. Y. Acad. Sci., 127*, Art.1, 127

Owen, R. B., Jr., (1969). Heart rate, a measure of metabolism of blue winged teal. *Comp. Biochem. Physiol., 31*, 431.

Poppano, A. J. (1972). Increased susceptibility to blockade by tetrodotoxin during embryonic development. *Circ. Res., 31*, 379.

Purton, M. D. (1971). Pressure changes during the avian cardiac cycle. *J. Anat., 108*, 620 (Proceedings).

Rakalska, Z. (1964). Electrocardiogram of young cockerels. *Bull. Vet. Inst. Pulawy (Poland), 5*, 145.

Ringer, R. K., H. S. Weiss, and P. D. Sturkie. (1955). Effect of sex and age on blood pressure in the duck and pigeon. *Am. J. Physiol., 183*, 141.

Ringer, R. K., H. S. Weiss, and P. D. Sturkie. (1957). Heart rate of chickens as influenced by age and gonadal hormones. *Am. J. Physiol., 191*, 145.

Soliman, F. F. A., and T. M. Huston. (1972). The photoelectric plethysmography technique for recording heart rate in chick embryos. *Poultry Sci., 51*, 651.

Speralakis, N., and K. Shigenobu. (1972). Changes in membrane properties of chick embryonic hearts during development. *J. Gen. Physiol., 60*, 430.

Ssinelnikow, R. (1928). Die herznerven der vogel. *Z. Anat. Entwickl., 86*, 540.

Sturkie, P. D. (1948). Effects of changes in position of the heart of the chicken on the electrocardiogram. *Am. J. Physiol., 154*, 251.

Sturkie, P. D. (1949). The electrocardiogram of the chicken. *Am. J. Vet. Res., 10*, 168.

Sturkie, P. D. (1950). Abnormal electrocardiograms of chickens produced by potassium deficiency and effects of certain drugs on the abnormalities. *Am. J. Physiol., 162*, 538.

Sturkie, P. D. (1952). Further studies of potassium deficiency in the chicken. *Poultry Sci., 31*, 648.

Sturkie, P. D. (1963). Heart rate of chickens determined by radiotelemetry during light and dark periods. *Poultry Sci., 72*, 797.

Sturkie, P. D. (1965). "Avian Physiology," 2nd Ed. Ithaca, N.Y.: Cornell University.

Sturkie, P. D. (1970). Effects of reserpine on nervous control of heart rate in chickens. *Comp. Gen. Pharmacol. 1*, 336.

Sturkie, P. D. (1973). Effects of cadmium on ECG, blood pressure, and hematocrit of chickens. *Avian Dis., 17*, 196.

Sturkie, P. D., and J. Chillseyzn. (1972). Heart rate changes with age in chickens. *Poultry Sci., 51*, 906.

Sturkie, P. D., and W. G. Hunsaker. (1957). Role of estrogen in sex difference of the electrocardiogram of the chicken. *Proc. Soc. Exp. Biol. Med., 94*, 731.

Sturkie, P. D., and D. W. Poorvin. (1973). The avian neurotransmitter. *Proc. Soc. Exp. Biol. Med., 143*, 644.

Sturkie, P. D., E. P. Singsen, L. D. Matterson, A. Kozeff, and E. L. and Jungherr. (1954). The effects of dietary deficiencies of vitamin E and the B complex vitamins on the electrocardiogram of chickens. *J. Vet. Res., 15*, 457.

Sturkie, P. D., Yu-Chong-Lin, and N. Ossorio. (1970). Effects of acclimatization to heat and cold on heart rate in chickens. *Am. J. Physiol., 219*, 34.

Swank, R. L., and O. A. Bessey. (1941). Avian thiamine deficiency: Characteristic symptoms and their pathogenesis. *J. Nutr., 22*, 77.

Szabuniewicz, M. (1967). The electrocardiogram of the chicken. *Southwestern Vet., 20*, (4).

Tigerstedt, R. (1921). "Physiologie des Kreislaufes", vol. 2. Berlin and Leipzig.

Tummons, J. L. (1970). Nervous control of heart rate in the domestic fowl. Ph.D. thesis, Rutgers University, New Brunswick, New Jersey.

Tummons, J. L., and P. D. Sturkie. (1968). Cardioaccelerator nerve stimulation in chickens. *Life Sci., 7*, 377.

Tummons, J. L., and P. D. Sturkie. (1969). Nervous control of heart rate during excitement in the adult White Leghorn cock. *Am. J. Physiol., 216*, 1437.

Tummons, J. L., and P. D. Sturkie. (1970). Beta adrenergic and cholinergic stimulants from the cardioaccelerator nerve of the domestic fowl. *Z. Vergl. Physiol., 68*, 268.

Vogel, J. A., and P. D. Sturkie. (1963). Effects of starvation on the cardiovascular system of chickens. *Proc. Soc. Exp. Biol. Med., 112*, 111.

Whittow, G. C., P. D. Sturkie, and G. Stein, Jr. (1965). Cardiovascular changes in restrained chickens. *Poultry Sci. 44*, 1452.

Woods, J. J. (1971). Studies on the distribution and action of serotonin in the avian cardiovascular system. Ph.D. thesis, Rutgers University, New Brunswick, New Jersey.

Yousuf, N. (1965). The conducting system of the heart of the house sparrow, *Passer domesticus. Anat. Rec., 152*, 235.

# 6

# Respiration

## M. R. Fedde

The respiratory system has the primary functions of providing oxygen ($O_2$) to the blood, removing carbon dioxide ($CO_2$) from the blood, and eliminating heat from the body. This chapter is concerned only with its function in the exchange of gases between air and blood. The topics covered include: (1) the structure of the system; (2) the mechanisms that force gases past exchange surfaces; (3) the factors involved in exchange of $O_2$ and $CO_2$ between gas and blood; (4) the reaction of these gases with blood; and (5) the manner in which the system is controlled.

## STRUCTURE OF THE RESPIRATORY SYSTEM

### Adult Morphology

The morphology of the avian respiratory system, especially the lung and extensions therefrom, is markedly different from that of other vertebrates (Figure 6–1). The general features of the system are presented here, but details of the respiratory systems of many species of birds may be obtained from King (1966a, 1975), King and Molony (1971), and Duncker (1971, 1972, 1974).

The upper airways originate at the external nares and mouth and continue into the nasal and buccal cavities. These cavities communicate with the oropharynx and the larynx, which continues into the trachea. The trachea branches at the syrinx, the vocal organ, into two extrapulmonary primary bronchi that enter the lungs. The lungs are rather rigid structures from which emanate thin-walled air sacs. The air sacs fill most of the body cavity not occupied by other viscera and also penetrate into

the interior of many bones and subcutaneous regions outside the coelom. The gas volumes of the lungs and various air sacs in domestic chickens and ducks are shown in Table 6–1.

The lungs are the gas-exchanging organs of the respiratory system. They do not expand and contract during the respiratory cycle, as do mammalian lungs. Instead, gas moves through the avian lungs during the respiratory cycle, on its way to and from the air sacs. The tubular system of a lung consists of three bronchial subdivisions; the intrapulmonary part of the primary bronchus, various secondary bronchi (Table 6–2), and many parabronchi.

The general arrangement of the primary and secondary bronchi in most birds is shown in Figure 6–2, although there is some variation among species. The extrapulmonary primary bronchus enters the hilus of the lung on the septal (ventromedial) surface; from that point on, it is called the intrapulmonary primary bronchus. The first set of secondary bronchi (medioventral bronchi) arises near the hilus. The medioventral bronchi branch over the septal surface of the lung and parabronchi emanate from their surfaces. The cervical air sac arises from the first medioventral bronchus. The first, second, and third medioventral bronchi form the main connections to the clavicular air sac, whereas the third medioventral bronchus forms the main connection to the cranial thoracic air sac. These air sacs form a cranial group, all of which have a direct connection to a medioventral bronchus.

The intrapulmonary primary bronchus then curves through the lung toward the costal (dorsolateral) surface and gives off a second set of secondary bronchi (mediodorsal bronchi) from its dorsal surface. The mediodorsal bronchi branch

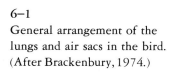

6–1

General arrangement of the lungs and air sacs in the bird. (After Brackenbury, 1974.)

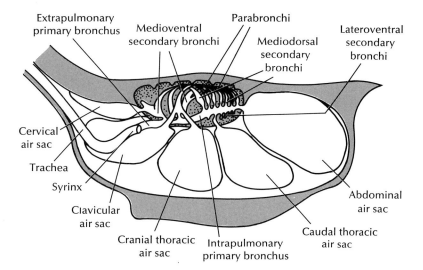

*Table 6–1* Volumes of lungs and air sacs

| | Species: | *Gallus domesticus* | | | | | | Domestic duck |
|---|---|---|---|---|---|---|---|---|
| | Reference: | King (1966a) | | Burton and Smith (1968) | | Scheid and Piiper (1969) | Duncker (1972)[a] | Scheid et al. (1974b) |
| | Sex: | M | F | M | F | F | – | – |
| No. of birds | | 10 | 10 | 9 | 8 | 13 | – | 4 |
| Weight (kg) | | 3.7 | 2.9 | 2.3 | 1.7 | 1.6 | – | 2.5 |
| Anatomical state | | Maximum capacities | | Recently killed | | Spontaneous respiration | – | Spontaneous respiration |
| Method of study | | Resin cast | | Bouyancy | | Inert gas washout | Silicone rubber casts | Inert gas washout |
| Trachea | | – | – | – | – | – | 1.3% | – |
| Both cervical sacs (ml) | | 30 | 20 | – | – | – | 2.7% | – |
| Clavicular sac (ml) | | 95 | 55 | – | – | – | 8.0% | 113.3 |
| Both cranial thoracic sacs (ml) | | 90 | 50 | – | – | – | 16.0% | 108.6 |
| Both caudal thoracic sacs (ml) | | 30 | 24 | – | – | – | 12.3% | 143.2 |
| Both abdominal sacs (ml) | | 180 | 110 | – | – | – | 48.5% | 92.2 |
| Both lungs (ml) | | 70 | 35 | 18.6 | 14.6 | – | 11.2% | – |
| Skeleton (ml) | | 7 | 4 | – | – | – | – | – |
| Total respiratory system vol. (ml) | | 502 | 298 | – | – | 170 | – | 531.5 |

[a]Volumes are percentages of the total respiratory system volume.

*Table 6–2*  *Terminologies most recently used for the secondary bronchi in the avian lung*

| King (1966a) | Duncker (1971) | ICAAN[a] |
|---|---|---|
| Craniomediales | Ventrobronchi | Medioventrales |
| Caudodorsales | Dorsobronchi | Mediodorsales |
| Caudoventrales | Laterobronchi | Lateroventrales |
| Caudolaterales | – | Laterodorsales |

[a]Terminology adopted by the International Committee on Avian Anatomical Nomenclature at Liverpool, England, July 22–26, 1974.

over the costal surface of the lung, with parabronchi emanating from their surfaces. The parabronchi from those two sets of secondary bronchi join to form a series of rather parallel tubes called the "paleopulmo" (Figure 6–3a). These are the only parabronchi in penguins and emus, birds that have the simplest bronchial arrangement found so far in any avian species.

A third set of secondary bronchi (lateroventral bronchi) leave the intrapulmonary primary bronchus from the side opposite to the mediodorsal bronchi (Figure 6–2). These bronchi pass along the ventral part of the costal surface of the lung and the second (sometimes the first or third) forms the direct connection to the caudal thoracic air sac. The intrapulmonary primary bronchus then courses to the caudal border of the lung and enters the abdominal air sac. The caudal thoracic and abdominal air sacs therefore form a caudal group of air sacs that arises from the lateroventral bronchi and the intrapulmonary primary bronchus.

In most birds, an additional set of secondary bronchi (laterodorsal bronchi, not shown in Figure 6–2) and an additional network of parabronchi are present (Figure 6–3b). The additional network of parabronchi has been called the "neopulmo." The neopulmo is poorly developed in such birds as storks, cormorants, and cranes, where it arises from the intrapulmonary primary bronchus and the lateroventral bronchi and connects to the caudal thoracic and abdominal air sacs. It is more extensive in pigeons, ducks, geese and gulls, where parabronchi may originate from the initial segments of the mediodorsal bronchi. In these birds, the main trunks of the mediodorsal secondary bronchi are visible on the costal surface of the lung. In woodcocks, pheasants, quail, chickens, and songbirds, the neopulmo is so extensive that the secondary bronchi are displaced into the substance of the lung and are no longer visible from the outer surface. The neopulmo also has connections to the clavicular and cranial thoracic air sacs in those species. However, even in birds in which it is most extensively developed, the neopulmo never exceeds 20–25% of the total lung volume.

At various places on the surface of the lung, called ostia, parabronchi are collected by tubes, called saccobronchi. The saccobronchi are similar in caliber to secondary bronchi and connect to the air sacs. These parabronchial connections to the air sacs have been referred to as recurrent bronchi in past literature.

There may be 300–500 parabronchi in the lung of a chicken (King and Cowie, 1969). They range in length from 1 to 4 cm (Payne, 1960). The variation in length occurs in the neopulmonic parabronchi

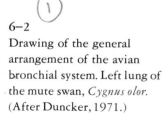

6–2

Drawing of the general arrangement of the avian bronchial system. Left lung of the mute swan, *Cygnus olor.* (After Duncker, 1971.)

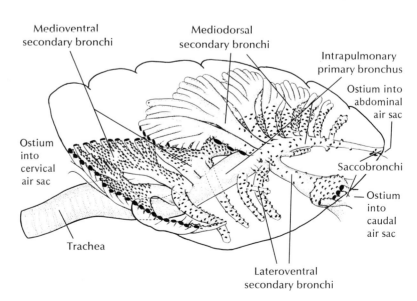

Medioventral secondary bronchi

Mediodorsal secondary bronchi

Intrapulmonary primary bronchus

Ostium into abdominal air sac

Ostium into cervical air sac

Saccobronchi

Ostium into caudal air sac

Trachea

Lateroventral secondary bronchi

126

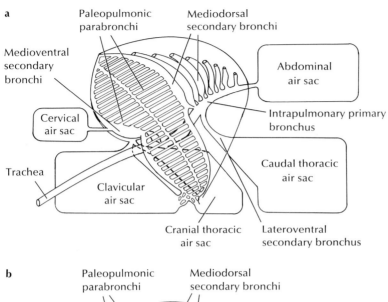

a

Paleopulmonic
parabronchi

Mediodorsal
secondary bronchi

Medioventral
secondary
bronchi

Abdominal
air sac

Cervical
air sac

Intrapulmonary primary
bronchus

Trachea

Clavicular
air sac

Caudal thoracic
air sac

Cranial thoracic
air sac

Lateroventral
secondary bronchus

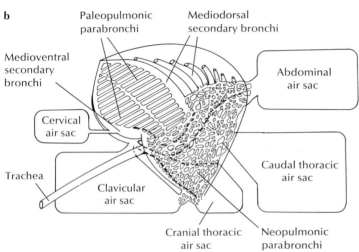

b

Paleopulmonic
parabronchi

Mediodorsal
secondary bronchi

Medioventral
secondary
bronchi

Abdominal
air sac

Cervical
air sac

Trachea

Clavicular
air sac

Caudal thoracic
air sac

Cranial thoracic
air sac

Neopulmonic
parabronchi

6-3
Scheme of the development of
the parabronchial system in
birds. (a) Only paleopulmonic
parabronchi are present (penguin
and emu). (b) Highly developed
neopulmonic parabronchial
net in addition to paleopulmonic
parabronchi (woodcocks,
pheasants, quail, chicken, and
song birds). (After Duncker,
1972.)

but the length and the diameter of the paleopulmonic parabronchi are constant throughout the
lung of a given species and range between 0.5 and
2.0 mm in different species (Duncker, 1974).

A series of tubular subdivisions (atria and
infundibula) extend from the walls of the parabronchi. The smallest set of tubes in the lung, the
air capillaries, invaginate the parabronchial mantle
from the infundibula. The air capillaries are an-
astomosing cylindrical tubes with diameters ranging
from 3 $\mu$m in songbirds to 10 $\mu$m in penguins,
swans, and coots (Duncker, 1971). Gas exchange occurs across the walls of the air capillaries, which
course in a radial direction from the parabronchial
lumen toward the periphery of the tissue mantle.
Likewise, blood capillaries from branches of the
pulmonary artery arise at the periphery of the tissue
mantle of a parabronchus and course toward the

lumen. The interlacing of blood and air capillaries
provides a large surface area for gas exchange. The
arterialized blood from the blood capillaries is
then collected in venules just under the epithelium
of the parabronchial lumen and eventually reaches
the pulmonary vein.

The avian lung contains an abundance of smooth
muscle. Circular, oblique, and longitudinal layers
of smooth muscle are in the primary bronchus and
initial segments of secondary bronchi. The musculature further distal in the secondary bronchi is
organized in narrow, spiral bands that are especially thick where they surround the origin of the parabronchi. The smooth muscle appears to be able to
reduce the diameter of the parabronchial lumen
and to close the lumen of the atria when strongly
activated by acetylcholine or efferent neural activity in the vagi (King and Cowie, 1969).

## Embryological Development

The first appearance of the lungs of the chick embryo comes in the early part of the third day of development (Locy and Larsell, 1916a,b). At their beginning, the primitive lungs are paired and consist of two shallow pouches that open widely into the floor of the pharynx. The bronchial system develops from the lung pouches, which are lined by endoderm. At the end of the fourth day of incubation, the trachea becomes differentiated from the caudal portion of the laryngotracheal groove, and at the distal end of the lung tube there is an enlargement that later becomes the abdominal air sac.

The secondary bronchi begin to develop in the sixth day. On the ninth day of development, the lung has increased in size dorsoventrally and occupies a more lateral position in the thoracic cavity. The lung has begun to press against the ribs and exhibits shallow furrows where the lung substance has grown around the bodies of the ribs. The five air sacs are formed and project beyond the surface of the lung. On the tenth day, outgrowths from the abdominal and caudal thoracic air sacs appear (called "recurrent bronchi" by Locy and Larsell, 1916a,b), which eventually ramify and anastomose with parabronchi in various parts of the lung. By 10½ days of incubation, similar outgrowths appear from all air sacs except the cervical sacs.

The parabronchi are fully formed by the eighteenth day of incubation, and the air capillaries are fully developed between the nineteenth and twenty-first days of development. There is no "bronchial tree" in the adult birds' lung; instead, there is established a network of intercommunicating passages forming bronchial circuits.

## MECHANICS OF BREATHING

### Forces that Move Gases Through the Lungs

As indicated earlier, the avian respiratory system is differentiated into two components: the lungs, which function in gas exchange, and the air sacs, which function to move gas through the lungs during inspiration and expiration. The forces required to move gas through the lungs are derived from the action of the respiratory muscles (Table 6–3). The inspiratory muscles act to increase the volume of the body cavity (and therefore of the air sacs) and thereby create subatmospheric pressure within the sacs. Air then enters the mouth and nostrils of the bird and passes through the lungs and into the air sacs. Conversely, the expiratory muscles, which are active throughout expiration, reduce the volume of the body cavity and thereby increase the pressure in the air sacs, forcing gas from the sacs back through the lungs and out the nostrils and mouth. The air sacs therefore function as bellows, the pressure and volume are modulated by the muscles of respiration, with the result that gas is forced through the lung during both inspiration and expiration.

Through the action of the respiratory muscles, the volume of the body cavity is altered by movement in both the dorsoventral and lateral direc-

*Table 6–3* *Respiratory muscles of the chicken[a]*

| Inspiratory | Expiratory |
| --- | --- |
| Scalenus | External intercostals of fifth and sixth spaces |
| External intercostals (except in fifth and sixth spaces) | Internal intercostals of third to sixth spaces |
| Internal intercostal in second space | Costisternalis pars minor |
| Costisternalis pars major | External abdominal oblique |
| Levatores costarum | Internal abdominal oblique |
| Serratus dorsalis | Transversus abdominis |
| | Rectus abdominis |
| | Serratus ventralis |
| | Costopulmonary muscles |

[a]Data from electromyographic studies of Kadono *et al.* (1963) and Fedde *et al.* (1964a,b,c). For innervation of the muscles, see deWet *et al.* (1967).

128 tions (Figure 6–4). The expansion of the cavity during inspiration results from the arrangement of the two articulations of each vertebral rib with the thoracic vertebra, so that when the rib is moved cranially by inspiratory muscles it must also move ventrally and laterally (Zimmer, 1935; King and Molony, 1971). The sternum, coracoids, and furcula are simultaneously moved ventrally and cranially, pivoting at the shoulder joint (Figure 6–4).

Birds have no muscular diaphragm as exists in mammals and the thoracic and abdominal cavities are functionally continuous. The lungs do not collapse when air enters these cavities (pneumothorax), as occurs during certain common surgical procedures (i.e., caponization). Furthermore, by cannulation of one or more of the air sacs on each side of the bird, the lungs can be unidirectionally, artificially ventilated by passing air into the trachea, through the lungs, and out to the atmosphere through the air sac cannulae (Fedde *et al.*, 1969). Equally effective ventilation results if air is passed into the air sac cannulae and out through the trachea. Air sac diverticula extend into many of the bones of birds. If the humerus is fractured, air can move freely from the atmosphere through the humerus to the lungs and into other air sacs, allowing the bird to ventilate the lungs even though the trachea is occluded.

Intrathoracic pressure changes during a respiratory cycle in birds are also considerably different from those of mammals. Those pressures are essentially the same as those inside the air sacs and are higher than atmospheric pressure during expiration (0.60 cm $H_2O$ at midexpiration in anesthetized chickens) and subatmospheric during inspiration (−1.40 cm $H_2O$ at midinspiration).

## Impedances to Breathing

**Deformation of the thoracic cage and abdominal wall.** Work is required by both the inspiratory and expiratory muscles to overcome the elasticity of the thoracic cage and abdominal wall. Both inspiration and expiration are active processes and depend on contraction of respiratory muscles. When all respiratory muscles are relaxed, the sternum rests approximately midway between its position at the peak of inspiration and that at the peak of expiration. This "resting" position suggests that elastic recoil of the thoracic cage aids the inspiratory muscles during the first half of inspiration and aids the expiratory muscles during the first half of expiration. Nevertheless, the inspiratory muscles become active near the beginning of inspiration and the expiratory muscles become active slightly before the end of inspiration. This way, the alternate action of these muscles creates a smooth transition between the two phases of the cycle (Fedde *et al.*, 1964a,b).

The compliance (volume change produced by a unit of pressure change) of the respiratory system is a measure of its elasticity. Because the lungs in birds are relatively stiff, the compliance is mainly determined by the air sacs and surrounding body walls. Compliance of the respiratory system has been measured in chickens with their skeletal muscles relaxed by succinylcholine (Scheid and Piiper, 1969). A maximum compliance of 9.5 ml/cm $H_2O$ occurred in the transmural pressure range of −10 to 0 cm $H_2O$, whereas 6.5 ml/cm $H_2O$ occurred in the pressure range of 0–10 cm $H_2O$. The total compliance of the respiratory system of *Columba livia* (domestic pigeon) is 2.75 ml/cm $H_2O$ over a trans-

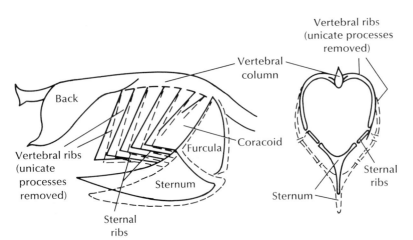

6–4

Changes in the position of the thoracic skeleton during breathing in a standing bird. Solid lines represent thoracic position at the end of expiration; dotted lines, at the end of inspiration. (After Zimmer, 1935).

mural pressure range of 0–6 cm $H_2O$ (Kampe and Crawford, 1973).

**Deformation of the lungs and air sacs.** Unlike the extremely elastic mammalian lungs, the avian parabronchial lungs are quite rigid. Definitive data demonstrating the degree of expansion of the lungs during inspiration is lacking, although various opinions have been expressed (see King, 1966a, for review). Duncker (1971) has provided arguments, based both on anatomical data and on consideration of the surface forces at the gas–liquid interface of the air capillaries, that the volume of the avian lung remains constant throughout the respiratory cycle. His arguments imply that the lungs remain slightly stretched at all times by their surrounding structures and, as they do not change in volume, their recoil does not aid the expiratory muscles during expiration.

It is also likely that stretch of the thin-walled air sacs does not require a significant amount of work during inspiration or that their recoil aids expiration.

**Surface forces at the gas–liquid interface.** In mammals, the inspiratory muscles must provide work during expansion of the lungs to overcome the surface forces that exist at the gas–liquid interfaces, especially in the alveoli. The surface forces, therefore, create an impedance to breathing in those animals. A surface-active material (surfactant), secreted onto the inner surface of the alveoli, acts to reduce the surface forces.

A surfactant (phospholipid) also exists in the air capillaries of the avian lung (see Duncker, 1971, for review). However, the diameter of the air capillaries is so small that even with surfactant the surface forces do not become sufficiently low so that available muscular forces can reexpand them during inspiration if their diameters have been reduced during expiration. Air capillaries therefore probably do not change volume during the respiratory cycle and, therefore, surface forces do not provide a significant impedance to breathing in birds. The major function of the surfactant may be to prevent transudation so that air capillaries remain filled with air.

The stability of the air capillaries may result from the forces exerted on a given air capillary by all of its neighbors. Those forces may be visualized using the stress distribution model developed for mammalian lungs (Mead et al., 1970). They could be quite high and would tend to make all air capillaries the same size. They would also prevent a given air capillary from disappearing, if it became slightly smaller, or from rupturing, if it became slightly larger than its neighbors.

**Resistance to air flow.** The tubular component of the respiratory system imposes a resistance to the flow of gas. This resistance is defined as the ratio of driving pressure across the respiratory system (in cm $H_2O$) to gas flow through the system (in liters/sec). Driving pressure can be determined by direct measurement of air sac pressure, and gas flow can be measured with a body plethysmograph or with a pneumotachograph. Airway resistance varies from 4 to 20 cm $H_2O$/liter/sec during quiet breathing in the unanesthetized goose (Cohn and Shannon, 1968; Brackenbury, 1972, 1973) and appears to be greater during inspiration than expiration. Airway resistances of 40 cm $H_2O$/liter/sec at midinspiration and 30 cm $H_2O$/liter/sec at midexpiration have been found for the anesthetized chicken (Fedde, unpublished observations). The higher airway resistance may be caused by the effect of convergence of the caudal part of the intrapulmonary primary bronchus on the inspiratory gas stream, whereas the lower resistance may result from the effect of the divergence of the caudal part of the intrapulmonary primary bronchus on the expiratory gas stream (Brackenbury, 1972).

## Pattern and Direction of Gas Flow Through the Avian Lung

The pattern and direction of gas flow through the complex tubular network of the avian lung has inspired much study and speculation. Various conclusions came from early studies (see Bretz and Schmidt-Nielsen, 1971, for review). The movement of gas within the lungs of various species of birds has been measured directly (Brackenbury, 1971; Bretz and Schmidt-Nielsen, 1971; Scheid and Piiper, 1971). The measurements show unequivocally that during both inspiration and expiration gas moves *unidirectionally* from the intrapulmonary primary bronchus to the mediodorsal secondary bronchi and into the parabronchi of the paleopulmo, as originally proposed by Bethe (1925) and Hazelhoff (1943) (Figure 6–5). However, gas moves *bidirectionally* through the neopulmo and through the direct connections to the caudal air sacs (caudal thoracic and abdominal sacs) during both inspiration and expiration.

Gas does not appear to flow from the intrapulmonary primary bronchus through the medioventral bronchi directly to the cranial air sacs (cervical, clavicular, and cranial thoracic sacs) during inspiration (Schmidt-Nielsen et al., 1969; Bouverot

130 and Dejours, 1971; Bretz and Schmidt-Nielsen, 1972). Gas that reaches the cranial air sacs must therefore pass through the paleopulmonic parabronchi and undergo exchange with the blood. Part of the gas that reaches the caudal air sacs during inspiration passes through the neopulmonic parabronchi and is thereby exposed to gas-exchange surfaces; part of it may reach the air sacs by passing through direct connections and therefore may not be exposed to exchange surfaces. Such gas movement is responsible for the lower $O_2$ concentration and higher $CO_2$ concentration in the cranial air sacs compared with the caudal air sacs (Table 6-4).

On expiration, gas passes simultaneously from all air sacs to the trachea, but over different pathways. Gas from the caudal air sacs passes through the neopulmo in the opposite direction from that in inspiration; part of it then moves into the mediodorsal bronchi, through the paleopulmonic parabronchi, through the medioventral bronchi to the intrapulmonary primary bronchus, and out the trachea (Figure 6-5). Part of the gas may also enter the trachea without passing through the paleopul-

mo. Gas from the cranial air sacs passes directly out through the medioventral bronchi to the intrapulmonary primary bronchus and trachea without making contact with gas-exchange surfaces.

Gas that enters the neopulmo during most of inspiration is similar in composition to air (after dead space gas from the trachea and primary bronchi has been washed into the air sacs); the composition of the gas that enters those parabronchi during expiration is similar to that in the caudal air sacs (high $O_2$ low $CO_2$, Table 6-4). Gas that enters the paleopulmo during most of inspiration (after the dead space gas mentioned above has been washed into the air sacs) is also similar in composition to air. During expiration, however, the gas that enters those parabronchi is a mixture, part of which has been exposed to the exchange surfaces in the neopulmo and part of which comes directly from the caudal air sacs. The concentration of $O_2$ in that mixture would be lower than that in the caudal air sacs but higher than that in end-expiratory gas, whereas the concentration of $CO_2$ would be higher than that in the caudal air sacs but lower than that

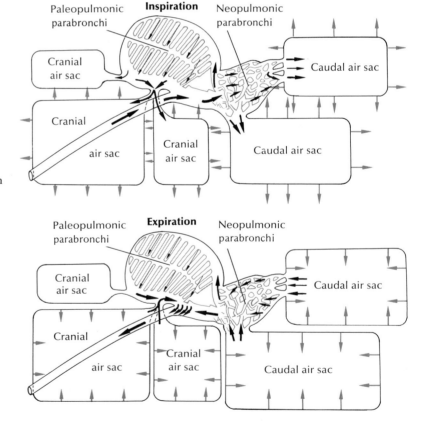

6-5
Schematic representation of the pathway of gas flow through the paleopulmonic and neopulmonic parabronchi during inspiration and during expiration. (After Duncker, 1971.)

*Table 6-4* *Partial pressure of $O_2$ and $CO_2$ in air sacs and end-expiratory gas of indicated species of birds*

| | References[a]: (1)<br>Species: Goose<br>Posture: Upright<br>Anesthesia: None | (2)<br>Chicken<br>Upright<br>None | (3)<br>Chicken<br>Prone<br>General | (4)<br>Duck<br>Upright<br>None |
|---|---|---|---|---|
| Clavicular | | | | |
| $P_{CO_2}$, torr | 35 | 44.0 | 45.2 | 39.2 |
| $P_{O_2}$, torr | 100 | 83.9 | – | 99.4 |
| Cranial thoracic | | | | |
| $P_{CO_2}$, torr | 35 | 41.6 | – | 35.7 |
| $P_{O_2}$, torr | 100 | 99.1 | – | 104.3 |
| Caudal thoracic | | | | |
| $P_{CO_2}$, torr | 28 | 24.2 | – | 18.9 |
| $P_{O_2}$, torr | 115 | 120.3 | – | 123.9 |
| Abdominal | | | | |
| $P_{CO_2}$, torr | 28 | 14.7 | 27.9 | 17.5 |
| $P_{O_2}$, torr | 115 | 130.0 | – | 126.7 |
| End expiratory | | | | |
| $P_{CO_2}$, torr | 35 | 36.7 | 43.4 | 35.7 |
| $P_{O_2}$, torr | 100 | 94.3 | – | 100.1 |

[a] (1) Cohn and Shannon (1968), Figure 6; (2) Piiper *et al.* (1970); (3) Bouverot and Dejours (1971); (4) Vos (1934), composition of gas was given as percentage. Partial pressures were calculated by assuming a mean barometric pressure of 760 torr and a water vapor pressure of 60 torr.

in end-expiratory gas. Therefore, the gas that enters both sets of parabronchi during both inspiration and expiration contains relatively high $O_2$ concentration and low $CO_2$ concentration.

The proportion of the gas expelled from the caudal air sacs that leaves the lungs through the intrapulmonary primary bronchus without passing over the exchange surfaces of the paleopulmo is not known (Schmidt-Nielsen *et al.*, 1969; Bretz and Schmidt-Nielsen, 1971; Scheid *et al.*, 1972). It is possible that the volume of gas through that channel could be varied by changes in the contraction of intrapulmonary smooth muscle. This feature may serve to redistribute gas between gas-exchange and gas nonexchange surfaces during various degrees of activity by the bird or during hyperventilation (Bouverot *et al.*, 1974a).

The end-expiratory gas is therefore a complex mixture of gases from cranial air sacs, parabronchi, and caudal air sacs. Its composition depends on the relative contribution and composition of each constituent gas. The concentration of $CO_2$ is remarkably constant throughout expiration in chickens and ducks (Bouverot and Dejours, 1971). This finding can be explained if the expired gas results from the compilation of gas mixtures of different but fixed compositions, with the proportion of each remain-

ing constant during the entire period of expiration.

Hazelhoff (1943) proposed that the passage of gas through mediodorsal bronchi and parabronchi in a unidirectional manner resulted from aerodynamic conditions. The shape and curvature of the intrapulmonary primary bronchus and the angle of departure and configuration of the secondary bronchi at their origin from the intrapulmonary primary bronchus may all contribute to the aerodynamic conditions involved. Possible mechanisms for unidirectional flow have been discussed (Brackenbury, 1972; Scheid *et al.*, 1972).

## MOVEMENT OF GAS FROM PARABRONCHI TO BLOOD
### Area Available for Gas Transfer

The exchange of $O_2$ and $CO_2$ between gas and blood occurs across the walls of the air and blood capillaries. Air and blood capillaries occupy approximately 50% of the total lung volume in the domestic fowl, carrion crow, and domestic pigeon but somewhat less (approximately 35%) in the Canada goose and in *Cygnus olor* (mute swan) (Duncker, 1972). The diffusion barrier between gas and blood is extremely thin in birds, frequently

132 between 0.1 and 0.2 μm thick (King and Molony, 1971). A large area of each air capillary is exposed to blood (Figure 6−6).

With the advent of morphometric techniques (Weibel, 1963), accurate estimates of the area available for gas exchange in the lungs have been possible. The effective gas-exchange surface area (the surface area of air capillaries opposed to blood capillaries) in several species of birds ranges from 188 mm²/mm³ of air−blood capillary tissue in the turkey to 302 mm²/mm³ in the domestic pigeon (Duncker, 1972). When these values are converted to exchange surface per unit body weight, the domestic hen has 17.9 cm² of exchange surface per gram of body weight; the Canada goose, 18.3 cm²/g; the mute swan, 39.8 cm²/g; and the domestic pigeon, 40.3 cm²/g. The data indicate that the size of the exchange surface per unit volume of the avian lung is at least ten times that of the lung of man (Weibel, 1963) and may be even higher for small flying birds, such as hummingbirds (Stanislaus, 1937).

## Movement of Gas into Air Capillaries and Blood

Even though the air capillaries of one parabronchus may anastomose with those from an adjacent parabronchus (Fischer, 1905; Duncker, 1971), the

6−6 Gas exchange area in the chicken. See text for explanation. (After King and Molony, 1971.)

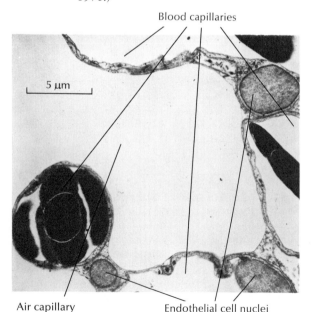

Blood capillaries

5 μm

Air capillary          Endothelial cell nuclei

lack of a pressure difference between the parabronchi suggests that gas moves into the air capillaries by diffusion. Furthermore, a $P_{CO_2}$ difference between a parabronchus and the air capillaries of only 0.5 torr would be required in resting birds to account for the required volume of exchange of this gas (Zeuthen, 1942; Salt and Zeuthen, 1960). Such a low pressure gradient implies that the diffusion resistance from a parabronchus to the air capillaries is extremely low and that the required movement of gas can occur entirely by diffusion.

The major impedance to $O_2$ movement between parabronchi and blood probably occurs in the tissue and fluid layers interposed between the lumen of the air capillaries and the hemoglobin molecules. The carbon monoxide (CO) diffusing capacity of chicken lungs indicates that 0.80 ml/min/torr of CO can diffuse across the exchange surface. From that value, an $O_2$ diffusing capacity of 1.0 ml/min/torr can be calculated (Piiper et al., 1969). That value should be considered a minimum; the diffusing capacity may be much higher in strong flying birds (Scheid and Piiper, 1970). Further, the diffusing capacity per unit gas-exchange surface area can be calculated using these data and the morphometric data of Duncker (1972). Values of 0.45 ml $O_2$/min/torr/m² have been calculated by Piiper and Scheid (1973) and have been found to exceed that in the dog (0.31 ml $O_2$/min/torr/m²). The diffusing capacity for $CO_2$ appears to be at least three times higher than for $O_2$ (Scheid and Piiper, 1970).

## Arrangement of Parabronchi with Respect to Blood Capillaries

From the experimental observation that end-expired gas contained a higher $CO_2$ percentage than gas in the humeral diverticulum of the clavicular air sac (which has very low ventilation), Zeuthen (1942) proposed that the individual blood capillaries were in contact with gas contained in only a small length of a parabronchus. He hypothesized that the partial pressure of $O_2$ in the parabronchial gas should progressively decline and that of $CO_2$ progressively increase as the gas flows along the parabronchus, whereas the partial pressures of these gases in the arterialized blood should be a complex mixture of the partial pressures in the capillary blood bathing the various segments of the parabronchus. Scheid and Piiper (1970) made an analysis of gas exchange in the avian lung; their study indicated a parabronchial−blood capillary arrangement, which they called a cross-current exchange system, as shown in Figure 6−7. In a cross-

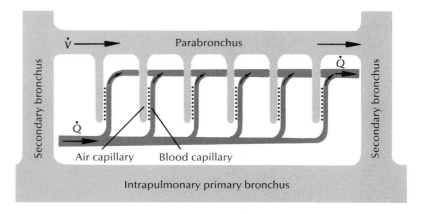

current exchange system, the blood flows effectively at right angles to the parabronchial axis. Furthermore, the partial pressure of $CO_2$ in the end-parabronchial gas may be higher than that in arterial blood (and the partial pressure of $O_2$ may be lower than that in arterial blood) if functional inhomogeneity, shunt, and diffusion limitations are minimal.

6–8 Partial pressures of $CO_2$ and $O_2$ in gas and blood of ducks with normal and reversed parabronchial ventilation. MD, mediodorsal secondary bronchi; MV, medioventral secondary bronchi; $E$, end-expiratory gas tension; $I$, inspired gas tension; $\bar{v}$, gas tension of mixed venous blood; $a$, gas tension of arterial blood. (After Scheid and Piiper, 1972.)

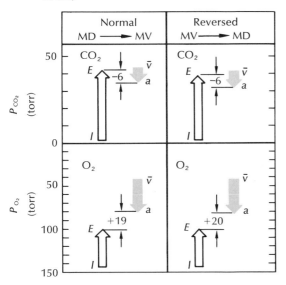

6–7 Model of the arrangement of blood capillaries within a paleopulmonic parabronchial unit of the avian lung (cross-current exchange system). A parabronchus lies parallel to the intrapulmonary primary bronchus. Air capillaries depart from the parabronchus (atria and infundibuli have been omitted) and are in gas exchange contact with the blood capillaries. Respired gas flows through the parabronchus at a constant rate, $\dot{V}$, and the composition of the gas changes along the parabronchus as $CO_2$ and $O_2$ are exchanged with the blood. The blood flow to the parabronchus, $\dot{Q}$, is uniformly distributed over the parabronchial length and is directed at a 90° angle to the longitudinal axis of the parabronchus. (After Scheid and Piiper, 1970.)

As predicted by theory, end-expiratory $CO_2$ is higher than that in arterial blood in birds, whereas $O_2$ is lower than that in arterial blood (Figure 6–8). Furthermore, in a cross-current exchange system, gas-exchange efficiency is not related to the direction of gas flow, relative to blood flow, through the parabronchus (Figure 6–8). The neopulmo, which has gas passing through it in both directions, can therefore serve equally well as a gas exchanger during both inspiration and expiration.

The gas-exchange efficiency of the cross-current system in the bird lung, as indicated by the amount of ventilation required to produce a certain degree of arterialization of the blood, is greater than the uniform pool exchange system of the mammalian lung but not so great as the countercurrent exchange system of fish gills (Piiper and Scheid, 1972). Bird lungs therefore have the potential to extract more $O_2$ from a given volume of inspired air than do mammal lungs.

134

## Arrangement of Air Capillaries with Respect to Blood Capillaries

Air capillaries radiate from the infundibula of the parabronchi toward the periphery of the parabronchial unit. Similarly, blood capillaries originate from branches of the pulmonary artery at the periphery of the unit and course inward toward the parabronchial lumen, where the venules are formed just beneath the epithelium. A single air capillary and a single blood capillary exhibit a countercurrent-type arrangement, as shown in Figure 6–9. In a countercurrent system, capillary blood equilibrates with increasing $P_{O_2}$ along its course and enters the venules after contact with gas with a $P_{O_2}$ close to that in the parabronchial lumen. This arrangement may aid gas transfer in the avian lung by enhancing the equilibration of capillary blood with parabronchial gas when there is a diffusion gradient of $P_{O_2}$ and $P_{CO_2}$ along the air capillary, as may exist during flight (Zeuthen, 1942).

## DISPOSITION OF GASES IN BLOOD

When $O_2$ moves from air capillaries into blood, a small portion physically dissolves in the blood but most complexes with the iron in hemoglobin. Likewise, $CO_2$ is present in the blood in several forms: in chemical combination with hemoglobin and other plasma proteins; in the form of bicarbonate ions; and in physical solution. It diffuses from pulmonary capillary blood into air capillaries at the same time that $O_2$ is diffusing into the blood.

### Forms in Which $O_2$ is Carried in Blood

**Dissolved $O_2$.** According to Henry's law, the concentration of a gas in solution at equilibrium is directly proportional to its partial pressure in the gas phase. For $O_2$, therefore, $[O_2] = \alpha_{O_2} \cdot P_{O_2}$, where $[O_2]$ is its concentration in aqueous solution, $P_{O_2}$ is its partial pressure, and $\alpha_{O_2}$ is its solubility coefficient, expressed as millimoles of $O_2$ per liter blood per torr (Piiper et al., 1971). $\alpha_{O_2}$ is not yet known for avian blood but it probably is similar to that for whole human blood (0.00124 mmole/liter/torr at 15 g hemoglobin per 100 ml of blood and 41°C; Bartels et al., 1971). If this is so, avian blood contains 0.102 mmole $O_2$/liter in the physically dissolved form at a $P_{O_2}$ of 82 torr, which is approximately the $P_{O_2}$ in arterial blood of unanesthetized, undisturbed chickens and ducks (Kawashiro and Scheid, 1975).

**Chemically bound $O_2$.** Most of the $O_2$ in blood is chemically bound to hemoglobin to form oxyhemoglobin ($HbO_2$). The bond is rather weak and $O_2$ is easily released when blood reaches tissues that contain a lower partial pressure. The heme component of avian hemoglobin is usually considered to be similar to that of mammals. If this is so, 1 g of hemoglobin can combine with 1.34 ml of $O_2$ (0.060 mmole of $O_2$) when all hemes are fully saturated. If the amount of hemoglobin is known, therefore, its oxygen capacity can be readily calculated. The total $O_2$ content can be determined by adding the quantity of dissolved $O_2$ in the blood to the $O_2$ capacity of hemoglobin.

Not all of the hemes on a hemoglobin molecule have the same affinity for $O_2$. That relationship is exhibited by the sigmoid shape of the *in vitro* oxyhemoglobin dissociation curve (Figure 6–10), which relates the percent saturation of hemoglobin to the partial pressure of $O_2$.

The effective or *in vivo* $O_2$ dissociation curve (Figure 6–11) has been obtained in unanesthetized, undisturbed ducks by using the $O_2$ dissociation curves in Figure 6–10, Haldane and Bohr effect factors, the buffer value of whole blood, ar-

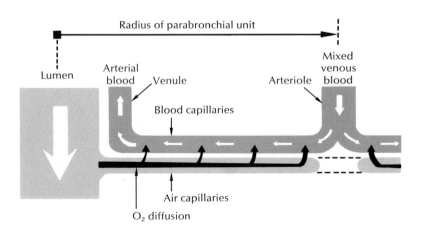

6–9
Model of the arrangement of a single air capillary and a single blood capillary in the avian lung. (After Piiper and Scheid, 1973.)

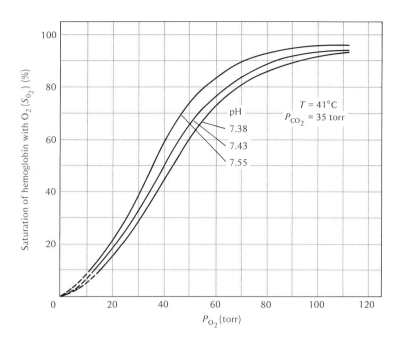

**6–10**

Oxyhemoglobin dissociation curves determined on duck blood. Bohr effect is demonstrated by the shift of the curve to the right as pH decreases. (After Scheipers *et al.,* 1975.)

terial values of $P_{O_2}$ (82 torr), pH (7.49), and body temperature (41.1°C). Figure 6–11 illustrates the changes in saturation of hemoglobin with changes in $P_{O_2}$ of the blood in the body as the blood loses its $O_2$ in the tissues and gains $O_2$ in the lungs during the concomitant changes in $P_{CO_2}$ and pH. Hence, *in vivo,* when the arterial blood has a $P_{O_2}$ of 82 torr, hemoglobin is 91% saturated. If 100 ml of arterial blood has 12 g of hemoglobin, therefore, it would contain 0.663 mmole $O_2$ (0.653 mmole of $O_2$ bound to hemoglobin + 0.010 mmole of $O_2$

physically dissolved). As the blood passes through the tissue capillaries, $O_2$ diffuses from the blood and the $P_{O_2}$ equilibrates with that in the tissues. Because the hemes give up their $O_2$ readily as the $P_{O_2}$ drops between 70 and 20 torr, a large amount of $O_2$ can be delivered to the tissues with a rather small reduction in $P_{O_2}$. If the mixed venous blood, as represented by the blood in the pulmonary artery, has a $P_{O_2}$ of 39 torr (Piiper *et al.,* 1970), the hemoglobin is only about 46% saturated, and 100 ml of blood contains 0.337 mmole of $O_2$. Therefore,

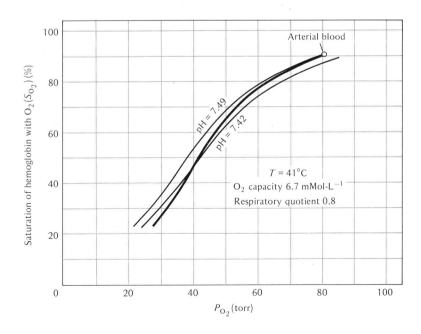

**6–11**

Effective or *in vivo* oxyhemoglobin dissociation curve for blood of an unanesthetized, undisturbed duck (heavy line). For reference, iso-pH dissociation curves derived as in Figure 6–10 are drawn through the arterial point of the same ducks (pH = 7.49) and the point of half saturation, $S_{O_2} = 50\%$ (pH = 7.42). (After Scheipers *et al.,* 1975.)

136    the 100 ml of blood will deliver 0.326 mmole of $O_2$ to the tissues under those conditions.

## Factors Influencing the Affinity of Hemoglobin for $O_2$

The partial pressure of carbon dioxide and the hydrogen ion concentration have an important influence on hemoglobin's affinity for oxygen. The effect of increasing concentrations of both compounds on the oxyhemoglobin dissociation curve, called the Bohr effect, is to shift the curve to the right, thereby increasing the ease with which hemoblobin gives up its $O_2$. Hemoglobin can release almost all of its $O_2$ (3–4% saturation) while maintaining $P_{O_2}$ values of 28–30 torr during prolonged dives by diving birds because of the increase in acidity of the blood (Andersen and Lövö, 1967). As long as a small amount of $O_2$ remains bound to hemoglobin during a dive, therefore, the driving pressure of $O_2$ can remain high enough to prevent damage to the central nervous system and other vital organs. The Bohr effect factor ($\Delta \log P_{50}/\Delta pH$, where $P_{50}$ is the $P_{O_2}$ at which hemoglobin is half-saturated and is hence a measure of the $O_2$ affinity of hemoglobin) is −0.53 for duck blood (Scheipers et al., 1975); −0.566 for pigeon (Lutz et al., 1973); −0.471 for geese (Danzer and Cohn, 1967); −0.48 for the herring gull (Clausen et al., 1971); and −0.505 for the penguin (Lenfant et al., 1969). The change in $P_{50}$ is −4.8 torr for a pH change of 0.1 unit in the range between 7.4 and 7.5 for the duck.

The presence of certain organic phosphates that bind to hemoglobin in the avian red blood cells, especially myoinositol 1,3,4,5,6-pentaphosphate 4 (Johnson and Tate, 1969), influences the affinity of hemoglobin for $O_2$ (Bartlett, 1970). When these compounds increase in concentration inside the red cell, as they may during hypoxia or ascent to high altitude, hemoglobin decreases its affinity for $O_2$ and the oxyhemoglobin dissociation curve shifts to the right.

Apparently because of the high metabolic rate of the nucleated erythrocytes, which possess virtually all enzymes typical of metabolically active cells (Bell, 1971), avian blood consumes $O_2$ at a rate at least ten times faster than does mammalian blood (Besch, 1966). It has recently been argued that the high rate of $O_2$ consumption produces large errors in determining the oxyhemoglobin dissociation curve when the classical Van Slyke method is used to measure $O_2$ content and that the errors have led to the belief that avian hemoglobin has considerably less affinity for $O_2$ than does mammalian hemoglobin (Lutz et al., 1973). However, Scheipers et al. (1975) have demonstrated that the classical Van Slyke method can be used successfully to determine the oxyhemoglobin dissociation curve and that the $P_{50}$ is identical to that determined by the technique used by Lutz et al. (1973). However, the slope of the upper part of the curves determined by Lutz et al. (1973) appear to be too steep and, thus, to deviate from that deemed theoretically possible for a tetramer hemoglobin molecule (Scheipers et al., 1975). Hemoglobin from larger birds seems to have more affinity for $O_2$ than does hemoglobin from smaller birds (Lutz et al., 1974). $P_{50}$ values for various birds are shown in Table 6–5.

## Forms in Which $CO_2$ Is Carried in Blood

If the solubility coefficient of $CO_2$ at 41°C is 0.0278 mmole $CO_2$ per liter of blood per torr (value given for bovine plasma by Bartels et al., 1971), and the arterial $P_{CO_2}$ is 38 torr (unanesthetized, undisturbed duck; Kawashiro and Scheid, 1975), there are 1.056 mmoles of $CO_2$ physically dissolved in a liter of blood. The remainder of the $CO_2$ is carried in blood either bound to the proteins (mostly hemoglobin) as carbamino compounds or as the bicarbonate ion, most of which is in the plasma.

The $CO_2$ dissociation curve of avian blood (Figure 6–12), unlike the oxyhemoglobin dissociation curve, tends to be more linear in the physiological range. The degree of oxygenation of hemoglobin greatly influences the quantity of $CO_2$ that the blood contains (the Haldane effect). When oxy-

*Table 6–5* Oxygen half-saturation pressure ($P_{50}$) for hemoglobin of indicated species of birds[a, b]

| Species | Body mass (g) | $P_{50}$ (torr) |
|---|---|---|
| Rhea americana (rhea) | 29700 | 20.7 |
| Anas platyrhynchos (mallard) | 2760 | 35.2 |
| Gallus domesticus (chicken) | 2420 | 35.1 |
| Phasianus colchicus (pheasant) | 795 | 34.7 |
| Columba livia (pigeon) | 300 | 29.5 |
| Coturnix coturnix (quail) | 40 | 42.4 |
| Passer domesticus (sparrow) | 25 | 41.3 |

[a]From Lutz et al. (1974)

[b]Cells not hemolyzed. Temperature = 41°C, pH = 7.5, $P_{CO_2}$ = 35 torr.

6-12

Carbon dioxide dissociation curves from the duck. Upper (deoxygenated blood) and lower (oxygenated blood) curves are derived from *in vitro* equilibration of blood samples. Heavy line is the effective or *in vivo* dissociation curve from unanesthetized, undisturbed animals and illustrates the change in $CO_2$ content ($C_{CO_2}$) in the blood as it changes from arterial blood to venous blood in the tissue capillaries. (After Scheipers *et al.*, 1975.)

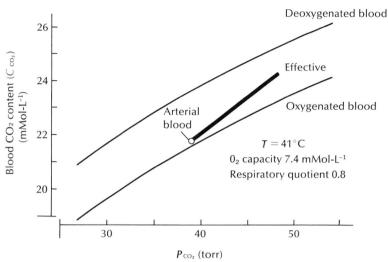

gen is removed from hemoglobin as it passes through the tissue capillaries, the reduced hemoglobin binds more hydrogen ions. This allows the formation of additional $HCO_3$, which in turn increases the amount of $CO_2$ carried by the blood. When $O_2$ is added to the hemoglobin in the lung capillaries, the hydrogen ion is driven from the hemoglobin molecule, thereby causing $CO_2$ to be formed from $HCO_3$. The $CO_2$ then diffuses into the air capillaries, to be removed from the lungs by the ventilation.

The change in the quantity of $CO_2$ in the blood as arterial blood is converted to venous blood in the tissue capillaries is shown as the heavy curve in Figure 6-12. That curve represents the effective or *in vivo* carbon dioxide dissociation curve.

The *in vivo* buffering characteristics of blood from chickens and mammals appear quite similar despite differences in hemoglobin concentration (12 g% for chicken, 15 g% for man), plasma protein concentration (30-35 g/liter for chicken, 70 g/liter for man) and body temperature (40-41°C for chicken, 37-38°C for mammals) (Nightingale and Fedde, 1972). The buffering ability of blood of both birds and mammals *in vivo* is about one-half (12.5-14.5 meq/liter per pH unit), that of blood equilibrated with $CO_2$ *in vitro*. Buffer values for duck's whole blood and for true plasma are 19.3 and 22.9 meq/liter per pH unit, respectively (Scheipers *et al.*, 1975).

## Arterial Blood Gases and pH

Special caution must be used in the handling of avian blood for blood gas measurements. Blood gases and pH must be determined immediately af-

ter withdrawal of the blood from the bird because of the high metabolic rate of avian blood (Fedde and Kuhlmann, 1974; Scheid and Kawashiro, 1975). If the blood cannot be analyzed within one minute after withdrawal, the metabolic rate can be essentially halted by placing the syringes in an ice bath. The blood gas electrodes should be set at the body temperature of the bird because correction factors for the influence of temperature on these variables have not been determined for avian blood. Furthermore, the conventional $P_{O_2}$ electrode will generally not provide a true reading of the $P_{O_2}$ in avian blood (Nightingale *et al.*, 1968); rather, the reading will be lower, by a variable factor, than the true $P_{O_2}$ in the blood. To obtain the true $P_{O_2}$ in a blood sample, a correction factor must be determined by equilibrating a sample of the blood with a gas of known $P_{O_2}$ and obtaining a reading of the $P_{O_2}$ from the equilibrated blood. The correction factor is the ratio of the $P_{O_2}$ reading in the equilibrated blood to the $P_{O_2}$ in the equilibrating gas. The true $P_{O_2}$ in the unknown sample is then obtained by dividing the $P_{O_2}$ reading of the unknown sample by the correction factor.

Few studies have determined the arterial blood gas and pH values in unanesthetized, undisturbed birds. A technique to collect arterial blood under such conditions has recently been developed (Scheid and Slama, 1975); the values found for chickens and ducks are shown in Table 6-6. Higher values of $P_{O_2}$ and lower values of $P_{CO_2}$, which are generally reported for unanesthetized but restrained birds, probably result from hyperventilation caused by the unnatural experimental situation.

Other blood gas values reported for unanesthe-

6. Respiration

*Table 6–6* *Arterial blood gases and pH in unanesthetized undisturbed birds*

| Bird | $P_{O_2}$ (torr) | $P_{CO_2}$ (torr) | pH |
|------|------|------|------|
| White pelican[a] | — | 28.5 | 7.50 |
| Goose (in lay)[a] | — | 24.5 | 7.53 |
| Duck[a] | — | 29.9 | 7.50 |
| Duck[b] | 82 | 38 | 7.49 |
| Turkey vulture[a] | — | 27.5 | 7.51 |
| Black Bantam hen[a] | — | 29.9 | 7.48 |
| White Rock rooster[a] | — | 29.2 | 7.53 |
| White Leghorn hen[b] | 82 | 33 | 7.52 |
| Herring gull[a] | — | 27.2 | 7.56 |
| Pigeon[a] | — | 28.5 | 7.52 |
| Roadrunner[a] | — | 24.5 | 7.58 |

[a]Calder and Schmidt-Nielsen (1968).

[b]Kawashiro and Scheid (1975).

tized, lightly restrained chickens (Piiper *et al.*, 1970) are: mixed venous $P_{O_2}$, 40.8 torr; mixed venous $P_{CO_2}$, 39.3 torr; arterial $O_2$ content, 10.0 vol%; mixed venous $O_2$ content, 4.3 vol%; arterial $CO_2$ content, 42.2 vol%; and mixed venous $CO_2$ content, 45.8 vol%. Values for additional species can be obtained from Sturkie (1965).

## CONTROL OF BREATHING

### Factors that Influence Ventilation

Chemical and neural factors involved in the modulation of avian respiration have been reviewed by Jukes (1971). He clearly points out the labile nature of respiratory rate and tidal volume and, therefore, the amount of ventilation the lungs receive. Experimental difficulties in obtaining reliable data include especially (1) excitement of unanesthetized birds when they are restrained or in any way manipulated in a foreign environment; (2) attachment of recording devices to the trachea, which not only disturbs an unanesthetized bird but also may alter the airway resistance and dead space volume and thereby severely alter normal ventilation; and (3) anesthetization, which suppresses the central nervous system and thus reduces ventilation to a variable and noncontrollable degree.

Overcoming such difficulties would likely eliminate much of the variability reported and allow much more rapid advances in our understanding of the function of the respiratory system.

**Carbon dioxide.** Inhalation of $CO_2$ by unanesthetized birds increases tidal volume and min-

ute volume but has variable effects on respiratory rate, sometimes increasing and sometimes decreasing or causing no change (Andersen and Lövö, 1964; Fowle and Weinstein, 1966; Johnston and Jukes, 1966; Jones and Purves, 1970; Bouverot *et al.*, 1974b). When the inspired $CO_2$ reaches sufficiently high concentrations (6–12%), ventilation is suppressed, probably by either its anesthetic action or its action on upper respiratory nociceptors. In anesthetized chickens that are unidirectionally ventilated, apnea is produced when intrapulmonary $CO_2$ concentrations fall below 3–4% (Ray and Fedde, 1969). In those birds, when the $CO_2$ concentration is increased above 3–4%, respiratory amplitude continuously increases even though $CO_2$ concentration may reach 20%. Respiratory rate, however, is relatively unaffected by inspired $CO_2$ concentrations above those that produce apnea. In the spontaneously breathing, anesthetized chicken, inhalation of $CO_2$ reduces the rate and increases the depth of respiration (Richards and Sykes, 1967). $CO_2$ therefore produces a strong respiratory drive in both unanesthetized and anesthetized birds, primarily by increasing tidal volume.

The mechanism by which $CO_2$ stimulates ventilation has not been fully elucidated. Receptors in several locations in the body may be potentially involved (see p. 139). However, in unanesthetized ducks, ventilation is approximately doubled when increased $CO_2$ concentrations are inhaled in the absence of measurable differences in arterial $P_{CO_2}$ (Jones and Purves, 1970). Such evidence, coupled with the extremely rapid ventilatory response to sudden changes in intrapulmonary $CO_2$ concentration (Peterson and Fedde, 1968), suggests that receptors that detect airway gas concentration are involved in the control mechanism.

**Oxygen.** Inhalation of 100% $O_2$ by unanesthetized ducks decreases ventilation, compared to ventilation during breathing of air (Jones and Purves, 1970; Jukes, 1971; Bouverot *et al.*, 1974b). Ducks therefore appear to have a hypoxic chemoreflex drive of ventilation under normal air-breathing conditions.

Reduced concentration of inhaled $O_2$ in either unanesthetized or anesthetized birds generally does not stimulate an increase in ventilation until the inhaled concentration reaches 14–12% (Butler, 1967; Ray and Fedde, 1969). When the arterial $P_{O_2}$ falls to 60 torr or lower, ventilation is increased primarily by an increase in respiratory frequency (Jones and Holeton, 1972; Bouverot *et al.*, 1974b). The mechanism for stimulation of ventilation by hypoxia appears to differ markedly in both sensitivity and in action from the mechanism that deals with changes in carbon dioxide.

**Stimulation of peripheral nerves.** Stimulating almost any peripheral nerve will affect ventilation, especially in an unanesthetized animal. Electrical stimulation of the skin of unanesthetized pigeons, chickens, or ducks produces an increase in total ventilation, tidal volume, and respiratory frequency that is independent of additional stimulation by various levels of inspired $CO_2$ (Fowle and Weinstein, 1966). Furthermore, under certain conditions respiration in birds can be paced by periodic electrical shocks applied to the toes (D. R. Jones, personal communication). Both visual and auditory cues also elicit a ventilatory response from awake birds (Fowle and Weinstein, 1966). It is apparent, therefore, that neural input from many sources impinges on the respiratory neuronal pool either directly or via the cerebral cortex.

Electrical stimulation of the central end of the cut vagus nerve causes a wide variety of effects on ventilation depending on many factors, especially on the frequency and strength of the stimulus (see King, 1966b, McLelland, 1970, for reviews). Recent studies in pigeons and chickens, using controlled stimulus parameters, indicate that a weak stimulus $(1-3$ V; $5-25$ Hz; 1-msec duration) applied to the central end of either the right or left vagus at any phase of the breathing cycle increases respiratory frequency and slightly decreases respiratory depth (Sinha, 1958; Richards, 1969; McLelland, 1970). Stronger stimuli (higher voltages or frequencies) inhibit respiration.

Section of both vagi in birds markedly decreases respiratory frequency and increases respiratory amplitude (Fedde *et al.,* 1963; Richards, 1968; McLelland, 1970). Stimulating the central end of one of the cut vagi with the weak stimulus mentioned above prevents the changes in respiratory rate and amplitude that follow bilateral vagotomy. It also permits initiation and maintenance of thermal panting in the chicken in response to increasing body temperature (Richards, 1968, 1969; McLelland, 1970). The vagi contain afferent fibers the neural activity of which is essential to maintain normal, rhythmic respiration.

**Temperature.** Increases in body temperature produce thermal polypnoea, which results in hyperventilation. If the hyperventilation is of sufficient magnitude, intrapulmonary $CO_2$ concentration decreases and pronounced alkalosis occurs (Linsley and Burger, 1964; Calder and Schmidt-Nielsen, 1968; Bouverot *et al.* 1974a). The ventilatory drive

from the panting center is very strong and can overcome the inhibition of respiration produced by low intrapulmonary $CO_2$ concentrations. The panting response appears to have priority over other mechanisms associated with the control of gas exchange.

Bilateral section of the vagi prevents panting in the chicken but not in the pigeon (Richards, 1968); apparently panting is controlled by different types of central mechanisms in these birds.

**Noxious gases.** Inhaling any one of several types of noxious gases (sulfur dioxide, ammonia vapor, acetic acid vapor) slows breathing or produces apnea (Eaton *et al.,* 1971; Callanan *et al.,* 1974). Furthermore, simply allowing cold, dry air or cold water to come into contact with the upper respiratory system (upper trachea and larynx) also slows breathing or produces apnea (Eaton *et al.,* 1971; Bamford and Jones, 1974). There appear to be irritant receptors in the upper respiratory system that are strongly stimulated by such substances.

### Components of a Control System

The various components in a control system must be fully recognized and analyzed before the system can be thoroughly understood.

**Controlled variable.** The most important consideration in defining the components of a control system is the identification of the controlled variable or variables, i.e., the variables to be kept at some long-term homeostatic level. For example, the average concentration of $CO_2$ in the intrapulmonary gas may be a controlled variable. The arterial $P_{CO_2}$ and therefore the $P_{CO_2}$ of blood perfusing the body tissues is dictated by the concentration of $CO_2$ in the exchange areas of the lungs.

**Receptor system.** The controlled variable must activate some receptor system which detects the magnitude of the variable. Birds apparently have several such receptor systems, most of which are not fully understood.

*Intrapulmonary $CO_2$ receptor system.* One of the most important receptor systems that appears to be involved in the control of breathing is the intrapulmonary $CO_2$ receptor system. It recently has been demonstrated in several species of birds (Fedde and Peterson, 1970; Peterson and Fedde, 1971; Fedde *et al.,* 1974a; Osborne and Burger, 1974). These receptors decrease their discharge frequency as the intrapulmonary $CO_2$ concentration increases (Figure $6-13$); they are not stimulated by stretching the

140 respiratory system. They discharge rhythmically during spontaneous breathing and during ventilation with a reciprocating pump; some receptors have peak discharge frequencies during inspiration, some during expiration, and some are biphasic with peak discharge frequencies during both phases of the respiratory cycle (Fedde *et al.*, 1974a). The intrapulmonary $CO_2$ receptors apparently reside primarily in the gas-exchange areas of neopulmonic and paleopulmonic parabronchi and monitor the $CO_2$ load returning to the lungs in the mixed venous blood (Banzett, 1974; Burger *et al.*, 1974; Scheid *et al.*, 1974a). The ultrastructure of afferent nerve endings in the avian lung and their possible relationship to intrapulmonary $CO_2$ receptors have recently been discussed (King *et al.*, 1974).

*Carotid body.* Receptors in the carotid body (see Chapter 4) play a definite role in controlling breathing in birds. Intravenous injection of sodium cyanide ( a chemical that stimulates chemoreceptor cells in the mammalian carotid body) into the arteries perfusing the carotid body in the chicken increases ventilation, primarily by increasing respiratory frequency (Magno, 1973). Bouverot and Leitner (1972) found vagal afferent fibers in the chicken, which have receptors sensitive to injections of sodium cyanide into the blood and to changes in arterial $P_{O_2}$ and $P_{CO_2}$. These receptors are thought to be in the carotid bodies and to sample arterial blood. Surgical denervation of the carotid bodies in ducks eliminates the ventilatory response to hypoxia or hyperoxia and produces a slight hypoxia (average arterial $P_{O_2}$ of 79 torr) and a hypercapnia when the ducks breath air (Jones and Purves, 1970; Bouverot *et al.*, 1974b). It appears likely that the carotid bodies contain receptors responsible for detecting low arterial $P_{O_2}$, and possibly elevated arterial $P_{CO_2}$, and that they initiate a ventilatory drive during eupneic breathing.

6–13 Discharge frequency of an intrapulmonary $CO_2$ receptor during unidirectional, artificial ventilation in which the $CO_2$ concentration in the ventilating gas varied from 0 to 12.4%. (After Fedde *et al.*, 1974a.)

*Central nervous system.* Receptors in the central nervous system also appear to be affected by changes in arterial $P_{CO_2}$. Apnea can be produced in unidirectionally ventilated chickens following bilateral, cervical vagotomy when intrapulmonary $CO_2$ concentration is reduced below 3%; however, unlike the nonvagotomized chicken, in which apnea occurs within 0.5 sec, apnea occurs only after a delay of 5–6 sec. Such a delay would allow blood containing low $CO_2$ to reach the brain and produce an effect on receptors there (Peterson and Fedde, 1968).

*Pulmonary stretch receptors.* Pulmonary stretch receptors in birds have been postulated by many investigators (see Fedde, 1970, for review; Molony, 1972; Leitner, 1972; Leitner and Roumy, 1974). The apneic response following inflation of the respiratory system with air has been equated with the Hering-Breuer reflex. However, the intrapulmonary $CO_2$ receptors are strongly activated during inflation with air because air has a low $CO_2$ concentration and discharge of the intrapulmonary $CO_2$ receptors initiates apnea. Eaton *et al.* (1971) has demonstrated that the apneic response to inflation with air is essentially abolished by use of a gas containing 6–8% $CO_2$, which inhibits most of the $CO_2$ receptors. Therefore, although the same basic ventilatory response to inflation with air occurs in birds as in mammals, i.e., apnea, its mechanism of action in birds is apparently through activation of the intrapulmonary $CO_2$ receptors. That the apneic response is elicited by intrapulmonary mechanoreceptors, which are activated by changes in the caliber of bronchi induced by changes in intrapulmonary $CO_2$ concentration, remains to be proved (Leitner and Roumy, 1974).

Afferent activity in some fibers in the avian vagus is phasic with respiration but not influenced by intrapulmonary $CO_2$ (Fedde *et al.*, 1974b; Molony, 1974). The receptors appear to be mechanoreceptors but their location and their effect on the control of breathing are unknown.

*Other possible receptors.* Anatomical descriptions have been made of other possible peripheral chemoreceptors that lie (1) in the connective tissue between the ascending aorta and the pulmonary

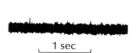

0      6.3      12.4

1 sec

artery; (2) on the dorsal and lateral surfaces of the aorta, the brachiochephalic arteries, and the pulmonary arteries; (3) in the adventitia and media of the pulmonary trunk at the site of its junction with the right ventricle; and (4) in the wall of the pulmonary artery near the hilus of the lung (see Fedde, 1970, for review). The literature contains no studies on the functions of those structures and their physiological significance remains unknown.

**Afferent pathway.** The afferent pathway from the intrapulmonary $CO_2$ receptors to the brain is via the vagus nerves and, to a lesser degree, via sympathetic nerves (Burger *et al.*, 1974). The glossopharyngeal and the vagus nerves both supply the carotid body (Adams, 1958; Fedde, 1970). Many other nerves also contain afferent fibers the activity of which influences breathing.

**Central centers.** Ablation or stimulation of many regions of the avian brain has pronounced effects on respiration as anticipated from consideration of many types of peripheral inputs that alter respiratory rate and amplitude. Few of the sites, however, appear to be in telencephalic regions. Complete extirpation of the cerebrum of the pigeon has no influence on panting (area rostral to 1 in Figure 6–14): neither do hyperstriatal lesions. Additionally, stimulation of the archistriatum (amygdala) or any other telencephalic site produces no influence on respiratory rate (Cohen, 1967; Kotilainen and Putkonen, 1972).

Transection of the midbrain (designated by 2 in Figure 6–14) causes panting to cease immediately or prevents it from occurring; however, this transection does not prevent cyclic respiratory movements of between 60 and 70 per minute. Lesions of the ventromedial tegmentum in pigeons appear to increase respiratory rate (Durkovic and Cohen, 1969). Stimulating the septal and preoptic areas induces polypneic panting with a moderate increase in respiratory frequency and some reduction in amplitude (Kotilainen and Putkonen, 1974). The panting center appears to be in the rostral–dorsal region of the midbrain; however, recent experiments also suggest that this area may be homologous with the pneumotaxic center in the mammalian pons (Richards, 1970, 1971).

Stimulating rather large areas in the lateral thalamus, rostral to and surrounding the nucleus rotundus, produces apneic responses in which respiration is usually stopped at the end of a normal inspiration and the sternum moves to the neutral resting position (Kotilainen and Putkonen, 1974). This apneic response appears indistinguishable from the response produced by reducing intrapulmonary $CO_2$ concentration.

When the brain is transected more caudally (3 in Figure 6–14), respiration is influenced. Stimulating a continuous midline area in this region produces prolonged apnea (Kotilainen and Putkonen, 1974). Furthermore, apnea can be produced by stimulating more lateral regions in the mesencephalic pretectal area.

When the brain is transected just caudal to the pons (4 in Figure 6–14), respiration ceases completely. Responses to stimulation of the hindbrain appear to be more associated with eupneic respiration than with polypneic panting or vocalization. Apparently, therefore, the central respiratory neuronal pool, or so-called "respiratory" center, is in the region of the pons and rostral part of the medulla oblongata.

The exact mechanism by which afferent im-

6–14
Location of regions of the pigeon brain involved with respiratory control. (See text for explanation of numbers.) (After von Saafeld, 1936.)

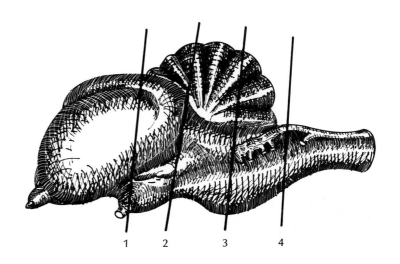

142 pulses from peripheral receptors act on the central respiratory neuronal pool is not yet known. A possible mechanism for inhibitory receptors, such as the intrapulmonary $CO_2$ receptors, has been proposed by Kunz and Miller (1974a): impulses from them may induce hyperpolarization of medullary pacemaker neurons and thereby inhibit the neurons. When the afferent discharge decreases or ceases, the transmembrane potential (prepotential) of the pacemaker cells may tend to drift toward threshold levels of depolarization. The rate of change of the prepotential may depend on such additional extracellular factors as temperature, $P_{CO_2}$, $P_{O_2}$, and pH of the extracellular fluid of the brain. The characteristics of the prepotential of the pacemaker cells, the level of depolarization required to reach threshold, and the afferent impulses from peripheral receptors all would determine the discharge frequency of the pacemaker cells.

Much more work is needed with neurophysiological recording techniques to define the central respiratory cells' location and mode of activation.

**Respiratory muscles.** Motoneurons emanating from various segments of the spinal cord to respiratory muscles control the rate and amplitude of their contraction and thereby the ventilation of the respiratory system. Ventilation of the gas-exchange region of the lung, in turn, determines the intrapulmonary $CO_2$ concentration and therefore the degree of activation of intrapulmonary $CO_2$ receptors. A negative-feedback mechanism may therefore operate to control the $CO_2$ concentration in the body (Kunz and Miller, 1974b).

## Normal Values of Some Respiratory Variables

Specific values for respiratory rate, tidal volume, and minute volume for various birds are shown in Table 6–7. Additional values for resting respiratory rate for many species have been compiled by Calder (1968). Because there are approximately 86,000 species of birds, ranging in weight from 2 to 150,000 g, respiratory variables vary widely.

The relationship between some respiratory variables and body weight has been useful in predicting the magnitude of the variable from known body weights (Lasiewski and Calder, 1971; Lasiewski, 1972). The allometric relationship is based on a power function equation of the form $Y = aW^b$, where $Y$ is some variable, $W$ is the body weight in kilograms, and $a$ and $b$ are empirically derived constants. The key to success in deriving the constants is measuring respiratory variables accurately. Some respiratory variables, especially tidal volume, are extremely difficult to measure under truely undisturbed conditions. Tidal volume measurements used by Lasiewski and Calder (1971) to derive the constants for their allometric equation were obtained, in most cases, from restrained birds with a facemask or a cannulated trachea. Indeed, most of the values given in Table 6–7 suffer from the same problem. Plethysmography has been more recently

*Table 6–7*  *Values of various respiratory parameters in resting, unanesthetized birds*

| Species | Weight (kg) | $f^a$ (respirations per min) | $V_T^a$ (ml) | $\dot{V}^a$ (ml/min) | Comments |
|---|---|---|---|---|---|
| Duck (1)[b] | | | | | |
| Muscovy | 2.16 | 10.5 | 69 | 700 | Endotracheal tube, |
| Pekin | 2.4 | 8.2 | 98 | 807 | pneumotachograph |
| Duck (2)[b] | | | | | |
| Pekin | 2.01 | 11.9 | 55 | 650 | Resting in plethysmograph |
| Pigeon (3)[b] | 0.38 | 26 | 4.6 | 118 | Face mask |
| Chicken (4)[b] | | | | | |
| Male | 4.2 | 17 | 46 | 777 | Tracheal cannula, valves, |
| Female | 3.4 | 27 | 31 | 766 | spirometer |
| Chicken (5)[b] | | | | | |
| Female | 1.6 | 23.0 | 33.0 | 760 | Tracheal cannula, valves, spirometer |
| Goose (6)[b] | 4.5–9.0 | 12.6 | 112.5 | 1418 | Face mask, pneumotachograph |

[a] $f$, respiratory frequency; $V_T$, tidal volume; $\dot{V}$, minute ventilation.

[b] (1) Jones and Holeton (1972); (2) Bouverot *et al.* (1974b); (3) Hart and Roy (1966); (4) King and Payne (1964); (5) Piiper *et al.* (1970); (6) Cohn and Shannon (1968, Fig. 3).

used to measure tidal volume in unanesthetized ducks in a resting condition without facemasks or tracheal cannulation (Bouverot *et al.*, 1974b). Tidal volumes for ducks weighing from 2.01 to 2.6 kg were considerably larger (55–63 ml body temperature, pressure, saturated) than values predicted from the allometric equations for birds that size (28–37 ml). However, the technique of relating respiratory variables to body weight appears to have considerable promise in predicting a variable for a given individual when more reliable data become available.

# REFERENCES

Adams, W. E. (1958). "The Comparative Morphology of the Carotid Body and Carotid Sinus." Springfield, Ill.: Charles C. Thomas, p. 171.

Andersen, H. T., and A. Lövö. (1964). The effect of carbon dioxide on the respiration of avian divers (ducks). *Comp. Biochem. Physiol.*, 12, 451.

Andersen, H. T., and A. Lövö. (1967). Indirect estimation of partial pressure of oxygen in arterial blood of diving ducks. *Resp. Physiol.*, 2, 163.

Bamford, O. S., and D. R. Jones. (1974). On the initiation of apnoea and some cardiovascular responses to submergence in ducks. *Resp. Physiol.*, 22, 199.

Banzett, R. B. (1974). Physiological parameters which determine PCO$_2$ at the intrapulmonary chemoreceptor site in *Gallus domesticus*. Ph.D. thesis, University of California, Davis, California.

Bartels, H., C. Christoforides, J. Hedley-Whyte, and L. Laasberg. (1971). Solubility coefficients of gases. In "Biological Handbooks: Respiration and Circulation" (P. L. Altman and D. S. Dittmer, Eds.). Bethesda, Maryland: Federation of American Societies for Experimental Biology, p. 18. .

Bartlett, G. R. (1970). Patterns of phosphate compounds in red blood cells of man and animals. In "Advances in Experimental Medicine and Biology," Vol. 6, "Red Cell Metabolism" (G. J. Brewer, Ed.). New York: Plenum Press, p. 245.

Bell, D. J. (1971). Metabolism of the erythrocyte. In "Physiology and Biochemistry of the Domestic Fowl," Vol. 2 (D. J. Bell and B. M. Freeman, Eds.). New York: Academic Press, p. 863.

Besch, E. L. (1966). Respiratory activity of avian blood cells. *J. Cell Physiol.*, 67, 301.

Bethe, A. (1925). Atmung: Allgemeines and Vergleichendes. In "Handbuch der normalen und pathologischen Physiologie." (A. Bethe, G. V. Bergmann, G. Embden, and A. Ellinger, Eds). Berlin: Springer Verlag, Bd. 2, p. 1.

Bouverot, P., and P. Dejours. (1971). Pathway of respired gas in the air sacs-lung apparatus of fowl and ducks. *Resp. Physiol.*, 13, 330.

Bouverot, P., and L.-M. Leitner. (1972). Arterial chemoreceptors in the domestic fowl. *Resp. Physiol.*, 15, 310.

Bouverot, P., N. Hill, and Y. Jammes. (1974b). Ventilatory responses to CO$_2$ in intact and chronically chemodenervated Peking ducks. *Resp. Physiol.*, 22, 137.

Bouverot, P., G. Hildwein, and D. LeGoff. (1974a). Evaporative water loss, respiratory pattern, gas exchange and acid-base balance during thermal panting in Pekin ducks exposed to moderate heat. *Resp. Physiol.*, 21, 255.

Brackenbury, J. H. (1971). Airflow dynamics in the avian lung as determined by direct and indirect methods. *Resp. Physiol.*, 13, 319.

Brackenbury, J. H. (1972). Physical determinants of air flow pattern within the avian lung. *Resp. Physiol.*, 15, 384.

Brackenbury, J. H. (1973). Respiratory mechanics in the bird. *Comp. Biochem. Physiol.*, 44A, 599.

Brackenbury, J. H. (1974). Pressure relationships of airflow in the avian respiratory system, and their influence on haemodynamics. Ph.D. thesis, University of Cambridge, Churchill College, England.

Bretz, W. L., and K. Schmidt-Nielsen. (1971). Bird respiration: Flow patterns in the duck lung. *J. Exp. Biol.*, 54, 103.

Bretz, W. L., and K. Schmidt-Nielsen. (1972). The movement of gas in the respiratory system of the duck. *J. Exp. Biol.*, 56, 57.

Burger, R. E., J. L. Osborne, and R. B. Banzett. (1974). Intrapulmonary chemoreceptors in *Gallus domesticus*: Adequate stimulus and functional localization. *Resp. Physiol.*, 22, 87.

Burton, R. R., and A. H. Smith. (1968). Blood and air volumes in the avian lung. *Poultry Sci.*, 47, 85.

Butler, P. J. (1967). The effect of progressive hypoxia on the respiratory and cardiovascular systems of the chicken. *J. Physiol. (London), 191*, 309.

Calder, W. A. (1968). Respiratory and heart rates of birds at rest. *Condor, 70*, 358.

Calder, W. A., and K. Schmidt-Nielsen. (1968). Panting and blood carbon dioxide in birds. *Am. J. Physiol., 215*, 477.

Callanan, D., M. Dixon, J. G. Widdicombe, and J. C. M. Wise. (1974). Responses of geese to inhalation of irritant gases and injections of phenyl diguanide. *Resp. Physiol., 22*, 157.

Clausen, G., R. Sanson, and A. Storesund. (1971). The HbO$_2$ dissociation curve of the fulmar and the herring gull. *Resp. Physiol., 12*, 66.

Cohen, D. H. (1967). The hyperstriatal region of the avian forebrain: A lesion study of possible functions, including its role in cardiac and respiratory conditioning. *J. Comp. Neurol., 131*, 559.

Cohn, J. E., and R. Shannon. (1968). Respiration in unanesthetized geese. *Resp. Physiol., 5*, 259.

Danzer, L. A., and J. E. Cohn. (1967). The dissociation curve for goose blood. *Resp. Physiol., 3*, 302.

deWet, P. D., M. R. Fedde, and R. L. Kitchell. (1967). Innervation of the respiratory muscles of *Gallus domesticus*. *J. Morphol., 123*, 17.

Duncker, H.-R. (1971). The lung air sac system of birds. A contribution to the functional anatomy of the respiratory apparatus. *Ergebn. Anat. Entwickl.-Ges., 45*(6), 1.

Duncker, H.-R. (1972). Structure of avian lungs. *Resp. Physiol., 14*, 44.

Duncker, H.-R. (1974). Structure of the avian respiratory tract. *Resp. Physiol., 22*, 1.

Durkovic, R. G., and D. H. Cohen. (1969). Effect of caudal midbrain lesions on conditioning of heart- and respiratory-rate responses in the pigeon. *J. Comp. Physiol. Psychol., 69*, 329.

Eaton, J. A. Jr., M. R. Fedde, and R. E. Burger. (1971). Sensitivity to inflation of the respiratory system in the chicken. *Resp. Physiol., 11*, 167.

Fedde, M. R. (1970). Peripheral control of avian respiration. *Federation Proc., 29*, 1664.

Fedde, M. R., and D. F. Peterson. (1970). Intrapulmonary receptor response to changes in airway-gas composition in *Gallus domesticus*. *J. Physiol. (London), 209*, 609.

Fedde, M. R., and W. D. Kuhlmann. (1974). PO$_2$ changes during analysis of chicken arterial blood. *Comp. Biochem. Physiol., 50A*, 633.

Fedde, M. R., R. E. Burger, and R. L. Kitchell. (1963). The effect of anesthesia and age on respiration following bilateral, cervical vagotomy in the fowl. *Poultry Sci., 42*, 1212.

Fedde, M. R., R. E. Burger, and R. L. Kitchell. (1964a). Electromyographic studies of the effects of bodily position and anesthesia on the activity of the respiratory muscles of the domestic cock. *Poultry Sci., 43*, 839.

Fedde, M. R., R. E. Burger, and R. L. Kitchell. (1964b). Electromyographic studies of the effects of bilateral, cervical vagotomy on the action of the respiratory muscles of the domestic cock. *Poultry Sci., 43*, 1119.

Fedde, M. R., R. E. Burger, and R. L. Kitchell. (1964c). Anatomic and electromyographic studies of the costopulmonary muscles in the cock. *Poultry Sci., 43*, 1177.

Fedde, M. R., R. N. Gatz, H. Slama, and P. Scheid (1974a). Intrapulmonary CO$_2$ receptors in the duck: I. Stimulus specificity. *Resp. Physiol., 22*, 99.

144

Fedde, M. R., P. D. deWet, and R. L. Kitchell. (1969). Motor unit recruitment pattern and tonic activity in respiratory muscles of *Gallus domesticus. J. Neurophysiol., 32,* 995.

Fedde, M. R., R. N. Gatz, H. Slama, and P. Scheid. (1974b). Intrapulmonary $CO_2$ receptors in the duck: II. Comparison with mechanoreceptors. *Resp. Physiol., 22,* 115.

Fischer, G. (1905). Vergleichende anatomische Untersuchungen über den Bronchialbaum der Vögel. *Zoologica, 19,* H. 45, 1.

Fowle, A. S. E., and S. Weinstein. (1966). Effect of cutaneous electric shock on ventilatory response of birds to carbon dioxide. *Am. J. Physiol., 210,* 293.

Hart, J. S., and O. Z. Roy. (1966). Respiratory and cardiac responses to flight in pigeons. *Physiol. Zool., 39,* 291.

Hazelhoff, E. H. (1943). Bouw en functie van de vogellong. *Verslag van de gewonne vergaderingen der Afdeeling Natuurkunde van de Nederlanse Akademie van Wetenschappen* (Amsterdam), *52,* 391. [English translation: Structure and function of the lung of birds. *Poultry Sci., 39,* 3 (1951).]

Johnson, L. F., and M. E. Tate. (1969). Structure of "phytic acids." *Can. J. Chem., 47,* 63.

Johnston, A. M., and M. G. M. Jukes. (1966). The respiratory response of the decerebrate domestic hen to inhaled carbon dioxide–air mixture. *J. Physiol. (London), 184,* 38P.

Jones, D. R., and G. F. Holeton. (1972). Cardiovascular and respiratory responses of ducks to progressive hypocapnic hypoxia. *J. Exp. Biol., 56,* 657.

Jones, D. R., and M. J. Purves. (1970). The effect of carotid body denervation upon the respiratory response to hypoxia and hypercapnia in the duck. *J. Physiol. (London), 211,* 295.

Jukes, M. G. M. (1971). Control of respiration. In "Physiology and Biochemistry of the Domestic Fowl," Vol. I (D. J. Bell and B. M. Freeman, Eds.). London: Academic Press, p. 171.

Kadono, H., T. Okada, and K. Ono. (1963). Electromyographic studies on the respiratory muscles of the chicken. *Poultry Sci., 42,* 121.

Kampe, G., and E. C. Crawford, Jr. (1973). Oscillatory mechanics of the respiratory system of pigeons. *Resp. Physiol., 18,* 188.

Kawashiro, T., and P. Scheid. (1975). Arterial blood gases in undisturbed resting birds: Measurements in chicken and duck. *Resp. Physiol., 23,* 337.

King, A. S. (1966a). Structural and functional aspects of the avian lungs and air sacs. In "International Review of General and Experimental Zoology," Vol. 2 (W. J. L. Felts and R. J. Harrison, Eds.). New York: Academic Press, p. 171.

King, A. S. (1966b). Afferent pathways in the vagus and their influence on avian breathing: A review. In "Physiology of the Domestic Fowl" (C. Horton-Smith and E. C. Amoroso, Eds.). London: Oliver and Boyd, p. 302.

King, A. S. (1975). Aves, respiratory system. In "The Anatomy of the Domestic Animals," 5th Ed. (R. Getty, Ed.). Philadelphia: Saunders, Chapter 64.

King, A. S., and A. F. Cowie. (1969). The functional anatomy of the bronchial muscle of the bird. *J. Anat., 105,* 323.

King, A. S. J. McLelland, R. D. Cook, D. Z. King, and C. Walsh. (1974). The ultrastructure of afferent nerve endings in the avian lung. *Resp. Physiol., 22,* 21.

King, A. S., and V. Molony. (1971). The anatomy of respiration. In "Physiology and Biochemistry of the Domestic Fowl," Vol. 1 (D. J. Bell and B. M. Freeman, Eds.). New York: Academic Press, p. 93.

King, A. S., and D. C. Payne. (1964). Normal breathing and the effects of posture in *Gallus domesticus. J. Physiol. (London), 174,* 340.

Kotilainen, P. V., and P. T. S. Putkonen. (1972). Respiratory arrest and bradycardia during anterolateral diencephalic stimulation in the chicken. *Acta Physiol. Scand., 85,* 286.

Kotilainen, P. V., and P. T. S. Putkonen. (1974). Respiratory and cardiovascular responses to electrical stimulation of the avian brain with emphasis on inhibitory mechanisms. *Acta Physiol. Scand., 90,* 358.

Kunz, A. L., and D. A. Miller. (1974a). Pacing of avian respiration with $CO_2$ oscillation. *Resp. Physiol., 22,* 167.

Kunz, A. L., and D. A. Miller. (1974b). Effects of feedback delay upon the apparent damping ratio of the avian respiratory control system. *Resp. Physiol., 22,* 179.

Lasiewski, R. C. (1972). Respiratory function in birds. In "Avian Biology," Vol. II (D. S. Farner and J. R. King, Eds.). New York: Academic Press, p. 287.

Lasiewski, R. C., and W. A. Calder, Jr. (1971). A preliminary allometric analysis of respiratory variables in resting birds. *Resp. Physiol., 11,* 152.

Leitner, L.-M. (1972). Pulmonary mechanoreceptor fibres in the vagus of the domestic fowl. *Resp. Physiol., 16,* 232.

Leitner, L.-M. and M. Roumy. (1974). Vagal afferent activities related to the respiratory cycle in the duck: Sensitivity to mechanical, chemical and electrical stimuli. *Resp. Physiol., 22,* 41.

Lenfant, C., G. L. Kooyman, R. Elsner, and C. M. Drabek. (1969). Respiratory function of blood of the Adélie penquin *Pygoscelis adeliae. Am. J. Physiol., 216,* 1598.

Linsley, J. G., and R. E. Burger. (1964). Respiratory and cardiovascular responses in the hyperthermic domestic cock. *Poultry Sci., 43,* 291.

Locy, W. A., and O. Larsell. (1916a). The embryology of the bird's lung based on observations of the domestic fowl. Part I. *Am. J. Anat., 19,* 447.

Locy, W. A., and O. Larsell. (1916b). The embryology of the bird's lung based on observations of the domestic fowl. Part II. *Am. J. Anat., 20,* 1.

Lutz, P. L., I. S. Longmuir, and K. Schmidt-Nielsen. (1974). Oxygen affinity of bird blood. *Resp. Physiol., 20,* 325.

Lutz, P. L., I. S. Longmuir, J. V. Tuttle, and K. Schmidt-Nielsen. (1973). Dissociation curve of bird blood and effect of red cell oxygen consumption. *Resp. Physiol., 17,* 269.

Magno, M. (1973). Cardio-respiratory responses to carotid body stimulation with NaCN in the chicken. *Resp. Physiol., 17,* 220.

McLelland, J. (1970). The innervation of the air passages of the avian lung and observations on afferent vagal pathways concerned in the regulation of breathing. Ph.D. thesis, University of Liverpool, Liverpool, England.

Mead, J., T. Takishima, and D. Leith. (1970). Stress distribution in lungs: a model of pulmonary elasticity. *J. Appl. Physiol., 28,* 596.

Molony, V. (1972). A study of vagal afferent activity in phase with breathing and its role in the control of breathing in *Gallus domesticus.* Ph.D. thesis, University of Liverpool, Liverpool, England.

Molony, V. (1974). Classification of vagal afferents firing in phase with breathing in *Gallus domesticus. Resp. Physiol., 22,* 57.

Nightingale, T. E., and M. R. Fedde. (1972). Determination of normal buffer line for chicken blood. *Resp. Physiol. 14,* 353.

Nightingale, T. E., R. A. Boster, and M. R. Fedde. (1968). Use of the oxygen electrode in recording $PO_2$ in avian blood. *J. Appl. Physiol., 25,* 371.

Osborne, J. L., and R. E. Burger. (1974). Intrapulmonary chemoreceptors in *Gallus domesticus. Resp. Physiol., 22,* 77.

Payne, D. C. (1960). Observations on the functional anatomy of the lungs and air sacs of *Gallus domesticus.* Ph.D. Thesis, University of Bristol, Bristol, England.

Peterson, D. F., and M. R. Fedde. (1968). Receptors sensitive to carbon dioxide in lungs of chicken. *Science, 162,* 1499.

Peterson, D. F., and M. R. Fedde. (1971). Avian intrapulmonary $CO_2$-sensitive receptors: A comparative study. *Comp. Biochem. Physiol., 40A,* 425.

Piiper, J., and P. Scheid. (1973). Gas exchange in avian lungs: Models and experimental evidence. In "Comparative Physiology" (L. Bolis, K. Schmidt-Nielsen, and S. H. P. Maddrell, Eds.). Amsterdam: North-Holland Publishing Co., p. 161.

Piiper, J., and P. Scheid. (1972). Maximum gas transfer efficacy of models for fish gills, avian lungs and mammalian lungs. *Resp. Physiol. 14,* 115.

Piiper, J., P. Dejours, P. Haab, and H. Rahn. (1971). Concepts and basic quantities in gas exchange physiology. *Resp. Physiol., 13,* 292.

Piiper, J., K. Pfeifer, and P. Scheid. (1969). Carbon monoxide diffusing capacity of the respiratory system in the domestic fowl. *Resp. Physiol., 6,* 309.

Piiper, J., F. Drees, and P. Scheid. (1970). Gas exchange in the domestic fowl during spontaneous breathing and artificial ventilation. *Resp. Physiol. 9,* 234.

Ray, P. J., and M. R. Fedde. (1969). Responses to alterations in respiratory $PO_2$ and $PCO_2$ in the chicken. *Resp. Physiol., 6,* 135.

Richards, S. A. (1968). Vagal control of thermal panting in mammals and birds. *J. Physiol. (London), 199,* 89.

Richards, S. A. (1969). Vagal function during respiration and the effects of vagotomy in the domestic fowl *(Gallus domesticus). Comp. Biochem. Physiol., 29,* 955.

Richards, S. A. (1970). A pneumotaxic centre in avian brain. *J. Physiol. (London), 207,* 57.

Richards, S. A. (1971). Brain stem control of polypnoea in the chicken and pigeon. *Resp. Physiol., 11,* 315.

Richards, S. A., and A. H. Sykes. (1967). The effects of hypoxia, hypercapnia and asphyxia in the domestic fowl *(Gallus domesticus). Comp. Biochem. Physiol., 21,* 691.

Salt, G. W., and E. Zeuthen. (1960). The respiratory system. In: "Biology and Comparative Physiology of Birds," Vol. 1 (A. J. Marshall, Ed.). New York: Academic Press, p. 363.

Scheid, P., and J. Piiper. (1969). Volume, ventilation and compliance of the respiratory system in the domestic fowl. *Resp. Physiol., 6,* 298.

Scheid, P., and J. Piiper. (1970). Analysis of gas exchange in the avian lung: Theory and experiments in the domestic fowl. *Resp. Physiol., 9,* 246.

Scheid, P., and J. Piiper. (1971). Direct measurement of the pathway of respired gas in duck lungs. *Resp. Physiol., 11,* 308.

Scheid, P., and J. Piiper. (1972). Cross-current gas exchange in avian lungs: Effects of reversed parabronchial air flow in ducks. *Resp. Physiol., 16,* 304.

Scheid, P., and T. Kawashiro. (1975). Metabolic changes in avian blood and their effects on determination of blood gases and pH. *Resp. Physiol., 23,* 291.

Scheid, P., and H. Slama. (1975). Remote-controlled device for sampling arterial blood in undisturbed animals. *Pflügers Arch., 356,* 373.

Scheid, P., H. Slama, R. N. Gatz, and M. R. Fedde. (1974a). Intrapulmonary $CO_2$ receptors in the duck: III. Functional localization. *Resp. Physiol., 22,* 123.

Scheid, P., H. Slama, and J. Piiper. (1972). Mechanisms of unidirectional flow in parabronchi of avian lungs: Measurements in duck lung preparations. *Resp. Physiol., 14,* 83.

Scheid, P., H. Slama, and H. Willmer. (1974b). Volume and ventilation of air sacs in ducks studied by inert gas wash-out. *Resp. Physiol., 21,* 19.

Scheipers, G., T. Kawashiro, and P. Scheid. (1975). Oxygen and carbon dioxide dissociation of duck blood. *Resp. Physiol., 24,* 1.

Schmidt-Nielsen, K., J. Kanwisher, R. C. Lasiewski, J. E. Cohn, and W. L. Bretz. (1969). Temperature regulation and respiration in the ostrich. *Condor, 71,* 341.

Sinha, M. P. (1958). Vagal control of respiration as studied in the pigeon. *Helv. Physiol. Acta, 16,* 58.

Stanislaus, M. (1937). Untersuchungen an der Kolibrilunge. *Z. Morphol. Okol. Tiere, 33,* 261.

Sturkie, P. D. (Ed). (1965). "Avian Physiology," 2nd Ed. Ithaca, New York: Cornell University Press.

von Saafeld, E. (1936). Untersuchungen über das Hacheln bei Tauben. *Z. Vergl. Physiol., 23,* 727.

Vos, H. J. (1934). Über den Weg der Atemluft in der Entenlunge. *Z. Wiss. Biol. Vergl. Physiol., 21,* 552.

Weibel, E. R. (1963). "Morphometry of the Human Lung." Berlin: Springer-Verlag.

Zeuthen, E. (1942). The ventilation of the respiratory tract in birds. *Kgl. Danske Videnskab. Selskab. Biol. Medd., 17,* 1.

Zimmer, K. (1935). Beiträge zur Mechanik der Atmung bei den Vögeln in Stand und Flug. *Zoologica, 33,* (5 Heft 88), 1.

# 7

# Regulation of Body Temperature

## G. C. Whittow

# INTRODUCTION

Birds, like mammals, are "homeotherms," which means that they maintain a relatively constant deep-body temperature. Birds are also "endotherms," a term indicating that they are able to increase their body temperature by generating a considerable amount of heat within their tissues instead of relying on heat gained directly from their surroundings (Whittow, 1966).

However, they differ conspicuously from mammals in a number of different ways that have a direct bearing on their energy metabolism and the manner in which they regulate their body temperature. The plumage of birds provides them with a very effective insulation, and most birds are able to fly. The disposition of fat tends to be different in birds and mammals, with implications as far as their tissue insulation is concerned. The salt glands of some birds enable them to avoid many of the consequences of dehydration, as a result of evaporative heat loss, but the absence of sweat glands in birds places the onus of evaporative cooling on their respiratory mechanisms. Finally, the development of the embryo in an egg outside the body puts a different perspective on the ontogeny of thermoregulation in birds.

It is not my intention to provide an exhaustive treatment of thermoregulation in birds, but to present the general principles of physiological and behavioral temperature regulation, with special reference to birds. The reader's attention is directed also to an earlier review of temperature regulation in birds (Whittow, 1965a), and to more recent reviews by Dawson and Hudson (1970), by Freeman (1971), and by Calder and King (1974).

# HEAT BALANCE

Some of the heat produced in the tissues by metabolic activity is stored in the body and thereby contributes to the high body temperature of birds. Most of the heat, however, is lost to the environment. This simple statement can be amplified to form the following equation, which provides a rational framework for the discussion of temperature regulation in birds.

$$M = E \pm R \pm C \pm K \pm S$$

where $M$ = metabolic heat production, $E$ = evaporative heat loss (always positive, implying heat loss from the body), and $S$ = heat storage in the body

The preparation of this chapter was supported by a grant (GB-29287X) from the National Science Foundation.

147

(positive if the heat content of the body increases). The nonevaporative heat-loss parameters are $R$ = heat loss by radiation (positive if heat is lost to the environment), $C$ = heat loss by convection (positive if heat is lost to the environment). $K$ = heat loss by conduction (positive if heat is lost to the environment). This equation pertains to a bird at rest.

In most previous publications on temperature regulation, the kilocalorie (kcal) has been the unit of heat most frequently used. Recently, by international agreement among physiologists interested in temperature regulation, it was decided to replace the kilocalorie with the joule (J). In place of kilocalories per hour to describe heat transfer per unit time, the watt (W) was proposed. The data herein on birds, however, have not been converted from the kilocalorie.

# HEAT STORAGE (*S*)

The quantity of heat stored in the body of a bird, in a given time, may be calculated with the aid of the following equation:

$$S = \Delta \overline{T_b} \times \text{body weight (kg)} \times 0.83$$

where $S$ = heat stored (kcal) over the specified time period, $\Delta \overline{T_b}$ = change in *mean* body temperature (°C) over the same period, and 0.83 is the mean specific heat of the body tissues (kcal/kg/°C).

The mean body temperature $(\overline{T_b})$ is exactly that, i.e., the mean of a large number of temperatures measured both on the surface and deep within the body. This is obviously both a difficult and an impractical quantity to measure. It may be derived, with some loss of accuracy but with considerably greater facility, from the consideration that the body of a bird consists of an inner "core" at a relatively high temperature and an outer "shell" at a lower, more variable temperature.

The core temperature may be measured by inserting a thermistor or thermocouple probe into the rectum or stomach. The shell temperature is estimated by averaging the temperatures taken at several different sites on the surface of the skin and applying weighting factors to the skin temperature of each site commensurate with the surface area of each site (Richards, 1971a). The mean body temperature is then computed by taking the average of, say, the rectal temperature $(T_{re})$ and the mean skin temperature $(\overline{T_s})$, $T_{re}$ and $\overline{T_s}$ being multiplied by other weighting factors appropriate to the amount of tissue at core and shell temperature, respectively. These factors have not been determined experimentally for birds, but in mammals in a warm environment the mean body temperature $(\overline{T}_b)$ is given by the expression $\overline{T}_b = 0.1\,\overline{T}_s + 0.9\,T_{ty}$, where $T_{ty}$ is the deep-body temperature recorded from the external auditory meatus (Hardy et al., 1971).

Changes in the quantity of heat stored within the body constitute an important thermoregulatory mechanism, particularly during exposure to hot environments. The increased rate of heat storage results in a rise in the deep-body temperature; the temperature gradient between the bird and the air increases and so, therefore, does the nonevaporative heat loss from the bird to its environment. If the ambient temperature is higher than that of the bird itself, the bird gains heat from the environment. This happens when the bird is exposed to direct solar radiation but it occurs particularly under desert conditions, where the temperature of the sand and also of the air may exceed the bird's temperature. In these circumstances, heat storage results in an increased body temperature and this in turn, leads to a reduction in the temperature gradient between the bird and its environment. Consequently, heat gain from the environment diminishes.

The storage of heat within the body also implies a saving of water, under hot conditions, simply because the alternative to storage of the heat is its dissipation by evaporative moisture loss. It is appropriate, therefore, that many desert birds become more hyperthermic when they are dehydrated and when their body water balance is more precarious (Dawson, 1954).

The amount of heat stored cannot be such that the body temperature rises to lethal levels, which in many birds seems to be between 46°C and 47°C (Baldwin and Kendeigh, 1932; Randall, 1943; Dawson, 1954). The limitation of heat storage is effected by the thermoregulatory control mechanisms, which are discussed later in this chapter. It is important to emphasize, however, that the curtailment of heat storage is usually achieved at the expense of an increased water loss and an enhanced risk of dehydration. Moreover, because the extent of heat storage is determined by tissue mass, small birds with a relatively high heat production are at a disadvantage in comparison with large birds.

## BODY TEMPERATURE

### Measurement

Probably the best single measure of deep-body temperature in birds is obtained by inserting a flexible thermistor or thermocouple probe into a pe-

ripheral artery, such as the femoral, and threading the probe toward the heart until its tip lies in free flowing blood in the aorta. The blood leaving the heart is mixed blood from all the tissues of the body that are perfused with blood. Consequently, the temperature of the blood in the aorta is as close to the mean body temperature as can be achieved by a single measurement (Whittow, 1971; Woods and Whittow, 1974). Insertion of a thermistor or thermocouple into the hypothalamus is also a good index of deep-body temperature, and it has the additional advantage that it provides information on the temperature of that part of the brain which not only senses changes of deep-body temperature but also integrates information from temperature receptors throughout the body. In the chicken, the temperature of the hypothalamus is lower than that in the colon by 0.7°C (Richards, 1971a), and there is evidence that the arterial blood flowing to the hypothalamus is cooled by venous blood returning from the skin and nasal mucosa.

In practice, and particularly under field conditions, a simpler procedure is called for. Rectal temperature is commonly used, and most of our informaton on the body temperature of birds is in terms of rectal temperature. In recent years, telemetry techniques have been applied to the measurement of body temperature in birds. In one application, the birds swallows a small capsule that transmits information on the gut temperature (Shallenberger et al., 1974). The advantage of this technique is that the bird is unencumbered by wires and its body temperature may be studied in natural surroundings with minimum disturbance to the behavior of the bird.

### In Different Species

In general, the deep-body temperature of birds is higher than that of mammals, although there are many exceptions to this generalization, as Dawson and Hudson (1970) have pointed out. The relatively high body temperature of birds may be related to the effectiveness of their plumage as insulation and, in the case of passerines, to a higher level of heat production (see section on heat production).

There are differences in body temperature between different species of birds (Table 7–1), and some of these differences may be connected with the birds' size, for the body temperature of large birds is lower than that of small species (McNab, 1966). This may be related to the relatively high heat production of many small birds (see section on heat production). Again there are exceptions to this rule; e.g., the body temperature of hummingbirds is

*Table 7-1   Deep-body temperature (T_b) of selected birds, at rest, under thermoneutral conditions*

| Species | Body weight (kg) | $T_b$ (°C) | Reference |
|---|---|---|---|
| *Struthio camelus* (ostrich) | 100.0 | 38.3 | Crawford and Schmidt-Nielsen (1967) |
| *Dromiceius novae-hollandiae* (emu) | 38.3 | 38.1 | Crawford and Lasiewski (1968) |
| *Rhea americana* (rhea) | 21.7 | 39.7 | Crawford and Lasiewski (1968) |
| Domestic goose | 5.0 | 41.0 | McNab (1966) |
| *Spheniscus humboldti* (Peruvian penguin) | 3.9 | 39.0 | Drent and Stonehouse (1971) |
| Domestic turkey | 3.7 | 41.2 | McNab (1966) |
| Domestic pigeon | 3.0 | 42.2 | McNab (1966) |
| Domestic chicken | 2.4 | 41.5 | Richards (1970) |
| Domestic duck | 1.9 | 42.1 | McNab (1966) |
| *Lagopus lagopus* (willow ptarmigan) | 0.573 | 39.9 | West (1972a) |
| *Lophortyx californicus* (California quail) | 0.139 | 41.3 | Brush (1965) |
| *Hesperiphona vespertina* (evening grosbeak) | 0.060 | 41.0 | West and Hart (1966) |
| *Colius striatus* (speckled mousebird) | 0.053 | 39.0 | Bartholomew and Trost (1970) |
| *Acanthis flammea* (common redpoll) | 0.015 | 40.1 | West (1972b) |
| *Taeniopygia castanotis* (zebra finch) | 0.012 | 40.3 | Calder (1964) |

low, although they are small birds, but they are also birds that may become torpid under appropriate conditions (see section on thermoregulation during topor). It may be significant also, that many of the large birds that have low body temperatures are flightless birds, such as *Apteryx* (kiwi), or flightless diving birds, such as the penguins.

## Circadian Rhythm

The deep-body temperature of birds fluctuates during the course of a day. Circadian rhythms of body temperature are important because they reveal the extent to which the bird stores heat and the degree to which the thermoregulatory control mechanisms permit the body temperature to change. One of the factors that determines the extent of the fluctuation is the size of the bird, the variation in temperature ranging from 8°C in hummingbirds (Lasiewski, 1964), to less than 1°C in the ostrich (Crawford and Schmidt-Nielsen, 1967). In general, the body temperature is highest when the bird is most active, and this is true for both diurnal and nocturnal species. Because the highest body temperatures of nocturnal birds occur during the night when the environmental temperature is lowest, it may be argued that the rhythm of body temperature is independent of the environ-

mental temperature; however, this is not the case because the fluctuation of body temperature in birds subjected to a constant high environmental temperature is reduced (Wilson, 1948; Dawson, 1954).

The daily cycle of body temperature is clearly keyed to the photoperiod, and seasonal changes in the temperature cycle may be correlated with corresponding changes in day length (Veghte, 1964). A circadian rhythm of body temperature was absent in a 5-month-old emperor penguin (*Apdenodytes forsteri*) during the 24-hr antarctic day, in spite of the concurrent fluctuation of environmental temperature (Goldsmith and Sladen, 1961). Experimently, the circadian rhythm of body temperatures may be reversed by changing the times of illumination (Koskimies, 1950). Nevertheless, the persistence of a daily temperature cycle in *Scardafella inca* (Inca doves) kept in complete darkness suggests that endogenous factors may be involved, at least in some species (MacMillen and Trost, 1967a). In a carefully controlled study on the chicken Aschoff and v. Saint Paul (1973) found that the mean level of body temperature, its range of oscillation, and the activity of the bird were related to the light intensity. The oscillation in temperature persisted, although with a reduced amplitude, under conditions of constant dim light (Aschoff et al., 1973).

150     The circadian rhythm of body temperature in chickens was reduced in amplitude following the administration of thiouracil (Washburn *et al.,* 1962), suggesting that an underlying variation of thyroid activity was involved. Clearly, a change in body temperature must be achieved by variations in either heat production, or heat loss, or both. Dehydration results in a more pronounced circadian rhythm of deep-body temperature in birds (Dawson, 1954), as it does in mammals (see Whittow, 1971), under hot conditions. The reasons for this have not been established, but a diminished sensitivity of thermally sensitive neurons in the hypothalamus or an impaired circulatory response to thermal stimuli are possible explanations. In chickens, cyanosis of the comb develops during dehydration, suggesting that the circulation is inadequate (Wilson and Edwards, 1952).

### Environmental Temperature

For most birds, there is a range of environmental temperature over which the deep-body temperature remains essentially constant. The extent of this range depends, among other things, on the size of the bird and the amount of plumage. At high air temperatures the body temperature increases, the air temperature at which this occurs depending on the degree to which evaporative cooling mechanisms are used (Figure 7–1). At low air temperatures, shivering may increase heat production to the extent that deep-body temperature increases (see section on heat production).

### Acclimation and Acclimatization

The term "acclimation" generally refers to changes induced by prolonged exposure to a particular temperature, usually under laboratory conditions. "Acclimatization" refers to seasonally induced changes or to changes resulting from climatic variations, usually out of doors (Carlson and Hsieh, 1970). The rectal temperatures of chickens acclimated to an air temperature of 31°C were significantly higher than those of birds kept at 0°C, both in males and females (Whittow *et al.,* 1966). Similarly, Harrison and Biellier (1969) reported lower rectal temperatures of hens at an air temperature of 5°C and higher rectal temperatures at 35°C, compared to values under control conditions (21°C).

### Dehydration

The body temperature of dehydrated *Struthio camelus* (African ostrich) increased, during exposure

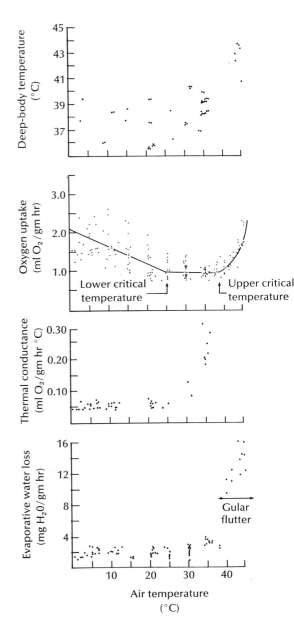

7–1 Deep-body temperature, oxygen uptake, thermal conductance, and evaporative water loss of *Speotyto cunicularia* (burrowing owl) in relation to air temperature. (After Coulombe, 1970).

to heat (45°C), in contrast to the behavior of the normally hydrated bird (Crawford and Schmidt-Nielsen, 1967). This phenomenon has been observed in the turkey (Haller and Sunde, 1966) and in mammals (see Whittow, 1971), and it is related to reduced respiratory evaporative cooling (see later section on evaporation heat loss).

# HEAT PRODUCTION (M)

## Measurement

The heat production of a bird may be computed from the measured oxygen uptake. The bird is enclosed in a chamber through which air is drawn at a constant and known rate. The air leaving the chamber is analyzed for its oxygen and carbon dioxide content. From the rate of air flow and the difference in the oxygen and carbon dioxide content of the air entering and leaving the chamber, the oxygen consumption and carbon dioxide production can be calculated. Romijn and Lokhorst (1961) have proposed the following formula for the calculation of heat production in chickens:

$$M = 3.871 O_2 + 1.194 CO_2$$

where $M$ = heat production (kcal), $O_2$ = oxygen consumption (liters) and $CO_2$ = carbon dioxide production (liters).

Although the equation incorporates a number of simplifications, described by Whittow (1965b), the error involved in its use is less than 1.5%, according to Romijn and Lokhorst (1961). Many investigators do not measure the carbon dioxide production of the bird. In order to convert data for oxygen uptake to heat units, an assumption is made regarding the respiratory quotient (RQ) of the bird, and it is assumed further that the caloric equivalent of oxygen is 4.8 kcal/liter $O_2$ (see Brush, 1965). Consequently the heat production is obtained by multiplying the oxygen uptake by 4.8.

A further technical error is introduced when the carbon dioxide production and RQ are not measured. This is because the volume of air leaving the chamber is always less than the volume entering the chamber, simply because less carbon dioxide is produced than oxygen is consumed, when the RQ is less than 1. The magnitude of the error introduced when this factor is ignored is less than 4.5%, according to Depocas and Hart (1957), who outline a number of procedures for eliminating this error. In place of the "open-circuit" technique described in the preceding paragraphs, a closed-circuit method may be used. In this procedure, the air is recirculated, rather than voided, and a measured quantity of oxygen is admitted to the system in proportion to that used by the bird (Waring and Brown, 1965). The method is accurate but precautions must be taken to correct for changes in temperature and pressure within the system.

The methods described above are a form of "indirect calorimetry," the term "indirect" implying that heat is not measured directly; instead, it is computed form the measured rate of oxygen consumption. "Direct calorimetry" involves the enclosure of the animal in some form of calorimeter and the measurement of the temperature change of the air circulating through the calorimeter, in addition to the rate of heat loss through the walls of the calorimeter. Calorimeters really measure the total amount of heat lost from the animal; but if the body temperature does not change during the course of the measurements, the heat loss is the same as the heat production. The most recent development in calorimetric technique has been the "gradient-layer" calorimeter, which was first developed by Benzinger and Kitzinger (1949) to measure energy exchanges in man. Gradient-layer calorimetry, which was described in an earlier edition (see Whittow, 1965b), has been used mainly for the study of domestic birds (Roller and Dale, 1962; Deshazer, 1967). Davidson *et al.* (1968) compared the heat loss from chickens measured directly in a gradient layer calorimeter with the heat loss estimated from the comparative slaughter technique. The direct technique gave values 3–12% below those determined from the relationship heat loss = metabolized energy – tissue energy gain.

## In Different Species

The resting heat production (see Chapter 8) of a number of birds is shown in Table 7–2. The heat production (kcal/hr) of large birds is greater than that of small ones (Table 7–2). However, the heat production per unit body weight (kcal/g/hr) is less in large birds. These are generalizations that apply equally well to mammals. The relationship between heat production and body weight for nonpasserine birds is as follows:

$$M = 78 W^{0.72}$$

where $M$ = heat production (kcal/24 hr) and $W$ = body weight (kg).

This relationship is very similar to that for mammals. The relationship between heat production and body weight is different in passerine birds (Lasiewski and Dawson, 1967; Dawson and Hudson, 1970), which are mainly small species ($W <$ 0.1 kg). The reason for this has not been elucidated. There are other exceptions to the relationship given above.

Aschoff and Pohl (1970a,b) have proposed that the relationship between the resting heat production and body weight in birds should be reassessed and that separate equations be computed for birds tested during the time of day that they are normally active, "activity time," and for the period when they are normally at rest, "rest time."

*Table 7–2   Resting heat production (M) of selected birds under thermoneutral conditions*

| Species | Body weight (kg) | M (kcal/hr) | Reference |
|---|---|---|---|
| *Struthio camelus* (ostrich) | 100.0 | 97.916 | Crawford and Schmidt-Nielsen (1967) |
| *Dromiceius novae-hollandiae* (emu) | 38.3 | 43.166 | Crawford and Lasiewski (1968) |
| *Rhea americana* (rhea) | 21.7 | 32.958 | Crawford and Lasiewski, (1968) |
| Domestic goose | 5.0 | 11.666 | Crawford and Lasiewski (1968) |
| *Spheniscus humboldti* (Peruvian penguin) | 3.9 | 8.166 | Drent and Stonehouse (1971) |
| Domestic turkey | 3.7 | 7.666 | Dawson and Hudson (1970) |
| Domestic chicken | 2.4 | 6.833 | Dawson and Hudson (1970) |
| Domestic duck | 1.9 | 6.541 | Dawson and Hudson (1970) |
| *Corvus corax* (raven) | 0.866 | 3.954 | Dawson and Hudson (1970) |
| *Lagopus lagopus* (willow ptarmigan) | 0.573 | 3.111 | West (1972a) |
| *Lophortyx californicus* (California quail) | 0.139 | 0.724 | Brush (1965) |
| *Cyanocitta cristata* (northern blue jay) | 0.081 | 0.733 | Dawson and Hudson (1970) |
| *Colius striatus* (speckled mousebird) | 0.053 | 0.301 | Bartholomew and Trost (1970) |
| *Acanthis flammea* (common redpoll) | 0.015 | 0.285 | West (1972b) |
| *Taeniopygia castanotis* (zebra finch) | 0.012 | 0.187 | Calder (1964) |

### Circadian Rhythm

There is a variation in heat production of birds during the course of the day that is independent of the effects of food intake, although food consumption contributes to the rhythm in birds that are fed (Eriksson and Kivimäe, 1954; Figure 7–2). In the chicken, the heat production is highest in the forenoon and lowest at approximately 8:00 p.m. The reduction in the heat production at night amounts to 18–30% in the chicken, but to as much as 49% in the English sparrow (King and Farner, 1961). The fluctuation is in fact, greater in small than in large birds. Deighton and Hutchinson (1940) concluded that the circadian rhythm in fasting Light Sussex fowls was not entirely the result of changes in activity.

Reversal of the daily photoperiod was followed by an inversion of the time relations of the circadian fluctuation in heat production (Fill, 1942). Aschoff and Pohl (1970a) have summarized the situation succinctly in the following way: "the metabolism of starving birds, sitting motionless in the dark, has a profound diurnal rhythm."

### Environmental Temperature

The oxygen uptake and heat production of many birds varies with environmental temperature, in a manner similar to that depicted in Figure 7–1. The range of environmental temperature over which the oxygen uptake remains essentially constant (25°–37°C in Figure 7–1), is the thermoneutral zone. This is a range of air temperature defined by the upper and lower critical temperatures. The range of air temperatures over which birds are in a thermoneutral condition varies from a few degrees centigrade in some small birds, to 28°C (2°–30°C) in penguins (Drent and Stonehouse, 1971). At air temperatures higher than the upper critical temperature, the oxygen consumption increases, usually, as a result of an increased body temperature. The increased temperature of the tissues results in a generalized acceleration of chemical reactions and consequently in an increased oxygen requirement and heat production (van't Hoff-Arrhenius effect).

The heat production also increases at air temperatures below the lower critical temperature, but the mechanism in this instance is quite different: the animal shivers and thereby produces heat. *Carduelis flammea* (common redpoll) is able to increase its heat production over fivefold during exposure to cold (Pohl and West, 1973). The rate at which the oxygen uptake increases in response to exposure to low air temperatures depends on the insulation of the tissues and plumage: the greater the insulation, the lower the rate of increase in oxygen uptake. As the insulation of small birds is generally

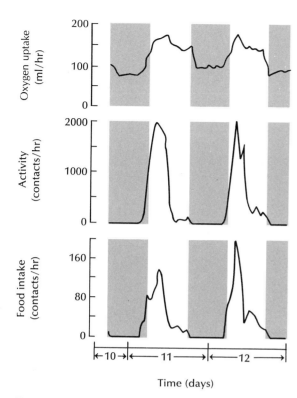

Figure 7–1. When the heat production of *Hesperiphona vespertina* (evening grosbeak) was measured at night at different temperatures, there was no well-defined thermoneutral zone. Heat production and insulation changed simultaneously at ambient temperatures below 30°C (West and Hart, 1966).

## Acclimation and Acclimatization

In many birds tested during the winter, the lower critical temperature has shifted to the left; i.e., the lower critical temperature has diminished compared with birds tested under summer conditions (Table 7–3). In addition, the slope of the relationship between oxygen uptake and air temperature is less. These differences reflect an underlying increase in insulation (see sections on heat transfer and heat loss) in the birds tested in winter. These phenomena are illustrated in *Lagopus lagopus* (willow ptarmigan), an arctic species, in which the summer critical temperature was 7.7°C and the winter one was −6.3°C, close to the lowest known value for any bird (West, 1972a). The well-defined lower critical temperature implies that the insulation has reached a maximum at the lower critical temperature and that it does not increase further at air temperatures below the lower critical temperature. One consequence of this is that if a line is drawn through the values for heat production obtained below the lower critical temperature, and if this line is extrapolated to zero heat production, it transects the horizontal (temperature) axis at the deepbody temperature of the bird. This simply means that when the insulation is constant the heat loss from the bird is proportional to the difference in temperature between the bird and the air surrounding it, an expression of Fourier's law. It follows from this that the heat flow is zero when the air is at the same temperature as the bird.

The situation described in the preceding para-

7–2 Variation in the oxygen uptake, activity, and food intake of *Fringilla coelebs* (chaffinch) during alternating 12-hr periods of light and dark (shaded area). Activity and food intake are expressed in terms of the frequency of operation of microswitches (contacts per hour) actuated by hopping and feeding activity, respectively. (After Aschoff and Pohl, 1970b.)

less effective than that of large ones (see section on nonevaporation heat loss), the rate of increase in heat production below the lower critical temperature is usually greater in small birds.

The level of heat production, both within the thermoneutral zone and below the lower critical temperature, as well as the value for the lower critical temperature itself vary with the experimental conditions (Pohl, 1969; Aschoff and Pohl, 1970a,b). Among the factors known to influence the values are (1) whether the measurements are made at night or during the day, (2) the level of activity of the bird, (3) the intensity and duration of the light, (4) the environmental conditions to which the bird is adapted before the tests, and (5) the level of food intake.

The change in heat production with temperature does not always follow the pattern illustrated in

*Table 7–3* *Resting heat production (M) and lower critical temperatures ($T_{lc}$) of acclimatized common redpolls[a]*

|  | $M$ (kcal/hr) | $T_{lc}$ (°C) |
|---|---|---|
| Winter |  |  |
| Day | 0.406 | 7 |
| Night | 0.348 | 11.5 |
| Summer |  |  |
| Day | 0.249 | 23.5 |
| Night | 0.227 | 21.0 |

[a]Adapted from Pohl and West (1973).

graph obtains when birds acclimatized to winter and summer conditions are subjected to a number of environmental temperatures, each exposure lasting for only a few hours. If the birds are first acclimated to each air temperature by prolonged exposure and are then tested at that temperature, the relationship between heat production and air temperature may be quite different. There is no clearly defined thermoneutral zone, and the heat production below the lower critical temperature is not proportional to the temperature difference between the bird and its environment. Therefore, a line drawn through the values for heat production does not extrapolate to body temperature at zero heat production, but to a temperature considerably higher than body temperature. This means that the effective insulation changes with decreasing air temperature in the acclimatized animal. This seems to be true for large birds, such as the willow ptarmigan (550 g), but not for small birds, such as the common redpoll (14 g), according to West (1972b).

Some birds experience an increased heat production within the thermoneutral zone, during the cold season of the year (Gelineo, 1968). This is a feature of the common redpoll (Pohl and West, 1973; Table 7–3). There was an associated increase in thyroid activity, suggesting that the calorigenic effect of thyroid hormone was involved in the response. Other birds have the ability to maintain higher metabolic rates below their lower critical temperatures, in winter. The evening grosbeak illustrates this effect, according to West (1965).

Experimental exposure to cold in the laboratory, as opposed to seasonally induced changes, produces reasonably clearcut results. There is an increase in basal metabolic rate, which may amount to 85% in *Chrysomitris spinus* (siskin) after acclimation to cold (Gelineo, 1964). Neither Hart (1962) nor Chaffee *et al.* (1963) were able to obtain evidence for "nonshivering thermogenesis," an increased heat production in the absence of shivering, such as occurs in many mammals during acclimation to cold.

Nevertheless, nonshivering thermogenesis cannot be entirely discounted. Evidence of increased thyroid activity in the cold-acclimated domestic fowl (Hahn *et al.* 1966) is compatible with nonshivering thermogenesis. El-Halawani *et al.* (1970) and Jansky *et al.* (1969) provide further support for this mode of heat production in the cold-acclimated bird. Lin and Sturkie (1968) obtained evidence for an increased rate of catecholamines secretion in cold-acclimated chickens and an inhibition of synthesis in birds chronically exposed to heat. Whether the catecholamines are involved in thermogenesis in cold-acclimated birds, however, requires further experimental proof.

The metabolic response of birds to high air temperatures, in relation to season, has not been studied as extensively as have the reactions to low air temperature. Wallgren (1954) found that the basal heat production of *Emberiza c. citrinella* (yellow buntings) did not vary seasonally. In contrast, the heat production of a population of *Passer domesticus* (house sparrows) in Houston, Texas was lower than that of populations in the cooler climates of Michigan and Colorado (Hudson and Kimsey, 1966).

Continued exposure to constant high temperatures in the laboratory results in a diminution in heat production in several species of birds (Hoffman and Shaffner, 1950; Gelineo, 1955; Harrison and Bieller, 1969). In the chicken and *Coturnix coturnix japonica* (Japanese quail), this has been attributed to a diminution in thyroid activity (Hoffman and Shaffner, 1950; Huston *et al.*, 1962; McFarland *et al.*, 1966). The response to high temperatures is suppressed if the temperature is allowed to fluctuate (Wallgren, 1954). Clearly the metabolic responses of birds to both natural and artificial changes of environmental temperature are varied and complex.

## HEAT TRANSFER WITHIN THE BODY

### Pathways

Heat produced in such deep-seated organs as the liver must be transported to the skin surface or the mucosa lining the upper respiratory tract before it can be lost to the environment. This transfer of heat occurs along three distinct pathways.

**Conduction.** Conduction through the tissues takes place by direct transfer of energy from molecule to molecule. The rate of conductive heat transfer depends on the thickness of the layer of tissue (fat, skin, muscle) that the heat must traverse and on the thermal conductivity of the tissue components:

|  | Fat | Skin | Muscle |
|---|---|---|---|
| Thermal conductivity (kcal/m/hr/°C) | 0.18 | 0.29 | 0.43 |

Although fat has the lowest thermal conductivity, its role as a barrier to heat flow is not as important in birds as it is in many mammals because some birds, e.g., the chicken, do not have a substantial layer of fat beneath the skin. Instead, the fat deposition is localized in discrete areas in the abdominal cavity. Quite unlike the chicken in this respect are birds that have adapted to life in the water, notably penguins and ducks. Heat loss to water is considerably greater than that to air at the same temperature. Consequently, a layer of subcutaneous fat, as in mammals, serves to limit heat loss in aquatic species, particularly in penguins, which encounter both very cold water and extremely low air temperatures. Some birds, such as pelicans, have a considerable subcutaneous pneumaticity that may provide additional insulation (Bartholomew and Dawson, 1954).

Convection. Heat transfer by conduction within the body is most important under cold conditions, when the blood flow through the skin is minimal. Within the thermoneutral zone, the more important avenue of heat transfer is by way of the bloodstream, a type of "internal convection." The blood acquires heat in the heat-producing tissues and conveys it to the skin. The skin temperature rises and heat loss to the environment increases.

Countercurrent heat exchange. Heat transfer between the core and the skin surface is also influenced by a process of countercurrent heat exchange in the limbs. The warm arterial blood entering the limb gives up some of its heat to the cool blood returning in the veins from the distal parts of the limbs. This heat is returned to the core. The temperature of the distal parts of the limbs diminishes, and so does the heat loss from the limb to its surroundings. It is easy to see that this process increases the amount of tissue making up the shell. In a warm environment, the venous return from the distal parts of the limbs occurs by way of superficial veins, so that the arterial blood entering the limb is not cooled until it reaches the skin. The advantage of the countercurrent system is that blood flow and oxygen supply to the distal parts of the extremities may be maintained without incurring a high level of heat loss. In other words, the supply of nutrients to the tissues of the extremities is separated from the delivery of heat to them.

Countercurrent heat exchange is strikingly illustrated in the wood stork, a species in which heat conservation is facilitated by the presence in the leg of a special vascular structure, the rete mirabile (Kahl, 1963). In this structure the arteries and veins divide to form a network of intermingling vessels in which arteries and veins are in close apposition to each other. Such a complex structure is not essential for countercurrent heat exchange to occur but it does increase its effectiveness.

## Cold Vasodilatation

Curtailment of heat transfer from the deep tissues to the extremities, by the mechanism described in the preceding paragraph, obviously entails the risk of the peripheral tissues freezing if the environmental temperature is low enough. This possibility is circumvented by the intermittent flow of warm blood to the distal extremities, a phenomenon known as "cold vasodilatation," and first described by Grant and Bland (1931) in the foot of the chicken. Subsequently, it has been reported in the foot of the Antarctic emperor penguin (Goldsmith and Sladen, 1961), a species inhabiting one of the harshest environments on earth.

## Tissue Insulation

In practice, it is difficult both to measure and to distinguish between the avenues of heat transfer within the body. It is much easier to consider the heat transfer as a single process $(H)$, as follows:

$$H = (T_b - \overline{T}_s) h_T$$

where $H$ = heat flow from the core to the skin surface (kcal/m²/hr), $T_b$ = rectal temperature or some other index of core temperature (°C), $\overline{T}_s$ = mean skin temperature (°C; see section on heat storage), and $h_T$ = tissue conductance (kcal/m²/hr/°C).

The tissue conductance is a measure of the "ease" with which heat flows from the core to the skin surface. The reciprocal of the conductance is the tissue insulation, $I_T$. Substituting $I_T$ for $h_T$ in the above equation yields:

$$H = \frac{(T_b - \overline{T}_s)}{I_T}$$

Note that the heat flow is directly proportional to the temperature gradient $(T_b - \overline{T}_s)$, which may be regarded as the "driving force," and inversely proportional to the insulation of the tissues, which may be considered as offering "resistance" to heat flow.

Experimentally, $H$ is usually determined from the measured heat production $(M)$ after any heat stored $(S)$ within the body together with the heat loss by evaporation of moisture from the respiratory tract $(E_{ex})$ are subtracted. The rationale of these corrections is that neither heat stored within the body nor that lost from the respiratory tract flows to the skin.

156 Very little information is available on the tissue insulation of birds, largely because most investigators have computed the total insulation of the bird. Variations in the tissue insulation are effected largely by changes in the blood flow to the skin. Tissue insulation is maximal when the blood flow through the skin is lowest and it tends to be minimal when the cutaneous blood flow is high. In general, the tissue insulation of the feathered areas changes little with variations in environmental temperature. Marked changes in the tissue insulation of unfeathered skin sites, such as the comb and feet, occur, however (Richards, 1971a). The effectiveness of changes in tissue insulation in the unfeathered extremities is brought out by Steen and Steen (1965), who reported that less than 10% of the heat production of gulls and herons is lost from the legs at low ambient temperatures. However, all of the heat production may be lost to water at 35°C if only the legs are immersed.

## Changes in Tissue Insulation During Acclimation and Acclimatization

Winter fattening is a common phenomenon in small birds that winter in cold climates (King and Farner, 1966). The deposition of fat was greater in pigeons acclimated to an air temperature of 10°C than in those acclimated to 29°C, suggesting a difference in the tissue insulation under the two conditions. Rautenberg (1969a) reported that the skin temperature of the trunk and extremities was higher in cold-acclimated than in heat-acclimated pigeons. He attributed this difference to an increased peripheral blood flow in the cold-acclimated birds, which would be consistent with a diminution of tissue insulation. An increase in the tissue insulation of the legs of cold-acclimatized ring-necked pheasants appeared to be brought about by the operation of the countercurrent heat exchange mechanism (Ederstrom and Brumleve, 1964; see above).

## HEAT LOSS

### Nonevaporative

**Pathways.** Heat transported from the tissue where it is produced to the surface of the body may be lost from the surface to the environment by both evaporative and nonevaporative means. The latter, as its name implies, does not involve the evaporation of water. Nonevaporative heat loss, or "sensible" heat loss as it is sometimes called, may occur by three distinct processes.

*Radiation (R).* Heat, in the form of electromagnetic waves, is transferred from the body to surfaces in the environment that are at temperatures lower than those of the skin. The intervening air is not involved. Of course, if the temperature of the surroundings is higher than that of the skin of the bird, the bird gains heat by radiation. This frequently occurs, particularly under desert conditions, and it ought to be borne in mind that whenever a bird is exposed to direct sunlight there is a radiant heat gain. Total radiant heat exchange (R, in kcal/hr) from a bird may be expressed by the following equation:

$$R = \sigma \epsilon_s \epsilon_r (\overline{T}_s^4 - T_r^4) A$$

where $\sigma$ is a constant (the Stefan–Boltzmann constant) with a value of $4.96 \times 10^{-8}$ kcal/m²/hr/°K⁴; $\epsilon_s$ is the emittance of the surface of the bird, i.e., the ratio of the actual emission of heat from the surface to that of a "perfect black body" at the same temperature; $\epsilon_r$ is the emittance of the environmental surfaces; $\overline{T}_s$ is the mean surface temperature of the bird (°K); $\overline{T}_r$ is the mean radiant temperature of the environment (°K); and $A$ is the effective radiating area (m²).

The emissivity of the skin and feathers of birds is very close to that of a perfect black body (Jordan and Dale, 1961) with respect to radiation of long wavelengths (see below). Provided that the difference in temperature between the skin and feathers, on the one hand, and the environmental surfaces, on the other, is not too large (<20°K), heat exchange by radiation may be represented by a simpler equation than that given above:

$$R = h_r (\overline{T}_s - \overline{T}_r)$$

where $h_r$ is the radiation heat transfer coefficient, equal to $4\sigma T^3 A$ ($T$ = mean of $\overline{T}_s$ and $\overline{T}_r$ in °K). The color of the plumage may have a significant effect on the amount of heat lost by the bird under conditions of solar radiation (Hamilton and Heppner, 1967; Heppner, 1970). White *Poephila castanotis* (zebra finches) exposed to artificial sunlight produced 23% less heat in a cool environment (10°C) after their plumage had been dyed black. The difference in the energy production of birds of different colors represents mainly heat gained by the bird's feathers in the visible and near-infrared parts of the spectrum, because, as indicated above, plumage and skin of different colors behave essentially as black bodies with regard to infrared radiation. The mechanism by which solar radiation modifies the heat production of birds depends on the temperature of the outer layers of the plumage. If the temperature of the plumage exceeds that of the skin, heat is gained from the environment by the bird. If the temperature of the feathers increases as a result of solar radiation but remains below the skin temperature, heat loss from the bird is simply reduced. In either situation, the bird need produce less heat to maintain its body temperature.

*Convection (C).* Heat loss by convection involves the actual movement of molecules of the air. Air in contact with the skin warms, becomes less dense, and rises, being replaced by cooler, denser air. This is "natural convection." If the bird is exposed to moving air, or if the bird itself is actually moving through the air, considerably more heat may be lost. Provided that the air velocity is not too high, such "forced convection" is roughly proportional to the square root of the air velocity. Convective heat loss (kcal/m²/hr) may be expressed simply as follows:

$$C = h_c(\overline{T_s} - T_a)$$

where $h_c$ is the convective heat transfer coefficient (kcal/m²/hr/°C), incorporating dimensionless numbers describing the flow and thermal properties of the air and the size and shape of the animal. $\overline{T_s}$ is the mean surface temperature and $T_a$ is the air temperature.

*Conduction (K).* Heat loss by conduction involves the transfer of energy from molecule to molecule but, unlike convection, there is no actual gross translocation of molecules. Because of the low thermal conductivity and specific heat of air, heat loss by conduction to the air is small. Conductive heat loss is important in special circumstances, e.g., in water, which has a high thermal conductivity and specific heat compared with air. The equation for heat transfer by conduction ($K$, in kcal/m²/hr) is:

$$K = h_k(\overline{T_s} - T_a)$$

where $h_k$ is the conductive heat transfer coefficient (kcal/m²/hr/°C). The conductive heat transfer coefficient depends on the thermal conductivity of the medium to which heat is being lost, i.e., water or nest materials, and, in the case of air and water, on the thickness of the "boundary" layer of air or water adjacent to the skin or feathers. The thickness of the boundary layer in turn varies with the roughness and shape of the animal's surface, as well as with the velocity of the air or water movement adjacent to the animal.

**Respiratory nonevaporative heat loss.** A special instance of nonevaporative heat loss is the warming of inspired air to body temperature by a process of convection and conduction in the upper respiratory tract. The warming of the air as it enters the nasal passage removes heat from the nasal mucosa, the temperature of which falls. When the air is exhaled, cooling of the air occurs in the nasal passages, so that some of the heat is regained by the mucosa. This is another example of a countercurrent heat exchange system and it has important implications as far as respiratory evaporative heat loss is concerned. The temperature of the exhaled air depends on the surface area and width of the nasal passages, and different birds vary significantly in this respect (Schmidt-Nielsen *et al.*, 1970). In the cactus wren (*Camphylorhyncus brunnelcapillum*) 81% of the heat added to the inhaled air is recovered in this way at an air temperature of 15°C, and 91% is recovered at an air temperature of 30°C (Schmidt-Nielsen *et al.*, 1970). However, desert birds did not appear to be different from other birds in this respect. The following equation describes respiratory nonevaporative heat loss ($H_{resp}$, in kcal/hr) in birds:

$$H_{resp} = \dot{V}_E \rho C_p (T_{ex} - T_{in})$$

where $\dot{V}_E$ is the respiratory minute volume (liters/hr), $\rho$ is the density of air (g/liter), $C_p$ is the specific heat of air (kcal/g/°C), $T_{ex}$ is the temperature of expired air (°C), and $T_{in}$ is the temperature of inspired air (°C).

**Insulation of the plumage.** The plumage of birds provides a very effective barrier to heat loss from the skin surface to the surrounding air. The down feathers trap air in which little convective movement occurs, and the distal parts of the contour feathers provide a windproof covering. The feathers are covered with a thin layer of oil secreted by the preen gland, and the spaces between the finest divisions of the feather structure are extremely small. Both factors render the plumage of birds relatively resistant to wetting (Hutchinson, 1954). The insulation provided by the plumage is greater in large than in small birds (Herreid and Kessel, 1967). This probably reflects the fact that large birds are able to carry a heavier load of feathers than are small birds. In addition, the radial distribution of feathers around the torso and extremities of a small bird results in a less compact insulation than is the case in large birds (see Hutchinson, 1954; Whittow, 1971). The insulation of the plumage may be varied by the activity of the ptilomotor nerves, which supply the arrectores plumorum muscles. These are smooth muscles and the available evidence suggests that their innervation may be cholinergic (Jenkinson and Blackburn, 1968). Birds evidently have an elaborate structural system for controlling feather movements.

Birds fluff out their feathers during exposure to cold (Hutchinson, 1954). This increases the insulation provided by the feathers; when *Troglodytes aedon aedon* (eastern house wrens) were prevented from fluffing their feathers, their body temperature decreased more rapidly than did that of control birds (Baldwin and Kendeigh, 1932). The ambient temperature at which the feathers of *Streptopelia risoria* (Barbary dove) are fully raised is higher in birds deprived of food or water (McFarland and Baher, 1968; McFarland and Budgell, 1970), presumably because their heat production is below normal. The lower critical temperature of defeathered California quail was higher than that of birds with plumage, again reflecting a diminution in insulation (Brush, 1965). In fowls with poor or scant plumage, the level of heat production was higher than in controls (Benedict *et al.*, 1932; Romijn and Lokhorst, 1961); this effect could also be produced in normal chickens by removing the plumage (Hoffman and Shaffner, 1950). The higher heat production was probably related to the poor insulation in these birds.

Some birds elevate certain of their feathers during exposure to solar radiation. The raised scapulars of *Sula dactylatra* (masked Booby) illustrate this response; its purpose appears to be to permit a better circulation of air through the plumage and thus to enhance heat loss (Bartholomew, 1966).

Kendeigh (1934) found that the weight of the winter plumage was about 30% greater than that of the summer plumage, in *Passer domesticus* (English sparrow) (see also West, 1962). Experimentally, the weight of the plumage could be reduced by acclimating chickens to a warm environment (Fisher *et al.*, 1965). Coulombe (1970) found that the emissivity of the plumage of the owl was greater in winter than in summer.

**Overall insulation.** More information is available on the total insulation and its converse, total conductance, of birds than on the separate insulation of the tissues and feathers, because the former is simpler to compute. Calculations of tissue insulation and the insulation of the plumage require that the mean skin temperature ($\overline{T_s}$) be measured. The total insulation $I$. in °C-m²-hr/kcal, which consists of the tissue insulation, the insulation of the plumage and the insulation of a layer of still air immediately contiguous to the outer surface of the plumage and bare skin, may be derived from the following equation:

$$I = \frac{(T_b - T_a)}{(M \pm S - E)}$$

where $T_b$ is deep-body temperature (°C), $T_a$ is air temperature (°C), $M$ is heat production (kcal/m²/hr), $E$ is total evaporative heat loss (kcal/m²/hr), and $S$ is heat storage (kcal/m²/hr).

Table 7–4 presents data for the total thermal conductance of birds with different body weights. With some exceptions the thermal conductance of

***Table 7–4*** *Total thermal conductance (h) of birds, at rest, at the lower critical air temperature[a]*

| Species | Body weight (kg) | $h$ (kcal/m²/hr/°C) |
|---|---|---|
| *Struthio camelus* (ostrich) | 100.0 | 2.9 |
| Domestic goose | 5.0 | 1.46 |
| *Spheniscus humboldti* (Peruvian penguin) | 3.9 | 0.81 |
| Domestic chicken | 3.3 | 1.32 |
| Domestic pigeon | 0.315 | 1.77 |
| *Geococcyx californianus* (roadrunner) | 0.285 | 1.80 |
| *Speotyto cunicularia* (burrowing owl) | 0.143 | 1.03 |
| *Lophortyx californicus* (California quail) | 0.138 | 1.64 |
| *Cyanocitta cristata* (northern blue jay) | 0.081 | 1.54 |
| *Chordeiles minor* (common nighthawk) | 0.075 | 1.49 |
| *Hesperiphona vespertina* (evening grosbeak) | 0.055 | 1.53 |
| *Colius striatus* (speckled mousebird) | 0.050 | 1.35 |
| *Passer domesticus* (house sparrow) | 0.025 | 2.04 |
| *Taeniopygia castanotis* (zebra finch) | 0.012 | 2.54 |
| *Calypte costae* (Costa's hummingbird) | 0.003 | 1.97 |

[a]Modified from Dawson and Hudson (1970) and Drent and Stonehouse (1971).

small birds is greater, and the insulation is therefore less, than that of large birds. This is partly because of the smaller amount of plumage carried by the small birds, as discussed previously. However, a similar relationship exists between body weight and insulation in defeathered birds (Herreid and Kessel, 1967), indicating that small birds also have less tissue insulation. This is probably because of differences in the thickness of the skin and fat layers, but it may also reflect differences in the degree to which the cutaneous blood flow can be varied in birds of different weight. In addition, the laws of heat transfer through both tissue and plumage indicate that heat is conducted more rapidly through a small bird, with small radii of curvature of its torso and appendages, than in a large bird. The increase in the thermal insulation of birds with increasing body size occurs more steeply than does the decrease in heat production per unit body weight. The consequence of this is that the lower critical temperature diminishes with increasing body size. However, even quite large arctic species such as *Lagopus leucuous* (white-tailed ptarmigan) and *Branta nigricens* (black brant) have lower critical temperatures in excess of 0°C (Irving *et al.*, 1955; Dawson and Hudson, 1970). The lower critical temperatures of many birds inhabiting cold regions of the world are well above the temperatures they regularly encounter under natural conditions in winter. The birds must therefore augment their rate of heat production and they must increase their food intake when food is likely to be most scarce and the daylight hours for feeding most limited. Nevertheless, the performance of some birds is extremely impressive. For instance, the lower critical temperature of a small arctic bird, the common redpoll, weighing approximately 14 g, is 9°C; yet the bird is able to survive exposure to −50°C for 3 hr (Pohl and West, 1973). Small birds are not able to increase their insulation sufficiently during exposure to cold, and an increased heat production is the principal means by which they are able to maintain body temperature (Pohl and West, 1973). The common redpoll is apparently able to increase heat production during the day and to increase insulation at night, during the winter. However, Steen (1958) interpreted his experimental results to mean that many small birds are able to secure shelter from their cold environment at night. Mac-Millen (1974) found that two congeneric species of Hawaiian honeycreepers behaved quite differently at environmental temperatures below the lower critical temperature. In one species *(Loxops virens)* the thermal conductance varied below the lower critical temperature. In the other species *(Loxops parva)* the thermal conductance was constant but the body temperature diminished.

Data compiled by Dawson and Hudson (1970) reveal that birds can vary their total insulation two- to fivefold over a range of environmental temperatures. The highest value for insulation reported in the literature is that of the *Spheniscus humboldti* (Peruvian penguin; Drent and Stonehouse, 1971).

Scholander *et al.* (1950) obtained evidence that the insulation of arctic birds is superior to that of tropical species, and the thermal conductance of *Speotyto cunicularia* (burrowing owls) acclimatized to winter conditions was lower than that of summer-adapted birds (Coulombe, 1970). The owls appeared to have more extensive plumage in winter and this probably contributed in large part to their lower thermal conductance.

### Evaporative *(E)*

**Total.** Evaporation of moisture may occur from the surface of the skin or from the respiratory tract. Total evaporative heat loss *(E)* may be represented as follows:

$$E = E_{ex} + E_{sw}$$

where $E_{ex}$ is evaporative heat loss from the respiratory tract and $E_{sw}$ is evaporative heat loss from the skin.

The partition of evaporative heat loss into its respiratory and cutaneous components has not been achieved in many birds (Figure 7–3). The technique is discussed in a later section. Total evaporative water loss may be measured simply by recording the weight loss of the animal over an accurately measured period of time, making appropriate corrections for the weight loss contingent on respiratory gas exchange (oxygen, carbon dioxide). The technique is discussed by Lasiewski *et al.* (1966a,b). If the metabolic weight loss is ignored, the total evaporative water loss *(E)*, in kcal/hr. becomes:

$$E = \dot{m}\lambda$$

where $\dot{m}$ is weight loss (kg/hr) and $\lambda$ is the latent heat of vaporization (kcal/kg).

The latent heat of vaporization is the heat that must be removed from the body in order to evaporate 1 kg of water. The value varies with temperature. An approximate value is 580 kcal/kg $H_2O$.

When the air temperature equals the body temperature of the bird, heat can be lost only by evaporation of moisture.

**Cutaneous ($E_{sw}$).** Cutaneous evaporative water loss may be measured by enclosing the bird in a

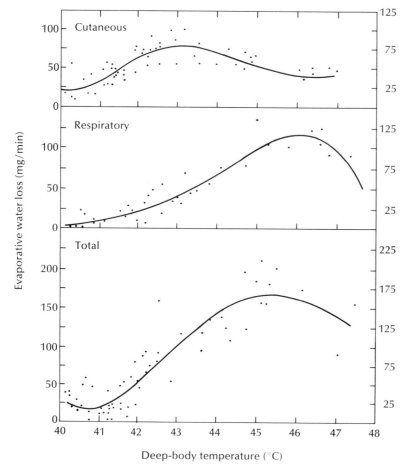

7–3

Partition of total evaporative water loss from *Columba livia* (pigeon), at different deep-body temperatures, into its respiratory and cutaneous components. (After Smith, 1969; courtesy of Dr. Richard M. Smith.)

chamber containing a flexible partition through which the bird's head is inserted. The purpose of this is to separate respiratory from cutaneous moisture loss. Both compartments within the chamber are ventilated with air at a known flow rate, and the humidity of the air entering and leaving the two compartments is recorded. This method also, of course, permits the quantitative evaluation of respiratory evaporative water loss

The total transfer of heat from the skin to the air by evaporation ($E_{sw}$, in kcal/hr/m$^2$) is described by the following equation:

$$E_{sw} = h_e (\theta_s P_{ws} - \theta_a P_{wa})\lambda$$

where $h_e$ is the evaporative heat transfer coefficient, a function of air movement, viscosity, density, and thermal conductivity (kg/hr/m$^2$/mm Hg); $\theta_s$ is the relative humidity at the skin surface (%); $\theta_a$ is the relative humidity of the air (%); $P_{ws}$ is the saturated aqueous vapor pressure of skin at $T_s$ (mm Hg); and $P_{wa}$ is the saturated aqueous vapor pressure of air at $T_a$ (mm Hg).

Neither sweat glands nor sebaceous glands are present in the skin of birds (Jenkinson and Blackburn, 1968). The amount of moisture that may be lost from the skin under hot conditions is therefore limited. Nevertheless, it may amount to considerably more than hitherto believed, at least in some birds. For example, Smith and Suthers (1969) and Smith (1969, 1972) obtained evidence that although the maximal cutaneous water loss from the pigeon was less than the maximal respiratory water loss, under certain conditions the actual cutaneous water loss exceeded that from the respiratory tract (Figure 7–3). This occurred in the early stages of hyperthermia and it reflected the fact that, whereas the cutaneous water loss increased rapidly when the birds were exposed to heat, respiratory water loss increased more slowly; it did not, in fact, reach its maximum until a deep-body temperature of 46°C was attained. Similarly, Bernstein (1971) found that at an air temperature of 35°C, cutaneous evaporative water loss exceeded respiratory loss in *Excalfactoria chinensis* (painted quail) and evidence for a significant water loss from the skin of the chicken was obtained by van Kampen (1971). An explanation for the high rates of cutaneous water loss in birds must await further investigation. Smith (1969) has postulated that the thin, vascular skin of birds and possibly a high rate of filtration of fluid from the blood capillaries in the skin may permit higher rates of water loss than in mammals. It is pertinent that cutaneous evaporative water loss in *Taeniopygia castanotis* (zebra finch) was reduced by depriving the birds of drinking water (Lee and Schmidt-Nielsen, 1971).

**Respiratory ($E_{ex}$).** Respiratory evaporative heat loss ($E_{ex}$) in kcal/hr may be represented as follows:

$$E_{ex} = \dot{V}(\rho_{ex} - \theta_a\rho_{in})\lambda$$

where $V$ is respiratory minute volume (liter/hr), $\rho_{ex}$ is kilograms of water per liter air saturated with water vapor at the temperature of expired air, $\theta_a$ is the relative humidity of inspired (ambient) air, $\rho_{in}$ is kilograms $H_2O$ per liter air saturated at ambient air temperature, and $\lambda$ is the latent heat of vaporization of water (kcal/kg). Respiratory evaporative cooling is extremely important in birds and almost without exception, birds exhibit some form of panting.

*Thermal polypnea.* Thermal polypnea involves an increase in the respiratory minute volume; this leads to an increase in respiratory evaporative heat loss. The increased respiratory minute volume is brought about by an increase in respiratory frequency, while the tidal volume decreases (Figure 7-4). This particular pattern of respiration permits a maximal increase in respiratory minute volume and respiratory evaporative cooling with minimal disturbance of the blood gases, because the increased ventilation is limited to the respiratory dead space, in which gas exchange between blood and air does not occur. However, as the body temperature of the bird increases to high levels, the respiratory frequency reaches a maximal value and subsequently declines. This change in respiratory frequency is accompanied by an increase in tidal volume, while the minute volume increases further. At very high temperatures the respiratory minute volume declines also (Figure 7-4). This change in the pattern of breathing is characteristic of many hyperthermic panting animals, including mammals. It represents the breakdown of thermal polypnea, and the possible mechanism for it has been discussed in detail elsewhere (Whittow, 1971).

The extensive air sac system of birds appears to endow them with an unsurpassed means of direct-

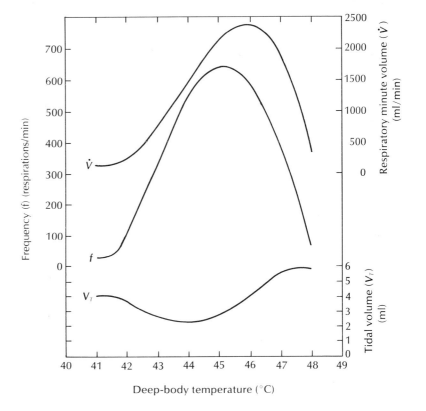

7-4
Respiratory minute volume ($\dot{V}$), frequency ($f$), and tidal volume ($V_T$) of the pigeon in relation to deep-body temperature ($T_b$). The data were obtained from birds enclosed in a body plethysmograph. (After Smith, 1972.)

162 ing the increased ventilation to parts of the respiratory tract that do not participate in the exchange of gas between blood and air while, at the same time, permitting evaporative heat loss to occur. Paradoxically, with the exception of the ostrich (Schmidt-Nielsen et al., 1969), they do not appear to take advantage of this anatomical arrangement. In other words, birds incur a reduction in the level of carbon dioxide in the blood (Calder and Schmidt-Nielsen, 1966, 1968), and the reduction in tidal volume simply minimizes the hyperventilation of the air spaces in the lung where gas exchange takes place.

The initiation of thermal polypnea varies in character in different birds. In some birds, e.g., the domestic fowl and Phalacrocorax auritus (double-crested cormorant), the respiratory frequency increases steadily with increasing heat load (Whittow et al., 1964; Bartholomew et al., 1968). In other birds, e.g., the ostrich and Geococcyx californianna (road runner) (Schmidt-Nielsen et al., 1969; Calder and Schmidt-Nielsen, 1967), the respiratory frequency changes in response to heat from the normal low rate to a high value, which does not change thereafter. This value matches the resonant frequency of the entire respiratory system (Crawford and Kampe, 1971) in many birds. At this frequency the energy cost of panting is low, amounting to that required to keep the respiratory system oscillating at its natural frequency. If the frequency of thermal polypnea is constant in these birds, then they can vary evaporative cooling only by intermittent operation of the panting mechanism, or by modulation of tidal volume. The energy cost of panting, however, can be substantial in some birds. Dawson estimated that 40% of the heat dissipated by panting in the cardinal (Richmondena cardinalis) merely offsets the heat produced by the respiratory muscles (see Dawson and Hudson, 1970).

The amount of heat that birds may lose by respiratory evaporative cooling is considerable, many birds being quite capable of dissipating all the heat that they produce by respiratory evaporation in a hot environment (Table 7–5). Not all birds have effective mechanisms of evaporative cooling however. Notable exceptions are two species of Hawaiian honey-creepers (Loxops), which were comparatively heat intolerant (MacMillen, 1974).

*Gular flutter.* This is an evaporative heat loss mechanism in addition to thermal polypnea. Some birds are able to vibrate the floor of their mouth cavities, the gular area. The gular flutter is actuated by flexure of the hyoid apparatus, and the gular area becomes conspicuously suffused with blood. The advantage of gular flutter over thermal polypnea is twofold. In the first place, the air movement is restricted to surfaces that do not participate in gas exchange, so that the dangers of hyperventilation are circumvented. Second, the energy cost of moving the gular area is considerably less than that of moving the larger thoracic cavity. Consequently,

*Table 7–5* *Evaporative heat loss (E), expressed as a percentage of heat production, at high air temperatures $(T_a)$[a]*

| Species | Body weight (kg) | $T_a$ (°C) | $E$ (%) |
|---|---|---|---|
| Struthio camelus (ostrich) | 100.0 | 44.5 | 100 |
| Gallus domesticus (Bedouin fowl) | 1.427 | 48 | 159 |
| Columbia livia (rock dove) | 0.315 | 44.5 | 118 |
| Geococcyx californianus (roadrunner) | 0.285 | 44.5 | 137 |
| Speotyto cunicularia (burrowing owl) | 0.143 | 44.1 | 95 |
| Chordeiles minor (common nighthawk) | 0.075 | 43.5 | 148 |
| Colius striatus (speckled coly) | 0.044 | 44 | 99 |
| Excalfactoria chinensis (painted quail) | 0.043 | 43.5 | 116 |
| Scardafella inca (Inca dove) | 0.042 | 43.5 | 108 |
| Phalaenoptilus nuttallii (poorwill) | 0.040 | 43.5 | 175 |
| Passer domesticus (house sparrow) | 0.025 | 44.5 | 106 |
| Carpodacus mexicanus (house finch) | 0.020 | 44.5 | 130 |
| Poephila gouldiae (Gouldian finch) | 0.014 | 44.5 | 105 |
| Taeniopygia castanotis (zebra finch) | 0.012 | 43.5 | 123 |
| Calypte costae (Costa's hummingbird) | 0.003 | 40 | 66 |

[a]From Dawson and Hudson (1970); Coulombe (1970); and Marder (1973).

the heat loss contingent on gular flutter is not offset to any large extent by the heat produced in the muscles that move the hyoid apparatus.

It is significant that birds which gular flutter are the most effective in losing heat by evaporative means. Especially proficient at gular fluttering are such birds as the caprimulgids, which have a large gular area. *Phalaenoptilus nuttallii* (poorwill) and *Eurostopodus guttatus* (Australian spotted nightjar) are able to lose heat in excess of three times the amount of heat that they produce, at high air temperatures (Lasiewski, 1969; Dawson and Hudson, 1970). This is facilitated in the poorwill by an unusually low heat production.

In some species, the rate of gular flutter increases with increasing heat load; in others, the flutter frequency remains constant (Dawson and Hudson, 1970; Weathers, 1972). In the latter instance, the contribution of gular flutter to evaporative cooling is augmented by an increase in the duration of episodes of gular flutter, by increasing the amplitude of the flutter movements, or by increasing the area of the gular region involved (Dawson and Hudson, 1970).

In birds that demonstrate both gular flutter and thermal polypnea, the frequencies of the two movements are not necessarily the same. The frequency of gular flutter is usually higher than that of thermal polypnea (Bartholomew *et al.*, 1968), in keeping with the smaller mass of the gular–hyoid structure (Calder and Schmidt-Nielsen, 1967). It seems likely that gular flutter occurs at the resonant frequency of the gular region and in several species, gular flutter commences before thermal polypnea (Bartholomew *et al.*, 1968). However, this was not true for the pigeon or *Tyto alba* (barn owl) (Weathers, 1972).

*Acclimation, acclimatization.* The respiratory frequency of female chickens acclimated to an air temperature of 31°C was significantly higher than that of birds acclimated to 0°C (Whittow *et al.*, 1966). So also was the rectal temperature. Substantially similar conclusions may be drawn from the work of Harrison and Biellier (1969). In Hillerman and Wilson's (1955) study, the respiratory frequency remained elevated in the heat-acclimated birds after the deep-body temperature had returned to control levels, suggesting that the increased respiratory frequency was not necessarily related to an increased deep-body temperature. In pigeons, there was no difference in the threshold of mean body temperature for thermal polypnea, between cold- and warm-acclimated birds (Rautenberg, 1969a).

There appears, therefore, to be an increased sensitivity of the control mechanism for thermal polypnea as a result of acclimation to heat Evaporative water loss was higher in *Speotyto cunicularia* (burrowing owl) during the summer than in winter (Coulombe, 1970).

*Dehydration.* Respiratory frequency and evaporation were less in the dehydrated ostrich during exposure to heat than in the hydrated ostrich (Crawford and Schmidt-Nielsen, 1967). Pulmocutaneous and excretory water loss were also reduced in zebra finch when the birds were exposed to heat in the dehydrated state (Calder, 1964).

## Partition of Heat Loss

Using a gradient-layer calorimeter, several investigators have partitioned the heat loss from chickens at different environmental temperatures. The results are summarized in Figure 7–5. At low environmental temperatures, most of the heat produced is lost by nonevaporative means, convection or radiation being the major pathways, depending on the rate of air movement. As the air temperature increases, the proportion of heat lost by evapora-

7–5

Partition of heat loss from *Gallus domesticus* (domestic fowl), recorded in a gradient-layer calorimeter, into its evaporative and nonevaporative components, at different environmental temperatures. Data are from Roller and Dale (1962) and Deshazer (1967; broken lines).

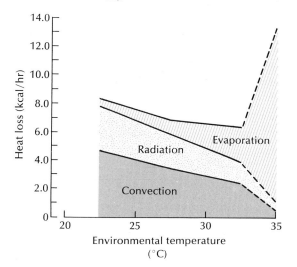

164 tion increases; at an air temperature of 35°C, evaporative heat loss may amount to almost all of the heat loss (see also Table 7–5). For a hummingbird sitting on its nest, Calder (1973) estimated that radiative heat loss was 8.7–35% of the total heat loss, whereas convective heat loss amounted to 43.5–46%.

## BEHAVIORAL THERMOREGULATION

Thermoregulatory behavior usually involves movement of the entire bird or part of the bird, such as a limb, in response to a change of either environmental or body temperature and it requires conscious effort. Only recently has quantitative information become available on the effectiveness of thermoregulatory behavior in birds.

The most conspicuous thermoregulatory behavior of birds is migration to warmer or cooler areas. Some of the more obvious responses of birds to intense desert heat are to soar at altitudes where air temperature and radiant heat are less than at ground level, or to seek shade, or to reduce activity in the hottest part of the day (Dawson and Hudson, 1970). Many tropical sea birds face extremely demanding conditions during the nesting season. Air temperatures are high, solar radiation is intense, and there is no shade. The birds supplement their physiological responses by a number of behavioral adjustments. For example, *Sula dactylatra* (masked booby) orients its body so that its back is to the sun, thereby placing its feet and gular area in the shade of its body (Bartholomew, 1966). In addition, the wings are held away from the body and the scapular feathers are elevated, both responses facilitating convective heat loss to the air. *Mycteria americana* (wood stork) when hot, resorts to the bizarre expedient of directing its liquid excrement onto its long legs, which are cooled by evaporation of the water in the excrement (Kahl, 1963). The chicken achieves a similar end result, in a more socially acceptable way, by splashing water over its comb and wattles (Wilson, 1949).

In a cold environment, the chicken reduces its surface area, and hence its heat loss, by "hunching" (Hutchinson, 1954). An additional reduction in heat loss, amounting to 12% in the chicken (Deighton and Hutchinson, 1940), may be achieved by tucking the head under a wing. If the chicken chooses to sit, it can reduce heat loss from the unfeathered legs and feet, a saving of 20–50% compared with the standing position (Deighton and

Hutchinson, 1940; Deshazer 1967). Penguins, in addition to squatting, rest only their tarsometatarsal joints on the ground, thus minimizing conductive cooling to the ice (Goldsmith and Sladen, 1961). Huddling is an effective means of reducing heat loss but it is probably not widespread among adult birds.

Birds make less use of burrows and shelters as a protection against cold than do mammals. One species that does is *Lagopus lagopus* (willow ptarmigan), which utilizes burrows in the snow to protect itself from the rigors of the climate (Dawson and Hudson, 1970).

Budgell (1971) succeeded in training barbary doves to press a switch in order to turn on a heater. In this way, the birds were able to control their environmental temperature, and it is interesting that they maintained their environmental temperature at approximately 33°C, which is within the thermoneutral zone.

## CONTROL MECHANISMS

There is evidence that both peripheral temperature receptors and temperature-sensitive neurons in the central nervous system are involved in the regulation of body temperature, heat production, and heat loss in birds.

When chickens are exposed to a cold environment, shivering can be detected before any change occurs in the deep-body temperature (Randall, 1943). This observation is consistent with the control of heat production by thermal receptors in the periphery. The only known peripheral cold receptors in birds are in the beak, innervated by the trigeminal nerve (Necker, 1972), but there may well be others elsewhere. There is also good evidence that the heat production may be influenced by changes in the temperature of thermoreceptors in the central nervous system, i.e., by changes of deep-body temperature. For example, localized heating of the anterior hypothalamus–preoptic region of the brain of *Passer domesticus* (house sparrow) results in a diminution of heat production, whereas cooling the same region has the opposite effect (Mills and Heath, 1972a). Bilateral lesions in the anterior hypothalamus–preoptic region significantly impaired the maintenance of body temperature in a cold environment (Mills and Heath, 1972b). In the domestic fowl (*Gallus*) lesions of the anterior hypothalamus abolished the shivering response (Kanematsu *et al.*, 1967; Lepkovsky *et al.*, 1968), but shivering could not be elicited by local-

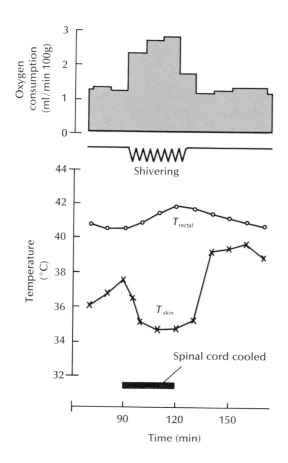

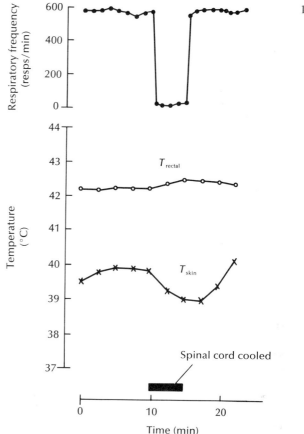

ized cooling of the anterior hypothalamus of *Columba* (pigeon) and there was no increase in oxygen consumption (Rautenberg *et al.,* 1972). However, localized cooling of the spinal cord resulted in both shivering and an increased oxygen consumption (Rautenberg, 1969b; Figure 7–6). Rautenberg (1971) presented evidence that heat production in the pigeon is regulated by a "proportional controller," a type of control system which implies that the magnitude of the effector response (in this instance, heat production) is proportional to the extent to which body temperature (spinal cord temperature, in the pigeon) deviates from a certain value, the "set point." In the pigeon, the set point varied with changes in skin temperature.

There is clear evidence in the chicken that the tissue insulation of the unfeathered comb and feet may diminish in response to infrared irradiation of the thorax and abdomen, before the deep-body temperature increases, indicating that changes in tissue insulation may be effected by stimulation of peripheral thermal receptors (Richards, 1970). So far, peripheral warm receptors have been described

7–6 Effect of localized cooling of the spinal cord of the pigeon. Left: oxygen consumption, rectal temperature, and skin temperature of the foot; air temperature = 29.5°C. Right: respiratory frequency, rectal temperature, and skin temperature of the foot; air temperature = 38°C. (After Rautenberg *et al.,* 1972.)

only in the beak in birds (Necker, 1972). However, cooling the spinal cord or the brainstem of the pigeon elicits a reduced blood flow and an increased tissue insulation in the foot (Figure 7–6; Rautenberg *et al.,* 1972). Localized heating of the spinal cord evokes a diminution of the tissue insulation of the bare extremities of the pigeon (Rautenberg, 1969b). It is obvious that changes in tissue insulation may be effected by variations in both central and peripheral temperatures and that central ther-

166 moreceptors are present both in the spinal cord and in the brain.

The control of ptilomotor activity seems also to be invested in the anterior hypothalamus–preoptic region in the house sparrow. Localized heating of this region diminished the degree of fluffing of the feathers in birds exposed to a cold environment (Mills and Heath, 1972b). Cooling the anterior hypothalamus of the pigeon resulted in erection of the feathers. A similar effect was elicited by localized cooling of the spinal cord (Rautenberg *et al.,* 1972).

There is evidence that both thermal polypnea and gular flutter can occur in response to exposure to solar radiation before an increase in deep-body temperature takes place (Howell and Bartholomew, 1962; Shallenberger *et al.,* 1974). Whether this is an effect specific to solar radiation is not known, but it is known that exposure of the domestic fowl to an increased air temperature in the absence of a radiant heat load results in thermal polypnea only after the deep-body temperature has increased (Randall, 1943; Richards, 1970, 1971a; Woods and Whittow, 1974). Although there is little evidence that an increase in skin temperature per se can provoke an increased respiratory frequency, there is an indication that skin temperature can influence thermal polypnea after it has become established (see above references).

Thermal polypnea has also been produced in *Passer domesticus* (house sparrow) by localized heating of the preoptic–anterior hypothalamic region of the brain alone (Mills and Heath, 1972b), and by exposing the sparrows to high air temperatures. It could be inhibited by localized cooling of the same region in the brain (Mills and Heath, 1972b). In the pigeon, localized heating of the anterior hypothalamic region was relatively ineffective in producing thermal polypnea (Rautenberg *et al.,* 1972) but localized heating of the spinal cord induced panting in the pigeon, which could be inhibited by localized cooling of the spinal cord (Figure 7–6; Rautenberg; 1969b; Rautenberg *et al.,* 1972). Panting could occur in the hyperthermic chicken after transection of the brain caudal to the hypothalamus (Richards, 1971b) but it could not be evoked after damage to the midbrain, indicating that the temperature-sensitive neurons were there. However, bilateral lesions in the hypothalamus abolished the polypneic response of chickens to heat (Feldman *et al.,* 1957; Lepkovsky *et al.,* 1968). Additional experiments must be performed on other species in order to determine whether there is a wide variation in the relative role of the hypothalamus and the spinal cord in the regulation of panting in different species.

The role of the vagus nerves in the regulation of thermal polypnea is difficult to decipher. Panting occurs in the vagotomized pigeon (Sinha, 1959), but not in the chicken (Hiestand and Randall, 1942). However, stimulation of the central ends of the vagi combined with heat exposure reinstated the capacity for thermal polypnea (Richards, 1969). It seems probable that the vagi do not convey thermal information but that they permit the respiratory apparatus to perform at high frequencies, if a thermal stimulus for a high frequency is also present.

Behavioral thermoregulatory responses in birds seem to be regulated by the anterior hypothalamus–preoptic region of the brain, rather than by peripheral receptors. For example, in the chicken, drooping of the wings in response to heat was abolished by lesions in the hypothalamus (Lepkovsky *et al.,* 1968). In barbary doves, also, thermoregulatory behavior was controlled by hypothalamic rather than peripheral temperature, and the control mechanism appeared to operate as a simple "on–off" system (Budgell, 1971).

## THERMOREGULATION DURING FLIGHT

One of the most exciting developments in the physiology of temperature regulation in birds in recent years has been the feasibility of obtaining information from flying birds. The most important feature of the thermal physiology of flight is the greatly increased heat production. The metabolic rate of *Calypte costae* (Costa's hummingbird) during hovering flight was seven times the standard rate (Lasiewski, 1963). The flight metabolism of *Columbia livia* (rock doves) exceeded that during rest by a factor of 8.2 (LeFebvre, 1964). A similar increment in oxygen uptake during flight has been recorded in *Melopsitacus undulatus* (budgerigar) and in the *Larus atricilla* (laughing gull), by Tucker (1966; 1972). For very short periods of flight, the oxygen uptake of *Hesperiphora vespertina* (evening grosbeak), *Larus delawarensis* (ring-billed gull), and *Anas rubripes* (black duck) was 12–13 times the resting values (Berger *et al.,* 1970). The metabolic rate varies with the flight speed. In the budgerigar the metabolic rate during level flight was lowest at a speed of 35 km/hr, increasing at lower and higher speeds. In the laughing gull the minimal metabolic rate occurred at a flight speed of 30 km/hr (Tucker, 1968; 1972).

Some of the heat produced during flight is stored in the bird. Elevations of body temperature amounting to 1.5°–2.6°C have been described after flight (see Dawson and Hudson, 1970). In fact, the budgerigar became overheated after flying for less than 20 min through air at 36°–37°C, in a wind tunnel, and it would not fly further (Tucker, 1968).

The total thermal conductance of birds during flight appears to be more than five times that of birds at rest (Hart and Roy, 1967; Tucker, 1968, 1972). A flying bird, with its wings outstretched, has a relatively large surface area. Moreover, it exposes poorly feathered areas—under the wings, for example. In addition, the air movement past a flying bird greatly enhanced convective cooling. Tucker (1968) estimated that even at an air temperature of 30°C nonevaporative heat loss accounted for 82% of the total heat loss in the budgerigar flying at a speed of 35 km/hr.

At higher air temperatures, most heat is lost by evaporative cooling (Tucker, 1968). A considerable increase in respiratory minute volume occurs in *Columba livia* (rock dove) during flight (Hart and Roy, 1966), and this subserves the increased oxygen requirements of the flying bird in addition to promoting heat loss. The respiratory minute volume during flight was 20 times that when the bird was at rest the increase being brought about largely by an increase in respiratory frequency (Hart and Roy, 1966). The increased ventilation during flight was effected by an increased respiratory tidal volume, in addition to an increased respiratory frequency, in the three species studied by Berger *et al.* (1970). The increase in ventilation was also less in these species than in the rock dove; it was, in fact, proportional to the oxygen consumption. An augmented cutaneous evaporative heat loss is also likely to occur in flying birds, according to Smith (1969), and there is clearly a need to partition total evaporative water loss into its respiratory and cutaneous components during flight.

Some birds are flightless, and it is illuminating to compare their temperature regulation during the only strenuous activity of which they are capable, i.e., running, with that of flying birds. The temperature regulation of *Rhea americana*, trained to run on a treadmill, has been examined by Taylor and his colleagues (Taylor *et al.*, 1971). The rhea dealt with the heat produced during exercise by storing a considerable proportion of it. This raised the bird's temperature, which in turn facilitated nonevaporative heat loss. Cutaneous evaporation did not increase, and although respiratory evaporation was augmented it played a minor role in the heat balance during running. There are, therefore, some basic similarities between the thermoregulatory responses of flying and running birds. Perhaps the major difference is the greater use of evaporative cooling in the flying bird at high air temperatures.

# THERMOREGULATION DURING TORPOR

Representatives of several orders of birds have the extraordinary facility to allow their body temperature to diminish in certain circumstances, i.e., to become torpid. The particular circumstance that induces torpor seems to be a curtailment of the bird's energy supply. Many birds that are able to become torpid feed on insects or nectar, both of which may become temporarily unavailable. However, this conclusion should be tempered by Jaeger's (1949) observation that a dormant poorwill, found under natural conditions, was quite heavy and clearly in good nutritional condition. Furthermore, *Colius striatus* (speckled mousebird), which does not feed on either insects or nectar and which is not particularly small, may become torpid (Bartholomew and Trost, 1970). It is likely that some birds become torpid on a daily basis, during the inactive part of their circadian cycle. Inca doves deprived of either water or food, experienced a pronounced nocturnal hypothermia (MacMillen and Trost, 1967a). Seasonal dormancy has been observed only in the Caprimulgidae.

Very little is known about the physiological mechanisms by which a bird becomes torpid. By analogy with the situation in mammals, entrance into torpor is initiated as a cardiovascular event whereby blood is diverted from heat-producing tissues (Hudson, 1973; Whittow, 1973). Heat production decreases and cooling occurs passively. It is known that body cooling is facilitated in *Patagonia gigas* (giant hummingbird), and in the poorwill, by inhibition of the shivering mechanism (Bartholomew *et al.*, 1962; Lasiewski *et al.*, 1967). The rate of entry into torpor is inversely related to body weight (Lasiewski and Lasiewski, 1967). This is not surprising in view of the relatively greater thermal conductance and surface area of small birds. The metabolic rate of torpid birds may be only one-fiftieth of the basal rate at "normal" body temperature, and water loss is also reduced, amounting to one-tenth to one-third of that in homeothermic hummingbirds (Lasiewski and Lasiewski, 1967).

Birds vary in their tolerance of low body temperatures. For example, the poorwill and *Caprimulgus europaeus* (nightjar) survived body temperatures of 5°–8°C (Bartholomew *et al.*, 1957; see also Dawson and Hudson, 1970), which are lethal to hummingbirds (Lasiewski, 1963). However, it is important to draw a distinction between the body temperature that torpid birds can tolerate and the temperature from which they can arouse on their own. The latter temperature appears to be of the

168 order of 13°–20°C (Dawson and Hudson, 1970). The body temperature of many torpid birds tends to approximate that of the environment, and lowering the environmental temperature does not appear to stimulate thermoregulatory mechanisms that prevent the body temperature from falling further. For example, a poorwill could be subjected to an air temperature of 15°C, from which it would eventually arouse. If the temperature were lowered to and held at 5°C, however, the bird would eventually die, simply because it would be unable to arouse, on the one hand, and to remain torpid indefinitely, on the other. There is one exception to this generalization: Hainsworth and Wolf (1970) found that *Eulampis jugularis* (tropical hummingbird) maintained its body temperature at 18°–20°C in the face of a lowered air temperature by increasing its heat production. The thermal conductance of the tissues and plumage was the same in the torpid as in the nontorpid bird. Substantially similar results were obtained for two other species of hummingbirds (Wolf and Hainsworth, 1972), and it was shown that the regulated level of body temperature was related to the minimal environmental temperature encountered by the species under natural conditions.

Rewarming of a torpid bird is accomplished by vigorous shivering. The rate of rewarming is inversely related to body size, as is the rate of entry into torpor. This places a limitation on the capacity of birds of increasing size to indulge in short-term torpidity. Daily torpor is therefore practicable only in small birds.

## ONTOGENY OF THERMOREGULATION

### Embryo

The responses of the embryo to changes of environmental temperature are a legitimate consideration in this chapter because the egg may be exposed to excessive heat or cold, depending on the attentiveness of the parent birds during the incubation period. The chicken embryo is unable to regulate its own temperature during the early stages of incubation. From the nineteenth day of incubation, however, the embryo is able to respond to a small reduction in ambient temperature by a transient rise in metabolic rate (Romijn, 1954; Freeman, 1971). The metabolic response to cold appears to be associated with an increased thyroid activity (Hoffman and Shaffner, 1950). The respiratory quotient (RQ) increases, an indication of the metabolism of glycogen, and the temperature of the egg remains above that of the environment. The embryos of *Larus occidentalis* (western gulls) also appear to be able to regulate their body temperatures to some extent (Bartholomew and Dawson, 1952).

Fortunately, the embryos of many species are able to withstand temporary periods of hypothermia when the adult is away from the nest (Baldwin and Kendeigh, 1932). Moreng and Bryant (1955) demonstrated that the 1-day-old chick embryo can survive an exposure of 76 hr to air at 0°C, although the normal incubation temperature for the chicken is 39°–40°C. The lower lethal temperature of the chicken's egg is from −2.2°C to −1.1°C. During the first 5 days of incubation of the chicken's egg, its upper lethal temperature is 42.2°C. By the eighth day, the upper lethal temperature has increased to 45.6°–47.8°C, and it remains at this level for the remainder of the incubation period. The eggs of the Eastern house wren appear to have a similar upper lethal temperature (Baldwin and Kendeigh, 1932).

During the first 10 days of incubation the evaporative heat loss from the chicken's egg exceeds the heat production, so that the temperature of the egg may be slightly below the air temperature. Toward the end of the incubation period the major channel of heat loss from the egg is nonevaporative (Romijn and Lokhorst, 1956, 1960).

### Chick

Birds vary enormously in their thermoregulatory capacities immediately after hatching. Precocial species, e.g., the chick of the domestic chicken, are covered with down and they are able to respond effectively to heat and to cold. In contrast, altricial birds, e.g., the Passeriformes, are naked when hatched and they have little ability to regulate their body temperature at air temperatures below 35°C or above 40°C. Other birds, e.g., the shearwaters, are intermediate between precocial and altricial species in their thermoregulatory capacities (Dawson and Hudson, 1970).

**Precocial species.** Immediately after hatching, the body temperature of the chick of the domestic fowl may diminish to below 30°C (Freeman, 1971). The down feathers are wet in the newly hatched chick, and evaporative cooling probably explains the decrease in body temperature. Thereafter, the body temperature increases to reach the adult level, at about 3 weeks. The increase results in part from an increase in the chick's metabolically active mass and metabolic rate, without a commensurate increase in surface area (Freeman, 1971).

The chick responds to cold exposure with an increase in heat production. However, the maximal increase in heat production in the newly hatched laughing gull during exposure to cold was only 1.5 times the level in the thermoneutral zone (Dawson *et al.,* 1972). Although the newly hatched chick is capable of shivering (Freeman, 1971), it may also augment heat production without shivering, i.e., by nonshivering thermogenesis. The main source of energy appears to be carbohydrate, although free fatty acids are also mobilized (Freeman, 1967). Propranolol, a β-adrenergic blocking agent that inhibits nonshivering thermogenesis in mammals (see Hull, 1973), also interferes with the response of newly hatched chicks to cold (Wekstein and Zolman, 1968). However, the mechanism of nonshivering thermogenesis in young birds is not fully understood and it may differ in some respects from that in mammals; there is evidence of thyroid involvement in birds (Freeman, 1971). Furthermore, norepinephrine, which plays a role in cold thermogenesis in the newborn mammal, lowers body temperature and heat production in the domestic chick (Allen and Marley, 1967). The lower critical temperature of the chick decreases with age, and the rate of increase in heat production below the critical temperature diminishes (Barott and Pringle, 1946). Both of these changes are consistent with a diminution in the relative surface area and an increase in insulation with growth. The upper critical temperature is also higher in the chick. This conforms with the relatively greater surface area of the chick and its lower insulation, both features promoting heat loss in a hot environment. The minimal thermal conductance of the hatchling laughing gull was similar to the predicted value for an adult bird (Dawson, *et al.,* 1972).

The newly hatched chick responds to heat exposure with an identifiable thermal polypnea (Randall, 1943), which commences at a lower body temperature in the newly hatched chick than in the adult. The maximal respiratory frequency during exposure to heat is higher in the chick than in the adult. This is probably related to the size of the bird and, in particular, to the mass of the thorax (Whittow, 1973). Hatchling laughing gulls were able to dissipate 131% of their heat production at an air temperature of 45°C (Dawson et al., 1972).

Little is known about the role of peripheral and central thermoreceptors in the regulation of body temperature in the chick. The nestling *Phaethon rubricauda* (red-tailed tropic bird) placed in the sun pants before the deep-body temperature increases (Howell and Bartholomew, 1962), indicating that stimulation of peripheral receptors alone is sufficient to elicit panting. Infusion of catecholamines into the hypothalamus of chicks of the domestic fowl resulted in a decrease in their body temperature and oxygen consumption (Marley and Stephenson, 1970). Intravenous injection of tryptamine and 5-hydroxytryptamine had the opposite effect (Allen and Marley, 1967). It is possible that the amines are involved as transmitter substances in the hypothalamus.

**Altricial birds.** Newly hatched altricial species are essentially naked; they are unable to maintain their body temperature or to increase their heat production in the face of a lowered environmental temperature. They develop the capacity to do both after approximately 6 days, in the nestling *Pooecetes gramineus* (vesper sparrow; Dawson and Hudson, 1970). In the intervening time between hatching and the development of effective thermogenesis, altricial birds rely heavily on the protection of their parents. The acquisition of thermoregulatory ability seems to be related largely to the growth of heat-producing tissue, notably skeletal muscle. Such growth is accompanied by the development of the plumage and a reduction in the surface area relative to body mass. These factors help curtail heat loss and therefore facilitate the regulation of body temperature. However, there is evidence that body temperature can be sustained in a cool environment before the plumage is fully developed. Breitenbach and Baskett (1967) concluded that in *Zenaidura macroura* (mourning dove) heat loss is actually increased at one stage of feather development, when the "blood quills" provide an increased vascularized surface from which heat may be lost. Some species develop their thermoregulatory capability before others (Ricklefs and Hainsworth, 1968). Although newly hatched altricial species are vulnerable, the altricial condition does present some energetic and evolutionary advantages (Dawson and Hudson, 1970). The altricial state is a very efficient one from an energetic point of view.

Many altricial birds are hatched under very hot conditions. Some, such as *Bubulcus ibis* (cattle egret), have evaporative cooling mechanisms operative on the first day of hatching (Dawson and Hudson, 1970). Nevertheless, this potential is probably only realized under survival conditions, in the event that the parent must leave the nest. Ordinarily, altricial nestlings, such as *Sula sula,* that are hatched into a very hot environment are closely brooded by the parents (Howell and Bartholomew, 1962).

## 170  CONCLUSIONS

The relatively high deep-body temperature, the absence of sweat glands, the very effective insulation provided by the plumage, and the widespread incidence of gular flutter distinguish the thermoregulatory physiology of birds. Many birds become torpid on occasion, and most birds are able to fly. The physiology of temperature regulation during flight and during torpor are perhaps the most dramatic aspects of thermoregulation in birds. Although there are many good descriptions of thermoregulatory behavior in birds, there are few quantitative data on the effectiveness of behavioral thermoregulation. The application of thermal modeling techniques (Birkebak, 1966; Gates, 1970) to birds promises to provide ecologically useful predictions of heat loss under widely different environmental conditions.

## REFERENCES

Allen, D. J., and E. Marley. (1967). Effect of sympathomimetic and allied amines on temperature and oxygen consumption in chickens. Brit. J. Pharmacol. Chemother., 31, 290.

Aschoff, J., and H. Pohl. (1970a). Der Ruheumsatz von Vögeln als Funcktion der Tageszeit und der Körpergrösse. J. Ornithol., 111, 38.

Aschoff, J., and H. Pohl. (1970b). Rhythmic variations in energy metabolism. Fed. Proc., 29, 1541.

Aschoff, J., and U. von Saint Paul. (1973). Circadian rhythms of brain temperature in the chicken, measured at different levels of constant illumination. Jap. J. Physiol., 23, 69.

Aschoff, C., J. Aschoff, and U. von Saint Paul. (1973). Circadian rhythms of chicken brain temperatures. J. Physiol., 230, 103.

Baldwin, S. P., and S. C. Kendeigh. (1932). Physiology of the temperature of birds. Sci. Publ. Cleveland Mus. Nat. Hist., 3, 1.

Barott, H. G., and E. M. Pringle. (1946). Energy and gaseous metabolism of the chicken from hatch to maturity as affected by temperature. J. Nutr., 31, 35.

Bartholomew, G. A. (1966). The role of behavior in the temperature regulation of the masked booby. Condor, 68, 523.

Bartholomew, G. A., and W. R. Dawson. (1952). Body temperatures in nestling western gulls. Condor, 54, 58.

Bartholomew, G. A., and W. R. Dawson. (1954). Temperature regulation in young pelicans, herons and gulls. Ecology, 35, 466.

Bartholomew, G. A., and C. H. Trost. (1970). Temperature regulation in the speckled mousebird, Colius striatus. Condor, 72, 141.

Bartholomew, G. A., T. R. Howell, and T. J. Cade. (1957). Torpidity in the white-throated swift, anna hummingbird, and poorwill. Condor, 59, 145.

Bartholomew, G. A., J. W. Hudson, and T. R. Howell. (1962). Body temperature, oxygen consumption, evaporative water loss, and heart rate in the poor-will. Condor, 64, 117.

Bartholomew, G. A., R. C. Lasiewski, and E. C. Crawford, J. (1968). Patterns of panting and gular flutter in cormorants, pelicans, owls and doves. Condor, 70, 31.

Benedict, F. G., W. Landauer, and E. L. Fox. (1932). The physiology of normal and frizzle fowl with special reference to basal metabolism. Univ. Conn. ,Storrs. Agr. Expt. Sta. Bull., No. 177, p. 15.

Benzinger, T. H., and C. Kitzinger. (1949). Direct calorimetry by means of the gradient principle. Rev. Sci. Instr., 20, 849.

Berger, M, J. S. Hart, and O. Z. Roy. (1970). Respiration, oxygen consumption and heart rate in some birds during rest and flight. Z. Vergl. Physiol., 66, 201.

Bernstein, M. H. (1971). Cutaneous and respiratory evaporation in the Painted Quail, Excalfactoria chinensis, during ontogeny of thermoregulation. Comp. Biochem. Physiol., 38A, 611.

Birkebak, R. C. (1966). Heat transfer in biological systems. In "International Review of General and Experimental Zoology," Vol. 2 (W. J. F. Felts and R. J. Harrison, Eds.). New York: Academic Press, p. 269.

Breitenbach, R. P., and T. S. Baskett. (1967). Ontogeny of thermoregulation in the mourning dove. Physiol. Zool., 40, 207.

Brush, A. H. (1965). Energetics, temperature regulation and circulation in resting, active and defeathered California quail, Lophortyx Californicus. Comp. Biochem. Physiol., 15, 399.

Budgell, P. (1971). Behavioral thermoregulation in the barbary dove (Streptopelia risoria). Anim. Behav., 19, 524.

Calder, W. A. (1964). Gaseous metabolism and water relations of the zebra finch (Taeniopygia castanotis). Physiol. Zoöl., 37, 400.

Calder, W. A. (1973). An estimate of the heat balance of a nesting hummingbird in a chilling climate. Comp. Biochem. Physiol., 46A, 291.

Calder, W. A., and J. R. King. (1974). Thermal and caloric relations of birds. In "Avian Biology," Vol. IV (D. S. Farner and J. R. King, Eds.). New York: Academic Press, p. 259.

Calder, W. A., and K. Schmidt-Nielsen. (1966). Evaporative cooling and respiratory alkalosis in the pigeon. Proc. Natl. Acad. Sci. (U.S.), 55, 750.

Calder, W. A., and K. Schmidt-Nielsen. (1967). Temperature regulation and evaporation in the pigeon and the roadrunner. Am. J. Physiol., 213, 883.

Calder, W. A., and K. Schmidt-Nielsen. (1968). Panting and blood carbon dioxide in birds. Am. J. Physiol., 215, 477.

Carlson, L. D., and A. C. L. Hsieh. (1970). "Control of Energy Exchange." New York: Macmillan, p. 95.

Chaffee, R. R. J., W. W. Mayhew, M. Drebin, and Y. Cassuto. (1963). Studies on thermogenesis in cold-acclimated birds. Can. J. Biochem. Physiol., 41, 2215.

Coulombe, H. N. (1970). Physiological and physical aspects of temperature regulation in the burrowing owl, Speotyto cunicularia. Comp. Biochem. Physiol., 35, 307.

Crawford, E. C., and G. Kampe. (1971). Resonant panting in pigeons. Comp. Biochem. Physiol., 40A, 549.

Crawford, E. C., Jr, and R. C. Lasiewski. (1968). Oxygen consumption and respiratory evaporation of the emu and rhea. Condor, 70, 333.

Crawford, E. C., Jr., and K. Schmidt-Nielsen. (1967). Temperature regulation and evaporative cooling in the ostrich. Am. J. Physiol., 212, 347.

Davidson, J., W. R. Hepburn, J. Mathieson, and J. D. Pullar. (1968). Comparisons of heat loss from young cockerels by direct measurement and by indirect assessment involving body analysis. Brit. Poultry Sci., 9, 93.

Dawson, W. R. (1954). Temperature regulation and water requirements of the brown and Abert towhees, Pipilo fuscus and Pipilo aberti. Univ. Calif. Publ. Zool., 59, 81.

Dawson, W. R. (1958). Relation of oxygen consumption and evaporative water loss to temperature in the cardinal. Physiol. Zool., 31, 37.

Dawson, W. R., and J. W. Hudson. (1970). Birds. In "Comparative Physiology of Thermoregulation," Vol. I (G. C. Whittow, Ed.). New York: Academic Press, p. 223.

Dawson, W. R., J. W. Hudson, and R. W. Hill. (1972). Temperature regulation in newly hatched laughing gulls (Larus atricilla). Condor, 74, 177.

Deighton, T., and J. C. D. Hutchinson. (1940). Studies on the metabolism of fowls. II: The effect of activity on metabolism. J. Agri. Sci., 30, 141.

Depocas, F., and J. S. Hart. (1957). Use of the Pauling oxygen analyser for measurement of oxygen consumption of animals in open-circuit systems and in a short-lag, closed-circuit apparatus. J. Appl. Physiol., 10, 388.

Deshazer, J. A. (1967). Heat loss variations of the laying hen. Ph.D. Thesis, North Carolina State University, Raleigh, North Carolina.

Drent, R. H., and B. Stonehouse. (1971). Thermoregulatory responses of the Peruvian penguin, Spheniscus humboldti. Comp. Biochem. Physiol., 40A, 689.

Ederstrom, H. E., and S. J. Brumleve. (1964). Temperature gradients in the legs of cold-acclimatized pheasants. *Am. J. Physiol., 207,* 457.

El-Halawani, M. El-S., W. O. Wilson, and R. E. Burger. (1970). Cold acclimation and the role of catecholamines in body temperature regulation in male Leghorns. *Poultry Sci., 49,* 621.

Eriksson, S., and A. Kivimäe. (1954). Diurnal variation of food consumption and carbon dioxide production in laying hens. *Acta Agri. Scand., 4,* 71.

Feldman, S. E., S Larsson, M. K. Dimick, and S. Lepkovsky. (1957). Aphagia in chickens. *Am. J Physiol., 191,* 259.

Fill, W. (1942). Der Einfluss des Lichtes auf Stoffwechsel und Geschlechtsreife bei Warmblutern. *Z. Wiss. Zool., 155,* 343.

Fisher, H., P. Griminger, and H. S. Weiss. (1965). Body composition and atherosclerosis in cocks after long exposure to heat and cold. *J. Appl. Physiol., 20,* 591.

Freeman, B. M. (1967). Some effects of cold on the metabolism of the fowl during the perinatal period. *Comp. Biochem. Physiol., 20,* 179.

Freeman, B. M. (1971). Body temperature and thermoregulation. In "Physiology and Biochemistry of the Domestic Fowl," Vol. 2 (D. J. Bell and B. M. Freeman, Eds.). London: Academic Press, p. 1115.

Gates, D. M. (1970). Animal climates (Where animals must live). *Environ. Res., 3,* 132.

Gelineo, S. (1955). Température d'adaptation et production de chaleur chez les oiseaux de petite taille. *Arch. Sci. Physiol., 9,* 225.

Gelineo, S. (1964). Organ systems in adaptation: the temperature regulating system. In "Handbook of Physiology," Sec. 4. "Adaptation to the Evironment" (D. B. Dill, E. F. Adolph, and C. G. Wilber, Eds.). Washington, D.C.: American Physiological Society.

Gelineo, S. (1968). The heat production of goldfinches and canaries in summer and winter. In "Quantitative Biology of Metabolism" (A. Locker, Ed.). New York: Springer-Verlag, p. 102.

Goldsmith, R., and W. J. L. Sladen (1961). Temperature regulation of some Antarctic penguins. *J. Physiol. (London), 157,* 251.

Grant, R. T., and E. F. Bland. (1931). Observations on arteriovenous anastomoses in human skin and in the bird's foot with special reference to the reaction to cold. *Heart, 15,* 385.

Hahn, D. W., T. Ishibashi, and C. W. Turner. (1966). Alteration of thyroid hormone secretion rate in fowls changed from a cold to a warm environment. *Poultry Sci., 45,* 31.

Haller, R. W., and M. L. Sunde. (1966). The effects of withholding water on the body temperature of poults. *Poultry Sci., 45,* 991.

Hainsworth, F. R., and L. L. Wolf. (1970). Regulation of oxygen consumption and body temperature during torpor in a hummingbird, *Eulampis jugularis. Science, 168,* 368.

Hamilton, W. J., and F. Heppner. (1967). Radiant solar energy and the function of black homeotherm pigmentation: An hypothesis. *Science, 155,* 196.

Hardy, J. D., J. A. J. Stolwijk, and A. P. Gagge. (1971). Man. In "Comparative Physiology of Thermoregulation," Vol. II (G. C. Whittow, Ed.). New York: Academic Press, p. 327.

Harrison, P. C., and H. V. Biellier. (1969). Physiological response of domestic fowl to abrupt changes of ambient air temperature. *Poultry Sci., 48,* 1034.

Hart, J. S. (1962). Seasonal acclimatization in four species of small wild birds. *Physiol. Zoöl., 35,* 224.

Hart, J. S., and O. Z. Roy. (1966). Respiratory and cardiac responses to flight in pigeons. *Physiol. Zoöl., 39,* 291.

Hart, J. S., and O. Z. Roy. (1967). Temperature regulation during flight in pigeons. *Am. J. Physiol., 213,* 1311.

Heppner, F. (1970). The metabolic significance of differential absorption of radiant energy by black and white birds. *Condor, 72,* 50.

Herreid, C. F., and B. Kessel. (1967). Thermal conductance in birds and mammals. *Comp. Biochem. Physiol., 21,* 405.

Heistand, W. A., and W. C. Randall. (1942). Influence of proprioceptive vagal afferents on panting and accessory panting movements in mammals and birds. *Am. J. Physiol., 138,* 12

Hillerman, J. P., and W. O. Wilson. (1955). Acclimation of adult chickens to environmental temperature changes. *Am. J. Physiol., 180,* 591.

Hoffmann, E., and C. S. Shaffner. (1950). Thyroid weight and function as influenced by environmental temperature. *Poultry Sci., 29,* 365.

Howell, T. R., and G. A. Bartholomew. (1961). Temperature regulation in Laysan and black-footed albatrosses. *Condor, 63,* 185.

Howell, T. R., and G. A. Bartholomew. (1962). Temperature regulation in the red-tailed tropic bird and the red-footed booby. *Condor, 64,* 6.

Hudson, J. W. (1973). Torpidity in mammals. In "Comparative Physiology of Thermoregulation," Vol. III (G. C. Whittow, Ed.). New York: Academic Press, p. 97.

Hudson, J. W., and S. L. Kimsey. (1966). Temperature regulation and metabolic rhythms in populations of the House Sparrow, *Passer domesticus. Comp. Biochem. Physiol., 17,* 203.

Hull, D. 1973. Thermoregulation in young mammals. In "Comparative Physiology of Thermoregulation" Vol. III (G. C. Whittow, Ed.). New York: Academic Press, p. 167.

Huston, T. M., H. M. Edwards, Jr., and J. J. William. (1962). The effects of high environmental temperature on thyroid secretion rate of domestic fowl. *Poultry Sci., 41,* 640.

Hutchinson, J. C. D., (1954). Heat regulation in birds. In "Progress in the Physiology of Farm Animals," Vol. I (J. Hammond, Ed.). London: Butterworths Scientific Publ., p. 299.

Irving, L., H. Krog, and M. Monson. (1955). The metabolism of some Alaskan animals in winter and summer. *Physiol. Zool. 28,* 173.

Jaeger, E. C. (1949). Further observations on the hibernation of the poor-will. *Condor, 51,* 105.

Jansky, L., R. Bartuňkova, J. Kōckova, J. Mejsnar, and E. Zeisberger. (1969). Interspecies differences in cold adaptation and nonshivering thermogenesis. *Fed. Proc., 28,* 1053.

Jenkinson, D. McE., and P. S. Blackburn. (1968). The distribution of nerves, monoamine oxidase and cholinesterase in the skin of poultry. *Res. Vet. Sci., 9,* 429.

Jordan, K. A., and A. C. Dale. (1961). The measurement of heat transmission components of chickens. Paper No. 61-402, Annual Meeting American Society of Agricultural Engineers, Ames, Iowa.

Kahl, M. P. (1963). Thermoregulation in the wood stork, with special reference to the role of the legs. *Physiol. Zoöl., 36,* 141.

Kanematsu, S., M. Kii, T. Sonoda, and Y. Kato. (1967). Effects of hypothalamic lesions on body temperature in the chicken. *Jap. J. Vet. Sci., 29,* 95.

Kendeigh, S. C. (1934). The role of environment in the life of birds. *Ecol. Monogr., 4,* 229.

King, J. R., and D. S. Farner. (1961). Energy metabolism, thermoregulation and body temperature. In "Biology and Comparative Physiology of Birds," Vol. 11 (A. J. Marshall, Ed). New York: Academic Press, p. 215.

King, J. R., and D. S. Farner. (1966). The adaptive role of winter fattening in the white crowned sparrow with comments on its regulation. *Am. Nat., 100,* 403.

Koskimies, J. 1950. The life of the swift, *Micropus apus* (L) in relation to the weather. *Ann. Acad. Sci. Fenn. Ser. A, 4* (15), 1.

Lasiewski, R. C. (1963). Oxygen consumption of torpid, resting, active, and flying hummingbirds. *Physiol. Zoöl., 36,* 122.

Lasiewski, R. C. (1964). Body temperatures, heart and breathing rate and evaporative water loss in hummingbirds. *Physiol. Zoöl., 37,* 212.

Lasiewski, R. C. (1969). Physiological responses to heat stress in the poor-will. *Am. J. Physiol., 217,* 1504.

Lasiewski, R. C., and W. R. Dawson. (1967). A reexamination of the relation between standard metabolic rate and body weight in birds. *Condor, 69,* 13.

Lasiewski, R. C., and R. J. Lasiewski. (1967). Physiological responses of the blue-throated and Rivoli's hummingbirds. *Auk, 84,* 34.

Lasiewski, R. C., A. L. Acosta, and M. H. Bernstein. (1966a). Evaporative water loss in birds—I. Characteristics of the open flow method of determination, and their relation to estimates of thermoregulatory ability. *Comp. Biochem. Physiol., 19,* 445.

Lasiewski, R. C., A. L. Acosta, and M. H. Bernstein. (1966b). Evaporate water loss in birds—II. A modified method for determination by direct weighing. *Comp. Biochem. Physiol., 19,* 459.

172

Lasiewski, R. C., W. W. Weathers, and M. H. Bernstein. (1967). Physiological responses of the giant hummingbird, *Patagonai gigas. Comp. Biochem. Physiol., 23,* 797.

Lee, P., and K. Schmidt-Nielsen. (1971). Respiratory and cutaneous evaporation in the zebra finch: effect on water balance. *Am. J. Physiol., 220,* 1598.

LeFebvre, E. A. (1964). The use of $D_2O^{18}$ for measuring energy metabolism in *Columbia livia* at rest and in flight. *Auk, 81,* 403.

Lepkovsky, S., N. Snapir, and F. Furuta. (1968). Temperature regulation and appetitive behavior in chickens with hypothalamic lesions. *Physiol. Behav., 3,* 911.

Lin, Y. C., and P. D. Sturkie. (1968). Effect of environmental temperatures on the catecholamines of chickens. *Am. J. Physiol., 214,* 237.

MacMillen, R. E. (1974). Bioenergetics of Hawaiian honeycreepers: the amakihi *(Loxops virens)* and the anianiau *(L. para.)* *Condor, 76,* 62.

MacMillen, R. E., and C. H. Trost. (1967). Thermoregulation and water loss in the inca dove. *Comp. Biochem. Physiol., 20,* 263.

MacMillen, R. E., and C. H. Trost. (1967a). Nocturnal hypothermia in the inca dove, *Scardafella inca. Comp. Biochem. Physiol., 23,* 243.

Marder, J. (1973). Temperature regulation in the bedouin fowl *(Gallus domesticus). Physiol. Zoöl., 46,* 208.

Marley, E., and J. D. Stephenson. (1970). Effects of catecholamines infused into the brain of young chickens. *Brit. J. Pharmacol., 40,* 639.

McFarland, D. J., and E. Baher. (1968). Factors affecting feather posture in the barbary dove. *Anim. Behav., 16,* 171.

McFarland, D., and P. Budgell. (1970). The thermoregulatory role of feather movements in the barbary dove *(Streptopelia risoria). Physiol. Behav., 5,* 763.

McFarland, L. Z., M. K. Yousef, and W. O. Wilson. (1966). The influence of ambient temperature and hypothalamic lesions on the disappearance rates of thyroxine-$I^{131}$ in the Japanese quail. *Life Sci., 5,* 309.

McNab, B. K. (1966). An analysis of the body temperatures of birds. *Condor, 68,* 47.

Mills, S. H., and J. E. Heath. (1972a). Responses to thermal stimulation of the preoptic area in the house sparrow, *Passer domesticus. Am. J. Physiol., 222,* 914.

Mills, S. H., and J. E. Heath. (1972b). Anterior hypothalamic/preoptic lesions impair normal thermoregulation in house sparrows. *Comp. Biochem. Physiol., 43A,* 125.

Moreng, R. E., and R. L. Bryant. (1955). The tolerance of the chicken embryo to periods of low temperature exposure. *Poultry Sci., 34,* 1342.

Necker, R. (1972). Response of trigeminal ganglion neurons to thermal stimulation of the beak in pigeons. *J. Comp. Physiol., 78,* 307.

Pohl, H. (1969). Some factors influencing the metabolic response to cold in birds. *Fed. Proc., 28,* 1059.

Pohl, H., and G. C. West. (1973). Daily and seasonal variation in metabolic response to cold during rest and forced exercise in the common redpoll. *Comp. Biochem. Physiol., 45A,* 851.

Randall, W. C. (1943). Factors influencing the temperature regulation of birds. *Am. J. Physiol., 139,* 56.

Rautenberg, W. (1969a). Untersuchungen zur Temperaturregulation wärme-und kälteakklimatisierter Tauben. *Z. Vergl. Physiol., 62,* 221.

Rautenberg, W. (1969b). Die Bedeutung der zentralnervösen Thermosensitivität für die Temperaturregulation der Taube. *Z. Vergl. Physiol., 62,* 235.

Rautenberg, W. (1971). The influence of the skin temperature on the thermoregulatory system of pigeons. *J. Physiol. (Paris), 63,* 396.

Rautenberg, W., R. Necker, and B. May. (1972). Thermoregulatory responses of the pigeon to changes of the brain and the spinal cord temperatures. *Pflügers Arch., 338,* 31.

Richards, S. A. (1969). Vagal function during respiration and the effects of vagotomy in the domestic fowl *(Gallus domesticus). Comp. Biochem. Physiol., 29,* 955.

Richards, S. A. (1970). The role of hypothalamic temperature in the control of panting in the chicken exposed to heat. *J. Physiol. (London), 211,* 341.

Richards, S. A. (1971a). The significance of changes in the temperature of the skin and body core of the chicken in the regulation of heat loss. *J. Physiol. (London), 216,* 1.

Richards, S. A. (1971b). Brain stem control of polypnoea in the chicken and pigeon. *Resp. Physiol., 11,* 315.

Ricklefs, R. E., and F. R. Hainsworth. (1968). Temperature regulation in nestling cactus wrens: The development of homeothermy. *Condor, 70,* 121.

Roller, W. L., and A. C. Dale. (1962). Heat losses from Leghorn layers at warm temperatures. Paper No. 62-428, Annual Meeting of the American Society of Agricultural Engineers, Washington, D. C.

Romijn, C. (1954). Development of heat regulation in the chick. Section Papers, 10th World's Poultry Congress, p. 181.

Romijn, C., and W. Lokhorst. (1956). The caloric equibrium of the chicken embryo. *Poultry Sci., 35,* 829.

Romijn, C., and W. Lokhorst. (1960). Foetal heat production in the fowl. *J. Physiol., (London), 150,* 239.

Romijn, C., and W. Lokhorst. (1961). Climate and poultry: Heat regulation in the fowl. *Tijdschr. Diergeneesk., 86,* 153.

Schmidt-Nielsen, K., F. R. Hainsworth, and D. E. Murrish. (1970). Counter-current heat exchange in the respiratory passages: effect on water and heat balance. *Resp. Physiol., 9,* 263.

Schmidt-Nielsen, K., J. Kanwisher, R. C. Lasiewski, J. E. Cohn, and W. L. Bretz. (1969). Temperature regulation and respiration in the ostrich. *Condor, 71,* 341.

Scholander, P. F., R. Hock, V. Walters, and L. Irving. (1950). Adaptation to cold in artic and tropical mammals and birds in relation to body temperature, insulation and abasal metabolic rate. *Biol. Bull., 99,* 259.

Shallenberger, R. J., G. C. Whittow, and R. M. Smith. (1974). Body temperature of the nesting red-footed booby *(Sula sula). Condor, 76,* 476.

Sinha, M. P. (1959). Observations on the organization of the panting center in avian brain. Abstracts, *21st Intl. Congr Physiol. Sci.,* Buenos Aires, p. 254.

Smith, R. M. (1969). Cardiovascular, respiratory, temperature and evaporative water loss responses of pigeons to varying degrees of heat stress. Ph.D. Thesis. University of Indiana, Bloomington, Indiana

Smith, R. M. (1972). Circulation, respiratory volumes and temperature regulation of the pigeon in dry and humid heat. *Comp. Biochem. Physiol., 43A,* 477.

Smith, R. M., and R. A. Suthers. (1969). Cutaneous water loss as a significant contribution to temperature regulation in heat-stressed pigeons. *Physiologist, 12,* 358.

Steen, J. (1958). Climatic adaptation in some small northern birds. *Ecology, 39,* 625.

Steen, I., and J. B. Steen. (1965). The importance of the legs in the thermoregulation of birds. *Acta Physiol. Scand., 63,* 285.

Taylor, C. R., R. Dmi'el, M. Fedak, and K. Schmidt-Nielsen. (1971). Energetic cost of running and heat balance in a large bird, the rhea. *Am. J. Physiol., 221,* 597.

Tucker, V. A. (1966). Oxygen consumption of a flying bird. *Science, 154,* 150.

Tucker, V. A. (1968). Respiratory exchange and evaporative water loss in the flying budgerigar. *J. Exp. Biol., 48,* 67.

Tucker, V. A. (1972). Metabolism during flight in the laughing gull, *Larus artricilla. Am. J. Physiol., 222,* 237.

van Kampen, M. (1971). Some aspects of thermoregulation in the White Leghorn fowl. *Intl. J. Biometeorol., 15,* 244.

Veghte, J. H. (1964). Thermal and metabolic responses of the gray jay to cold stress. *Physiol. Zoöl., 37,* 316.

Wallgren, H. (1954). Energy metabolism of two species of the genus Emberiza as correlated with distribution and migration. *Acta Zool. Fenn., 84,* 1.

Waring, J. J., and W. O. Brown (1965). A respiration chamber for the study of energy utilization for maintenance and production in the laying hen. *J. Agri. Sci. Cambridge, 66,* 139.

Washburn, K. W., P. B. Siegel, R. J. Freund, and W. B. Gross. (1962). Effect of thiouracil on the body temperatures of White Rock females. *Poultry Sci. 41,* 1354.

Weathers, W. W. (1972). Thermal panting in domestic pigeons,

*Columbia livia,* and the barn owl, *Tyto alba. J. Comp. Physiol., 79,* 79.

Wekstein, D. R., and J. F. Zolman. (1968). Sympathetic control of homeothermy in the young chick. *Am. J. Physiol., 214,* 908.

West, G. C. (1962). Responses and adaptation of wild birds to environmental temperature. In "Comparative Physiology of Temperature Regulation," Part 3 (J. P. Hannon and E. Viereck, Eds.). Fort Wainwright, Alaska. Arctic Aeromedical Laboratory, p. 291.

West, G. C. (1965). Shivering and heat production in wild birds. *Physiol. Zoöl., 38,* 111.

West, G. C. (1972a). Seasonal differences in resting metabolic rate of Alaskan ptarmigan. *Comp. Biochem. Physiol., 42A,* 867.

West, G. C. (1972b). The effect of acclimation and acclimatization on the resting metabolic rate of the common redpoll. *Comp. Biochem. Physiol., 43A,* 293.

West, G. C., and J. S. Hart. (1966). Metabolic responses of evening grosbeaks to constant and to fluctuating temperatures. *Physiol. Zoöl., 39,* 171.

Whittow, G. C. (1965a). Regulation of body temperature. In "Avian Physiology," (2nd ed.) (P. D. Sturkie, Ed.). Ithaca, N. Y.: Cornell University Press, p. 186.

Whittow, G. C. (1965b). Energy metabolism. In "Avian Physiology," (2nd ed.) (P. D. Sturkie, Ed.). Ithaca, N.Y.: Cornell University Press, p. 239.

Whittow, G. C. (1966). Terminology of thermoregulation. *Physiologist, 9,* 358.

Whittow, G. C. (1971). Ungulates. In "Comparative Physiology of Thermoregulation," Vol. II (G. C. Whittow, Ed.). New York: Academic Press, p. 191.

Whittow, G. C. (1973). Evolution of thermoregulation. In "Comparative Physiology of Thermoregulation," Vol. III (G. C. Whittow, Ed.). New York: Academic Press, p. 201.

Whittow, G. C., P. D. Sturkie, and G. Stein, Jr. (1964). Cardiovascular changes associated with thermal polypnea in the chicken. *Am. J. Physiol., 207,* 1349.

Whittow, G. C., P. D. Sturkie, and G. Stein, Jr. (1966). Cardiovascular differences between cold-acclimatized and heat-acclimatized chickens. *Res. Vet. Sci., 7,* 296.

Wilson, W. O. (1948). Some effects of increasing environmental temperatures on pullets. *Poultry Sci., 27,* 813.

Wilson, W. O. (1949). High environmental temperatures as affecting the reaction of laying hens to iodized casein. *Poultry Sci., 28,* 581.

Wilson, W. O., and W. H. Edwards. (1952). Response of hens under thermal stress to dehydration and chilled drinking water. *Am. J. Physiol., 169,* 102.

Wolf, L. L., and F. R. Hainsworth. (1972). Environmental influence on regulated body temperature in torpid hummingbirds. *Comp. Biochem. Physiol., 41A,* 167.

Woods, J. J., and G. C. Whittow. (1974). The role of central and peripheral temperature changes in the regulation of thermal polypnea in the chicken. *Life Sci., 14,* 199.

# 8

# Energy Metabolism

## G. C. Whittow

# INTRODUCTION

The reader of the preceding chapter is aware that the physiology of temperature regulation cannot be considered without considerable reference to many different aspects of energy metabolism. Nevertheless, there are some features of energy metabolism that are not directly related to thermoregulation and that usually occur over an extended period of time. These aspects of energy metabolism are discussed in this chapter. They include, *inter alia*, energy storage during growth and premigratory fattening, the energy cost of egg production, and the regulation of energy intake. In the particular instance of domestic birds, these considerations are often of economic importance; in wild birds, considerations of energy expenditure and intake are frequently a matter of survival in an adverse environment.

# ENERGY BALANCE

Apart from the radiant energy gained from the sun, or from very hot surfaces in the environment, the energy requirements of birds are met entirely by the chemical energy contained in their food. The fate of the *gross energy* of the food may be depicted as follows (modified from King and Farner, 1961):

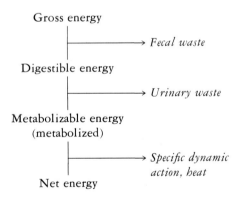

A portion of the energy contained in the substances absorbed from the gut (the *digestible energy*) is excreted by the kidney, largely as uric acid. The energy retained in the body is the *metabolized energy* (some authors refer to this as the *"metabolizable"* energy), whereas the fecal and urinary waste are collectively known as the *excretory energy* (Kendeigh, 1949, 1970). Not all of the metabolized

The preparation of this chapter was supported by grant (GB-29287X) from the National Science Foundation.

energy is available for growth, maintenance, the performance of work, storage, or for such other special functions as the production of eggs. The absorption of energy from the gastrointestinal tract is followed, soon after its absorption, by an increase in heat production. This heat is referred to variously as the *heat increment*, the *calorigenic effect*, or the *specific dynamic action* (SDA) of the diet. When the body weight is constant, i.e., the bird is not storing energy, the metabolized energy is referred to as the *existence energy* (Kendeigh, 1949, 1970; Owen, 1970). If the bird gains weight or is producing eggs, the metabolized energy is clearly greater than the existence energy and the difference between the two is identified as the *productive energy* (Kendeigh, 1949).

The *net energy* represents the metabolized energy minus the specific dynamic action and the heat liberated coincidentally to storage and work. If the bird performs work, some of the net energy is transformed into work; if energy is stored, a portion of the net energy is incorporated into tissue. If no work is performed and if the body weight and composition do not change, then all the metabolized energy appears as heat.

# THE MEASUREMENT OF ENERGY EXCHANGE

Energy balance studies are comparatively simple to perform on domestic birds and on wild birds kept under laboratory conditions. The amount of food consumed and of feces and urine produced, together with their respective energy contents, may readily be determined, yielding the gross energy, digestible energy, excretory energy, and metabolized energy. The disposition of the metabolized energy may be estimated from the energy content of the eggs produced or fat deposited. The rate of energy expenditure of a bird may be determined from its oxygen consumption by the techniques described in Chapter 7. However, these techniques do require the bird to be in an enclosure. Its activity is therefore circumscribed by the dimensions of the chamber in which it is confined.

Under natural conditions, it is clearly impossible to compile a comprehensive energy budget of a bird, but the energy expenditure may be estimated over a given period of time by several different techniques. One method requires the labeling of the body water of the bird with stable isotopes of hydrogen and oxygen (deuterium and $^{18}O_2$, respectively). Samples of body water are taken after a specified period of time, and the change in the con-

176 centration of the isotopes is determined. The turn-over rate of $O_2$ is greater than that of deuterium because, whereas the latter is lost only in water, the $O_2$ is lost both as water and as carbon dioxide. The difference between the two rates of loss is a measure of the carbon dioxide production which, in turn, reflects the rate of energy exchange (LeFebvre, 1964).

A technique that has been used to estimate the energy expenditure of free-living birds under natural conditions promises to be used a great deal more in the field. The procedure may be described as a "time and energy budget" and in principle is extremely simple. A careful note is kept of the bird's activities, which are classified into three or more such categories as sleep, flight, and nonflying activity. From the percentage time that the bird devotes to a particular activity and the known oxygen uptake for that activity, it is possible to arrive at a figure for the heat production of the bird without interfering with the bird's normal activity. Moreover, it is possible to partition the energy expenditure into the categories of activity used. The energy costs of the different activities are derived from laboratory determinations of the energy expenditure of birds. Clearly, the precision of the method is increased if such determinations are performed on the same species studied in the field. Utter and LeFebvre (1973) recently compared the method with the $D_2O^{18}$ technique, in *Progne subis* (purple martin) and reported excellent agreement.

Interest in the use of heart rate as an indication of energy expenditure is growing. The advantage of this is that heart rate can be measured by telemetry, so that information on the metabolic activity of free-flying birds may be obtained. The disadvantage of using heart rate in this way is that heart rate may be influenced by many factors not directly related to heat production. Nevertheless, Owen (1969) obtained some useful correlations between heart rate and existence metabolism in *Anas discors* (blue-winged teal).

## GROSS ENERGY INTAKE

As birds derive their energy from the food that they eat, the regulation of food intake is of paramount importance to an understanding of energy exchange. This aspect of energy metabolism is discussed in detail in Chapter 9. Among the factors that affect energy intake is environmental temperature. For example, the gross energy intake of *Taeniopygia castanotis* (zebra finch) increased linearly with decreasing environmental temperature (Figure 8–1).

## Effects of Energy Deprivation

When birds are deprived of food, their heat production diminishes. The RQ decreases also, because fat is preferentially metabolized during starvation (Koskimies, 1950). Minimal RQ values are attained in the chicken after a 48-hr period of starvation (Mitchell and Haines, 1927; Barott and Pringle, 1946). In smaller birds, the fasting RQ is attained after a shorter fast. For example, *Columba* (pigeon) requires 28 hr and the ortolan and yellow bunting only 3 hr (Benedict and Riddle, 1929; Wallgren, 1954). The glycogen reserves of pigeons are depleted within 24 hr of the start of a fast (Wallgren, 1954). Young *Micropus apue* (swifts) lost 60% of their body weight during a fast, whereas adults lost 38% before death (Koskimies, 1950). The young birds were heavier initially, and had greater fat deposits than adults. Next to adipose tissue, liver and muscle incurred the greatest losses of weight during the fast. In the pigeon, adipose tissue lost 93%; spleen, 71%; pancreas, 64%; liver, 52%; heart, 45%; and muscle, 42% of their respective initial weights during a fast (Kleiber, 1961).

## Effects of the Level of Energy Intake

When chickens are fed a sufficient amount of food to maintain constant body weight, on a so-called "maintenance diet," their heat production is approximately 50% greater than their "standard" metabolic rates (Mitchell, 1962). The standard or basal metabolic rate is the metabolic rate determined under carefully controlled conditions with the bird at rest, in a postabsorptive state, and within the thermoneutral zone of environmental temperature (see Chapter 7).

The concept of basal metabolic rate was developed in connection with work on human subjects. The requisite conditions are often difficult to attain for animals. A more appropriate index for animals is the metabolic rate at a specified level of food intake, with the animal resting or at a minimal level of activity. At an air temperature of 23°C the resting metabolic rate was 18% higher than the fasting rate in the White Leghorn chicken (Berman and Snapir, 1965). Tasaki and Sakurai (1969) noted a marked difference in standard metabolic rate between two populations of adult chickens. When the birds were fed a maintenance ration, however, their "resting" metabolic rates were practically identical. On a maintenance diet, some of the increased heat production over and above that of fasting birds is the result of greater activity. After a single meal, the heat production of chickens remained elevated for between 24 and 48 hr (Mitchell and Haines, 1927). According to Mellen *et al.* (1954), male chickens on a high-energy diet have a higher standard metabolic rate than do those on a low-energy diet, which these investigators have attributed to differences in body composition as a result of feeding. Freeman (1963) found that the effect of feeding a high-energy, high-protein diet to chicks persisted for some time after the diet of the birds had been changed. Not only the energy content but also the ratio of protein to energy in the diet has an influence on the heat production of chickens. A reduction of the dietary protein/energy ratio results in an increase in heat production (Davidson, 1965).

## EXCRETORY ENERGY

Inverse relationships between the excretory energy and ambient temperature (Figure 8–1) have been described by Zimmerman (1965), El-Wailly (1966), and Brooks (1968). This relationship was demonstrable in Alaskan redpolls under conditions of both constant and fluctuating temperatures and at winter and summer photoperiods (Brooks, 1968). Seasonal variations in the excretory energy occurred in the willow ptarmigan, the calorific value of the guano being lowest during the late-summer molt (West, 1968).

## METABOLIZED ENERGY

In view of the inverse relationships between gross energy intake and excretory energy, on the one hand, and environmental temperature, on the other, it is not surprising that such a relationship also exists between metabolized energy and ambient temperature (Figure 8–2). In the case of Alaskan redpolls, this relationship was evident at constant and fluctuating temperatures and at winter and summer photoperiods (Brooks, 1968). The efficiency of utilization of the food (metabolized energy/gross energy) decreased initially, in the redpolls at low air temperatures, but it increased again with prolonged exposure. A diminution in the efficiency of utilization with decreasing air temperature was apparent in zebra finch (El-Wailly, 1966; Figure 8–1) and also in the redpolls.

## NET ENERGY, SPECIFIC DYNAMIC ACTION

The net energy is approximately 84% of the metabolized energy in the chicken (Waring and Brown, 1965). In the chick, the net energy was

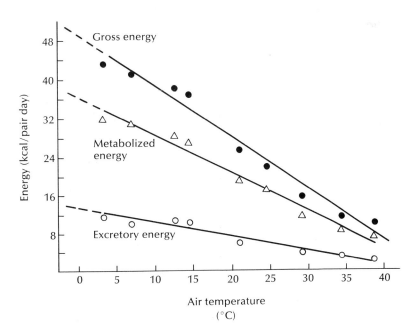

8–1

The effect of air temperature ($T_a$) on the gross energy intake, metabolized energy, and excretory energy of a pair of *Taeniopygia castanotis* (zebra finches). (After El-Wailly, 1966.)

178 maximal at an environmental temperature of 32°C (Kleiber and Dougherty, 1934). The calorigenic effect (specific dynamic action, SDA) of protein resulted in a rate of heat production 15–18% above the expenditure of basal energy in the chicken (Barott et al., 1938). The heat is thought to be derived from the stimulation of metabolism by some of the absorbed food molecules or by the intermediary metabolites. The magnitude of the specific dynamic action depends on a number of factors which have been discussed by Whittow (1965).

## EXISTENCE ENERGY (ACTIVITY)

The existence energy is a more useful measure of energy metabolism than is the minimal, resting, or "standard" metabolism (see Chapter 7; Kendeigh, 1970). The existence energy measures the energy expenditure associated with normal everyday activities. Kendeigh (1970) presented equations describing the relationship between existence energy and environmental temperature in a number of species of caged birds. No zone of thermal neutrality was evident. The energy cost of cage existence, over and above the standard metabolism, was calculated to be equivalent to 26–31% of the standard metabolism.

A different relationship between existence energy and environmental temperature in blue-winged teal examined out of doors, as opposed to that indoors, was thought to be associated with the difficulty in adjusting to rapidly fluctuating temperatures out of doors (Owen, 1970). However, in Alaskan redpolls, Brooks (1968) demonstrated an inverse relationship between existence energy and environmental temperature in birds exposed to either constant or fluctuating temperatures and at winter and summer photoperiods.

The existence energy clearly includes the energy cost of activity. Consequently, factors that influence activity will ipso facto alter the existence energy. Activity is the most potent single factor affecting energy expenditure. The activity of birds is influenced by both photoperiod and environmental temperature. For example, Carpodacus mexicanus (house finch) awakened later when the air temperature was low and the day length was long (Enright, 1966). The circadian rhythm of activity (see Chapter 7) in the house finch was slowed by low environmental temperature, but the effect was obvious only at relatively high light intensities. Seasonal variations in the activity of the willow ptarmigan

are dramatic (West, 1968). In the roadrunner, activity was less on overcast than on clear days, and the birds were most active in the evening (Kavanau and Ramos, 1970).

*Nest building, incubation.* El-Wailly (1966) calculated that the existence energy of the zebra finch increased during nest building and also during incubation of the eggs. Moreover, the increase was greater at lower air temperatures. The energy cost of incubation, of course, includes a considerable transfer of heat from the bird to the eggs.

*Energy cost of feeding.* The energy that a bird expends in order to procure food must obviously offset, to a variable extent, the energy derived from the food. This is an important consideration in hummingbirds, which feed while hovering, because hovering is very expensive from an energetic point of view. Hainsworth and Wolf (1972a) reported that the energy required to hover for a given time was greater in large than in small hummingbirds. This may very well set an upper limit on body size for hummingbirds that hover in order to obtain food. This problem is exacerbated for a bird at high altitude, where the ambient temperature is lower and the energy requirements greater. The production of nectar, on which hummingbirds feed, and its concentration are lower at high elevations, so that a bird must devote more time and energy to the acquisition of food than at low altitude. Hainsworth and Wolf (1972b) obtained values of 0.02–0.12 kcal expended in foraging for each kilocalorie of food energy ingested in hummingbirds. Time and energy budgets constructed for hummingbirds revealed that a large part (26–64%) of the energy expenditure of these birds was accounted for by foraging (Wolf and Hainsworth, 1971).

*Energy cost of prolonged flight.* Many migrating birds perform prodigious feats of endurance flight. *Pluvialis dominica fulva* (golden plover) (Tucker, 1969; 1971), for instance, migrates between the Aleutian Islands and Hawaii, a distance of 2,400 miles entirely over the ocean, with no opportunity to feed *en route*. The fuel for long-distance flight is largely fat; before migration some birds may accumulate fat equivalent to 50% of their body weight, and most of this has been metabolized at the end of the migratory flight (Tucker, 1971). Indeed, fat is the only feasible source of energy for a migrating bird because of its high energy content per unit weight. If the bird stored energy in the form of glycogen, it would have to carry a mass of glycogen eight times that of fat of equivalent energy content (Tucker, 1971). As the bird flies and consumes fuel, its weight diminishes and its rate of fuel consumption decreases also.

The energy cost of moving a unit weight of bird a given distance diminishes with the size of the bird. This means that large birds can fly a greater distance for the expenditure of a given amount of fuel than is the case for small birds (Tucker, 1971). This conforms with records of the distance over which birds migrate. For example, hummingbirds weighing 5 g are able to cross the Gulf of Mexico (Lasiewski, 1962), whereas golden plovers (200 g) cross 2400 miles of ocean (Tucker, 1971). Tucker's (1971) calculations of the energy cost of flight, in conjunction with the known energy reserves of birds, explain the ability of birds to fly great distances, but the margin of safety is apparently small for land birds flying over the ocean.

The most efficient speed of flight for a bird depends on the nature of the flight. If the bird needs to stay aloft for long periods of time while searching for food, it ought to fly at the speed that has the minimal energy cost. In *Larus atricilla* (laughing gull) this was 19 miles/hr (8.5 m/sec; Tucker, 1969). A migrating bird, in contrast, needs to cover the maximal distance on a given amount of fuel. This is accomplished at a flight speed at which the ratio power expenditure/flight speed is minimal. In the laughing gull this speed was 13.0 m/sec (Tucker, 1969). Calculations of the flight performance of birds are complex because of the variations in wind speed and direction that a bird encounters under natural conditions, the aerodynamic efficiency of formation flight in some birds (Lissaman and Schollenberger, 1970), vertical air movements, and probably other factors also.

## PRODUCTIVE ENERGY (ENERGY STORAGE)

The storage of energy in the form of avian tissue is often important to the commercial poultryman (eggs, muscle) and always important biologically.

### Growth

**Embryo.** The heat production of the chicken's egg increases continuously throughout the incubation period (Table 8–1). However, there is a rapid increase after the tenth day coincident with evidence for incipient thyroid activity, suggesting a

*Table 8–1  Heat production (M) and respiratory quotient (RQ) of a chicken's egg during incubation at an air temperature of 37.7°C[a]*

| Day of incubation | M (kcal/hr) $\times 10^3$ | RQ |
|---|---|---|
| 1 | – | 1.63 |
| 2 | 1.125 | 0.84 |
| 3 | 1.575 | 1.00 |
| 4 | 3.708 | 1.00 |
| 5 | 3.708 | 0.94 |
| 6 | 5.792 | 0.86 |
| 7 | 7.500 | 0.80 |
| 8 | 11.500 | 0.92 |
| 9 | 15.667 | 0.88 |
| 10 | 24.333 | 0.85 |
| 11 | 37.000 | 0.81 |
| 12 | 54.000 | 0.74 |
| 13 | 71.917 | 0.69 |
| 14 | 91.500 | 0.71 |
| 15 | 104.583 | 0.69 |
| 16 | 111.792 | 0.69 |
| 17 | 113.167 | 0.67 |
| 18 | 119.708 | 0.69 |
| 19 | 112.417 | 0.73 |
| 20 | 130.167 | – |

[a]From Romijn and Lokhorst (1960).

causal relationship between these two phenomena (Romijn and Lokhorst, 1960). The respiratory quotient (RQ) of the egg of the domestic fowl decreases during the incubation period (Table 8–1). The main source of energy for the embryo is fat and, in fact, most of the energy stored in the yolk is in the form of lipid (Romijn and Lokhorst, 1969; Freeman, 1971). The humidity of the air surrounding the egg appears to have an important effect on the energy metabolism of the embryo (Romijn and Lokhorst, 1962). After the fifteenth day of incubation, an increase in the atmospheric humidity results in a diminution in the rate of diffusion of oxygen into the egg, and part of the heat production of the embryo is then derived from anaerobic sources. Recent work has drawn attention to the importance of the gas conductance of the egg shell in the rate of diffusion of oxygen into the egg and, therefore, to its oxygen consumption (Rahn, Paganelli, and Ar, 1974).

The oxygen consumption increases further at the time of hatching and it has been postulated that this increase is the result of a hormonal stimulus (Freeman, 1962, 1964). McNagg *et al.* (1972) ob-

180   tained evidence for a sudden increase in thyroid secretory activity in the Japanese quail embryo at this time, again implicating thyroid hormone in the calorigenic response. However, the onset of pulmonary respiration and pipping activity must also contribute to the increased heat production.

Chick. Within a few hours of hatching, an additional increase in heat production occurs as a correlate of the greatly increased heat loss of the chick (see Chapter 7). Subsequently, the oxygen uptake increases as the chick grows, the highest value per unit body weight occurring at about 15 days (Figure 8–2). It then decreases until the adult level is reached. It is interesting that the thyroxine secretion rate was also highest at 2 weeks of age (Tanabe, 1965). In some rapidly growing passerine species, an increase in heat production above the adult level is not evident (Dawson and Evans, 1957). Although there is a general parallelism between growth and metabolic rate, the time of the highest growth rate may not coincide with the time of the greatest metabolic rate in all species. For example, Riddle *et al.* (1932) have pointed out that the stage of most rapid growth in the pigeon is at 3 days after hatching, whereas the highest rate of metabolism occurs at 11 days. During the perinatal period, yolk lipid continues to be the major source of energy. Approximately 5 g of yolk remain after hatching, and this is ordinarily utilized within 5 days; however, the yolk sac is not essential for the chick to survive.

The rate of growth of male chickens is greater than that of females, but the energy equivalent of the growth increments is greater in pullets than in cockerels (Mitchell, 1962; Freeman, 1963). This may be a result of the greater ability of the hen to fatten during growth, because the energy equivalent of the gained body weight varies directly with the fat content of the increased body weight. The difference between the male and the female chicken in this respect is largely abolished if the males are caponized (Mitchell, 1962). If testosterone propionate is administered to pullets, their rate of growth increases to equal that of cockerels. Male turkeys also grow at a greater rate than do females (Asmundson and Pun, 1954).

The increase in body weight during growth mainly involves the synthesis of protein. According to Kielanowski (1965), the energy cost of protein deposition in chickens is 7.74 kcal of metabolized energy per gram of protein. The deposition of 1 g of fat required 15.64 kcal of metabolized energy. The main factor determining the amount of fat deposited is the protein content of the diet in relation to the total energy; the greater the protein/energy ratio, the lower the fat content of the bird (Mitchell, 1962). Methionine-deficient chicks

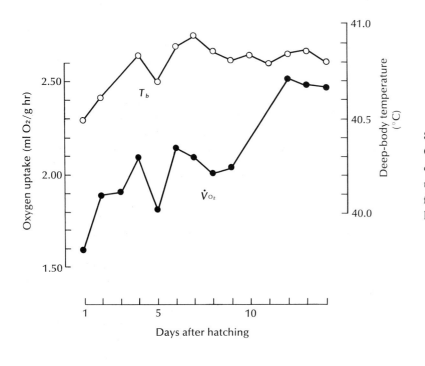

8–2
Oxygen uptake ($V_{O_2}$) and deep-body temperature ($T_b$) of the chick of the domestic fowl for the first 14 days after hatching. (After Freeman, 1965.)

gained more fat but less protein than did chicks that received supplementary methionine (Hill, 1965). The percentage utilization of the metabolized energy of the diet for gains in tissue energy is significantly increased in chickens by the addition of supplementary methionine to the diet (Davidson, 1965). Chickens utilize metabolized energy derived from animal fat as efficiently as they do energy from starch (Davidson, 1965). Royama (1966) determined that 70–80% of the digestible energy of nestling great tits was available for growth.

The growth of young chicks is adversely affected by exposure to hot weather. The impaired growth is partly caused by diminished food intake but also by less efficient food conversion (Kleiber and Dougherty, 1934; Osbaldiston and Sainsbury, 1963a). The optimal environmental temperature for growth in chicks seems to be approximately 35°C. The composition of the gained body substance during growth is also influenced by the environmental temperature. For example, the amount of fat stored per gram body weight increase was maximal at an environmental temperature of 32°C and was less at temperatures of 21° or 40°C (Kleiber and Dougherty, 1934). Growth rates of chicks are adversely affected by cold winds (Wilson et al., 1957), probably because heat loss is accelerated under these conditions and energy otherwise available for growth is used to maintain the body temperature.

A reduction in thyroid activity as a result of the administration of thiouracil is associated with a reduced rate of growth (Mellen and Hill, 1953; see also Chapter 18). The reduced rate of growth is probably related to the reduced metabolic rate.

**Adult.** In the adult bird, energy is stored partly as glycogen in liver and muscle, but mainly as fat. Birds fed a high-energy diet deposit more fat than those on a low-energy diet (Mellen et al., 1954).

The caloric equivalent of a change in body weight of 1 g was estimated to be 5.0 kcal in the blue-winged teal (Owen, 1970). The body weight and percentage of fat were lower in chickens that were allowed access to food for only 2 hr a day (meal eaters) than in birds fed ad libitum (nibblers), according to Leveille and Hanson (1965). The rate of lipogenesis from acetate and of fatty acid synthesis from glucose were greater in meal eaters than in nibblers.

In the adult fowl, carbohydrate provides 87% of the bird's energy, protein supplying the remainder (Freeman, 1971). The diet of mature birds varies

enormously under natural conditions. Some birds subsist on seeds or other plant material; others eat insects, fish, reptiles, or mammalian tissues. Many birds, particularly migratory species, change their diet seasonally (Seel, 1966). Unfortunately, very little is known about the implications of these dietary variations as far as energy metabolism is concerned.

Lesions in the ventromedial area of the hypothalamus of male chickens produced hyperphagia and obesity (see Chapter 9). The fat was laid down in the abdomen, muscle, and other tissues but not in the liver.

The composition of their subcutaneous fat depends on the environmental temperature at which chickens are kept (Fisher et al., 1962). The fat was more unsaturated in birds at 0°C than at 21°C or 32°C. The body weights of adult chickens fed ad libitum were similar at environmental temperatures of 2°C and 21°C, but significantly lower at 32°C (Fisher et al., 1965). These differences in body weight reflected differences in the total body fat content.

### Premigratory Fattening

An increase in body weight has been observed in a number of species of birds prior to migration (Wallgren, 1954; King and Farner, 1965). Presumably, one of the main functions of the accumulated fat is to provide a reserve of energy for the migratory flight. The increase in the body weight of *Emberiza hortulana* (ortolan bunting) before migration was associated with only a very slight increase in the metabolic rate. The metabolic rate per unit of lean body weight was unchanged during the fattening period, indicating that the deposition of fat had no accelerator effect on the metabolic processes. On the contrary, the lower oxygen uptake of *Fringilla montifringilla* (brambling) during the migratory season was considered to permit the diversion of energy away from heat production and into the deposition of fat (Pohl, 1971), although this may not be true for other species. The fat is mainly deposited in the abdomen and beneath the skin (Johnston, 1973); this involves an increase in the fat content of the cells and not an increased number of cells.

An increased food intake is the principal source of calories for lipogenesis preceding the spring migration (King and Farner, 1965). The hyperphagia seems to be induced by the increasing vernal photoperiod. In *Zonotrichia leucophrys gambelii* (white-crowned sparrow), Meier and Farner (1964)

182 were able to simulate premigratory fattening by increasing the duration of the daily photoperiod. The effect appeared to be mediated by prolactin and gonadotropin.

Zimmerman (1965) found that the caloric value of the excreta decreased in *Spiza Americana* (dickcissel) during premigratory hyperphagia, a factor favoring the efficiency of deposition of fat. A diminished capacity for fatty acid oxidation in the premigratory *Sternus roseus* (starling) is consistent with the bird's predilection to lay down fat rather than to metabolize it (George and Vallyathan, 1964).

### Egg Production

The metabolized energy was significantly increased during the egg-laying period in the zebra finch (El-Wailly, 1966) and so was the efficiency of food utilization. It also increased in the willow ptarmigan during the egg-laying period (West, 1968). The energy-demanding activities of this species, such as the seasonal change of weight, molting, egg laying, thermoregulation, and gross activity, occur sequentially so that the total energy requirement tends to be uniform throughout the year (West, 1968). In chickens, the efficiency of converting dietary energy to eggs was not affected by the energy content of the diet (Brown *et al.*, 1965). The percentage of the metabolized energy that was diverted to egg production in chickens was increased by 20%, however, by feeding the birds only for two 2½-hr periods each day as opposed to *ad libitum* feeding (Polin and Wolford, 1973). This increased productive efficiency was achieved at the expense of body fat stores. Force feeding the birds so that their energy intake was 150% of that during *ad libitum* feeding resulted in a reduction in the efficiency of egg production.

Although there are no differences in the utilization of energy between sexes, different breeds of chickens vary in the efficiency with which they convert their diet into tissue (Begin, 1967). The energetic efficiency of egg production in chickens has been discussed by Mitchell (1962) and is comparable to that of growth on an ordinary diet.

The diminished egg production often observed in a hot environment is often related to the lower energy intake (Wilson, 1949; Payne, 1966). Squibb *et al.* (1959), however, could not demonstrate an inhibitory effect of high environmental temperature on egg production under natural conditions, provided daily fluctuations of temperature occurred. Similar results were obtained by Mueller (1967). Birds have the highest productivity at environmental temperatures within the thermoneutral range, because their energy requirements for thermoregulatory purposes are at a minimum then (Osbaldiston and Sainsbury, 1963b).

The energy cost of incubation amounted to 28% of the productive energy in *Spizella arbores* (tree sparrow) (West, 1960) and 17–51% in *Troglodytes aedon* (house wren) (Kendeigh, 1963). In the zebra finch, the energy cost of incubation increased with a decrease in air temperature (El-Wailly, 1966), a not unexpected finding as the cost of incubation is largely the replacement of heat transfered directly to the egg.

### Molting

The standard metabolic rate increases during molting. In the ortolan bunting, the increase was 26% (Wallgren, 1954). Perek and Sulman (1945) observed an increase of 45% during the molt in the chicken. The greatest increase in metabolic rate coincides with the regeneration of the flight feathers (Koch and de Bont, 1944). The increase in metabolic rate during the molt is less in young birds than in adults (Wallgren, 1954). Molting is associated with an increase in thyroid activity, which is probably one of the causes of the increase in metabolic rate. Loss of feathers, naturally or artificially, causes an increase in heat production and heat loss (Hoffman and Shaffner, 1950). The frizzle chicken is a breed characterized by scanty plumage and its heat production is greater than that of normal fowls (Benedict *et al.*, 1932); it also possesses a relatively high rate of thyroid activity. The metabolized energy of the willow ptarmigan was low during molting. However, as the excretory energy was also low, the efficiency of extracting energy from the food was high during molting (West, 1968). The productive energy of dickcissel also increased during molting.

## CONCLUSIONS

The regulation of energy intake by birds has many of the features observed in mammals. The crop provides a distinctive food storage organ in some species (Chapter 9). Energy conservation in other birds is promoted by periods of torpidity. Many birds change the nature of their diet completely during the course of the year. There is need for determining the energy contents of different diets and the effect of these diets on the heat production of the birds that consume them. The energy cost of flight, the most characteristic activity of birds, has now been determined in several species. Procedures are available for estimating the energy expenditure of birds living freely under natural conditions.

# REFERENCES

Asmundson, V. S., and C. F. Pun. (1954). Growth of bronze turkeys. *Poultry Sci. 33,* 981.

Barott, H. G., and E. M. Pringle. (1946). Energy and gaseous metabolism of the chicken from hatch to maturity as affected by temperature. *J. Nutr., 31,* 35.

Barott, H. G., J. C. Fritz, E. M. Pringle, and H. W. Titus. (1938). Heat production and gaseous metabolism of young male chickens. *J. Nutr., 15,* 145.

Begin, J. J. (1967). The relation of breed and sex of chickens to the utilization of energy. *Poultry Sci., 46,* 379.

Benedict, F. G., and O. Riddle. (1929). The measurement of the basal heat production of pigeons. II: Physiological technique. *J. Nutr., 1,* 497.

Benedict, F. G., W. Landauer, and E. L. Fox. (1932). The physiology of normal and frizzle fowl with special reference to basal metabolism. *Univ. Conn (Storrs) Agr. Expt. Sta. Bull. No. 177,* p 15.

Berman, A., and N. Snapir. (1965). The relation of fasting and resting metabolic rates to heat tolerance in the domestic fowl. *Brit. Poultry Sci., 6,* 207.

Brooks, W. S. (1968). Comparative adaptations of the Alaskan redpolls to the arctic environment. *Wilson Bull, 80,* 253.

Brown, W. O., J. J. Waring, and E. Squance. (1965). A study of the effect of variation in the calorie-protein ratio of a medium energy diet and a high energy diet containing sucrose on the efficiency of egg production in caged layers. *Brit. Poultry Sci., 6,* 59.

Davidson, J. (1965). The efficiency of conversion of dietary metabolizable energy to tissue energy in young chickens as measured by body analysis. In "Energy Metabolism" (K. L. Blaxter, Ed.). London: Academic Press, p. 333.

Dawson, W. R., and F. C. Evans. (1957). Relation of growth and development to temperature regulation in nestling field and chipping sparrows. *Physiol. Zool., 30,* 315.

El-Wailly, A. J. (1966). Energy requirements for egg-laying and incubation in the zebra finch, *Taeniopygia castanotis. Condor, 68,* 582.

Enright, J. T. (1966). Influences of seasonal factors on the activity onset of the house finch. *Ecology, 47,* 662.

Fisher, H., P. Grimanger, and H. S. Weiss. (1965). Body composition and atherosclerosis in cocks after long exposure to heat and cold. *J. Appl. Physiol., 20,* 591.

Fisher, H., K. G. Hollands, and H. S. Weiss. (1962). Environmental temperature and composition of body fat. *Proc. Soc. Exp. Biol. Med., 110,* 832.

Freeman, B. M. (1962). Gaseous metabolism in the domestic chicken. II: Oxygen consumption in the full-term and hatching embryo, with a note on a possible cause for "death in shell." *Brit. Poultry Sci., 3,* 63.

Freeman, B. M. (1963). The gaseous metabolism of the domestic chicken. III: The oxygen requiremens of the chicken during the period of rapid growth. *Brit. Poultry Sci., 4,* 169.

Freeman, B. M. (1964). The emergence of the homeothermic-metabolic response in the fowl *(Gallus domesticus). Comp. Biochem. Physiol., 13,* 413.

Freeman, B. M. (1965). The relationship between oxygen consumption, body temperature and surface area in the hatching and young chick. *Brit. Poultry Sci., 6,* 67.

Freeman, B. M. (1971). Metabolic energy and gaseous metabolism. In "Physiology and Biochemistry of the Domestic Fowl," Vol. 1 (D. J. Bell and B. M. Freeman, Eds.). London: Academic Press, p. 1115.

George, J. C., and N. V. Vallyathan. (1964). Capacity for fatty acid oxidation by the breast muscle of the Starling (*Sturnus ro-seus*) in the pre- and postmigratory periods. *Can. J. Physiol. Pharmacol., 42,* 447.

Hainsworth, F. R., and L. L. Wolf. (1972a). Power for hovering flight in relation to body size in hummingbirds. *Am. Nat., 106,* 589.

Hainsworth, F. R., and L. L. Wolf. (1972b). Crop volume, nectar concentration and hummingbird energetics. *Comp. Biochem. Physiol., 42A,* 359.

Hill, F. W. (1965). Utilization of energy for growth by chicks. In "Energy Metabolism" (K. L. Blaxter, Ed.). London: Academic Press, p. 327.

Hoffman, E., and C. S. Shaffner. (1950). Thyroid weight and function as influenced by environmental temperature. *Poultry Sci., 29,* 365.

Johnson, D. W. (1973). Cytological and chemical adaptations of fat deposition in migratory birds. *Condor, 75,* 108.

Kavanau, J. L., and J. Ramos. (1970). Roadrunners: Activity of captive individuals. *Science, 169,* 780.

Kendeigh, S. C. (1949). Effect of temperature and season on energy resources of the English sparrow. *Auk, 66,* 113.

Kendeigh, S. C. (1963). Thermodynamics of incubation in the house wren. Proc. 13th Intl. Ornithol. Congr., 1962, p. 884.

Kendeigh, S. C. (1970). Energy requirements for existence in relation to size of bird. *Condor, 72,* 60.

Kielanowski, J. (1965). Estimates of the energy cost of protein deposition in growing animals. In "Energy Metabolism" (K. L. Blaxter, Ed.). London: Academic Press, p. 13.

King, J. R., and D. S. Farner. (1961). Energy metabolism, thermoregulation and body temperature. In "Biology and Comparative Physiology of Birds," Vol. 2 (A. L. Marshall, Ed.). London: Academic Press, p. 215.

King, J. R., and D. S. Farner. (1965). Studies of fat deposition in migratory birds. *Ann. N. Y. Acad. Sci., 131,* 422.

Kleiber, M. (1961). "The Fire of Life: An Introduction to Animal Energetics." New York: John Wiley & Sons.

Kleiber, M., and J. E. Dougherty. (1934). Influence of environmental temperature on the utilization of food energy in baby chicks. *J. Gen. Physiol., 17,* 701.

Koch, H. J., and A. F. de Bont. (1944). Influence de la mue sur l'intensite de metabolisme chez le pinson, *Fringilla coelebs coelebs* L. *Ann. Soc. Zool. Belg., 75,* 81.

Koskimies, J. (1950). The life of the swift, *Micropus apus* (L) in relation to the weather. *Ann. Acad. Sci. Fenn. Ser., 4,15.,* 1.

Lasiewski, R. C. (1962). The energetics of migrating hummingbirds. *Condor, 64,* 324.

LeFebvre, E. A. (1964). The use of $D_2O^{18}$ for measuring energy metabolism in *Columba livia* at rest and in flight. *Auk, 81,* 403.

Leveille, G. A., and R. W. Hanson. (1965). Influence of periodicity of eating in the chicken. *Am. J. Physiol., 209,* 153.

Lissaman, P. B. S., and C. A. Schollenberger. (1970). Formation flight of birds. *Science, 168,* 1003.

McNabb, R. A., R. L. Stouffer, and F. M. A. McNabb. (1972). Thermoregulatory ability and the thyroid gland: their development in embryonic Japanese quail (*Coturnix c. japonica*). *Comp. Biochem. Physiol., 43A,* 187.

Meier, A. H., and D. S. Farner. (1964). A possible endocrine basis for premigratory fattening in the white-crowned sparrow, *Zonotrichia leucophrys gambelii* (Nuttall). *Gen. Comp. Edocrinol., 4,* 584.

Mellen, W. J., and F. W. Hill. (1953). Effects of thiouracil, thyroprotein and estrogen upon the basal metabolism and thyroid size of growing chickens. *Poultry Sci., 32,* 994.

Mellen, W. F., F. W. Hill, and H. H. Dukes. (1954). Studies of the energy requirements of chickens. 2: Effect of dietary energy level on the basal metabolism of growing chickens. *Poultry Sci., 33,* 791.

Mitchell, H. H. (1962). "Comparative Nutrition of Man and Domestic Animals," Vol. 1. New York: Academic Press.

Mitchell, H. H., and W. T. Haines. (1927). The basal metabolism of mature chickens and the net-energy value of corn. *J. Agri. Res., 34,* 927.

Mueller, W. J. (1967). The effect of two levels of methionine on the biological performance of laying pullets in controlled environments. *Poultry Sci., 46,* 82.

184

Osbaldiston, G. W., and D. W. B. Sainsbury. (1963a). Control of the environment in a poultry house. Part II. Broiler house experiments. *Vet. Rec., 75,* 193.

Osbaldiston, G. W., and D. W. B. Sainsbury. (1963b). Control of the environment in a poultry house — The principles and practice, Part I. *Vet. Rec., 75,* 159.

Owen, R. B. (1969). Heart rate, a measure of metabolism in blue-winged teal. *Comp. Biochem. Physiol., 31,* 431.

Owen, R. B. (1970). The bioenergetics of captive blue-winged teal under controlled and outdoor conditions. *Condor, 72,* 153.

Payne, G. C. (1966). Practical aspects of environmental temperature for laying hens. *World Poult. Sci. J., 22,* 126.

Perek, M., and F. Sulman. (1945). The basal metabolic rate in molting and laying hens. *Endocrinology, 36,* 240.

Pohl, H. (1971). Seasonal variation in metabolic functions of bramblings. *Ibis, 113,* 185.

Polin, D., and J. H. Wolford. (1973). Factors influencing food intake and caloric balance in chickens. *Fed. Proc., 32,* 1720.

Rahn, H., C. Y. Paganelli, and A. Ar. (1974). The avian egg: air-cell gas tension, metabolism and incubation time. *Resp. Physiol., 22,* 297–309.

Riddle, O., T. C. Nussman, and F. G. Benedict. (1932). Metabolism during growth in a common pigeon. *Am. J. Physiol., 101,* 251.

Romijn, C., and W. Lokhorst. (1960). Foetal heat production in the fowl. *J. Physiol., (London) 150,* 239.

Romijn, C., and W. Lokhorst. (1962). Humidity and incubation. Section Papers, 12th World Poultry Congress, p. 136.

Royama, T. (1966). Factors governing feeding rate, food requirement and brood size of nestling great tits *Parus major. Ibis, 108,* 313.

Seel, D. C. (1966). Food, feeding rates and body temperature in the nestling house sparrow *Passer domesticus* at Oxford. *Ibis, 111,* 36.

Squibb, R. L., G. N. Wogan, and C. H. Reed. (1959). Production of White Leghorn hens subjected to high environmental temperatures with wide diurnal fluctuations. *Poultry Sci., 38,* 1182.

Tanabe, Y. (1965). Relation of thyroxine secretion rate to age and growth rate in the cockerel. *Poultry Sci., 44,* 591.

Tasaki, I., and H. Sakurai. (1969). *Mem. Lab. Anim. Nutr., Nagoya Univ.* (Cited by Freeman, 1971.)

Tucker, V. A. (1969). The energetics of bird flight. *Sci. Am., 220,* 70.

Tucker, V. A. (1971). Flight energetics in birds. *Am. Zool., 11,* 115.

Utter, J. M., and E. A. LeFebvre. (1973). Daily energy expenditure of purple martins (*Progne subis*) during the breeding season: estimates using $D_2O^{18}$ and time budget methods. *Ecology, 54,* 597.

Wallgren, H. (1954). Energy metabolism of two species of the genus *Emberiza* correlated with distribution and migration. *Acta Zool. Fenn., 84,* 1.

Waring, J. J., and W. O. Brown. (1965). A respiration chamber for the study of energy utilization for maintenance and production in the laying hen. *J. Agri. Sci., Cambridge, 65,* 139.

West, G. C. (1960). Seasonal variation in the energy balance of the tree sparrow in relation to migration. *Auk, 77,* 306.

West, G. C. (1968). Bioenergetics of captive willow ptarmigan under natural conditions. *Ecology, 49,* 1035.

Whittow, G. C. (1965). Energy metabolism. In "Avian Physiology" (2nd ed.) (P. D. Sturkie, Ed.). Ithaca, N. Y.: Cornell University Press, p. 239.

Wilson, W. O. (1949). High environmental temperatures as affecting the reaction of laying hens to iodized casein. *Poultry Sci., 28,* 581.

Wilson, W. O., C. F. Kelly, R. F. Lourenzen, and A. E. Woodward. (1957). Effect of wind on growth of fryers after two weeks of age. *Poultry Sci., 36,* 978.

Wolf, L. L., and F. R. Hainsworth. (1971). Time and energy budgets of territorial hummingbirds. *Ecology, 52,* 980.

Zimmerman, J. L. (1965). Bioenergetics of the dickcissel, *Spiza americana. Physiol. Zool., 38,* 370.

# 9

Alimentary Canal:
Anatomy, Prehension,
Deglutition, Feeding,
Drinking, Passage
of Ingesta, and
Motility

P. D. Sturkie

## 186  ANATOMY OF THE ALIMENTARY CANAL

The organs of the digestive tract of the bird include the beak, mouth, salivary glands, tongue (but not teeth), pharynx, esophagus, crop, proventriculus, gizzard, intestines, ceca, rectum, and cloaca (see Figure 9–1). The lengths of various parts of the tract vary with size of the bird, type of food eaten, and other factors. Birds eating coarse, fibrous food tend to have especially large digestive tracts, and grain-eating birds have larger tracts than carnivores do.

For details concerning anatomical and histological variations and peculiarities of different wild species, see Ziswiler and Farner (1972); for domestic species, see Calhoun (1954).

**Mouth and pharynx.** There is no sharp line of demarcation between the mouth and pharynx, and there is no soft palate in most birds. The hard palate is pierced by a median slit, which communicates with the nasal cavities. The cavity of the mouth is lined with stratified squamous epithelium.

Salivary glands are present and usually tubular but may be simple or branched. In general, species that ingest slippery aquatic food have poorly developed glands and those eating dry food have well-developed ones. The glands of some species (sparrow and others) contain appreciable amounts of amylase, whereas others, such as the chicken and turkey, do not (Jerrett and Goodge, 1973).

**Esophagus and crop.** The esophagus of most birds is relatively long (15–20 cm in the adult chicken). Its diameter is greater in those species ingesting large and bulky items (fish) and lesser in insectivorous and grain-eating species (Ziswiler and Farner, 1972). The esophagus has external longitudinal and internal circular muscles, and mucous glands are abundant.

The size and shape of crops vary according to the eating habits of the species. The gland may be unilobular, bilobed, or spindle shaped. The crops of certain grain-eating birds are bilobed and large, and in some species are very large; in certain others, such as insectivores, they are rudimentary or absent.

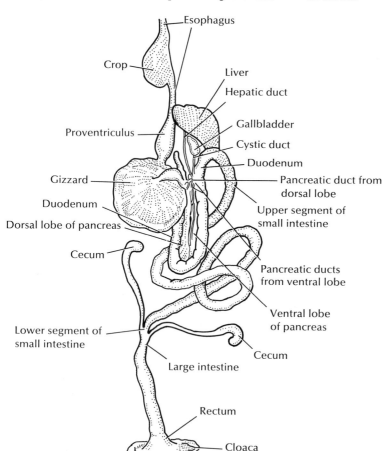

9–1

Digestive tract of the chicken.

The crops of doves and pigeons are especially adapted to produce crop milk, and the proliferation of the crop epithelium and milk secretion are induced by prolactin. These birds regurgitate the crop milk to feed their young. The crop has essentially the same structure as the esophagus.

Proventriculus. The proventriculus or glandular stomach is a fusiform organ and varies in size with the species. It is relatively small in many species but may be quite large and distensible in such species as storks, albatrosses, gulls, and cormorants. The proventriculus is lined with mucous membrane, which contains the gastric glands. These glands in most species contain only one cell (the chief cell), which secretes both acid and pepsin. The chief cells contain zymogen or pepsinogen granules, in varying amounts, depending on the state of digestion, that are precursors of pepsin. These granules increase on starvation and decrease immediately after feeding.

Gizzard. The gizzard or muscular stomach (where food is ground and macerated) of grain eaters is characterized by a massive muscular development and a thick keratinoid-like lining. The gland of species eating soft food is less muscular and may be long, saccular, and distensible (Ziswiler and Farner, 1972).

The main body of the gizzard is made up of two thick, opposed, lateral muscles, the ends of which are attached to a central aponeurosis and two thin anterior and posterior intermediary muscles (Hill, 1971). The glandular layer of the gizzard is composed of simple tubular glands. The so-called keratinoid lining of the gizzard has undergone more detailed studies, which suggest that it is protein in nature instead of keratin (Webb and Colvin, 1964). Innervation of the gizzard is discussed under gizzard motility (see also Chapter 1).

Small intestine. The small intestine consists of the duodenum (loop) and a jejunum and ileum, according to the terminology of some authors; beyond the duodenum there are no delimited areas in the small intestine. Some authors refer to the upper and lower ileum as corresponding to the jejunum and ileum in mammals. The remnant of the attachment of the yolk stalk may be found about midway along the small intestine. In relation to body length, the intestines of birds are shorter than those of mammals; however, there is considerable variation in the length, which is influenced by food habitat. It is longer in herbivores and grain eaters and shorter in carnivores.

The mucosa of the small intestine is characterized by crypts of Lieberkühn of varying degrees of development. In carnivorous birds there are well-developed and fingerlike villi; in herbivores the villi are flattened and leaflike (Ziswiler and Farner, 1972). The epithelium usually consists of simple columnar cells with many goblet cells. The layers or coats from the epithelial surface outward form the muscularis mucosae and a thin submucosa containing a few blood vessels and nerves. Brunner's glands are absent in the chicken (Calhoun, 1954), but in some species tubular glands that are similar to or homologous with Brunner's glands of mammals may be present (Ziswiler and Farner, 1972). Lymphocytes, which are present in large numbers in the lamina propria, are distributed diffusely or in isolated lymph follicles or in Peyer's patches.

Ceca, large intestine, and cloaca. The ceca are situated at the juncture of the small and large intestines. In some species (grain eaters) they are large, prominent and paired, whereas in some species they may be single, rudimentary, or absent (Browne, 1922). Guarding the entrance of the ceca into the intestine are the muscular ileocecal valves. The ceca may be histologically similar to the intestine, except that villi are not as tall; or may be quite glandular and exhibit a high degree of secretory activity (owls); or they may be of the lympho-epithelial type as present in may passerine species (Ziswiler and Farner, 1972).

The large intestine extends from the ceca to the cloaca and it is relatively short in most species except in the *Rhea americana,* where it is long. There is no sharp line of demarcation between the rectum and colon as in mammals. Histologically it is similar to the small intestine except for differences in size of villi.

The cloaca is the common opening into which empties the large intestine (coprodaeum), and the urinary and reproductive tracts (urodaeum). These, in turn, empty into the proctodaeum, which opens externally through the anus. At the junction of the large intestine and the cloaca is a dorsal projection known as the bursa of Fabricius, a prominent lymphoid organ.

Circulation of blood in the digestive tract. The esophagus and crop receive arterial blood from branches of the external carotid arteries and are drained by branches of the jugular veins. (See Figures 4–1 and 4–2 in Chapter 4.)

The coeliac artery branches to supply the proventriculus, gizzard (Nishida *et al.,* 1969), liver, pancreas, duodenum, and spleen. The anterior mesen-

188  teric artery supplies the remainder of the small intestine, and the caudal mesenteric artery supplies the large intestine, rectum, and cloaca.

The hepatic portal vein, carrying venous blood to the liver, receives blood from the gastroduodenal vein, which in turn receives blood from the proventriculus, gizzard, duodenum, and spleen. The anterior mesenteric vein courses in the mesentery of the small intestines and also drains into the hepatic portal veins. The coccygeomesenteric vein is a large vein located in the mesentery of the hind gut, which it drains. It anastomoses with the hepatic portal and renal portal veins. Blood in the coccygeomesenteric vein may flow into the hepatic portal and to the liver or reverse its direction of flow via the renal portal to the kidney and thence to the vena cava (Akester, 1967; Clarkson and Richards, 1966; Purton, 1970). For further details, see Chapters 4 and 14.

**Innervation.** Details on the nerves involved are considered in detail in the pertinent subsections of the section on food passage and in Chapter 1.

## PREHENSION, DEGLUTITION, AND APPETITE

### Prehension

The manner in which food is grasped, picked up, carried to the mouth, mixed with saliva and manipulated before swallowing (deglutition) varies with the different species depending on their feeding habits (see Ziswiler and Farner, 1972). In general, the food mass or bolus and water are forced downward in some species (goose, chicken, duck, and many others) by gravity and by negative pressure in the esophogus as the bird raises its head and extends its neck. These birds do not possess a soft palate, which in certain mammals and birds (pigeon) aids in forcing the bolus downward. The pigeon and hummingbird, however, can drink with the head down, like a horse, and develop considerable suction.

### Deglutition

In many species, particularly grain eaters, food particles are swallowed whole and pass to the crop. After a short sojourn here they pass on to the proventriculus and thence to the gizzard, or muscular stomach, where grinding and maceration of hard food, particularly grains, are completed. Raptors, such as the horned owl and hawks, regurgitate pellets of indigestible material. The mechanism of this phenomenon is not clear and needs to be further investigated (Balgooyen, 1971; Grimm and Whitehouse, 1963; see also section on motility in the small intestine).

### Feed Intake and Appetite Regulation

Animals eat to satisfy (1) energy requirements and (2) volume receptors, or to attain the state of fullness or satiety. The amount of feed consumed depends on many factors, including size and age, environmental temperature, activity, stage in the reproductive cycle, appearance and taste of food, and availability of water. Accurate records of feed intake of individual wild and even domestic birds are scarce for various reasons. The quantity eaten may be expressed as a percentage of body weight per 24 hr. This figure for White Leghorn females (weighing 1.8 kg) and laying approximately 65% averaged 6.4% of body weight (Sturkie, unpublished). The amount for males is about 50% less per unit of body weight. Small birds consume more per unit of body weight than large ones.

Some investigators believe that energy requirements and, ultimately, adipose tissue stores are the main regulators of appetite or food intake. When the amount of fat in the tissues increases above a given level, or set point, this causes a decrease in feed intake and promotes lipolysis (Mu et al., 1968). Conversely, when the fat level is below the set point, feed intake increases and lipogenesis and fat deposition are accelerated. Feed intake and body weight stabilize when the fat depots match the level called for by the new set point (Lepkovsky, 1973). The intake of feed and, indirectly, the size of fat depots are regulated by the appropriate centers in the hypothalamus (Brobeck, 1957). Hyperphagia resulting from lesions of the ventromedial nucleus is produced because a new set point becomes operative (Lepkovsky and Yasuda, 1966; Lepkovsky, 1973)

There is general agreement that the satiety and appetite centers of mammals are located in the ventromedial and lateral nucleus of hypothalamus, respectively; based on lesions of the brain there is evidence for these centers in birds (Feldman et al., 1957; Lepkovsky and Yasuda, 1966; Ackerman et al., 1960). Smith (1969), in chickens, and Kuenzel (1972), in *Zonotrichia albicollis,* reported that lesions in the ventromedial nucleus (VMN) at the base of the third ventricle, above the optic chiasma and supraoptic decussation, caused hyperphagia. Lesions in the lateral hypothalamus just slightly caudal to the region of the VMN resulted in aphagia.

The results of stimulations of these hypothalamic areas are questionable. Stimulation of these areas in chickens by Phillips and Youngnen (1971) and in mallard ducks by Maley (1969) failed to evoke clearcut results. Ackerman *et al.* (1960), however, reported that stimulation of the lateral hypothalamus of pigeons caused hyperphagia although Goodman and Brown (1966) could not confirm these results in the same species. Tweeton *et al.* (1973) conducted an extensive study involving stimulation at 625 different sites in the anterior hypothalamus and supra- and preoptic areas of brains of 68 chickens. These areas were discrete and located according to well-known and numbered chicken brain coordinates described by van Tienhoven and Juhusz (1962); the positions of the electrodes were verified histologically. Increased feed intake was elicited from only six sites and none of these led to normal feeding of mash during the stimulations. The reasons for the poor results with stimulations are unknown.

Gold thioglucose, which produces lesions in the ventromedial nucleus of mammals, was ineffective in *Coturnix coturnix Japonica* (Japanese quail) (Carpenter *et al.,* 1969)

The mechanisms by which the hypothalamus or brain regulate feed intake are not clear. Lepkovsky (1973) marshalled evidence in favor of the view that energy requirements and, particularly, adipose tissue stores are the set points for the hypothalamus. He reported that continued forced feeding of chickens twice normal nutrient requirements made the birds obese. When the force feeding ceased, the birds refused to eat for 7–10 days until they lost weight and depleted their adipose stores to such level as to trigger the feeding center. He believed that testosterone was one of the adjustors of the set point. Hill and Dansky (1954) amply demonstrated that energy requirements influenced feed intake by varying caloric intake or nutrient density of feed. The difference in energy intakes between birds of same weight and performance (egg laying), however, suggested that other factors were also operative. One of these is volume of feed eaten or stimulation of volume receptors in the crop and esophagus. Polin and Wolford (1973) performed experiments showing that volume of feed, and not mainly energy requirements or fat deposits, was an important stimulator of feed intake. They studied groups of chickens, some of which were fed *ad libitum,* some *ad libitum* and force fed, and some force fed 150% of the *ad libitum* group. The increase in blood lipids and adipose tissue reflected the increased feed intake. When force feeding was discontinued within 2–3 days and *ad libitum* feeding was resumed, there was no difference in the feeding patterns (amount eaten), although there were considerable differences in fat depots among the groups.

It is well known that obese chickens do not have lower feed intake and that increasing nutrient density but not volume causes obesity. Polin and Wolford (1973) cite these as evidence of volume receptors that are influenced by rate of filling, capacity, and discharge of feed. Hormones or other factors may regulate the set point at which the receptors operate. That emptiness, fullness, or distension of the digestive tract of mammals influence feed intake is well known. Sturkie and Joiner (1959) placed lesions or small foreign bodies in the rectums of chickens, which decreased feed intake drastically. The effect presumably was mediated through the hypothalamus.

## Water Consumption

Water consumption is influenced by size and age of bird, environmental temperature, type and amounts of food consumed, and other factors. Dunston and Buss (1969) reported that normal adult male chickens consumed water in the amount of 5.5% of body weight in 24 hr. In young growing birds (3–4 weeks) the figure was 18–20%. Adult laying chickens eat more feed than males but also consume more water (13.6% of body weight) and with a water/feed ratio of 2.1 (Sturkie, unpublished). As less feed is eaten, less water is consumed except when the ambient temperature is high.

Water consumption has been determined on hens at frequent intervals for an 8-month period (Howard, 1968). The amounts consumed varied considerably but increased significantly on days that hens laid and most during the 12 hr preceding oviposition. For Brown Leghorns, the amounts consumed averaged 115 g per day on days when not laying and 225 g per day when laying (Howard 1975). Bartholomew and Cade (1963), in an extensive review of water consumption of wild birds, reported an inverse relationship between water intake and body size. The figure for most species in the absence of temperature stress ranged from 5 to 30% of body weight, but some few exhibited signs of excessive drinking (polydipsia). The polydipsia may result from an abnormality of the thirst center in the brain and is primary; the resulting polyuria is secondary. The polydipsia resulting from a lack of antidiuretic hormone of the posterior pituitary,

190 however, is secondary to the primary polyuria or diabetes insipidus. Lesions in or removal of the posterior lobe of chickens cause this condition (Shirley and Nalbandov, 1956). Hereditary polydipsia (probably primary) has been reported in chickens by Dunston and Buss (1969; Dunston et al., 1972). A similar abnormality has been reported in mockingbirds by Dunston (1970).

Lack of drinking (adipsia) has been produced in pigeons (Ackerman et al., 1960), in Zonotrichia albicollis (Kuenzel, 1972), and in chickens (Lepkovsky and Yasuda, 1966) by lesions in the lateral hypothalamus, the same area in which aphagia was produced. Stimulation in this area in the pigeons caused polydipsia (Ackerman et al., 1960). Lesions in the ventral medial hypothalamus (VMH) of Zonotrichia also caused polydipsia (Kuenzel, 1972).

## PASSAGE OF INGESTA THROUGH THE TRACT

### Rate

The rate of food passage through the alimentary canal is influenced by the consistency, hardness, and water content of the food and by the amount consumed (Ihnen, 1928; Halnan, 1949). Dry food remains in the crop longer than wet food. The figures of the different investigators vary considerably in this regard (Sturkie, 1965).

A better idea of the speed of food passage is gained by radiography, by the first appearance after feeding of feed in feces, and by feeding certain foods impregnated within chromic oxide, which serves as a marker. Experiments indicate that this dye can be detected in the feces within 2.5 hr after feeding and that most of it may be recovered in the feces within 24 hr of administration (Dansky and Hill, 1952).

When radioactive barium was administered to chickens, approximately half of the food ingested was excreted within 4–5 hr (Imabayashi et al., 1956).

Food passes faster through young chicks than through adults (Thornton et al., 1956), and the rate of passage through the adult turkey is similar to that of the chicken (Hillerman et al., 1953). Factors that affect the overall motility of the tract also influence the rate of food passage.

### Motility

**Crop and esophagus.** The crop undergoes contractions that vary considerably in rhythm and amplitude and that are influenced by the nervous state of the animal, by hunger, and by other factors. Extreme excitement, fear, or struggling may inhibit or retard crop contractions in the chicken and pigeon (Rogers, 1915; Henry et al., 1933; Ashcraft, 1930; Paterson, 1927). Hunger produced restlessness and irregular crop activity in normal and decerebrate pigeons and chickens, but fear had no effect on crop activity of the decerebrate pigeon (Rogers, 1915). Paterson (1927), however, reported that crop motility in hungry decerebrate pigeons was fairly regular. Crop contractions are studied by placing balloons in the crop or by attaching appropriate recorders on the crop.

Peristaltic contraction begins in the esophagus and spreads down the crop to the gizzard (Halnan, 1949). It usually occurs in groups of varying number and speed, depending on state of hunger, amount of feed in the crop, and other factors. The waves usually appear in groups of from two to 15 and at intervals of from 1 to 40 min, according to Ashcraft (1930), and at intervals of one per minute according to Groebbels (1932).

The frequencies of these waves for chickens starved for 1.5, 10, and 27 hr were 13, 55, and 75 per hour, respectively (Groebbels, 1932). When the gizzard and crop are full, crop contractions may cease in the pigeon for 30–40 min (Paterson, 1927; Rogers, 1915). According to Akahori et al., (1967; 1971a) crop movements occur at intervals of 5–10 min, based on studies with balloons and action potentials.

Within 1–2 hr after feeding the pigeon, peristaltic waves appear in groups of three or four and at intervals of 15–20 min. After 5–12 hr, they appear in groups of 6–20 and at intervals of 10–30 min. In the hungry bird with an empty crop, the contractions occur in groups of 8–16 and at intervals of 10–60 min.

When food leaves the crop and goes down the esophagus, it may not enter the proventriculus or gizzard if the latter are contracting. Part of the bolus may move in a retrograde direction to the crop. (Vonk and Postma, 1949). Regurgitation of crop milk to the mouth is normal in pigeons and doves.

The pressure in the hen's crop ranges from 7 to 18 cm $H_2O$ (Groebbels, 1932).

*Nervous control of esophagus and crop.* The motility of the esophagus and crop is under nervous control. These organs receive parasympathetic excitatory fibers from the vagus, according to Ihnen (1928), and also both excitatory and inhibitory fibers from the sympathetic system, according to Nolf (see Ziswiler and Farner, 1972, for references). Stimulation of the peripheral end of the left vagus causes contraction in the left side of the crop (cephalic and dorsal region), and stimulation of the right vagus causes contraction of the right side (Ihnen, 1928). Transection of the right vagus alone has little effect on crop motility, but ligation of the left vagus inhibits motility and particularly the ability of the crop to empty itself (Mangold, 1929). According to Ihnen, the left vagus nerve apparently controls the peristaltic movements of the esophagus, for after ligation of this nerve these movements are abolished. According to Hanzlik and Butt (1928), stimulation of the vagus produces contraction in the circular muscles of the crop; stimulation of the sympathetics causes contraction of the longitudinal muscles. These authors believe that the latter have little influence on normal crop motility.

However, more recent data indicate that few adrenergic nerves could be demonstrated histochemically in the esophagus, and sympathetic nerve stimulation of crop and esophagus was ineffective (see Chapter 1). Everett (1968), who studied isolated crops and esophaguses, reported that they responded to such drugs as acetylcholine, epinephrine, histamine, and 5HT, in a manner similar to mammalian smooth muscle; the effects of these drugs were blocked by the appropriate antagonist. For results of further studies of these agents on the chicken esophagus, see Bartlett and Hassan (1968) and the section on drug sensitivity.

**Proventriculus.** Apparently few observations have been made on motility of the grandular stomach, although a number of studies have been conducted on gastric secretion. The passage of food to the proventriculus from the crop and from it to the gizzard is influenced by movements in the crop and gizzard. Normally, food remains in the proventriculus for a short time. Ashcraft (1930) reported that waves of contraction in chickens were fairly regular, rhythmic, and of high amplitude, with the rate averaging about 1 per minute in the hungry chicken; the rate is higher in males than females (Ikegami, 1938), which is attributed to male sex hormones.

**Gizzard.** Motility has been studied extensively by Akahori et al. (1968; 1969; 1971a,b), Bennett (1969a,b), Dziuk and Duke (1972) Duke et al., (1972), and Duke and Evanson (1972). Much of the older work is reviewed by Sturkie (1965), Groebbels (1932), and Mangold (1929).

The gizzard exhibits regular rhythmic contractions. Motility has been studied by observing the organ in the opened bird, by fluoroscopic examination, by placing balloons attached to a suitable

*Table 9–1  Frequency of contractions in gizzard (waves per minute)*

| Species | Age (weeks) | | |
|---------|------|------|------|
|         | 1–2  | 3–8  | 9–20 |
| Chickens | 5 | 4–4.3 | 3.2–3.5 |
| Quails | 1–20 | 6.4–7.8 | – |

manometer and recording device in the gizzard, or by inserting pressure transducers attached to open-tipped, fluid-filled tubes into the gizzard, (Duke et al., 1972). Another method involves the study of action potentials following normal activity, after the administration of certain drugs, or during electrical stimulation.

The contractions or grinding sounds of the gizzard can be heard in the bird with a stethoscope, particularly when coarse or hard food and grit are present (Groebbels, 1932).

The frequency of contractions appears to vary little in the hen and ranges from two to three per minute, according to most investigators (Ashcraft, 1930; Mangold, 1929; Henry et al., 1933). To what extent the state of hunger influences the frequency is not clear. Henry et al., (1933) and also Mangold (1929) reported a slightly higher frequency in fed birds as compared with those that had been starved. However, Rossi's results (see Groebbels, 1932) showed the opposite effect, but this was not confirmed in chickens and quails by Akahori et al., (1971b), who showed that after starvation frequency of contractions was reduced by about one half.

Frequency of contractions tends to decrease with age in quails and chickens but it is greater in quails (Table 9–1; from Akahori et al., 1971a).

The duration of contractions in chickens ranges, in most cases, from 20 to 30 sec and is influenced by hunger as well as by the type of feed (Mangold, 1929).

The amplitude of the gizzard movements is greater when grit is present (Groebbels, 1932). Grit remains in the gizzard for a considerable time and is not ordinarily passed out with the feed (Browne, 1922).

Pastea et al. (1968) have described four different stages of activity of the gizzard of chickens and turkeys. In stage 1, contraction begins with an increase in pressure, which reaches a peak in stage 2, declines in stage 3, and reaches a low in stage 4, which is the relaxation phase. The duration of the contraction wave (stages 1–3) is about 6 sec and the relaxation phase, 4, is 14 sec, or a total of 20 sec for the complete cycle.

Five phases of contraction and relaxation of the turkey gizzard, with involvement of the proventriculus and duodenum, have also been described. These are summarized in Table 9–2. The duration of the cycles was approximately the same in fed and fasted turkeys, but the number of cycles was lower in the fasted ones.

In another study, Duke et al. (1972) reported on the frequency, duration, and amplitude of contractions and electropotential changes in turkeys (Table 9–3). The pressures Duke et al. have reported are considerably lower than those reported for chickens and other species by Mangold and coworkers, by Kato, and by others (see Mangold, 1929) who reported pressures as follows in mm Hg: buzzard, 8–26; duck, 180; hen, 100–150; goose, 265–280. The pressure is much lower in carnivores, such as the buzzard, where the gizzard is poorly developed. Such hard, fibrous feeds as barley produce higher gizzard pressure than do softer ones, such as wheat. The amplitude of contractions is greater in males than females.

Dziuk and Duke (1972) also reported that almost all of the contractile activity of the upper duodenum was correlated with that of the stomach, a finding earlier reported by Nolf for the chicken.

Duke and Evanson (1972) showed that motility in glandular and muscular stomachs of turkeys could be inhibited by distending the duodenum with a balloon and by introduction of mineral oil and other liquids. Distension produced almost instant inhibition, suggesting a neural reflex, whereas the liquids caused inhibition much later, indicating a humoral mediation. The introduction of fat into the duodenum also decreased motility, and Duke and Evanson (1972) presumed that enterogasterone was released (see Chapter 10)

*Nervous control of the gizzard.* The gizzard receives extrinsic fibers from the vagus and the sympathetic system. Nolf, and also Doyon (reviewed by Groebbels, 1932, and Burnstock, 1969), reported the presence of excitatory and inhibitory fibers in the vagus.

Recent studies involving anatomical, histochemical, and electrophysical techniques demonstrated the existence of pre- and postganglionic cholingergic excitatory fibers in the vagus and also in the perivascular sympathetic trunks. There are also some nonadrenergic inhibitory fibers running in the vagus, which are apparently of sympathetic origin. The nonadrenergic nerve fibers running to gizzard muscle appear to be associated only with ganglion cells or blood vessels (see Bennett, 1969a,b,c; Bennett and Cobb, 1969a,b).

There is an extensive myenteric plexus (Bennett

**Table 9–2**  *Phases of contraction and relaxation of turkey gizzard*[a]

Numbers (1)–(5) represent order of occurrence; cont. = contraction, relax. = relaxation.

| Phase | Duration (sec) | Thin muscle | Thick muscle | Proventriculus | Duodenum |
|---|---|---|---|---|---|
| A | 4 | (1) Onset cont. | (2) Complete cont. | (3) Closure of gastric isthmus | — |
| B | 4 | (2) Maximum cont. (3) Onset relax. | (1) Relax | — | (4) Opening of pyloris and flow of ingesta from gizzard to duodenum |
| C | 2 | (1) Onset cont. | | (4) Opening of gastric isthmus (5) Ingesta enters from gizzard | (2) Cessation of flow from gizzard and closure of pyloris (3) Cont. of duodenum |
| D | 2 | (2) Relax. | (1) Cont. (continued) | — | — |
| E | 12 | — | (1) Cont. (continued) (4) Onset relax. | (2) Onset of cont. (3) Flow of ingesta to gizzard (5) Contraction completed | — |
| Total | 24 | | | | |

[a]From Dziuk and Duke (1972).

*Table 9—3    Contraction in turkey gizzard*[a]

|  | Frequency (cycles/min) | Duration (sec) | Pressure (mm Hg) | Amplitude (mV) |
|---|---|---|---|---|
| Proventriculus | 3.3 | 7.3 | 34.4 | — |
| Gizzard — thin muscle | 3.3 | 5.6 | 42.5 | — |
| Gizzard — thick muscle | 3.3 | 9.4 | 61.6 | 1.0 |
| Duodenum (lower) | 3.4 | 4.6 | 25.0 | 0.9 |

[a]Data from Duke *et al.* (1972).

and Cobb, 1969b), involving Auerbach's plexus, that lies immediately below the serosal layer of the gizzard and that is responsible for the basic automatic rhythmic movements persisting after extrinsic nerve denervation (Nolf and others). A plexus comparable to Meissners' in mammals is absent in birds (Bennett and Cobb, 1969b). The excitatory fibers, which are cholinergic, are blocked by atropine (Nolf) or hyoscine (Bennett, 1969a).

**Small intestine.** The intestines of birds undergo peristaltic and segmenting movements (Vonk and Postma, 1949; Mangold, 1929; Groebbels, 1932). This has been demonstrated by *in vitro* studies. The peristaltic wave proceeds aborally. The movements are influenced by a combination of neural, humoral, and such mechanical factors as amount of ingesta and movements in the stomachs. Factors affecting local blood flow, as histamine, 5HT, and catecholamines, also influence motility. There is some evidence suggesting that 5HT may initiate peristaltic waves (Burnstock, 1969). Perfusion of intestine with 5HT changes motility considerably by increasing smooth muscle contraction (Sturkie, unpublished).

Regurgitation of the duodenal contents into the gizzard and crop has been reported, and this suggests reverse peristalsis. Pellet regurgitation in certain raptors, mentioned in the section on deglutition, may also be an example of reverse peristalsis. Kostuch and Duke (1975) and Duke *et al.* (1975) have studied gastric motility and digestion in a number of raptor species, employing radio telemetry. Based on the amplitude, frequency, and duration of pressure waves, the authors describe three phases of digestion as mechanical, chemical, and pellet formation and egestion. Contractions begin in the glandular stomach, proceed then to the muscular stomach, and finally enter the duodenum. The egestion phase appears to be comparable more to regurgitation, as in ruminants, than to vomition.

The innervation of the intestine is extensive, including extrinsic and intrinsic fibers and a myenteric system, consisting of Auerbachs' and Meissners' plexuses. The extrinsic nerve consists of pre- and postganglionic cholinergic fibers that may be vagal or symphathetic in origin. Recent studies on isolated innervated chicken intestines by Everett (1968) indicate that the perivascular sympathetic nerves contain cholinergic excitatory and both adrenergic and nonadrenergic inhibitory nerve fibers (see also Chapter 1).

Coaxial stimulation of the gut excites mainly parasympathetic fibers, whereas stimulation of the perivascular nerves or nerve trunk excites mainly preganglionic nerves (Everett, 1968; Bolton, 1971). Catecholamines antagonize the effects of cholinergic nerve stimulation (see Bolton, 1971). Histamine has a direct contracting effect on the chicken intestine. It can normally overcome the relaxing effect of catecholamines it releases but if histamine dosage is small, only the effect of the catecholamines is apparent (Everett and Mann, 1967)

**Large intestine.** Few studies have been made on the motility of the large intestine. Yasukawa (1959), employing balloons, reported peristaltic and antiperistaltic waves in the large intestine, the latter occurring at intervals of from 5.6 to 6.3 sec.

According to Burnstock (1969), there is no evidence for a sacral parasympathetic nerve supply to the gut of birds, and recent evidence cited by Bolton (1971) suggests that parasympathetic nerves supply cholinergic nerves to all parts of the tract of birds. Whether these are exclusively vagal in origin is not stated.

Remak's nerve is a long nerve extending from the duodenum to the cloaca. The origin, homology, and function of this nerve are controversial. Some investigators consider the nerve sympathetic in origin, whereas others (Yntema and Hammond, 1952) claim that it is a derivative of the sacral parasympathetic system (see Bennett and Malmfors, 1970, for review).

**Ceca.** According to Browne (1922), the ceca undergo peristalsis, the wave passing from the intestinal junction to the blind end of the organ, and the ceca are filled in this manner. Other workers have suggested that they are filled by antiperistaltic movements of the intestines or by pressure in the

194 latter. During antiperistalsis the colonic contents do not go into the small intestine, presumably because the ileocecal valve must be closed at this time. Little is known concerning the physiology of these valves in the filling and emptying of the ceca.

According to Yasukawa (1959) these antiperistaltic movements may begin at the apex of the ceca and end at the proximal end or enter into the large intestine. Recent confirmation of retrograde flow of ingesta from colon to ceca has been reported by Akester et al. (1967) and by Nechay et al. (1968).

The contents of the ceca are homogeneous and pultaceous in consistency and are usually chocolate colored. Cecal contents or droppings can be readily distinguished from rectal feces, and this has been used in determining when the ceca are evacuated. The ratio of cecal to rectal evacuations for the hen ranges from 1 to 7.3 after the feeding of barley, to 1 – 11.5 after the ingestion of corn (Röseler, 1929).

**Cloaca.** Colonic contents are discharged into the coprodaeum of the cloaca, which is at times relaxed and at others very active (Akester et al., 1967). It contracts vigorously to expel contents and also undergoes continuous peristaltic movements.

## Sensitivity of Various Segments of the Intestine to Drugs

The response of isolated segments of the esophagus (Bartlett and Hassan, 1968) and intestine and ceca (Everett, 1968) to drugs has been described. Nagora-Stasiak and Pytasz (1968) made an extensive study of the response of the duodenum, jejunum, cecum, and rectum of several species to acetylcholine, histamine, and epinephrine. The jejunum and ceca exhibited marked sensitivity to the drugs and the duodenum and rectum were less sensitive. Gallinaceous species (chickens and turkeys) were more sensitive to epinephrine and acetytcholine and aquatic species (ducks and geese) were more sensitive to histamine.

The normal motility of the tract in intact animals, and also its response to drugs is influenced by activity, sleep, presence of food in the tract, and other factors. Food in the tract decreases motility, whereas sleep decreases the frequency of contractions but increases their amplitude.

## REFERENCES

Ackerman, B., B. Anderson, E. Fabricius, and L. Svesson. (1960). Observations on central regulation of body temperature and of food and water intake in the pigeon (Columba livia). Acta. Physiol. Scand., 50, 328.

Akahori, F., M. Matsuura, and K. Arai. (1971a). Studies on the movement of the alimentary canal. VI. Physiological values in growing female chicks and quails. Bull. Azabu Vet. Coll., No. 22, p. 25. [English summary.]

Akahori, F., M. Matsuura, and K. Arai. (1971b). Studies on the movement of the alimentary canal. V. Effect of starvation upon the movement of gizzard in quails. Bull. Azabu Vet. Coll., No. 22, p. 15.

Akahori, F., M. Matsuura, and K. Arai. (1968). Studies on the movement of the alimentary canal. II. Changes in movement of the gizzard with growth of chicks. Bull. Azabu Vet. Coll., No. 18, p. 73.

Akahori, F., M. Matsuura, and K. Arai. (1967). Studies on the movement of the ailmentary canal. I. Movement of the crop and gizzard. Bull. Azabu Vet. Coll., No. 16. p. 55.

Akahori, F., M. Matsuura, and K. Arai. (1969). Studies on the movement of the alimentary canal. III. Movement of the gizzard of chickens under starvation. Bull. Azabu Vet. Coll., No. 20, p. 1.

Akester, A. R. (1967). Renal portal shunts in the kidney of domestic fowl. J. Anat., 101, 569.

Akester, A. R., R. S. Anderson, K. J. Hill, and G. W. Osbaldiston. (1967). A radiographic study of urine flow in the domestic fowl. Brit. Poultry Sci., 8, 209.

Ashcraft, D. W. (1930). Correlative activites of the alimentary canal of fowl. Am. J. Physiol., 93, 105.

Balgooyen, T. G. (1971). Pellet regurgitation of captive sparrow hawks. Condor, 73, 382.

Bartholmew, G. A., and T. J. Cade. (1963). The water economy of land birds. Auk, 80, 504.

Bartlett, A. L., and T. Hassan. (1968). Some actions of histamine and 5HT on isolated chicken esophagus. Brit. J. Pharmacol. Chemother., 32, 156.

Bennett, T. (1969a). The effects of hyoscine and anticholinesterases on cholinergic transmission to the smooth muscle cells of the avian gizzard. Brit. J. Pharmacol., 37, 585.

Bennett, T. (1969b). Studies on avian gizzard. Histochemical analysis of extrinsic and intrinsic innervation. Z. Zellforsch., 98, 188.

Bennett T. (1969c). Nerve mediated excitation and inhibition of the smooth muscle cells of avian gizzard. J. Physiol. (London), 204, 669.

Bennett, T. and J. L. S. Cobb. (1969a). Studies on avian gizzard morphology and innervation of smooth muscle. Z. Zllforsch., 96, 173.

Bennett, T., and J. L. S. Cobb. (1969b). Studies on avian gizzard: Auerbach's plexus. Z. Zellforsch., 99, 109.

Bennett T., and J. Malmfors. (1970). The adrenergic nervous system of domestic fowl. Z. Zellforsch., 106, 22.

Bolton, T. B. (1971). Physiology of nervous system. In "Physiology and Biochemistry of Fowl," Vol. 2 (D. J. Bell, and B. M. Freeman, Eds.). London: Academic Press, Chapter 28, p. 675.

Brobeck, J. R. (1957). Neural control of hunger, appetite, and satiety. Yale J. Biol. Med., 29, 565.

Browne, T. G. (1922). Some observations on the digestive system of the fowl. J. Comp. Pathol. Ther., 35, 12.

Burnstock, C., (1969). Evolution of the autonomic innervation of visceral and cardiovascular systems in vertebrates. Pharmacol. Rev., 21, 247.

Calhoun, M. (1954). "Microscopic Anatomy of the Digestive System." Ames, Iowa: Iowa State College Press.

Carpenter, J. W., C. M. Stein, A. Silverstein, and A. van Tienhoven. (1969). The effect of gold thioglucose on food consumption and reproduction of the Japanese quail. Poultry Sci., 48, 574.

Clarkson, M. J., and T. G. Richards. (1966). Liver blood flow in the turkey. In "Physiology of Domestic Fowl" (C. H. Smith, and E. C. Amoroso, Eds.). Edinburgh: Oliver and Boyd, Chapter 33.

Dansky, L. M., and F. W. Hill. (1952). Application of the chromic oxide indicator method to balance studies with growing chickens. J. Nutr., 47, 449.

Duke, G. E., and O. A. Evanson. (1972). Inhibition of gastric motility by duodenal contents of turkeys. Poultry Sci., 51, 1625.

Duke, G. E., H. E. Dziuk, and O. A. Evanson. (1972). Gastric pressure and smooth muscle electrical potential changes in turkeys. *Am. J. Physiol., 222,* 167.

Duke, G. E., A. A. Jegers, G. Loff and O. A. Evanson. (1975). Gastric digestion in some raptors. *Comp. Biochem. Physiol., 50,* 649.

Dunston, W. A. (1970). Excessive drinking (polydipsia) in a Galapagos mockingbird. *Comp. Biochem. Physiol., 36,* 143.

Dunston, W. A., and E. G. Buss. (1969). Abnormal water balance in a mutant strain of chickens. *Science, 161,* 167.

Dunston, W. A., E. G. Buss, W. H. Sawyer, and H. W. Sokol. (1972). Herditary polydipsia and polyuria in chickens. *Am. J. Physiol., 222,* 1167.

Dziuk, H. E., and G. E. Duke. (1972). Cineradiographic studies of gastric motility in turkeys. *Am. J. Physiol., 222,* 159.

Everett, S. D., (1968). Pharmacological responses of the isolated innervated intestine of the chick. *Brit J. Pahrmacol. Chemother., 33,* 342.

Everett, S. D., and S. P. Mann. (1967). Catecholamine release by histamine from the isolated intestine of the chick. *Eur. J. Pharmacol., 1,* 310.

Feldman, S. E., S. Larsson, M. K. Dimick, and L. Lepkovsky. (1957). Aphagia in chickens. *Am. J. Physiol., 191,* 259.

Goodman, I. J., and J. L. Brown. (1966). Stimulation of positively and negatively reinforcing sites in the avian brain. *Life Sci., 5,* 693.

Grimm, R. J., and W. M. Whitehouse. (1963). Pellet formation in a great horned owl. A roentgenographic study. *Auk, 80,* 310.

Groebbels, F. (1932). "Der Vogel. Erster Band: Atmungswelt und Nahrungswelt." Berlin: Verlag von Gebrüder Borntraeger.

Halnan, E. T. (1949). The architecture of the avian gut and tolerance of crude fiber. *Brit. J. Nutr., 3,* 245.

Hanzlik, P. J., and E. M. Butt. (1928). Reactions of the crop muscles under tension, with a consideration of the antomical arrangement, innervation and other factors. *Am. J. Physiol., 85,* 271.

Henry, K. M., A. J. MacDonald, and H. E. Magee. (1933). Observations on the functions of the alimentary canal in fowls. *J. Exp. Biol., 10,* 153.

Hill, K. J. (1971). The physiology of digestion. In "Physiology and Biochemistry of the Domestic Fowl," Vol. 1 (D. J. Bell and B. M. Freeman, Eds). London: Academic Press, Chapter 2. p. 25.

Hill, F. W., and Dansky. (1954). Studies of the energy requirements of chickens. I. The effects of dietary energy level in growth and feed consumption. *Poultry Sci., 33,* 112.

Hillerman, J. P., F. H. Kratzer, and W. D. Wilson. (1953). Food passage through chickens and turkeys and some regulating factors. *Poultry Sci., 32,* 332.

Howard, B. R. (1968). Drinking activity of hens in relation to egg laying. *Proc. 24th Intl. Cong. Physiol. Sci., 7,* 202.

Howard, B. R. (1975). Water balance of the hen during egg formation. *Poultry Sci., 54,* 1046.

Ihnen, K. (1928). Beiträge zur Phusiologie des Kropfes bei Huhn und Taube I: Bewegung und Innervation des kroptes. *Arch. Ges. Physiol. (Pflügers), 218,* 767.

Ikegami, Y. (1938). The function of the testes and the stomach movement. *Jap. J. Gastroenterol., 10,* 103 (*Biol. Abs.,* 14547, 1940).

Imabayashi, K., M. Kametaka, and T. Hatano. (1956). Studies on digestion in the domestic fowl. *Tokyo, J. Agri. Res., 2,* 99.

Jerrett, S. A., and W. R. Goodge. (1973). Evidence for amylase in avian salivary glands. *J. Morphol., 139,* 27.

Kostuch, T. E., and G. E. Duke (1975). Gastric motility in great horned owls. *Comp. Biochem. Physiol. 51,* 201.

Kuenzel, W. J. (1972). Dual hypothalamic feeding system in a migratory bird, *Zonotrichia albicollis. Am. J. Physiol., 223,* 1138.

Lepkovsky, S. (1973). Hypothalamic adipose tissue interrelationships. *Fed. Proc., 31,* 1705.

Lepkovsky, S., and M. Yasuda. (1966). Hypothalamic lesions, growth and body composition of male chickens. *Poultry Sci., 45,* 582.

Maley, M. J. (1969). Electrical stimulation of agonistric behavior in the mallard. *Behavior, 34,* 138.

Mangold, E. (1929). "Hanbuch der Ernährung und des Stoffwech-

sels der landswirtschaflichen Nutztiere." Berlin: Zweiter Band, Verlag von Julius Springer.

Mu, J.Y., T. H. Yin, C. L. Hamilton, and J. R. Brobeck. (1968). Variability of body fat in hyperphagic rates. *Yale J. Biol. Med., 41,* 133.

Nechay, B. R., S. Boyarsky, and P. Catacutan-Labay. (1968). Rapid migration of urine into intestine of chick. *Comp. Biochem. Physiol., 26,* 369.

Nishida, T., Y. K. Paik, and M. Yasuda. (1969). LVIII. Blood vascular supply of the glandular stomach and the muscular stomach. *Jap. J. Vet. Sci., 31,* 51. (English summary.)

Pastea, E., A. Nicolau, and I. Rosca. (1968). Dynamics of the digestive tract in hens and ducks. *Acta. Physiol. Hung., 33,* 305.

Paterson, T. L. (1927). Crop movements in the pigeon. *J. Lab. Clin. Med., 12,* 1003.

Phillips, R. E., and O. M. Youngren. (1971). Brain stimulation and species typical behavior. Activities evoked by electrical stimulation of the brains of chickens. *Anim. Behav., 19,* 757.

Polin, D., and J. H. Wolford. (1973). Factors influencing food intake and caloric balance in chickens. *Fed. Proc., 32,* 1720.

Purton, M. D. (1970). Blood flow in liver of domestic fowl. *J. Anat., 106,* 189.

Rogers, F. T. (1915). The hunger mechanism in birds (preliminary report). *Proc. Soc. Exp. Biol. Med., 13,* 119.

Röseler, M. (1929). Die Bedeutung der Blinddärme des Haushuhnes fur die Resorption der Nahrung und Verdauung der Rohfaser. *Z. Tierz. Zücht, 13,* 281.

Shirley, H. V., and A. V. Nalbandov. (1956). Effects of neurohypohysectomy in domestic chickens. *Endocrinology, 58,* 477.

Smith, C. J. V. (1969). Alterations in the food intake of chickens as a result of hypothalamic lesions. *Poultry Sci., 48,* 475.

Sturkie, P. D. (Ed.). (1965). "Avian Physiology" (2nd ed.). Ithaca, N. Y.: Cornell University Press.

Sturkie, P. D., and W. P. Joiner. (1959). Effects of foreign bodies in cloaca and rectum of the chicken on feed consumption. *Am. J. Physiol., 197,* 1337.

Thorton, P. A., P. J. Schaible, and L. F. Wolterink. (1956). Intestinal transit and skeletal retention of radioactive strontium in the chick. *Poultry Sci., 35,* 1055.

Tweeton, J. R., R. E. Phillips, and F. W. Peek. Feeding behavior elicited by electrical stimulation of the brain of chickens, *Gallus gallus. Poultry Sci., 52,* 165.

van Tienhoven, A., and L. P. Juhasz. (1962). The chicken telencephalon, diencephalon, and mesencephalon in sterotaxic coordinates. *J. Comp. Neurol., 118,* 185.

Vonk, H. H., and N. Postma. (1949). X-ray studies on the movements of the hen's intestine. *Physiol. Comp. Oecol., 1,* 15.

Webb, T. E., and J. R. Colvin. (1964). The composition, structure and mechanism of formation of the lining of the gizzard of the chicken. *Can. J. Biochem., 42,* 59.

Yasukawa, M. (1959). Studies in movements of large intestine VII: Movements on large intestine of fowls. *Jap. J. Vet. Sci., 21,* 1. (English summary.)

Yntema, C. L., and W. S. Hammond. (1952). Experiments on the origin and development of the sacral autonomic nerves in chick embryo. *J. Exp. Zool., 129,* 375.

Ziswiler, V., and D. S. Farner. (1972). Digestion and digestive system. "Avian Biology," Vol. II (D. S. Farner and James R. King, Eds). London: Academic Press, p. 343.

# 10

## Secretion of Gastric and Pancreatic Juice, pH of Tract, Digestion in Alimentary Canal, Liver and Bile, and Absorption

P. D. Sturkie

# SECRETION OF GASTRIC JUICE

## Collection

Gastric juice free from food may be obtained by starving the bird. Little is secreted under such conditions, unless some other stimulus is employed. Even under starvation conditions the juice, although free from food, may contain intestinal juice unless the proventriculus or the gizzard is cannulated. In order to study the stimulating effects of food ingestion on the rate of secretion and the composition of pure gastric juice, one of two methods may be used: (1) preparation of a fistula or opening of the esophagus, so that when food is ingested it does not pass to the stomach but drops out of the opening (sham feeding); or (2) preparation of a pouch of the stomach, with an intact nerve and blood supply, that opens to the outside through the body wall (Pavlov or Heidenhain pouch). Food entering the main stomach, but not the pouch, stimulates both stomachs, and pure juice is collected from the pouch.

Most of the studies on the gastric juice of birds are based on samples collected by cannulation of the proventriculus (Friedman, 1939; Long, 1967; Burhol and Hirschowitz, 1970,1971a,b). Such birds may or may not be hydrated. Some researchers have collected gastric juice by aspiration of stomach contents through catheters inserted by way of the mouth and crop or by insertion of needles into the gizzards of fed birds (Farner, 1943a; Collip, 1922). Usually birds are starved for 18 hr or until the crop is empty. This tends to decrease water consumption and leads to dehyration, which also decreases gastric secretion. To obtain fairly steady-state secretion, therefore, birds are usually hydrated (Long, 1967; Burhol and Hirschowitz, 1970,1971a,b).

## Composition

Gastric juice is composed principally of water, with smaller amounts of hydrochloric acid, certain salts, pepsin, and mucin. The composition varies with the rate of secretion and other factors (Tables 10–1 and 10–2). The pH of mixed gastric juice collected from the gizzard of the live bird averages about 2.0 (Farner, 1943a; Kokas *et al.*, 1971). Total acidity and HCl in the gastric juice of fed chickens averages 59.2 and 25.0 meq/liter, respectively (Farner, 1943b). In chickens starved for 12–24 hr the figures are highly variable (Cheney, 1938); similar variability was reported for the pigeon by Friedman (1939). More recent data from Long (1967) reveal an acid concentration of 93 meq for total acidity for starved but hydrated unanesthetized chickens (Table 10–1). Mean hydrogen ion concentration in similarly treated chickens was reported to be 123.1 meq (Table 10–2). Actually, chickens produce more HCl per kilogram body weight than does man or many other laboratory animals (Long, 1967; Burhol and Hirschowitz, 1972a,b).

The pepsin content of avian gastric juice found by earlier workers was highly variable (Friedman, 1939; Sturkie, 1965). More recent data from Long (1967) on chickens show that pepsin concentration per milliliter, units (247) is lower than in monkeys or rats, but that the pepsin output per kilogram body weight per hour (2430 units) is highest of all the species previously named (Table 10–2). Burhol and Hirschowitz (1972) reported a much higher concentration of pepsin (1550 units/ml) under basal conditions (Table 10–2). The reason for these discrepancies is not known.

Likewise, the basal secretion rates of $H^+$, $Cl^-$,

*Table 10–1  Gastric secretion and composition in chickens[a]*

Basal secretion, and after histamine (400 $\mu$g/kg subcutaneously) birds starved, unanesthetized, and hydrated

| Measure | Unit | Basal | Histamine |
| --- | --- | --- | --- |
| Volume | ml/hr | 15.4 | 38.8 |
| | ml/hr/kg | 8.8 | 22.2 |
| Pepsin output | Pu/hr | 4256 | 8148 |
| | Pu/hr/kg | 2430 | 4656 |
| Pepsin concentration | Pu/ml | 247 | 210 |
| Acid output | meq/hr | 1.37 | 5.6 |
| | meq/hr/kg | 0.78 | 3.2 |
| Acid concentration | meq/liter | 93 | 145 |

[a]From Long (1967).

**Table 10-2**  *Effects of histamine (dose response) on mean concentration of gastric juice of chickens*[a]

Birds starved for 18 hr and anesthetized with Penthrane

| Concentration (meq/liter) | Basal | Histamine ($\mu$g/kg/hr)(s.c. infusion) | | | | |
| | | 75 | 150 | 300 | 600 | 1200 |
|---|---|---|---|---|---|---|
| $H^+$ | 123.1 | 140.6 | 157.0 | 153.9 | 161.8 | 161.1 |
| $Cl^-$ | 147.1 | 161.6 | 171.1 | 170.8 | 176.0 | 176.0 |
| $K^+$ | 9.6 | 9.9 | 11.2 | 10.7 | 11.0 | 11.4 |
| $Na^+$ | 16.9 | 13.3 | 5.9 | 8.8 | 4.6 | 5.7 |
| Pepsin (Pu/ml) | 1550 | 2200 | 1810 | 2070 | 2540 | 2130 |

[a]From Burhol and Hirschowitz (1972).

and $K^+$ (Table 10-2) are higher than in a number of mammals (Burhol and Hirschowitz, 1972).

### Factors Affecting Gastric Secretion

A number of factors influence gastric secretion, including food in the tract, degree of hydration, anesthesia, excitement, nervous control, and certain drugs and hormones.

**Food.** Starvation or withholding of food for 12-24 hr was reported to decrease the flow of gastric juice in pigeons, chickens, and ducks (see Sturkie, 1965) but the results were variable and if birds were not hydrated this might have been as important as their lack of food. Fedorovskii and Konopleva (1959) studied gastric secretion in geese with Pavlov pouches before and after starvation on different diets. The volume secreted within 30 min was variable depending on diet and time food was withheld. Green clover stimulated the greatest secretion, meat and bone meal caused less, and oats caused the least amount secreted. The pH of gastric juice was lower (1.71) when oats were fed; it was 3.71 after feeding clover and 4.2 after feeding meat and bone meal. The stimulating effect of food as it enters the stomach (gastric phase) is therefore like that in mammals.

Employing the esophageal fistula and sham feeding, where food does not reach the stomach, Karpov (1919) and Collip (1922) reported an increase in gastric secretion in geese and chickens. The sensation of eating therefore evokes the discharge of impulses from the gastric secretory center in the brain, probably via nerve fibers in the vagus to gastric glands (cephalic phase of secretion). Farner (1969) reported that sham feeding with an esophageal fistula above the crop in chickens gave equivo-

cal results but was stimulatory when the fistula was below the crop. He concluded that the cephalic phase of secretion was absent in chickens. Psychic stimulation of gastric secretion in ducks by auditory stimuli has been reported by Walter (1939). The act of swallowing caused a reflex stimulation of gastric secretion according to Collip (1922).

**Drugs and hormones.** *Histamine.* The basal secretion of gastric juice and the effects of histamine on secretion are shown in Tables 10-1 and 10-2.

These results indicate that the chicken produces a greater volume of gastric juice, with more acid and pepsin output, on a body weight basis than does man, monkey, or rat (Long, 1967). Table 10-2 presents the results from Burhol and Hirschowitz (1972) on the basal secretion and effects of histamine on concentrations of $H^+$, $Cl^-$, $K^+$, and pepsin. In both studies the chickens were injected or infused subcutaneously with saline but the birds of Burhol and Hirschowitz (1972) were anesthetized and those of Long (1967) were not.

It can be observed from Tables 10-1 and 10-2 that histamine produces an increase in most of the parameters except $Na^+$, which decreases (Table 10-2). Some of the older data (see Sturkie, 1965) indicated a decrease in pepsin activity and some an increase (Friedman, 1939). Long's (1967) data show a decrease, whereas the extensive data from Burhol and Hirschowitz (1972) show an increase.

Log dose response curves for volume, $H^+$, $Cl^-$, $K^+$, and pepsin output were S shaped (Figures 10-1) and exhibited Michaelis-Menten kinetics (Burhol and Hirschowitz, 1972). These values were plotted according to the linear transformation of Dowd and Riggs:

$$V = -k\frac{V}{S} + V_{max};$$

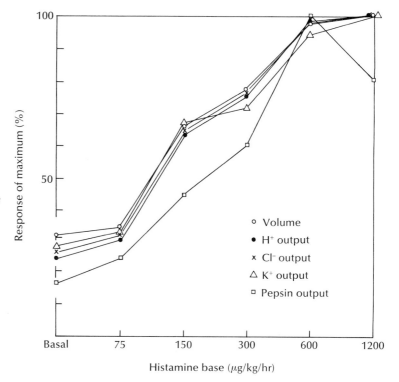

**10–1**

Dose secretion relationship for output of $H^+$, $Cl^-$, $K^+$, and pepsin expressed in percentage of their respective maxima. Histamine infused subcutaneously at given rates. (After Burhol and Hirschowitz, 1972.)

where $V$ = observed response, $S$ = dose and $V_{max}$ = calculated constant, numerically equal to dose required to elicit half maximal response ($S_{50}$ dose). The $S_{50}$ values for volume, $H^+$, $Cl^-$ and $K^+$ were similar, ranging from 148 to 164 $\mu$g histamine per kilogram per hour; the figure for pepsin output was 225 (see Figure 10–1).

*Pentagastrin.* Earlier work by Collip (1922) had indicated that crude extracts of gastrin stimulated gastric secretion. Pentagastrin in doses of 12.5, 25, 50, 100, 200, and 400 $\mu$g/kg body weight were injected subcutaneously into chickens and gastric juice was collected and measured (Burhol and Hirschowitz, 1970). The responses to pentagastrin were similar to those of histamine. The equation describing the log dose response to histamine also applied to pentagastrin. Neither histamine nor pentagastrin appears to be capable of differentially affecting gastric secretion of HCl and pepsin coming from the same gastric cell.

*Cholinergic agents.* Pilocarpine (500 $\mu$g/kg) produces a secretion of moderate volume and peptic activity in the pigeon (Friedman, 1939). Acetylcholine (100 $\mu$g/kg) in the pigeon induces the secretion of small amounts of gastric juice that is very rich in pepsin (Friedman, 1939) but Friedman's data on volume are inconclusive. Both pilocarpine and mecholyl also increased gastric secretory flow rate (Kokas *et al.*, 1967).

Urecholine infused subcutaneously at a dose of 200 $\mu$g/kg/hr increased gastric secretion significantly, although not greatly; it increased pepsin output considerably. Maximum response in volume was obtained with dosages of 1600–3200 $\mu$g/kg/hr but it was less effective than histamine (Burhol and Hirschowitz, 1971a).

Ruoff and Sewing (1970) reported that large doses of carbachol gave responses similar to histamine.

*Cholecystokinin–pancreozymin.* Cholecystokinin–pancreozymin is a substance similar to gastrin that is known to stimulate gastric secretion in birds (Burhol and Hirschowitz, 1971b).

*Glucagon.* Dosages of 25 $\mu$g glucagon per kilogram intravenously to chickens decreased gastric secretion to one-third of the basal level (Kokas *et al.*, 1971) and decreased pepsin output significantly. When glucagon was administered following histamine the increase in gastric secretion was less than when histamine alone was given. A similar effect of glucagon following pentagastrin administration was also observed, suggesting that glucagon blocked the pentagastrin stimulatory effect as it did in dogs. No significant effect was observed on pepsin output.

*Insulin.* Hypoglycemia was induced in chickens by insulin (Long, 1967) but insulin did not produce a stimulation of gastric secretion, as has been reported in certain mammals.

*Secretin.* Perfused at rates of 24 and 48 units/kg/hr to chickens, secretin reduced volume of secretion and acid significantly and also reduced pepsin output (Burhol and Hirschowitz, 1971c; see also Kokas *et al.,* 1967).

*Anesthesia.* The type and depth of anesthesia affects gastric secretion. Nembutal anesthesia drastically reduces flow (Friedman, 1939; Ruoff and Sewing, 1970). Urethane, however, did not significantly depress secretion (Kokas *et al..* 1971).

Methoxyflurane (Penthrane), although less effective than nembutal, reduced volume of gastric secretion following histamine approximately one-half and decreased acid and pepsin output significantly (Kessler *et al.,* 1972).

*APP.* A new polypeptide hormone has been isolated from the chicken pancreas by Hazelwood *et al.* (1973; see Chapter 11, p. 606), which exerts a "gastrin-like" secretogogic action on the proventriculus, inducing marked increases in acid and pepsin secretion as well as volume of gastric juice.

*Fats and enterogastrone.* Lipid administration in mammals tends to decrease gastric secretion by inhibiting gastrin release. Chickens do release gastrin, and its derivative, pentagastrin, is very effective in stimulating gastric secretion as mentioned above. Infusion of triolein into the duodenum of chickens did not affect acid or pepsin secretion (Long, 1967). This suggests that chickens may not have the hormone enterogasterone, which is released in mammals when fat enters the duodenum and which reduces gastric secretion. However, data from Lepkovsky *et al.* (1970) show that the chicken has this hormone. More data are needed.

In the chicken, which has only one type of gastric cell, the chief cell, most of the substances previously mentioned that affect volume and acid secretion also affect pepsin output in like manner. This is unlike the situation in most mammals, which have different cell types involved in the secretion of the acid and pepsin.

## Nervous Control of Gastric Secretion

The results obtained after administration of cholinergic agents suggest that the secretion of pepsin, acid, and volume of flow to a lesser extent are controlled by vagus nerves. Atropine administration to pigeons (Friedman, 1939) or chickens (Long, 1967) inhibits or decreases gastric secretion.

The negative effect obtained with epinephrine suggests that the sympathetic nerves to the stomach play a minor role in gastric secretion. Few studies, however, have dealt with stimulation of nerves to the stomach. One study by Kokas *et al.* (1967) showed that peripheral stimulation of the vagus at 10–15 V and a frequency of 10–25 per second for 10 sec did not affect gastric secretion, for reasons not clear. However, vagal stimulation in *Columba* (pigeon) (Friedman, 1939) and chicken (Collip, 1922) was effective in increasing gastric secretion. Gibson *et al.* (1974) have demonstrated that electrical stimulation of the chickens vagus at levels of 5–50 V, at 10 pulses per second, and at a duration of 1 msec produced a graded response (linear) in the secretion of acid and pepsin. The threshold stimulus was 13.6 V for acid secretion and 13.9 V for pepsin. The response to vagal stimulation was greater than the response to cholinergic agents.

## SECRETION OF PANCREATIC AND INTESTINAL JUICE

### Secretion of Pancreatic Juice

**Collection.** Pancreatic juice and bile are emptied into the distal end of the duodenal loop. Pure juice is obtained by cannulating one of the three ducts, preferably the main or larger one; however, certain difficulties are involved. If only one duct is cannulated it does not always remain open; it may become plugged or blocked particularly if the cannula causes irritation. If even the one duct remains patent the amount of juice collected probably represents no more than one-third to one-half of the total secreted. More recent methods of cannulation reported by Dal Borgo *et al.* (1968a) and Hulan *et al.* (1972) indicate that the cannulated main duct may remain patent for 30 days and in some instances for 90 days (Hulan *et al.* 1972). Pancreatic juice is pale yellow in color and has a pH of 6.4–6.8.

**Factors affecting secretion.** White Leghorn chickens 14–20 weeks of age secreted 15–20 ml of pancreatic juice per chicken per 24 hr when the main pancreatic duct was cannulated; one bird continued to secrete for a period of 3 months (Hulan *et* al., 1972). Chickens 3 weeks of age secreted 9.7 ml/day/kg when fed a diet containing autoclaved soybean meal; this value was 11.7 when the meal was unheated (Dal Borgo et al., 1968b). These figures are based on a 3-hr collection period during the lighted hours. Little or no juice was secreted at night. Varying levels of fat in the diet did not influence the rate of pancreatic juice secretion (Niess et al., 1972). One-year-old chickens with the main pancreatic duct cannulated secreted 0.4–0.8 ml/hr but this rate increased considerably (3.0 ml/hr) immediately after feeding (Ivanov and Gotev, 1962). Kokue and Hayama (1972) reported that pancreatic secretion was not influenced appreciably by starvation and vagotomy.

Secretin has been isolated from the duodenum and other segments of the small intestine of chickens and pigeons but not from the large intestine, rectum, or cloaca (Koschtojanz et al., 1933). A crude extract of rat intestine containing secretin caused a copious secretion of pancreatic juice in the chicken (Heatley et al., 1965). Factors affecting enzyme secretion are discussed under digestion in the intestine.

## Secretion of Intestinal Juice

The chicken, as well as some other avian species, possess glands of Lieberkühn that secrete juice into the duodenum. When intestinal juice is collected from a duodenal loop from which bile and the secretions of the proventriculus and pancreas have been excluded, it has a light straw color and contains mucus and some proteolytic, amylolytic, and lipolytic enzymes. The basal secretory rate, based on a 2–4 hr period, averaged 1.1 ml/hr per bird (adults weighing 2.5–3.5 kg), and the pH ranged from slightly acid to slightly alkaline (Kokas et al., 1967). Administration of secretin increased the rate to 3.4 ml/hr. Pilocarpine and vagal stimulation had no appreciable effect on amount of secretion, but the secretion was more viscous in character. Mecholyl increased the rate of secretion and the content of solids and mucus. Histamine had little or no effect on secretion rate but tended to decrease the enzyme concentration and mucus.

## HYDROGEN ION CONCENTRATION OF THE DIGESTIVE TRACT

The hydrogen ion concentration or pH of the digestive tract is dependent mainly on the amount of HCl secreted in the proventriculus and on the action of bile and pancreatic juice, which tend to neutralize the acid or increase pH in certain parts of the tract.

The alimentary tract pH of several species of birds has been determined (see Sturkie, 1965; Herpol, 1966, 1967; Herpol and van Grembergen, 1967). Most workers are agreed that all parts of the tract are acid, with the highest pH recorded in the intestines and the lowest in the gizzard and the proventriculus.

The values for different parts of the tract of several species are shown in Table 10–3. The figures on chickens and pigeons are based on reports by Farner (1942), Herpol (1966), and Herpol and van Grembergen (1967), which agree except in some organs, such as the proventriculus, crop, duodenum, and rectum. The figures based on live birds with electrodes inserted into the organs may be different from those on dead animals. The work of Winget et al. (1962) clearly demonstrates that the digestive tract pH is ever changing, not static. The pH in the intestines exhibited a curvilinear response to duration of starvation, and a similar response was observed in the proventriculus.

Avian bile from the gall bladder has a pH of 5.9 (chicken) to 6.8 depending on species, according to Farner (1942), but bile from the cannulated bile ducts of chickens has a much higher pH (7.68), according to Lin et al. (1974). The reason for the discrepancy is not known.

The pH of the tract is not influenced appreciably by different diets (see Sturkie, 1965). Ingestion of large amounts of basic salts tends to increase pH as expected. Acidity of the tract may be increased after large volumes of milk are drunk (Ashcraft, 1930; Farner, 1943b).

The age of chickens (1 day to adulthood) had no significant influence on the pH of digestive tract organs (Herpol, 1966).

## DIGESTION

Relatively few recent studies have been made on enzymatic digestion in birds. Digestion involves all of the physical and chemical changes that ingested food must undergo before it can be absorbed in the intestines. These processes include swallowing; maceration; grinding of food in the gizzard; and the action of digestive enzymes from the saliva, stomach, intestines, and pancreas; of bile from the liver; of hydrochloric acid from the stomach; and also of bacteria.

Ingested carbohydrates must be converted into the simple sugars, the monosaccharides, before they can be absorbed (see Chapter 11). Some of the

*Table 10–3*  *The pH of contents of the digestive tract of avian species*[a]

| | Chicken | Pigeon | Pheasant | Duck | Turkey |
|---|---|---|---|---|---|
| Crop | 4.51 | 6.3 (H) 4.28 | 5.8 | 4.9 | 6.0 |
| Proventriculus | 3.17 (*) 4.80 1.4 (**) | 1.4 (H) 4.80 1.0 (**) | 4.7 | 3.4 | 4.7 |
| Gizzard | 4.74 2.50 (HG) | 2.00 | 2.0 | 2.3 | 2.2 |
| Duodenum | 5.7–6.0 | 6.4 (H) 5.2–5.4 | 5.6–6.0 | 6.0–6.2 | 5.8–6.5 |
| Jejunum | 5.8–5.9 | 5.3–5.9 | 6.2–6.8 | 6.1–6.7 | 6.7–6.9 |
| Ileum | 6.3–6.4 | 6.8 (H) 5.6 | 6.8 | 6.9 | 6.8 |
| Rectum or colon | 6.3 | 5.4 6.6 (H) | 6.6 | 6.7 | 6.5 |
| Ceca | 5.7 | — | 5.4 | 5.9 | 5.9 |
| Bile | 7.7 (L) 5.9 | — — | — 6.2 | — 6.1 | — 6.0 |
| Mouth | 6.7* | | | | |
| Crop | 6.4* | | | | |
| Small intestine | 6.7* | | | | |
| Large intestine | 7.1* | | | | |

[a]Based on the work of Farner (1942) (unmarked), Lin *et al.* (1974) (L), Herpol (1966) (H), and Herpol and van Grembergen (1967) (HG) on dead birds, and on live birds by Winget *et al.* (1962) (*) and Herpol (1966) (**).

enzymes concerned in the breakdown of the complex carbohydrates are amylase, lactase, maltase, and invertase.

The fats are hydrolyzed to fatty acids and glycerol before absorption into the small intestines (see also Chapter 13). This is accomplished by the action of bile, which emulsifies the fats, and of lipase, a fat-splitting enzyme.

Ingested proteins are hydrolyzed to amino acids, in which form they are absorbed in the intestines (see also Chapter 12). In this process the primary protein derivatives, which are insoluble, are broken down to the secondary proteins, mainly proteoses, peptones and peptides. Although these are soluble, normally they are not absorbed but are converted finally into amino acids. The enzymes involved in the cleavage of proteins in the bird are pepsin from the stomach, trypsin and chymotrypsin from the pancreas, and carboxypeptidases, aminopeptidases, and dipeptidases (De Rycke, 1962). Lactase, which is present in mammals, is absent in chickens and this may be the reason that lactose is not hydrolyzed and is poorly absorbed in the intestinal tract (Rutter *et al.,* 1953).

In the digestion of fats, carbohydrates, and proteins, a number of intermediary products are formed. Textbooks of nutrition and biochemistry should be consulted for details.

## Digestion in the Mouth, Esophagus, and Crop

The amylase, ptyalin, is present in the saliva and in scrapings from the mouth and esophagus of the fowl (Shaw, 1913; Leasure and Link, 1940); although its content is not as high as in human saliva (Leasure and Link, 1940), enough of it is present to hydrolyze starch to sugar within 1 hr (Shaw, 1913). However, Jerrett and Goodge (1973) reported the presence of amylase in salivary glands of sparrows but none in these glands of chickens and turkeys. Bhattacharya and Ghose (1971) reported high levels of amylase in the salivary glands of certain species and its absence in others. Jung and Pierre (1933) found little or no conversion of starch into sugar in the crop of chickens and concluded that saliva played a very minor role in enzymatic digestion.

The presence of enzymes in the crop and their role in digestion have been subjects of controversy. A number of workers have reported the presence of proteolytic and amylolytic enzymes in the crop or its contents, whereas others have not (see Sturkie, 1965). The presence of such enzymes in crop tissue, however, does not mean that they play a significant role in digestion, nor does their presence in the contents of the crop prove that they are normally produced there; they may come from the feed itself, as has been demonstrated. Bolton (1965) and Pritchard (1972) reported that certain carbohydrates are degraded in the crop and the breakdown was attributed to enzymes of dietary origin or bacterial fermentation. Regurgitation of the contents from the proventriculus, gizzard, and duodenum, including bile, into the crop has been demonstrated, so it is likely that some of the enzymes found in the crop come from the duodenum and proventriculus. Surgical removal of the crop does not affect feed consumption or growth of chickens (Fisher and Weiss, 1956).

Absorption from the crop has been considered minimal, or absent, the report of Leasure and Foltz (1940) revealed that botulinus toxin introduced into the crop was not absorbed. However, Soedarmo *et al.* (1961) demonstrated that glucose but not xylose was absorbed in appreciable quantities from the crop.

### Digestion in the Proventriculus

The proteolytic enzyme, pepsin, is preformed in the chief cells of the proventriculus as pepsinogen, and its presence has been reported by many workers (see Sturkie, 1965). Before birds are fed, the pepsinogen granules are abundant in the gastric mucosa; shortly after feeding they virtually disappear, however, indicating that they are concerned in digestion. More recent evidence from Herpol (1964, 1967) indicates that pepsin is present in the proventriculus of all grain-eating species investigated and even in the gizzard of certain carnivorous species such as *Falco tinnunculus* (falcon) and *Buteo buteo* (buzzard) (Herpol, 1964). The concentration of the enzyme is greater in carnivores than in grain eaters and is considerably higher in the proventriculus of pigeons than in that of chickens (Herpol, 1964). Significant amounts of dipeptidase and small amounts of carboxypeptidase have been discovered in the proventriculus mucosa and pancreatic extracts of chickens (De Rycke, 1962).

Based on the recent work of Green and Llewellin (1973), there are at least five chicken pepsinogens. Some of these are derived, and one of them (fraction 4) appears to be pure and is converted to only one pure pepsin; this seems to be the same simple pepsin that was reported by Levchuk and Orekhovich (1963). It appears that the latter workers' fractions 1 and 2 represent Green's and Llewellen's (1973) fractions 3 and 4. The molecular weight of fraction 4, pepsinogen, is 36,000 and that of pure pepsin is 34,000. Chicken pepsin is unique in having a single thiol group, and it is unusually

stable for long periods at a high pH (7). However, the pH optimum for activity was near 2.0, at least for hemoglobin digestion (Levchuk and Orekhovich, 1963). Assays of chicken pepsin, based on milk clotting and the hydrolysis of bisphenyl sulfite expressed as a percentage of specific activity of crystalline pig pepsin, were 58% for milk clotting at a pH of 6.2 and 92% for hydrolysis of the sulfite at pH 3.6 (Green and Llewellin, 1973).

### Digestion in the Gizzard

Pepsin is always present in the contents of the gizzard, and the pH of the latter is 2–3.5. This pH is more nearly optimum for peptic digestion than is that in other parts of the tract, even the proventriculus; this may suggest that some or most of peptic digestion occurs in the gizzard. However, removal of the gizzard, the chief function of which is grinding food, has little effect upon digestion if the food is soft (Fritz *et al.*, 1936). This suggests that some peptic digestion may take place in the intestine, where the pH is usually much higher (6–7), or that most of the protein digestion is accomplished by other enzymes (trypsin, etc.), which are more active at this pH than pepsin is. The optimum activity of these enzymes in the mammal, however, is at pH 7.5–8.5.

Although amylolytic enzymes have been reported in the epithelium of the gizzard (see Sturkie, 1965), there is no real evidence for digestion of carbohydrates in this organ.

**Grit and digestion.** Grit is essential for optimum digestion because it increases the motility and grinding action of the gizzard and the digestibility of coarse feed, which may be increased by 10% (Titus, 1955). Grit is not indispensable, however, as its absence does not influence growth and reproduction adversely (Sturkie, 1965). Lesions of the epitheleal lining of the gizzard comparable to peptic ulcers in mammals have been reported in chickens. The possible mechanisms involved are not known but are considered (Sturkie, 1965). It is known that certain feedstuffs decrease their incidence (Titus, 1955).

### Digestion in the Small Intestine

**Pancreatic enzymes.** The pancreas of birds, like that in mammals, contains amylolytic, proteolytic, and lipolytic enzymes. These enzymes have been reported in ground whole intestines and pancreases of Aves (see Sturkie, 1965, for review of older liter-

204  ature). Recent studies have shown these enzymes to be present in pure avian pancreatic juice and to be secreted by the pancreas.

The distribution of trypsin, chymotrypsin, and amylase in the tissues, pancreas, duodenum, jejunum, ileum, and cecum of the goose has been determined by Nitsan et al. (1973), as shown in Table 10–4. The concentration of the enzymes is highest in the pancreas and next highest, for the proteolytic enzymes, in the ileum and then the jejunum. Increasing the protein in diet from 16 to 28% had little effect except that it increased the chymotrypsin activity in the duodenum and jejunum. Force feeding (fattening) reduced the concentration of most of the enzymes.

Bird (1971) determined the distribution of trypsin and amylase in different segments of the chicken duodenum (males 14–16 weeks old). The first three-quarters of the duodenum contained 45% of trypsin, with 55% in the remaining quarter. The figure for amylase was 23%; most of the enzyme activity in the duodenum is therefore in the last quarter, or near the point where pancreatic ducts empty into the duodenum.

Highly purified chicken chymotrypsin and turkey trypsin have been extracted from the pancreas. Less purified samples of chicken trypsin and turkey chymotrypsin have also been obtained (Ryan, 1965). The molecular weight of turkey trypsin was 22,500 (by light scattering) and the amino acid analysis indicated its similarity to mammalian trypsin. Chicken chymotrypsin (MW 20,000) exhibited esterase activity almost twice that of bovine $\alpha$-chymotrypsin but only two thirds of the protease activity (Ryan et al., 1965). Ryan and Tomimatsu (1965) also precipitated a crystalline protein having a molecular weight of 41,000 from the avian pancreas. Whether the protein is a structural one, a fragment of another pancreatic component, or an enzyme is not yet known. Proteolytic activity of the pancreases

and other digestive organs of a number of avian species was determined by Herpol (1967).

Kishida and Liener (1968) made a further study of crystalline turkey trypsin with respect to the sequence of amino acids and end groups. They found many structural similarities with bovine and porcine trypsin.

The amylolytic activity of pancreatic juice has been studied a great deal but apparently such enzymes have not been purified or crystallized. Amylase activity in various organs of avian species has been studied by Bhattacharya and Ghose (1971). Two types of amylases have been isolated from chicken pancreas (fast and slow acting types) and these types are inherited (Heller and Kulka, 1968).

Dietary changes influence the enzyme activity of pancreatic juice. Increased intake of carbohydrates and fat in the diet increases the amylase and lipase activity of pancreatic juice (Hulan and Bird, 1972). Unheated or raw soybean meal in the diet decreased the specific activities of amylase, lipase, and chymotrypsin in pancreatic juice but had no effect on trypsin activity (Dal Borgo et al., 1968b; see also Lepkovsky and Furuta, 1970).

Ovomucin from chicken egg elbumen contains an inhibitor of trypsin and chymotrypsin that has a molecular weight of 46,500 (Tomimatsu et al., 1966). Levels of pancreatic amylase and intestinal maltase as influenced by age, growth, and development have been studied by Laws and Moore (1963).

Sucrose activity increases in chick embryo intestines and reaches a maximum at 19 days; it then decreases at 20 days and rises after hatching in the ileum and jejunum and decreases in the duodenum. The injection of hydrocortisone caused a significant increase in sucrose activity (Brown, 1971).

Pancreozymin, which stimulates pancreatic secretion of juice and enzymes in mammals, had no significant effect on amylase activity of chicken pancreas (Niess et al., 1972) or in pigeons in most

*Table 10–4*  Level of digestive enzymes of geese fed a 16% protein diet in units per gram of tissues $(\mu/g)^a$

|  | Weight (units/g) | Trypsin (units/g) | Chymotrypsin (units/g) | Amylase (units/g) |
|---|---|---|---|---|
| Pancreas | 4.95 | 165.0 | 1680.0 | 368.0 |
| Duodenum | 4.03 | 8.08 | 12.0 | 5.98 |
| Jejunum | 6.3 | 11.8 | 16.7 | 5.84 |
| Ileum | 4.5 | 13.3 | 24.3 | 5.28 |
| Ceca | 4.2 | 10.2 | 10.05 | 0.42 |

[a]From Nitsan et al. (1973).

instances (Webster and Tyor, 1966); apparently, however, there was an increase in proteolytic enzyme activity or protein synthesis in the pigeon pancreas.

**Cholinergic compounds.** Metacholine administered to pigeons increases secretion of pancreatic juice and amylase (Webster, 1968, 1969), as it does in mammals. Apparently no studies have been conducted on the effects of vagal stimulation.

Atropine has been reported to block the effect of cholinergic agents on mammalian and also pigeon pancreas slices with respect to enzyme secretion (Hokin and Hokin, 1953). Further studies by Morissett and Webster (1970) on the effects of atropine suggest that the effects of atropine are not clearcut but atropine may have a direct metabolic effect on acinar cells apart from its cholinergic blocking effect. Atropine produced a great increase in the amylase content of the pancreas that was associated with a decreased rate of secretion (which was not measured) or an increased rate of synthesis; the evidence is against the latter.

**Enterokinase.** Because fat introduced into the duodenum does not appear to release enterokinase (Long, 1967), it has been assumed that the bird lacks this enzyme. Experiments by Lepkovsky *et al.* (1970), however, prove conclusively that the chicken pancreas does have enterokinase. Its concentration averaged about 90 units/g of dry matter (intestinal contents) in normal birds and decreased when raw soybean meal was fed. Moreover, in depancreatized birds there was little or none of the enzyme present.

## Digestion in the Ceca and Large Intestine

Presumably, little or no digestion takes place in the large intestines of birds other than in the ceca, but there is evidence of water resorption in the large intestine and rectum (see Chapter 14).

Digestion in the ceca has been reviewed by Mangold (1929, 1934), Groebbels (1932), Halnan (1949), and Sturkie (1965). There is considerable evidence in favor of the ceca as the site of digestion of crude fiber (Mangold, 1934) (see section on digestibility, below). Radeff (1928) and Henning (1929) determined the coefficients of digestibility of crude corn fiber before and after surgical removal of the ceca of hens. The coefficients for corn before cecectomy were 17.1 (Radeff, 1928) and 19.7 (Henning, 1929), and 0.0 after the operation. The figures for oats and wheat with ceca intact were

9.25 and 5.7, respectively, and after the operation they were 1.31 and 1.4, respectively. The digestibility of fiber in pigeons, a species with rudimentary ceca, is less than in chickens (Mangold and Hock, 1938; Radeff, 1928). Microbial decomposition of cellulose in the cecum is primarily fermentative (Beattie and Shrimpton, 1958).

Surgical removal of the ceca has no ill effects, but it may reduce the amount of water absorbed. After cecectomy the water content of the feces is higher than before (Röseler, 1929), but the operation did not affect the digestion of amino acids (Payne *et al.,* 1971).

## Digestibility of Feedstuffs

In order to determine the digestibility coefficient of each nutrient in the feed, it is necessary to determine the composition of the feed, to collect the feces unmixed with urine, and to determine the quantities of nutrients present or undigested. Separation of feces and urine in birds presents difficulties because the two are voided together in the cloaca. To separate the two therefore involves surgery or the preparation of an artificial anus or exteriorizing of the ureters (Chapter 14). If feces and urine are collected together, a correction for the amount of nitrogen in the urine must be made. The results thus obtained compare favorably with determinations made on uncontaminated feces. An alternative method of determining digestibility is the use of chromic oxide, an undigestible marker that can be mixed in the feed. Its concentration in the feed, digestive tract, and feces can then be determined, as well as that of the nutrient under consideration, without having to collect accurately all feces and urine. The ratio of the concentrations in the feed and feces is a measure of the percent of digestibility (Dansky and Hill, 1952; Nakahiro, 1966).

Except for crude fiber the coefficients of digestibility of common feedstuffs for birds compare favorably with those of mammals (Titus, 1955). Unfortunately, no recent studies have been conducted but most old data indicate that crude fiber is digested in avian species, although to a considerably lesser extent than in mammals. However, the coefficients of digestibility of crude fiber are highly variable, even within the same species and with the same variety of grain (Mangold, 1934; see also Groebbels 1932). These figures range from zero to 29% for crude fiber of wheat, with most figures ranging from 3 to 10%. Cellulose, lignin, and pentosans from corn fodder are almost completely indigestible.

**LIVER AND BILE**

The avian liver is large and bilobed. A hepatic duct from each lobe leads to the duodenum. The left hepatic duct communicates directly with the duodenum, but the right one may have a branch going to the gall bladder or may be enlarged locally as a gall bladder; hence, in its terminal part it serves as a cystic duct. The gall bladder, which is not present in all species, serves as a storage and concentrating organ.

**Production and action of bile.** The main digestive function of the liver relates to the production and action of bile. Avian bile is slightly acid (Table 10–3). Amylase is found in chicken bile, and its activity in bile from the gall bladder is greater than in bile from the liver. It is present in all chickens above 8 weeks of age but is absent in some at 4 weeks (Farner, 1943c). Little is known about the function of bile in birds but it presumably aids in the absorption of fats by its emulsifying action and its activating effects on pancreatic lipase and in the digestion of carbohydrates by virtue of the amylase present in it.

Few studies have been conducted on the secretion of bile. The research by Clarkson *et al.* (1957) revealed that White Leghorn cockerels (14 weeks of age) secrete approximately 1 ml of bile per hour and about 9.5 ml/kg per 24 hr according to Capaul and Garbini (1965). The administration of gallogen and of sulfarlem, both substances reported to increase bile secretion in mammals, was followed by a slight increase in secretion (after feeding gallogen) and by a very large increase, viz., 200 or 300% (after feeding sulfarlem). Lin *et al.* (1974) reported bile flow of 20.1 $\mu$l/kg/min, or 1.2 ml/kg/hr in White Leghorn chickens (age 10–18 weeks).

Haslewood (1964) reported that among ten wild species of birds investigated, chenodeoxycholic acid was the chief bile acid; in carnivorous birds, however, cholic and allocholic acids predominate (see also Haslewood, 1968). The common deoxycholic acid in mammalian bile has not been detected in the bile of chickens. In the domestic fowl, maintained germ-free, cholic, allocholic, and chenodeoxycholic acids were the only ones observed; others in addition to these were found in chickens raised in the presence of bacteria, however, suggesting that some are artifacts arising from the action of intestinal flora.

The bile salts glycocholate and taurocholate are readily absorbed by different segments of small intestine, but the rate of absorption increased toward the distal end (Lindsay and March, 1967).

After obstruction of both bile ducts, there was a significant elevation in the plasma of unconjugated and conjugated bilirubin; the bilirubin levels were 40 times higher than the level of biliverdin, whereas normally (no duct ligation) there is little difference in levels of the two (Lind *et al.*, 1967).

Lin *et al.* (1974) reported that endogenous secretion rates for biliverdin and bilirubin were 14.7 and 0.9 $\mu$g/kg/min, respectively. Excretory rates for total endogenous bile pigments were greater than in other nonavian species, and bilirubin accounted for only 6% of the total. Because the chicken has very low levels of liver glucuronyl transferase and little or no biliverdin reductase, biliverdin is the major bile pigment excreted by the avian liver, and the synthesis of bilirubin is limited by biliverdin reductase activity.

**Other functions of the liver.** The liver is involved in the metabolism of protein, fats, and carbohydrates (Chapters 12, 13, and 11) and in the detoxication of metabolities. The liver is also the site of lipogenic enzyme production, which is influenced by diet (Pearce, 1972). There are pronounced sex differences in blood levels of plasma proteins, lipids, and calcium of birds. These are primarily the effects of the female sex hormone, estrogen, on the liver in the formation and retention of and clearance of these substances.

One method of determining the functional state of the liver is its rate of clearance of, or its ability to extract, sodium bromsulphthalein (BSP) from the blood and to excrete it in the bile. Campbell (1957) reported that laying hens or estrogenized males or capons clear BSP at a slower rate than normal males or capons. The reason for the difference is not clear, but the author suggested that the ability of the liver cells to clear the dye may have been impaired by estrogen, and this may be associated with the increased fat content of liver resulting from estrogen. In contrast, Nordstrom (1966) reported a greater clearance rate in laying females and that this was associated with higher levels of lipid in females livers (Nordstrom and Smith, 1967). The differences of these authors have not been reconciled and further studies are needed.

**ABSORPTION**

The methods used to study absorption involve the ingestion or administration, *in vivo,* of nonabsorbable markers, such as chromic oxide, barium sulfate, yttrium,[91] and others. *In vitro* techniques involve uptake of substances in the isolated gut, usually everted. Most absorption takes place in the small intestine by (1) diffusion in accordance with a concentration gradient or (2) active transport against a concentration gradient. Some substances may be (3) carrier mediated, in which case their transport (glucose) is dependent on another actively transported substance (Na).

The detailed mechanisms involved in absorption and transport of carbohydrates, lipids, and proteins are discussed in Chapters 11, 13 and 12. The absorption of water and certain electrolytes is discussed here briefly.

Calcium. In laying chickens each egg laid contains approximately 2 g of calcium. The ingestion, absorption, and turnover of calcium must therefore be very high in order to supply the calcium required for shell formation (see also Chapter 16). The rate of absorption is greatest in the duodenum and jejunum and lowest in the ileum (Hurwitz and Bar, 1965). Absorption was higher when calcium was being deposited on the shell than when no calcium was deposited, but there were no significant differences during periods of early and late calcification, when it is believed that the rate of calcium deposition is different (see Chapter 16). The absorption of phosphorus followed a pattern similar to calcium.

Hurwitz and Bar (1969) studied changes in electropotential difference (ECPD) between the lumen of the intestine and blood and its relationship to calcium absorption. When the Ca content of diet was high, the ECPD was always positive in the duodenum and jejunum, where most absorption occurs; this indicates a mechanism of simple diffusion. When the Ca level in the diet of chicks was low (0.3%) the ECPD was negative, suggesting that absorption was against the concentration gradient and therefore active transport was involved. Adams and Norman (1970) likewise found Ca absorption in the isolated chick ileum to be active under certain conditions. There is a gradual increase in calcium absorption capacity in female chickens at the onset of laying and the increase is related to an increase in duodenal calcium-binding protein, which also occurs at the onset of laying (Hurwitz and Bar, 1971). However, this relationship applies only for a while, and not after sustained egg laying; this indicates that other factors are also involved.

Water and sodium. Water is absorbed in small and large intestines, including the rectum and cloaca (Lepkovsky et al., 1967; Hart and Essex, 1942; Skadhauge, 1967; Hill and Lumijarvi, 1968; Crocker and Holmes, 1971). Water is passively transport-

ed and its movement is associated with the active transport of sodium.

Crocker and Holmes (1971) determined the absorption of water and Na in different isolated segments (everted gut technique) of the intestine from jejunum to ceca (segments I–V) of Pekin ducks. One group of ducks had been maintained on fresh water and the other received 60% sea water. There were no differences in the absorption of water and Na in these segments of the ducks maintained on salt-free water, but the ducks adapted to sea water had higher rates of absorption in the more proximal segments, I, II, III (jejunum and upper ileum) and lower in the distal ones. Moreover, the salt water adapted birds secreted more Na from the nasal glands; when they were given spironolactone, however, which inhibits the adrenal hormone aldosterone, these ducks behaved as ducks kept on salt-free water and secreted no Na through the nasal glands. These results show that the secretion of the nasal glands is influenced by the amount of Na absorbed and that the latter stimulates the glands to increased secretion of Na (see also Chapter 14).

## REFERENCES

Adams, T. H., and A. W. Norman. (1970). Studies on the mechanism of action of calciferol. I. Basic parameters of vitamin D-mediated calcium transport. J. Biol. Chem., 245, 4421.

Ashcraft, D. W. (1930). Correlative activities of the alimentary canal of fowl. 93, 105.

Beattie, J., and D. H. Shrimpton. (1958). Surgical and clinical techniques for in vitro studies of intestinal microflora of domestic fowls. Quart. J. Exp. Physiol., 43, 399.

Bhattacharya, S., and K. C. Ghose. (1971). Influence of food on amylase system in birds. Comp. Biochem. Physiol., 40B, 317.

Bird, F. H. (1971). Distribution of trypsin and amylase activities in the duodenum of the domestic fowl. Brit. Poultry Sci., 12, 373.

Bolton, W. (1965). Digestion in crop. Brit. Poultry Sci., 6, 97.

Brown, K. M. (1971). Sucrose activity in the intestine of the chick; Normal development and influence of hydrocortisone, actinomycin D, cycloheximide and puromycin. J. Exp. Biol, 177, 493.

Burhol, P. G., and B. I. Hirschowitz. (1970). Single subcutaneous doses of histamine and pentagastrin in gastric fistula chickens. Am. J. Physiol., 218, 1671.

Burhol, P. G., and B. I. Hirschowitz. (1971a). Gastric stimulation by subcutaneous infusion of urecholine in fistula chickens. A comparison to histamine and pentagastrin. Scand. J. Gastroenterol., 6, (Suppl. 11), 25.

Burhol, P. G., and B. I. Hirschowitz. (1971b). Gastric stimulation by subcutaneous infusion of cholecystokinin—pancreozymin in fistula chickens. Scand. J. Gastroenterol., 6(Sup. 11), 41.

Burhol, P. G., and B. I. Hirschowitz. (1971c). Gastric inhibition by subcutaneous infusion of secretin in fistula chickens. Scand. J. Gastroenterol. 6 (Suppl. 11), 49.

Burhol, P. G., and B. I. Hirschowitz. (1972). Dose responses with subcutaneous infusion of histamine in gastric fistula of chickens. Am. J. Physiol., 222, 308.

Campbell, J. G. (1957). Studies on the influence of sex hormones

208

on avian liver. I. Sexual differences in avian liver clearance curves. *J. Endocrinol. 15*, 339.

Capaul, E. G., and J. D. Garbini. (1965). Secretion and filtration pressure of bile in fowls. [Abstract] *Vet. Bull., 36* (10), 674.

Cheney, G. (1938). Gastric acidity in chicks with experimental gastric ulcers. *Am. J. Digest. Dis., 5*, 104.

Clarkson, T. B., J. S. Kin, and N. H. Warnock. (1957). A comparison of the effect of gallogen and sulfarlem on the normal bile flow of the cockerel. *Am. J. Vet. Res., 18*, 187.

Collip, J. B. (1922). The activation of the glandular stomach of the fowl. *Am. J. Physiol., 59*, 435.

Crocker, A. D., and W. N. Holmes. (1971). Intestinal absorption in ducklings maintained on fresh water and hypertonic saline. *Comp. Biochem. Physiol., 40A*, 203.

Dal Borgo, G., P. C. Harrison, and J. McGinnis. (1968a). A method for cannulation of pancreatic ducts in young chicks. *Poultry Sci., 47*, 1818.

Dal Borgo, G. A., J. Salman, M. H. Pubols, and J. McGinnis. (1968b). Exocrine function of the chick pancreas as affected by dietary soybean meal and carbohydrate. *Proc. Soc. Exp. Biol. Med., 129*, 877.

Dansky, L. M., and F. W. Hill. (1952). Application of the chromic oxide indicator method to balance studies with growing chickens. *J. Nutr., 47*, 449.

De Rycke, P. (1962). Onderzoek over exopeptidasen bijhet kwiken. *Natuurwetensch. Tijdschr. (Ghent), 43*, 82.

Farner, D. S. (1942). The hydrogen ion concentration in avian digestive tracts. *Poultry Sci., 21*, 445.

Farner, D. S. (1943a). Gastric hydrogen ion concentration and acidity in the domestic fowl. *Poultry Sci., 22*, 799.

Farner, D. S. (1943b). The effect of certain dietary factors on gastric hydrogen ion concentration and acidity in the domestic fowl. *Poultry Sci., 22*, 295.

Farner, D. S. (1943c). Biliary amylase in the domestic fowl. *Biol. Bull., 84*, 240.

Farner, D. S. (1960). Digestion and digestive system. In "Biology and Comparative Physiology of Birds" (A. J. Marshall, Ed.). New York: Academic Press, Chapter 11.

Fedorovskii, N. P., and V. I. Konopleva. (1959). Physiology of gastric digestion in the goose. *Plicevodstuo, 10*, 39. (Abstracted in *World Poultry Sci.), 17*, 61, 1961.)

Fisher, ., and H. S. Weiss. (1956). Feed consumption in relation to dietary bulk. The effect of surgical removal of crop. *Poultry Sci., 35*, 418.

Friedman, M. H. F. (1939). Gastric secretion in birds. *J. Cell. Comp. Physiol., 13*, 219.

Fritz, J. C., W. H. Burrows, and W. H. Titus. (1936). Comparison of digestibility of gizzardectomized and normal fowls. *Poultry Sci., 15*, 289.

Gibson, R. G., H. W. Colvin, J., and B. I. Hirschowitz. (1974). Kinetics of gastric response in chickens to graded electrical vagal stimulation. *Proc. Soc. Exp. Biol. Med., 145*, 1058.

Green, M. L., and J. M. Llewellin. (1973). The purification and properties of a single chicken pepsinogen fraction and pepsin derived from it. *Biochem. J., 133*, 105.

Groebbels, F. (1932). "Der Vögel. Erster Band: Atmungswelt and Nahrungswelt." Berlin: Verlag von Gebrüder Borntraeger.

Halnan, E. T. (1949). The architecture of avian gut and tolerance of crude fiber. *Brit. J. Nutr., 3*, 245.

Hart, W. M., and H. E. Essex. (1942). Water metabolism of the chicken with special reference to cloaca. *Am. J. Physiol., 136*, 657.

Haslewood, G. A. D. (1964). The biological significance of chemical differences in the bile salts. *Biol. Rev., 39*, 537.

Haslewood, G. A. D. (1968). Evolution and bile salts. In "Handbook of Physiology," Sec. VI, "Alimentary Canal," Vol. 5, Washington, D. C.: American Physiological Society, p. 2375.

Hazelwood, R. L., S. D. Turner, J. R. Kimmel, and H. G. Pollock. (1973). Spectrum effects of a new polypeptide (third hormone?) isolated from the chicken pancreas. *Gen. Comp. Endrocrinol., 21*, 485.

Heatley, N. G., F. McElheny, and L. Lepkovsky. (1965). Measure-

ment of rate of flow of pancreatic secretion in anesthetized chicken. *Comp. Biochem. Physiol., 16*, 29.

Henning, H. J. (1929). *Landw. Versuchsstat., 108, 253.* (Cited by Groebbels, 1932.)

Heller, H., and R. G. Kulka. (1968). Amylase isoenzymes in the developing chick pancreas. *Biochem. Biophys. Acta, 165*, 393.

Herpol, C. (1964). Activite proteolytique de l'appareil gastrique d'-oiseaux granivores et carnivores. *Ann. Biol. Anim. Biophys., 4*, 239.

Herpol, C. (1966). Influence de l'ago sur le pH dans le tube de gallus domesticus. *Ann. Biol. Anim. Biophys., 6*, 495.

Herpol, C. (1967). Etude de l'activite proteolytique des divers organes du système digestif de quelques especes d'oiseaux en rapport avec leur regime alimentaire. *Z. Vergl. Physiol., 57*, 209.

Herpol, C., and G. van Grembergen. (1967). La signification du pH dans le tube digestif de gallus domesticus. *Ann. Biol. Anim. Biochem. Biophys., 7*, 33.

Hill, F. W., and D. H. Lumijarvi. Evidence for an electrolyte-conserving function of the colon in chickens. *Fed. Am. Soc. Exp. Biol., 27*, 421. (Abst. 1165.)

Hokin, L. E., and M. R. Hokin. (1953). Enzyme secretion and the incorporation of $^{32}P$ into phospholipids of pancreas slices. *J. Biol. Chem., 203*, 967.

Hulan, H. W., and F. H. Bird. (1972). Effect of fat level in isonitrogenous diets on composition of avian pancreatic juice. *J. Nutr., 102*, 459.

Hulan, H. W., G. Moreau, and F. H. Bird. (1972). A method for cannulating the main pancreatic duct of chickens: The continuous collection of avian pancreatic juice. *Poultry Sci., 51*, 531.

Hurwitz, S., and A. Bar. (1965). Absorption of calcium and phosphorus along the gastrointestinal tract of the laying fowl as influenced by dietary calcium and egg shell formation. *J. Nutr. 86*, 433.

Hurwitz, S., and A. Bar. (1969). Relation between the lumen blood–electrochemical potential difference of calcium, calcium absorption and calcium binding protein in the intestine of the fowl. *J. Nutr., 99*, 217.

Hurwitz, S., and A. Bar. (1971). Relationship of duodenal Ca binding protein to calcium absorption in the laying fowl. *Comp. Biochem. Physiol., 41*, 735.

Ivanov, N., and R. Gotev. (1962). Untersuchungen über die aussensekretorische Tätigkeit der Bauchspeicheldrüse bei Hühnen. *Arch. Tierernähr., 12*, 65.

Jerrett, S. A., and W. R. Goodge. (1973). Evidence for amylase in avian salivary glands. *J. Morphol., 139*, 27.

Jung, L., and M. Pierre. (1933). Sur le rôle der la salive chez les oiseaux granivores. *Comp. Rend. Soc. Biol., 113*, 115.

Karpov, L. V. (1919). [in Russian:] *Russ. Physiol. J. 2*, 185. [*Physiol. Abs. 5*, 469, 1920.]

Kessler, C. A., B. I. Hirschowitz, P. G. Burhol, and G. Sachs. (1972). Methoxyflurance (penthrane) anesthesia effect on histamine stimulated gastric secretion in the chickens. *Proc. Soc. Exp. Biol. Med., 139*, 1340.

Kishida, T., and I. Liener. (1968). Further characterization of turkey trypsin: End groups and sequence of histidine containing peptides. *Arch. Biochem. Biophys., 126*, 111.

Kokas, E., S. H. Kaufman, and J. C. Long. (1971). Effect of glucagon on gastric and duodenal secretion in chickens. *Z. Vergl. Physiol., 74*, 315.

Kokas, E., L. Phillips, Jr., and W. D. Brunson, J. (1967). The secretory activity of the duodenum in chickens. *Comp. Biochem., Physiol., 22*, 81.

Kokue, E., and T. Haymana. (1972). Effects of starvation and feeding in the endocrine pancreas of chicken. *Poultry Sci., 51*, 1366.

Koschtojanz, I., M. Mirjeeff, P. Korjvieff, and S. Otschakowskaja. (1933). Zun Frage der Spezifitat des Sekpetins: Vergleichende Physiologische Untersuchung. *Z. Vergl. Physiol., 18*, 112.

Laws, B. M., and J. H. Moore. (1963). Some observations on pancreatic amylase and intestinal maltese of the chick. *Can. J. Biochem. Physiol., 41*, 2107.

Leasure, E. E., and V. D. Foltz. (1940). Experiments on absorption in the crop of chickens. *J. Am. Vet. Med. Assoc., 96*, 236.

Leasure, E. E., and R. P. Link. (1940). Studies on missing leasures. The saliva of the hen. *Poultry Sci., 19*, 131.

Lepkovsky, S., and F. Furuta. (1970). Lipase in pancreas and intestinal contents of fed, heated, and raw soybean diets. *Poultry Sci., 49*, 192.

Lepkovsky, S., S. E. Feldman, and I. M. Sharon. (1967). In "Handbook of Physiology, Vol. 1, Sect. 6 (C. F. Code, Ed.). Baltimore: Williams and Wilkins, p. 117.

Lepkovsky, S., F. Furuta, M. J. Dimeck, and I. Yamashina. (1970). Enterokinase and the chicken pancreas. *Poultry Sci., 49*, 421.

Levchuk, T. P., and V. N. Orekhovich. (1963). Production and some properties of chick pepsin. *Biokhimiya, 28*, 1004.

Lin, G. L., J. A. Himes, and C. E. Cornelius. (1974). Bilirubin and biliverdin excretion by the chicken. *Am. J. Physiol., 226*, 881.

Lind, G. W., R. R. Gronwall, and C. E. Cornelius. (1967). Bile pigments in the chicken. *Res. Vet. Sci., 8*, 280.

Lindsay, O. B., and B. E. March. (1967). Intestinal absorption of bile salts in the cockerel. *Poultry Sci., 46*, 164.

Long, J. F., (1967). Gastric secretion in unanesthetized chickens. *Am. J. Physiol., 212*, 1303.

Mangold, E. (1929). "Handbuch der Ernährung und des Stoffwechsels der Landwirt Schaftlichen Nutztiere: Zweiter band." Berlin: Verlag von Julius Springer.

Mangold, E. (1934). The digestion and utilization of crude fiber. *Nutr. Abstr. Rev., 3*, 647.

Mangold, E., and A. Hock (1938). Die Verdaulichkeit der Futtermittel bei der Taube. *Arch. F. Geflügel., 12*, 334.

Morissett, J., and P. D. Webster. (1970). Effects of atropine on pigeon pancreas. *Am. J. Physiol., 219*, 1286.

Nakahiro, Y. (1966). Studies on the method of measuring the digestibility of poultry feed. *Mem. Fac. Agri. Kagawa University*, No. 22. [Summary in English.]

Niess, E., C. A. Ivy, and M. C. Nesheim. (1972). Stimulation of gallbladder emptying and pancreatic secretion in chicks by soybean whey protein. *Proc. Soc. Exp. Biol. Med., 140*, 291.

Nitsan, Z., I. Nir, Y. Dror, and I. Bruckental. (1973). The effect of forced feeding and dietary protein level on enzymes associated with digestion, protein and carbohydrate metabolism in geese. *Poultry Sci., 52*, 474.

Nordstrom, J. O. (1966). Avian liver function studies. Ph.D. Thesis, University of California, Davis, Calif.

Nordstrom, J. O., and A. H. Smith. (1967). BSP clearance and fatty infiltration of liver in the domestic fowl. *Physiologist, 10*, 264.

Payne, W. L., R. R. Kifer, D. G. Snyder, and G. F. Combs. (1971). Investigation of apparent amino acid digestibility of fish meal protein using a cecaectomized adult male chickens. *Poultry Sci., 50*, 143.

Pearce, J. (1972). Effect of diet and also physiological state on some enzymes of carbohydrate metabolism in the liver of the domestic fowl, *Biochem. J., 130* (1), 21, (Proceedings.)

Pritchard, P. J. (1972). Digestion of sugars in the crop. *Comp. Biochem. Physiol., 43A*, 195.

Radeff, T. (1928). Die Verdaulichkeit der Rohfaser und die Funktion der Blinddärme beim Haushuhn. *Arch. f. Geflügel., 2*, 312.

Röseler, M. (1929). Die Bedentung der Blinddärme des Haushuhnes für die Resorption der Nahrung und Verduung der Rohtaser. *Z. Tierz. Zücht., 13*, 281.

Rouff, H. J., and K. F. Sewing. (1970). Die Wirkung von Histamine Carbacol, Pentagastrin and Huhnergastrinextrakten auf die Magensekretion von nicht narkotisierten Hühnern mit einer Magenfistel. *Naunynschmiedbergs. Arch. Pharmakol., 267*, 170.

Rutter, W. J., P. Krichevsky, H. M. Scott, and R. H. Hansen. (1953). The metabolism of lactose and galactose in the chick. *Poultry Sci., 32*, 706.

Ryan, C. A. (1965). Chicken chymotrypsin and turkey trypsin. I. Purification. *Arch. Biochem. Biophys., 110*, 169.

Ryan, C. A., and Y. Tomimatsu. (1965). A crystalline avian pancreatic protein. *Arch. Biochem. Biophys., 111*, 461.

Ryan, C. A., J. J. Clary, and Y. Tomimatsu. (1965). Chicken chymotrypsin and turkey trypsin. II. Physical and enzyme properties. *Arch. Biochem. Biophys., 110*, 175.

Shaw, T. P. (1913). Digestion in the chick. *Am. J. Physiol., 31*, 349.

Skadhauge, E. (1967). *In vivo* perfusion studies of the cloacal water and electrolyte resorption in the fowl. *Comp. Biochem. Physiol., 23*, 483.

Soedarmo, D., M. R. Kare, and R. H. Wasserman. (1961). Observations on the removal of sugar from the mouth and crop of the chicken. *Poultry Sci., 40*, 123.

Sturkie, P. D. (Ed.). (1965). "Avian Physiology" (2nd ed.). Ithaca, N. Y.: Cornell University Press.

Titus, H. W. (1955). "The Scientific Feeding of Chickens" (3rd ed.). Danville, Ill.: The Interstate Press.

Tomimatsu, Y., J. J. Clary, and J. J. Bartulovich. (1966). Physical characterization of oviinhibitor, a trypsin and chymotrypsin inhibitor from chicken egg white. *Arch. Biochem. Biophys., 115*, 36.

Walter, W. G. (1939). Bedingte Magensaftsekretlon bei der Ente. *Acta Brev. Neerl. Physiol., 9*, 56.

Webster, P. D. (1968). Effect of metacholine on pancreatic amylase synthesis. *Gastroenterology, 55*, 375.

Webster, P. D. (1969). Effect of stimulation of pancreatic amylase secretion and nuclear RNA synthesis. *Proc. Soc. Exp. Biol. Med., 132*, 1072.

Webster, P. D., and M. P. Tyor. (1966). Effect of intravenous pancreozymin on amino acid in vitro by pancreatic tissue. *Am. J. Physiol., 211*, 157.

Winget, C. M., G. C. Ashton, and A. J. Cawley. (1962). Changes in gastrointestinal pH associated with fasting in laying hen. *Poultry Sci., 41*, 1115.

# 11

# Carbohydrate Metabolism

## R. L. Hazelwood

# GENERAL INTRODUCTION

**Current literature.** Since the previous edition of this text, much new information pertinent to a better understanding of normal avian carbohydrate metabolism has been gathered. Use of newly designed methodology, of more sensitive techniques, and of the "molecular approach" allow for reevaluation of the results of older experiments as well as for progress in understanding avian carbohydrate phenomena at a lower level of (organismic) organization. Emphasis has been placed on the cell, on the intracellular cooperation of organelles, and on the existence, location, and design of receptor sites. Unfortunately, the majority of this work has been restricted to but a few of the many available avian species. Most of our knowledge of avian carbohydrate metabolism is derived from studies completed on "domestic" avian forms, such as *Gallus domesticus* (chicken), duck, goose, and, to a lesser extent, *Columba* (pigeon).

Of particular note are the many monographs, texts, and treatises dealing with the physiology and biochemistry of both the embryo and the adult bird that have been published since 1965. For example, the reader is referred to Romanoff (1967) for a quantitative analysis of the developing avian embryo of many species; to Bell and Freeman (1971) for detailed descriptions of the biochemical basis for physiological function of most avian tissues; and to Farner and King (1972 and 1973) for an erudite discussion of the physiological regulatory patterns associated with organ systems and metabolism in general. Certain avian tissues have received concentrated treatment relative to an integration of structure, function, and metabolism within a narrow area. An example of the latter research is the excellent review by Drummond (1967) on avian muscle dynamics and metabolism.

**Future needs.** The understanding of many aspects of avian carbohydrate metabolism has lagged behind that of equivalent relationships in mammalian systems. Tools are at hand, however, and the basic information available to gain greater insight into the cellular factors that govern carbohydrate metabolism within Aves. The role of cyclic-3′,5′-AMP as a possible second (hormone) messenger, the isolation and characterization of any tissue receptor site involved in carbohydrate metabolism regulation, and the physiological "triggers" for hormonal release in altering carbohydrate metabolism are yet to be defined in avian systems. Still, the trend of experimental design at the present is in these directions. The results obtained therefrom can in all probability aid our understanding of the interrelationships of fat, carbohydrate, and protein in providing cellular substrate to the bird, enabling it to meet the diverse energy–metabolic requirements ranging from preparation for migratory flight to egg production.

## PATTERNS OF CARBOHYDRATE METABOLISM

### Biochemical Pathways Available for Carbohydrate Metabolism

All evidence available documents the fact that the major glycogenic, glycogenolytic, and glycolytic pathways found and described in mammals exist and are operative in Aves. For example, *d*-glucose (180–240 mg per 100 ml), *d*-fructose (1–3 mg per 100 ml), and *d*-galactose (< 1 mg per 100 ml) are the major circulating forms of carbohydrates found in birds. Virtually no carbohydrate can be found within the erythrocyte. Plasma glucose increases constantly during chicken embryogenesis to reach a level of about 160–180 mg per 100 ml at the time of hatching and continues to increase for several weeks, reaching adult levels of 200–240 mg per 100 ml by 2 months of age. During this time, and for several months thereafter in the chicken, the hematocrit steadily decreases (Bell and Sturkie, 1965).

### Embryonic Pathways

Although the avian embryo possesses all the critical enzymes involved in the anaerobic degradation of glucose, hexokinase (liver) and glucokinase activities are virtually nonexistent (for phosphorylating glucose) until late in embryogenesis. However, hepatic carbohydrate can be utilized by the developing embryo as a result of steady increasing levels of phosphofructokinase, fructose-1,6-diphosphate aldolase, glyceraldehyde-3-phosphate dehydrogenase, phosphohexose isomerase, pyruvate kinase, and enolase. Most of these enzyme activities increase continuously up to a week or two after hatching, only then to decrease thereafter to relatively low levels in adulthood. In contrast, hexokinase activity increases greatly after hatching and reaches peak levels which are three to four times greater than that of glucokinase during adulthood (Bell, 1971; Hazelwood, 1972). All other glycolytic enzymes apparently decrease as the bird gets older. In addition to the aforementioned enzymes Goodridge (1968a) has observed decreases in activity levels of liver α-glycerophosphate dehydrogenase with age of the chick. It therefore appears that the enzymatic potential to metabolize glucose matures with embryonic age, readying the newly hatched chick for the rather abrupt nutritional switchover from high-lipid diet (yolk) to that of high-carbohydrate diet (starter mash).

## Glycogen Metabolism

Although the synthetases and the phosphorylases required for glycogenesis and glycogenolysis, respectively, can be detected within liver and muscle tissue during the first week of incubation, glycogen levels wax and wane throughout the entire incubation period as various glycogenic and/or glycogenolytic hormones are released by concomitantly maturing endocrine tissues. Hepatic glycogen levels generally increase with embryonic age despite a very marked depression at day 13–14; concomitantly, glucose-6-phosphatase, $\beta$-glucuronidase, phosphorylases a and b, and UDPG synthetase activities increase throughout the remaining embryogenic period (for details, see Hazelwood, 1965). Liver glycogen levels reach peak levels 1 day prior to hatching only to fall to about one-sixth of these 1 day after hatching (Freeman, 1969); cardiac glycogen falls about 60% over the same time period, indicating the impact of hatching on energy sources. Liver glycogen levels remain low for several weeks, increasing to adult levels only several months later. During this time they are subjected not only to diurnal rhythms but also (in females) to marked depressions at the time of ovulation and molting (see later sections). Plasma glucose continues to increase during the critical pre–post hatching metabolic switchover from a high-lipid diet to one high in carbohydrate content.

## Aerobic and Anaerobic Degradation of Carbohydrate

Estimates of the levels of malate and succinic dehydrogenases, along with those of cytochrome oxidase, allow for an evaluation of activity of the tricarboxylic acid cycle (oxidative glucose degradation). Such observations indicate increased cycle activity throughout chick embryogenesis and, especially in liver tissue, continued increase in these levels as the bird approaches adulthood (Goodridge, 1968b). Anaerobic glycolysis and the tricarboxylic acid cycle appear to be the major routes of energy release from carbohydrate degradation in adult birds (Figure 11–1). An alternate pathway of glucose 6-phosphate metabolism, although firmly established as existing in many mammalian tissues, is not so well

documented in avian tissues. The direct oxidative path of glucose degradation is sometimes referred to as the hexose monophosphate (or pentose phosphate) shunt, and has been established to be very active during the first week of incubation of the avian embryo. Such activity allows for a bypassing of the "classic" anaerobic glycolytic pathway by the direct oxidation of three glucose 6-phosphate molecules, leading to pentoses, three-carbon phosphate, and $CO_2$ (Figure 11–1). In addition to reformation of glucose 6-phosphate from some of the pentoses and recombination of glyceraldehyde 3-phosphate, the pentoses are available for nucleotide and nucleic acid synthesis. The reduced NADP liberated is available for lipid and steroidogenesis. Activity of the pentose cycle varies from embryonic tissue to tissue but generally only peaks at high levels between day 8 and day 15; it has subsided markedly to barely detectable levels by hatching time (Pearce and Brown, 1971; Hazelwood, 1965, 1972). Contributions by this direct oxidative degradation of glucose in providing energy, substrates, or cofactors to birds after hatching appears to be minimal at best (see below).

## Gluconeogenesis

Gluconeogenesis provides glucose or intermediary substrates of glycolysis (derived originally from noncarbohydrate sources) for eventual degradation. Conversion of alanine, glycine, serine, aspartate, and glutamate to pyruvate, oxaloacetate, or $\alpha$-ketoglutarate occurs primarily in the liver (to a lesser extent in kidney) and has been found to be quite active during avian embryogenesis as well as during posthatch life, and particularly during periods of food deprivation. Key enzymes (see Figure 11–1) for gluconeogenesis include glucose-6-phosphatase, fructose-1,6-diphosphatase, pyruvate carboxylase, phosphoenolpyruvate carboxykinase, and selective enzymes concerned with the oxidative conversion of amino acids to their corresponding $\alpha$-keto acids (amino acid oxidases, transaminases, and dehydrogenases). Because of the steady absorption of yolk components (relatively low carbohydrate content) by the avian embryo, gluconeogenesis is important for providing energy for morphogenesis up to the time of hatching. After hatching, the dietary composition of birds is altered greatly in favor of a relatively high-carbohydrate diet; as a result, the gluconeogenic enzyme activity levels fall precipitiously at this time. Comparison of activities of gluconeogenic enzymes in chicken tissue indicates a 66% decrease in glucose-6-phosphatase from hatching time to adulthood, and a decrease of 50% over

**11-1**

Metabolism of glycogen and simple sugars. Controlled reactions are by the number: (1) glucokinase, (2) glucose-6-phosphatase, (3) phosphoglucomutase, (4) UDPG-pyrophosphorylase, (5) branching enzyme + glycogen synthetase, (6) adenylcyclase, (7) Dephosphophosphorylase kinase, (8) galactokinase + UDPG, (9) glucose-6-phosphate dehydrogenase, (10) phosphohexosisomerase, (11) fructose-1,6-diphosphatase, (12) hexokinase (fructokinase), (13) pyruvate kinase, (14) pyruvate carboxylase, (15) Phosphoenolypyruvate carboxykinase. Reactions governed by enzymes with italicized numerical designations are reactions essential to gluconeogenesis (see text) and therefore circumvent certain critical energy barriers to a simple reversal of glycolysis.

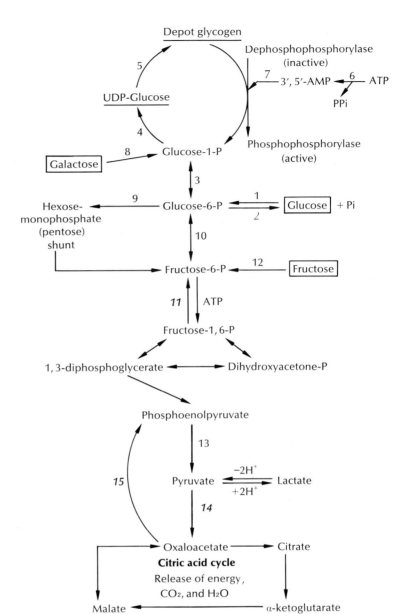

the same time span for fructose-1,6-diphosphatase activity (Wallace and Newsholme, 1967). Studies made comparing granivorous with carnivorous birds have confirmed earlier reports, which indicated that the carnivores can withstand prolonged periods of fasting without alterations of blood glucose. The very nature of the normal diet of the black vulture (dead carcasses) suggests an effective gluconeogenic mechanism for providing glucose substrates. Such has been found to be the case by Migliorini *et al.* (1973), wherein comparisons of enzyme levels/activities of vulture liver with that

of chicken liver were made. These workers concluded that whereas liver glycogen is depleted modestly during a fasting period in vultures, muscle glycogen is markedly decreased and the critical gluconeogenic enzymes (see above), especially PEP carboxykinase, are increased markedly (three to five times). Even in the fed state the carnivorous bird had much higher hepatic enzyme levels than did the chicken, levels that were augmented disproportionately greater than those observed in the fasting chicken liver. Similar results were observed in other carniverous forms (e.g., the horned owl).

## Differences in Carbohydrate Metabolism Between Birds and Mammals

Differences exist between Aves and Mammalia relative to the time of life during which a given metabolic pathway contributes most to the organisms intermediary metabolism as well as to the quantitative contribution by such a pathway to total body energy requirements. Differences between mammalian and avian forms in this regard are therefore differences of when, where, and how much rather than of what.

Probably best documented is the difference in contribution of the pentose (hexose monophosphate) shunt to the overall metabolism of Aves. Although the pentose shunt "enzymatic machinery" is present in most avian tissues, it contributes most during periods of growth and differentiation. For example, pentose shunt activity is highest in the avian embryo, particularly between day 8 and 15, and is largely restricted to intestinal and cardiac muscle as well as to brain and other neural tissue. Degradation of glucose via this pathway exceeds by far that routed over the glycolytic paths. After hatching, however, the pentose phosphate shunt is virtually inoperative in most tissues, particularly the liver (O'Hea and Leveille, 1969). The adult mammalian liver relies heavily on the end products of hexose monophosphate activity. Because the avian liver is responsible for over 90% of the total organismic fatty acid synthesis, it must rely on other pathways for the substrates and cofactors required for lipogenesis. Mammalian erythrocytes metabolize glucose preferentially via the pentose phosphate pathway but nucleated avian erythrocytes utilize mainly the aerobic glycolytic scheme to sustain their metabolism.

## Uronic Acid Pathway

Another oxidative path for glucose 6-phosphate that, although reported to exist in adult mammals and birds, is prevalent in the avian embryo is the uronic acid pathway. Even in the absence of detectable amounts of insulin, the avian embryo is capable of synthesizing glycogen and glucuronic acid using hepatic urindine-diphosphoglucuronyl transferase and synthetase. The uronic pathway favors the synthesis of UDP glucuronic acid by converting the sixth carbon of glucose 1-phosphate to glucuronic acid. This intermediate is an important substrate for steroid hormone conjugation and for precursors of cartilage structural elements. Furthermore, in contrast to mammals, birds employ the UDP glucuronic acid as a substrate for ascorbic acid synthesis

in the liver. In many respects, and with emphais on the foregoing reactions, the avian embryonic liver is quite similar to the adult (but not fetal) mammalian liver.

## Erythrocyte Metabolism

Enzymes essential for the aerobic metabolism of organic acid metabolites of glucose exist in the nucleated avian erythrocyte, and the synthesis of porphoryn-related compounds essential to hemoglobin formation is aided greatly by the oxidation of these substrates. The alternating "peaks" and "valleys" of energy release via the Krebs cycle in the avian RBC during incubation probably reflect activity of globin and hemoglobin synthetic pathways in primitive cell lines. Such a demand for a ready source of energy is evident when it is considered that the RBC of a 5-day chick embryo may complete the ribosomal synthesis of a single polypeptide chain (required in the hemoglobin molecule) in less than 2 min! Mammalian erythrocytes, lacking a nucleus, mitochrondria, RNA, and Kreb's cycle enzymes, are incapable of hemoglobin synthesis after the reticulocyte stage has passed. As a result, maintenance of its biconcave shape, of the membrane-associated sodium pump, and of the reactions for the required reduction of pyridine nucleotides all rely on anaerobic glucose metabolism and/or the hexose monophosphate shunt. The latter pathway appears to be very important in meeting the energy needs of the mature mammalian erythrocyte. The fact that very little glucose resides as such within the avian RBC indicates a very efficient utilization of what substrate is available, or a high intracellular transfer rate of extracellular glucose concomitant with an equal rate of degradation. Absence of Kreb's cycle activity in the avian cell relegates fatty acid contributions, and to a large extent that of protein degradation, to maintenance of erythrocytic structural integrity and function.

## Skeletal Muscle Metabolism

Drummond (1967) presented the metabolic requirements for vertebrate muscular effort in detail. He has also elucidated the microcellular events that subserve such activity in cardiac, smooth, and skeletal muscle energetics and that favor the prolonged, often nonstop, flight of migratory avian species. For example, examination of the white muscle fibers ("light meat") and the red fibers ("dark meat") indicates that the former generally have a relatively poor vascular supply, very low levels of myoglobin, high Embden–Myerhoff pathway enzyme content, and few mitochondria and lipid droplets. Additionally, these white skeletal muscle fibers contain very large deposits of glycogen. Apparently, such fibers are geared for anaerobic work, probably of an explosive nature of short duration. Histochemical, biochemical, and enzymatic evaluation of red muscle fibers presents a converse picture to that observed in white fibers, with the added feature that low glycogen and high fatty acid levels obtain. Coincident with the latter observation is the finding that lipases, fatty acid oxidases, and Kreb's cycle oxidative enzymes are found in abundance in the red (but not the white) skeletal muscles. Clearly, these muscles appear structurally and enzymatically best equipped to utilize noncarbohydrates as a metabolic fuel during activity. Such would be the case when sustained flight (in contrast to bursts of activity) occurred. Certainly, such fatty acid utilization and/or gluconeogenesis is employed by the red skeletal muscle fibers of many species during migration. Experimental studies have verified the preferential use of different muscle fuels in relation both to the fiber type and to the physical task normally performed by that muscle (Drummond, 1967; George and Berger, 1966).

## CARBOHYDRATE, LIPID, AND PROTEIN INTERRELATIONSHIPS

The role of gluconeogensis and/or fatty acid degradation to sustain circulating plasma glucose levels (or to provide energy release directly by oxidation) is important to vertebrates. The avian class is no exception. As seen in Figure 11–2, there are obvious specific points of entry of end products or intermediates of both protein and fat metabolism into the general metabolic scheme. (See also Chapter 12 and 13.) The end result may be a reformation of tissue glycogen (available for subsequent hydrolysis), of circulating glucose (available for intracellular translocation at sites distant from its formation), or oxidation to $CO_2$ and $H_2O$ (and energy release) at the original cell level.

### Aminio Acid Metabolism

Alanine, glycine, cysteine, and serine (or threonine) resulting from protein degradation within avian cells may enter the glycolytic pathway and, depending on local enzyme–substrate kinetics, may form (via pyruvate) acetyl-CoA preparatory to engagement in the oxidative Krebs cycle or "recombine" to form either glucose or glycogen (Figure

11–2). These possibilities emphasize the importance of high-protein diets, which lead to the formation of an abundance of these L-amino acids ("glycogenic" amino acids). Arginine, glutamine, histidine, and proline can be modified to glutamic acid, which in turn undergoes deamination to form the corresponding $\alpha$-keto acid, $\alpha$-ketoglutarate. L-Asparagine, after conversion to L-aspartate, contributes its entire four-carbon skeleton to form oxaloacetate, thus entering the metabolic caldron. Other amino acids (e.g., phenylalanine, tyrosine) may be converted to enter these major gluconeogenic pathways or may be converted directly to acetyl-CoA.

### Lipid Metabolism

The conversion of lipid substrates to glucose, glycogen and/or $CO_2$, and $H_2O$ with energy release is apparent also in Figure 11–2. The step by step $\beta$ oxidation of fatty acids leads to the ultimate formation of acetyl-CoA and acyl-CoA. The latter is used to "activate" a free fatty acid preparatory to $\beta$ oxidation. Thus, metabolism of lipid leads to a "push forward" on the Kreb's tricycle, leading to a greater energy evolvement per unit weight metabolized. Such a sequence of events "spares" carbohydrate depots to a large extent, rather than resynthesizing or replenishing them. It is evident that interconversion of foodstuffs (or direct usage of noncarbohydrates for energy availability) to carbohydrate affords birds considerable latitude in meeting metabolic demands within an ever-changing environment. The hepatic gluconeogenetic capacity of the owl, vulture, raven, and kestrel, for example, attests to the composition of the normal diet of these species and makes possible the maintenance of adequate circulating glucose simultaneous with oxidation of metabolites to release energy. The preferential utilization of fatty acids by certain muscle fibers (particularly red muscle) allows for a more efficient liberation of energy concomitant with sparing of existing (although limited) carbohydrate supplies as is seen during migratory flights.

## ABSORPTION AND DISTRIBUTION OF CARBOHYDRATE

### Intestinal Transport of Sugars

Careful *in vitro* experimentation in the late 1950's and much of the 1960's has validated and extended much of the early *in vivo* data pertaining to avian carbohydrate absorption. The organismic approach, sometimes modified to employ large in-

216

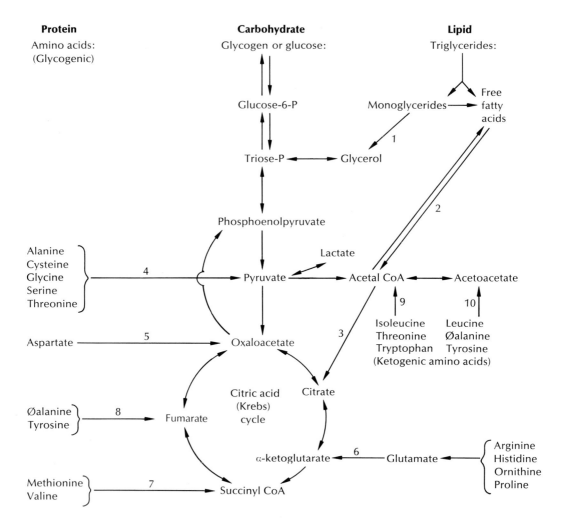

11-2 Interrelationships of protein, fat, and carbohydrate metabolism in Aves. Steps number 1, 2, and 3 indicate the principle gluconeogenic pathways for fat substrate (step 1) or for the release of energy within the avian cell (steps 2 and 3). Steps 4, 5, and 6 are the principle routes of entry of amino acids for gluconeogenesis. Steps 4, 5, 6, 7, and 8 also indicate entry of individual "glycogenic amino acids," whereas steps 9 and 10 indicate entry of "ketogenic amino acids," which also may be considered glycogenic in characteristic.

testinal loops *in situ,* has been replaced by studies employing isolated gut tissue rings, scraped intestinal mucosal cells, and everted (gut) sac prepara-

tions. Collectively, the data obtained indicate that active transport (energy dependent and against concentration gradients) of monosaccharides and possibly disaccharides occurs *in ovo* as well as throughout adulthood (Fearon and Bird, 1968; Bogner, 1966). Apparently, the absorption rate for various carbohydrates by the avian gut are generally higher than for most mammals when related to unit gut dimension (Bogner, 1966). When compared to mammals of equal body size, the avian rate of carbohydrate absorption is virtually identical as is the rate of individual monsaccharide absorption (D-galactose $\geq$ D-glucose, both $>$ D-xylose, which is $>$ D-fructose). The active transport of such sugars is readily apparent by day 18 in the chick embryo gut, appears to be most active in the middle segment of the small intestine, and increases in activity for at least 2 weeks after hatching. The increased activity occurs via increasing the number of carrier molecules rather than by altering the affinity of the carrier for sugar substrate (Bogner and Haines, 1964; Hudson *et al.*, 1971; Ziswiler and Farner, 1972). Reduction in oxygen availability, inhibition of simultaneous Na⁺ transport, and/or the simultaneous presence of competitive sugars (i.e., galactose vs. glucose) reduce chicken intestinal transport of monosaccharides (Holdsworth and Wilson 1967; Alvarado and Monreal, 1967).

## Distribution of Monosaccharides

Once transported from the mucosal (lumen) to the serosal (vascular) side, the carbohydrates are carried mainly in the plasma (over 98%); in fact, the very low levels of galactose and fructose in blood can be detected only in plasma. Carried to the liver via the portal vein, carbohydrates are subject to polymerization and storage, or anaerobic and oxidative glycolysis, or conversion to the lipoid moiety by pathways described above. Ultimately, of course, whether or not lipogenesis occurs, the substrate is degraded to $CO_2$ and $H_2O$ and energy is released. The metabolism of fructose and galactose by avian tissues has been studied in depth because of certain differences from mammalian metabolism of these sugars; a more detailed discussion of these two sugars is found below and in Hazelwood (1965, 1972) and Pearce and Brown (1971). Hepatic glycogen is synthesized quickly in birds after ingestion and absorption of glucose. In fact, even in the fasted chicken much of the ¹⁴C label on a test glucose meal appears in the glycogen molecule (within the first postprandial 2 hr), only to be released subsequently to the circulation (Lepkovsky *et al.*, 1960).

## Circadian and Temperature Effects

**Circadian.** Even under normal absorptive conditions, cyclic alterations in liver glycogen levels occur. The embryonic liver demonstrates at least two cycles a day, whereas the adult bird exhibits a more true circadian rhythm. Alterations (decrement with darkness) in liver weight and fat, and glycogen contents have been reported for many birds (blackbirds, starlings, chickens, etc.) when analyses are carried out 12 hr apart under otherwise identical conditions. Actually, if the day–night light pattern is reversed by 12 hr, hepatic glycogen levels are altered accordingly. Tweist and Smith (1970) have studied in detail the whole blood glucose rhythms in chickens under controlled lighting conditions. They found that daylight glucose levels averaged about 20–30 mg % higher than nighttime blood glucose levels. Quantitative assessment of blood and

plasma gludose and liver glycogen (as a major source of blood glucose), therefore, should always be made with care taken toward the impact of circadian and photoperiod rhythms (Smith, 1972).

**Temperature.** Ambient temperature, as well as circadian rhythm and hematocrit alterations, also has been shown to influence liver glycogen and plasma carbohydrate levels. Studies on 1-day-old chicks indicate that exposure to cold (20°C) leads to a nonshivering thermogenic response that probably does not depend on adrenal catecholamine release (Freeman, 1966). Metabolically, cold-exposed chicks respond with increased oxygen consumption, decreased plasma glucose levels (20%), decreased liver glycogen levels (50–70%), and increased free fatty acid levels (40%); again, in contrast to mammals, such responses probably are mediated by the liver rather than by increased adrenal medullary secretions (Freeman, 1966, 1967). Although adult birds subjected to cold environments respond with increased adrenal catecholamine biosynthesis and release (Lin and Sturkie, 1968), when they are subjected to heat stress no evidence of altered synthesis or release has been garnered. However, marked hepatic glycogenolysis (after a few minutes lag time) occurs in pigeons exposed to 48°C for a few hours concomitant with a modest rise in plasma glucose. Hepatic glycogenolysis occurs with either type deviation from "normal" ambient temperature, therefore, and plasma glucose alterations are not necessarily consistent with adrenomedullary secretory patterns. Although the basis (liver?) for these thermogenic and/or thermoglycemic responses is yet to be established it is known that double vagotomy abolishes the plasma glucose response of chickens exposed to heat stress (Hazelwood, 1965).

# PANCREATIC CONTROL OF AVIAN CARBOHYDRATE METABOLISM

## Insulin

Insulin can be extracted from a variety of avian organs (liver, kidney, spleen, etc.), yet the primary site of insulinogenesis probably is the pancreatic $\beta$ cell. Disquieting evidence exists indicating that the pancreas may not be the only source of the hormone. Such reports are from observations employing pancreatropic sulfonylureas in depancreatized fowl or use of alloxan and streptozotocin in normal, intact birds (for reviews see Langslow and Hales, 1971; Assenmacher, 1973; Hazelwood, 1972, 1973). The goose (and probably the owl)

218 behave more like mammals in their diabetic response to extirpation of the pancreas (reviewed by Hazelwood, 1965). The possibility that varying degrees of "completeness" of pancreatectomy is basic to these diverse reports (except the work done on the owls and geese) has been suggested by various workers (see Chapter 21; also Langslow and Hales, 1971; Hazelwood 1972, 1973). More work is needed to resolve the question surrounding a possible nonpancreatic source of insulin in Aves.

**Chemistry of avian insulin.** Evidence at hand indicates that avian insulin is synthesized at the pancreatic β-cell ribosomes as a "large" insulin molecule, namely as a proinsulin, which has a MW of 9100 daltons. Avain proinsulin is a single-chain polypeptide from which is cleaved the double-chain molecule containing two disulfide crosslinking bonds, as seen in Figure 11–3. Part of the A chain originally is connected by a biologically inert C peptide (connecting peptide) to the B chain. There is evidence indicating that considerable difference exists between the duck C peptide and that established for mammalian counterparts.

11–3 Comparison of the structure of chicken insulin with that of several established mammalian insulin structures. Turkey insulin is identical with the chicken molecule and duck insulin differs from chicken by substitution of Glu and Pro at position 8 and 10, respectively, on the A chain, and Thr at position 30 on the B chain.

After cleavage from the C peptide, the biologically active double-chain insulin molecule is condensed, forming β-cell granules enclosed by sac membranes. Different "pools" of stored avian insulin probably exist but when stimulated by the appropriate physiological stimulus, equimolar ratios of C peptide and the active hormone are released to the circulation. Largely through the efforts of Mirsky and Kawamura (1966), Smith (1966), and Kimmel *et al.* (1968), the isolation, homogeneity, amino acid composition and structure, and the phylogenetic placement of chicken insulin have been established. As indicated in Figure 11–3, the structure of chicken insulin is remarkably similar to that of most mammalian insulin structures, the A chain containing 21 amino acids and the B chain containing 30 amino acids. The alterations and replacements indicated in Figure 11–3 are moderate, indeed, and probably do not confer any conformational change to the avian molecule. In fact, chicken insulin differs structurally no more from established mammalian insulin structures than the latter do among themselves (Smith, 1966).

Biologically, the chicken insulin molecule is equally effective *in vitro* and *in vivo* when compared with pork, beef, and sheep insulins (Hazelwood *et al.,* 1968). Turkey insulin structure appears to be identical with that of chicken insulin, whereas duck insulin differs from the chicken molecule in the presence of glutamine and proline at positions 8 and 10, respectively, on the A chain and by threonine at position 30 on the B chain (Marhussen and Sundby, 1973). The primary peripheral receptor site for chicken insulin appears to be all three types of muscle, probably the liver and, to a much

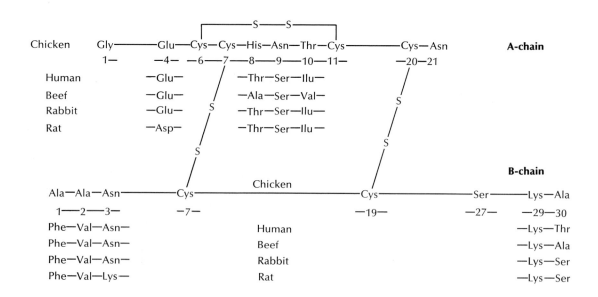

lesser degree, the adipocyte. The result is hypoglycemia caused by the intracellular translocation of glucose and probably by a permissive synergistic effect with that of glucagon (see Hazelwood, 1973).

## Avian Glucagon

Glucagon is secreted by the $\alpha_2$ cell of the avian pancreas; these reside in the so-called "dark islets," which also contain $\alpha_1$ cells (see Chapter 21). Most workers feel that a "proglucagon" molecule is synthesized first, that subsequently the inactive portion of the molecule is cleaved, and that the active hormone is therefore released as a single-chain polypeptide (Figure 11−4). Unlike the insulin content of the avian pancreas (which is approximately one-fifth to one-eighth that of mammalian tissue), the glucagon content appears to be at least four to eight times greater than levels found in equivalent amounts of mammalian pancreata (Langslow and Hales, 1971; Hazelwood, 1972, 1973).

All mammalian glucagon structures are identical, each possessing the same amino acid sequence of 29 residues. Three avian glucagon structures have been elucidated, two species differing from the known mammalian hormone by one residue (chicken and turkey) and one species (duck) differing by two residues (Figure 11−4). Although the aforementioned differences in sequence involve but one residue each, the substitution may be looked on as of considerable significance. Virtually no modification or substitution can be made in the mammalian structure without marked loss of biological activity. However, substitution in the mammalian hormone by serine for asparagine occurs in the chicken and turkey glucagon molecules at position 28 and provides the bird with a hormone that is extremely potent, regardless of what vertebrate species is employed as a test subject. Duck glucagon is similar in sequence to that of turkey and chicken but, additionally, has a threonine at position 16, replacing serine (Sundby and Frandsen, 1972). These singular substitutions have little effect on the physiological activity of the avian glucagons but they definitely lessen favorable cross-reactivity in immunoassay systems (Hazelwood, 1973).

Once released from the pancreatic "dark islets," avian glucagon appears to act on adenylcyclase enzyme associated with the plasma membrane. This enzyme cyclizes ATP, yielding adenosine 3',5'-monophosphate (cyclic AMP), which readily accumulates intracellularly. Cyclic AMP, often referred to as the "second messenger," then communicates the glucagon message internally to evoke a final path of hormone response, one of the minor effects

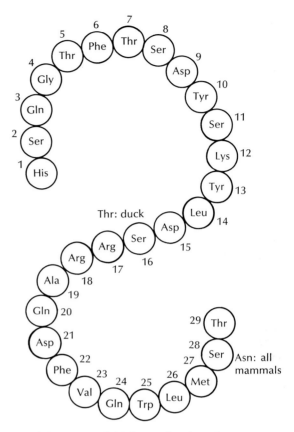

11−4 Structure of chicken and turkey glucagon polypeptides. Reported structures for all mammals are identical and differ from the chicken amino acid sequence only by one substitution, that of Asn for Ser at position 28. Duck glucagon has a replacement of Thr at position 16 to differ from the chicken.

being hepatic glycogenolysis and attendant hyperglycemia.

## Avian Pancreatic Polypeptide (APP)

The third avian pancreatic endocrine elaboration only recently has come under close biological scrutiny. Although all the classical criteria for a true hormone have not been met, this avian pancreatic secretion provokes both metabolic and digestive−secretogogic responses (Hazelwood *et al.*, 1973). The cellular origin of this avian pancreatic polypeptide (APP) is a cell extremely similar to the $\alpha_1$ type. Once released by the pancreas, the relatively high APP levels presented to the hepatocyte exert a carbohydrate and lipid effect; after perfusing the liver the peripherally "diluted" hormone exerts a gastric secretogogic effect specifically at the avian proventriculus (Hazelwood 1972; Hazelwood *et al.,* 1973; Chapter 10).

Structurally, APP has been established to be a linear polypeptide (MW 4200 daltons), distinct from other pancreatic hormones (Kimmel *et al.,* 1968, 1975) by the lack of disulfide linkages and by the presence of four proline, one isoleucine, and a cluster of basic residues near the tyrosine amide terminus (Figure 11–5). Interestingly, Lin and Chance (1972) have reported finding a very similar polypeptide of identical length in bovine, ovine, porcine, and human pancreata (Figure 11–5).

### Endogenous "Triggers" of Pancreatic Hormone Release

**Insulin.** Mechanisms of islet cell release of insulin in mammals have been studied extensively using perfused organ preparations, perifused islet preparations, and microdissected islet cells. What is known about the release of avian insulin, however, is based mainly on data obtained at the organismic level by the injection of "physiological" substances, and these studies have been carried out only in chickens and ducks.

Progressive fasting has little effect (also see below) on plasma insulin levels in ducks and chickens (Langslow and Hales, 1971); the injection of enough glucose to provoke a marked hyperglycemia doubles or triples normal insulin levels within 20 min in chickens. A similar response is observed

in response to an induced hyperaminoacidemia; both glucose and amino acids are more effective as insulin releasers when administered intravascularly than when given *per os* (Langslow and Hales, 1971; Hazelwood, 1973). Such observations contrast with those garnered from studies in mammals.

Evidence indicating endocrine regulation of insulin release from the chicken and duck β cell appears equivocal. Marked elevation of plasma glucose and free fatty acid (FFA) levels in response to glucagon injection, or the hyperglycemia (only) induced by epinephrine injections, are without effect on insulin release (Langslow and Hales, 1971). Contrarily, in ducks Mialhe (1969) reported an insulinogenic effect of infused glucagon that was disproportionate to the degree of hyperglycemia produced. Vagal stimulation and/or acetylcholine administration is without effect on the chicken insulin release mechanism.

**Glucagon.** Glucagon release from the avian $\alpha_2$ cells has been studied only in the duck (physiological stimulators) and in the chicken (exogenous provacators). The meager data available indicate that insulin injection increases, whereas glucose decreases, glucagon release and circulating plasma levels in ducks (Samols *et al.,* 1969). Pancreozymin (CKK) and free fatty acids are also effective releasers of pancreatic glucagon in the duck.

**APP.** No studies have been reported relative to hormone control of APP release.

### Pancreatectomy

Attempts to alter avian pancreatic content and/or release of hormones have been carried out for over 80 years, the methods ranging from classic surgical extirpation as employed in 1893 by Minkowski to the more recent use of α- or β-cytotoxic agents. Early reports were that "total" pancreatectomy was without permanent influence on carbohydrate metabolism in all graniverous and most carniverous avian forms. Recent attempts to remove

11–5 Structure of avian pancreatic polypeptide (APP): the relationship of this third pancreatic "hormone" with known mammalian homologs. These structures are readily distinguished from those of insulin, glucagon, C peptide, and gastrin. Major differences among several other mammalian pancreatic polypeptides appear to center around position 6, where either Gln or Val replaces Thr of the chicken molecule.

| | 1 | 2 | 3 | 4 | 5 | 6 | 7 | 8 | 9 | 10 | 11 | 12 | 13 | 14 | 15 | 16 | 17 | 18 |
|---|---|---|---|---|---|---|---|---|---|---|---|---|---|---|---|---|---|---|
| Chicken | Gly | Pro | Ser | Gln | Pro | Thr | Tyr | Pro | Gly | Asp | Asp | Ala | Pro | Val | Glu | Asp | Leu | Ilu |
| Bovine | Ala | — | Leu | Glu | — | Gln | — | — | — | — | — | — | Thr | Pro | — | Gln | Met | Ala |

| | 19 | 20 | 21 | 22 | 23 | 24 | 25 | 26 | 27 | 28 | 29 | 30 | 31 | 32 | 33 | 34 | 35 | 36 |
|---|---|---|---|---|---|---|---|---|---|---|---|---|---|---|---|---|---|---|
| Chicken | Arg | Phe | Tyr | Asp | Glu | Leu | Gln | Gln | Tyr | Leu | Asn | Val | Val | Thr | Arg | His | Arg | TyrNH$_2$ |
| Bovine | Gln | Tyr | Ala | Ala | — | — | Arg | Arg | — | Ilu | — | Met | Leu | — | — | Pro | — | — |

all pancreas (including the superior splenic isthmus) in the chicken, duck, and goose have been made, however, and the result has been a severe defect in carbohydrate metabolism that ultimately leads to hypoglycemic crisis and death (see reviews by Langslow and Hales, 1971; Hazelwood 1971, 1972; Assenmacher, 1973). Such observations imply that a regulatory endocrine mechanism has been upset by surgical removal of all pancreas.

Langlsow and Freeman (1972) employed partial pancreatectomy in young chickens to observe the effects on plasma glucose, FFA, and insulin levels. Hypoglycemia, instead of hyperglycemia, ensued and persisted for 72 hr; free fatty acids fell markedly also, glucose tolerance was impaired severely, and plasma insulin levels were decreased by 75%, which level persisted for 72 hr. Although such observations place a severe challenge to those workers who propose a secondary, nonpancreatic source of insulin in Aves, it is disquieting that any measurable insulin remains after 72 hr considering the very short half-life of the chicken hormone.

Pancreatectomy therefore reduces, but does not necessarily abolish, plasma insulin levels; however, assayable glucagon levels fall more precipitously, although not to nondetectable quantities. When the splenic lobe is intentionally left intact in chickens after partial pancreatectomy, the immediate transient hyperglycemia disappears within 4–5 days, a time course closely followed by the return of plasma insulin levels to normal. No information is available on the day-to-day postoperative fluctuations in glucagon levels after surgical ablation of the avian pancreas. Present data indicate that glucagon is the most important pancreatic hormone in regulating avian carbohydrate metabolism. Pancreatectomy in chickens also markedly reduces plasma APP levels to levels barely detectable by immunoassay techniques. However, as in the case of postoperative insulin levels, APP concentrations gradually increase to reach normal levels by day 4–5 after partial (95%) pancreatectomy.

## Pancreatropic and Pancreatoxic Agents

Intravenous or intracardiac injection of the $\beta$-cytotropic sulfonylurea, tolbutamide, produces a profound fall in blood glucose and free fatty acids in pigeons, geese, ducks, and chickens but not in owls (see reviews by Langslow and Hales, 1971; Hazelwood, 1972, 1973). Surprisingly, however, FFA levels decrease prior to that of glucose and no evidence of an inhibition of the adipokinetic effect caused by previous glucagon injection can be observed (Grande, 1971). Tolbutamide produces a

quick fall in duck plasma glucagon concomitant with a prompt increase in circulating insulin levels (Samols et al., 1969). These observations, when considered with those of Mirsky and Gitelson (1957) in enterectomized chickens and with those of Hazelwood (1958) in hepatect-pancreatectomized chickens, indicate the possibility of a secondary source of insulin in Aves. For example, tolbutamide injected into either of the above two surgical preparations results in an hypoglycemia, the onset, the nadir, and the duration of which equals that observed in similarly injected intact chickens. The fact that the insulin response to tolbutamide observed in ducks (Samols et al., 1969) was measured by immunoassay precludes explaining the hypoglycemic response of depancreatized preparations as being caused by an innate hypoglycemic action of tolbutamide. Also, injection of the sulfonylurea—which is considered a potent "release trigger" of preformed insulin—into chickens is without effect on circulating catecholamines; in contrast, injection of chicken insulin provokes an immediate and a marked increase in plasma epinephrine levels (Pittman and Hazelwood, 1973). The sulfonylurea may therefore release insulin from sequestered peripheral receptor–binding sites.

Attempts to stimulate or to destroy the glucagon-producing $\alpha_2$ cells have not been numerous, either because of the resistance of the avian dark ($\alpha$) islet to a particular experimental approach, or because of the toxicity of the cytotoxic agents employed. However, "total" pancreatectomy, in which special care is taken to remove the two main pancreatic lobes harboring most of the $\alpha_2$ cells, has been carried out in the chicken, duck, and goose (Hazelwood, 1973; Assenmacher, 1973). Such operations provoke a profound hypoglycemic crisis, quickly resulting in death of the bird unless glucose or glucagon is provided. $\alpha$-cytotoxic agents (such as Synthalin A or cobalt salts) cause a transient hyperglycemia and increased fatty acid levels, followed by a profound hypoglycemia. The hepatic glycogenolysis witnessed, however, is probably not caused by the $\alpha$-toxic nature of the agents. For example, mild destruction and/or degranulation of the chicken pancreatic $\alpha_2$ cell in response to Synthalin A does not support the marked metabolic effects observed; neither are these effects obtained by partial (85%) pancreatectomy (Langlsow and Freeman, 1973; Langslow, et al., 1973).

Colbalt salts, but not those of nickel or iron, have been reported to be $\alpha$-cytotoxic in mammals and some birds. However, careful reevaluation of these early reports indicate a disparity in experimental results observed and the use of this metal as

222 a glucagon release trigger is open to serious question (Freeman and Langslow, 1973).

Alloxan and streptozotocin have been employed unsuccessfully as potential diabetogenic agents in various species of birds. Although potent diabetogenic agents in all mammals, these two substances fail to destroy adequate insulinogenic ($\beta$ tissue) cells to produce a transitory, much less a permanent, diabetic state in pigeons, ducks, chickens, geese, owls, or various carniverous forms (Lukens, 1948; Hazelwood, 1965, 1972; Langslow and Hales, 1971). As a consequence, plasma insulin levels are unaltered by these two substances. Diazoxide, which inhibits insulin release in many mammals, causes a mild hyperglycemia in chickens concomitant with a modest depression of plasma insulin levels over a period of several hours (Langslow and Hales, 1971). More effective in producing a transitory diabetic state is the injection of an antiinsulin antibody. Mirsky et al. (1964) presented evidence that antiporcine insulin antibody (produced in guinea pigs), when injected into intact or "pancreatectomized" ducks, causes a prompt and marked hyperglycemia. The blood glucose of intact ducks returned to normal within 3 hr; however, a marked hyperglycemia remained in the operated ducks for at least 6 hr. These observations indicate that the insulin molecule, indeed, is essential for normal carbohydrate metabolism in ducks and inadequate insulin availability (as produced by the antibody–insulin interaction) precipitates an acute "diabetic" state.

Pharmacologic identification of specific receptor types within individual $\beta$ cells of the avian pancreas has received little investigative attention. However, as in the mammalian $\beta$ cell, available evidence suggests that when activated or stimulated the $\beta$-adrenergic receptor encourages release of insulin from the smaller (less than 2% of the total available) of two insulin "pools." Finally, there is a growing body of evidence indicating that the pancreatic content of insulin in Aves is about 20% of that found in mammals, that the small compartment reacts "sluggishly" to a glucose challenge, and that the insulinogenic reserve is considerably less than that observed in mammals (see review by Hazelwood, 1973).

### Temperature Effects

Ambient temperature is known to alter circulating glucose levels and hepatic glycogen depots in domestic fowl. Hyperthermia (if vagi are intact) induces hyperglycemia; hypothermia causes hypoglycemia; and hepatic glycostatic mechanisms move in the direction of homeostatic maintenance of normal blood glucose levels, even in the embryo. These alterations in plasma glucose and hepatic glycogen levels in response to ambient temperature changes do not depend on an intact pancreas; moreover, the observed effect of adrenal catecholamine release (in response to cold) would be expected to cause blood glucose and liver glycogen levels to change in ways opposite to those observed. Evidently, the changes observed are a reflection of altered rates of carbohydrate reactions independent of endocrine secretions, with hepatic glycogenolysis supporting normal plasma glucose availability.

### Circulation and Mechanism of Pancreatic Hormone Action

**Insulin.** Once released from the $\beta$ cell, avian insulin circulates normally at widely variable levels, depending on species, time of day, state of nutrition, and degree of physical activity. Most studies have been carried out in chickens and the data obtained indicate a "normal" circulating level of insulin of 30–40 $\mu$U/ml (1–2 ng/ml) plasma in 4- to 6-week-old chicks and 60–90 $\mu$U/ml plasma in 10- to 24-week-old adults. Ducks, which have a normoglycemia some 50–70 mg % below that of chickens, have plasma insulin levels approximately one-half those of young chickens. Data on insulin levels in other avian forms are not available. Chicken insulin has a half-life of 5–7 min and although a specific transport–binding protein has not been associated with the hormone, there is an indication that a small portion of the circulating molecule is associated with a heat-labile protein (Hazelwood, 1973). Certainly, injection of heterologous insulins into Aves leads to a complex binding of the hormone in the plasma, thus reducing the activity of the nonavian molecule markedly.

Chicken insulin is equally active, if not more so, as the major mammalian insulins at the peripheral tissue receptor site. Although the configuration of the avian insulin receptor site is yet to be elucidated, the receptivity of the chick embryonic heart to insulin has been observed. An "insulin-sensitive" cardiac membrane develops between days 7 and 8 in the chick embryo, allowing for the favorable intracellular translocation of glucose from the surrounding media. Before this time glucose uptake and metabolism is a function of media concentration (Guidotti and Foa, 1961). These observations, in conjunction with the effect of insulin on amino acid transport (with or without glucose), indicate a prime effect at the cell membrane, similar to that proposed for mammalian insulins and target tissues (Guidotti et al., 1966, 1968; Morgan and Neely, 1972). Goodridge (1968a,b) has provided the only other evidence of receptor site – hormone interaction as related to age; alterations in adipose tissue response to insulin can be detected when 19-day chick embryos are compared with 3-week-old chicks. Whether this represents a maturation of a tissue receptor site (as with the "cardiac membrane") or whether it represents an alteration in background "endocrine noise" that has prepared the adipocyte for insulin interaction is yet to be elucidated. The little evidence available indicates that avian insulin probably initiates specific cytoarchitectural changes favoring the intracellular translocation of glucose antecedant to its phosphorylation and subsequent metabolism (Hazelwood, 1972, 1973). In addition, insulin is not antilipolytic and, in some ways, appears to set the hormonal background for a synergistic action with glucagon.

**Glucagon.** Avian glucagon has been studied only very recently and, at that, largely from a molecular structure and composition point of view and as a potential regulator of insulin release in ducks and chickens. The only "metabolic" studies with crystalline avian (chicken) glucagon indicate an hepatic glycogenolytic action identical (but probably more powerful) to that observed with equivalent amounts of nonhomologous glucagons (Hazelwood et al., 1973). At this time, therefore it must be assumed that avian glucagon, which circulates in the 16-hr fasted duck at levels of 1 – 1.5 ng/ml (three to four times higher than humans), exerts its action at the periphery by interacting with membrane-bound adenyl cyclase. Although the half-life of avian glucagon is yet to be determined, its effects are usually rapid and transient, cyclyzing adenosine triphosphate (ATP) to form cyclic 3',5'-AMP, the so-called "second messenger" of hormone action. The quality of action is intrinsic to the particular cell involved, and the quantity of action is proportional to the amount of cyclic AMP formed initially concomitant with the amount of AMP-destructive phosphodiesterase available. Glucagon activation of adenyl cyclase, therefore, results in transmission of the hormone message intracellulary where cyclic AMP probably mediates all known effects of glucagon on liver, adipose tissue, heart, and probably the pancreas (Exton et al., 1972). Such effects include diverse activities as hormone release (pancreas), $Ca^{2+}$ and $K^+$ release (liver), lipolysis (adipose and hepatic tissue), protein catabolism (liver), and glycogenolysis (liver).

**APP.** Avian pancreatic polypeptide (APP) is released from the pancreas probably as a result of specific diet constituent(s) rather than of the physical presence of food. Neural pathways do not ap-

pear important to pancreatic APP activity, and once in circulation, the polypeptide is available at levels of 4 – 12 ng/ml plasma in the postabsorptive young chicken (Langlsow et al., 1973b). Fasting of chickens reduces these plasma levels by at least 50% within 24 hr and refeeding returns the APP levels quickly (within 20 – 30 min) to normal levels or above. APP induces hepatic glycogenolysis and probably fatty acid synthesis concomitant with hypoglycerolemia. A profound proventricular secratogogic effect of APP also has been reported (Hazelwood et al., 1973). This latter action is not mediated by release of gastric histamine and probably reflects a direct effect of APP on the chief cells of the proventriculus (Turner and Hazelwood, 1973).

## Peripheral Tissue Responses to Pancreatic Hormones

The most important organismic levels of impact for pancreatic hormones (in decreasing order of significance to the bird) are the liver, skeletal muscle, adipose tissue, cardiac muscle, and the erythrocyte.

**Liver.** Hepatic glycogen is markedly influenced by insulin injection in all avian species examined. The injection of (bovine) insulin at low or high doses into young or old, fed or fasted chickens causes a rapid hypoglycemia and, in fed birds only, a marked glycogenetic response, liver glycogen reaching levels 200 – 300% higher than fed control levels (reviewed by Hazelwood, 1965). These observations have been confirmed many times, by many workers, employing avian as well as nonavian insulin in a variety of bird species. They are summarized in Table 11 – 1. Although hepatic glucose uptake is not absolutely dependent on insulin presence, the fact remains that this hormone facilitates sugar transport in liver tissue and that intracellularly it increases glucokinase and glycogen synthetase activity. The end result is a lowering of blood glucose antecedent to increased hepatic synthesis and deposition of glycogen. The proteinaceous effects of insulin in Aves are similar to those observed in mammals; gluconeogenesis is drastically reduced as a result of decreased activity of those major enzymes that favor transformation of noncarbohydrate substrate to plasma glucose.

Both glucagon and APP cause glycogen hydrolysis in liver tissue, the former by the well-known cyclic AMP – phosphorylase activation sequence, and the latter by an unknown mechanism. However, only glucagon-induced hepatic glycogenolysis leads to an hyperglycemia; APP is without effect on

**Table 11−1**  *Tissue response of the chicken to insulin injections*[a]

| Type of bird | | Insulin dose (iv) (units/kg) | Hours since injection | Blood glucose (mg/100 ml) | Tissue glycogen (mg/100 g) | |
|---|---|---|---|---|---|---|
| Age (weeks) | Fed or fasted | | | | Liver | Pect. muscle (P) or heart (H) |
| 50–70 | Fed | — | — | 196 ± 6 | 4862 ± 526 | 152 ± 6  (H) |
| | Fed | 1 | 1/2 | 137 ± 5 | 4566 ± 600 | 148 ± 7  (H) |
| | Fed | 10 | 1/2 | 152 ± 6 | 4102 ± 622 | 158 ± 4  (H) |
| | Fed | 1 | 1 | 125 ± 7 | 4271 ± 714 | 139 ± 6  (H) |
| | Fed | 10 | 1 | 132 ± 8 | 3590 ± 801 | 146 ± 5  (H) |
| | Fed | 1 | 3 | 155 ± 7 | 3866 ± 682 | 138 ± 7  (H) |
| | Fed | 10 | 3 | 114 ± 11 | 3112 ± 542 | — |
| 6 | Fed | — | — | 196 ± 4 | 2404 ± 121 | 1150 ± 47 (P) |
| | Fasted 24 hr | — | — | 182 ± 4 | 364 ± 36 | 773 ± 30 (P) |
| | Fasted 24 hr | 1 | 2 | 87 ± 5 | 154 ± 32 | 763 ± 24 (P) |
| | Fasted 24 hr | 2 | 2 | 66 ± 5 | 132 ± 21 | 814 ± 10 (P) |
| | Fasted 24 hr | 5 | 2 | 49 ± 7 | 192 ± 23 | 844 ± 41 (P) |
| 4 | Fed | — | — | 188 ± 2 | 2550 ± 195 | 1168 ± 64 (P) |
| | Fed | 60 | 24 | 226 ± 10 | 4950 ± 202 | — |
| | Fasted 24 hr | — | — | 148 ± 2 | 260 ± 22 | 773 ± 20 (P) |
| | Fasted 24 hr | 120 | 24 | 182 ± 8 | 434 ± 119 | — |
| | Fasted 48 hr | — | — | 153 ± 4 | 326 ± 34 | 889 ± 26 (P) |
| | Fasted 48 hr | 120 | 24 | 201 ± 10 | 494 ± 82 | — |
| | Fasted 72 hr | — | — | 169 ± 3 | 248 ± 35 | 157 ± 15 (H) |
| | Fasted 72 hr | 120 | 24 | 223 ± 12 | 412 ± 64 | — |

[a]Data compiled from Opdyke (1942), Golden and Long (1942), Hazelwood and Lorenz (1959), Hazelwood (1960–1966, unpublished), and Pittman and Hazelwood (1968–1970, unpublished).

blood glucose levels, suggesting that the hydrolyzed polysaccharide is shunted to other pathways, presumably to fatty acid synthesis (Hazelwood *et al.,* 1973). Like mammalian muscle, avian skeletal and cardiac muscle do not contain phosphatase; activation of the phosphorylase system preparatory to splitting the $\alpha$-1,4-glucosyl linkages of muscle glycogen therefore results in three- and two-carbon fragment intermediates, which in turn are "fed" into the Krebs cycle; they do not contribute glucose molecules to the circulation.

Glucagon is known also to favor increased gluconeogenesis, mainly in the liver of birds, by increased levels and/or activity of phosphopyruvate carboxykinase. For example, avian hepatic cells respond to glucagon by increased amino acid uptake, increased gluconeogenesis, and a disposition toward ureogenesis from endogenous proteinaceous substrates. Even though the protein effects of glucagon are readily duplicated by cyclic AMP, the precise effect of glucagon on proteolysis is yet to be established.

Liver lipid metabolism is treated more thoroughly in Chapter 13. In contrast to the liver of mammals, the avian liver plays a major role in lipogenesis, deriving a large majority of the carbon skeletons required in the structure of fatty acids from ingested fructose, glucose, galactose, and mannose. Over 90% of the total body lipogenesis occurs in the avian liver, with very little contribution by the hexose monophosphate shunt in making available reducing equivalents for lipid formation (Annison, 1971; Hazelwood, 1972; and Chapter 13 for reviews).

Neither homologous nor heterologous insulins are antilipolytic in either *in vitro* or *in vivo* avian liver tissue systems. Instead, this hormone produces a profound ketonemia, hypertriglyceridemia, and hyperglycerolemia in young and adult chickens (but not owls or geese), all at the expense of liver and adipose depot sites (Heald *et al.,* 1965; Lepkovsky *et al.,* 1967; Langslow *et al.,* 1970; Grande, 1969, 1970). Hypoglycemia occurs, regardless of other species' variations, in response to insulin. Partial (85%) pancreatectomy in chicks also reduces plasma glucose and free fatty acids and severely impairs tolerance to glucose loads, but it has no effect whatsoever on the bird's hypertriglyceridemic and hyperglycemic responses to injected glucagon (Langslow and Freeman, 1972).

The major lipid effect of insulin may well be the potentiation of glucagon activity at both adipocyte and hepatocyte levels. The powerful avian response to the lipolytic action of glucagon is generally considered to be caused by activation of an intracellular lipase, resulting in mobilization of depot lipids and in lipemia. Minute amounts of glucagon also increase blood glucose and free fatty acids rapidly and markedly in ducks, geese, owls, and turkeys. This response is not prevented by simultaneous injection of insulin but it is depressed (at least in geese) by previous hepatectomy (Grande, 1969; Grande and Prigge, 1970). Actually, the lipolytic action of glucagon is so powerful in most birds that the liver "pulls out" circulating triglycerides, provided by the adipokinetic action on peripheral fatty tissues, and deposits them in the hepatocyte (Grande and Prigge, 1970). Glucagon also appears to inhibit the hepatic release of lipids. The infusion of either glucose or epinephrine fails to duplicate this action of glucagon, indicating that increased blood glucose levels per se are not responsible for the accumulation of lipid in the avian liver. Actually, the plasma free fatty acid, rather than plasma glucose, response to glucagon injections is better correlated in birds with varying doses of this pancreatic hormone (Grande, 1968).

**Skeletal muscle.** Glycogen levels of muscle increase slowly and steadily the first 13–14 days of embryonic life in chicks and then increase abruptly at days 14–18. Hexokinase levels of skeletal muscle parallel in activity those of glycogen levels and both begin a slow, steady decrease after day 18 to reach so-called "adult" glycogen and enzyme levels within the first 3 weeks of posthatch life.

The fact that high levels of both chicken and mammalian insulin are required to encourage glucose uptake and incorporation into muscle glycogen seems to indicate the relative refractoriness of avian abdominal muscle *in vitro* to this pancreatic hormone. However, the comparison of chicken insulin with several mammalian insulins in rat hemidiaphragm bioassays yielded results indicating that the avian hormone is as potent as the mammalian hormones in promoting glucose uptake by this thin skeletal muscle (Hazelwood *et al.*, 1968). Such apparent contradictions emphasize the importance of considering the hormone—receptor site complex when interpreting results because no hormone works in a physiologic vacuum.

**Adipose tissue.** Recent work on avian adipose tissue has clearly indicated the relatively minor role played by this tissue in avian carbohydrate and lipid metabolism (see Chapter 13). Although liver carbohydrate metabolism is closely tied to frequency and quality of dietary intake, fat deposits are relatively impervious to nutritional manipulation.

Glucagon is a powerful lipolytic agent in chick adipose tissue; in contrast to observations in mammals, insulin is not antilipolytic in birds. Instead it apparently intensifies glucagon's lipolytic action *in vitro* and *in vivo* (Langslow and Hales, 1969). Metabolism of glucose by fat depot cells is not markedly altered in the presence of insulin. The major effect of pancreatic hormones on avian adipose tissue therefore appears to be a rapid and marked glucagon activation of specific lipases (although not necessarily as a result of cyclic AMP mediation) which may be intensified by the synergistic presence of insulin (Grande *et al.*, 1972).

What role APP plays in adipose tissue metabolism is yet to be established, although data presented to date suggest a possible adipogenetic effect at the expense of depot glycogen (Hazelwood *et al.*, 1973).

**Cardiac muscle.** Glycogen accumulation within the embryonic chick myocardium occurs as early as day 3 and is known to be 20 times greater than in any other tissue. This glycogen moiety continues to increase up to day 13, only to decrease daily thereafter until hatching time. Such maxima and minima in levels of cardiac muscle glycogen reflect, in all probability, the onset of insulin secretion, the differentiation of cardiac lipases, and after day 13 the equalizing effects of various glycogenolytic hormones which are at that time becoming abundant. The end result is likely greater utilization of fatty acids by the embryonic heart, thereby sparing glycogen until day 13; subsequently, glucagon and circulating catecholamines increase and mobilize depot glycogen.

Fasting for 48 hours increases adult chicken cardiac glycogen levels from 100 mg per 100 g tissue to three times these levels; they decrease precipitously after fasting is ended. Such effects have been recorded in rats also and are dependent on hypophyseal release of growth hormone, which provides increased tissue lipolysis and spares glycogen. All other tissue glycogen depots are reduced markedly by fasting. Glucagon increases cardiac glycogen levels of nonfasted chickens but is without effect on these increasing levels in fasted chickens (Hazelwood and Lorenz, 1959).

**Erythrocytes.** The avian erythrocyte contains very little glucose; yet these cells contain nuclei and the enzymatic machinery to degrade (aerobic) glucose to final end products and release energy. They also consume very little, if any, glucose al-

226 though they actively take up oxygen (see review by Bell, 1971). The maintenance of avian erythrocytic function can therefore be expected to depend on some other form of energy substrate during the cell's life span. Fatty acid metabolism is the most likely contributor to the cell's viability, although critical evidence is lacking. Insulin is without effect on glucose uptake by chick erythrocytes. No data are available at this time on the possible effects of glucagon and/or APP on erythrocytic metabolism.

**Glycogen body.** The glycogen body is a pea-shaped, opaque structure located within the vertebral column, dorsal to the spinal cord, at the emergence of the sciatic plexus. As the name implies, this structure is heavily endowed with glycogen, e.g., up to 80% of its lipid-free weight. The molecular structure of the glycogen moiety of this avian body is consistent with what is known about glycogen molecules in other avian and mammalian tissues. The glycolytic enzymes are present in proximity with the glycogen granules but the carbohydrate levels are resistant to dietary, metabolic, and hor-monal manipulation (see review in Hazelwood, 1965, 1972). The significance of this glycogen-laden structure in birds therefore remains obscure and, until contrary evidence is presented it must be presumed to lie outside the avian metabolic–hormonal sphere.

## Summary of Pancreatic Control

Generally, birds have been reported to be very resistant to exogenous insulin, even to pharmacologic (convulsive producing) doses, and the essentiality of insulin in regulating normal carbohydrate metabolism has been questioned (Table 11–2). Evidence now accumulated indicates definite roles for insulin in Aves, one of facilitating glucose transport, one of adjusting tissue sensitivity to the impact of other hormones, and one of (intermediary) metabolism of circulating glucose. Insulin is essential for full expression of the metabolic effects observed at the cellular level (Hazelwood, 1973).

Birds respond quickly and markedly to the glycogenolytic and hypertriglyceridemic effects of

*Table 11–2  Avian resistance to heterologous insulin*

**A. Comparative lethal doses[a]**

| Species injected | Number of observations | Body weight (kg) | Lethal or convulsive dose (units/kg body wt.) |
|---|---|---|---|
| Chicken | 60 | 3.00 | 5000 |
| Canary | 24 | 0.12 | 2396 |
| Pigeon | 67 | 0.30 | 705 |
| Duck | 26 | 2.12 | 157 |
| Rabbit[b] | 49 | 1.89 | 5 |

**B. *In vivo* insulin sensitivity curves[c] (White Leghorn chicks, fed, 5 weeks old)**

| Crystalline insulin preparation | Dose injected | Number of observations | Plasma glucose (mg %): minutes after injection | | | | | | |
|---|---|---|---|---|---|---|---|---|---|
| | | | 0 | 20 | 40 | 60 | 80 | 100 | 120 |
| None | 0.2 ml NaCl | 14 | 202 | 204 | 204 | 192 | 194 | 206 | 206 |
| Chicken | 0.02 units/kg | 14 | 200 | 195 | 178 | 172 | 164 | 176 | 180 |
| Beef | 0.02 units/kg | 12 | 198 | 190 | 191 | 190 | 192 | 194 | 196 |
| Chicken | 0.2 units/kg | 14 | 206 | 176 | 171 | 168 | 162 | 169 | 184 |
| Beef | 0.2 units/kg | 12 | 206 | 176 | 175 | 174 | 182 | 181 | 194 |
| Chicken | 1.0 units/kg | 16 | 202 | 147 | 127 | 114 | 112 | 134 | 140 |
| Beef | 1.0 units/kg | 12 | 205 | 163 | 143 | 140 | 145 | 163 | 178 |
| Chicken | 2.0 units/kg | 16 | 199 | 157 | 84 | 82 | 80 | 74 | 60 |
| Beef | 2.0 units/kg | 12 | 196 | 166 | 128 | 138 | 128 | 131 | 136 |

[a]Taken from Chen *et al.* (1945).
[b]Used as reference species for establishing Standard International Unit.
[c]Compiled from Hazelwood *et al.* (1968) and Hazelwood (unpublished, 1966–1968).

glucagon; insulin appears to potentiate glucagon's adipokinetic effects.

The metabolic impact of APP remains to be clarified.

## HYPOPHYSEAL SECRETIONS AND CARBOHYDRATE METABOLISM

### Growth Hormone (GH) and Adrenocorticotropic Hormone (ACTH)

Growth and adrenocorticotropic hormones are among the most frequently employed hypophyseal hormones in studies devoted to investigating pituitary gland control of avian carbohydrate metabolism.

Injection of purified GH preparations into chicks does not alter plasma glycemic or liver glycogen levels; injected into adult nonfasted birds, pure GH encourages cardiac glycogenesis and increases glycogen levels by at least 100% 1 hr after injection, or by 300% after three once-daily injections (Hazelwood and Lorenz, 1959).

ACTH is virtually without effect on avian carbohydrate metabolism unless injected at supraphysiological levels. The evidence available indicates that all gluconeogenic and glycogenic effects observed after administration of ACTH are the result of corticosterone, and to a lesser extent hydrocortisone, released from the adrenal cortex (see Chapter 20). Hyperglycemia occurs within a few hours after ACTH injection to adult chickens; it is followed by hepatic glycogenesis as a result of inhibition of liver glycogenolytic enzymes.

Removal of the anterior pituitary gland in growing chickens leads to decreased body weights but greatly increased hepatic glycogen levels (King, 1969). However, in adult chickens the operation leads to a marked obesity, which reflects a defect in lipolysis concomitant with altered peripheral utilization of carbohydrate secretions. The injection of bovine GH or ACTH in small to large doses is without carbohydrate or lipid effects in adult chickens.

### Reproductive Hormones (FSH, LH, and LTH)

All attempts to study the carbohydrate metabolic effects of the gonadotrophic hormones have been made with what mammalian preparations as are/have been available. From such studies it is evident that FSH and LH have no direct action on the regulation of plasma glucose or tissue glycogen levels. What effects are observed can be attributed to hormonal secretions from the specific target (gonadal) tissues involved. Prolactin, however, may have a direct effect on avian carbohydrate metabolism. Hypophysectomy triples liver glycogen levels in pigeons. Injection of crystalline prolactin into pigeons and chicks results in marked hepatic lipogenesis (from glucose substrates) but is without much effect on abdominal fat pad lipid metabolism. Considered with Miller's (1942) study, wherein he has found that prolactin injections to pigeons (intact and hypophysectomized) increase size, number, and activity of pancreatic $\alpha_1$ cells, these data indicate a possible hypophyseal nontrophic hormone regulation of intermediary metabolism.

The strong possibility exists that prolactin release from pituitary may play a more significant regulatory role on carbohydrate metabolism than previously regarded. This release, which is known to occur in the vernal premigratory or nesting periods, may cause the well-known broodiness, cropsecretory activity, hyperphysical activity, restlessness, hyperphagia, etc., associated with these conditions. The release may also induce hyper-$\alpha_1$-cell activity and possible release of APP. Prolactin is known to act as an antiinsulin agent, to reduce pancreatic insulin levels, and to reduce the insulin sensitivity of pituoprivic mammals. Further research work is needed.

## PERIPHERAL ENDOCRINE CONTROL OF CARBOHYDATE METABOLISM

### Adrenal Cortical and Medullary Secretions

The relative absence of plasma cortisone in birds and the marked insensitivity of Aves to the carbohydrate effects of injected cortisone contrast greatly with observations made in mammals. Crude extracts of adrenal tissue (ACE) have been reported to cause modest plasma and tissue carbohydrate changes in normal pigeons and in ones lacking pancreatic, pituitary, thyroidal, or adrenal tissue; more marked glycemic and hepatic glycogenic increases occur in chickens. However, the composition of such adrenal extracts is open to question and the results obtained therein are subject to reevaluation. Greenman and Zarrow (1961) demonstrated the glycogenic efficacy of corticosterone and hydrocortisone (singly) in chicks and adult Leghorn chickens (Table 11-3). These data once again verify the relative impotency of cortisone *in vivo* as a regulator of avian tissue carbohydrate levels.

"Steroid diabetes" has been produced in young

*Table 11−3*  Blood glucose and liver glycogen responses to various adrenal steroids in the domestic fowl

| Group | Daily dose (mg) | Blood glucose[a] (mg/100 ml) | | Group | Liver glycogen[c] (mg/100 g liver) | |
|---|---|---|---|---|---|---|
| | | Initial | Maximum[b] | | Total dose | 10 hr postinjection |
| Control | — | 170 | 175 | Control | — | 248 |
| Hydrocortisone | 1.0 | 174 | 202 | Hydrocortisone | 25 $\mu$g | 356 |
| Hydrocortisone | 2.5 | 171 | 335 | Hydrocortisone | 50 $\mu$g | 662 |
| Hydrocortisone | 5.0 | 181 | 546 | Hydrocortisone | 100 $\mu$g | 738 |
| Corticosterone | 5.0 | 159 | 448 | Cortisone | 4 mg | 280 |
| Cortisone | 10.0 | 190 | 203 | Cortisone | 8 mg | 325 |
| Cortisone | 20.0 | 174 | 199 | Cortisone | 16 mg | 326 |
| Cortisone | 40−50 | 166 | 221 | Corticosterone | 200 $\mu$g | 348 |
| Desoxycorticosterone | 5 | 150 | 227 | Corticosterone | 400 $\mu$g | 466 |
| Stilbesterol | 1−2 | 181 | 193 | Corticosterone | 800 $\mu$g | 741 |

[a]Adult hens.
[b]Usually 1−3 days after start of daily injections.
[c]Chicks, 300−600 g, fasted 24 hr.

(8-weeks) cockerels by Stamler *et al.* (1954). "Depancreatized" cockerals injected daily with hydrocortisone and compared with uninjected birds exhibited an hyperglycemia (410 vs. 239 mg%), a lipemia (cholesterol: 1502 vs. 692 mg%), retarded body growth (942 vs. 1824g) and, in some injected birds, glycosuria. The hyperglycemia and the hepatic glycogen deposition observed by other workers are a reflection of glucocorticoid-induced gluconeogenesis. Nitrogen excretion increases in response to injected corticosterone and liver glycogen stores increase as protein (depot) catabolism continues. The glycogenic effect of the steroids is probably a direct one and the inhibitory effect on glycolytic enzymes is probably secondary. The hyperglycemia originates from glucogenic amino acids and is facilitated by an increased hexose phosphatase activity, thereby delivering "free" glucose to the plasma. Free fatty acids are elevated concomitantly (Heald *et al.,* 1965).

Epinephrine and norepinephrine are glycogenolytic and hyperglycemic agents in both mammals and birds. Most of the carbohydrate effects, however, are attibuted to the methylated form, epinephrine. This hormone is a powerful $\beta$-receptor activator and stimulates cyclization of ATP, resulting in marked liver and skeletal muscle glycogenolysis and lactic acidemia. Epinephrine is glycogenolytic and hyperglycemic in ducks, pheasant, pigeons, owls, chickens, and geese, and to a lesser extent, in turkeys and quail (Assenmacher, 1973). The observation by Hazelwood and Lorenz (1959) that daily injections of protamine zinc insulin into chickens leads to an hyperglycemic rebound 24 hr later, which is abolished by adrenal $\beta$-adrenergic blocking agents, implicates a compensatory catecholamine discharge. That this may, indeed, be a physiological homeostatic mechanism to make adequate blood glucose levels available is indicated further by the observation that exogenous insulin induces not only hypoglycemia in adult chickens but also a concomitant depression of circulating norepinephrine and elevation of epinephrine levels (Pittman and Hazelwood, 1973).

### Thyroid and Parathyroid Hormones

Early reports that thyroxine is an essential hormone in maintaining avian normoglycemic levels have been amply confirmed. As has been found in mammals, thyroid gland removal results in a mild hypoglycemia in doves, pigeons (Riddle and Opdyke, 1947), and ducks (Ensor *et al.,* 1970) but is without effect on skeletal muscle and glycogen body glycogen levels. Plasma glucose levels of chickens appear less influenced by thyroid extirpation. Chicks injected with iodine-131 or fed prophylthiouracil (while on a low-iodine diet) respond with both enlarged livers and glycogen levels 50 times greater than control chicks levels (Snedecor, 1968).

Contrarily, injection of thyroid hormone $T_3$ or $T_4$) either to fasted pigeons or to chicks leads to a delayed, although marked mobilization of hepatic glycogen, concomitant with a glycogenic action cardiac and skeletal muscle and an attendent hyperglycemia. The enzyme pattern as modified by injections of thyroxine in chicks has been studied in detail by Raheja *et al.* (1971a,b).

Earlier reports that parathyroidal extracts cause hyperglycemia in chicks and pigeons are open to question and merit reevaluation because of the "purity" of preparation then available. Highly purified forms of these two hormones had negative effects.

## Gonadal Hormones

Sex differences in circulating glucose levels of whole blood but not plasma in chickens have been reported, male birds having lower glucose levels than females (see Sturkie, 1965). Castration at an early age equates these glucose levels, whereas androgen injection into capons returns the male to levels of plasma glucose below those of female control chickens. Studies have indicated that the packed cell volume of chicken blood markedly changes in response to androgen injection; for example, administration of testosterone to capons increases the hematocrit, lowering the plasma compartment percentage and therefore the amount of organic substances (glucose, etc.) dissolved therein.

## EFFECTS OF FASTING AND ALTERED DIETARY INTAKE

### Effects of Starvation

The initial impact of the fasting state is depletion of hepatic glycogen to one-tenth (or even less) fed levels during the first 24–36 hr. Muscle glycogen is much more stable after starvation; however, the replenishment of these depots after muscular exercise or use is markedly delayed and diminished. In contrast, cardiac muscle glycogen levels increase during starvation, probably as a result of preferential fatty acid utilization and the resultant carbohydrate sparing.

As avian glycogen depots are mobilized during periods of food deprivation, levels and activity of glucose-6-phosphatase, pyruvate carboxylase, and phosphoenolpyruvate carboxykinase increase. This allows stabilization of blood glucose at levels high enough to support some activity but still somewhat lower than normal, fed blood glucose levels. Such gluconeogenic activity is accomplished at the expense of protein stores (see protein deprivation) and lipid depots (Langslow *et al.,* 1970); increased nitrogen excretion occurs and increased free fatty acid levels appear in the plasma. The plasma glu-

cose levels fall early during the fasting period, however, only to rise subsequently toward (but not to reach) normal nonfasted levels as a result of increased gluconeogenesis as the period of deprivation exceeds 48–72 hr.

In Aves, the injection of insulin consistently elevates plasma free fatty acids concomitant with intracellular translocation of glucose (Heald *et al.,* 1965; Lepkovsky *et al.,* 1967 Langslow *et al.,* 1970). Normally, circulating free fatty acid levels are dependent largely on intracellular availability of carbohydrate in most vertebrates. Therefore, any dietary, hormonal, or physiological manipulation acting to decrease available glucose substrate also encourages increased lipolysis, resulting in increased plasma levels of fatty acids. Because avian adipocytes, unlike those of mammals, are resistant to the lipolytic action of the catecholamines released and because depancreatized chickens (Lepkovsky *et al.,* 1967) respond similarly to intact control birds, release of glucagon by injected insulin cannot be cited as a reasonable explanation for the resulting hyperglyceridemia and hyperfattyacidemia. In birds (pigeons, finches, and chicks and in both intact and hypophysectomized adult chickens) fasting elevates circulating free fatty acids and decreases blood glucose (Heald *et al.,* 1965; Lepkovsky *et al.,* 1967; Langslow *et al.,* 1970). In this respect, birds react to starvation in a manner indistinguishable from mammals, yet the mechanism of response must be different considering that epinephrine in physiological amounts is without effect on avian adipose depots (Langslow and Hales, 1969). It appears that the more mild plasma glucose excurisons during starvation of birds are a result of fatty acid mobilization and utilization as well as of increased gluconeogenesis at the expense of protein stores. Both mechanisms provide substrate to sustain the avian organism and thereby both either "spare" plasma glucose or add to the circulating pool of carbohydrate by metabolic conversions. In both mammalian and avian heart muscle glycogen levels actually double or triple in response to a 48–72 hr fast (Hazelwood and Lorenz, 1959).

### Protein Deprivation

Fasting is known to decrease insulin availability, and therefore glucose availability, in most vertebrates. Gluconeogenesis is stimulated markedly in birds in response to fasting; however, if fasted chicks are fed a diet free of protein but high in dextrose, the high plasma lysine and threonine levels usually observed are reduced toward normal concentrations. Insulin injections similarly reduce

230 plasma amino acid levels of fasted pullets (Shao and Hill, 1967). Evidently, the intracellular availability of dextrose facilitates the curtailment of rampant protein catabolism during fasting. Urinary carbohydrate excretion increases as dietary protein intake decreases.

### Lactose Tolerance

Feeding diets varying in quantities of the disaccharide lactose as well as of the pentoses l-arabonose or *d*-xylose to chickens results in marked depression of growth, diarrhea, reduced egg production and feed efficiency, retardation of liver and intestine size and cellularity, and depletion of liver and skeletal muscle glycogen levels. Blood glucose rises, as do cholesterol and uric acid levels (Wagh and Waibel, 1966). It therefore appears that absorption of these sugars, pentoses particularly, does not meet the energy substrate needs of the chicken and, as a result, protein catabolism and free fatty acid metabolism are accelerated. Intracellular translocation of glucose appears to be hindered also.

### Fructose Metabolism

Diets containing high levels of fructose are tolerated well by domestic fowl. Metabolism of fructose by the avian (chicken) liver occurs rapidly and efficiently and is unimpeded by the simultaneous availability of glucose. This is not the case in mammals. That avian liver metabolism of fructose is more efficient than that of glucose is indicated by a respiratory quotient exceeding unity when liver tissue is incubated with fructose as substrate, by the finding that sucrose replacement of glucose in the diet leads to higher hepatic cholesterol levels, and by the observation that hepatic lipogenesis by tissue slices in a fructose media exceeds that observed when glucose replaces fructose (Heald, 1963; Hawkins and Heald, 1966; Pearce and Brown, 1971). It therefore appears that metabolism of fructose and its conversion to lipid rank high in metabolic priority for domestic fowl. The speed with which chickens phosphorylate fructose to fructose-1-phosphate appears to explain the efficacy with which avian liver forms acetyl-CoA from this sugar and does so to a greater extent than that from glucose.

### Galactose Toxicity

Studies on galactose metabolism in domestic fowl have been numerous because of the readily observable toxicity that subsequently develops. Such experimental interest is furthered by reports that the gut absorption coefficient for galactose exceeds that of glucose, although both hexoses are transported by active processes. Dietary levels of galactose below 10% are innocuous, physiologically, in domestic fowl; above 10%, however, dietary galactose induces a central nervous system disorder characterized by epileptiform convulsions. Replacement of 50% of the diet with galactose in chickens leads to high blood galactose levels, normal blood glucose and muscle glycogen levels, lowered hepatic glycogen levels, severe renal dysfunction and damage, convulsive seizures, and ultimately death. Female birds are more sensitive to galactose toxicity than are males (Mayes *et al.*, 1970). Accumulation of brain galactose-1-phosphate apparently is caused by a reduction in galactose-1-phosphate uridyltransferase activity. In addition to a reduction in the levels of all glycolytic intermediates in the brain of galactose-fed chickens, there is also a significant reduction in ATP and phosphocreatine. The growing body of evidence, therefore, indicates that the complete metabolism of galactose by the intoxicated chicken is not the result of a single enzyme or cofactor and that the accumulation of tissue galactose-1-phosphate suppresses normal glucose oxidation (see reviews by Hazelwood, 1965; Pearce and Brown, 1971). The above effects may ultimately be traced to the molecular level, considering the well-known competition of glucose with galactose for the same carrier (transport) molecule in vertebrate systems.

## REFERENCES

### *General Reviews*

Bell, D. J., and B. M. Freeman (Eds.). (1971). "Physiology and Biochemistry of the Domestic Fowl," Vols. I, II, and III. London: Academic Press.

Drummond, G. I. (1967). Muscle metabolism. *Fortschr. Zool., 18,* 359.

Farner, D. S., and J. R. King (Eds.). (1972) and (1973). "Avian Biology," Vols. II and III. New York: Academic Press.

George, J. C., and A. J. Berger. (1966). "Avian Myology." New York: Academic Press.

Romanoff, A., (1967). "Biochemistry of the Avian Embryo." New York: John Wiley & Sons.

### *Selected Papers*

Alvarado, F., and J. Monreal. (1967). Na+-Dependent active transport of phenylglucosides in the chicken intestine. *Comp. Biochem. Physiol., 20,* 471.

Annison, E. F. (1971). Lipid and acetate metabolism. In "Physiology and Biochemistry of the Domestic Fowl," Vol. I (D. J. Bell and B. M. Freeman, Eds.). London: Academic Press, Chapter 12.

Assenmacher, I. (1973). The peripheral endocrine glands. In "Avian Biology," Vol. III (D. S. Farner, and J. R. King, Eds.). New York: Academic Press, Chapter 3.

Bell, D. J. (1967). Some monosaccharides in hen's urine. *Comp. Biochem. Physiol., 20,* 523.

Bell, D. J. (1971). Plasma glucose. In "Physiology of the Domestic Fowl," Vol. 2 (D. J. Bell and B. M. Freeman, Eds.). London: Academic Press, Chapter 39.

Bell, D. J., and P. D. Sturkie (1965). In "Avian Physiology" (2nd ed.) (P. D. Sturkie, Eds.). Ithaca, N. Y.: Cornell University Press, Chapter 2.

Bogner, P. H. (1966). Development of sugar transport in the chick intestine. *Biol. Neonat., 9,* 1.

Bogner, P. H., and I. A. Haines. (1964). Functional development of active sugar transport in the chick intestine. *Am. J. Physiol., 207,* 37.

Chen, K. K., R. C. Anderson, and N. Maze. (1945). Susceptibility of birds to insulin as compared with mammals. *J. Pharmacol. Exp. Ther., 84,* 74.

Ensor, D. M., D. H. Thomas, and J. G. Phillips. (1970). Possible role of thyroid in extrarenal secretion following a hypertonic saline load in the duck. *J. Endocrinol. 46,* X (Abst.).

Exton, J. H., G. A. Robison, and E. W. Sutherland. (1972). Glucagon and cyclic AMP. In "Handbook of Physiology," Sect. 7, "Endocrinology," Vol. I (N. Breinkel and D. F. Steiner, Eds.). Baltimore: Williams and Wilkins, Chapter 27.

Fearon, J. R., and F. H. Bird. (1968). Site and rate of active transport of D-glucose in the intestine of the fowl at various initial glucose concentrations. *Poultry Sci., 47,* 1412.

Freeman, B. M. (1966). The effects of cold, nor-adrenaline and adrenaline upon the oxygen consumption and carbohydrate metabolism of the young fowl. *Comp. Biochem. Physiol., 18,* 369.

Freeman, B. M. (1967). Some effects of cold on the metabolism of the fowl during the perinatal period. *Comp. Biochem. Physiol., 20,* 179.

Freeman, B. M. (1969). The mobilization of hepatic glycogen in *Gallus domesticus* at the end of incubation. *Comp. Biochem. Physiol., 28,* 1169.

Freeman, B. M., and D. R. Langslow. (1973). Responses of plasma glucose, free fatty acids and glucagon to cobalt and nickel chlorides by *Gallus domesticus. Comp. Biochem. Physiol., 46A,* 427.

Goodridge, A. G. (1968a). Lipolysis *in vitro* in adipose tissue from embryonic and growing chicks. *Am. J. Physiol., 214,* 897.

Goodridge, A. G. (1968b). Metabolism of glucose-U-¹⁴C *in vitro* in adipose tissue from embryonic and growing chicks. *Am. J. Physiol., 214,* 897.

Goodridge, A. G. (1968c). Citrate-cleavage enzyme, malic enzyme and dehydrogenases in embryonic and growing chicks. *Biochem. J., 108,* 663.

Golden, W. R. C., and C. N. H. Long. (1942). The influence of certain hormones on the carbohydrate levels of the chick. *Endocrinology, 30,* 675.

Grande, F. (1968). Effect of glucagon on plasma free fatty acids and blood sugar in birds. *Proc. Soc. Exp. Biol. Med., 128,* 532.

Grande, F. (1969). Lack of insulin effect on free fatty acid mobilization produced by glucagon in birds. *Proc. Soc. Exp. Biol. Med., 130,* 711.

Grande, F. (1970). Effects of glucagon and insulin on plasma free fatty acids and blood sugar in owls. *Proc. Soc. Exp. Biol. Med., 133,* 540.

Grande, F. (1971). Effect of tolbutamide on plasma-free fatty acids and blood sugar in birds. *Proc. Soc. Exp. Biol. Med., 137,* 548.

Grande, F., and W. F. Prigge (1970). Glucagon infusion, plasma FFA and triglycerides, blood sugar, and liver lipids in birds. *Am. J. Physiol., 218,* 1406.

Grande, F., W. F. Prigge, and M. de Oya. (1972). Influence of theophylline on the adipokinetic effect of glucagon *in vivo. Proc. Sco. Exp. Biol. Med., 141,* 774.

Greenman, D. L., and M. X. Zarrow. (1961). Steroids and carbohydrate metabolism in the domestic bird. *Proc. Soc. Exp. Biol. Med., 106,* 459.

Guidotti, G., and P. Foa. (1961). Development of an insulin-sensitive glucose transport system in chick embryo hearts. *Am. J. Physiol., 201,* 869.

Guidotti, G., A. Borghetti, G. Gaja, L. Loreti, G. Ragnotti, and P. Foa. (1968). Amino acid uptake in the developing chick embryo heart. *Biochem. J., 107,* 565.

Guidotti, G. G., L. Loreti, G. Gaja, and P. P. Foa. (1966). Glucose uptake in the developing chick embryo heart. *Am. J. Physiol., 211,* 981.

Hawkins, R. A., and P. J. Heald. (1966). Lipid metabolism and the laying hen: IV. The synthesis of triglycerides by slices of avian liver. *Biochim, Biophys. Acta, 116,* 41.

Hazelwood, R. L. (1958). The peripheral action of tolbutamide in the fowl. *Endocrinology, 63,* 611.

Hazelwood, R. L. (1965) Carbohydrate metabolism. In "Avian Physiology" (2nd ed.) (P. D. Sturkie, Ed.). Ithaca, N.Y.: Cornell University Press, Chapter 12.

Hazelwood, R. L. (1971). Endocrine control of avian carbohydrate metabolism. *Poultry Sci., 50:*9.

Hazelwood, R. L. (1972). The intermediary metabolism of birds. In "Avian Biology," Vol. II, (D. S. Farner and J. R. King, Eds.). New York: Academic Press, Chapter 8.

Hazelwood, R. L. (1973). The avian endocrine pancreas. *Am. Zool., 13,* 699.

Hazelwood, R. L., and F. W. Lorenz. (1959). Effects of fasting and insulin on carbohydrate metabolism of the domestic fowl. *Am. J. Physiol., 197,* 47.

Hazelwood, R. L., J. R. Kimmel, and H. G. Pollock. (1968). Biological characterization of chicken insulin activity in rats and domestic fowl. *Endocrinology, 83,* 1331.

Hazelwood, R. L., S. D. Turner, J. R. Kimmel, and H. G. Pollock. (1973). Spectrum effects of a new polypeptide (third hormone?) isolated from the chicken pancreas. *Gen. Comp. Endocrinol., 21,* 485.

Heald, P. J. (1963). The metabolism of carbohydrate by liver of the domestic fowl. *Biochem. J., 86,* 103.

Heald, P. J., P. M. McLachlan, and K. A. Rookledge. (1965). The effects of insulin, glucagon and adrenocorticotropic hormone on the plasma glucose and free fatty acids of the domestic fowl. *J. Endocrinol., 33,* 83.

Holdsworth, C. D., and T. H. Wilson. (1967). Development of active sugar and amino acid transport in the yolk sac and intestine of the chicken. *Am. J. Physiol., 212,* 233.

Hudson, D. A., R. J. Levin, and D. H. Smyth. (1971). Absorption from the alimentary tract. In "Physiology and Biochemistry of the Domestic Fowl," Vol. I (D. J. Bell and B. M. Freeman, Eds.). London: Academic Press, Chapter 3.

Kimmel, J. R., L. J. Hayden, and H. G. Pollock. (1975). Isolation and characterization of a new pancreatic polypeptide hormone. *J. Biol. Chem.,* in press.

Kimmel, J. R., H. G. Pollock, and R. L. Hazelwood. (1968). Isolation and characterization of chicken insulin. *Encodrinology, 83,* 1323.

King, D. B. (1969). Effect of hypophysectomy of young cockerels, with particular reference to body growth, liver weight and liver glycogen level. *Gen. Comp. Endocrinol., 12,* 242.

Langslow, D. R., and B. M. Freeman. (1972). Partial pancreatectomy and the role of insulin in carbohydrate metabolism in *Gallus domesticus. Diabetologia, 8,* 206.

Langslow, D. R., and B. M. Freeman. (1973). Investigations into the mode of action of Synthelin A in *Gallus domesticus. Comp. Biochem. Physiol., 46A,* 447.

Langslow, D. R., and C. N. Hales. (1969). Lipolysis in chicken adipose tissue *in vitro. J. Endocrinol., 43,* 285.

Langslow, D. R., and C. N. Hales. (1971). The role of the endocrine pancreas and catecholamines in the control of carbohydrate and lipid metabolism. In "Physiology and Biochemistry of the Domestic Fowl," Vol. I (D. J. Bell and B. M. Freeman, Eds.). London: Academic Press, Chapter 21.

Langslow, D. R., E. J. Butler, C. N. Hales, and A. W. Pearson. (1970). The response of plasma insulin, glucose and nonesterified fatty acids to various hormones, nutrients and drugs in the domestic fowl. *J. Endocrinol., 46,* 243.

Langslow, D. R., B. M. Freeman, and K. D. Buchanan. (1973a). Responses of plasma glucose, free fatty acids, glucagon and insulin to Synthalin A by *Gallus domesticus Comp. Biochem. Physiol., 46A,* 437.

Langslow, D. R., J. R. Kimmel, and H. G. Pollock. (1973b). Studies of the distribution of a new avian pancreatic polypeptide and insulin among birds, reptiles, amphibians and mammals. *Endocrinology, 93,* 558.

Lepkovsky, S., A. Chari-Bitron, R. Lemmon, R. Ostwald, and M. Dimick. (1960). Metabolic and anatomic adaptations in

232

chickens "trained" to eat their daily food in two hours. *Poultry Sci., 39,* 385.

Lepkovsky, S., M. K. Dimick, F. Furuta, N. Sapir, R. Park, N. Narita, and K. Komatsu. (1967). Response of blood glucose and plasma free fatty acids to fasting and to injection of insulin and testosterone in chickens. *Endocrinology, 81,* 1001.

Lin, T. M., and R. E. Chance. (1972). Spectrum gastronintestinal actions of a new bovine pancreas polypeptide (BPP). *Gastroenterology, 62,* 852. (Abstr.)

Lin, Y. C., and P. D. Sturkie. (1968). Effect of environmental temperatures on the catecholamines of chickens. *Am. J. Physiol., 214,* 237.

Lukens, F. D. W. (1948). Alloxan diabetes. *Physiol. Rev., 28,* 304.

Marhussen, J., and F. Sundby. (1973). Duck insulin: Isolation, crystallization and amino acid sequence. *Intl. J. Peptide Protein Res., 5,* 37.

Mayes, J. S., L. R. Miller and F. K. Myers. (1970). The relationship of galactose-1-phosphate accumulation and uridyl transferase activity to the differential galactose toxicity in male and female chicks. *Biochem. Biophys. Res. Comm., 39,* 661.

Mialhe, P. (1969). Some aspects of the regulation of carbohydrate metabolism in birds. In "Progress in Endocrinology (C. Gual, Eds.). Intl. Congr. Ser. No. 184. Amsterdam: Excerpta Med. Foundation, p. 158.

Migliorini, R. H., C. Linder, J. L. Moura, and J. A. Veiga. (1973). Gluconeogenesis in a carnivorous bird (black vulture). *Am. J. Physiol., 225,* 1389.

Miller, R. A. (1942). Effects of anterior pituitary preparations and insulin on islet cells of the pigeon pancreas. *Endocrinology, 31,* 535.

Mirsky, I. A., and S. Gitelson. (1957). Comparison of the hypoglycemic action of tolbutamide in the fowl and other species. *Endocrinology, 61,* 148.

Mirsky, I. A., and S. Gitelson. (1958). The diabetic response of geese to pancreatectomy. *Endocrinology, 63,* 345.

Mirsky, I. A., and K. Kawamura. (1966). Heterogeneity of crystalline insulin. *Endocrinology, 78,* 1115.

Mirsky, I. A., R. Jinks, and G. Perisutti. (1964). Production of diabetes mellitus in the duck by insulin antibodies. *Am. J. Physiol., 206,* 133.

Morgan, H. E., and J. R. Neely. (1972). Insulin and membrane transport. In "Handbook of Physiology," Sect. 7, "Endocrinology," Vol. 1, "Endocrine Pancreas" (D. F. Steiner and N. Freinkel, Eds.). Baltimore: Williams and Wilkins Co., Chapter 20.

Nelson, N., S. Elgart, and I. A. Mirsky. (1942). Pancreatic diabetes in the owl. *Endocrinology, 31,* 119.

O'Hea, E. K., and G. A. Leveille. (1968). Lipogenesis in isolated adipose tissue of the domestic chick. *Comp. Biochem. Physiol., 26,* 111.

O'Hea, E. K., and G. A. Leveille. (1969). Lipid biosynthesis and transport in the domestic chick *(Gallus domesticus). Comp. Biochem. Physiol., 30,* 149.

Opdyke, D. F. (1942). Response of fasted and non-fasted chicks to insulin. *Endocrinology, 31,* 363.

Pearce, J., and W. O. Brown. (1971). Carbohydrate metabolism. In "Physiology and Biochemistry of the Domestic Fowl" Vol. 1 (D. J. Bell and B. M. Freeman, Eds.). London: Academic Press, Chapter 11.

Pittman, R. P., and R. L. Hazelwood. (1973). Catecholamine response of chickens to exogenous insulin and tolbutamide. *Comp. Biochem. Physiol., 45A,* 141.

Raheja, K. L., J. G. Snedecor, and R. A. Freedland. (1971a). Activities of some enzymes involved in lipogenesis, gluconeogenesis, glycolysis and glycogen metabolism in chicks from day of hatch to adulthood. *Comp. Biochem. Physiol., 39B,* 237.

Raheja, K. L., J. G. Snedecor, and R. A. Freedland. (1971b). Effect of propylthiouracil feeding on glycogen metabolism and malic enzyme in the liver of the chick. *Comp. Biochem. Physiol., 39B,* 833.

Riddle, O., and D. F. Opdyke. (1947). The action of pituitary and other hormones on the carbohydrate and fat metabolism of young pigeons. *Carnegie Inst. Publ., 569,* 49.

Samols, E., J. Tyler, and P. Mialhe. (1969). Suppression of pancreat-

ic glucagon release by the hypoglycemic sulfonylureas. *Lancet, 2,* 174.

Shao, T. C.I and D. C. Hill. (1967). A comparison of the effect of dietary fat and carbohydrate on free amino acids in blood *plasma of chicks. Can. J. Physiol. Pharmacol, 45,* 225.

Smith, C. J. V. (1972). Blood glucose levels in young chickens: the influence of light regimes. *Poultry Sci., 51,* 268.

Smith, L. (1966). Species variation in the amino acid sequence of insulin. *Am. J. Med., 40,* 662.

Snedecor, J. G. (1968). Liver hypertrophy, liver glycogen accumulation, and organ-weight changes in radio-thyroidectomized and goitrogen-treated chicks. *Gen. Comp. Endocrinol., 10,* 277.

Stamler, J., R. Pick, and L. N. Katz. (1954). Effects of cortisone, hydrocortisone and corticotrophin on lipemia, glycemia and atherogenesis in cholesterol-fed chicks. *Circulation, 10,* 237.

Sundby, F., and E. K. Frandsen. (1972). Crystallization and amino acid sequence of duck glucagon. *Fed. Eu. Biol. Sci. Letters, 26,* 39.

Turner, S. D., and R. L. Hazelwood. (1973). Does histamine play a role in the secretogogic effect of avian pancreatic "gastrin"? *Proc. Soc. Exp. Biol. Med., 144,* 852.

Tweist, G., and C. J. Smith. (1970). Circadian rhythm on blood glucose level of chickens. *Comp. Biochem. Physiol., 32,* 371.

Wagh, P. V., and P. E. Waibel. (1966). Metabolizability and nutritional implications of 1-arabinose and *d*-xylose for chicks. *J. Nutr., 90,* 207.

Wallace, J. C., and E. A. Newsholme. (1967). A comparison of the properties of fructose 1,6-diphosphatase, and the activities of other key enzymes of carbohydrate metabolism, in the livers of embryonic and adult rat, sheep and domestic fowl. *Biochem. J. 104,* 378.

Ziswiler, V., and D. S. Farner. (1972). Digestion and the digestive system. In "Avian Biology," Vol. II (D. S. Farner and J. R. King, Eds.). New York: Academic Press, Chapter 6.

# 12

## Protein Metabolism

Paul Griminger

234 The "Elementary Compendium of Physiology for the Use of Students," the first modern textbook of physiology, appeared in 1817. The author, Francois Magendie, expounded the idea of a division of the "proximate principles of animals" into nitrogenous and nonnitrogenous matter. Twenty years later, Gerardus Mulder of Utrecht coined the term "protein" on the, albeit erroneous, supposition that such nitrogen-rich organic compounds as fibrin, egg albumen, and gluten contained a common basic component. The discovery of the real basic components of protein, the amino acids, stretched over more than a century, culminating with the discovery of threonine by Rose in 1935. For detailed historical accounts of these developments, McCollum (1957) and Munro (1964) should be consulted.

One-fifth to one-quarter of the fat-free body of mammals and birds is protein (Mitchell *et al.,* 1931; Griminger and Gamarsh, 1972). Because of variations in body fat content (mostly between 5 and 20%), which are only partially balanced by adjustments in water content, whole body protein is somewhat more variable.

In birds, as much as 20 to 30% of the body protein may be found in the feathers. Other structural proteins are found in bone, muscle, and skin. The regulatory role of protein is exemplified by enzymes, plasma proteins, and such transport proteins as hemoglobin. Proteins can also play a functional role by supplying energy in the course of their degradation; this is of special importance for carnivorous species. There are clearly more similarities than differences among the protein metabolism of mammals, birds, and reptiles, and the principal differences are in the nature of the end products. As described in more detail in the section on nitrogen excretion, the principal end product is urea in mammals and uric acid or related compounds in birds and reptiles.

Much of the available information on avian protein metabolism has been derived from experiments with *Gallus domesticus* (chicken), although *Columba* (pigeon) and other domestic species have received their share of attention. Information on wild species is extremely scanty, and this is a fertile field of comparative biochemical research for the future.

## ABSORPTION

The digestion of dietary protein and the hydrolysis to amino acids have been discussed in Chapter 11. The amino acids enter the organism by way of the portal circulation almost entirely in the free form. It should be understood that not all of the amino acids absorbed are derived from the proteins in the ingesta. As is the case in mammals, an appreciable amount of amino acids is contributed by the hydrolysis of desquamated intestinal mucosal epithelial cells and of digestive enzymes. It has been estimated that the mucosal cells of the jejunum of very young chicks are replaced in approximately 48 hr, somewhat more slowly in the more proximal and distal parts of the intestinal tract (Imondi and Bird, 1966).

### The Absorptive Process

Kratzer (1944) concluded from a series of experiments that amino acid absorption in the chick was a function of the rate of diffusion and was not controlled by any cellular metabolism. More recent work is at variance with this view, indicating an active absorption process. Contradictory viewpoints and some of the problems incurred in absorption have been discussed by Bird (1968). In general, the transport pathways in avian intestine seem to be similar to those of mammals, although they differ in detail. Absorption occurs by attachment to a specific site, presumably on the mucosal epithelial membrane, and when different sites appear to be involved, it is usual to speak of different "pathways." Lerner (1971) concluded from his experiments and those of others that in the chicken there are at least three separate absorptive pathways for neutral amino acids: a system for methionine and related aliphatic compounds, one for glycine, and one for proline and related amino acids. There is, furthermore, a distinct pathway for basic amino acids. It is less clear whether a specific pathway exists for the absorption of the acidic amino acids.

The existence of pathways for groups of amino acids entails competition among the members of a group in the absorptive process. Among the neutral amino acids, methionine and leucine inhibited the transport of alanine and of glycine in jejunal sacs of chicken intestine incubated *in vitro* (Sheerin and Bird, 1972). In other *in vitro* experiments leucine was a strong inhibitor of arginine uptake, whereas the influence of arginine on leucine uptake was slight. Methionine inhibited the absorption of leucine and phenylalanine competitively. However, methionine also inhibited glutamic acid, a member of the acidic amino acid family (Tasaki and Takahashi, 1966). Apparently the absorption sites exhibit preference rather than exclusiveness. The complexity of absorption mechanisms is highlighted by the findings of Burrill and Lerner (1972) that proline uptake occurs partly in a leucine-shared system and partly in one shared with other cyclic secondary amino acids. Additional and separate evidence on the heterogeneity of the neutral amino acid transport system across the avian intestinal wall was obtained by the same group (Miller *et al.*, 1973) by the use of model amino acids specially synthesized for this purpose.

The natural isomers (L-amino acids) are generally more rapidly absorbed than the D forms. A common but L-preferring site exists for the transport of both isomers. Other neutral L-amino acids have a high affinity for this site, whereas the D-isomers, except for D-methionine, have a very low affinity (Lerner and Taylor, 1967). Both L- and D-amino acids therefore seem to be transported actively, albeit at different rates, and, to a degree, in competition with each other.

By the use of a pyridoxine antagonist, Tasaki and Yokota (1970) have shown that the absorption of amino acids from the chick intestine is vitamin B$_6$ dependent.

### Absorption Rates and Sites

Nitrogenous compounds disappear rapidly from the intestine of chickens. In 6-week-old birds, four-fifths of the nitrogen leaving the duodenum was shown to have been removed from the gut in the adjacent section (upper jejunum) of the intestinal tract (Bird, 1968).

The more distal segments may play a more important role in the absorption of amino acids derived from endogenous protein, because the latter is not digested as rapidly as exogenous protein, an observation not restricted to birds (Crompton and Nesheim, 1969). These authors also noted that in Khaki Campbell ducks, the central portion of the intestinal tract (the middle fifth of the total intestinal length) contains the largest quantity of free amino acids. When segments of everted chicken intestine were incubated with lysine, the duodenum, jejunum, and ileum accumulated the amino acid at a similar rate, whereas ceca and colon–rectum slices accumulated appreciably less amino acid in the same period of time (Wakita *et al.*, 1970). With-

in the jejunum, the proximal third accumulated the greatest amount of glutamic acid, methionine, or lysine. The absorption of amino acids can therefore take place in essentially all sections of the avian small intestine, albeit at varying rates.

Because of incomplete hydrolysis and a consequent relative scarcity of free amino acids, actual amino acid absorption in the duodenum is slight; it is again low in the distal parts of the small intestine, for the bulk of amino acids have been absorbed previously. This is demonstrated in Table 12–1, which shows the cumulative percent protein digested and absorbed by 3-week-old chicks receiving high-protein (20%) and low-protein (14.4%) diets. This digestive study was based on the ratio of trichloroacetic acid nonextractable nitrogen to yttrium-91 and the absorption study on the ratio of total nitrogen to yttrium-91, the latter serving as a reference substance in both cases.

If the natural flow of ingesta is impeded by artificial separation of sections of the gastrointestinal tract, absorption can occur even in the most proximal parts. Teekell *et al.* (1967) found that threonine was absorbed from the crop and gizzard as well as from the proventriculus and the duodenum when these sections were ligated and injected with [¹⁴C] threonine. However, absorption at the latter two locations was appreciably greater than from the crop and gizzard.

The hydrogen ion concentration in the gut lumen influences the rate of absorption. Using Thiry-Vella fistulas and five pH levels from 2.6 to 10, Ivanov and Ivanov (1962) observed maximum absorption of a protein hydrolyzate at a pH of 6.8 from the small intestine of adult chickens.

## AMINO ACIDS

### Essential Amino Acids

It is customary to classify amino acids as essential and nonessential. Clearly, all amino acids nor-

*Table 12–1* *Cumulative digestion and absorption of protein nitrogen in 3-week-old chickens on a low (14%) and high (20%) protein diet*[a]

| Section | Length (cm) | Cumulative digestion (%) | | Cumulative absorption (%) | |
|---|---|---|---|---|---|
| | | Low-protein | High-protein | Low-protein | High-protein |
| Duodenum | 23 | 58.6 | 62.6 | 3.9 | 11.5 |
| Upper jejunum | 22.5 | 75.8 | 79.8 | 55.0 | 57.4 |
| Lower jejunum | 22.5 | 85.5 | 84.1 | 70.8 | 69.9 |
| Upper ileum | 23.5 | 90.9 | 90.5 | 79.5 | 78.5 |
| Lower ileum | 23.5 | 92.3 | 93.2 | 82.9 | 83.8 |

[a]Adapted from Hurwitz *et al.* (1972).

236 mally found in tissues are biologically essential and the classification really pertains to their dietary essentiality. Eight amino acids are considered essential for all higher animals (Table 12–2). Chickens, turkeys, and probably other domestic fowl require arginine in addition to these eight; growing and egg-producing fowl require histidine as well. Cystine and tyrosine are synthesized from methionine and phenylalanine, respectively, and their adequacy therefore depends on the supply of these

**Table 12–2** *Nutritionally essential amino acids*

| For maintenance of all species of higher animals | |
| --- | --- |
| Isoleucine | Phenylalanine |
| Leucine | Threonine |
| Lysine | Tryptophan |
| Methionine | Valine |

| For growth and/or maintenance of many species | |
| --- | --- |
| Histidine | Arginine |

| Under certain conditions | |
| --- | --- |
| Cystine | Tyrosine |
| Glycine | Proline |

12–1 Ornithine cycle. Enzyme systems: (1) carbamyl phosphate synthetase, (2) ornithine transcarbamylase, (3) argininosuccinate synthetase, (4) succinase, (5) arginase.

two essential amino acids. Glycine (or serine) has been considered essential for optimum growth by several authors, as discussed by Hewitt and Lewis (1972), and proline improves growth of chicks during their second week (Greene *et al.*, 1962). A mixture of glycine, proline, and glutamic acid that supplies one-third of the dietary nitrogen adequately meets the needs for all nutritionally dispensible amino acids (Stucki and Harper, 1961).

## Metabolic Pathways

**Ornithine cycle.** Starting in the 1960's, investigations of avian liver and kidney enzyme systems have thrown light on some of the peculiarities of avian amino acid metabolism.

In mammalian liver, reversal of the reactions of ornithine catabolism can lead to ornithine synthesis. Ornithine, by way of the urea cycle, can serve as a source of arginine (Figure 12–1). The effectiveness of this pathway for the supply of arginine varies among mammalian species, and is very low, if it exists at all, in chickens and probably other birds. Chickens cannot synthesize ornithine except from arginine and cannot convert ornithine to citrulline. This conversion requires carbamyl phosphate, which is synthesized in the liver of ureotelic ani-

mals from ammonia, biotin-activated carbon dioxide, and ATP in the presence of carbamylphosphate synthetase. In the chicken, this key enzyme is absent (Tamir and Ratner, 1963). When citrulline is provided, however, arginine can be synthesized in the avian kidney.

Young chicks can convert ornithine and therefore arginine to proline (Figure 12–2). However, the amount of proline synthesized in this manner is insufficient for adequate growth (Austic, 1973a). Proline synthesis by this pathway is not stimulated by excess arginine or ornithine, and ornithine-δ-transaminase as well as the conversion of Δ¹-pyrroline-5-carboxylic acid may be the rate-limiting reaction.

In experiments by Shen *et al.* (1973a), exogenous α-ketoglutaric acid greatly stimulated the *in vitro* conversion of ornithine to both Δ¹-pyrroline-5-carboxylic acid and proline. Employing ¹⁴C-labeled glutamic acid the same authors also demon-

12–2 Proline synthesis from ornithine. Enzyme systems: (1) ornithine-δ-transaminase, (2) pyrolline-5-carboxylic acid dehydrogenase, and (3) pyrolline-5-carboxylic acid reductase.

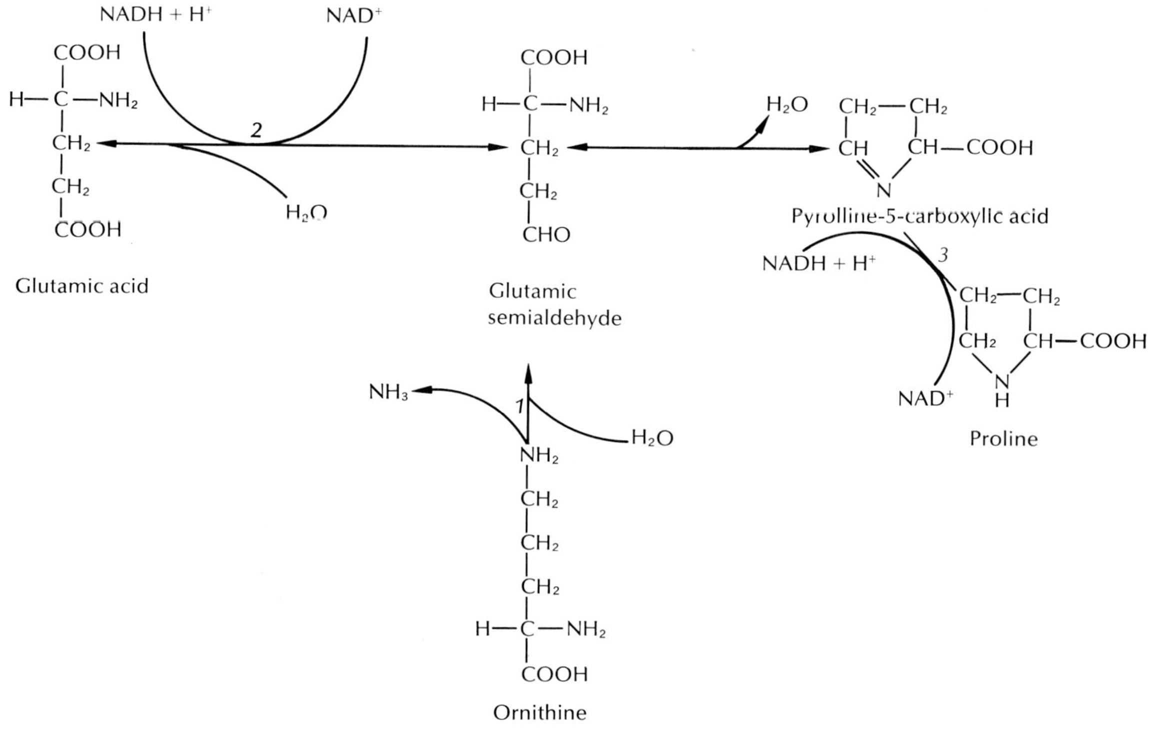

238 strated *in vivo* and *in vitro* that glutamic acid can be converted to proline (Shen *et al.,* 1973b).

**Glycine.** There is no agreement about the ability of the chicken to satisfy its glycine needs by synthesis alone. Graber and Baker (1973) estimated from their experiments that 60–70% of the glycine needed for maximal growth of chicks could be synthesized. Earlier work from the same laboratory had shown that sarcosine and betaine could be demethylated, or glycolic acid aminated, to yield glycine and that dietary serine could completely replace glycine. However, on the basis of growth studies as well as the lack of effect of excess threonine on plasma glycine levels, their claim was disputed by D'Mello (1973).

**Cystine and tyrosine.** It is well established that tyrosine (hydroxyphenylalanine) has a sparing effect on phenylalanine, as does cystine on methionine, because tyrosine can be readily synthesized from phenylalanine and cystine from methionine. If there is ample dietary intake of tyrosine or cystine, the actual requirement for methionine and phenylalanine is reduced. This sparing effect, of course, is limited to the requirement for the two nonessential amino acids, and they cannot replace the basic needs for phenylalanine and methionine. An exception to this was claimed by Ishibashi (1972), who maintained adult White Leghorn males in positive nitrogen balance on a phenylalanine-free, tyrosine-containing diet. There was some body weight loss, however. Tracer studies indicated some conversion of tyrosine to phenylalanine, but the rate of conversion seemed quite insufficient to compensate for the lack of dietary phenylalanine.

The addition of an oxygen atom to phenylalanine in the synthesis of tryosine increases the molecular weight by approximately 10%. In theory this means that more tyrosine for protein synthesis can be provided per unit of weight by dietary phenylalanine than by dietary tyrosine, if a similar efficiency of absorption is assumed for the two amino acids. The experimental work of Sasse and Baker (1972) shows that there is at least equivalency in the efficiency with which these two amino acids supply tyrosine for protein synthesis.

In the conversion of methionine to cysteine in mammals, removal of a methyl group first leads to homocysteine. The addition of serine results in cystathione, which is then split into cysteine and $\alpha$-ketobutyrate, with the loss of one amino group. It is assumed that birds utilize the same pathway. During protein synthesis cystine is created by the formation of disulfide bonds between two cysteine molecules. In the final analysis, two molecules of methionine are therefore required for each molecule of cystine in protein; therefore 100 g dietary methionine are required to produce 80.5 g of cystine. Indeed, experiments in our laboratory indicate that less dietary methionine than cystine, per unit of weight, is required to satisfy the cystine requirement of adult birds for nitrogen balance. Graber and Baker (1971), in contrast, found that the molar efficiency of methionine, 1/2-cystine, and cysteine were alike and that, on a weight basis, less of a methionine–cystine combination was needed than of methionine alone. The problem is made somewhat more complex by the absorption rates of the two amino acids. Although there are no comparative measurements in birds, it is possible that the rate of absorption of L-cystine is lower than that of L-methionine. Furthermore, cystine probably must be split into cysteine for incorporation into peptides, to be recombined later.

Dietary guanidoacetic acid accelerates the conversion of methionine to cysteine, whereas creatine, betaine, and choline have the opposite effect. The latter compounds accentuate the symptoms of nutritional muscular dystrophy in vitamin E-deficient chicks, and the acceleration of the conversion reduces their severity. Hathcock and Scott (1966) considered this additional proof that cysteine, not methionine, was the metabolically active sulfur amino acid aiding in the prevention of nutritional muscular dystrophy in vitamin E-deficient chicks.

The conversion of methionine to cystine is more efficient in White Leghorns than in Black Australorps, an Australian breed of domestic chickens, but contrary to earlier reports the latter are able to convert methionine to cystine in significant amounts (Miller *et al.,* 1960).

The methionine hydroxy analog can replace methionine in the diet of chickens. The conversion of the hydroxy analog into methionine involves the formation of a keto acid as an intermediate (Gordon and Sizer, 1965). This keto acid also serves as an intermediate in the conversion of D- to L-methionine (Figure 12–3). The amino group of leucine, and probably also that of other amino acids, participates in the transamination reaction.

When most of the methionine is supplied by the L-methionine of protein-containing foods, as is the case with birds eating natural feed, equimolar levels of the OH analog are approximately equivalent to methionine in nutritional value. In amino acid diets, however, L-methionine is superior to DL-methionine, and the latter is superior to the OH analog (Smith, 1966). The efficiency of conversion may depend on the availability of suitable amino group donors, which in practical terms may mean a surplus of certain amino acids.

12–3
The amination of methionine
hydroxy analog.

Hydroxy analog      Keto acid      Leucine      Methionine

## Amino Acid Isomers

Although most ingested D-amino acids can probably be catabolized to yield energy, incorporation into structural or functional proteins requires prior conversion to the corresponding L-isomer. It is generally assumed that this involves conversion to an α-ketoacid by action of liver or kidney D-amino acid oxidase, followed by transamination. D-amino acids may be absorbed less efficiently than the corresponding L-isomers; furthermore, they differ in their susceptibility to attack by D-amino acid oxidase; the conversion also depends on the total amount of D-isomers present. The ingestion of significant amounts of several D-amino acids causes a growth depression that may be a result of competition for the oxidase. According to Kamath and Berg (1964) D-amino acids ingested by rats fall into several categories: those fully, or nearly fully, convertible to the L-amino acid (methionine and tryptophan, respectively); those with intermediate replacement value (phenylalanine, arginine, histidine); those with very little replacement value for the L isomer (leucine, valine); and those essentially without replacement value (lysine, isoleucine, threonine). Sugahara and coworkers (1967) developed a similar classification for the growth-promoting value of 16 D-amino acids in chickens. Among the essential amino acids, they assigned equal or nearly equal replacement values for the L-isomers to D-methionine, D-phenylalanine, D-leucine, and D-proline. They considered D-valine to have half the replacement value; D-tryptophan, D-isoleucine, and D-histidine to have little replacement value; and the D-isomers of lysine, threonine, and arginine to have none. These categories not only differ substantially from those mentioned above for rats but some details are also at variance with the experience of other researchers. For example, Fisher et al. (1957) observed relatively poor utilization of D-phenylalanine, listed above in the high replacement value category.

In general, the nitrogen from D-amino acids is used as efficiently, or only slightly less efficiently, than that from excess indispensable L-amino acids for the synthesis of dispensable amino acids, depending on the criteria used (Featherstone et al., 1962). An excess of nonessential D-amino acids, however, may cause varying amounts of growth depression (Maruyama et al., 1972). D-Serine seems to be deaminated in chicken liver and kidney by serine dehydratase: even at the 2% level it did not depress growth. D-alanine depressed growth at the 1.5% level, and D-aspartic acid was deleterious even at only 1% of the diet. Accumulations of the latter two amino acids in the plasma pool indicated a limited capacity for their oxidation.

## Amino Acid Imbalance and Toxicity

Excessive intake of one or more of the essential amino acids may cause growth depression and, in some cases, specific symptoms. The terms "imbalance," "antagonism," and "toxicity" are used to describe variations of this condition. According to Harper et al. (1970), an amino acid imbalance is created when amino acids other than the growth-limiting one are added to a low-protein diet, causing depression in food intake and growth. It can be readily prevented by supplementation with the limiting amino acid. Amino acid antagonism, in contrast, can be alleviated by supplements of structurally similar amino acids but not by supplementation with the amino acid that is limiting in the basal diet. The term "toxicity" applies to conditions where an adverse effect is caused by a large surplus of an individual amino acid. An imbalance, in contrast, is created where the excess of one or more amino acids can be overcome by increasing the level of the limiting amino acid. Fisher et al. (1960) have a different definition for an amino acid imbalance. The addition of a protein or amino acid supplement may decrease the ratio of the most limiting amino acid to the sum total of

240 available amino acids. If this decrease is such that the amount of the most limiting amino acid is below the minimum requirement for optimum performance, an "imbalance" is created.

The literature on the effects of the ingestion of disproportionate amounts of amino acids in various species prior to 1970 has been excellently reviewed by Harper *et al.* (1970). Of special interest in birds is the antagonism between arginine and lysine. Excess dietary lysine decreases arginine efficacy by accentuating the arginine deficiency (Allen and Baker, 1972). It was later shown that the antagonism was not at the absorption level (Kardivel and Kratzer, 1974).

Kidney arginase synthesis can be induced by elevated levels of tissue and plasma lysine. An excess of cations (potassium acetate) reduces kidney arginase activity; when arginine is the limiting amino acid, this excess consequently increases arginine as well as lysine incorporation into protein (Stutz *et al.*, 1972). The authors hypothesize that the excess cations may reduce lysine transport into kidney cells and therefore diminish the subsequent induction of kidney arginase. Other workers (as reviewed by Austic and Nesheim, 1972) have discussed urinary losses of arginine caused by competition of lysine with arginine for renal tubular reabsorption, and the depression of liver transamidinase activity caused by excess lysine (*see* also Chapter 14). Transamidinase is the enzyme system responsible for the transfer of the amidine group of arginine to glycine in the synthesis of glycocyamine (guanidoacetic acid) which, in the presence of "active" methyl groups and ATP, forms phosphocreatine. It is therefore not surprising that excess arginine increases the demand for methyl groups, and a concommitant growth depression may be the expression of a relative deficiency of methionine, choline, or other factors needed to supply these methyl groups (Keshavarz and Fuller, 1971).

Lysine–arginine antagonism as well as the growth-depressing effect of excess leucine apparently do not operate on the level of appetite regulation (Harper *et al.*, 1970; D'Mello and Lewis, 1971). An excess of leucine specifically increases the requirement for isoleucine and valine (Bray, 1970).

**Inherited response to deficiency.** The growth response of chickens on an arginine-deficient diet is more variable than that of chickens subjected to a comparable deficiency of other amino acids. An inherited growth potential on arginine-low diets was demonstrated in a random-bred flock by Griminger and Fisher (1962) and between different strains by Nesheim and Hutt (1962). The latter

workers believed that the inherited differences were polygenic. Kidney arginase was found to increase in response to casein-based, arginine-deficient diets in high-requirement strains but not in those having a low requirement (Nesheim *et al.*, 1971). The increased arginase activity alone, however, cannot explain the different ability to grow on arginine-low diets, because a substantial growth differential still remains when arginase activity is suppressed by feeding 0.5% α-aminoisobutyric acid. High-requirement chicks, in response to the casein diet, also have a much higher lysine–arginine plasma ratio, which is believed to depress feed intake. It was indeed shown that the low-requirement strain had a higher level of lysine-ketoglutarate reductase, the initial degradation enzyme of lysine (Wang *et al.*, 1973).

**Methionine toxicity.** Methionine has repeatedly been shown to be the most toxic amino acid when ingested in excess (Boorman and Fisher, 1966). Information on methionine toxicity in rats has been reviewed by Harper *et al.* (1970); the effect of high levels of methionine and related compounds on chickens was described by Griminger and Fisher (1968) and on guinea pigs by Hardwick *et al.* (1970).

## Metabolic Transformations of Amino Acids

Because the dietary essential and semiessential amino acids, plus a source of amino nitrogen such as glutamic acid, ensures the wellbeing of birds, there must be provisions for the biosynthesis of serine, alanine, aspartic acid, asparagine, glutamic acid, glutamine, and especially for collagen synthesis, hydroxylysine, and hydroxyproline. Not only is there similarity in the metabolic pathways of nitrogenous compounds in various vertebrate species and, beyond that, in all animal species, but avian tissues have been used as a basis for the observations of many investigators and have thus become the source of a body of generalized information on pathways of amino acid metabolism.

Of special importance among the metabolic transformations are transamination, the transfer of an amino group from one carbon skeleton to another, and deamination, culminating in the excretion of the amino group. Amino group transfers are catalyzed by pyridoxal 6-phosphate-containing enzyme systems. An example of transamination is the transfer of an amino group from ornithine to α-ketoglutaric acid to form glutamate, a reaction catalyzed by ornithine-α-transaminase (Figure 12–2).

More frequently cited are the transaminases that remove the $\alpha$-amino group of an amino acid, such as aspartate transaminase, which catalyzes an exchange of an amino group between a five- and a four-carbon amino acid. In this sequence, glutamic acid is deaminated to $\alpha$-ketoglutarate, while oxaloacetate is aminated to aspartate, or vice versa (I). Glutamic acid can also be either deaminated or synthesized without involvement of a receptor or donor acid (II). Such deamination initiates the complete catabolism of glutamate and removal of ammonia and is mediated by glutamate dehydrogenase, an enzyme containing nicotinic acid. Glutamic acid therefore plays a central role in a complex system regulating amino nitrogen metabolism. Although oxidative deamination, mediated by L-amino oxidases, has also been observed in avian tissues, it is not clear whether it plays a significant role in avian nitrogen metabolism.

Glutamate + $\alpha$-ketoglutarate
$$= \text{oxaloacetate} + \text{asparate} \quad (I)$$
Glutamate + $NAD^+$ + $H_2O$
$$= \alpha\text{-ketoglutarate} + NADH + H^+ + NH_4^+ \quad (II)$$
Glutamate + ATP + $NH_4^+$
$$= \text{glutamine} + ADP + P_i \quad (III)$$

Carbamylphosphate synthetase (CPS), which is found in mammals and in some other classes of animals, is absent in chickens (Figure 12–1). The uptake of ammonia, however, can be catalyzed by other enzyme systems. One of these is glutamate dehydrogenase, in a reversal of the reaction (II) mentioned above. Another is glutamine synthetase (III). In this reaction, ammonia combines with glutamate in the presence of $Mg^{++}$ and of adenosine triphosphate as a source of energy to yield glutamine.

Carbamyl phosphate is an essential precursor of uridylic acid, which in turn is the precursor for other pyrimidines utilized in the synthesis of ribo- and deoxyribonucleic acids. The absence of the enzyme synthesizing this compound has been given as the reason for the lack of arginine synthesis in birds. Clearly, however, birds do synthesize pyrimidines. Jones (1970) offers a possible solution to this dilemma. Apparently there are two types of CPS. One of these, CPS I, is located in the mitochondria and is not found in Aves. It occurs in conjunction with ornithine transcarbamylase (Figure 12–1), which is also found in low concentration in birds. Their livers, however, contain CPS II, which occurs with aspartate transcarbamylase in the soluble supernatant. Although not active in the synthesis of arginine and, eventually, urea, CPA II may provide carbamyl phosphate for pyrimidine synthesis. This hypothesis requires further confirmation.

## Amino Acid Degradation

The deaminated carbon skeletons of amino acids can serve as a source of energy for the organism. They are converted to intermediates that ultimately form either glycogen or fat and are, accordingly, classified as glucogenic or ketogenic. Leucine belongs to the latter group, whereas isoleucine, lysine, phenylalanine, tyrosine, and threonine may be either ketogenic (by way of acetyl-CoA) or glycogenic. All other amino acids are considered glycogenic.

Part of the tryptophan ingested by chickens—as well as by the rabbit, rat, dog, man, pig, and probably other species—is converted to nicotinic acid. Fisher et al. (1955) observed that 50 mg dietary L-tryptophan replaced approximately 2.5 mg nicotinic acid; few biochemical details of this pathway have been published for the chicken, but there is reason to believe that it is similar to that established for mammals. Kment and Steininger (1961) also observed increased formation of serotonin (5-hydroxytryptamine) when supplemental tryptophan was given to adult chickens. Serotonin occurs in relatively high levels in birds (see Chapter 3).

Contradictory evidence regarding the utilization of excess threonine for glycine synthesis has been previously presented (p. 238). Although this amino acid does not participate in transamination reactions, carbon-14 from labeled threonine can be found in the carbon chains of several amino acids within hours of administering them orally to chicks (Teekell et al., 1967).

Lysine is degraded in chicken liver by an L-amino acid oxidase and lysine-ketoglutarate reductase, leading to the formation of pipecolic acid and saccharopine, respectively. Carbon-14 studies indicate that the saccharopine pathway may be the major one for the in vivo degradation of L-lysine in chicks (Wang and Nesheim, 1972). Both metabolites are subsequently converted to $\alpha$-amino adipate and eventually to $CO_2$. D-Lysine is catabolized via pipecolate, which is further metabolized. In this the chicken differs from the rat, and probably other mammals, which excrete pipecolate in the urine without further catabolism (Grove and Roghair, 1971). These authors think that the rapid elimination of the catabolic products of both lysine isomers speaks against a conversion of D- to L-lysine; however, if the capacity to catabolize D-amino acids readily were common to birds, it would be useful for the utilization of D-amino acids found in insects and other lower animal forms ingested by birds. There seems to be a similar difference between birds and mammals in the degradation of D-hydroxylysine (Hiles et al., 1972).

242    Proline is probably oxidized to glutamate and then to α-ketoglutarate. Austic (1973b) has studied the effect of dietary proline on (single comb White Leghorn) chicken enzyme systems involved in this pathway; he observed that in the absence of dietary proline, increased levels of liver pyrolline-5-carboxylic acid dehydrogenase were present (Figure 12–2). Although it is unclear why this increase occurs, it is possible that it reflects an increase in the activities of the enzyme complex for proline synthesis.

Brown (1970) has tabulated many of the enzyme systems found to be involved in nitrogen metabolism in avian tissues.

**Biogenic amines.** Most of these biologically important compounds are products of the degradation of amino acids or their derivatives. Histamine, produced by the decarboxylation of histidine, is a potent gastric secretagog. It stimulates the production of hydrochloric acid as well as of pepsin. The increase in gastric secretion in the chicken in response to histamine is more pronounced than that of several mammals tested (see Chapter 10). High doses of histamine, such as may be formed by microbial spoilage of fish meal, can be deleterious to chickens (Shifrine et al., 1959).

Serotonin arises from the conversion of tryptophan by tryptophan hydroxylase to 5-hydroxytryptophan, followed by the action of L-aromatic amino acid decarboxylase. The serum, tissue, and intestinal levels of this amine in several species of birds have been tabulated by Brown (1970) and by Sturkie et al. (1972). Part of the serotonin is acetylated by serotonin-N-acetyltransferase to N-acetylserotonin. Hydroxyindole-O-methyltransferase, which is highly localized in the pineal glands of mammals and birds, effects the methylation to melatonin,

with S-adenosylmethionine serving as a methyl donor. Melatonin is a pineal hormone to which many different actions have been ascribed in various species (Axelrod, 1974).

Norepinephrine, a hormone produced by the adrenal medulla, results from the decarboxylation of dihydroxyphenylalanine (DOPA), which is an oxidation product of phenylalanine (Figure 12–4). The conversion of tyrosine to DOPA requires the presence of the enzyme tyrosine hydroxylase. Norepinephrine differs from epinephrine in that the primary amine of the latter is methylated by the enzyme phenylethanolamine N-methyltransferase; the methyl donor for this conversion is S-adenosylmethionine (Iversen, 1967). Chemically, these two hormones are classed as catecholamines, because they are derivatives of catechol (o-dihydroxybenzene). The effects of catecholamines are discussed elsewhere (Chapter 4).

Taurine is a derivative of cysteine. It is found in bile of birds as a conjugate with cholic, chenodeoxycholic, and other bile acids (see Chapter 10).

Examples of other amines in tissues are the neurohormones acetylcholine and γ-aminobutyrate. In the intestinal tract bacteria synthesize amines, including histamine, tyramine, putrescine, and cadaverine, by decarboxylation of histidine, tyrosine, ornithine, and lysine, respectively.

**Other derivatives of amino acids.** Thyroxine is an iodinated derivative of tyrosine that occurs only in thyroglobulin, a protein elaborated by the thyroid gland. Its mode of action is described in Chapter 18. Thyroid tissue also contains triiodothyronine and mono- and diiodotyrosine.

Melanin is a dark pigment of skin and feathers that is derived from tyrosine by way of phenylalanine-3,4-quinone (Figure 12–4). The early stages of

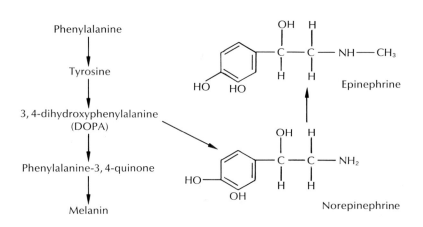

12–4
Abbreviated pathway of epinephrine and melanin synthesis.

synthesis require the copper-containing enzyme tyrosinase (*o*-diphenol oxidase). The final steps of melanin synthesis are obscure. The term "melanin" has been used for the quinonoid pigment as well as for an aggregate of the pigment and several enzyme systems in a protein matrix.

## NITROGEN EXCRETION

Urea is the major nitrogenous end product of mammalian metabolism. In humans, this compound accounts for 80–90% of the urinary nitrogen. In chickens, uric acid is the excretory vehicle for four-fifths of the metabolized N, whereas ammonia N accounts for 10–15% of total N. Chickens, and birds in general, are therefore said to be uricotelic, whereas man is ureotelic. Consequently, whereas blood levels of urea in mammals exceed uric acid levels by a factor of 10–20, levels of these two nitrogenous compounds are of approximately equal magnitude in birds. Urea, creatine, and amino acids are found in bird urine in lesser amounts, and creatinine may not be found. The major nitrogenous compounds in urine of chickens have been determined by a number of workers and details are presented in Chapter 14. The sites of synthesis of uric acid are the kidneys and liver (See Chapter 10).

Folk (1969), who subjected the urine of many different species to x-ray analysis, claims that bird urine does not consist largely of uric acid. It is possible of course, that the dry samples used by Folk consisted of urates rather than uric acid, which does not invalidate the finding that uric acid is the major excretory pathway for nitrogen in avian metabolism.

The steps that lead to the synthesis of urea from amino acid nitrogen in mammals include the removal of ammonia by transamination and oxidative decarboxylation, the transport of ammonia, and the synthesis of carbamyl phosphate (Figure 12–1), which enters the ornithine–urea cycle. As has been mentioned previously, birds lack carbamylphosphate synthetase and therefore cannot use this route to dispose of the ammonia. It has also been mentioned that there must be some facility to synthesize carbamyl phosphate for the synthesis of pyrimidines. Purines, however, derive their nitrogen from glutamine, glycine, and aspartate. Birds therefore use the pathway of purine synthesis, which also exists in other classes of the animal kingdom, as the major excretory pathway for nitrogen. There is one further difference between birds and saurian reptiles (i.e., lizards), on the one hand, and most species of other classes: uric acid is ex-creted as such and not broken down further. In mammals other than the primates, uricase decarboxylates uric acid to allantoin, and in some animals a further breakdown of allantoin occurs.

The renal clearance of uric acid and of other nitrogenous substances is discussed in detail in Chapter 14.

Although many of the excretory products that are the result of detoxification reactions are similar to those found in mammals, birds also make use of a conjugation with ornithine (Nesheim and Garlich, 1963). Ornithuric acid (dibenzoyl ornithine) and dinicotinyl ornithine are examples of such conjugations.

Studies of the end products of digestion and metabolism in birds are complicated by the mixing of feces and urine prior to voiding. One may use chemical methods to separate the excreta, create an artificial anus, and canulate or exteriorize the ureters. The problem as well as the methods, none of which is without drawbacks, are discussed in Chapters 10 and 13.

Some urea and ammonia have been found in the ceca and colon of Brown Leghorn chickens. Although some of the avian intestinal microorganisms can produce urea and ammonia from substrates present, retroperistaltic movement of urine from the cloaca cannot be excluded as a source of these products (Bell and Bird, 1966).

When an organism cannot, by dietary means, obtain sufficient amounts of an essential amino acid, it catabolizes body protein to obtain this amino acid. This process naturally leads to an increased excretion of nitrogen, in birds mostly as uric acid. With increasing dietary levels of the limiting amino acid, uric acid excretion decreases per unit of nitrogen (protein) consumed, until a plateau is reached when the birds' needs are fulfilled. In this manner, the level of uric acid excreted per unit of nitrogen consumed can serve as a measure of the avian amino acid requirement (Miles and Featherstone, 1974).

## BLOOD PROTEINS AND AMINO ACIDS

### Plasma Proteins

Most plasma proteins are synthesized in the liver from amino acids derived from the food or the catabolism of tissues. Their presence in the plasma is short lived, and as much as half of the plasma proteins may escape daily from the capillaries by filtration. Replenishment of these proteins is essential to exert a colloidal osmotic pressure in order

244

to aid in the preservation of blood volume and to help maintain the blood pH within a narrow range. The plasma also contains specialized proteins, such as prothrombin and fibrinogen, which act in the hemostatic mechanism. It is also essential, however, that the proteins be able to pass through the capillary walls to fulfill their extravascular tasks; they provide antibodies to control infections, transport protein-bound hormones and other compounds to their target organs, and are the major source of cellular metabolic protein.

Chickens can produce high levels of precipitating antibodies following injections of heterogenous serum proteins, a fact that makes them useful for immunological investigations. The demonstrable passage of antibodies to the egg yolk offers a mechanism of transfer of maternal antibodies to the offspring. However, the antibodies disappear rapidly; the half-life of $\gamma$-globulin in newly hatched chicks is only about 3 days and is progressively less as the bird matures (Patterson et al., 1962). The level of antibody production is influenced by such nutritional factors as protein and amino acids, and optimal antibody production may not be obtained at the same nutrient level as optimum growth (Fisher et al., 1964; Bhargave et al., 1971). It is of interest that the chicken, a good producer of antibodies, also has a relatively high level of $\gamma$-globulin.

Measurements of plasma proteins are frequently based on the determination of amino and imino nitrogen multiplied by 6.25. This factor is a good estimate of the ratio of the weighted average of the molecular weights of the amino acids of plasma proteins to the molecular weight of nitrogen and is therefore a good estimate of the polypeptide component of the plasma proteins. Plasma proteins, however, may include significant nonpeptide components, such as carbohydrates and lipids, which contain little or no nitrogen. This problem, as well as other assay methods, has been reviewed by Bell and Sturkie (1965) and by Martinek (1970).

**Plasma protein fractions.** Fractionations of plasma or serum proteins are frequently based on differences in ionic mobility of the various fractions, a process known as electrophoresis. This may be carried out in a buffered solution, as in the classic method devised by Tiselius ("free" electrophoresis), or on filter paper or starch gel ("zone" electrophoresis). If only the major components are to be determined, salting-out procedures may be satisfactory. Advantages and disadvantages of various methods have been discussed in the reviews by

Bell and Sturkie (1965) and Martinek (1970), and a comparison of electrophoretic techniques for chicken serum protein fractionation has been published by Torres-Medina et al. (1971). Gel electrophoresis appears superior to the other electrophoretic methods of fractionating avian plasma or serum. Five main fractions of plasma proteins can be discerned in all systems. These fractions correspond to albumin and four globulin fractions of mammalian plasma: $\alpha_1$, $\alpha_2$, $\beta$, and $\gamma$. Immunophoresis can aid greatly in the identification of the proteins. By this method, Tureen et al. (1966) identified 12 different proteins in chickens from 1 to 210 days of age.

Several workers have reported distinct prealbumin fractions. Tureen et al. (1966) found these to decrease after 8 days of age, and exist in traces only after 18 days. Harris and Sweeney (1969) noted prealbumins in adult males and Elliott and Bennett (1971) observed a prealbumin peak in all female samples, but none in males.

Albumins are believed to act as a protein reserve and a protein source at times of subnormal intake. In their normal role, however, albumins also act as carriers of many nutrients, including mineral elements, vitamins, and fatty acids. In the chicken, albumins are also carriers of thyroid hormones.

Transferrin, an iron-binding protein, behaves electrophoretically as a $\gamma_1$-globulin in the chicken, whereas mammalian transferrin exhibits the mobility of $\beta_1$-globulin (Torres-Medina et al., 1971). Most of the copper in serum is bound to ceruloplasmin, an $\alpha_2$-globulin found in chickens in lower levels than in other species investigated. Its concentration has been increased to several times the normal level by such induced stress as an infection with Salmonella gallinarum (Starcher and Hill, 1966).

Lipoproteins consist of lipids bound mostly by noncovalent forces to $\alpha$- or $\beta$-globulins; most of these lipids can therefore be extracted relatively easily by organic solvents. The major function of plasma lipoproteins is the transport of lipids, predominantly triglycerides but including a variety of other compounds, such as cholesterol, fat-soluble vitamins, and phospholipids (Schumaker and Adams, 1969).

Immunoglobulins are synthesized by the cells of the reticuloendothelial system in response to a variety of antigenic stimuli that are ever present in the interior and exterior environment of all living organisms. In the electrophoretic pattern of fractionation, part of the $\beta_2$- and essentially all of the $\gamma$-globulins are immunoproteins.

In the chicken plasma electrophoretic pattern, fibrinogen appears as a separate peak in the γ-globulin range (Sturkie, 1965). Fibrinogen, prothrombin, and other proteins that are an integral part of the hemostatic mechanism are discussed in Chapter 3.

**Plasma protein levels.** On the tenth day of embryonic development, chick as well as *Phasianus colchicus* (ring-neck pheasant) serum protein is relatively low in albumin, which increases rapidly in subsequent days relative to globulin (Weller, 1966). In one series of measurements, total serum proteins in chickens increased from 2.68 g per 100 ml at 1 week of age to 4.63 g per 100 ml at 12 weeks (Morgan and Glick, 1972). In the much faster maturing *Coturnix coturnix japonica* (Japanese quail) Atwal *et al.* (1964) measured levels between 2 and 3 g per 100 ml in 2-day-old chicks, and between 3.3 and 6.1 g per 100 ml at 50 days for both sexes. Nirmalan and Robinson (1971) obtained 2.7 g for 2-week-old *Coturnix* and 3.1–3.7 g for adult birds. Figures for mature birds of several species are shown in Table 12–3. To permit comparison of the data from various sources, prealbumin and albumin are combined as "albumin" and all globulin fractions as "globulin." It is probably correct to assume that in the determinations by Sturkie and Newman (1951) as well as those by Balasch *et al.* (1973) the "globulin" fraction includes fibrinogen. Dabrowsky (1966), using a salting-out method, determined plasma fibrinogen separately. The average fibrinogen values obtained—from 0.30 g per 100 ml for *Corvus corone cornix* (crow) to 0.80 g per 100 ml for *Pica pica pica* (magpie)—were not, for the purpose of this table, included in the "globulin" fraction. The total plasma protein levels in the species listed in Table 12–3 are remarkably similar. There is considerably more variation in the albumin and globulin values and their ratio to each other. Although some of this variation may come from methodology and insufficient sample size, the existence of genuine differences between species or larger groupings cannot be excluded. There is, however, appreciable variation within zoological classes. Whereas adult chickens and many other birds have an albumin/globulin ratio of less than 1, this is not the case with some of the species shown in Table 12–4, or the pigeon and the turkey. In mammals, horse, swine, and cattle have low levels of albumin relative to globulin, whereas the opposite is true for many other species, including man and the rat (Altman and Dittmer, 1961). Additional data for various breeds of domestic chickens as well as a number of other species, have been listed by Sturkie (1965).

**Factors affecting plasma proteins.** The state of hydration or dehydration, or hemorrhage, influences the level of plasma proteins, as does the level of protein nutrition (Leveille and Sauberlich, 1961), sex, and the stage of development.

Grant and Anastassiadis (1962) found the serum protein levels of female Leghorn chickens to be higher than those of males and those of mature birds higher than of immature ones. The injection of combinations of gonadal hormones to immature pullets increased the level of serum proteins. In other data quoted by Sturkie (1965) the increase in plasma proteins in response to estrogen administration is shown to be caused by an appreciable increase in the globulin fractions.

Changes in plasma proteins induced by egg formation are discussed in Chapter 16.

## Plasma Nonprotein Nitrogen (NPN)

On precipitation of plasma proteins, a number of nitrogenous substances remain in the protein-free fluid. Quantitatively, these substances constitute only a small fraction of the total plasma nitrogen. They are nevertheless of great physiological importance. Roughly half of the nonprotein nitrogen (NPN) is present as amino acids; the other half includes urea, urates, creatine, ammonia and a host of lesser components, many of them unidentified. Whereas avian erythrocytes contain, on a volume basis, about six times as much NPN as the plasma, all of the urates are found in plasma (Bell *et al.*, 1959).

Uric acid concentrations in plasma are greatly influenced by such factors as age, sex, and reproductive and nutritional status, whereas urea and ammonia appear relatively unaffected. Featherstone (1969) found that increasing protein from 25% to 75% of the diet did not significantly change plasma ammonia but did increase plasma uric acid fourfold and free plasma amino acids by one-third. It was shown in other experiments with chicks subjected to similar treatment that the plasma uric acid level increase was in agreement with changes in levels of liver xanthine dehydrogenase, an enzyme responsible for uric acid formation.

**Free plasma amino acids.** The free plasma amino acids of domestic fowl have been determined by various authors, frequently in response to different amino acid or protein intake levels. For

*Table 12-3* Some measurements of total plasma (or serum) proteins, "albumins," "globulins," and "A/G" ratio in various species of birds[a]

| Species | Sex | Total protein (g/100 ml) | "Alb" (g/100 ml) | "Glob" (g/100 ml) | A/G (g/100 ml) | References |
|---|---|---|---|---|---|---|
| **Galliformes** | | | | | | |
| *Gallus gallus domesticus* (chicken) | M | 4.00 | 1.66 | 2.33 | 0.71 | Sturkie and Newman (1951) |
| | F | 5.24 | 1.97 | 3.27 | 0.60 | Sturkie and Newman (1951) |
| *Meleagris gallopavo* (S) | M | 4.40 | 2.69 | 1.35 | 1.98 | Lynch and Stafseth (1953) |
| *Numida meleagris* (Guinea fowl) | M | 3.52 | 1.45 | 1.98 | 0.73 | Balasch *et al.* (1973) |
| *Phasianus colchicus* (pheasant) | M | 4.90 | 2.29 | 2.62 | 0.87 | Balasch *et al.* (1973) |
| *Alectoris graeca* (rock partridge) | M | 4.66 | 1.66 | 2.98 | 0.56 | Balasch *et al.* (1973) |
| *Gallus gallus gallus* (bankiva) | M and F | 4.43 | 1.95 | 2.47 | 0.79 | Balasch *et al.* (1973) |
| *Pavo christatos* (peacock) | M and F | 4.36 | 2.41 | 1.94 | 1.24 | Balasch *et al.* (1973) |
| *Penelope waenieri* (guan) | M and F | 3.69 | 2.03 | 1.60 | 1.22 | Balasch *et al.* (1973) |
| **Passeriformes** | | | | | | |
| *Corvus frugilegus* (rook) | M and F | 4.10 | 0.81 | 2.69 | 0.30 | Dabrowsky (1966) |
| *Corvus corone cornix* (crow) | M and F | 4.40 | 1.30 | 2.80 | 0.46 | Dabrowsky (1966) |
| *Coleus monedula spermologus* (jackdaw) | M and F | 4.60 | 1.20 | 2.80 | 0.43 | Dabrowsky (1966) |
| *Pica pica pica* (magpie) | M and F | 4.30 | 1.00 | 2.50 | 0.40 | Dabrowsky (1966) |
| *Garrulus glandarus* (jay) | M and F | 4.80 | 1.12 | 3.16 | 0.35 | Dabrowsky (1966) |

[a]Plasma except for *Meleagris gallopavo*, where serum (S) was used; in the Passeriformes samples. (Dabrowsky, 1966), fibrinogen (0.30–0.80 g/100 ml) was not included in the globulin fraction; it was, apparently, in the other plasma samples. A/G = albumin/globulin ratio.

*Table 12–4  Hydroxyproline content of skin, muscle, and comb in male Leghorn chickens[a]*

| Age (months) | Muscle[b] | Skin (% dry weight) | Comb |
|---|---|---|---|
| Day old | 0.23 | 2.33 | – |
| 1 | 0.20 | 4.11 | 3.7 |
| 3 | 0.34 | 5.24 | 5.9 |
| 6 | 0.36 | 8.16 | 5.8 |
| 12 | 0.33 | 6.60 | 5.1 |
| 38 | 0.56 | 6.45 | 6.3 |

[a]Adapted from Fisher and Griminger (1963); mean values for 8–10 birds.
[b]Pectoralis major.

data on very young chicks, Zimmerman and Scott (1967) may be consulted, and levels for adult cockerels have been tabulated by Ohno and Tasaki (1972) and Desmarais and Pare (1972). The latter authors showed differences in individual plasma amino acid levels in different strains of adult chickens, indicating that heredity plays an important role in the free plasma amino acid levels of mature chickens.

## MISCELLANEOUS PROTEINS AND DERIVATIVES

### Structural Proteins

It can be assumed that the structural proteins of birds, such as muscle and collagen, are similar to those of mammals. The comb and wattles of mature chickens are epidermal appendages, and their similarity with skin is indicated by their hydroxyproline content, which is indicative of collagen content (Table 12–4).

**Feathers.** Although feathers generally constitute only 5–10% of body weight, up to one-third of the total protein of a bird may be feather keratin. Harrap and Woods (1967) have listed the amino acid composition of feathers and feather parts of several species. Serine, glycine, and proline are the most abundant amino acids in feathers and methionine, histidine, lysine, and tryptophan occur at rather low levels. It should be noted, however, that tryptophan also occurs in relatively low concentrations in muscle tissue.

Three classes of pigments participate, in addition to optical effects from feather structure, in the coloration of bird plumage. The carotenoids are nonnitrogenous lipochromes, largely derived from the food, and are responsible for shades from yellow to red. Melanins, depending on type and concentration, have an effect ranging from orange-brown to black. The heme-related coproporphyrin III provides a reddish color to plumage and egg shells, and copper–uroporphyrin III complex (turacin) lends an intense red coloration to feathers (Völker, 1965). Phorphyrin in feathers and egg shells causes fluorescence in ultraviolet light.

### Other Proteins and Peptides

The plasma proteins have been discussed in this chapter under blood proteins and hemoglobin has been taken up in Chapter 3. Cytochromes of some bird species were analyzed and found to be very similar, but not identical, to those of mammals. A complete amino acid sequence of chicken heart cytochrome c was published by Chan and Margoliash (1966).

Histones are basic proteins that occur in the nuclei of higher plants and animals. They are believed to control protein biosynthesis by controlling messenger RNA formation through partial blocking of the DNA molecule. Information on the composition of avian histones has been reviewed by Brown (1970).

**Polypeptide hormones.** The neurohypophyseal hormones vasopressin and oxytocin each consist of eight amino acids. Their structure and mode of action is discussed in Chapter 15. Adrenocorticotropic hormone (ACTH) consists of 39 amino acids, of which only the first 23 are necessary for activity. Other hormones secreted by the anterior pituitary, such as growth hormone and the tropic hormones, contain larger numbers of amino acids, and the hormones of the latter group, especially, are classified as proteins; they are discussed in detail in the appropriate chapters.

Another protein hormone is insulin, produced by the β-cells of the pancreas. Fowl insulin differs from porcine insulin (which is very similar to human insulin) in the sequence of only six of the 51 constituent amino acids. The $\alpha_2$ cells of the pancreas produce glucagon, a polypeptide hormone consisting of 29 amino acids. These endocrine secretions of the pancreas are discussed in Chapter 10. Secretin, one of the hormones stimulating pancreatic secretion, consists of 27 amino acid residues, with about half in the same position as in glucagon. The activities of this hormone, secreted in the walls of the intestine, are described in Chapter 11. The digestive enzymes, as well as the metabolic enzymes, are protein in nature. There is reason to believe that the chemical properties of avian digestive enzymes closely resemble those of their mammalian counterparts (see Chapter 10).

## ENDOCRINE INFLUENCES ON PROTEIN METABOLISM

Hormones may have a stimulatory or depressing effect on the metabolism of nitrogenous compounds, and they may consequently be considered anabolic or catabolic with reference to protein. This type of classification has a disadvantage because the entire organism may not be affected, and a given hormone may stimulate or inhibit protein metabolism in various organs or tissues to a different degree; nevertheless, the classification is in general use.

Thyroid hormone stimulates protein accretion of some organs but causes, at the same time, a loss of carcass protein. A direct effect on the incorporation of amino acids into rat liver microsomes has been observed by Roche *et al.* (1962). Adrenal corticosteroids increase mobilization, and therefore breakdown, of protein, creating a less favorable nitrogen balance. The liver, however, may increase in net protein content, utilizing some of the amino acids available from the catabolism of muscle protein. Growth hormone promotes positive nitrogen balance, lowers blood nonprotein nitrogen, and increases protein synthesis: the latter may be caused by an increase in the rate of amino acid incorporation into messenger RNA, constituting an action on the genetic level.

Hormones that effect the metabolism of carbohydrates indirectly also influence lipid and protein metabolism. Whereas insulin, by its effect on glucose metabolism, helps to provide the energy necessary for protein synthesis, it may also have a direct effect on amino acid transport and uptake by muscle cells. Glucagon, perhaps because of a direct action on the liver, increases protein and amino acid metabolism (Leathem, 1964). Further interrelationships are discussed in Chapter 11.

With some exceptions, notably for the gonadal hormones, information about endocrine effects on avian nitrogen metabolism is scanty; for an illuminating discussion of the hormonal control of protein metabolism in general, with special stress on the action of growth hormone, the reader is directed to a chapter on endocrine control systems by Morgan (1973).

**Androgens.** These anabolic steroid hormones possess a cyclopentanoperhydrophenantrene nucleus with a 19-carbon skeleton. The principal androgen in birds, as well as in most mammals, is testosterone. It is believed to be synthesized from progesterone and pregnenolone via androstenedione (Ozon, 1972) in the interstitial cells of the testes as well as in the ovaries. For further details see Chapters 15 and 16.

Metabolically, the androgens increase protein synthesis, at the same time decreasing the rate of amino acid catabolism and thus causing a general increase in muscle mass. This stimulation of muscle growth is much more apparent in some muscles than in others. A direct connection between the level of androgen activity and muscle mass development (myotropic activity) has long been suspected, but the action is subject to a pronounced species dependence (Krűskemper, 1968). The stimulation of the striated musculature, however, is only one phase of the anabolic action of androgen and the increase in nitrogen retention may exceed the amount explainable by the effect on sexual organs and the musculature.

Howes (1962) reported growth stimulation of three synthetic anabolic steroids on young male and female chickens when they were raised on wire floors but not when they were raised on litter. He found this effect to be more apparent with lower protein levels. Adult castrated male *Phasianus colchicus* (pheasant) responded to the injection of testosterone cyclopentylproprionate, prolactin, or corticosterone with increased food intake, but only the testosterone increased adrenal heart and body weights significantly (Nagra *et al.,* 1963).

**Estrogens.** These aromatic $C_{18}$ steroids are formed from androgens (Chapter 16). The principal naturally occurring estrogens in the chicken, isolated from the ovaries and excreta, are 17-β-estradiol and estrone (Sturkie, 1965; Chapter 15). A number of synthetic estrogens are available, the best known being diethylstilbesterol, which although not steroidal in nature, nevertheless exerts potent estrogenic effects.

Although the most pronounced effect of estrogens is on lipids and minerals, they also affect nitrogen metabolism. They induce the formation of vitellin, a phospholipoprotein not normally found in males or immature females, which binds calcium to a nondiffusable protein–calcium complex. The blood calcium is also raised by estrogenic activity, which is important for birds approaching egg formation. Estrogens, furthermore, cause an increase in serum proteins and a peculiar type of bone growth in which the marrow cavities become almost filled with spongy bone (Nalbandov, 1964).

Further discussion on the effect of estrogens can be found in Chapters 13 and 16.

# REFERENCES

Allen, N. K., and D. H. Baker. (1972). Effect of excess lysine on the utilization of and requirement for arginine by the chick. *Poultry Sci., 51,* 902.

Altman, P. L., and D. S. Dittmer (Eds.). (1961). "Blood and Other Body Fluids." Biological Handbooks. Washington, D. C.: Federation of American Societies of Experimental Biology.

Atwal, O. S., L. Z. McFarland, and W. O. Wilson. (1964). Hematology of *Coturnix* from birth to maturity. *Poultry Sci., 43,* 1392.

Austic, R. E. (1973a). Conversion of arginine to proline in the chick. *J. Nutr. 103,* 999.

Austic, R. E. (1973b). Influence of proline deficiency on enzymes of proline metabolism in the chick. *Poultry Sci., 52,* 801.

Austic, R. E., and M. C. Nesheim. (1972). Arginine and creatine interrelationships in the chick. *Poultry Sci., 51,* 1099.

Axelrod, J. (1974). The pineal gland: a neurochemical transducer. *Science, 184,* 1341.

Balasch, J., L. Palacios, S. Musquera, J. Palomeque, M. Jimenez, and M. Alemany. (1973). Comparative hematological value of several galliformes. *Poultry Sci., 52,* 1531.

Bell, D. J., and T. P. Bird. (1966). Urea and volatile base in the caeca and colon of the domestic fowl: the problem of their origin. *Comp. Biochem. Physiol., 18,* 735.

Bell, D. J., W. M. McIndoe, and D. Gross. (1959). Tissue components of the domestic fowl. 3. The nonprotein nitrogen of plasma and erythrocytes. *Biochem. J., 71,* 355.

Bell, D. J., and P. D. Sturkie. (1965). Chemical constituents of blood. In, "Avian Physiology" (2nd ed.) (P. D. Sturkie, Ed.). Ithaca, N. Y.: p. 32. Cornell University Press.

Bhargava, K. K., R. P. Hanson, and M. L. Sunde. (1971). Effects of threonine on growth and antibody production in chicks infected with Newcastle disease virus. *Poultry Sci., 50,* 710.

Bird, F. H. (1968). Role of the avian small intestine in amino acid metabolism. *Fed. Proc., 27,* 1194.

Boorman, K. N., and H. Fisher. (1966). The arginine–lysine interaction in the chick. *Brit. Poultry Sci., 7,* 39.

Bray, D. J. (1970). The isoleucine and valine nutrition of young laying pullets as influenced by excessive dietary leucine. *Poultry Sci., 49,* 1334.

Brown, G. W., Jr. (1970). Nitrogen metabolismn of birds. In "Comparative Biochemistry of Nitrogen Metabolism," Vol. 2 (J. W. Campbell, Ed.). New York: Academic Press, p. 711.

Burrill, P., and J. Lerner. (1972). A distinct component of proline transport in chicken small intestine. *Comp. Biochem. Physiol., 42A,* 437.

Chan, S. K., and E. Margoliash. (1966). Amino acid sequence of chicken heart cytochrome c. *J. Biol. Chem., 241,* 507.

Crompton, D. W. T., and M. C. Nesheim. (1969). Amino acid patterns during digestion in the small intestine of ducks. *J. Nutr., 99,* 43.

Dabrowski, Z. (1966). Electrophoretic studies of blood serum proteins of birds of the crow family (Corvidae). *Acta Biol. Cracoviensio, Ser. Zool., 9,* 259.

Desmarais, M., and J. P. Pare. (1972). Genetic analysis of free plasma amino acids in pure strains of mature chickens. *Poultry Sci., 51,* 751.

D'Mello, J. P. F. (1973). Aspects of threonine and glycine metabolism in the chick. *Nutr. Metab., 15,* 357.

D'Mello, J. P. F., and D. Lewis. (1971). Amino acid interactions in chick nutrition. 4. Growth, food intake and plasma amino acid patterns. *Brit. Poultry Sci., 12,* 345.

Elliott, J. W., and J. Bennett. (1971). Genic determination of a protein in the immunoglobulin region in the chicken. *Poultry Sci., 50,* 1365.

Featherston, W. R. (1969). Nitrogenous metabolites in the plasma of chicks adapted to high protein diets. *Poultry Sci., 48,* 646.

Featherston, W. R., H. R. Bird, and A. E. Harper. (1962). Ability of the chick to utilize D- and excess L-indispensable amino acid nitrogen in the synthesis of dispensable amino acids. *J. Nutr., 78,* 95.

Fisher, H., and P. Griminger. (1963). Aging and food restriction: changes in body composition and hydroxyproline content of selected tissues. *J. Nutr., 80,* 350.

Fisher, H., P. Griminger, G. A. Leveille, and R. Shapiro. (1960). Quantitative aspects of lysine deficiency and amino acid imbalance. *J. Nutr., 71,* 213.

Fisher, H., J. Grun, R. Shapiro, and J. Ashley. (1964). Protein reserves: evidence for their utilization under nutritional and disease stress conditions. *J. Nutr., 83,* 165.

Fisher, H., D. Johnson, Jr., and G. A. Leveille. (1957). The phenylalanine and tryosine requirement of the growing chick with special reference to the utilization of the D-isomer of phenylalanine. *J. Nutr., 62,* 349.

Fisher, H., H. M. Scott, and B. C. Johnson. (1955). Quantitative aspects of the nicotinic acid-tryptophan interrelationship in the chick. *Brit. J. Nutr., 9,* 340.

Folk, R. L. (1969). Spherical urine in birds: petrography. *Science, 166,* 1516.

Gordon, R. S., and I. W. Sizer. (1965). Conversion of methionine hydroxy analogue to methionine in the chick. *Poultry Sci., 44,* 673.

Graber, G., and D. H. Baker. (1971). Sulfur amino acid nutrition of the growing chick: quantitative aspects concerning the efficacy of dietary methionine, cysteine and cystine. *J. Anim. Sci., 33,* 1005.

Graber, G., and D. H. Baker. (1973). The essential nature of glycine and proline for growing chickens. *Poultry Sci., 52,* 892.

Grant, D. L., and P. A. Anastassiadis. (1962). Effects of reproductive stage, sex, and gonadal hormones on hexosamine and protein levels of avian and bovine sera. *Can. J. Biochem. Physiol., 40,* 639.

Greene, D. E., H. M. Scott, and B. C. Johnson. (1962). The role of proline and certain non-essential amino acids in chick nutrition. *Poultry Sci., 41,* 116.

Griminger, P., and H. Fisher. (1962). Genetic differences in growth potential on amino acid deficient diets. *Proc. Soc. Exp. Biol. Med., 111,* 754.

Griminger, P., and H. Fisher. (1968). Methionine excess and chick growth. *Poultry Sci., 47,* 1271.

Griminger, P., and J. L. Gamarsh. (1972). Body composition of pigeons. *Poultry Sci., 51,* 1464.

Grove, J. A., and H. G. Roghair. (1971). The metabolism of D- and L-lysine in the chicken. *Arch. Biochem. Biophys., 144,* 230.

Hardwick, D. F., D. A. Applegarth, D. M. Cockcroft, P. M. Ross, and R. J. Calder. (1970). Pathogenesis of methionine-induced toxicity. *Metabolism, 19,* 381.

Harper, A. E., N. J. Benevenga, and R. M. Wohlhueter. (1970). Effects of ingestion of disproportionate amounts of amino acids. *Physiol. Rev., 50,* 428.

Harrap, B. S., and E. F. Woods. (1967). Species differences in the proteins of feathers. *Comp. Biochem. Physiol., 20,* 449.

Harris, G. C., and M. J. Sweeney. (1969). Electrophoretic evaluation

250    of blood sera proteins of adult male chickens. *Poultry Sci.,* *48,* 1590.

Haslewood, G. A. D. (1967). "Bile Salts." London: Methuen & Co.

Hathcock, J. N., and M. L. Scott. (1966). Alterations of methionine to cysteine conversion rates and nutritional muscular dystrophy in chicks. *Proc. Soc. Exp. Biol. Med., 121,* 908.

Hewitt, D., and D. Lewis. (1972). The amino acid requirements of the growing chicken. I. Determination of amino acid requirements. *Brit. Poultry Sci.,13,* 449.

Hiles, R. A., C. J. Willett, and L. M. Henderson. (1972). Hydroxylysine metabolism in rats, mice, and chickens. *J. Nutr., 102,* 195.

Howes, J. R. (1962). Avian growth as influenced by the oral administration of anabolic steroids. *Poultry Sci., 41,* 1651. (Abstr.)

Hurwitz, S., N. Shamir, and A. Bar. (1972). Protein digestion and absorption in the chick: effect of *Ascaridia galli. Am. J. Clin. Nutr., 25,* 311.

Imondi, A. R., and F. H. Bird. (1966). The turnover of intestinal epithelium in the chick. *Poultry Sci., 45,* 142.

Ishibashi, T. (1972). Protein metabolism in the fowl. Part IV. Possibility of conversion of tyrosine to phenylalanine in the adult rooster. *Agri. Biol. Chem., 36,* 596.

Ivanov, N., and C. Ivanov. (1962). Die Eiweissresorption im Hühnerdarm in Abhängkeit von der Wasserstoffionenkonzentration im Darm und dem Kohlendioxydgehalt des Blutes. *Arch. Tierern., 12,* 109.

Iversen, L. L. (1967). "The Uptake and Storage of Noradrenaline in Sympathetic Nerves." London: Cambridge University Press.

Jones, M. E. (1970). Vertebrate carbamyl phosphate synthetase I and II. Separation of the arginine-urea and pyrimidine pathways. In "Urea and the Kidney" (B. Schmidt-Nielson, Ed.). Amsterdam: Excerpta Medica Foundation.

Kadirvel, R., and F. H. Kratzer. (1974). Uptake of L-arginine and L-lysine by the small intestine and its influence on arginine-lysine antagonism in chicks. *J. Nutr., 104,* 339.

Kamath, S. H., and C. P. Berg. (1964). Antagonism of poorly invertible D-amino acids toward growth promotion by readily invertible D-amino acids. *J. Nutr., 82,* 237.

Keshavarz, K., and H. L. Fuller. (1971). Relationship of arginine and methionine to creatine formation in chicks. *J. Nutr., 101,* 855.

Kment, A., and A. Steininger. (1961). Untersuchungen über den 5-Hydroxytryptamin (Serotonin)- Gehalt tryptophangefütterter Hühner. *Wien. Tierärztl. Monatsschr., 6,* 389.

Kratzer, F. H. (1944). Amino acid absorption and utilization in the chick. *J. Biol. Chem., 153,* 237.

Krüskemper, H.-L. (1968). "Anabolic Steroids." New York: Academic Press.

Leathem, J. H. (1964). Some aspects of hormone and protein metabolic interrelationships. In "Mammalian Protein Metabolism," Vol. 1 (H. N. Munro and J. B. Allison, Eds.). New York: Academic Press. p. 343.

Lerner, J. (1971). Intestinal absorption of amino acids *in vitro* with special reference to the chicken: a review of recent findings and methodological approaches in distinguishing transport systems. University of Maine, Orono, Tech. Bull. 50.

Lerner, J., and M. W. Taylor. (1967). A common step in the intestinal absorption mechanisms of D- and L-methionine. *Biochem. Biophys. Acta, 135,* 991.

Leveille, G. A., and H. E. Sauberlich. (1961). Influence of dietary protein level on serum protein components and cholesterol in the growing chick. *J. Nutr., 74,* 500.

Lynch, J. E., and H. J. Stafseth. (1953). Electrophoretic studies on the serum proteins of turkeys. I. The composition of normal turkey serum. *Poultry Sci., 32,* 1068.

Martinek, R. G. (1970). Review of methods for determining proteins in biologic fluids. *J. Am. Med. Technol., 32,* 177.

McCollum, E. V. (1957). "A History of Nutrition." Boston: Houghton Mifflin Co.

Miles, R. D., and W. R. Featherston. (1974). Uric acid excretion as an indicator of the amino acid requirement of chicks. *Proc. Soc. Exp. Biol. Med., 145,* 686.

Miller, D. S., D. Houghten, P. Burrill, G. R. Herzberg, and J. Lerner. (1973). Specificity characteristics in the intestinal absorption of model amino acids in domestic fowl. *Comp. Biochem. Physiol., 44A,* 17.

Miller, E. C., J. S. O'Barr, and C. A. Denton. (1960). The metabo-

lism of methionine by single comb White Leghorn and Black Australorp chicks. *J. Nutr., 70,* 42.

Mitchell, H. H., L. E. Card, and T. S. Hamilton. (1931). A technical study of the growth of White Leghorn chickens. *Agr. Expt. Sta. Bull.* No. 367, University of Illinois, Urbana.

Morgan, H. E. (1973). Hormonal control of growth and protein metabolism. In "Best and Taylor's Physiological Basis of Medical Practice" (9th ed.) (J. R. Brobeck, Ed.). Baltimore: Williams and Wilkins, p. 7.

Morgan, G. W., Jr., and B. Glick. (1972). A quantitative study of serum proteins in bursectomized and irradiated chickens. *Poultry Sci., 51,* 771.

Munro, H. N. (1964). Historical introduction: the origin and growth of our present concepts of protein metabolism. In "Mammalian Protein Metabolism," Vol. 1 (H. N. Munro and J. B. Allison, Eds.). New York: Academic Press.

Muruyama, K., M. L. Sunde, and A. E. Harper. (1972). Effect of D-alanine and D-aspartic acid on the chick. *J. Nutr., 102,* 1441.

Nagra, C. L., R. P. Breitenbach, and R. K. Meyer. (1963). Influence of hormones on food intake and lipid deposition in castrated pheasants. *Poultry Sci., 42,* 770.

Nalbandov, A. V. (1964). "Reproductive Physiology." San Francisco: W. H. Freeman and Company.

Nesheim, M. C., and J. D. Garlich. (1963). Studies on ornithine synthesis in relation to benzoic acid excretion in the domestic fowl. *J. Nutr., 79,* 311.

Nesheim, M. C., and F. B. Hutt. (1962). Genetic differences among White Leghorn chicks in requirements of arginine. *Science, 137,* 691.

Nesheim, M. C., R. E. Austic, and S. H. Wang. (1971). Genetic factors in lysine and arginine metabolism of chicks. *Fed. Proc., 30,* 121.

Nirmalan, G. P., and G. A. Robinson. (1971). Haematology of the Japanese quail (*Coturnix coturnix japonica*). *Brit. Poultry Sci., 12,* 475.

Ohno, I., and I. Tasaki. (1972). Effect of dietary lysine level on plasma free amino acids in adult cockerels. *J. Nutr., 102,* 603.

Ozon, R. (1972). Androgens in fishes, amphibians, reptiles, and birds. In "Steroids in Nonmammalian Vertebrates" (D. R. Idler, Ed.). New York: Academic Press.

Patterson, R., J. S. Youngner, W. O. Weigle, and F. J. Dixon. (1962). Antibody production and transfer to egg yolk in chickens. *J. Immunol., 89,* 272.

Roche, J., R. Michel, and T. Kamei. (1962). Action des hormones thyroidiennes sur l'incorporation de la leucine marqueé dans les protéines des microsomes hépatiques in vitro. *Biochem. Biophys. Acta, 61,* 647.

Sasse, C. E., and D. H. Baker. (1972). The phenylalanine and tyrosine requirements and their interrelationship for the young chick. *Poultry Sci., 51,* 1531.

Schumaker, V. N., and G. H. Adams. (1969). Circulating lipoproteins. *Ann. Rev. Biochem., 38,* 113.

Sheerin, H. E., and F. H. Bird. (1972). Studies on the competitive absorption of neutral L-amino acids from the avian small intestine. *J. Nutr., 102,* 1563.

Shen, T. F., H. R. Bird, and M. L. Sunde. (1973a). Conversion of glutamic acid to proline in the chick. *Poultry Sci., 52,* 676.

Shen, T. F., H. R. Bird, and M. L. Sunde. (1973b). Relationship between ornithine and proline in chick nutrition. *Poultry Sci., 52,* 1161.

Shifrine, M., L. E. Ousterhout, C. R. Grau, and R. H. Vaughn. (1959). Toxicity to chicks of histamine formed during microbial spoilage of tuna. *Appl. Microbiol., 7,* 45.

Smith, R. E. (1966). The utilization of L-methionine, DL-methionine and methionine hydroxy analogue by the growing chick. *Poultry Sci., 45,* 571.

Starcher, B., and C. H. Hill. (1966). Isolation and characterization of induced ceruloplasmin from chicken serum. *Biochim. Biophys. Acta, 127,* 400.

Stucki, W. P., and A. E. Harper. (1961). Importance of dispensable amino acids for normal growth of chicks. *J. Nutr., 74,* 377.

Sturkie, P. D. (Ed.). (1965). "Avian Physiology" (2nd ed.). Ithaca, N.Y. Cornell University Press.

Sturkie, P. D., and H. J. Newman. (1951). Plasma proteins of chickens as influenced by time of laying, ovulation, number of blood samples taken and plasma volume. *Poultry Sci., 30,* 240.

Sturkie, P. D., J. J. Woods, and D. Meyer. (1972). Serotonin levels in blood, heart, and spleen of chickens, ducks, and pigeons. *Proc. Soc. Exp. Biol. Med., 139,* 364.

Stutz, M. W., J. E. Savage, and B. L. O'Dell. (1972). Cation – anion balance in relation to arginine metabolism in the chick. *J. Nutr., 102,* 449.

Sugahara, M., T. Morimoto, T. Kobayashi, and S. Ariyoshi. (1967). The nutritional value of D-amino acid in the chick nutrition. *Agri. Biol. Chem., 31,* 77.

Tamir, H., and S. Ratner. (1963). Enzymes of arginine metabolism in chicks. *Arch. Biochem. Biophys., 102,* 249.

Tasaki, I., and N. Takahashi. (1966). Absorption of amino acids from the small intestine of domestic fowl. *J. Nutr., 88,* 359.

Tasaki, I., and H. Yokota. (1970). Effect of deoxypyridoxine on the intestinal amino acid absorption in the chicken in situ. *Jap. J. Zootech. Sci., 41,* 104.

Teekell, R. A., E. N. Knox, and A. B. Watts. (1967). Absorption and protein biosynthesis of threonine in the chick. *Poultry Sci., 46,* 1185.

Torres-Medina, A., M. B. Rhodes, and H. C. Mussman. (1971). Chicken serum proteins: a comparison of electrophoretic techniques and localization of transferrin. *Poultry Sci., 50,* 1115.

Tureen, L. L., K. Warecka, and P. A. Young. (1966). Immunophoretic evaluation of blood serum proteins in chickens. I. Changing protein patterns in chickens according to age. *Proc. Soc. Exp. Biol. Med., 122,* 729.

Völker, O. (1965). Stoffliche Grundlagen der Gefiederfarben der Vögel. *Mitt. Naturforsch. Gesellsch. Bern, 22* (new series), 201.

Wakita, M., S. Hoshino, and K. Morimoto. (1970). Factors affecting the accumulation of amino acid by the chick intestine. *Poultry Sci., 49,* 1046.

Wang, S. H., and M. C. Nesheim. (1972). Degradation of lysine in chicks. *J. Nutr., 102,* 583.

Wang, S. H., L. O. Crosby, and M. C. Nesheim. (1973). Effect of dietary excesses of lysine and arginine on the degradation of lysine by chicks. *J. Nutr., 103,* 384.

Weller, E. M. (1966). Comparative development of pheasant and chick embryo sera. *Proc. Soc. Exp. Biol. Med., 122,* 264.

Zimmerman, R. A., and H. M. Scott. (1967). Plasma amino acid pattern of chicks in relation to length of feeding period. *J. Nutr., 91,* 503.

# 13

# Lipid Metabolism

Paul Griminger

# INTRODUCTION

Triglycerides, also called "neutral fats," are a source as well as a reserve of energy for all higher animals. Chemically, they are fatty acid esters of glycerol. Phospholipids are complex lipids found in all plant and animal tissues; they are especially abundant in nervous tissue and may constitute as much as 30% of the dry matter of the brain. On hydrolysis, some phospholipids yield glycerol, fatty acids, phosphoric acid, and a base such as choline (in phosphatidyl choline or "lecithin") or ethanolamine (in phosphatidyl ethanolamine), or the amino acid serine (in phosphatidyl serine); the latter two groups of phospholipids were originally classified as "cephalins." Other phospholipids yield glycerol, fatty acids, phosphoric acid, and the cyclic polyalcohol inositol (phosphatidyl inositol). Sphingomyelins, another important group, consist of the base sphingosine, a fatty acid, phosphoric acid, and choline.

A number of other compounds are generally included in the "lipid" group. Their normal characteristic is that they are extractable in such nonpolar organic solvents as benzene, ether, petroleum ether, and chloroform. To these belong the fatty acids (excluding those with very short carbon chains, such as acetic acid), the glycolipids, long-chain alcohols esterified with fatty acids (waxes), the steroids (including cholesterol and various hormones), and the fat-soluble vitamins.

## Lipid Needs and Intake

With the exception of certain unsaturated fatty acids, birds are not known to have a requirement for dietary lipid; this is probably true for most higher animals. At the same time, birds are capable of utilizing large amounts of dietary lipid. Fat intake varies widely in wild birds. In carniverous species and those eating seeds containing high levels of oil, fat may be close to half of the dry matter ingested. At the other extreme, in birds sustaining their needs from low-fat grains or nectar, it may be negligible. Under laboratory conditions, chickens can also adapt to considerable variation in fat intake. Fisher et al. (1961) gave an essentially fat-free ration to female chickens for 19 months; except for initial problems arising from the physical condition of the extremely dry feed, no difficulties were encountered, and eggs laid by these hens hatched normally. Vermeersch and Vanschoubroek (1968) in their excellent review indicated that levels of fat in the diet as high as 30% had no deleterious effect on growth. Good chick growth was also obtained by Renner (1964) when essentially all the nonpro-

tein calories in a diet were derived from lard, the latter exceeding 35% of the diet (by weight).

## Body Fat

Body fat is the most variable item among the major body constituents. It varies not only with species, sex, and age, but also with the level of nutrition. This is not surprising inasmuch as body fat acts, to a large extent, as an energy reserve. Complete utilization of body lipids does not occur, however. Even at the time of starvation to death from inanition, fat is not likely to drop significantly below 4% of total body weight; this level is probably necessary to protect tissues and organs. The lowest measurements made by Summers and Fisher (1962) in adult cockerels 1 and 2½ years of age after 4 weeks of starvation were 2.53 and 1.95% fat, respectively, of dry body weight (6.7 and 5.1% of total body weight).

At the other end of the scale, just prior to migration nearly half of the body weight of some species of migratory birds may consist of fat (Griminger and Gamarsh, 1972). Although the body fat composition is species specific, there do not appear to be qualitative differences between migrating and nonmigrating subspecies of the same nutritional background (Yablonkevich, 1972).

# LIPID SOURCES

A 60-g egg contains approximately 6 g of fat. This is roughly twice the amount that is absorbed from the intestinal tract of a hen fed commercial laying feed during the period of egg formation. Thus, an appreciable part of the egg lipid must be synthesized from nonlipid constituents. Dietary carbohydrates may also be converted to fat prior to use as a source of energy. This is of particular importance for migratory species of birds, because during migration energy stores may not be replenished for relatively long periods of time; to a lesser extent, it is also important for birds eating intermittently.

There are therefore two distinct sources for storage and organ lipids as well as those appearing in such products as eggs: absorption from the intestinal tract, and synthesis from nonlipid compounds.

## Absorption of Ingested Lipids

In the intestinal tract, triglycerides are hydrolyzed to diglycerides, monoglycerides, glycerol, and fatty acids. There is good evidence that the lymphatic system is the major route of absorption

254    in mammals for long-chain fatty acids and their glycerol esters (Allen, 1970). Conrad and Scott indicated as early as 1942 that in the laying hen fatty acids may be absorbed by the portal system rather than by way of the lymphatic system. More recent evidence is mentioned by Bensadoun and Rothfeld (1972). These authors also reported that in the presence of a lipoprotein lipase inhibitor, in a conscious but functionally hepatectomized chicken, long-chain fatty acids are absorbed in the form of triglycerides as the major component of a lipoprotein. The authors suggest the term "portomicrons" for the lipoproteins absorbed via the portal system, by analogy to the term "chylomicrons" chosen half of a century ago for the fat-rich particles absorbed by mammals via the lymphatic capillaries.

According to Renner (1965), the middle section of the small intestine is the most active site of fat absorption in the chicken. In mammals the jejunum seems to be the most important site, but with increasing levels of fat the role of the ileum increases in importance. Renner hypothesizes that this difference may be related to the location of the pancreatic and bile ducts, which enter the proximal part of the duodenum in the human, dog, and rat, but enter the distal end in the chick. The fat passing through the section following the duodenum may be hydrolyzed and emulsified for absorption at a more distal section, therefore, whereas in the mammals mentioned the digestive preparation for absorption may have already occurred in the duodenum. Whitehead's (1973) work indicates that in the hen, as opposed to the chick, fat can be absorbed in more proximate sections of the small intestine. The site of absorption in chickens was not found to be influenced by induced changes in the intestinal flora, although quantitative differences in fatty acid absorption were noted (Cole and Boyd, 1967).

**Degree.** Growing chickens were found to absorb 96% of soybean oil, 92% of lard, and 69% of tallow. Absorption of the respective hydrolyzed fats was lower in all cases (Renner and Hill, 1961). In the hen, absorption of tallow fed at low levels was in excess of 90%. There was some reduction at higher levels, especially when the level of free fatty acids was high (Shannon, 1971). Fedde *et al.* (1960) did not observe a decrease in apparent absorbability of four different fats when their dietary level was increased from 10–20%. Absorption improved with age, however, in every case being better at 7–8 weeks than at 1–2 weeks. Absorption of individual fatty acids by laying hens ranges from 82 to 94% (Hurwitz *et al.*, 1973). About 8 g of bile acids are secreted into the duodenum in 1 day, but close to 93% of this is reabsorbed in the small intestine.

**Sterols.** The ability of the chicken to absorb exogenous cholesterol has been demonstrated by Janacek *et al.* (1959). Absorption, at low levels of intake in excess of 50% of ingested amount, decreased with increasing intake. Various polysaccharides and resins can reduce the rate of absorption of cholesterol, as well as of lipids in general. Although more than one mechanism is likely to be responsible for this phenomenon, the binding of bile salts by these compounds seems to play an important role in the reduction of cholesterol absorption and the consequent lowering of blood cholesterol. The domestic chicken is frequently used as an experimental animal for testing the quantitative and qualitative aspects of the antihypercholesterolemic effect of various compounds (Griminger and Fisher, 1966; Fisher *et al.*, 1969).

Chickens also absorb plant sterols to some degree; campesterol was better absorbed than $\beta$-sitosterol by adult cockerels, but neither one was absorbed as well as cholesterol (Boorman and Fisher, 1966). Interference of one sterol with the absorption of another was also observed by Clarenburg *et al.* (1971), who obtained, under the special conditions of their experiment, 60% absorption of plant sterols in laying hens and 85% in nonlayers. Although it therefore appears that earlier observations of nonabsorbability of plant sterols by chickens were erroneous, the rate of absorption, especially in growing birds, is probably low. Further work is certainly needed in this area.

### Synthesis

**Fatty acids.** The end products of glycolysis, the oxidation of glucose by the Embden-Meyerhof pathway, are pyruvate and lactate (see also Chapter 11). Pyruvate is oxidatively decarboxylated by a complex enzyme system (pyruvate dehydrogenase complex) to "active" acetate, also called acetylated coenzyme A (acetyl-CoA). Condensing with oxaloacetate to form citric acid, acetyl-CoA can enter the citric acid cycle and become a source of energy. It can also be the starting point for the synthesis of fatty acids.

It should be recognized that carbohydrate is not the only source of acetyl-CoA, which is also an end product of the breakdown of fatty acids. It must be kept in mind, furthermore, that the Krebs cycle and fatty acid synthesis are not the only systems requiring acetyl-CoA. However, the following pathway plays a significant role in the metabolism of the living organism.

In the presence of $CO_2$, acetyl-CoA is carboxylated to malonyl-CoA. ATP and the biotin- and

$$CH_3 \quad\quad ATP \quad\quad \text{Acetyl-CoA} \quad\quad ADP + P_i \quad\quad CH_2{-}COOH$$
$$| \quad\quad\quad\quad\quad\quad \text{carboxylase} \quad\quad\quad\quad\quad\quad |$$
$$C{=}O \quad\quad\quad\quad\quad\quad\quad\quad\quad\quad\quad\quad\quad\quad\quad C{=}O$$
$$| \quad\quad\quad CO_2 \quad\quad \text{Biotin, } Mn^{2+} \quad\quad\quad\quad |$$
$$S{-}CoA \quad\quad\quad\quad\quad\quad\quad\quad\quad\quad\quad\quad\quad\quad S{-}CoA$$

$Mn^{2+}$-containing enzyme acetyl-CoA carboxylase are necessary for the reaction shown in the box above. According to Arinze and Mistry (1970), this enzyme is found in negligible amounts only in embryonic chicken liver but increases to adult levels about 20 days posthatching.

In birds and mammals, as well as in yeast, fatty acid synthetase, a multienzyme system, has been found to catalyze the synthesis of fatty acids further. The next step in this synthesis is the combination of malonyl-CoA and the acyl-carrying enzyme to the four-carbon compound acetoacetyl, a reaction that includes decarboxylation of the malonyl component. By a series of reductions and dehydrations, the acetoaceyl—enzyme complex is changed into the acyl enzyme complex (see below).

$$CH_3 \quad\quad\quad\quad\quad CH_3$$
$$| \quad\quad\quad\quad\quad\quad\quad |$$
$$C{=}O \quad\quad\quad\quad\quad CH_2$$
$$| \quad\quad\quad\quad\quad\quad\quad |$$
$$CH_2 \quad\quad\quad\quad\quad CH_2$$
$$| \quad\quad O \quad\quad\quad | \quad\quad O$$
$$\quad \backslash \!\! / \quad\quad\quad\quad\quad \backslash \!\! /$$
$$C \quad\quad\quad\quad\quad\quad C$$
$$\quad\quad \backslash \quad\quad\quad\quad\quad\quad\quad \backslash$$
$$\quad\quad\quad \text{Enzyme—SH} \quad\quad \text{Enzyme—SH}$$

*Acetoacetyl complex*      *Acyl complex*

The saturated acyl—enzyme complex then combines with another molecule of malonyl-CoA and the reaction series is repeated until, for example, palmitate (a 16-carbon acyl radical) has been formed.

The system requires the presence of NADPH + $H^+$, and in the case of yeast also of $FMNH_2$, which is recharged by NADPH + $H^+$. The avian synthetase does not seem to contain flavin. For a discussion of the enzyme systems involved and a list of pertinent references, see the review by Volpe and Vagelos (1973).

Whereas these reactions have been demonstrated in the particle-free fraction of cells, it is believed that another pathway for fatty acid elongation exists in the microsomes of pigeon liver (Stumpf, 1969).

Leveille (1969) reported that liver was the major site of fatty acid synthesis in the young chicken as well as the growing hen, in contrast to the mouse and the rat, in which adipose tissue plays an important role. Goodridge and Ball (1967) have made similar observations with young pigeons. When labeled acetate was injected into young chicks and the birds were killed 15 min later, 47% of the total fatty acid synthesis had taken place in the liver, 2% in the intestine, 7% in the skin, and 44% in the carcass (Yeh and Leveille, 1973a). Considering the relative weight of carcass and liver, the latter tissue must have been more than 20 times as active per unit of weight as the carcass in the synthesis of fatty acids.

Of interest is the observation by Shrago *et al.* (1971) that there is little fatty acid synthesis in adipose tissue of humans and that synthesizing activity decreases in rats with age. These authors conclude that the rat may be a poor experimental model for the study of the carbon pathway of fatty acid synthesis and the regulation of lipogenesis. It is possible that birds may constitute more suitable models for such studies.

Various nutritional factors can influence lipogenesis. A well-fed animal consuming a carbohydrate-rich diet produces a high level of fat. A high-fat diet as well as restriction of caloric intake, however, tends to decrease fat synthesis.

Feeding rats once daily for 2 hr rather than at times of their choice increases lipogenesis. In chickens, such regimens tend to cause an enlargement of the crop but do not increase lipogenesis (Lepkovsky *et al.*, 1960). The enlarged crop serves as a storage organ and the chicken, for all practical purposes, remains a nibbler rather than a meal eater. This can be circumvented by surgical removal of the crop. Young cropectomized chickens, however, find it difficult to consume sufficient feed to grow and deposit fat at the same rate as *ad libitum*-fed control birds, even if they are offered several meals a day (Griminger *et al.*, 1969).

**Cholesterol.** Synthesis of cholesterol takes place in several stages, acetyl-CoA being the original source of all carbon atoms. The location of the synthesis varies with species, age, and dietary treatment. In rats and monkeys, hepatic and intestinal cholesterogenesis account for over 90% of the synthesizing activity that can be detected under *in vitro* conditions in all tissues. According to Dietschy and Weis (1971), approximately equal amounts of cholesterol came from the liver and the gastrointestinal tract of rats on a cholesterol-low diet, whereas liver cholesterogenesis was almost nil in the cholesterol-fed rat and low in fasted animals. In the chicken, Yeh and Leveille (1973a) observed that during 15 min after the injection of carbon-labeled acetate, 64% of all cholesterol synthesis took place in the liver, 24% in the carcass, and about 6% in the intestine and skin.

Cholesterol is also synthesized in the thoracic as well as abdominal aorta of young chickens, but synthesis falls off rapidly as the birds mature. Apparently, cholesterol synthesis in aortic tissue is largely related to tissue growth (Dayton, 1961).

An increase in dietary protein decreased the fatty acid synthesis in liver and carcass, but not in the intestines, of young chicks; however, it increased the cholesterol synthesis in liver and intestine, albeit not in the carcass. There was a significant decrease in plasma cholesterol but an increase in carcass cholesterol, pointing to the possibility of a shift in cholesterol from plasma to liver (Yeh and Leveille, 1972). By administering $[^{14}C - 4]$ cholesterol, the same authors (1973b) showed that the hypocholesterolemic effect of high-protein intake was also mediated, at least in part, by a more rapid turnover of cholesterol, resulting in faster removal from the blood and excretion in the feces as cholesterol and bile acids.

**Effect of fat intake.** Hepatic lipogenesis is stimulated by high levels of dietary carbohydrate and reduced by high levels of dietary fat. The addition of 10% corn oil to the feed of young growing chickens reduced incorporation of labeled acetate into liver lipid by 38%. Significant reductions in the specific activities of citrate-cleavage enzyme and "malic" enzyme in response to increased fat intake were also observed (Pearce, 1971); a similar response of these adaptive enzymes to fat intake has been demonstrated in the rat. The response of citrate-cleavage enzyme to dietary intake has been discussed in detail by Lowenstein (1968).

Dietary fat has also been shown to reduce hepatic lipogenesis in mature female chickens (Balnave and Pearce, 1969). As a consequence of corn oil supplementation, total liver lipids were rapidly reduced and liver lipid synthesis from [$^{14}$C]acetate was depressed. Ovarian lipid was increased, probably because of the rapid growth of small follicles of 5–10 mm diameter. The changes in lipid synthesis

were accompanied by a marked decrease in the lipogenic enzymes acetyl-CoA carboxylase and, to a lesser extent, citrate-cleavage enzyme, which is in step with the assumption that acetyl-CoA carboxylase is the rate-limiting step in the biosynthesis of fatty acids. The activity of isocitrate dehydrogenase did not show a similar reduction, although such had been observed in other conditions in which hepatic lipogenesis was also reduced, namely starvation and alloxan diabetes. This could be taken to imply that isocitrate dehydrogenase is not intimately involved in fatty acid biosynthesis; perhaps it plays a role in the synthesis of glucose from noncarbohydrate precursors.

Tissue lipids are derived from dietary lipids as well as from lipogenesis; therefore, fat intake influences not only the quantity of lipogenesis, but also the quality of lipids in various tissues.

Each species, and each different tissue within a given species, has a certain constant fatty acid composition. Triglycerides derived from liponeogenesis (i.e., from carbohydrates and proteins) will fit the specific composition of a given tissue. The consumption of significant amounts of lipids, however, changes the fatty acid composition of tissue lipids to varying degrees. Because of the dynamic nature of adipose tissue and the lipid moieties of other tissues, changes continuously occur so that the fatty acid composition of a tissue may ultimately return to its constant composition. Continuous desaturation and saturation of fatty acids are therefore taking place. Changes in the liver fatty acid pattern of mature female chickens after ingestion of various fats over a period of 20 days were recorded by Vogtmann and Prabucki (1971). When growing chickens were reared over a period of 58 days on diets containing safflower oil, linoleic acid in the neutral fats of the breast muscle (pectoralis major) was approximately twice as high as was the case with several other dietary fats. Some other significant changes in neutral fats, as well as in the fatty acid composition of phospholipids of the same tissue, have also been noted (Marion *et al.*, 1967). As determined by Miller and Robisch (1969) fish oils influenced especially the fatty acids with unsaturation at the third, sixth, and ninth carbon, counted from the methyl end of the molecule (fatty acids of the ω-3, ω-6, and ω-9 families). Effects of dietary fat on egg lipids in the chicken and turkey are discussed by Couch and Saloma (1973) and Couch *et al.* (1973), respectively, who also list many of the earlier publications on this subject. Egg fatty acids of 22 avian species, without special consideration of diet, have been determined by Christie and Moore (1972a).

## ESSENTIAL FATTY ACIDS

The essential fatty acids (EFA) are those that are necessary for normal physiological function of the organism but that cannot be synthesized by the same. Although linoleic, linolenic, and arachidonic acids are usually listed under this heading, there is doubt that linolenic acid satisfies the conditions of the definition for EFA, cited here, for birds or most other higher animals. Linoleic acid can be converted to arachidonic acid by way of $\gamma$-linolenic ($\omega$-6, -9, -12) and $\Delta$-5, 8, 11-eicosatrienoic acid. Therefore, a dietary supply of linoleic acid apparently can satisfy all EFA needs of birds. Indeed, in a recent discussion of EFA in poultry nutrition, Balnave (1970) limited the term EFA to linoleic and arachidonic acids.

Although EFA appear in the tissues as constituent fatty acids of phospholipids and as cholesteryl esters, their major function may well be as precursors of prostaglandins. For more information on this family of 20-carbon unsaturated fatty acids, see Weeks (1974) and the reviews mentioned in his paper.

It is common knowledge that an EFA deficiency has detrimental effects on the size of a hen's egg. Studies with $^{14}C$ showed that in mature females about one-quarter of the dietary linoleate was deposited rapidly as ovarian fatty acid (Balnave, 1971a). In the male, a deficiency caused a decrease in the fertilizing capacity, as measured by the decline in the number of fertile eggs after a single insemination. Semen volume, sperm motility, and sperm count were not affected. A fatty acid profile of the semen showed not only an extremely low level of linoleic acid for the deficient group, but also a major shift in the 22-carbon acids, namely a large increase in docosadienoic and a decrease in docosatetraenoic acid (Lillie and Menge, 1968).

## BLOOD LIPIDS

The lipids circulating in the blood are derived from intestinal absorption, synthesis (mainly in the liver), or mobilization from fat depots. They may be classified into neutral lipids (triglycerides), phospholipids (phosphatides), cholesterol esters, free fatty acids, and lesser quantities of various fat-soluble compounds, such as the fat-soluble vitamins. As in other classes of animals, their concentration in birds is influenced by species, age, sex, nutrition, state of health, energy needs (including climatic conditions), and other factors.

Avian blood lipids are neither quantitatively nor qualitatively unique among those of vertebrate animals, except that very high levels are observed in the mature female during periods of egg formation. These may result, in part, from the lipoprotein complexes that transport the lipids synthesized in the liver to the ovary where they are deposited intact in the follicles (Christie and Moore, 1972b; see also Chapter 15).

Serum lipids of unsexed White Leghorn chicks from 1 to 15 weeks of age varied between 420 and 480 mg per 100 ml; cholesterol measured 116–134 mg, and phospholipids 124–188 mg per 100 ml (Rudas et al., 1972). Broiler-type pullets, 10 weeks old and weighing 2200 g, had 1010 mg total lipid per 100 ml 80 min after a meal containing 50 g dry matter, but only 572 and 578 mg, respectively, after 2 and 4 hours (Leclercq et al., 1974). Force feeding a meal of 130 g corn produced lipid levels that were approximately 30% higher, with most of the increase coming from a significant increase in the very low-density lipoprotein fraction. Analyzing whole blood lipids of laying hens, Balnave (1971b) recorded a level of $2548 \pm 89$ mg total lipids per 100 ml blood for 101 active layers, and $1112 \pm 87$ mg for females with quiescent ovaries. Christie and Moore (1972b) determined the major classes of lipids and types of phospholipids in the plasma of laying hens as well as the predominant fatty acids in the triglycerides and phospholipids (Table 13–1). For additional data on plasma lipids of various avian species, Bell and Sturkie (1965) should be consulted.

**Cholesterol.** Among other factors, heredity, age, and nutrition affect the blood cholesterol level. Estep et al. (1969) observed a decrease of serum cholesterol in cockerels from the sixth to the twelfth week, followed by an increase to the twentieth week. The low and high levels were 83 and 132 mg per 100 ml, respectively, Heritability, based on regression of offspring on sire, was estimated to be 0.26, and on dam, 0.04. A combined heritability estimate of the serum cholesterol level for three generations of two breeds of pigeons (Racing Homer and White Carneau) was $0.51 \pm 0.04$ (Patton et al., 1974).

The addition of 1% dietary cholesterol or 10% corn oil had no effect on serum cholesterol of young chickens. When both were given simultaneously, however, serum cholesterol was increased by a factor of three to four with a diet suboptimal in protein, and two to three times with a diet containing an optimal protein level (Marion et al., 1961). The effects of some dietary factors and drugs on plasma cholesterol levels in laying hens, as well

*Table 13–1* *Proportions of the major classes of lipids in the plasma of laying hens and their fatty acid composition*[a]

| Lipid | % (wt) of lipids | Phospholipids | % (mole) of phospholipids |
|---|---|---|---|
| Triglycerides | 59.7 | Phosphatidyl ethanolamine | 18.5 |
| Diglycerides | 4.3 | Phosphatidyl choline | 69.6 |
| Free fatty acids | 1.8 | Phosphatidyl inositol | 2.3 |
| Cholesterol esters | 2.4 | Sphingomyelin | 3.8 |
| Phospholipids | 31.8 | Lyso-phosphatidyl choline | 5.8 |

| | % of fatty acids | | |
| Fatty acid | Triglycerides | Phosphatidyl ethanolamine | Phosphatidyl choline |
|---|---|---|---|
| 16:0 | 28.5 | 19.7 | 35.0 |
| 18:0 | 4.6 | 21.1 | 10.2 |
| 18:1 | 49.9 | 14.3 | 28.7 |
| 18:2 | 11.4 | 7.0 | 12.7 |
| 20:4 | | 13.6 | 3.6 |
| 22:4 | | 2.0 | 0.6 |
| 22:6 | | 19.0 | 6.6 |

[a]Blood samples collected 2–3 hr after feeding (Christie and Moore, 1972b).

as on egg cholesterol levels, have been studied by Weiss *et al.* (1967). There is great variability in plasma cholesterol of hens of the same treatment. Various complex carbohydrates and related compounds can reduce the plasma cholesterol level of chickens made hypercholesterolemic by dietary cholesterol (Fisher and Griminger, 1967).

High cholesterol levels have been experimentally induced in various species. The White Carneau pigeon, and perhaps other strains of *Columba livia,* however, appear to be spontaneously hypercholesterolemic, even though they are consuming cholesterol-free, low-fat foods; average values of over 300 mg per 100 ml serum are found in this strain of pigeons (Wartman and Connor, 1973).

## ENDOCRINE INFLUENCES ON LIPID METABOLISM

Glucose is a major precursor of lipids synthesized in the body, especially in the case of birds and other animals that obtain sustenance from high-carbohydrate, low-fat seeds and other plant products. By its action on glucose transport, insulin therefore plays a principal role in the regulation of lipogenesis, with increased insulin output increasing the uptake of glucose. Secondary to increased glucose transport, insulin influences triglyceride

synthesis by regulating esterification through provision of substrate, $\alpha$-glycerol phosphate. The fatty acids required can be supplied by plasma fatty acids, by synthesis from glucose, and by hydrolysis of existing triglycerides. Triglyceride hydrolysis, preliminary to the uptake of triglyceride fatty acids by extrahepatic tissue, appears to be mediated by lipoprotein lipase, an enzyme stimulated by insulin and, directly or indirectly, by glucose. Epinephrine and other hormones that stimulate lipolysis inhibit lipoprotein lipase activity (see also Chapter 11).

The lipolytic enzyme apparently directly affected by hormonal action is triglyceride lipase. According to Neely and Oram (1973), at least 12 hormones are known to stimulate lipolysis in adipose tissue. These include the biogenic amines epinephrine and norepinephrine (Chapter 12), the polypeptide hormones glucagon, secretin, and ACTH (Chapter 12), and two hormones secreted by the adenohypophysis: the mucoprotein TSH (thyroid-stimulating hormone) and the glycoprotein LH (luteinizing hormone, a pituitary gonadotropin). It is not surprising, therefore, that triglyceride lipase is also referred to as "hormone-sensitive lipase." The action of these hormones is believed to be mediated by 3', 5'-adenosine monophosphate (cyclic AMP) and the lipolytic response reaches maximum within a very short time. An apparently different mechanism, involving a lag period of not less than an hour, is exerted by growth hormone and glucocorticoids, which also stimulate lipolysis.

In birds, catecholamines appear to be of less importance in the mobilization of free fatty acids than in mammals, and recent investigations indicate that glucagon may be the prime lipolytic hormone in Aves. Braganza *et al.* (1973), in a study of the influence of heat stress, measured free fatty acids in 15-min intervals after intramuscular injection of glucagon. There was a considerable increase after 15 min and a peak was reached after 30 min. At a level of 100 $\mu$g/kg, plasma free fatty acids increased by a factor of more than three in birds kept at 21°C, and by a factor of more than five in birds acclimated to 35°C, both groups averaging more than 1500 $\mu$eq of free fatty acids per liter of plasma.

As mentioned earlier, insulin acts as an important antilipolytic hormone by inhibiting release of glycerol and free fatty acids in adipose tissue and by stimulating the conversion of glucose to fat. The stimulation of lipoprotein lipase increases incorporation of circulating triglycerides into cells. These processes result in the sparing of existing triglycerides and an increased fat deposition.

In contrast to most mammalian species, where exogenous insulin causes a decrease in plasma free fatty acids, an increase has been observed in birds by several researchers (Nir and Levy, 1973). A single intravenous injection of 5 units/kg of bovine insulin raised plasma free fatty acids within a 3-hr period twofold in cockerels and threefold in domestic geese. In the latter species plasma tri-

glycerides also increased substantially (see also Chapter 11).

Another unique response of chickens is the increased hepatic lipogenesis after hypophysectomy (Kompiang and Gibson, 1973). In the rat, removal of the hypophysis reduces hepatic lipogenesis, whereas adipose tissue lipogenesis is reduced in both species.

**Estrogens and androgens.** The increase in blood lipids with egg formation (see also Chapter 16) is governed mainly by estrogen (Table 13–2). Testosterone propionate has no effect on the lipid level of whole blood of male or female *Cortunix cortunix japonica* (Japanese quail) (Nirmalan and George, 1972) and both testosterone and progesterone cause a small but significant decrease in the blood lipids of immature male chickens (Balnave, 1969). The increase in lipids is also reflected in the increase of its individual components. Using non-laying hens as controls and administering estrogen to 11-week-old pullets, van Tienhoven (1968) observed changes in blood composition as follows: total lipids, from 1100 to 14,200 mg per 100 ml; phospholipids, from 162 to 934 mg per 100 ml; cholesterol, from 235 to 1136 mg per 100 ml; and total vitamin A, from 5.1 to 46.8 $\mu$g per 100 ml.

Consideration of the uptake of [$^{14}$C]acetate into lipids helps to illustrate the effect of gonadal hormones on lipid metabolism. Injecting estradiol dipropionate, testosterone propionate, and progesterone on alternate days over a period of 10 days into immature male chicks, Balnave (1968) found

*Table 13–2*    *Effects of estrogens on blood lipids*

| Species and treatment | Total lipids (g/100 ml) | | Reference |
|---|---|---|---|
| | Control | Treated | |
| Duck (Pekin), male, estradiol 1 mg/day | 0.45 | 3.14 | Landauer *et al.* (1941) |
| Pigeon (White carneaux), both sexes, immature 0.25–0.5 mg estradiol/per day | 0.47 | 1.78 | McDonald and Riddle (1945) |
| *Coturnix coturnix japonica* (Japanese quail), immature, stilbesterol propionate 1 mg/day | | | |
| female | 1.97 | 15.1 | Nirmalan and George (1972) |
| male | 1.80 | 13.1 | Nirmalan and George (1972) |
| Chickens (Hyline 934), male estradiol dipropionate 2 mg/48 hr, immature | 0.55 | 3.80 | Balnave (1969) |
| Chickens (Shaver starcross 288), female estradiol dipropionate 5 mg/48 hr | | | |
| immature | 0.65 | 7.53 | Balnave (1971c) |
| mature | 2.52 | – | Balnave (1971c) |

260 that the overall lipid composition of the liver was changed significantly only by the estrogenic compound. Liver weight was increased by 30% and today liver lipids were doubled; blood lipids increased sevenfold, and there was a significant increase in the incorporation of injected [$^{14}$C]acetate into liver lipids. Although testosterone and progesterone did not affect the overall lipid composition of the liver, they caused a spurt of [$^{14}$C]acetate uptake 15 min after injection, followed by a rapid decrease in the $^{14}$C content of liver lipids and accompanied by a significant reduction in the level of circulating lipids in the blood. Testosterone and progesterone therefore appear to produce rapid synthesis as well as rapid degradation of liver lipids.

The increased blood lipids in the laying female appear necessary for the deposition of the relatively large amounts of fat needed for yolk formation (see Chapter 16). When blood lipids in male birds are increased by the injection of estrogens, some of the surplus lipids are stored in the tissues, making the bird fatter and more desirable as a source of human food. To this end, diethylstilbesterol or its dimethyl ether (dianisylhexane) may be injected or implanted; diethylstilbesterol is relatively ineffective when given orally (Sturkie, 1965). When implanted, about 2 mg/week must be absorbed to be effective, and treatment for 4–6 weeks was generally found to be optimum. A pellet ranging in size from 15–25 mg, depending on the size of the bird, is implanted in the skin, high on the neck or head, with an instrument especially designed for the operation.

Not only tenderness, but also grade can be improved by estrogens in chickens and turkeys by virtue of increased subcutaneous fat deposits as well as the smoother and softer skin. These improvements are accompanied by increases in abdominal and liver fat.

At the present time, use of estrogens in chickens grown for human consumption is not permitted in the United States, since there is suspicion that hormonal residues in the neck may have a carcinogenic effect on the consumer.

A sensitive biological assay for the determination of residual estrogens in tissues has been described by Umberger et al. (1958), and a method for the analysis of urinary 17-β-estradiol and estrone has been discussed by Mathur and Common (1969). Tritium-labeled dianisylhexane, which is a potent estrogen for chickens also when given orally, was used by DeSteiguer et al. (1962) to obtain information on the distribution of this compound in the tissues of treated birds (see also Chapter 16).

## MISCELLANEOUS

**Brown fat.** In well-nourished animals, adipose tissue has a glistening pale-yellow appearance; the fat is present in one large vacuole within the distended cell and the nucleus is eccentric. In contrast to this "white" fat, some mammals have, in certain locations, brown adipose tissue cells that contain multiple small fat droplets and a central nucleus. This brown fat is especially prominent in hibernating animals and those adapted to a cold environment. Since birds are relatively unstable thermoregulators, Johnston (1971) attempted to find brown adipose tissue in avian tissue. Preparing several hundred sections from 11 birds, ranging from *Archilochus colibris* (ruby-throated hummingbird) to *Coragyps atratus* (black vulture), he was unable to detect any brown adipose tissue.

**Fatty livers.** Some domestic birds are able to accumulate large amounts of fat in their livers. This is of value in the creation of fatty goose livers for the preparation of *paté de fois gras,* but is less welcome when it occurs in domestic laying hens. Force-fed geese may increase their liver weight sixfold while adding only two-thirds to their body weight. About half of the weight of these livers is fat, and although RNA and DNA in the total liver increases, it is decreased per unit of liver weight (Nitsan et al., 1973).

High intake of energy and limited exercise may be the cause of the so-called "fatty liver syndrome" of laying hens, which is frequently accompanied by reduced egg production. The accumulation of fat largely results from the deposition of neutral lipids as triglycerides. This increase in neutral fats is accompanied by a decrease in phospholipids, and an increase in oleic acid content is compensated by a decrease in linoleic acid (Ivy and Nesheim, 1973). A restriction in carbohydrate intake by about 10% has been found successful to prevent the syndrome and, by way of an endocrine stimulation, to increase egg production (Sallmann and Scholle, 1973).

**Atherosclerosis.** Human atherosclerosis is a major health problem of modern man, and the experimental study of the pathology of this degenerative disease requires the use of suitable animal models. Such models can be found in the class Aves. Several species have been shown to develop atherosclerosis spontaneously as well as to be suitable for the experimental induction and manipulation of this disease. Among these are certain strains of pigeons as well as the domestic chicken and turkey. Although spontaneous aortic disease is extremely widespread in the animal kingdom (Bohorquez and Stout, 1972), the close resemblance of avian atherosclerosis to the human disease has been recognized since the early part of the twentieth century (Siller, 1965). Cockerels respond to a prolonged (8–40 weeks) feeding of a high-cholesterol, high-fat, atherogenic diet by developing an intimal arterial process that closely resembles atherosclerosis in other species, including man (Pick and Katz, 1965). Under proper conditions, a regression of atherosclerosis can also be affected (Pick et al., 1965). Moderate food restriction lessens the degree of atherosclerotic involvement of the abdominal aorta (Griminger et al., 1963), as do various dietary supplements, ranging from pectin to antibiotics (Fisher et al., 1964, 1974). A degree of causal implication of hemodynamic factors, blood lipids, and thrombogenic mechanisms in spontaneous avian atherosclerosis has been demonstrated by Weiss et al. (1968), whereas Kakita et al. (1972) have shown that elevation of plasma cholesterol to excessively high levels induces atherosclerosis in cockerels in short-term experiments. Although it is not possible in these pages to do justice to the vast amount of observational and experimental work in this field, the references mentioned above can serve as a starting point for further reading on this subject.

# REFERENCES

Allen, R. S. (1970). Absorption. In "Duke's Physiology of Domestic Animals," (8th ed.,) (M. J. Swenson, Ed.). Ithaca, N. Y.: Cornell University Press. p. 538.

Arinze, J. C., and S. P. Mistry. (1970). Hepatic acetyl-CoA carboxylase, propionyl-CoA carboxylase and pyruvate carboxylase activities during embryonic development and growth in chickens. Proc. Soc. Exp. Biol. Med., 135, 553.

Balnave, D. (1968). The influence of gonadal hormones on the uptake of [¹⁴C] acetate by liver lipid fractions in the immature male chick. J. Endocrinol., 42, 119.

Balnave, D. (1969). The effects of certain gonadal hormones on the content and composition of lipids in the blood and liver of immature male chicks. Comp. Biochem. Physiol., 28, 709.

Balnave, D. (1970). Essential fatty acids in poultry nutrition. World's Poultry Sci. J., 26, 442.

Balnave, D. (1971a). The contribution of absorbed linoleic acid to the metabolism of the mature laying hen. Comp. Biochem. Physiol., 40A, 1097.

Balnave, D. (1971b). Relationship between blood linoleic acid and laying activity in the laying hen. J. Sci. Food Agri., 22, 467.

Balnave, D. (1971c). The influence of exogenous estrogens and the attainment of sexual maturity on fatty acid metabolism in the immature pullet. Comp. Biochem. Physiol., 40B, 189.

Balnave, D., and J. Pearce. (1969). Adaptation of the laying hen (Gallus domesticus) to dietary fat with special reference to changes in liver and ovarian lipid content and liver enzyme activity. Comp. Biochem. Physiol., 29, 539.

Bell, D. J., and P. D. Sturkie. (1965). Chemical constituents of blood. In "Avian Physiology" (2nd ed.) (P. D. Sturkie, Ed.). Ithaca, N. Y.: Cornell University Press.

Bensadoun, A., and A. Rothfeld. (1972). The form of absorption of lipids in the chicken, Gallus domesticus. Proc. Soc. Exp. Biol. Med., 141, 814.

Bohorquez, F., and C. Stout. (1972). Arteriosclerosis in exotic mammals. Atherosclerosis, 16, 225.

Boorman, K. N., and H. Fisher. (1966). The absorption of plant sterols by the fowl. Brit. J. Nutr., 20, 689.

Braganza, A. F., R. A. Peterson, and R. J. Cenedella. (1973). The effects of heat and glucagon on the plasma glucose and free fatty acids of the domestic fowl. Poultry Sci., 52, 58.

Christie, W. W., and J. H. Moore. (1972a). The lipid composition and triglyceride structure of eggs from several avian species. Comp. Biochem. Physiol., 41B, 297.

Christie, W. W., and J. H. Moore. (1972b). The lipid components of the plasma, liver and ovarian follicles in the domestic chicken (Gallus gallus). Comp. Biochem. Physiol., 41B, 287.

Clarenburg, R., I. A. K. Chung, and L. M. Wakefield. (1971). Reducing the egg cholesterol level by including emulsified sitosterol in standard chicken diet. J. Nutr., 101, 289.

Cole, J. R., Jr., and F. M. Boyd. (1967). Fat absorption from the small intestine of gnotobiotic chicks. Appl. Microbiol., 15, 1229.

Conrad, R. M., and H. M. Scott. (1942). Fat absorption in the laying hen. Poultry Sci., 21, 407.

Couch, J. R., and A. E. Saloma. (1973). Effect of diet on triglyceride structure and composition of egg yolk lipids. Lipids, 8, 385.

Couch, J. R., T. M. Ferguson, and B. M. Cornett. (1973). Egg yolk lipids and maternal diet in the nutrition of turkey embryo. Lipids, 8, 682.

Dayton, S. (1961). Decline in rate of cholesterol synthesis during maturation of chicken aorta. Proc. Soc. Exp. Biol. Med., 108, 257.

DeSteiguer, D., E. M. Hodnett, R. D. Morrison, and R. H. Thayer. (1962). The use of tritium for the determination of residual estrogen in the tissues of broilers fed 3,4-dianisyl-2-t-3-hexene. Poultry Sci., 41, 1815.

Dietschy, J. M., and H. J. Weis. (1971). Cholesterol synthesis by the gastrointestinal tract. Am. J. Clin. Nutr., 24, 70.

Estep, G. D., R. C. Fanguy, and T. M. Ferguson. (1969). The effect of age and heredity upon serum cholesterol levels in chickens. Poultry Sci., 48, 1908.

Fedde, M. R., P. E. Waibel, and R. E. Burger. (1960). Factors affecting the absorbability of certain dietary fats in the chick. J. Nutr., 70, 447.

Fisher, H., and P. Griminger. (1967). Cholesterol-lowering effects of certain grains and of oat fractions in the chick. Proc. Soc. Exp. Biol. Med., 126, 108.

Fisher, H., A. S. Feigenbaum and H. S. Weiss. (1961). Requirement of essential fatty acids and avian atherosclerosis. Nature (London), 192, 1310.

Fisher, H., P. Griminger, and C. P. Schaffner. (1969). Effect of polyene macrolides on cholesterol metabolism of the chick. Proc. Soc. Exp. Biol. Med., 132, 253.

Fisher, H., P. Griminger, and W. Siller. (1974). Effect of candicidin on plasma cholesterol and avian atherosclerosis. Proc. Soc. Exp. Biol. Med., 145, 836.

Fisher, H., P. Griminger, H. S. Weiss, and W. G. Siller. (1964). Avian atherosclerosis: retardation by pectin. Science, 146, 1063.

Goodridge, A. G., and E. G. Ball. (1967). Lipogenesis in the pigeon: in vivo studies. Am. J. Physiol., 213, 245.

Griminger, P., and H. Fisher. (1966). Anti-hypercholesterolemic action of scleroglucan and pectin in chickens. Proc. Soc. Exp. Biol. Med., 122, 551.

Griminger, P., and J. L. Gamarsh. (1972). Body composition of pigeons. Poultry Sci., 51, 1464.

Griminger, P., H. Fisher, and H. S. Weiss. (1963). Food restriction and spontaneous avian atherosclerosis. Life Sci., 6, 410.

Griminger, P., V. Villamil, and H. Fisher. (1969). The meal eating response of the chicken—species differences, and the role of partial starvation. J. Nutr., 99, 368.

Hurwitz, S., A. Bar, M. Katz, D. Sklan, and P. Budowski. (1973).

262

Absorption and secretion of fatty acids and bile acids in the intestine of the laying fowl. *J. Nutr.*, *103*, 543.

Ivy, C. A., and M. C. Nesheim. (1973). Factors influencing the liver fat content of laying hens. *Poultry Sci.*, *52*, 281.

Janecek, H. M., R. Suzuki, and A. C. Ivy. (1959). Endogenous excretion and capacity to absorb dietary cholesterol in the chicken. *Am. J. Physiol.*, *197*, 1341.

Johnston, D. W. (1971). The absence of brown adipose tissue in birds. *Comp. Biochem. Physiol.*, *40A*, 1107.

Kakita, C., P. J. Johnson, R. Pick, and L. N. Katz. (1972). Relationship between plasma cholesterol level and coronary atherosclerosis in cholesterol-oil fed cockerels. *Atherosclerosis*, *15*, 17.

Kompiang, I. P., and W. R. Gibson. (1973). Effect of hypophysectomy on lipogenesis and glycogenesis in cockerels. *Am. J. Physiol.*, *224*, 362.

Landauer, W., C. A. Pfeiffer, W. U. Gardner, and J. C. Shaw. (1941). Blood serum and skeletal changes in two breeds of ducks receiving estrogens. *Endocrinology*, *28*, 458.

Leclercq, B., I. Hassan, and J. C. Blum. (1974). The influence of force-feeding on the transport of plasma lipids in the chicken *(Gallus gallus L.)*. *Comp. Biochem. Physiol.*, *47B*, 289.

Lepkovsky, S., A. Chari-Bitron, R. M. Lemmon, R. C. Ostwald, and M. K. Dimick. (1960). Metabolic and anatomic adaptations in chickens "trained" to eat their daily food in two hours. *Poultry Sci.*, *39*, 385.

Leveille, G. A. (1969). *In vitro* hepatic lipogenesis in the hen and chick. *Comp. Biochem. Physiol.*, *28*, 431.

Lillie, R. J., and H. Menge. (1968). Effect of linoleic acid deficiency on the fertilizing capacity and semen fatty acid profile of the male chicken. *J. Nutr.*, *95*, 311.

Lowenstein, J. M. (1968). Citrate and the conversion of carbohydrate into fat. In "The Metabolic Roles of Citrate," Biochemical Society Symposium No. 27 (T. W. Goodwin, Ed.). New York: Academic Press, p. 61.

Marion, J. E., T. S. Boggess, Jr., and J. G. Woodroof. (1967). Effect of dietary fat and protein on lipid composition and oxidation in chicken muscle. *J. Food Sci.*, *32*, 426.

Marion, J. E., H. M. Edwards, Jr., and J. C. Driggers. (1961). Influence of diet on serum cholesterol in the chick. *J. Nutr.*, *74*, 171.

Mathur, R. S., and R. H. Common. (1969). A note on the daily urinary excretion of estradiol-17-β and estrone by the hen. *Poultry Sci.*, *48*, 100.

McDonald, M. R., and O. Riddle. (1945). The effect of reproduction and estrogen administration on the partition of calcium, phosphorus, and nitrogen in pigeon plasma. *J. Biol. Chem.*, *159*, 445.

Miller, D., and P. Robisch. (1969). Comparative effect of herring, menhaden, and safflower oils on broiler tissues fatty acid composition and flavor. *Poultry Sci.*, *48*, 2146.

Neely, J. R., and J. F. Oram. (1973). Control of fatty acid metabolism in adipose tissue. In "Best and Taylor's Physiological Basis of Medical Practice" (9th ed.) (J. R. Brobeck, Ed.). Baltimore: Williams and Wilkins, p. 7-123.

Nir, I., and V. Levy. (1973). Response of blood plasma glucose, free fatty acids, triglycerides, insulin and food intake to bovine insulin in geese and cockerels. *Poultry Sci.*, *52*, 886.

Nirmalan, G. P., and J. C. George. (1972). The influence of exogenous oestrogens and androgen on respiratory activity and total lipid of the whole blood of the Japanese quail. *Comp. Biochem. Physiol.*, *42B*, 237.

Nitsan, Z., I. Nir, Y. Dror, and I. Bruckental. (1973). The effect of forced feeding and of dietary protein level on enzymes associated with digestion, protein and carbohydrate metabolism in geese. *Poultry Sci.*, *52*, 474.

Patton, N. M., R. V. Brown, and C. C. Middleton. (1974). Familial cholesterolemia in pigeons. *Atherosclerosis*, *19*, 307.

Pearce, J. (1971). An investigation of the effects of dietary lipid on hepatic lipogenesis in the growing chick. *Comp. Biochem. Physiol.*, *40B*, 215.

Pick, R., and L. N. Katz. (1965). The morphology of experimental, cholesterol- and oil-induced atherosclerosis in the chick. In "Comparative Atherosclerosis" (J. C. Roberts, Jr., R. Straus, and M. S. Cooper, Eds.). New York: Harper & Row.

Pick, R., S. Jain, L. N. Katz, and P. Johnson. (1965). Effect of dietary protein level on regression of cholesterol-induced hypercholesterolemia and atherosclerosis of cockerels. *J. Atheroscler. Res.*, *5*, 16.

Renner, R. (1964). Factors affecting the utilization of "carbohydrate-free" diets by the chick. I. Level of protein. *J. Nutr.*, *84*, 322.

Renner, R. (1965). Site of fat absorption in the chick. *Poultry Sci.*, *44*, 861.

Renner, R., and F. W. Hill. (1961). Factors affecting the absorbability of saturated fatty acids in the chick. *J. Nutr.*, *74*, 254.

Rudas, B., G. Wick, and R. K. Cole. (1972). Serum lipid pattern in chickens of the obese strain. *J. Endocrinol.*, *55*, 609.

Sallmann, H.-P., and J. Schole. (1973). Untersuchungen zum Fettleberproblem der Legehenne. III. *Mitt. Zbl. Vet. Med. A*, *20*, 222.

Shannon, D. W. F. (1971). The effect of level of intake and free fatty acid content on the metabolizable energy value and net absorption of tallow by the laying hen. *J. Agri. Sci. Cambridge*, *76*, 217.

Shrago, E., J. A. Glennon, and E. S. Gordon. (1971). Comparative aspects of lipogenesis in mammalian tissues. *Metabolism*, *20*, 54.

Siller, W. G. (1965). Spontaneous atherosclerosis in the fowl. In "Comparative Atherpsclerosis" (J. C. Roberts, Jr., R. Straus, and M. S. Cooper, Eds.). New York: Harper & Row, p. 66.

Stumpf, P. K. (1969). Metabolism of fatty acids. *Ann. Rev. Biochem.*, *38*, 159.

Sturkie, P. D. (1965). Gonadal hormones. In "Avian Physiology" (2nd ed.) (P. D. Sturkie, Ed.). Ithaca, N. Y.: Cornell University Press.

Summers, J. D., and H. Fisher. (1962). The nutritional requirements of the protein-depleted chicken. V. Effect of depletion by starvation on body composition and subsequent energy needs of the adult rooster. *Z. Ernährungswiss.*, *3*, 48.

Umberger, E. J., G. H. Gass, and J. M. Curtis. (1958). Design of a biological assay method for the detection and estimation of estrogenic residues in the edible tissues of domestic animals treated with estrogens. *Endocrinology*, *63*, 806.

van Tienhoven, A. (1968). "Reproductive Physiology of Vertebrates." Philadelphia: W. B. Saunders Company.

Vermeersh, G., and F. Vanschoubroek. (1968). The quantification of the effect of increasing levels of various fats on body weight gain, efficiency of food conversion and food intake of growing chicks. *Brit. Poultry Sci.*, *9*, 13.

Vogtmann, H., and A. L. Prabucki. (1971). Über den Einfluss der Art des Futterfettes auf das Fettsäuremuster der Leberlipide sowie auf den Vitamin-A- und-E-Gehalt der Leber von Legehennen. *Intl. J. Vit. Nutr. Res.*, *41*, 33.

Volpe, J. J., and P. R. Vagelos. (1973). Saturated fatty acid biosynthesis and its regulation. *Ann. Rev. Biochem.*, *42*, 21.

Wartman, A. M., and W. E. Connor. (1973). The cholesterol balance and turnover in genetically hypercholesterolemic pigeons: their response to treatment with a hypocholesterolemic drug, cholestane-3β, 5α, 6β-triol. *J. Lab. Clin. Med.*, *82*, 793.

Weeks, J. R. (1974). Prostaglandins. *Fed. Proc.*, *33*, 37.

Weiss, H. S., H. Fisher, and P. Griminger. (1968). Interrelationship among plasma cholesterol, blood pressure, blood coagulation and spontaneous avian atherosclerosis. *Poultry Sci.*, *47*, 137.

Weiss, J. F., R. M. Johnson, and E. C. Naber. (1967). Effect of some dietary factors and drugs on cholesterol concentration in the egg and plasma of the hen. *J. Nutr.*, *91*, 119.

Whitehead, C. C. (1973). The site of fat absorption in the hen. *Proc. Nutr. Soc. 32*, 16A.

Yablonkevich, M. L. (1972). Composition of fatty acids in hypodermic fat depots in migrating and nonmigrating birds. *Dokl. Akad. Nauk SSSR (ser. Biol.)*, *206*, 1465.

Yeh, S-j. C., and G. A. Leveille. (1972). Cholesterol and fatty acid synthesis in chicks fed different levels of protein. *J. Nutr.*, *102*, 349.

Yeh, S-j. C., and G. A. Leveille. (1973a). Significance of skin as a site of fatty acid and cholesterol synthesis in the chick. *Proc. Soc. Exp. Biol. Med.*, *142*, 115.

Yeh, S-j. C., and G. A. Leveille. (1973b). Influence of dietary protein level on plasma cholesterol turnover and fecal steroid excretion in the chick. *J. Nutr.*, *103*, 407.

# 14

## Kidneys, Extrarenal Salt Excretion, and Urine

P. D. Sturkie

## 264 ANATOMY

The urinary organs consist of paired symmetrical kidneys and the ureters, which transport urine to the urodeum of the cloaca. A urinary bladder and a renal pelvis are absent in birds. The kidneys are located in the bony depressions of the fused pelvis. Each kidney is made up of three divisions, often called lobes, designated as cranial, middle, and caudal (Siller and Hindle, 1969). Each division is made up of lobules, comprised of a large cortical mass of tissue and a smaller medullary component (Figures 14–1, 14–2, and 14–3). It is more correct to consider the avian lobe as the total complement of lobules drained by a single ureteral branch (Siller, 1971).

### Nephrons and Glomeruli

The *nephrons* include the glomerulus and tubules of two main types: those with no loops of Henle, of the reptilian type, located exclusively in the cortex; and those of the mammalian type, with long or intermediate length loops, located in the medulla (Figure 14–1; Braun and Dantzler, 1972). The reptilian type (RT) nephrons, located at the surface of the kidney, are arranged in radial fashion around a core formed by the central efferent vein. The cylinders formed by the RT nephrons and central vein form repeating units of cortex grouped in radiating patterns and associated with a single,

smaller medullary cone (Figure 14–1; see also Poulson, 1965). The medullary tubules are less numerous and some have very long loops of Henle; others have shorter loops. The medullary cone is tapered because of the varying lengths of the loops of Henle and the successive fusion of the collecting ducts, leading to a single duct at the tip of the core (Braun and Dantzler, 1972). Sperber (1960) and Siller (1971) have reviewed the structure of the nephron in detail.

Siller and Hindle (1969) reported a one-to-one relationship between cortical and medullary lobules, based on sectioned material. However, different conclusions were reached by other investigators, including Poulson (1965) and Johnson and Mugaas (1970a,b), who proposed that each medullary lobule drains several cortical ones. This conclusion, according to Johnson *et al.* (1972), disregarded the cortical lobule as a branched structure, which gave misleading results. Their studies (Johnson *et al.,* 1972), based on injected specimens, indicated that "a typical cortical lobule" is associated with several medullary lobules. There is considerable overlap in organizational pattern, however; although a given medullary lobule may receive collecting ducts from a portion of only one cortical lobule, many instances are observed where the same medullary lobule is associated with parts of separate cortical lobules.

The *glomerulus,* which is structurally similar to that of mammals, includes a Bowman's capsule and

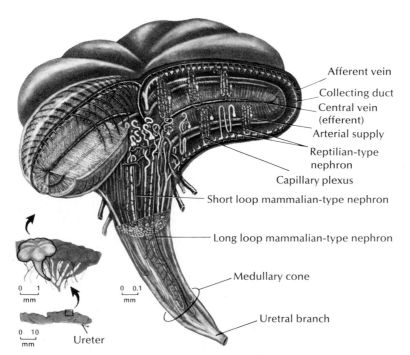

Afferent vein
Collecting duct
Central vein (efferent)
Arterial supply
Reptilian-type nephron
Capillary plexus
Short loop mammalian-type nephron
Long loop mammalian-type nephron
Medullary cone
Uretral branch
Ureter

14–1
A three-dimensional drawing of a section of avian kidney showing the types of nephrons present and their relationship to other renal structures. Interlobular veins designated as afferent veins, intralobular vein as central vein. (After Braun and Dantzler, 1972.)

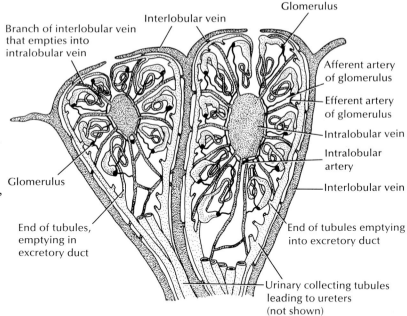

14–2
Diagram of the bird kidney showing the arrangement of the glomeruli and tubules in two lobules and blood vessels supplying them. (After Spanner, 1925.)

Branch of interlobular vein that empties into intralobular vein

Interlobular vein

Glomerulus

Afferent artery of glomerulus

Efferent artery of glomerulus

Intralobular vein

Intralobular artery

Interlobular vein

Glomerulus

End of tubules, emptying in excretory duct

End of tubules emptying into excretory duct

Urinary collecting tubules leading to ureters (not shown)

a juxtaglomerular apparatus with macula densa. The center of all glomeruli is occupied by a mass of mesangial cells, not present in mammals, around which the capillary loops are arranged in simple fashion (Siller and Hindle, 1969). The avian glomerulus is smaller and less vascular than the mammalian one, with fewer capillary loops (Sperber, 1960; see also Figure 14–3); it can therefore be expected to filter less per glomerulus. The number of glomeruli of certain birds, according to Marshall (1934) and others reviewed by him, are as follows:

|  | Body weight (g) | Number of glomeruli in both kidneys (thousands) |
|---|---|---|
| Chicken | 2500 | 840 |
| Duck | 3670 | 1989 |
| Goose | 5400 | 1659 |
| Pigeon | 232–420 | 274–535 |

The number of glomeruli ranges from 30,000 in small passerines to 200,000 in the chicken, according to Benoit (1950).

## Size

The kidneys of birds are relatively larger than those of mammals, ranging from 2 to 2.6% of body weight, depending on species (Benoit, 1950). Based on a study of 181 species, Johnson (1968) reported

that species weighing less than 100 g, weighing 100–1000 g, and weighing above 1000 g had kidney weights higher than 1%, exactly 1%, and less than 1%, respectively. The ratio of kidney to body weights (in mg/g) ranged from 6 to 21. The size of

14–3 Electron micrograph of a chicken glomerulus, showing afferent arteriole arising from intralobular artery (X) and the arrangement of capillary loops and efferent arteriole. (After Siller, 1971.)

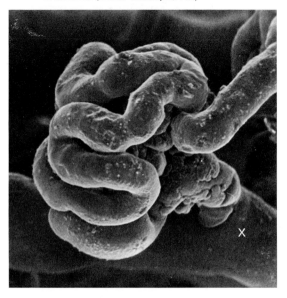

266 certain kidney components has been reported in 17 species of wild birds as follows by Johnson and Mugaas (1970b):

Diameter of cortical lobules, 0.36–1.72 mm
Diameter of medullary lobules, 0.12–0.97 mm
Number of collecting ducts entering lobules, 9–85
Diameter of thick limb of tubule, 18–35 $\mu$m
Diameter of thin limb of tubule, 11–22 $\mu$m

Certain measurements on individual nephrons of *Lophortyx gambel* (Gambel's quail) were made by Braun and Dantzler (1972) as follows:

| Type | Mammalian | | Reptilian |
|---|---|---|---|
| | Long loop | Short loop | |
| Length of proximal convoluted tubule (mm) | 3.6 | 3.4 | 1.6 |
| Length of Henles loop (mm) | 2.7 | 1.5 | – |
| Volume of glomeruli (nl) | 0.247 | 0.237 | 0.032 |

Measurements of chicken nephrons (see Sturkie, 1965) reveal similar dimensions as those for quail. The diameters for certain hen nephrons are as follows; glomerulus, 0.086 mm; proximal tubule, 0.062 mm; thick part of loop, 0.0349 mm; thin part of loop, 0.0186 mm;

## Circulation

The main blood vessels that supply and drain the lobule and the arrangement of these vessels within the lobules are shown in Figures 14–2 and 14–4 and also in Figure 4–1 in Chapter 4. There are three pairs of renal arteries; the anterior, arising directly from the aorta, and the middle and posterior ones, arising from the sciatic artery (Siller and Hindle, 1969) or external iliac artery (Figure 4–2, Chapter 4). The latter two branches supply the middle and posterior divisions (lobes) of the kidney. The femoral artery sends no branches to the kidney. Branches from the renal arteries become the intralobular arteries and these ramify to form the afferent arteriole to the glomeruli and the efferent artery leaving the glomeruli (Figure 14–2).

**Renal portal.** Birds, like reptiles, amphibia, and fish, have a renal portal circulation, but it is only since 1946 that the physiologic significance of this system has become evident. Sperber (1948, 1960)

has demonstrated that the renal portal veins carry blood to the kidney tubules and behave as arteries. When a substance normally secreted by tubules is injected into the leg vein (femoral vein or external iliac vein), it is excreted first by the tubules on the injected side before it gets into the general circulation. Apparently the tubules do not receive an afferent arterial blood supply directly but the efferent arterioles from the glomeruli anastomose with the capillary network of afferent veins; the peritubular blood is thus mixed with arterial and venous (renal portal) blood (Sperber, 1960). However, it is not possible from injection preparations to determine where the arteriole ends and the venous network begins (Siller and Hindle, 1969). These authors have reported that arterioles branching from the intralobular arteries may bypass the glomeruli and run directly to the peritubular capillary network. Ultimately the venous network empties into the central renal vein.

Located at the juncture of the renal vein and the iliac vein (renal portal) is a prominent valve that governs the flow of blood into the renal vein. This valve varies in shape and structure among the different species (Spanner, 1925, 1939). Little is known concerning its physiology except that pressure and flow relations in the renal portal veins and the renal veins may influence its opening and closing and therefore the relative amounts of afferent venous blood supplying the kidney by way of the interlobular veins and of extrarenal blood, which bypasses the kidney (see also Chapter 4). It is known that histamine and acetylcholine cause this valve to close in *in vitro* studies and epinephrine causes it to open (Rennick and Gandia, 1954). This valve is richly innervated with sympathetic and parasympathetic fibers (Akester and Mann, 1969). Akester (1967) has made a radiographic study of the renal portal system in the domestic chicken. After injection of both renal portal veins, the routes or courses the injectate and blood can take are as follows: (1) via the renal portal vein directly into the renal vein and thence to the vena cava (valves open) (this is the most common route); (2) via the caudal renal portal vein and the coccygeomesenteric vein and then toward the liver; (3) via the cranial renal portal vein and the vertebral venous sinuses. The coccygeomesenteric vein provides a link between the renal and hepatic portal systems. Blood flow may be shunted from the coccygeomesenteric vein away from the liver to the renal portal vein and from the latter to the coccygeomesenteric (Akester, 1967; Clarkson, 1961; Shimada and Sturkie, 1973; Sturkie and Abati, 1975; see also Chapter 4 and Figure 14–4).

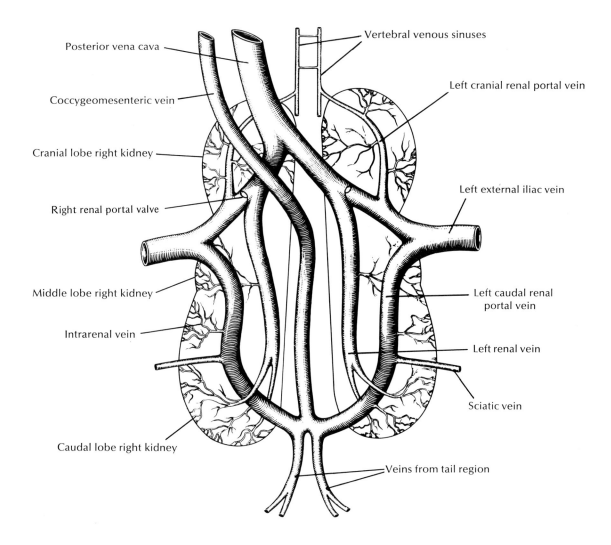

Posterior vena cava

Coccygeomesenteric vein

Cranial lobe right kidney

Right renal portal valve

Middle lobe right kidney

Intrarenal vein

Caudal lobe right kidney

Vertebral venous sinuses

Left cranial renal portal vein

Left external iliac vein

Left caudal renal portal vein

Left renal vein

Sciatic vein

Veins from tail region

## KIDNEY FUNCTION

The kidney performs three main functions: filtration, excretion or secretion, and absorption. It filters water and some substances normally used by the body from the blood, along with waste products of metabolism, which are voided in the urine. It conserves needed body water, glucose, and other substances by reabsorption. These processes make the kidney an important homeostatic mechanism whereby the body water and solutes are maintained at fairly constant levels.

Filtration takes place in the glomeruli, where crystalloids and substances with molecules of medium to small size pass through the capillary walls of the glomeruli into the capsule. The plasma proteins, which are composed of large molecules, do not normally pass through the capillary walls and

14-4 The principal veins concerned in the renal portal and hepatic portal systems of the chicken. Cranial and caudal renal portals also referred to as external and internal iliac veins respectively. (After Akester, 1967.)

are not filterable. Some of the filterable substances of the blood are sodium, potassium, chloride, inorganic phosphate, glucose, urea, creatinine, and uric acid. These substances have the same concentration in the capsular fluid as in the blood plasma and this is evidence of filtration.

The concentration of some of the substances in the urine may be higher or lower than that in the blood plasma. A lower concentration usually indicates that the substance is being reabsorbed by the kidney tubules. Glucose normally does not appear in the urine, but it is completely filterable and therefore must be reabsorbed. When the kidney tubule suffers impairment, such as follows administration of the glucoside, phlorizin, or when the blood sugar level is inordinately high, not all of the glucose that is filtered is reabsorbed and some appears in the urine.

The kidney tubules also reabsorb water, which aids in maintaining normal blood volume.

The concentration of certain substances in the tubules and urine may be higher than that in the plasma or glomerular filtrate. When the increased concentration cannot be accounted for by reabsorption of water from the tubules, it is evidence of tubule secretion.

In the aglomerular kidney of some marine teleosts, in which there is no filtration, the kidney tubules secrete the urine. Certain metabolites are excreted by the tubules, including uric acid in birds and reptiles and creatinine in fishes, chicken, anthropoid apes, and man. A number of foreign substances, such as Phenol Red, diodrast, and hippuran, when administered to mammals and birds, have a higher renal clearance than does inulin, indicating tubular secretion. Secretory activity is relatively a more important function in birds than mammals.

Energy is expended by the tubular cells in secretion and reabsorption. Reabsorption occurs even when the substance reabsorbed is many times more concentrated in blood than in the urine and is therefore not accomplished by simple diffusion.

Changes in arterial pressure do not appreciably affect secretion or reabsorption but do affect rate of filtration. The pressure required to drive the fluid through the glomerular blood vessels must be sufficient to overcome the pressure exerted by the capsular membrane and the osmotic pressure of blood colloids. The effective filtration pressure ($P_f$) therefore equals the pressure in the glomerular blood vessels ($P_b$) minus the capsular pressure ($P_c$) and the osmotic pressure of the blood colloids ($P_o$):

$$P_f = P_b - (P_o + P_c)$$

$P_b$ and $P_f$ can be estimated by determining the pressure required in the kidneys or ureters to stop urine flow. $P_b$ in the dog approximates 60% of mean arterial pressure. Recent direct determinations of $P_b$ in rat kidney indicate levels (45 mm Hg) considerably lower than indirect levels. The pressure required to stop urine flow in the chicken ureter may be as high as 32 mm Hg or as low as 7.5–15 mm Hg, according to Gibbs (1929a). Other factors affecting filtration are considered below.

## RENAL CLEARANCE

Renal clearance may be defined as the volume of blood that can be cleared of a given substance by excretion of urine for 1 min or the minimum volume of blood required to furnish the quantity of substances excreted in the urine in 1 min (Smith, 1951). The volume of blood cleared of a particular substance by the kidney in 1 min may be expressed as follows:

$U_x$ = concentration of $x$ in each milliliter of urine
$V$ = rate of urine formation (ml/min)
$P_x$ = concentration of $x$ in each milliliter of plasma
$U_x V$ = rate of excretion of $x$ (mg/min)

Then $U_x V / P_x$ = volume of plasma required to supply the quantity of $x$ excreted in each minute's time. Therefore $UV/P$ equals the clearance of a given substance, $x$ in the plasma.

The substance to be tested is usually infused at a constant rate, and urine samples are collected at regular and frequent intervals (usually at intervals of 2–7 min in the chicken). Blood samples are usually taken near the middle of the collection periods. The plasma concentrations are plotted against time and the exact values at the middle of each urine collection period are determined by interpolation.

Clearance therefore involves filtration ($C_F$), secretion ($T_S$), and reabsorption ($T_R$):

$$T_R = C_F P_x - U_x V$$

The point at which rate of reabsorption becomes constant and does not increase with increased plasma concentration (saturated) is known as the transport maximum ($T_m$). Tubular secretion,

$$T_S = U_x V - C_F P_x$$

### Filtration

**Inulin clearance and glomerular filtration rate (GFR).** A substance suitable for measuring glomerular filtration must be completely filterable and physiologically inert and must not be reabsorbed, excreted, or synthesized by the kidney tubules. Such a substance is inulin, a starchlike polymer containing 32 hexose molecules with a molecular weight of 5200. Inulin is neither reabsorbed nor excreted by the kidney tubules of mammals, amphibians, reptiles, or birds, and varies directly with the concentration of inulin in the plasma. Because $UV/P$ is constant and independent of plasma concentration, the clearance of inulin is a measure of glomerular filtration.

The ratio of the inulin clearance to the simultaneous clearance of other substances, such as urea, uric acid, creatinine, and Phenol Red, indicates whether the substance in question is reabsorbed or secreted by the kidney tubules. For example, a ratio of less than 1 indicates reabsorption and a ratio greater than 1 indicates excretion or secretion by the tubules. Figures on filtration (inulin clearance) and urine flow on a number of avian species are shown in Table 14–1.

Korr's (1939) data indicate that the rate of urine flow increases with inulin clearance and that both are influenced by the degree of hydration of the body, although hydration increases the filtration rate more than it does urine flow. However, the data of Pitts (1938) and Shannon (1938a), based on birds hydrated to a lesser extent, show only a slight increase in inulin clearance with urine flows from 0.4 to 1.8 ml/min; more recent data by Skadhauge and Schmidt-Nielsen (1967) on chickens also reveal a modest decrease in GFR from 2.13 to 1.73 ml/kg/min, following dehydration, even though urine flows decreased greatly from 0.298 to .018 ml/kg/min. GFR in the hydrated budgerigar was 4.43 $\mu$l/g/min and 3.24 in the dehydrated state (Krag and Skadhauge, 1972); urine flow averaged 0.028 and 0.105 $\mu$l/g/min in the dehydrated and hydrated states, respectively. GFR in mourning doves was about constant (2.6 ml/kg/min) at moderate to high rates of urine flow, but at low urine flows (below 0.15 ml/kg/min) it decreased with urine flow (Shoemaker, 1967). The state of hydration and urine flow also influence the GFR in ducks but not greatly because ducks drinking sea water and fresh water had GFR's of 2.1 and 2.5 ml/kg/min (Holmes et al., 1968). State of hydration and urine flow therefore do influence GFR in birds and lower forms but are not important factors in mammals. Arginine vasotocin, the antidiuretic hormone of Aves, decreased GFR in chickens (Ames et al., 1971) and in desert quail (Braun and Dantzler, 1974) and the excretion of $Na^+$ and $Cl^-$ but had no appreciable effect on urea (Ames et al., 1971). The GFR reduction in quail was attributed to a reduction in the number of filtering reptilian nephrons. Urine flow was reduced drastically.

An inulin clearance of 1.8 ml/kg of body weight per minute means that for a chicken weighing 2 kg, the fluid filtered through the kidneys in 1 min amounts to 3.6 ml and that in 1 hr to 216 ml or 5.18 liters in 24 hr. As approximately 130 ml of urine are voided by the chicken in 24 hr (Hester et al., 1940), most of the water filtered through the

*Table 14–1*   *Figures for inulin clearance in Aves*

| Species | Mean inulin clearance (ml/kg/min) | Condition | Mean urine flow (ml per bird or kg per minute) | References |
|---|---|---|---|---|
| Chicken | 1.84 | Hydration | 0.89 | Pitts (1938) |
| | 1.87 | Hydration | 0.90 | Shannon (1938a) |
| | 1.70 | Hydration | 1.20 | Shannon (1938b) |
| | 2.15 | Hydration | 1.13 | Pitts and Korr (1938) |
| | 1.37 | No water given | 0.33 | Korr (1939) |
| | 0.60 | Dehydrated 48–60 hr | 0.15 | Korr (1939) |
| | 2.45 | Bird very hydrated | 1.4 | Korr (1939) |
| | 3.00 | Laying hen not fasted | — | Sperber (1960) |
| | 1.96 | Not stated | 0.38 | Sykes (1960b) |
| | 1.81 | Fasted 18 hr, mild hydration | 0.92 | Berger et al. (1960) |
| Chicken | 1.73 | Dehydrated | 0.018 kg | Skadhauge and |
| | 2.12 | Hydrated | 0.298 kg | Schmidt-Nielsen |
| | 2.06 | Salt loaded (mild) | 0.181 kg | (1967a) |
| Duck | 2.1 | Sea water | 0.025 kg | Holmes et al. (1968) |
| | 2.5 | Fresh water | 0.023 kg | Holmes et al. (1968) |
| Seagull | 4.6 | Fresh water | — | Douglas (1966) |
| | 4.2 | Salt loading | — | Douglas (1966) |
| Doves | 2.6 | Mild hydration | — | Shoemaker (1967) |
| Budgerygah | 4.4 | Hydrated | 0.105 kg | Krag and Skadhauge (1972) |
| | 3.2 | Dehydrated | 0.028 kg | Krag and Skadhauge (1972) |

270 kidney (nearly 98%) is reabsorbed into the tubules; this figure is of the same order as that for man.

**GFR and salt loading.** Salt loading also affects GFR in birds with and without extrarenal mechanisms (nasal glands) for salt handling. Salt loading of chickens produced by infusing NaCl above 20 meq/kg of body weight (20–50 mg) decreased GFR at least 40% at higher loading and urine flow to the same magnitude. Initially there was an increase in urine flow with salt loading until the amount infused reached 40 meq (Dantzler, 1966). There was also an increase in urine and plasma osmolality. Braun and Dantzler (1972) have reported similar results in Gambel's quail and further demonstrated that the reptilian-type nephrons fail to filter salt during heavy salt loading. This substantiated the suggestion made by Dantzler (1966) that GFR was related to the number of functioning glomeruli. Filtration rates were determined on individual nephrons of the quail by Braun and Dantzler (1972), employing a modification of Hanssen's technique that involves the use of [14C]-labeled sodium ferrocyanide.

Moderate salt loading for chickens (12–15 mg/kg of NaCl) did not influence GFR (Skadhauge and Schmidt-Nielsen, 1967a) nor in ducks drinking sea water (Holmes et al., 1968) or quail (Braun and Dantzler, 1972). However, there was an increase in osmolality of the urine. Salt loads of 20–30 meq/kg in seagulls also had an inconsistent effect on the GFR (Douglas, 1966).

**Apparent tubular excretion fraction (ATEF).** Sperber (1948, 1960) demonstrated that the renal portal vein carried blood to avian renal tubules. When a substance was injected into the leg vein or iliac vein, the substance was first excreted by the tubules on the injected side or ipsilateral side before it got into the general circulation. This was determined by cannulating each ureter and collecting urine samples for determining the concentration of injected material. This technique has been used to demonstrate the tubular handling of various substances, $(x)$ and for determining the apparent tubular excretion fraction (ATEF), which represents the difference between the excretion rate $(E_x)$ (clearance) of the ipsilateral $(I,$ injected) and contralateral $(C)$ kidneys. Thus:

$$\text{ATEF} = \frac{E_{XI} - E_{XC} \times 100}{\text{Rate of infusion}}$$

The ATEF varies for different compounds at different concentrations. The ATEF of histamine, for example, ranges from 46 to 62% and for Phenol Red it is a little lower. The figures for other substances are as follows: choline, 23; PAH, 65; d-1-epinephrine, 38.

**Phenol Red clearance.** The dye Phenol Red is filtered and is secreted by the tubules of mammalian and avian species. Some of the dye is bound by the plasma proteins, and only the free dye is filterable. The amounts bound and free depend on the concentration of the dye in the plasma. At very low concentrations in chicken plasma (1 mg %), only 15–20% of the dye is free or filterable; at concentrations of 15 mg %, 60% is filterable, however, and at higher concentrations more is filterable because more is free (Pitts, 1938).

The ratio of free Phenol Red in the plasma to that in the urine is not constant and decreases after the concentration in the plasma has reached a certain point. At low plasma levels of the dye (1–3 mg %) the clearance ratio of Phenol Red to inulin ranges from 10:1 to 17:1 in the chicken (Pitts, 1938), as contrasted with ratios of 3.3:1 in man and 1.7:1 in the dog (Smith, 1951).

At high concentrations of the dye, the clearance ratio of Phenol Red to inulin approaches 1 (Figure 14–5). This means that as the plasma concentration reaches a certain point, proportionately less of the dye is excreted by the tubules and that the tubules have a limited capacity $(T_m)$ to excrete the dye. The absolute clearances of Phenol Red and inulin in the chicken at low plasma concentrations are 28 and 1.8 ml/min and at high concentrations (100 mg) they are 2.59 and 2.57, respectively (Pitts, 1938). The differences in the excretion of Phenol Red in relation to that filtered by the bird and mammal have been calculated by Smith (1951), who showed that the quantities of dye excreted by the tubules per milliliter of dye filtered for the dog, man, and chicken are 0.079, 0.21, and 0.62 mg, respectively. Phlorizin, which impairs or inhibits tubular function, depresses the excretion of Phenol Red in the chicken (Pitts, 1938); probenecid depresses the secretion of Phenol Red (Sanner, 1963). Different Phenol Red derivatives have different maximal transport rates (Sperber, 1954). Certain organic ions, such as tetraethylammonium (TEA), histamine, and piperidine, do not affect the tubular secretion of Phenol Red but they may influence the secretion of each other (Sperber, 1960).

**Urea clearance.** Urea is the chief nitrogenous constituent of the urine of mammals and represents the end product of protein metabolism, but uric acid is the chief nitrogenous constituent of urine in birds. Urea is the end product of purine metabolism in birds, yet it is handled by the avian kidney in a way similar to that in most mammals; it is completely filterable but it is partially reabsorbed by the kidney tubules, independently of the plasma concentration (Pitts and Korr, 1938). The chicken kidney contains arginase and can produce urea from plasma arginine, as was demonstrated by the infusion experiments of Owen and Robinson (1964).

The average urea clearance in the chicken is 1.50 ml/kg of body weight per minute, and the clearance ratio of urea to inulin is 0.74 (Pitts and Korr, 1938). This ratio is highly variable in turkeys, ranging from 1 to 0.02 (Skadhauge and Schmidt-Nielsen, 1967b); therefore the fraction of urea filtered that is resorbed or excreted in the urine can vary from 1 to 99% depending on conditions of hydration and salt loading. During hydration almost all of the filtered urea is excreted, and during dehydration nearly all (99%) is resorbed. In mammals on normal diets, the fraction of urea filtered that is excreted varies from 60% during hydration and water diuresis to 30–40% during antidiuresis (Skadhauge and Schmidt-Nielsen, 1967b). These authors (1967b) found that urea plays no role in the formation of a medullary osmotic gradient in the avian kidney, in contrast to the situation in mammals.

When urea is infused through the renal portal vein, unilateral diuresis occurs (Sykes, 1962). This may transiently increase the apparent clearance above the filtration rate on the infused side.

**Uric acid clearance.** Uric acid is synthesized in the liver and it is filtered by glomeruli and secreted by the kidney tubules. It is highly concentrated in the urine of birds and constitutes from 60 to 80% of the total nitrogen. Studies of uric acid clearance by Shannon (1938b) demonstrated that 87–93% of the chicken's uric acid is excreted by the tubules. The uric acid/inulin clearance ratio at moderate plasma uric acid concentrations (6–9 mg %) ranges from 7.5 to 15.8. These ratios are about the same as the Phenol Red/inulin ratios at low plasma levels of the dye. As the plasma level of uric acid is raised the ratio is depressed, until at a plasma uric acid level of 100 mg % the ratios range from 1.8 to 3.2. Actually, when clearance is plotted against plasma level of uric acid, the figure is similar to that for Phenol Red (Figure 14–5).

The absolute clearance of uric acid at plasma levels of 6–9 mg % is approximately 30 ml/kg/min (Shannon, 1938b). As the plasma level of uric acid increases, the amount filtered continues to increase; however, at very high plasma levels the ability of the tubules to secrete uric acid declines. The $T_m$ for uric acid is about 5 mg/min (Sykes, 1962). Sykes (1960a) reported the absolute clearance of uric acid in Sussex hens of 68.5 ml/min, or approximately 25 ml/kg at plasma levels under 5 mg %.

Clearances of about the same magnitude were reported by Nechay and Nechay (1959). The figures on uric acid reported by Sykes and by Nechay and Nechay are probably more reliable than some of the older data because they used a more reliable

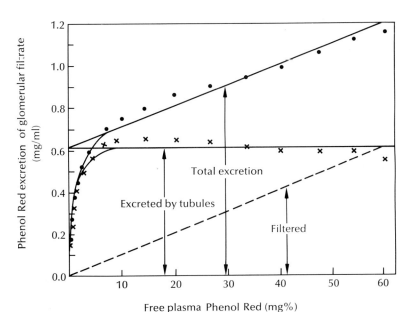

14–5

Excretion of Phenol Red by the chicken kidney in relation to concentration of free Phenol Red in plasma, indicating total excretion, that filtered, and that excreted by tubules. The amount of Phenol Red filtered increases with plasma concentration but this is not true for that excreted by tubules. (After Pitts, 1938.)

method (uricase) of uric acid determination. Most values (particularly on plasma) are lower with the uricase method. At similar plasma urate levels, the clearances of uric acid reported by Berger *et al.* (1960) suggest that the same cellular mechanism is involved in the tubular transport of PAH and uric acid. Increasing the plasma concentration of PAH depresses the clearance of uric acid. Further evidence that these substances compete in tubular transport is based on studies with drugs that depress uric acid secretion. These drugs likewise depress PAH transport. Such drugs as probenecid, sulfinpyrazone, and zoxazolamine, and high dosages of phenylbutazone, all of which increase uric acid secretion in man, depress its secretion in chickens (Berger *et al.*, 1960; Nechay and Nechay, 1959). In chickens these drugs depress secretion of uric acid, but in man they inhibit tubular reabsorption of it.

Clearances of uric acid in doves is about 25 ml/kg/min (Shoemaker, 1967) and of about the same magnitude in ducks (Stewart *et al.*, 1969). The site of tubular secretion of uric acid is not known but it appears in the collecting ducts and ureters in precipitated form.

Impaired renal clearance of uric acid of hereditary origin in chickens was reported by Austic and Cole (1972). Impaired clearance was associated with a high level of uric acid in the blood, which averaged 15 mg/100 ml compared to 8 mg/ml of a normal strain of chickens fed a standard diet. As protein level increased in the diet, the plasma level of uric acid increased to as high as 55 mg/100 ml in the high-uric acid strain and less in the low or normal strain. The renal clearance of uric acid of the high-uric acid strain was markedly less than the normal strain, and the rate of tubular secretion in the high-uric acid strain was only 40% of that of the normal strain.

**Creatinine and creatine clearance.** Creatinine is a normal constituent of the urine in mammals, but in birds the amount formed is negligible in relation to the amount of creatine. Clearance studies on birds, man, apes, and certain fishes indicate that the tubules of these species secrete creatinine. The creatinine/inulin ratio in the chicken at plasma concentrations of 9–12 mg % average 1.54 (Shannon, 1938a). At higher concentrations the ratio is depressed, and at concentrations of 200–230 mg % the ratios are 1.09 and 1.07, respectively. Sykes (1960b) reported that the absolute clearance of exogenous creatinine in hens is 3.90 ml/min at plasma concentrations ranging from 3.2 to 57.0 mg %, with a creatinine/inulin ratio of 1.46. The clearance of endogenous creatinine averaged 2.25

ml/min, with a creatinine/inulin ratio of 0.78. At normal or endogenous plasma levels (0.2–0.5 mg %), therefore, creatinine is not secreted but is reabsorbed. The ability of the kidney to clear the plasma of creatinine is therefore considerably lower than it is for uric acid, PAH, Phenol Red, and other substances.

The clearance of exogenous creatinine in hens averaged 6.70 ml/min, with a creatinine/inulin ratio of 2.2, at plasma concentrations of 2.8–13.3% (Sykes, 1960b). The mean clearance of endogenous creatine in hens is 3.90 ml, with a creatine/inulin ratio of 1.41.

The tubular secretion of creatinine can be inhibited by substances that inhibit the transport of either organic acids or bases, such as probenecid and priscoline, respectively, indicating transport by two systems (Rennick, 1967). Water diuresis increases creatinine clearance and urine flow (Dicker and Haslam, 1966).

**Clearance of other substances.** A number of other substances are known to be secreted by the kidney tubules of chickens. These include glucuronides of menthol and phenol; sulfuric esters of phenol, resorcinol, and hydroquinone (Sperber, 1960); tetraethylammonium (TEA) (Rennick *et al.*, 1954); thiamine and choline (Rennick, 1958); epinephrine (Rennick and Yoss, 1962); potassium (Rennick *et al.*, 1952; Orloff and Davidson, 1956; Sykes, 1961); histamine (Lindahl and Sperber, 1958); serotonin (Sanner and Wortman, 1962); acetylcholine and atropine (Acara *et al.*, 1973); and morphine (Watrous *et al.*, 1970; May *et al.*, 1967). The apparent tubular excretion fraction (ATEF) was determined on a number of these, as outlined previously, before and after administration of known metabolic blocking agents.

TEA is excreted at a very rapid rate and histamine, which has an ATEF ranging from 46 to 62%, is excreted less rapidly. The administration of certain organic bases (priscoline) depressed the secretion of histamine, suggesting that histamine has the same transport mechanism as the bases.

Serotonin (5-hydroxytryptamine), which is known to cause the release of histamine in chickens, appears to be secreted by the kidney tubules but not at an appreciable rate (Sanner and Wortman, 1962). Because excretion of serotonin might be influenced by its simultaneous destruction by monoamine oxidase, the effects of catron, an inhibitor of this enzyme, on serotonin excretion were studied. The inhibitor significantly increased the excretion rate of serotonin. Sanner (1963) has reported that serotonin is transported in the kidney tubule by the organic base system and is not influenced by pH. Reserpine did not influence the secretion of serotonin. Another substance, $d-1$-epinephrine, is secreted at a rate of about 75% of the excretion of PAH, which is very high. The ATEF of $d$-1-epinephrine averaged 38%. Probenecid, an inhibitor of the organic acid transport system, decreased the secretion of both epinephrine and PAH, but the secretion of the former was affected more (Rennick and Yoss, 1962).

Catechol produces a selective inhibition of epinephrine transport, suggesting a common transport pathway for the two (Quebbeman and Rennick, 1968). Although the tubular transport of injected catechol was previously found to be insensitive to both organic anion and cation competitors, the transport of the injected preformed conjugates of catechol, the glucuronide and sulfate, are sensitive to the organic anion competitor, probenecid (Rennick and Quebbemann, 1970). Catecholamines, catechol glucuronide, and preformed catechol sulfate were excreted at a site identical with that for PAH secretion, but injected catechol was excreted at a site distal to the site of PAH excretion.

Ferrocyanide and thiosulfate are secreted by kidney tubules (Sykes, 1960b). The tubules secrete acetylcholine by the organic cation transport mechanism (Acara and Rennick, 1972). Cholinesterase inhibitors enhanced the transport efficiency of acetylcholine. Atropine was also transported by the cation transport system and inhibited the transport of acetylcholine. Hemicholinium, which normally inhibits the synthesis of acetylcholine, did not inhibit the transport of acetylcholine but actually enhanced transport by 25% (Acara et al., 1973).

Novobiocin was found to inhibit the action of morphine-3, ethereal sulfate, and 5-hydroxyindole acetic acid (5HIAA) by inhibiting the organic anion transport system; however, it did not inhibit the action of 5HT or morphine. TEA and catechol transport were not affected but PAH transport was blocked (Fujimoto et al., 1973).

An inhibitor of the organic acid transport system, probenecid, had no effect on morphine transport but did block transport of morphine-3-ethereal sulfate (metabolite). The authors (Watrous et al., 1970) concluded that the site of action of probenecid was located at the border of peritubular cell.

## Renal Blood Flow

At low plasma concentrations certain substances are almost completely excreted by the tubules. The volume of the substance cleared per minute (see section on renal clearance for details) is therefore theoretically equal to the volume of plasma flowing through the kidney during the same time. In the bird, paraminohippuric acid (PAH), diodrast, and uric acid are very efficiently cleared from the plasma, and the clearance of these has been used to estimate renal plasma flow. Figures reported in the literature vary considerably, depending on the method used and on other factors, such as the variation caused by the presence of a renal portal circulation (see below). Sykes (1960) reported mean clearances of uric acid and PAH of 68.5 and 67.6 ml/min, respectively, for Light Sussex chickens ranging in weight from 2.3 to 2.9 kg; this gives a renal plasma flow of 23–30 ml/kg/min compared to 40 ml/kg/min reported by Skadhauge (1964). Other values include 27 ml/kg for ducks on fresh water (Holmes et al., 1968), and 25–30 ml/kg/min for mourning doves (Shoemaker, 1967). According to Sykes (1960a) there is less variation in the clearance of uric acid than there is for PAH, and uric acid may therefore be preferable for estimating plasma flow. Clearance of PAH decreases as the concentration increases above a given level (2 mg per 100 ml) and blood flow may therefore be underestimated. The transport maximum $(T_m)$ of PAH is reached in chickens when the blood level of PAH reaches 10–20 mg per 100 ml (Dantzler, 1966) and the amount secreted becomes constant. This value ranges from 1.08 to 1.93 mg/kg/min.

The ratio of inulin clearance to PAH clearance, the filtration fraction, is about 13% in doves (Shoemaker, 1967), 15% in chickens, and 11–15% in ducks (Holmes et al., 1968). This avian fraction is somewhat lower than that in mammals (20–25%), most likely because the arterial supply to the avian kidney is augmented with inflow of blood from the renal portal venous system (afferent). The relative contribution of this blood to the kidney circulation has not been determined (see also page 93).

## RENAL HANDLING OF ELECTROLYTES AND INORGANIC IONS

### Sodium Chloride

In birds without nasal glands sodium is handled by the kidney, but in those with salt glands 60–85 percent of the salt is eliminated by the nasal glands (see section on extrarenal salt excretion).

Sodium is the principal osmotically active electrolyte in the plasma and urine. It is actively absorbed in the intestine (see Chapter 10) and carried to the kidney, where it may be resorbed into the plasma or secreted by kidney tubules and excreted

274 in urine. This involves a renal concentration mechanism that depends on the size and orientation of Henle's loops. The solute is actively transported out of the ascending limb of Henle's loop; it then diffuses into the descending limbs and vasa recta and is carried to the tip of the medulla, where it is most concentrated. As urine water in water-permeable collecting tubules passes through the osmotic gradient in the medulla, water leaves the tubules and the urine is concentrated in the collecting ducts and ureters. The data of Emery et al. (1972), based on microcryoscopy, revealed an increasing concentration of NaCl from the cortex to the medulla; however, there was an actual decrease from this point to the deep medulla in the Savannah sparrow for reasons not clearly defined.

The renal concentrating ability depends on a countercurrent system in the medulla of mammals and also birds (Poulson, 1965; Skadhauge and Schmidt-Nielsen, 1967b). Differences in concentrating abilities of different mammalian species have been correlated with the lengths of the individual medullary loops of Henle involved but this is not true in birds (Poulson, 1965). However, it is positively correlated in birds with the number of Henle's loops and amount of medullary tissue generally (Poulson, 1965: Johnson and Mugaas, 1970b; Braun and Dantzler, 1972; Emery et al., 1972; Johnson and Ohmart, 1973).

Whether or not urine is osmotic, hypo-, or hyperosmotic depends on the degree to which the filtered solute is resorbed or excreted by the kidney and by the amount of filtered water that is excreted in the urine. The latter varies considerably depending on the degree of hydration. The amount of filtered solute resorbed or excreted is influenced by the loading of the solute and its transport maximum, $T_m$.

The habitat of avian species considerably influences their handling of water and electrolytes. Desert species subjected to long periods of insufficient water and species inhabiting salt marshes tend to conserve body fluids by increasing the rate of absorption of filtered water and the concentration of solutes. In such species the urine/plasma ratio of electrolytes and osmolality range from 2.3 to 5.8 (Poulson, 1965). *Passerculus sandwichensis rostratus* (Savannah sparrow), a water conserver, has a higher proportion of medullary nephrons than do nonconservers and is tolerant to NaCl solutions and sea water; however, it has little resistance to water deprivation and dehydration (Johnson and Ohmart, 1973). It appears that abundant medullary tissue may be also of adaptive value in the conservation of both water and electrolytes in some species,

whereas in other species it is important only in water conservation. Apparently factors other than quantity of medullary tissue are involved in these differences.

The presence of functional salt glands appears to be associated with increased weight of the renal mass of nonpasserine species (Hughes, 1970). Such species as the domestic chicken, the pigeon, and some marine species with salt glands have urine/plasma ratios of less than 1 to about 2, depending on conditions of hydration and salt loading. During dehydration birds are able to resorb more of the filtered water than most mammals (Skadhauge and Schmidt-Nielsen, 1967a). During water loading and diuresis the bird excretes more of the filtered water than do mammals. In birds, more NaCl is resorbed during dehydration than during hydration.

Shoemaker (1972) has tabulated the urinary concentrations of electrolytes in a number of avian species under varying conditions. The osmolalities of urine range in hydrated birds from 115 mosmoles/liter (for the chicken) to 512 for the mourning dove. Dehydration increased the figures to 538 mosmoles/liter in the chicken (Skadhauge and Schmidt-Nielsen, 1967a) to 607–848 in budgerigar (Krag and Skadhauge, 1972).

### Salt Loading

The osmolalities (mosmoles/liter) of urine after salt loading range from 362–450 in the chicken to 2000 in the salt marsh sparrow (Poulson and Bartholomew, 1962). Salt loading in ducks and gulls (with salt glands) indicates urine osmolalities similar to species without salt glands, particularly in the initial stages of loading; after this time, urine concentrations of salt decline, indicating that the nasal glands are excreting salt.

Details of the effects of dehydration, hydration, and mild salt loading on the osmotic and ionic composition of plasma and urine and on urine flow in chickens are shown in Table 14–2.

Acute water diuresis in desert quail produced by infusion of a dilute solution of glucose and salt caused a significant increase (more than 50%) in total kidney glomerular filtration rate (GFR) and in single nephron GFR of both mammalian- and reptilian-type nephrons. Despite the increase in GFR, urine flow rate was low and most of the birds excreted only 79% (average) of fluid infused during three 10-minute periods (Braun and Dantzler, 1975). These authors have reviewed their data and that of others.

May and Carter (1970) reported that cholinomimetric agents, when injected into the renal portal veins on one side, caused an increase in sodium and water excretion on that side. The effect was believed to be independent of the vasodilator effect and could be the result of direct inhibition of proximal tubule reabsorption of sodium.

Injection of an oncotically active substance, such as dextran or serum albumin, into the renal portal vein is followed by a reduction in kidney sodium excretion on the injected side and no change in the control side (Vereerstraeten and Toussaint, 1968). The effect is probably on the transport of sodium in the proximal tubule. It is known that corticosterones influence sodium retention and excretion (see Chapter 20).

## Calcium and Phosphates

The renal clearance of calcium in the laying hen was decreased slightly during the period of shell deposition on the egg and there was a significant increase in the clearance of phosphates (Prashad and Edwards, 1973).

Filtered phosphate is mainly reabsorbed, and its clearance, when compared to inulin, is about 0.1. After the administration of parathyroid hormone, which influences mobilization of calcium and phosphorus (see Chapter 19), the clearance of phosphate is over 3.00, indicating a high rate of secretion and possible inhibition of reabsorption (Levinsky and Davidson, 1957; Ferguson and Wolbach, 1967).

## Potassium

Potassium is an inorganic constituent that is filtered, reabsorbed, and secreted. Its level in the plasma is low and fairly constant (4–5 meq/liter); it is higher in urine (about 5–25 meq/liter), depending on conditions of hydration and loading (Table 14–2). Potassium is secreted in the fowl, but at a relatively low rate (Orloff and Davidson, 1956). The maximal rate of transport for one kidney (the one perfused) ranged from 60 to 85 $\mu$moles/min for a 2-kg chicken. Reducing $p_{CO_2}$ locally increases K excretion, and increasing $p_{CO_2}$ decreases it. A mercurial diuretic inhibited the excretion of K, and its virtual disappearance from the urine may indicate that the filtered K is entirely reabsorbed. Dehydration and salt loading increase its level in the urine.

Hydrochlorothiazide belongs to the sulphonamyl group of compounds and has been reported to have a diuretic action in turkeys. Sykes (1961) confirmed this and also reported that it increased the excretion of sodium and potassium in the urine.

Reserpine interferes with the diuretic action of theophylline and hydrochlorothiazide in chickens, according to Nechay and Sanner (1961).

Strophanthidin, a cardiac aglycone, has been reported to act directly on the kidney tubules of chickens and to inhibit the transport of potassium and hydrogen ions, as well as sodium ions (Orloff and Burg, 1960). Injection of the substance in the femoral vein caused an immediate increase in urine flow and in sodium excretion in the ipsilateral kidney. In some instances K excretion increased; in others it decreased. The drug inhibits sodium reabsorption and probably interferes with the secretion of potassium. The decrease in K excretion that occurred in some instances after administration of the drug is therefore interpreted as interference with secretion; it is proposed that in the chicken, as in other species, all or most of the filtered K is reabsorbed, and that subsequent secretion accounts for all or most of the K appearing in the urine.

## EXTRARENAL SALT EXCRETION

It had long been suspected that marine birds might be able to consume and handle salt water, but only in recent years has the mechanism responsible for this ability been discovered (Schmidt-Nielsen et al., 1958). Such birds have a specialized nasal gland that is able to secrete large quantities of NaCl. This gland has been reported and studied in several species, including cormorants (Schmidt-Nielsen et al., 1958), the brown pelican (Schmidt-Nielsen and Fange, 1958), the domestic duck (see Holmes et al., 1968; Holmes, 1972; Scothorne, 1959), the herring gull (Fange et al., 1958; Douglas, 1970), the Humboldt penguin (Schmidt-Nielsen and Sladen, 1958), roadrunner (Ohmart et al., 1970a,b), and in several other species reported by Shoemaker (1972), including ostriches, geese, flamingoes, and desert partridges.

### Anatomy of the Nasal Gland

The account that follows is mainly from Schmidt-Nielsen (1960). The existence of a nasal gland, so called, has been known for centuries. It is not, however, always located in the nose. In most marine birds it is located on the top of the head, above the orbit of the eye; it has also been called the supraorbital gland. On top of the skull of the gull are two flat, crescent-shaped "nasal" glands, located in the shallow depressions in the bone. Two ducts run from each side down to the nose, where they open into the vestibular concha. From the anterior nasal cavity, the secretion flows out through the nares and drips off from the tip of the beak. The gland consists of longitudinal lobes, which in cross-section show tubular glands radiating from a central canal. The gland receives its main arterial supply from the arteria ophthalmica interna. For further details on histology, see Ernest and Ellis (1969). The gland is innervated from the ganglion ethmoidale, which is supplied by a relatively large branch of the ophthalmic nerve and a small one from the facial nerve, as well as by sympathetic fibers. Stimulation of the parasympathetic nerve or branches going to the nasal gland produces an increase in volume of secretion rich in sodium (see Ash et al., 1969; Hakansson and Malcus, 1969). Acetylcholine also increases gland secretion and atropine blocks or depresses it (Fange et al., 1958; Ash et al., 1969). Acetylcholinesterase fibers are prominent and these disappear after denervation and nerve degeneration. Denervation abolished nasal secretion and changes in blood flow on geese following a salt load (Hanwell et al., 1971a,b). Stimulation of sympathetic nerves to the gland does not influence secretion directly but causes vasoconstriction (Fange et al., 1963).

Although a cholinergic mechanism is essential for normal nasal secretion, the latter is also dependent on an intact adenohypophysical–adrenocortical axis (Holmes, 1972). Removal of adenohypophysis reduces secretion of nasal gland of duck to about 5% of normal rate.

## Function of the Nasal Gland

Details of the anatomy and physiology of the nasal gland of a number of species have been reviewed by Shoemaker (1972) and Holmes (1972).

**Composition and rate of secretion.** The average ionic composition of the nasal secretion of a seagull is shown as follows, based on data of Schmidt-Nielsen (1960) in meq/liter.

| Na+ | K+ | Ca2+ and Mg2+ | Cl− | HCO3− |
|-----|-----|-----|-----|-----|
| 718 | 24 | 2.0 | 720 | 13 |

The variation in composition depends on the species involved, but the concentration of NaCl usually falls between one and two times that of sea water (Shoemaker, 1972). The concentrations are usually higher in marine species. Shoemaker (1972) has tabulated the concentration of ions in the nasal secretions and the maximum secretory rate following mild salt loading in some 19 species.

The usual concentration of Na in meq/liter for most species ranges from 500 to 700 but in some approaches 1000. Nasal secretion is not restricted to marine species but occurs also in certain terrestrial species such as *Ammoperdix heji* (desert partridge) and the ostrich. In these species nasal secretion occurred without osmotic stimulation but in response to high temperature (Schmidt-Nielsen et al., 1963). The chicken, pigeon, and many other species do not have nasal glands and handle all of their NaCl through the kidneys.

The amount or percentage of the intake of water and electrolytes excreted in the urine of ducks given fresh and salt water are as follows (Fletcher and Holmes, 1968):

| | Maintained on | |
|---|---|---|
| | Fresh water (%) | Salt water (%) |
| Water | 60.3 | 36.5 |
| Na+ | 59.5 | 10.0 |
| K+ | 71.3 | 71.3 |

The rate of secretion is more variable among species than is the concentration of fluid and is influenced by degree of salt loading and hydration. Data on rates of secretion are subject to greater variation because of difficulties of determining accurately flow rates. Secretion is usually collected by runoff from the beak into attached containers. Continuous secretion from moment to moment has been recorded by a new improved flowmeter (Hakansson and Malcus, 1969). The maximal secretory capacity of the nasal gland of herring gulls following initial electrical nerve stimulation for 3 min ranged from 0.280 to 0.375 ml/g/min of the tissue. These figures are about the same as those reported by Douglas (1970). Equal volumes were secreted from the two ducts of the glands. With continued secretion for periods of 1–2 hr, flow rate decreased to one-third to one-fourth the maximum level following electrical stimulation. These values are based on young herring gulls weighing approximately 1 kg, with salt glands weighing about 0.6 g per bird. The secretion therefore amounted to about 0.148–0.225 ml/min/kg of body weight, a figure similar to values reported for gulls by others (see the tabulation by Shoemaker, 1972) but lower than the value reported by Schmidt-Nielsen (1960) for herring gulls. Salt loading tends to increase the amount of secretion and the electrolyte concentration but to a lesser extent (Hanwell et al., 1971a; Holmes, 1972, and others).

The values reported by different investigators for different species vary from 0.074 to 0.50 ml/kg/min (Shoemaker, 1972). Hanwell *et al.* (1971a) reported secretion rates of 0.07–1.33 ml/g nasal tissue per minute in geese following different salt loads.

## Factors Affecting Nasal Secretion

The gland serves as an osmoregulator, for it responds to osmotic loads as well as to salt loads, although NaCl is the principal constituent affecting osmolality. A seagull that had ingested 134 ml of sea water containing 54 meq/liter of sodium, excreted most of the sodium through the salt gland, but some of it in the urine and feces within 175 min, as follows (Schmidt-Nielsen, 1960).

| Nasal secretion | | Cloacal excretion | |
|---|---|---|---|
| Volume (ml) | Sodium (meq/liter) | Volume (ml) | Sodium (meq/liter) |
| 56.3 | 43.7 | 75.2 | 4.41 |

Douglas (1970) reported that herring gulls receiving 80 ml of sea water containing 32.4 meq of Na excreted 66–74% of the Na load in the nasal fluid within 3.5–4 hr. The volume of nasal fluid ranged from 25.9 to 27.8 ml, or roughly 6 ml/hr. The volume of fluid excreted in the cloacal fluid was 80.1 ml in the unfasted bird and 38.2 ml in birds fasted for 24 hr before receiving the salt load. Fifteen to 18% of salt load was in the cloacal fluid.

Salt is therefore the principal stimulus to nasal secretion, and it is well known that progressive or extended salt loading increases the size of the gland and increases the size of cells in the gland (hyperplasia) (Ballantyne and Wood, 1969).

Oral administration of salt produces an increased (maximum) nasal secretion within 1½ hr, whereas the secretion begins almost immediately following intravenous administration.

Nonosmotic stimuli, such as physical stresses (temperature, light, sound), may induce salt gland secretion. Excitement decreases secretion in penguins (Douglas, 1968) and dehydration may decrease volume of nasal secretion (Douglas and Neely, 1969).

*Endocrines.* The stimulating effect of stresses may be exerted through the release of adrenal cortical steroids, a subject studied extensively in ducks by Holmes and co-workers and reviewed by him (Holmes and Wright, 1968: Holmes, 1972).

Although the normal triggering mechanism for nasal secretion may be osmoregulatory in nature, the final response is influenced by adrenocortical hormones. In the adrenalectomized salt-loaded duck there is no nasal secretion of NaCl (Phillips *et al.,* 1961), but it can be restored after administration of cortisol. Administration of cortisol, corticosterone, or ACTH to salt-loaded ducks increases nasal secretion (*see* Holmes, 1972). Moreover, adrenocortical hormones influence not only nasal secretion but also intestinal absorption of NaCl. Crocker and Holmes (1971) showed that ducks maintained on sea water as compared to fresh water had higher rates of Na transport and absorption (see Chapter 11) in the proximal parts of the small intestine and higher rates of nasal salt secretion. When salt water-adapted ducks received spironolactone, which inhibits aldosterone action, these ducks absorbed Na at the same rate as those in fresh water but did not secrete NaCl through the nasal gland. Aldosterone therefore not only influences intestinal absorption of Na, which is required in salt loading, but also the increased nasal secretion of salt. Nasal secretion is influenced also by thyroid hormones because it is decreased in the thyroidectomized duck given a salt load orally. This does not occur when salt is injected intravenously, indicating that the main effect is through a decreased absorptive capacity of the intestine (Ensor *et al.* 1970; see Holmes, 1972). Hypophysectomy reduces nasal secretion drastically; it can be restored with ACTH (Bradley and Holmes, 1971). Holmes (1975) has reviewed osmoregulation in marine birds.

Following a salt load in ducks or gulls there is an initial diuresis (renal phase), which is followed by nasal secretion and a progressive decrease in renal Na output as nasal secretion of Na progresses. As the Na is eliminated from the nasal gland this provides for an increase in osmotically free water and is a means of decreasing Na concentration in blood and urine. There is some evidence that separate mechanisms are involved in the handling of water and sodium by the salt gland (Inoue, 1963).

## Initiation and Control of Nasal Secretion

At the cellular level of nasal gland activity, $Na^+–K^+$, ATPase is most likely involved in increased nasal secretion, because it has been amply demonstrated that adaptation to salt loading results in a three- to fourfold increase (3 to 4 X) in ATPase activity (Fletcher *et al.,* 1967 and others; see Shoemaker, 1967; Holmes, 1972). When this activity is inhibited by administration of oaubain to the

**Table 14–2**  *Osmotic and ionic composition of plasma and urine of chickens (males), hydrated (H), dehydrated (D), and salt loaded (S) (12–15 meq/kg)*[a]

| | Osmolality (mosmoles/liter) | | | Na⁺ (meq/liter) | | | Cl⁻ (meq/liter) | | | K⁺ (meq/liter) | | |
|---|---|---|---|---|---|---|---|---|---|---|---|---|
| | D | H | S | D | H | S | D | H | S | D | H | S |
| Plasma | 341 | 312 | 338 | 163 | 151 | 166 | 130 | 119 | 142 | 4.7 | 4.6 | 4.7 |
| Urine | 538 | 115 | 362 | 133.6 | 37.7 | 161 | 70.2 | 27.4 | 140.6 | 18.8 | 5.61 | 25.43 |
| U/P | 1.58 | 0.37 | 1.06 | 0.82 | 0.25 | 0.97 | 0.54 | 0.23 | 0.99 | 8.53 | 1.22 | 5.41 |

| Urine flow (ml/min) | | | Percent of filtrate resorbed | | | Percent of filtered solute excreted | | |
|---|---|---|---|---|---|---|---|---|
| D | H | S | D | H | S | D | H | S |
| 17.9 | 298 | 181 | 99 | 85.8 | 87 | 1.76 | 4.12 | 6.8 |

[a] From Skadhauge and Schmidt-Nielsen (1967a).

**Table 14–3**  *Distribution of nitrogen in chicken urine as determined by various investigations, expressed as percent of total urinary nitrogen*[a]

| Uric acid N | Possible allantoin N | Other purines | NH₃ N | Urea N | Creatine and creatinine | Amino acid N | Undetermined | Reference |
|---|---|---|---|---|---|---|---|---|
| 82 | – | – | 5.6 | – | – | – | – | Katayama (cited in Sturkie, 1965) |
| 66 | – | – | – | – | 6.0 | – | – | Mayrs (1924) |
| 63 | – | – | 17.3 | 10.4 | 8.0 | – | 1.4 | Davis (1927) |
| 66 | 3.8 | 9.6 | 7.6 | 6.5 | 4.6 | – | 2.8 | Coulson and Hughes (1930) |
| 60 | – | 20.0 | – | – | – | 10.0[b] | – | Edwards and Wilson (1954) |
| 81 | – | – | 10.5 | 4.5 | 0.9 | 2.2 | 1.2 | Practical ration, O'Dell et al. (1960) |
| 76 | – | – | 15.4 | 5.6 | 0.2 | 1.7 | 1.2) | Purified diet, O'Dell et al. (1960) |
| 60 | – | – | 23 | 6.0 | 4.0 | 2.0 | – | Teekell et al. (1968) |

[a] From O'Dell et al. (1960) and Sturkie (1965).
[b] Amino nitrogen.

nasal gland, nasal secretion is also inhibited (Shoemaker, 1967). The level of potassium available in the media for ATPase activity is critical because deficiencies of potassium in chicken kidney slices depress ATPase activity (Dantzler, 1972). The evidence for volume receptors is not conclusive. If there are osmoreceptors, they appear not to be located in the brain or centrally, because intracarotid injections of saline (Hanwell *et al.,* 1971b) failed to elicit nasal secretion in the goose. Moreover the results of infusions of NaCl into the renal portal vein on nasal secretion were negative; however, because of the complicated circulation in the kidney and viscera of Aves, these authors do not rule out the possibility of receptors in the gut or renal portal blood vessels. Further studies are indicated.

Regardless of the nature and location of the receptors, the sensory (afferent) input goes to the central nervous system, which then relays the stimulus to the hypothalamus, pituitary, and adrenals and directly to the nasal gland via the seventh cranial nerve (efferent), to the ganglion ethmoidale, and thence to postganglionic (cholinergic) fibers that run to the gland to produce the final stimulus (secretion; see Holmes, 1972).

## URINE

### Collection and Amount of Urine Voided

The urine and feces of the bird are voided into the cloaca. In order to obtain urine free from fecal matter, therefore, it is necessary to cannulate the ureters or to separate the openings of the ureters or the rectum by surgery. Improved surgical techniques for exteriorizing the ureters (Dixon and Wilkinson, 1957) or the anus (Imabayashi *et al.,* 1956; Fussell, 1969; Paulson, 1969) have been reported. Uncontaminated urine in the cloaca may also be obtained by plugging the anal opening.

Most of the work relating to quantities of urine voided is based on short-period collections involving clearance studies, which calculations were made on the output for 24 hr. Most of those who cannulated the ureters and collected urine for short periods (usually 30–100 min) estimated the output of the adult chicken (weight about 2 kg) at from 500 to 1000 ml/day (Davis, 1927; Coulson and Hughes, 1930; Hester *et al.,* 1940). Short-period collections from exteriorized ureters gave similar estimates (Hester *et al.,* 1940).

The estimates of urine output based on short-period collections are obviously unduly high. An estimated output of 1000 ml in 24 hr is considerably higher than water consumption for the same period (50–250 ml). It was demonstrated by Hester *et al.,* (1940) and by Hart and Essex (1942) that such estimates are in error; the work of these authors showed the urine output from cannulated ureters to average 13.9 ml for the first 30 min but only 2.5 ml during the second 30 min. Estimates for 24 hr based on first collections therefore gave an output of 667 ml and on the second period one of 120 ml. These investigators and others showed that cannulation and handling of the bird causes diuresis, which persists for at least 30 min. In later experiments urine was collected in bags from exteriorized ureters for 24 hr; here the average output was 86.8 ml, with a range of 61–123.4 ml. In another experiment the output was as high as 180 ml. Urine collections made by Dixon (1958), from exteriorized ureters and after the rectum had been exteriorized show urine flows of 132 and 155 ml per 24 hr. Dixon's results are not in agreement with those of Dicker and Haslam (1966), who reported that birds with exteriorized ureters (Dixon's method) drank almost twice as much water after the operation as before (about 100 ml/kg per 24 hr). Urine collected by Ariyoshe and Morimoto (1956) from chickens with artificial anuses (cocks, weighing 2.5–3.0 kg) averaged 115 ml/per bird per 24 hr.

### Factors Affecting Urine Flow and Output

**Role of ureters.** The ureters tend to force or milk the urine along by peristaltic action. The peristaltic waves move caudally. The pressure they exert is considerable, and the urine may be forced along against a pressure as high as 30 mm Hg (Gibbs, 1929c). The ureters, according to Gibbs (1929c) appear to be under sympathetic control.

**Resorption of water.** Urine production is influenced significantly by the tubular resorption of water. As little as 6% of filtered water may be resorbed during water diuresis and as much as 99% at low rates of urine flow (Shoemaker, 1972). Mammals never resorb less than 90% of the filtered water, even when they are made diuretic (Skadhauge and Schmidt-Nielsen, 1967a).

**Diuresis.** Administration of water alone or of hypertonic solutions increases urine output, but dehydration decreases it (see also glomerular filtration and renal handling of electrolytes). Dicker and Haslam (1966) determined the effects of 50 ml/kg of water given orally on urine flow in chickens with exteriorized ureters. They reported that urine flow increased considerably (from less than 0.05 ml/kg/min to above 0.2 ml) within 15–20 min and reached a peak in 80 min; it then declined to almost the control level at 120 min after water administration. Changes in osmolality followed those of urine flow, decreasing from a control level of 490–520 mosmoles/liter to 60 at high urine flows.

Dilation of the crop by filling it with liquid paraffin caused diuresis similar to that produced by water; the mechanism for this effect is not known. Insertion of uretral cannulas are known to produce diuresis; in pigeons this lasts from 30 to 70 min, after which urine flow is stable at 0.4 ml/kg/hr (McNabb, *et al.*, 1970).

**Drugs and hormones.** A number of drugs and hormones affect urine and water consumption (see Chapter 10), some of which are discussed here. Urine flow is decreased by pitressin or pituitrin (Hester *et al.*, 1940) but increased by ether anesthesia and caffeine (Hester *et al.*, 1940). Atropine and pilocarpine have no appreciable effect on urine flow, according to Gibbs (1929b). The antidiuretic hormone arginine vasopressin, in mammals, and arginine vasotocin (AVT), its counterpart in birds, both produce antidiuresis in chickens, but the latter is considerably more potent (Munsick *et al.*, 1960). Unilateral antidiuresis can be produced by unilateral infusion of AVT into the portal vein (Skadhauge, 1964) demonstrating that AVT increases reabsorption of water in the collecting ducts and tubules.

A dose of 30 ng of AVT per kilogram was found to yield a maximum antidiuretic response in hydrated chickens (Ames *et al.*, 1971). The duration of effect ranged from 6 to 30 min, depending on dosage. Removal of the neural lobe of the hypophysis produces polyuria and polydipsia in chickens (see Chapters 10 and 17) and in ducks (Bradley *et al.*, 1971). Administration of arginine vasotocin in restored urine flow and excretion of NaCl to the normal levels.

Arecoline, pilocarpine, and propionylcholine (cholinomimetric agents) increased urine flow in chickens. The diuretic effect is believed to be independent of the vasodilating effect of these agents, because other vasodilating noncholinomimetic agents, papaverine and isoproterenol, had no significant effect (May and Carter, 1970). Acetylcholine (2.5–7.5 mg/kg/min), when infused unilaterally into the chicken's renal portal system increased excretion of water (urine flow), and NaCl which could be blocked by atropine at dosages of 10 μg/kg/min (Parmlee and Carter, 1968).

Angiotensin has a diuretic effect on the pigeon and its site of action appears to be the tubules (Langford and Fallis, 1966). Hydrochlorothiazide (HCZ) belongs to the sulphonamyl group of compounds and has been reported to have a diuretic action in turkeys (Sykes, 1961), increasing urine flow fivefold in these birds after a 25-mg dose. Reserpine (1 mg/kg) greatly reduced the diuretic effect of HCZ in chickens (Nechay and Sanner, 1961), as did theophylline, but had no effect on a mercurial diuretic, which is quite effective in chickens (Campbell, 1957).

**Submersion anuria.** Submersion of the head of the Aylesbury duck for 3–4 min resulted in an immediate cessation of urine flow under normal conditions and water diuresis was resumed 2 min after emersion. Asphyxia alone also resulted in anuria (Sykes, 1966).

**Laying cycle and urine flow.** There is an increase in urine flow a few hours before the first egg is laid, reaching a peak 1 hr before laying, which appears to be associated with an increased excretion of Na and P (Mongin and Lacassagne, 1967).

**Role of the cloaca in the absorption of urine water.** Many of the early investigators believed that water from ureteral urine was absorbed in the cloaca and rectum and that the cloaca served an important function in the conservation of water (for review of some of the early work, see Korr, 1939; Hester, *et al.*, 1940; Hart and Essex, 1942; Sturkie, 1965). Some of these workers observed an increase in the flow of urine collected from cannulated ureters or from the cloaca after the rectum was plugged.

Experiments by Hart and Essex (1942), based on long-term urine collections, suggest that some water is reabsorbed into the cloaca, but not appreciable amounts; the evidence for this conclusion is indirect (see Sturkie, 1965). Experiments by Dixon (1958), involving improved surgical techniques for exteriorizing the ureters and anus, indicate that little or no water was reabsorbed in the cloaca of the chicken. His data also indicated that surgical treatment had no significant effect on water consumption and urine flow. This is contrary to the work of Dicker and Haslam, (1966), Scheiber and Dziuk (1969), and others who have reported increased consumption of water and diuresis following surgery and cannulation and manipulation of ureters.

Weyrauch and Roland (1957) attempted to measure water reabsorption in the cloaca of the chicken by introducing a solution containing tracer isotopes into the cloaca and measuring the content of isotope in the bloodstream. The figures indicate that 7.6% of the isotope was absorbed within 4 hr. However, these studies really measure not cloacal absorption alone, but absorption into the anus and into the gut at a distance 10 cm above the anus.

Later data by Akester et al. (1967), Skadhauge (1968), and Nechay et al., (1968) on chickens; by Peaker et al., (1968) on ducks; and by Ohmart et al. (1970b) on the roadrunner, employing x rays or tracer isotopes, definitely showed that water is absorbed in the cloaca. The urine accumulated in the coprodaeum of the cloaca and was forced by antiperistaltic waves into the colon (Akester et al., 1967). The urine enters the bowel from the cloaca within 4 min after intravenous administration of a urographic contrast medium (Nechay et al., 1968). Absorption from the cloaca into the ceca of chickens with artificial anuses has been reported by Polin et al. (1967). The absorption of water and electrolytes can occur during hydration, dehydration, and salt loading in chickens and ducks (Peaker et al., 1968). Although less is absorbed during dehydration (Skadhauge, 1968), there appears to be no means of keeping ureteral urine from exposure to cloacal membranes and large intestine, across which the exchange of water and solutes may occur (Shoemaker, 1972). However, these rates of exchange are sufficiently low so that they can have only minor effects when urine is produced at moderate to high rates (Skadhauge, Schmidt-Nielsen, 1967a).

Skadhauge and Bradshaw (1974) have studied water consumption, urine flow, and ability to handle high levels of salt in *Taeniophygia castanotis* (zebra finch), which inhabits the semiarid zones of western Australia. These finches were able to consume greater quantities of salt water than domesticated finches, and their urine osmolality was 40% greater than in domesticated finches (1475 mosmole).

## Physical Characteristics of Urine

Bird urine is usually cream colored and contains thick mucoid material; the latter contains abundant uric acid, which is usually in the insoluble form. Under conditions of hydration the urine may be thin and watery. It is usually hypoosmotic but under certain conditions it may be hyperosmotic. The osmolality ranges from 115 mosmoles in hydrated (water-loaded) chickens, to 362 in salt-loaded (mildly) birds, to 538 in dehydrated birds (see Table 14–2 and section on the renal handling of electrolytes). The specific gravity of avian urine ranges from 1.0018 to 1.015 normally but increases or decreases depending on conditions of hydration and osmolality.

**Acid-base balance.** The pH of avian urine varies from 5.10 to 8.00, depending on stage of laying in females, hypoxia, and other factors. The pH of male urine is 6.4 (Ariyoshi and Morimoto, 1956). During the period when calcium is being deposited on the shell the pH of the urine is acid (5.3), and when the egg is laid or no Ca is being deposited it is alkaline (7.6) (Prashad and Edwards, 1973; see also Anderson, 1967). This is because the production of Ca for the shell results in an excess of hydrogen ions, which are buffered by blood, and there is a fall in blood bicarbonate and pH. This fall also occurs in the urine, and most of the bicarbonate is absorbed; there is also an increase in ammonia, phosphate, and titratable acidity (Anderson, 1967; Prashad and Edwards, 1973). Hypoxia occurring in the diving duck may lower pH of urine to 4.7 (Sykes, 1966). Although the chicken excretes from 1 to 2 g of uric acid per day, the uric acid and its salts are poorly dissociated and act as efficient buffers; however, the proportion of uric acid that can act as an acid or a base is not known (Sykes, 1971). A detailed review of acid–base balance in the urine has been presented by Sykes (1971).

**Nitrogenous constituents.** The principal differences in the chemical constituents of the urine in birds, as compared with that of mammals, are the preponderance of uric acid over urea and of creatine over creatinine in birds. Creatinine exists only in minute amounts in bird urine (Davis, 1927). O'Dell et al. (1960) have reviewed the literature and have presented new data on growing male chicks 5–6 weeks of age. Their results, and those of others, are presented in Table 14–3. In general, most of the investigators report a lower percentage of uric acid nitrogen in the urine than do O'Dell et al. (1960). The reason for the discrepancy is not clear, but certain differences did exist in the experiments performed. The results of O'Dell et al. were from growing chickens that were well adapted to the conditions of urine collection, whereas most of the previous work had been conducted on mature birds, some of which were under physiological stress during the collection periods. The determination of uric acid by O'Dell et al. was by the uri-

*Table 14–4*   *Uric acid content of some avian tissues*

| Species | Whole | Muscle blood | Kidney | Liver | Reference |
|---|---|---|---|---|---|
| Duck, normal | 6.7 | 1.8 | 70.5 | 22.2 | Folin *et al.* (1924) |
| Duck with ligated ureters | 224.0 | 30.2 | 354.0 | 101.0 | Folin *et al.* (1924) |
| Chicken, normal | 5.8 | — | — | — | Levine *et al.* (1947) |
| Chicken with ligated ureters | 304.0 | — | — | — | Levine *et al.* (1947) |

case method, which is highly specific and which was not used by most of the other investigators.

Starvation significantly decreases the amount of uric acid N in the urine (84–58%) and blood, and increases the level of ammonia (from 6.8 to 23.0%) according to Sykes (1971). Uric acid is only slightly soluble in water (0.39 mmole/liter of water) but its salts (urates) are considerably more soluble (Sykes, 1971). Uric acid and urates form colloidal solutions and in such form are transported through the tubules, collecting ducts, and ureters.

It is generally believed that the excretion of nitrogen as urates is a successful means of conserving water for birds and reptiles. Obviously, if uric acid were excreted in soluble form, the amount of urine water excreted would be very great. The figures reported are highly variable and range from 60 to 100 ml water per gram of uric acid, according to Korr (1939), and from 30 to 165, according to Hart and Essex (1942).

Uric acid was first believed to be synthesized mainly in the liver of birds, as was indicated by Minkowski in 1886 and by Edson *et al.*, (1936). It is now generally agreed that the kidney is also concerned in the synthesis of uric acid in the pigeon. Chou (1972) believes that the kidney produces nearly twice as much uric acid as the liver. The livers of chickens and pigeons produce hypoxanthine, which is then oxidized to xanthine and then to uric acid, in the kidney of the pigeon and in the liver of chickens, by xanthine oxidase.

The uric acid content of blood, liver, and kidneys of birds (in milligrams per 100 ml or 100 g) is given in Table 14–4. Ligation of the ureters of birds caused marked increases in the concentration of uric acid in the blood and tissues but not in the urine. Birds with ligated ureters usually died of uricemia within 12–24 hr (Folin *et al.*, 1924; Levine *et al.*, 1947).

# REFERENCES

Acara, M., and B. R. Rennick. (1972). Renal tubular transport of acetylcholine and atropine. Enhancement and inhibition. *J. Pharmacol. Exp. Ther., 182,* 1.

Acara, M., M. Kowalski, and B. R. Rennick. (1973). Enhancement by hemicholinium of choline and acetylcholine excretion by the renal tubule of the chicken. *J. Pharmacol. Exp. Ther., 185,* 254.

Akester, A. R. (1967). Renal portal shunts in the kidney of the domestic fowl. *J. Anat., 101,* 569.

Akester, A. R., and S. P. Mann. (1969). Adrenergic and cholinergic innervation of the renal portal valve in the domestic fowl. *J. Anat., 104,* 241.

Akester, A. R., R. S. Anderson, K. J. Hill, and G. W. Osbaldiston. (1967). A radiographic study of urine flow in the domestic fowl. *Brit. Poultry Sci., 8,* 209.

Ames, E., K. Steven, and E. Skadhauge. (1971). Effects of arginine vasotocin on renal excretion of Na⁺, K⁺, Cl⁻ and urea in the hydrated chicken. *Am. J. Physiol., 221,* 1223.

Anderson, R. S. (1967). Acid base changes in the excreta of the laying hen. *Vet. Rec., 80,* 314.

Ariyoshi, S., and H. Morimoto. (1956). Studies on nitrogen metabolism in the fowl. I. Separation of urine for nutritional balance studies. *Bull. Natl. Inst. Agri. Sci., Series G, No. 18,* 37.

Ash, R. W., J. W. Pearce, and A. Silver. (1969). An investigation into the nerve supply to the salt gland of the duck. *J. Exp. Physiol., 54,* 284.

Austic, R. E., and R. K. Cole. (1972). Impaired renal clearance of uric acid in chickens having hyper-uricemia and articular gout. *Am. J. Physiol., 223,* 525.

Ballantyne, B., and W. G. Wood. (1969). Mass and the function of the avian nasal gland. *Cytobios, 4,* 337.

Benoit, J. (1950). "Traité de zoologie," Tome XV. "Oiseaux" (P. P. Grasse, Ed.). Paris: Masson & Co., p. 341.

Berger, L., T. F. Yu, and A. B. Gutman. (1960). Effects of drugs that alter uric acid excretion in man on uric acid clearance in the chicken. *Am. J. Physiol., 198,* 575.

Bradley, E. L., and W. N. Holmes. (1971). The effects of hypophysectomy on adrenocortical function in the duck (*Anas platyrhynchos*). *J. Endocrinol., 49,* 437.

Bradley, E. L., W. N. Holmes, and A. Wright. (1971). The effects of neurohypophysectomy on the pattern of renal excretion of the duck. *J. Endocrinol., 51,* 57.

Braun, E. J., and W. H. Dantzler. (1972). Function of mammalian-type and reptilian type nephrons in kidney of desert quail. *Am. J. Physiol., 222,* 617.

Braun, E. J., and W. H. Dantzler. (1974). Effects of ADH on single nephron glomerular filtration rates and blood pressure on birds. *Am. J. Physiol., 226,* 1.

Braun, E. J., and W. H. Dantzler. (1975). Effects of water load on renal glomerular and tubular functions in desert quail. *Am. J. Physiol., 229,* 222.

Campbell, D. (1957). Excretion and diuretic action of mercurial diuretics. *Experientia, 13,* 327.

Chou, S. T. (1972). Relative importance of liver and kidney in synthesis of uric acid in chickens. *Can. J. Physiol. Pharmacol., 50,* 936.

Clarkson, M. J. (1961). The blood supply of the liver of the turkey and the anatomy of the biliary tract with reference to infection with *Histomonas meleagridis. Res. Vet. Sci., 2,* 259.

Coulson, E. J., and J. H. Hughes. (1930). Collection and analysis of chicken urine. *Poultry Sci., 10,* 53.

Crocker, A. D., and W. N. Holmes. (1971). Intestinal absorption in ducklings maintained on fresh water and hypertonic saline. *Comp. Biochem. Physiol., 40A,* 203.

Dantzler, W. H. (1966). Renal response of chickens to infusion of hyperosmotic sodium chloride solution. *Am. J. Physiol., 210,* 640.

Dantzler, W. H. (1972). Effects of incubations in low potassium and low sodium media on $Na^+-K^+$ ATPase activity in snake and chicken kidney slices. *Comp. Biochem. Physiol., 41B,* 79.

Davis, R. E. (1927). The nitrogenous constituents of hens urine. *J. Biol. Chem., 74,* 509.

Dicker, S. E., and J. Haslam. (1966). Water diuresis in the domestic fowl. *J. Physiol., 183,* 225.

Dixon, J. M. (1958). Investigation of urinary water reabsorption in the cloaca and rectum of hen. *Poultry Sci., 37,* 410.

Dixon, J. M., and W. S. Wilkinson. (1957). Surgical technique for exterioraization of the ureters of the chicken. *Am. J. Vet. Res., 18,* 665.

Douglas, D. S. (1966). Low urine salt concentrations in salt loaded gulls. *Physiologist, 9,* 171.

Douglas, D. S. (1968). Salt and water metabolism of the Adelie penguin. *Antarctic Res. Ser., 12,* 167.

Douglas, D. S. (1970). Electrolyte excretion in sea water loaded herring gulls. *Am. J. Physiol., 219,* 534.

Douglas, D. S., and S. M. Neely. (1969). The effect of dehydration on salt gland performance. *Am. Zool., 9,* 1095.

Edson, N. L., H. A. Krebs, and A. Motel. (1936). The synthesis of uric acid in the avian organism: *Biochem. J., 36,* 1380.

Emery, N., T. L. Poulson, and W. B. Kinter. (1972). Production of concentrated urine by avian kidneys. *Am. J. Physiol., 223,* 180.

Ensor, D. M., Thomas, D. H., and Phillips, J. G. (1970). The possible role of the thyroid in extrarenal secretion following a hypertonic saline load in the duck *(Anas platyrhynchos).* Proceedings of Society of Endocrinology. *J. Endocrinol. 46,* x.

Ernst, S. A., and R. A. Ellis. (1969). Development of surface specialization in secretory epithelium of avian salt gland in response to osmotic stress. *J. Cell. Biol., 40,* 305.

Fange, R., J. Krog, and O. Reite. (1963). Blood flow in avian salt gland studied by polarographic oxygen electrodes. *Acta Physiol. Scand., 58,* 40.

Fange, R., K. Schmidt-Nielsen, and M. Robinson. (1958). Control of secretion from the avian salt gland. *Am. J. Physiol., 195,* 321.

Ferguson, R. K., and R. A. Wolbach. (1967). Effects of glucose, phlorizin, and parathyroid extract on renal phosphate transport in chickens. *Am. J. Physiol., 212,* 1123.

Fletcher, G. L., and W. N. Holmes. (1968). Observations on the intake of water and electrolytes by the duck maintained on fresh water and on hypertonic saline. *J. Exp. Biol., 49,* 325.

Fletcher, G. L., I. M. Stainer, and W. N. Holmes. (1967). Sequential changes in the adenosinetriphosphatase activity and the electrolyte excretory capacity of the nasal glands of the duck *(Anas platyrhynchos)* during the period of adaptation to hypertonic saline. *J. Exp. Biol., 47,* 375.

Folin, O., H. Berglund, and C. Derick. (1924). The uric acid problem: an experimental study on animals and man, including gouty subjects. *J. Biol. Chem., 60,* 361.

Fujimoto, J. M., J. J. Lech, and R. Zamiatowski. (1973). A site of action of norobiocin in inhibiting renal tubular transport of drugs in the chicken. *Biochem. Pharmacol., 22,* 971.

Fussell, M. H. (1969). A method for the separation and collection of urine and feces in the fowl. *Res. Vet. Sci., 10,* 332.

Gibbs, O. S. (1929c). The function of the fowls ureters. *Am. J. Physiol., 87,* 594.

Gibbs, O. S. (1929a). The secretion of uric acid by the fowl. *Am. J. Physiol., 88,* 87.

Gibbs, O. S. (1929b). The effects of drugs on the secretion of uric acid in the fowl. *J. Pharmacol. Exp. Ther., 35,* 49.

Hakansson, C. H., and B. Malcus. (1969). Secretive response of electrically stimulated Nasal salt gland in herring gull. *Acta Physiol. Scand., 76,* 385.

Hanwell, A., J. L. Linzell, and M. Peaker. (1971a). Salt gland secretion and blood flow in geese. *J. Physiol. (London), 210,* 373.

Hanwell, A., J. L. Linzell, and M. Peaker. (1971b). Cardiovascular responses to salt loading in conscious domestic geese. *J. Physiol., 213,* 389.

Hart, W. M., and H. E. Essex. (1942). Water metabolism of the chicken with special reference to the role of the cloaca. *Am. J. Physiol., 336,* 657.

Hester, H. R., H. E. Essex, and F. C. Mann. (1940). Secretion of urine in the chicken. *Am. J. Physiol., 128,* 592

Holmes, W. N. (1972). Regulation of electrolyte balance in marine birds with special reference to the role of the pituitary adrenal axis in the duck. *Fed. Proc., 31,* 1587.

Holmes, W. N. (1975). Hormones and osmoregulation in marine birds. *Gen. Comp. Endocrinol., 25,* 249.

Holmes, W. N., and A. Wright. (1968). Some aspects of the control of osmoregulation and homeostasis in birds. Progress in Endocrinology. *Proc. 3rd Intl. Cong. Endocrinol.,* p. 237.

Holmes, W. N., G. L. Fletcher, and D. J. Steward. (1968). The patterns of renal electrolyte excretion in ducks, maintained on freshwater and on hypertenic saline. *J. Exp. Biol., 48,* 487.

Hughes, M. R. (1970). Relative kidney size in nonpasserine birds with functional salt glands. *Condor, 72,* 164.

Imbayashi, K., M. Kametaka, and T. Hatano. (1956). Studies on the digestion in the domestic fowl. I: "Artificial anus operation" for the domestic fowl and the passage of the indicator throughout the digestive tract. *Tohoku J. Agri. Res., 6,* 99.

Inoue, T. (1963). Nasal salt gland: Independence of salt and water transport. *Science, 142,* 1299.

Johnson, O. W. (1968). Some morphological features of avian kidneys. *Auk, 85,* 216.

Johnson, O. W., and J. N. Mugaas. (1970a). Some histological features of avian kidneys. *Am. J. Anat., 127,* 423.

Johnson, O. W., and J. N. Mugaas. (1970b). Quantitative and organizational features of avian renal medulla. *Condor, 72,* 288.

Johnson, O. W., and R. D. Ohmart. (1973). Some features of water economy and kidney microstructure in the large billed savannah sparrow. *Physiol. Zool., 46,* 276.

Johnson, O. W., G. L. Phipps, and J N Mugaas. (1972) Injection studies of cortical and medullary organization in the avian kidney. *J. Morphol. 136,* 181.

Korr, I. M. (1939). The osmotic function of the chicken kidney. *J. Cell. Comp. Physiol., 13,* 175.

Krag, B., and E. Skadhauge. (1972). Renal salt and water excretion in the budgerygah. *Comp. Biochem. Physiol., 41A,* 667.

Langford, H. G., and N. Fallis. (1966). Diuretic effect of angiotensin in the chicken. *Proc. Soc. Exp. Biol. Med., 123,* 317.

Levine, R., W. Q. Wolfson, and R. Lenel. (1947). Concentration and transport of true urate in the plasma of the azotemic chicken. *Am. J. Physiol., 151,* 186.

Levinsky, M. G., and D. G. Davidson. (1957). Renal action of parathyroid extract in the chicken. *Am. J. Physiol., 191,* 530.

Lindahl, K. M., and I. Sperber. (1958). Some characteristics of the renal tubular transport mechanism for histamine in the hen. *Acta Physiol. Scand., 42,* 166.

Marshall, E. K. (1934). Comparative physiology of vertebrate kidney. *Physiol. Rev., 14,* 133.

May, D. G., and M. K. Carter. (1970). Effect of vasoactive agents on urine and electrolyte excretion in the chicken. *Am. J. Physiol., 218,* 417.

May, D. G., J. M. Fujimoto, and C. E. Inturrisi. (1967). The tubular transport and metabolism of morphine of N-methyl-$^{14}$C by the chicken kidney. *J. Pharmacol. Exp. Ther., 157,* 626.

284

McNabb, F., M. Anne, and T. L. Poulson. (1970). Uric acid excretion in pigeons. *Comp. Biochem. Physiol., 33*, 933.

Mongin, P., and L. Lacassagne. (1967). Excretion urinaire chez la poule au moment de la ponte de son premier oeuf. *Compt. Rend. Acad. Sci. Paris, 264*, 2479.

Munsick, R. A., W. H. Sawyer, and H. B. Van Dyke. (1960). Avian neurohypophyseal hormones: pharmacological properties and tentative identification. *Endocrinology, 66*, 860.

Nechay, B. R., and L. Nechay. (1959). Effects of probenecid, sodium salicylate, 2,4 dinitrophenol and pyrazinamide on renal secretion of uric acid in chickens. *J. Pharmacol. Exp. Ther., 126*, 291.

Nechay, B. R., and E. Sanner. (1961). Interference of reserpine with diuretic action of theophylline and hydrochlorothiazide on the chicken. *Acta Pharmacol. Toxicol., 18*, 339.

Nechay, B. R., S. Boyarsky, and P. Catacutan-Labay. (1968). Rapid migration of urine into intestine of chickens. *Comp. Biochem. Physiol., 26*, 369.

O'Dell, G. L., W. D. Woods, O. A. Laerdal, A. M. Jeffay, and J. E. Savage. (1960). Distribution of the major nitrogenous compounds and amino acids in chicken urine. *Poultry Sci., 39*, 426.

Ohmart, R. D., T. E. Chapman, and L. Z. McFarland. (1970a). Water turnover in Roadrunners under different environmental conditions. *Auk, 87*, 787.

Ohmart, R. D., L. Z. McFarland, and J. P. Morgan. (1970b). Urographic evidence that urine enters the rectum and ceca of the roadrunner. *Comp. Biochem. Physiol., 35*, 487.

Orloff, J., and M. Burg. (1960). Effect of strophanthidin on electrolyte excretion in the chicken. *Am. J. Physiol., 199*, 49.

Orloff, J., and D. Davidson. (1956). Mechanism of potassium excretion in the chicken. *Fed. Proc., 15*, 452.

Owen, R. E., and R. R. Robinson. (1964). Urea production and excretion by the chicken kidney. *Am. J. Physiol., 206*, 1321.

Parmalee, M. L., and M. K. Carter. (1968). The diuretic effect of acetylcholine in the chicken. *Arch. Intl. Pharmacodyn. Ther., 174*, 108.

Paulson, G. D. (1969). An improved method for separate collection of urine, feces, and expiratory gases from the mature chicken. *Poultry Sci., 48*, 1331.

Peaker, M., A. Wright, S. J. Peaker, and J. G. Phillips. (1968). Absorption of tritiated water by cloaca of the domestic duck. *Physiol. Zool., 41*, 461.

Phillips, J. G., W. N. Holmes, and D. G. Butler. (1961). The effect of total and subtotal adrenalectomy on the renal and extrarenal response of the domestic duck *(Anas platyrhynchos)* to saline loading. *Endocrinology, 69*, 958.

Pitts, R. F. (1938). The excretion of phenol red by chickens. *J. Cell. Comp. Physiol. 11*, 99.

Pitts, R. F., and I. M. Korr. (1938). The excretion of urea by the bird. *J. Cell. Comp. Physiol., 11*, 117.

Polin, D., E. R. Wynosky, M. Loukides, and C. C. Porter. (1967). A possible urinary backflow to ceca revealed by studies on chicks with artifical anus and fed amprolium ¹⁴C. *Poultry Sci., 46*, 88.

Poulson, T. L. (1965). Counter current multipliers in avian kidneys. *Science, 148*, 389.

Poulson, T. L., and G. A. Bartholomew. (1962). Salt balance in the savannah sparrows. *Physiol. Zool., 35*, 109.

Prashad, D. N., and N. E. Edwards. (1973). Phosphate excretion in the laying fowl. *Comp. Biochem. Physiol., 46A*, 131.

Quebbeman, A. J., and B. R. Rennick. (1968). Catechol transport by the renal tubule in the chicken. *Am. J. Physiol., 214*, 1201.

Rennick, B. R. (1958). The renal tubular excretion of choline and thiamine in the chicken. *J. Pharmacol. Exp. Ther., 122*, 448.

Rennick, B. R. (1967). Transport mechanisms for renal tubular excretion of creatinine in the chicken. *Am. J. Physiol., 212*, 1131.

Rennick, B. R., and H. Gandia. (1954). Autonomic pharmacology of the smooth muscle valve in renal portal venous circulation in birds. *Fed. Proc., 13*, 396.

Rennick, B. R., and A. Quebbeman. (1970). Site of excretion of catechol and catecholamines: Renal metabolism of catechol. *Am. J. Physiol., 218*, 1307.

Rennick, B. R., and N. Yoss. (1962). Renal tubular excretion of DL-Epinephrine-2-¹⁴C in the chicken. *J. Pharmacol. Exp. Ther., 138*, 347.

Rennick, B. R., D. M. Calhoon, H. Gandia, and G. K. Moe. (1954). Renal tubular secretion of tetraethylammonium in the dog and chicken. *J. Pharmacol. Exp. Ther., 110*, 309.

Rennick, B. R., C. Latimer, and G. K. Moe. (1952). Excretion of potassium by the chicken kidney. *Fed. Proc., 11*, 132.

Sanner, E. (1963). Studies on the excretion mechanism of serotonin (5-hydroxytryptamine) in the chicken kidney. *Acta Physiol. Scand., 58*, 330.

Sanner, E., and B. Wortman. (1962). Tubular excretion of serotonin (5HT) in the chicken. *Acta Physiol. Scand., 55*, 330.

Scheiber, A. R., and H. E. Dziuk. (1969). Water ingestion and excretion in turkeys with a rectal fistula. *J. Appl., Physiol., 26*, 277.

Schmidt-Nielsen, K. (1960). The salt secreting gland of marine birds. *Circulation, 21*, 955.

Schmidt-Nielsen, K., and R. Fange. (1958). The function of the salt gland in the brown pelican. *Auk, 75*, 282.

Schmidt-Nielsen, K., and W. J. Sladen. (1958). Nasal salt secretion in the Humboldt penguin. *Nature (London), 181*, 1217.

Schmidt-Nielsen, K. A. Borut, P. Lee, and E. Crawford, J., (1963). Nasal salt excretion and possible function of the cloaca in water conservation. *Science, 142*, 1300.

Schmidt-Nielsen, K., C. E. Jorgensen, and H. Osaki. (1958). Extrarenal salt excretion in birds. *Am. J. Physiol., 193*, 101.

Scothorne, J. J. (1959a). The nasal glands of birds: a histological and histochemical study of the inactive gland in the domestic duck. *J. Anat., 93*, 246.

Shannon, J. A. (1938a). The excretion of exogenous creatinine by the chicken. *J. Cell. Comp. Physiol., 11*, 123.

Shannon, J. A. (1938b). The excretion of uric acid by the chicken. *J. Cell. Comp. Physiol., 11*, 135.

Shimada, K., and P. D. Sturkie. (1973). Renal portal circulation in chickens. *Jap. J. Vet. Sci., 35*, 57.

Shoemaker, V. H. (1967). Renal function in mourning dove. *Am. Zool., 7*, 736.

Shoemaker, V. H. (1972). Osmoregulation and excretion in birds. In "Avian Biology," Vol. II (D. S. Farner and J. R. King, Eds.). Chapter 9. New York: Academic Press.

Siller, W. G. (1971). Structure of the kidney. In "Physiology and Biochemistry of Domestic Fowl" (D. G. Bell and B. M. Freeman, Eds.). New York: Academic Press, Chapter 8.

Siller, W. G., and R. M. Hindle. (1969). The artificial blood supply to the kidney of the fowl. *J. Anat., 194*, 117.

Skadhauge, E. (1964). The effect of unilateral infusion of arginine vasotocin into the portal circulation of the avian kidney. *Acta Endocrinol., 47*, 321.

Skadhauge, E. (1968). The cloacal storage of urine in the rooster. *Comp. Biochem. Physiol., 24*, 7.

Skadhauge, E., and B. Schmidt-Nielsen. (1967a). Renal function in the domestic fowl. *Am. J. Physiol., 212*, 793.

Skadhauge, E., and B. Schmidt-Nielsen. (1967b). Renal medullary electrolyte and urea gradient in chickens and turkeys. *Am. J. Physiol., 212*, 1313.

Skadhauge, E. and S. D. Bradshaw. (1974). Saline drinking and cloacal excretion of salt and water in the zebra finch. *Am. J. Physiol., 227*, 1263.

Smith, H. W. (1951). "The kidney: Structure and function in health and disease." London: Oxford University Press.

Spanner, R. (1925). Der Pfortaderkreislauf in der Vogelniere. *Morphol. Jahrb., 54*, 560.

Spanner, R. (1939). Die Drosselklappe der veno-venosen Anastomose und ihre Bedeutung für den Abkürzungskreislauf in portocavalen. System des Vogels; zugleich ein Beitrag der epitheloiden Zellen. *Z. Anat. Entwicklungsges., 109*, 443.

Sperber, I. (1948). Investigations on the circulatory system of the avian kidney. *Zool. Bidrag (Uppsala), 27*, 429.

Sperber, I. (1954). Competitive inhibition and specificity of renal tubular transport mechanisms. *Arch. Intl. Pharmacol., 97*, 221.

Sperber, I. (1960). Excretion. In "Biology and Comparative Physiology of Birds" (A. J. Marshall, Ed). New York: Academic Press, Chapter 12.

Stewart, D. J. (1972). Secretion by salt gland during water deprivation in the duck. *Am. J. Physiol., 223,* 384.

Stewart, D. D., W. N. Holmes, and G. Fletcher. (1969). The renal excretion of nitrogenous compounds by the duck maintained on freshwater and hypertonic saline. *J. Exp. Biol., 359,* 127.

Sturkie, P. D. (1965). In "Avian Physiology" (2nd ed.) (P. D. Sturkie, ic, portal and renal portal veins of chickens. *Pflugers Archiv* in press.

Sturkie, P. D. (1965). In "Avian Physiology" (2nd ed.) (P. D. Sturkie, Ed.). Ithaca, N.Y.: Cornell University Press, Chapter 13.

Sykes, A. H. (1960a). The renal clearance of uric acid and *p*-amino hippurate in the fowl. *Res. Vet. Sci., 1,* 308.

Sykes, A. H. (1960b). The excretion of inulin, creatinine and ferrocyanide by the fowl. *Res. Vet. Sci., 1,* 315.

Sykes, A. H. (1961). The action of hydrochlorothiazide in the turkey. *Vet. Rec., 73,* 396.

Sykes, A. H. (1962). The excretion of urea following its infusion through the renal portal system of the fowl. *Res. Vet. Sci., 3,* 183.

Sykes, A. H. (1966). Submersion anuria in the duck. *J. Physiol., 184,* 16. (Proceedings)

Sykes, A. H. (1971). Formation and composition of urine. "Physiology and Biochemistry of the Fowl," Vol. 1 (D. J. Bell and B. M. Freeman, Eds.). New York: Academic Press, Chapter 9.

Teekell, R. A., C. E. Richardson, and A. B. Watts. (1968). Dietary protein effects on urinary nitrogen components of the hen. *Poultry Sci., 47,* 1260.

Vereerstraeten, P., and C. Toussaint. (1968). Role of peritubular oncotic pressure on sodium excretion by the avian kidney. *Pflügers Arch., 302,* 13.

Watrous, W. M., D. G. May, J. M. Fujimoto. (1970). Mechanism of renal tubular transport of morphine and morphine ethereal sulfate in the chicken. *J. Pharmacol. Exp. Ther. 172,* 224.

Weyrauch, H. M., and S. I. Roland. (1957). Electrolyte absorption from fowl's cloaca. *Trans. Am. Assoc. Genito-Urinary Surgeons, 49,* 117.

# 15

# Hypophysis

P. D. Sturkie

## INTRODUCTION—ENDOCRINE ORGANS

The endocrine glands or organs of the bird are (1) the hypophysis or pituitary, (2) the thyroids, (3) the parathyroids, (4) the adrenals, (5) the pancreas, (6) the testes and ovary (gonads), (7) the ultimobronchial glands, and (8) the intestine. The thymus and pineal bodies, which are sometimes classified as endocrine organs, are present in the bird but their functions are not clear.

The hypophysis is a master endocrine organ because it elaborates a number of hormones that in turn stimulate other glands to secrete hormones. The testes and ovary secrete androgen and estrogen respectively; these are discussed in Chapters 16 and 17 on reproduction in the female and the male. The hormones of the thyroids, the parathyroids and ultimobronchial glands, the adrenals, and the pancreas are considered in Chapters 18, 19, 20, and 21, respectively. A brief account of the intestinal hormone, secretin, is given in Chapter 10.

## ANATOMY OF THE HYPOPHYSIS

The avian pituitary includes an anterior lobe (adenohypophysis) and a posterior lobe (neurohypophysis) but has no intermediate lobe. The neurohypophysis produces two hormones, vasotocin and oxytocin, which are preformed and secreted by the neurosecretory cells in the supraoptic and paraventricular nuclei, and which migrate down fiber tracts to the neural lobe and median eminence.

The anterior pituitary is located in the saddle-like depression of the sphenoid bone (sella turcica) just posterior to the optic chiasma at the floor of the diencephalon. The anterior lobe (adenohypophysis) is separated from the posterior lobe (neurohypophysis) by a distinct connective tissue sheath. The neurohypophysis consists of an expanded distal portion, the infundibular process and stalk, which communicates with the third ventricle of the brain (Figure 15–1).

The anterior lobe or pars distalis is derived from Rathke's pouch and includes cephalic and caudal lobes, or divisions, based on cell types and functions. Although there is no direct vascular connection between the anterior and posterior lobes, there are areas where the tissues of these lobes are in contact.

The infundibulum, which is derived from the diencephalon, extends downward sending fibers to the posterior lobe and median eminence. The infundibular stem is in intimate contact with the pars tuberalis and with it forms the hypophyseal stalk. Fibers from the supraopticohypophyseal and tuberohypophyseal tracts pass through the median eminence, which is a prominent neurosecretory organ in birds (Figure 15–2) but the median eminence and posterior lobe are independent.

Details as to how stimuli from the hypothalamus reach the neural and anterior lobes are discussed in later sections.

The anterior lobes produces at least seven hormones, which are released and transported to the various target organs. These are the gonadotropic hormones (FSH, LH, and prolactin), the thyrotropic hormones (TSH), the growth hormone (GH), the adrenocorticotropic hormone (ACTH), and melanotropin (MSH).

The release of the anterior lobe hormones is caused by at least four or five specific factors or hormones originating from the hypothalamus, which are in turn influenced by the level of circulating anterior pituitary hormones and target organ hormones (feedback mechanism).

15–1 Diagrams of the pituitaries of the chicken and duck; sagittal sections. Large dots and small dots represent caudal and cephalic areas, respectively, of the anterior lobe. Solid black area, pars tuberalis; wavy lines, posterior lobe; parallel lines, area of third ventricle of brain. (After Rahn and Painter, 1941).

**Chicken**

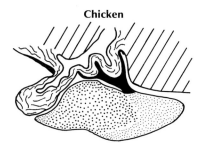

**Duck**

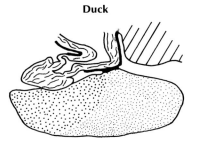

288

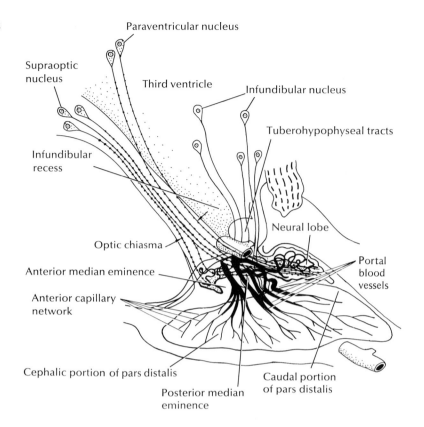

Paraventricular nucleus

Supraoptic nucleus

Third ventricle

Infundibular nucleus

Tuberohypophyseal tracts

Infundibular recess

Neural lobe

Optic chiasma

Portal blood vessels

Anterior median eminence

Anterior capillary network

Cephalic portion of pars distalis

Caudal portion of pars distalis

Posterior median eminence

**15-2**
Schematic parasagittal section through the infundibulum and hypophysis of white-crowned sparrow, showing fiber tracts from hypothalamus and portal blood vessels in the hypophysis. (After Oksche, 1965.)

## Hypothalamo—Hypophyseal Complex, Median Eminence, and Neurosecretory System

In recent years the structure and physiology of this complex have received much attention, which has served to explain many puzzling aspects of pituitary function. For more details on the structure of this system in several species, including chicken, pigeon, duck, Japanese quail, *Taeniophygia castanotis* (zebra finch), and white-crowned sparrow, consult the works of Farner and Oksche (1962), Farner *et al.*, (1967), Benoit and Assenmacher, (1951), Wingstrand (1951), Grignon (1956), Legait (1959), Vitums *et al.* (1964), and Kobayashi and Wada (1973). There are two neurosecretory systems in the avian hypothalamus, a posterior lobe component system and the anterior lobe component.

The posterior lobe system includes the neurosecretory cells of the supraoptic and paraventricular nuclei and the axons of these cells, which make up the supraoptic and paraventricular hypophyseal tracts. The anterior lobe system includes the infundibular nuclei (Figure 15–2) and axons of the tuberohypophyseal tract, and possibly others that extend into the pars tuberalis and median eminence but not directly into the pars distalis.

Evidence is presented later to show that this neurosecretory material or hypothalamic releasing factors from this system finds its way to the anterior lobe and stimulates it to release hormones. It is now abundantly clear that the releasing factors reach the pars distalis via the hypothalamohypophyseal portal blood vessels (Green, 1951; Vitums *et al.*, 1964).

The cells of the posterior lobe system are AF (aldehyde fuchsin) positive in their staining reaction and the cells of the anterior lobe system are AF negative.

Kobayashi and Wada (1973) state that the median eminence is exteriorly the portion covered by capillaries of the primary plexus of the hypophyseal portal veins, and interiorly it represents the basal portion of the hypothalamus occupied by the processes of the secretory ependymal cells. The pars tuberalis covers the primary plexus.

There are two distinct regions of the median eminence; anterior and posterior. Histologically there are five different cell types or layers and they are described in detail by Kobayashi and Wada (1973). These are (1) ependymal, (2) hypendymal, (3) fiber, (4) reticular, and (5) palisade. They are found in both the anterior and the posterior divisions, but the latter, which is closer to the posterior lobe, contains less AF-negative and more AF-positive material than the anterior median eminence.

Three main types of neurosecretory granules or vessels are present: (1) large granules (1500–2000Å), (2) smaller granules (about 1000Å) and (3) other granules. The large granules are abundant in the anterior median eminence and rare in the posterior, but the small granules are present in both divisions. The large granules may be carriers of neurohypophyseal hormones and the smaller ones (1000Å) of monamines. Other granules may be carriers of hypothalamic releasing factors (Kobayashi and Wada, 1973).

The significance of these hormones and monamines in the median eminence is not known. The anterior and posterior portal blood vessels collect blood from the anterior and posterior primary plexuses of these divisions of the median eminence (Green, 1951; Vitums et al., 1964). Because the cell types of the cephalic lobe may not be the same as those from the caudal lobe, it is possible that different adenohypophyseal hormone releasing factors go to the anterior and posterior median eminence. Blood from the primary capillary vessels is delivered to the pars distalis via the secondary capillary network (small blood vessels) (Figure 15–2).

## Cytology of Hypophysis

The cytology of avian pituitaries of chickens, ducks, white crowned sparrow, Coturnix. and pigeon have been studied in detail by a number of workers, such as Wingstrand (1951), Rahn and Painter (1941), Herlant et al. in 1960 (see Herlant, 1964), and Farner and co-workers (see Farner et al., 1967; Tixier-Vidal et al., 1968), and have been reviewed more recently by Farner et al. (1967) and Tixier Vidal and Follett (1973).

Seven different cell types can be recognized at least in Coturnix, only by employing several different staining techniques (Tixier-Vidal et al., 1968; Follett and Farner, 1966; Tixier-Vidal and Follett, 1973).

These cell types are described according to staining procedures as shown in Table 15–1. This presumes that each cell type secretes at least one hormone, a hypothesis that is not fully sustained (Tixier-Vidal and Follett, 1973).

Cell types of the pituitary may be classified according to the type of granules contained (Herlant, 1964). These are glycoprotein and simple protein granules. Of the seven cell types recognized in the avian pituitary, only five can easily be assigned to these classes (Tixier-Vidal and Follett, 1973).

The cell types containing glycoproteins and producing TSH, LH, and FSH stain prominently with basic types and are referred to as "basophils" in the older literature. These cells can be further differentiated by their staining reactions to PAS, Alcian Blue, and Orange G (see Table 15–1).

The $\alpha$ acidophil cells, with simple protein granules, normally stain strongly with acid dyes, but it is possible to distinguish two types of $\alpha$ cells. With Herlant's tetrachrome and with PAS methods, these cells can be further differentiated into acidophilic $\alpha$ cells and $\gamma$-glycoprotein cells (Tixier-Vidal and Follett, 1973).

The $\eta$ acidophils found in the cephalic lobe show an affinity for erythrosin in the tetrachrome stains of Herlant and Brooke (see Table 15–1). These cells correspond to the $A_2$ cells of Rahn and Painter and have been reported in ducks, pigeons, and sparrows.

The $\epsilon$ cells are believed to produce ACTH and are difficult to distinguish in normal birds. The cells are slightly acidophilic and PAS positive and have a distinct, although not strong, affinity for lead hematoxylin. They react best to Brooke's technique with a gray-rose color. These cells may correspond to the V cells of Mikami (1958) in the chicken. Because the granules of the V cells are also stainable with basic dyes, they are not true acidophils, according to Mikami. These cells have been distinguished in the duck, chicken, and sparrow (Tixier-Vidal and Follett, 1973; Mikami et al., 1969).

$\kappa$ cells are highly stainable but difficult to classify (see Table 15–1); they are believed to elaborate MSH.

Thus, at least seven cell types have been recognized in the pituitary, and although experimental evidence suggests a specialized secretory function for each cell (see Table 15–1) the evidence for secretory functional cell types is not conclusive. The best test is the immunocytological technique, which localizes the hormone within its cell, and this method has not yet been applied to Aves (Tixier-Vidal and Follett, 1973).

## Hypophysectomy

Hypophysectomy (hypox) has been performed in the pigeon, duck, chicken, and other species (see Benoit, 1950; Schooley, 1939; Nalbandov and Card, 1943; Rothschild, 1948, for details of the technique). The account in this section deals with the technique of hypophysectomy and its general effects. The specific effects of pituitary removal on reproductive organs, thyroids, and adrenals are considered in these chapters treating these subjects.

There are two principal approaches to the hypophysis: through the orbit, which entails removal of the eye (Benoit, 1950), and through the roof of

*Table 15-1* The hormones of the anterior lobe, releasing factors of hypothalamus (R), cell types in anterior lobe, and location and staining reaction

| Releasing factors: | ? | R | R | R | – | R | R |
|---|---|---|---|---|---|---|---|
| Anterior pituitary hormones: | TSH | LH | FSH | ACTH | MSH | STH | Prolactin |
| Type (chemical): | Glycoprotein | Glycoprotein | Glycoprotein | Polypeptide | Polypeptide | Protein | Protein |
| Cell types Location[a] | Δ ca and ce | γ ca | β ce | ε ce | κ ce | α ca | η ce |
| Stain[b] | | | | | | | |
| Herlant Tetrachrome | Very pale blue | Purple | Purple to blue | Purple to blue | Deep blue | Red-orange | Rose |
| Alcian Blue, PAS, Orange G | Pale blue | Yellow to brick red | Red-violet | Yellow to brick red | Very pale rose | Yellow | Very pale yellow |
| Brooke's technique | Very pale green | Brownish orange | Blackish | Rose | Light green | Yellow-orange | Rose |

[a] ca, caudal; ce, cephalic.
[b] From Tixier-Vidal *et al.* (1968) and Tixier-Vidal and Follett (1973).

the mouth and pharynx. Some workers have made the incision through the floor and roof of the mouth with beak and mouth closed (transbuccal); others have made the incision only through the roof of the mouth, with mouth opened and beak pulled backward (oral approach, Rothchild, 1948). The mortality following the operation is usually higher when the transbuccal approach is employed. The injury to the lower beak and mandible makes eating difficult and increases the chances for infection. These complications are avoided or minimized by employing the oral or parapharyngeal approach (Schooley, 1939). With the latter approach, the incision is made below the mouth, around the trachea, and through the palate. After the incision is made, the area is exposed and preparations are made for drilling through the bone. Burrs of suitable size and drill are necessary. After the gland is exposed, it may be removed by suction and/or destroyed by cautery.

All of the target organs that are influenced by pituitary hormones decrease in size following hypophysectomy and the effects on some of these are greater than others. Ablation of the gland in chickens decreases food consumption by one-half to two-thirds of normal.

## HORMONES OF THE ANTERIOR LOBE

### Gonadotropic Hormones

The anterior lobe produces the follicle stimulating hormone (FSH), the luteinizing hormone (LH), and prolactin. There is evidence that gonadotropins are produced in the duck and Japanese quail by the $\gamma$ cells in the caudal lobe and the $\beta$ cells in the cephalic lobe. In the white-crowned sparrow and chicken, however, the gonadotropic activity is localized in two cell types (types A and B), occuring in both cephalic and caudal lobes (Tixier-Vidal and Follett, 1973), which stain as basophils and are PAS positive. Castration causes pronounced changes in the gonadotropic cells.

There is no definite proof that distinct cell types produce LH and FSH, although in the duck it is believed that they are produced by the $\gamma$ and $\beta$ cells, respectively (see Table 15-1).

**Bioassays.** FSH and LH may be assayed by several methods, which are not completely specific for one or the other. These include the (1) ovarian enlargement method, mainly for FSH, and (2) the growth of testes, also principally but not specifically for FSH. Testicular uptake of $^{32}$P is a sensitive assay for FSH and LH but is not specific for either.

Burns (1970) has reported that neuraminidase (a bacterial enzyme) can selectively destroy pituitary FSH in mammals and also chickens. The $^{32}$P uptake then is a reflection of LH activity according to him. His results, however, were based on mammalian FSH and LH, and according to Tixier-Vidal and Follet (1973), Scanes (unpublished) has evidence that both chicken FSH and LH are equally susceptible to neuraminidase activity. Furr and Cunningham (1970) made a comparative study of assays supposedly specific for FSH and LH and those which measure the combined effects of the two. They compared the potencies of crude pituitary fractions and of purified fractions (Stockell-Hartree and Cunningham, 1969). They compared assays for ovarian growth (FSH), depletion of ovarian ascorbic acid (OAAD), LH, and $^{32}$P uptake and ovulation. They reported $^{32}$P uptake method by far the most sensitive for chicken gonadotropic fractions. The high sensitivity of this test appears to be dependent on the ratio of FSH and LH in the material, as the assay is more sensitive to cruder preparations containing both fractions.

The depletion of OAAD is considered specific for the assay of mammalian LH, and in much of the early work in chickens it was assumed to be specific for LH. However, it is now known that is is not specific in birds because the blood and pituitaries of Aves contain arginine vasotocin, which also depletes ovarian ascorbic acid (Jackson and Nalbandov, 1969a) and others. The OAAD method, however, is specific for purified avian LH fractions, (Follett et al., 1972).

Radioimmunoassay has been used for avian LH and is highly specific and sensitive (see Furr and Cunningham, 1970; Follett et al., 1972). Pituitary fractions containing FSH with high biologic activity showed little immunologic activity. The method measures immunoreactive LH in $25-200$ $\mu$l of plasma in chickens and quails and in a fraction of one pituitary. The principal disadvantage of the immunoassay is that the reaction derives from a part of the hormone molecule different from that which is biologically active. Boiling avian pituitary extracts destroys all biologic activity but only 53% of immunoreactivity (Follett et al., 1972).

**Factors affecting pituitary and plasma gonadotropin levels.** *Sex, age and reproductive stage.* Most workers, regardless of assay method, have reported differences in gonadotropic potency for the pituitaries of males and females at different ages and seasons. Male glands contain considerably more FSH and LH than do glands of laying females (Fraps, 1943). The gonadotropic potency of pituitaries of female chickens increases with age from 20

292 days to 126 days of age (Breneman, 1955). Based on chick testes weight, Nakajo and Imai (1961) reported the gonadotropic content in chick units as shown in Table 15−2. The gonadotropic potency of the cephalic and caudal lobes of *Coturnix coturnix japonica* (Japanese quail) appear to be about equal and increased with increasing light (Follett and Farner, 1966).

Employing the OAAD assay, which is not completely specific for LH in Aves, Tanaka *et al.* (1966b) estimated LH content of chicken pituitaries as follows:

|  | LH concentration ($\mu$g/100 mg pituitary) |
|---|---|
| Nonlaying hens | 2.0 |
| Laying hens |  |
| 0−3 hr after oviposition | 1.2 |
| 5−6 hr after oviposition | 2.2 |
| 8−9 hr after oviposition | 0.8 |

The authors show that the LH content of laying hens does not always differ from that of nonlaying hens. Heald *et al.* 1968a also studied pituitary LH (OAAD) at different intervals between successive clutches of eggs and their data indicated highly variable levels; however, the lowest level was at 4−8 hr prior to ovulation, which they considered the time when LH was released. These authors (Heald *et al.,* 1968b) reported that estrogen administration increases pituitary LH but not testosterone.

*Light−dark variation in LH or FSH.* Tanaka *et al.* (1966a) reported a diurnal variation in gonadotropic potency of pituitaries of Japanese quail, based on testes weight assay, depending on and influenced by amounts of light (L) and darkness (D) in a 24-hr period.

In birds exposed to 16L−8D, 14L−10D, or 6L−6D, a higher potency was found at the end of the light period than after 3 or 4 hr of darkness. It is well known that light stimulates the pituitary to secrete gonadotropins, particularly FSH (see Van Tienhoven and Planck, 1973).

Nicholls *et al.* (1973) employed radioimmunoassays to assay blood and pituitaries of Japanese quail exposed to different periods of light. They were placed on a regime of 20 hr light and 4 hr darkness for a number of days. There was an immediate increase in blood levels of LH within 2 days of light stimulation. The values were quite variable but changed little after 4−10 days of light exposure.

*Peaks of LH activity in pituitary and blood.* Peak levels of LH have been reported in the pituitary and plasma at different intervals before ovulation. These peaks are supposed to reflect times of release of LH from the gland. A decrease in LH level in the pituitary and an increase in the plasma indicate release time. Nelson *et al.* (1965) reported decreases in LH content of the pituitary and increases in the plasma at 20−21, 12−14, and 8 hr prior to ovulation of the $C_3$ follicle; this was confirmed by Bullock and Nalbandov (1967). Tanaka and Yoshioka (1967) reported pituitary LH peaks at 20 and 8 hr prior to $C_2$ ovulation but no peaks at 14 hr, based on OAAD activity.

These authors also reported a period following terminal ovulation when there were no changes in the pituitary concentration of LH but should have been if pituitary concentration and release and ovulation are closely related. Pituitary concentration may therefore be a poor reflection of circulating and physiologically active LH. Based on the sensitive radioimmunoassay for LH (Follett *et al.,* 1972), the pituitary of a laying quail contained 1878 ng equivalents of LH and the plasma level was 1.95 ng/ml; the circulating level of LH was only 0.5% of

*Table 15−2   Gonadotropic content in chickens*

| Breed | Reproductive stage | Gonadotropic content of anterior pituitary (chick units) | |
|---|---|---|---|
|  |  | Cephalic lobe | Caudal lobe |
| Nagoya | Nonlaying | 2.1 | 1.1 |
|  | Laying | 1.5 | 1.0 |
|  | Late broody | 0.7 | 0.3 |
| White Leghorn | Nonlaying | 2.5 | 1.1 |
|  | Laying | 1.5 | 1.0 |

the pituitary content. They reported plasma levels of LH in nanogram equivalents of avian $IRC_2$ (a highly purified avian LH preparation made by Stockell-Hartree and Cunningham, 1969) per milliliter in a Japanese quail and chicken as follows:

| | |
|---|---|
| Hypophysectomized chicken | 0.3 |
| Laying hen (two birds) | 0.52 and 0.96 |
| Female quail (long daylight) | 1.70 |
| Male quail | 20.7 |
| (castrate, long daylight) | |

Employing the radioimmunoassay on chickens, Furr et al. (1973) reported significantly higher levels of LH in the plasma 4–7 hr before ovulation than at any other time during the laying cycle. They reported plasma levels of LH at times before ovulation as follows:

| Hours before ovulation | LH (ng/ml) |
|---|---|
| 27 – 24 | 1.72 |
| 23 – 20 | 1.63 |
| 19 – 16 | 1.44 |
| 15 – 12 | 1.32 |
| 11 – 8 | 1.23 |
| 7 – 4 | 3.09 |
| 3 – 0 | 1.80 |

This one peak of LH was also confirmed by Wilson and Sharp (1973), who employed the same assay technique.

**Chemistry and physiology of FSH and LH.** Stockell-Hartree and Cunningham (1969) isolated and purified avian FSH and LH fractions. Extraction of acetone-dried chicken pituitary powder with 6% ammonium acetate, pH 5.1, in 40% ethanol resulted in a 20-fold concentration of FSH and LH activities. Their partial separation was achieved by chromatography on CM cellulose at pH 5.5 in 4 mM ammonium acetate (see Stockell-Hartree and Cunningham, 1971). The FSH fraction was further purified by chromatography to a 100-fold increase in potency and the LH fraction was concentrated 300-fold. The biological potencies of avian FSH and LH were considerably lower than those of the mammalian hormones.

It is well known that FSH stimulates the growth of ovarian follicles in females and the testes and maturation of spermatozoa in males. LH is known to cause ovulation in Aves and it is released from 6 to 8 hr prior to ovulation (for details on FSH and LH and their role in reproduction, see Chapters 16 and 17). It also acts on the Leydig cells of testes to produce androgen.

**Prolactin.** Prolactin, the hormone that causes milk secretion in mammals and crop-sac secretion in pigeons, causes broodiness in chickens. Highly purified preparations have been isolated from mammalian pituitaries, and details of the amino acid sequence in the substance have been reported; however, no such data are available for the avian hormone. Unlike mammals, where secretion of prolactin is inhibited by the hypothalamus, there is no inhibiting factor in the avian gland and there is evidence for an increasing or releasing factor (Meites and Nicoll, 1966). Nakajo and Imai (1961) have shown that the prolactin content of the pituitary tends to be inversely proportional to the level of FSH and LH. Meites and Nicoll (1966) demonstrated that hypothalamic extracts caused the release of prolactin from the pigeon pituitary in vitro. The pituitaries of broody chickens contain more prolactin than do those of nonbroody ones (Saeki and Tanabe, 1955); this has also been demonstrated in pigeons, and the gull (see Sturkie, 1965), the pheasant (Breitenbach and Meyer, 1959), and turkeys (Cherms et al., 1962). Riddle et al. (1935) first demonstrated that prolactin injected into hens caused broodiness and that the full expression of broodiness (clucking and nesting) was induced only in those breeds showing a natural tendency to go broody.

Nalbandov and Card (1942), working with the chicken, and Riddle and Bates (1939), with the pigeon, showed that different breeds and strains vary in the response to prolactin. Leghorn males (a nonbroody breed) require four to five times as much prolactin to produce broodiness as the Cornish, a naturally broody breed.

The prolactin content of pituitaries of adult male and female laying Japanese quails was not significantly different (2.0 – 2.6 Reece–Turner units per milligram of dried pituitary powder; Tanaka and Wilson, 1966).

There is an increase in pituitary prolactin during broodiness in California quail, and it is least during early incubating or setting when prolactin secretion is greatest (Jones, 1969). In certain species of phalarope only the male forms a brood patch and sits on the eggs, and the male pituitary contains more prolactin than the female (Höhn and Cheng, 1965). The changes in prolactin content of the duck pituitary, like those of FSH, exhibit an annual cyclic response; the content increases with increasing daily light or photostimulation (Gourdji, 1970).

The prolactin content of the cephalic and caudal areas of the anterior pituitaries of broody hens is about the same; it is much higher in the cephalic lobe of the nonbroody hen, however, where it remains fairly constant. The changes in the prolactin content of the caudal lobe are closely related to broodiness (Nakajo and Tanaka, 1956). Interruption of broodiness by electrical stimulation of the head decreased the prolactin content of the caudal area. For a review of the comparative action of prolactin among several species, including birds, see Bern and Nicoll (1968).

*Action.* Prolactin appears to play an important role in the regulation of fattening in migratory birds. Before migration many species accumulate large quantities of body fat. Meier *et al.* (1969) and Meier (1969) have shown a diurnal variation in the response to prolactin in the pituitary with highest levels at 6 hr after dawn, during the period of vernal migration. They believed that prolactin was released from the gland in the afternoon.

The antigonadal action of prolactin has been demonstrated in pigeons and chickens (see Sturkie, 1965) and in sparrows (Meier, 1969) and quail (Alexander and Wolfson, 1970). The testes and ovaries of sexually mature birds regress following prolactin administration, but the change can be prevented by simultaneous administration of FSH. Prolactin therefore acts by suppressing the output of FSH, which is necessary for gonad stimulation.

Broodiness in chickens can be terminated by estrogen administration (Sturkie, 1965), suggesting that this hormone prevents the release of prolactin by the pituitary. Although prolactin causes broodiness in hens, it does not in ring doves (Lehrman and Brody, 1961). These workers found, however, that progesterone induced incubation behavior, and they suggested that this behavior stimulated the secretion of prolactin. Prolactin may produce molting in the male, female, or capon chicken (Sturkie, 1965). The effect of prolactin on carbohydrate metabolism is discussed in Chapter 11. Prolactin has growth-promoting activity in pigeons (Hocker, 1969).

*Assays.* The crop-sac method has been widely used in assays for prolactin. There are a number of techniques, but all are based on stimulation and growth of the gland of the pigeon because this effect is produced only in the order Columbiformes. Three of these methods involve (1) the gross weight, (2) minimum stimulation, and (3) local stimulation (see Riddle and Bates, 1939; Meites and Turner, 1950).

The first is an objective method; the second is a subjective one, based on observed changes in the excised crop as examined by transmitted light. In the local stimulation method, prolactin is injected intracutaneously over the crop sac and only the small area at the site of the injection is affected. A single injection is made and the birds are autopsied after 48 hr. The excised crop is examined as in the minimum stimulation method. This method is very sensitive. As little as 0.1 gamma of the pure hormone produces a response. A shorter more sensitive modification of this method has been described by Grosvenor and Turner (1958). An international unit of prolactin is equal to 0.1 mg of pure prolactin. Because the response of the crop to prolactin exhibits a diurnal response (Meier, 1969), this must be considered in evaluating assays. The crop-sac method leaves much to be desired; it is variable and not overly sensitive. Radioimmunoassays have been used in mammalian species; these are very sensitive but as yet have not been developed for avian species.

**Release of gonadotropins from the hypophysis.** *Effects of light on FSH and LH.* The early, classic work of Benoit and associates (see Benoit, 1962, for review) has dealt with the mechanisms by which light stimulates the pituitary to release gonadotropins; this work has been reviewed by Farner and Oksche (1962) and by others (see Chapter 16). Benoit demonstrated that irradiation of the head and eyes stimulated the pituitary even when optic nerves were severed; when these organs were covered and other parts of the body were irradiated, however, the hypophysis was not stimulated. He and his group also found that the hypophysis could be stimulated by irradiating directly the hypothalamus or adjacent areas with light. Further evidence that the photoreceptor resides in the hypothalamus was revealed by Oishi and Lauber (1973) (see also Chapter 15 and 17).

They also reported that red and orange lights stimulated the hypophysis maximally, but that yellow, green, and blue lights (wavelengths 577, 546, and 436 nm) were relatively ineffective (Sturkie, 1965 for further details and Oishi and Lauber, 1973). The latter workers indicate that the pineal may be an auxillary photoreceptor, particularly of red light.

*Effects of hypothalamic lesions and extracts on FSH and LH.* There appear to be two separate cell types that secrete FSH and LH, and chromatographic separation of fairly pure avian FSH and LH pituitary fractions has been accomplished. This suggests the presence of separate releasing factors for these hormones. The first evidence that there are hypothalamic releasing factors in Aves was based on experiments involving lesions in the hypothalamus and severing of blood vessels between the hypothalamus and the hypophysis of ducks (Benoit and Assenmacher, 1951; Assenmacher, 1957; see reviews by Benoit, 1962; Farner *et al.*, 1967). Specifically, lesions in the area of the supraoptic and paraventricular nuclei interrupted normal sexual development in males. LH release and ovulation in the hen could be blocked by placing lesions in the same area (Ralph and Fraps, 1959; Opel and Fraps, 1961). Later evidence in the white-crowned sparrow by Wilson (1967) indicates that lesions in the tuberoinfundibular region also inhibits testicular growth; this has been confirmed by Stetson (1969) in the Japanese quail, and by Graber *et al.* (1967) on chickens.

Male chickens with bilateral lesions in the mammillary nuclei and the posterior part of the ventromedial nuclei behaved as though castrated, exhibiting completely atrophied testes and combs, evidence of inhibition of both FSH and LH-releasing factors (Ravona *et al.*, 1973). Another group, which had lesions placed in the posterior part of the mammillary nuclei, sometimes covering a part of the arcuate nuclei, behaved as castrates (lack of FSH) but had large combs (presence of LH).

In Japanese quail, permanent interruption of ovarian and testicular activity was produced by lesions in the entire median eminence or the anterior division, or posterior divisions of median eminence (Stetson, 1973). Interruption or injury to a number of pathways from the hypothalamus to the median eminence and anterior lobe therefore interferes with normal sexual development involving either or both FSH and LH. The gonadotropic releasing activity of the median eminence of laying hens at different stages of the ovulating cycle was determined by Tanaka *et al.* (1974). This activity varies with the cycle, with peaks of activity at 21 hr and 8–11 hr before ovulation of $C_2$.

Another approach to the study of releasing factors deals with extracts from different parts of the hypothalamus and median eminence injected into intact animals (Aves and mammals), or pituitaries incubated *in vitro* (free from hypothalamic control). Injection of chicken hypothalamic extracts into the anterior lobes of laying hens induced ovulation and this suggested a specific releasing factor for LH or LH-releasing factor (LRF) in the hypothalamus (Opel and Lenore, 1967), but injections of oxytocin and vasotocin were ineffective. These workers (Opel and Lenore, 1972) also reported that the releasing factor was not attributable to oxytocin or vasotocin found in the median eminence and that it appeared to be a low, molecular weight polypeptide distinct from median eminence hormones. Chicken hypothalamic extracts also caused the release of LH from rat pituitaries incubated *in vitro* (Jackson and Nalbandov, 1969a). Such extracts also released LH from cock pituitaries (Tanaka *et al.*,

1969). Both of these studies were based on OAAD activity, and it is now known that chicken hypothalami contain arginine vasotocin which has OAAD activity (Jackson and Nalbandov, 1969b); however, Tanaka *et al.* (1969) claim that most of the OAAD activity of their hypothalamic extracts resulted from LH, because after boiling, which normally destroys OAAD activity in hypothalamic extracts but not in posterior pituitary extracts (containing arginine vasotocin), there was no detectable LH activity remaining.

Ishii *et al.* (1970) reported that in the pigeon median eminence, OAAD activity results from arginine vasotocin. Avian hypothalamic extracts also stimulate the release of FSH from avian and rat pituitaries incubated *in vitro* (Kamiyoshi and Tanaka, 1969; Follett, 1970). Isolation and partial purification of specific FSH and LH releasing factors from the avian hypothalamus was accomplished by Jackson (1971a,b, 1972). Extracts of hypothalamus of rats and chickens were purified by ultrafiltration and chromatography. LRF activity was evaluated by release of LH from rat hypophysis *in vitro*, and LH was assayed by immunoassay. The elution patterns of rat and chicken fractions on ion exchange were distinctly different, indicating that the two LRF's are chemically distinct compounds, although there is an overlap in their activity. Synthetic ovine LH releasing factor, injected intravenously at dosages of 15–20 µg into chickens, induces premature ovulation consistently (van Tienhoven and Schally, 1972; see also Chapter 16). Jackson (1972) also isolated and partially purified FSH releasing factors (FRF) from rat and chicken hypothalami. The FRF of both rat and chicken hypothalamic extracts emerged from columns in the same fractions as the LRF's of these species, demonstrating the existence of an avian FRF and showing that the releasing factor was not the same in rats and chickens, although it was similar. The data suggest that similar compounds are responsible for LRF and FRF activities in both species (Jackson, 1972); whether these activities are attributable to identical or distinct compounds remains to be determined.

The release of LH appears to be related to plasma levels of estrogen, because the peak plasma level of LH associated with ovulation occurs about 2 hrs after the peak concentration of plasma estradiol is realized, suggesting an LH releasing role for estrogen (Senior and Cunningham, 1974, see also Chapter 16). Implants of estrogen into the hypothalamus or hypophysis prevented LH release and ovulation in Japanese quail (Stetson, 1972).

**Prolactin-releasing factor.** It is generally accepted that the secretion of prolactin by the pituitary of mammals is inhibited by the hypothalamus; when the connection between the pituitary and hypothalamus is interrupted by stalk transection or transplantation of pituitary, the release of prolactin is not inhibited. In chickens, however, there is no increase in prolactin secretion following transplantation of pituitary (Ma and Nalbandov, 1963). Moreover, chicken and quail hypothalamic extracts release prolactin from pigeon pituitaries cultured *in vitro* (Meites and Nicoll, 1966), indicating a positive releasing factor from the hypothalamus.

A prolactin-releasing factor has also been reported in the hypothalami of ducks (Gourdji and Tixier-Vidal, 1966) and turkey (Chen *et al.*, 1968). The concentration of the releasing factors varies with different reproductive states (Kragt and Meites, 1965). Very little is known about the chemistry of the releasing factor.

## Somatotropin (STH) or Growth Hormone (GH)

Growth hormone (GH) is a protein composed of a single polypeptide chain, which in humans has over 100 amino acid residues. Chemical similarities between human and avian GH are indicated by an immunologic cross-reaction between rat and chicken pituitary extracts (Hayashida, 1969). Papkoff and Hayashida (1972) purified GH from turtles and ducks and compared these to human GH. Both of these preparations stimulate growth in rats, based on the tibial epiphyseal plate assay in hypophysectomized rats. The purified duck preparation was examined by polyacrylamide gel disk electrophoresis. Analysis for terminal amino acids showed the presence of phenylalanine and leucine in the duck and turtle preparations, whereas most mammalian GH's show phenylalanine and bovine and ovine GH's also show alanine. Based on the amino acid composition, GH's from turtle, duck and human, all revealed close similarities for content of histidine, arginine, aspartic acid, threonine, and isoleucine. The turtle and duck have similar contents of lysine, alanine, leucine, tyrosine, and phenylalanine and human and turtle GH are also similar in their content of serine, glutamic acid, $\frac{1}{2}$-cystine, and valine.

Radioimmunoassays on these GH's, involving cross-reactions, indicated the specificity, distinctness, and similarities of these GH's (Papoff and Hayashida, 1972).

**GH level in pituitaries and activity.** Hypophysectomy in the growing chick retards growth, as it does in mammals (see Sturkie, 1965), indicating the existence of a pituitary growth hormone.

Hazelwood and Hazelwood (1961) assayed rat and chicken pituitaries in immature hypophysectomized rats and found that for equal amounts of dried pituitary, the rat hypophysis contained eight times as much growth hormone. The chicken extract not only produced growth but also decreased the hematocrit in the rat. Moudgal and Li (1961) have also reported growth hormone in the chick pituitary, based on the rat assay.

Mammalian growth hormone had no effect on the growth of young chickens, according to Libby *et al.* (1955) and Glick (1960). This hormone did increase the growth of the long bones in chick embryos (Blumenthal *et al.,* 1954). Enemar (1967) reported GH activity in the caudal lobe of the chick embryo by 15 days of development but none in the cephalic lobe. It appears that the hypophysectomized rat is not a suitable species for assaying avian growth hormone. Further studies on the effects of more purified avian GH preparations are needed.

There is some evidence that prolactin acts to promote growth in pigeons and in chickens (Huble, 1956). Schooley *et al.* (1941) claim to have obtained adequate growth in hypophysectomized pigeons with prolactin. Schlumberger and Rudolph (1959) have studied pituitary tumors of parakeets and have found that the tumors contained an active growth hormone that increases growth in rats and in parakeets. Moreover, mammalian growth hormones are effective in producing changes in the plasma proteins of parakeets according to Rudolph and Pehrson, (1961).

**GH-releasing factor.** A GH-releasing factor from pigeon hypothalamus was demonstrated by Muller *et al.* (1967) but further work is needed.

## Adrenocorticotropin (ACTH)

The avian pituitary, like that of mammals, contains ACTH. It first appears in the chick embryonic pituitary as early as 16 days and increases thereafter up to hatching time (Moszkowski, 1949). ACTH activity has been reported in the pituitaries of chickens, ducks, pigeons, seagulls, and others (see Chapter 20). There is abundant evidence also that mammalian ACTH can stimulate the adrenals of a number of avian species to elaborate cortical hormones (Chapter 20) and so can various stresses that induce a release of ACTH.

Mammalian ACTH has been purified and chemically characterized. However, this is not so in Aves, although chicken ACTH appears to be similar to that of mammals based on its response to certain chemicals, boiling, and depletion of adrenal ascorbic acid (Salem *et al.*, 1970a,b). Salem *et al.* (1970a) assayed the ACTH content in the laying hen pituitary gland by adrenal ascorbic acid depletion in hypophysectomized rats and reported levels of 401 mU (milliunits) of mammalian ACTH per milligram frozen pituitary. This amount is considerably higher than the figure reported by De Roos and De Roos (1964), which ranged from 65 to 100 mU per milligram of fresh tissue. Differences in experimental procedures may explain the difference (Salem *et al.*, 1970a).

**Assays.** These are discussed in detail in Chapter 20 and include changes in adrenal weight, adrenal ascorbic acid depletion, and determination of levels of adrenal corticoids in adrenal venous blood. Radioimmunoassays that have been developed for mammals are not yet available for Aves.

**Action.** The details concerning action of ACTH and the control of adrenal secretion are discussed in Chapter 20.

**ACTH-releasing factor.** There is evidence for an ACTH-releasing factor in the hypothalamus of chickens (Salem, 1970a,b), of ducks (Stainer and Holmes, 1969), and in the median eminence of pigeons (Peczely and Zboray, 1967; and Peczelyetal, 1970).

## Thyrotropin (TSH)

It has been known for many years that hypophysectomy greatly decreases thyroid activity, indicating the dependence of the thyroid on the anterior pituitary (see Ringer, 1965, and Chapter 18). TSH has been purified from a number of mammalian species and is a polypeptide of high molecular weight. Chicken TSH has been partially purified by Scanes and Follett (1972). It is a glycoprotein of large molecular weight, similar to its mammalian counterpart. These workers assayed pituitaries of hens and broilers for TSH as follows:

| | TSH as $\mu$g equivalents of NIH-TSH-S6 |
|---|---|
| Hens | 0.317 |
| Broilers | 0.509 |

**Location.** Mikami (1958) reported that the cephalic lobe of chickens contained more TSH than the caudal lobe, based on thyroid cell height, and similar results were obtained by Brasch and Betz (1971), based on a different assay. Radke and Chiasson (1974) demonstrated that the cephalic lobe

contained four times the amount found in the caudal lobe of chickens.

**Assays.** These techniques include the uptake or release of $^{131}I$ or $^{32}P$ by the thyroid, which are increased when the gland is stimulated by TSH. A measure of increased thyroid secretion rate is therefore also a measure of TSH secretion or release from the pituitary. Other assays include growth or change in the weight of the thyroid and/or an increase in the height of the epithelium of chick thyroid follicles (see Ringer, 1965, and Chapter 18 for review of details).

Radioimmunoassays for mammalian TSH are in use, but avian TSH has not been sufficiently purified to permit radioiodination (Follett *et al.*, 1972).

**Action.** More details on the action of TSH are considered in Chapter 18.

**TSH-releasing factor.** No avian releasing factor for TSH has as yet been isolated, but TSH secretion is influenced by the hypothalamus. Section of the portal blood vessels in the duck and pigeon (Assenmacher, 1959; Bayle *et al.*, 1966) or lesions of the hypothalamus (Assenmacher 1957) interfere with normal thyroid function. Later studies in the quail by McFarland *et al.* (1966) and on chickens by Takahara *et al.* (1967), who placed lesions in the anterior hypothalamus, revealed that thyroid weight and presumably thyroid secretion were diminished. Recent work by Kanematsu and Mikami (1970), who studied $^{131}I$ uptake of thyroid of chickens after hypothalamic lesions, revealed that TSH secretion is regulated by a region of anterior hypothalamus extending from the area ventrocaudally to the anterior commissure to the area dorsocaudally to the optic chiasma.

Synthetic TSH releasing factor (pyroglutamyl histidyl prolylamide) injected into young cockerels (intravenously) at a dose of $50-400$ $\mu$g per 100 g body weight was effective in releasing TSH immediately. Injection of thyroxine prior to releasing hormone blocked the effects of the latter (Newcomer and Huang, 1974).

## Melanotropin (MSH)

Melanotropin or intermedin is present in the intermediate lobe of mammals but is present in the anterior lobe of chickens (Kleinholz and Rahn, 1940) and ducks (Mialhe-Voloss and Benoit, 1954). The cephalic portion of the lobe of chickens is considerably more potent (20 times) than the caudal portion. Chen *et al.* (1940) reported that this hormone is present in the chick's hypophysis as

298 early as the fifth day. MSH causes an expansion of melanophores in the skin of the frog, chameleon, lizard, and fish. Kleinholz and Rahn (1940) used the hypophysectomized lizard, *Anolis carolinensis*, to assay the potencies of the pituitaries of several species for intermedin. They found that the cephalic portion of the anterior lobe of chickens was more potent in MSH than were equal weights of pituitary from the intermediate lobes of cattle. Tougard (1971) found a positive correlation between the concentration of MSH in the pituitary and the number of κ cells in the gland.

The function and chemical nature of MSH in Aves are not known.

### Hormone Feedback

This is another mechanism by which the output of anterior pituitary hormones is regulated. An increase in circulating levels of certain target organ hormones acting either directly or indirectly through the hypothalamus and releasing factors causes the pituitary to decrease its output of appropriate tropic hormones. This is particularly true of adrenal cortical hormones (Chapter 20), thyroxine (Chapter 18) and gonadal hormones (Chapters 16 and 17).

## NEUROHYPOPHYSIS

The avian neurohypophysis contains the hormones oxytocin and vasotocin (Munsick *et al.,* 1960; Munsick, 1964) and mesotocin (Acher, et al 1970). The structures of these are given below, showing the sequence of amino acids in the ring and side chains. Mesotocin has pharmacologic properties similar to those of oxytocin. Acher *et al.* (1970) suggested that oxytocin reported by others in avian pituitaries may have been introduced with mammalian neurophysin added to facilitate precipitation of chicken hormones. Further work, however, is needed to definitely determine whether one or more oxytocins are present.

### Oxytocin

The relative potencies of fowl neurohypophyseal extracts, including oxytocin and vasotocin, based on 11 different assays were reported by Munsick *et al.* (1960). The oxytocic content of neural lobes averaged 1.2 μg/mg of gland. Oxytocic activity is assayed by its effect on the uterus of hens or rats and by its depressor effect on avian blood pressure. The latter is a less sensitive assay than the uterus assay. Mesotocin is about 10% more active than oxytocin based on the avian blood depressor assay (Acher *et al.,* 1970) but slightly less active than the uterine assay.

### Arginine Vasotocin

Arginine vasotocin has extraordinary potency when assayed for its oxytocic activity, particularly on the uterus (Munsick *et al.,* 1960). It is the avian antidiuretic hormone (see Chapter 14) and it has a powerful effect in increasing water permeability of the frog bladder (an assay technique used by Sturkie and Lin, 1966). Munsick *et al.* (1960) reported that the concentration of arginine vasotocin in chicken pituitaries was ten times that of oxytocin; the anterior pituitary also contains arginine vasotocin (Jackson and Nalbandov, 1969b).

Tanaka and Nakajo (1962) demonstrated that the posterior lobe of laying hens contained the least amount of vasotocin coincident with laying time and suggested that this hormone was released into the blood at this time.

Sturkie and Lin (1966) reported that the concentration of vasotocin in the blood was greatest at the time of laying. In fact, the vasotocin activity before

---

CyS-Tyr-Ile-Glu(NH₂)-Asp(NH₂)-CyS-Pro-Leu-Gly(NH₂)
 1  2  3  4    5     6  7  8  9
*Oxytocin*

CyS-Tyr-Ile-Glu(NH₂)-Asp(NH₂)-CyS-Pro-Ile-Gly(NH₂)
*Mesotocin (8-isoleucine oxytocin)*

CyS-Tyr-Ile-Glu(NH₂)-Asp(NH₂)-CyS-Pro-Arg-Gly(NH₂)
*Vasotocin (8-arginine oxytocin)*

oviposition was 50–167 μU/ml of blood and immediately prior to and during oviposition it increased to 7059 μU (see also Chapter 16) Within 20 min after oviposition it decreased considerably and soon thereafter reached the resting level. They revealed also that stimuli which normally cause a release of vasotocin in mammals, such as intracarotid injection of saline, were without effect in chickens. Moreover, other agents, such as acetylcholine, nembutal, and uterine distension, which may cause premature oviposition, did not induce the release of vasotocin (Sturkie and Lin, 1967). Their experiments suggested that vasotocin probably was a stimulus for oviposition but that oviposition did not induce release of vasotocin. Stimulation of the brain preoptic area caused premature oviposition (Opel, 1966) and an increase in plasma vasotocin. Hens continue to lay, however, after complete removal of the posterior lobe, according to Shirley and Nalbandov (1956). Following such surgery, however, the anterior lobe and the median eminence are still intact and the latter contains vasotocin (Hirano, 1964; Jackson and Nalbandov, 1969b). Further details on the effects of oxytocic compounds on oviposition are presented in Chapter 16.

Injections of oxytocin (0.03 IU/kg) and arginine vasotocin (0.4 μg/kg) significantly increased the number of sexual mountings in cocks and male pigeons (Kihlstrom and Danninge, 1972).

# REFERENCES

Alexander, B., and A. Wolfson. (1970). Prolactin and sexual maturation in Japanese quail. Poultry Sci., 49, 632.

Acher, R., J. Chauvet, and M. T. Chauvet. (1970). Phylogeny of the neurohypophyseal hormones. The Avian active peptides. Eu. J. Biochem., 11, 509.

Assenmacher, I. (1957). Répercussions de lésions hypothalamiques sur le conditonement genital tu canard domestique. Compt. Rend. Acad. Sci. Paris, 245, 210.

Assenmacher, I. (1959). Regulations thryéotropes après section des veines portes hypophysaires chez le canard. Gumma J. Med. Sci., 8, 199.

Bayle, J. D., H. Astier, and I. Assenmacher. (1966). Activité thyroidienne du pigeon après hypophysectonnie ou autogreffe hypophysaire. J. Physiol. (Paris), 58, 459.

Benoit, J. (1950). "Traité de Zoologie," Tome XV, Oiseaux (P. P. Grasse, Ed.). Paris: Masson & Co., p. 316.

Benoit, J. (1962). Hypothalamo-hypophyseal control of the sexual activity in birds. Gen. Comp. Endocrinol., 1 (Suppl.), 254.

Benoit, J., and I. Assenmacher. (1951). Etude preliminarie de la vascularization de l'appareil hypophysaire du canard domestique. Arch. Anat. Microscop. Morphol. Exp., 40, 27.

Bern, H. A., and C. S. Nicoll. (1968). Comparative endocrinology of prolactin. Rec. Prog. Hormone Res., 24, 681.

Blumenthal, H. T., K. Hsieh, and T. Wang. (1954). The effect of hypophyseal growth hormone on the tibia of the developing chick embryo. Am. J. Pathol., 30, 771.

Brasch, M., and T. W. Betz. (1971). The hormonal activities associated with the cephalic and caudal regions of the cockerel pars distalis. Gen. Comp. Endocrinol., 16, 241.

Breitenback, R. P., and R. K. Meyer. (1959). Pituitary prolactin levels in laying, incubating and brooding pheasants. Proc. Soc. Exp. Biol. Med., 101, 16.

Breneman, W. R. (1955). "Reproduction in Birds: the Female." Mem. Soc. Endocrinol., No. 4. London: Cambridge University Press.

Bullock, D. W., and A. V. Nalbandov. (1967). Hormonal control of hens ovulation cycle. J. Endocrinol., 38, 407.

Burns, J. M. (1970). LH bioassay based on uptake of radioactive phosphorus of the chick testes. Comp. Biochem. Physiol., 34, 727.

Chen, C., E. J. Bixler, A. Weber, and J. Meites. (1968). Hypothalamic stimulation of prolactin release from the pituitary of turkey hens, and poults. Gen. Comp. Endocrinol., 11, 489.

Chen, G., F. K. Oldham, and E. M. K. Geiling. (1940). Appearance of the melanophore-expanding hormone of the pituitary gland in developing chick embryo. Proc. Soc. Exp. Biol. Med., 45, 810.

Cherms, F. L., R. B. Herrick, W. H. McShan, and W. C. Hymer. (1962). Prolactin content of the anterior pituitary gland of turkey hens in different reproductive stages. Endocrinology, 71, 389.

De Roos, R., and C. C. De Roos. (1964). Effects of mammalian corticotropin and chicken adenohypophyseal extracts on steroid-genesis by chicken adrenal tissue in in vitro. Gen. Comp. Endocrinol., 4, 602.

Enemar, A. (1967). Ontogeny of the hypophyseal growth promoting activity in the chick. J. Endocrinol., 37, 9.

Farner, D. S., and B. K. Follett. (1966). Light and other environmental factors affecting reproduction. J. Anim. Sci., 25 (Suppl.), 90.

Farner, D. S., and A. Oksche. (1962). Neurosecretion in birds. Gen. Comp. Endocrinol., 2, 113.

Farner, D. S., F. E. Wilson, and A. Oksche. (1967). Avian neuroendocrine mechanisms. In "Neuro-endocrinology," Vol. 2 (G. L. Martine and W. F. Ganong, Eds.). New York: Academic Press, p. 529.

Follett, B. K. (1970). Gonadotropin releasing activity in the quail hypothalamus. Gen. Comp. Endocrinol., 15, 165.

Follett, B. K., and D. S. Farner. (1966). Pituitary gonadotropins in the Japanese quail during photoperiodically induced gonadal growth. Gen. Comp. Endocrinol., 7, 125.

Follett, B. K., C. G. Scanes, and F. J. Cunningham. (1972). A radioimmunoassay for avian LH. J. Endocrinol., 52, 359.

Fraps, R. M. (1943). Potencies of anterior pituitary glands of mature chickens in the induction of ovulation in the hen. Anat. Rec., 87, 443.

Furr, B. J. A., and F. J. Cunningham. (1970). The biological assay of chicken pituitary gonadotropins. Brit. Poultry Sci., 11, 7.

Furr, B. J. A., R. C. Bonney, R. J. England, and F. J. Cunningham. (1973). LH and progesterone in peripheral blood during the ovulatory cycle of the hen. J. Endocrinol., 57, 159.

Glick, B. (1960). The effect of bovine growth hormone, DCA, and cortisone on weight of bunsa of Fabricius, adrenal glands, heart and body weight of young chickens. Poultry Sci., 39, 1527.

Gourdji, D. (1970). Prolactine et relations photosexuelles chez les oiseaux. Coll. Intl. Cent. Natl. Rech. Sci., 172, 233.

Gourdji, D. and A. Tixier-Vidal. (1966). Mise en évidence d'un contrôle hypothalamique stimulant de la prolactine hypophysaire chez le canard. Compt. Rend. Acad. Sci. (Paris), 263, 162.

Graber, J. W., A. I. Frankel, and A. V. Nalbandov. (1967). Hypothalamic center influencing the release of LH in the cockerel. Gen. Comp. Endocrinol., 9, 187.

Green, J. D. (1951). The comparative anatomy of the hypophysis with special reference to its blood supply and innervation. Am. J. Anat., 88, 225.

Grignon, G. (1956). "Developement du Complexe Hypothalamo-hypophysaire chez l'Embryon de Poulet." Nancy: Société d'Impressions Typographiques.

Grosvenor, C. E., and C. W. Turner. (1958). Assay of lactogenic hormone. Endocrinology, 63, 530.

Hayashida, T. (1969). Relatedness of pituitary growth hormone from various vertebrate classes. Nature (London), 222, 294.

Hazelwood, R. L., and B. S. Hazelwood. (1961). Effects of avian

300

and rat pituitary extracts on tibial growth and blood composition. *Proc. Soc. Exp. Biol. Med., 108*, 10.

Heald, P. J., K. A. Rookledge, B. E. Furnival, G. D. Watts. (1968a). Changes in LH content of anterior pituitary of the domestic fowl during the interval between clutches. *J. Endocrinol., 41*, 197.

Heald, P. J., K. A. Rookledge, B. E. Furnival, and G. D. Watts. (1968b). The effects of gonadol hormones on the levels of pituitary LH on the domestic fowl. *J. Endocrinol., 41*, 313.

Herlant, M. (1964). The cells of the adenohypophysis and their functional significance. *Intl. Rev. Cytol., 17*, 299.

Hocker, W. (1969). Über somatotrope prolactinwirkungen bei hypophysektomierten Tauben. *Zool. Anz. suppl., Bd. 33, Vertt. Zool. Ges., 5*, 278.

Höhn, E. O., and S. C. Cheng. (1965). Prolactin and the incidence of brood patch formation. *Nature (London), 208*, 197.

Hirano, I. (1964). Further studies on the neuro-hypophyseal hormones in the avian median eminence. *Endocrinol. Jap., 11*, 87.

Huble, J. (1956). Gonadal and hypophyseal interactions on the young fowl. *Acta Endocrinol., 23*, 101.

Ishii, S., A. K. Sarkar, and H. Kobayashi. (1970). Ovarian ascorbic acid depleting factor in pigeon median eminence. *Gen. Comp. Endocrinol., 14*, 461.

Jackson, G. L. (1971a). Avian LH releasing factor. *Endocrinology, 89*, 1454.

Jackson, G. L. (1971b). Comparison of rat and chicken LH releasing factors. *Endocrinology, 89*, 1460.

Jackson, G. L. (1972). Partial purification and characterization of chicken and rat FSH releasing factors. *Endocrinology, 91*, 1090.

Jackson, G. L., and A. V. Nalbandov. (1969a). LH releasing activity in the chicken hypothalamus. *Endocrinology, 84*, 1262.

Jackson, G. L., and A. V. Nalbandov. (1969b). Ovarian ascorbic acid depleting factors in the chicken hypophysis. *Endocrinology, 85*, 113.

Jones, R. E. (1969). Epidermal hyperplasia in the incubation patch of the California quail in relation to pituitary prolactin content. *Gen. Comp. Endocrinol., 12*, 498.

Kamiyoshi, M., and K. Tanaka. (1969). Changes in pituitary FSH concentrations during an ovulatory cycle of the hen. *Poultry Sci., 48*, 2025.

Kanematsu, S., and S. I. Mikami. (1970). Effects of hypothalamic lesions on protein, blood [131]iodine and thyroidal [131]I uptake in the chicken. *Gen. Comp. Endocrinol., 14*, 25.

Kihlstrom, J. E., and I. Dannige. (1972). Neurohypophyseal hormones and sexual behavior in males of the domestic fowl and the pigeon. *Gen. Comp. Endocrinol., 18*, 115.

Kleinholz, L. H., and H. Rahn. (1940). The distribution of intermedin: A new biological method of assay and results of tests under normal and experimental conditions. *Anat. Rec., 76*, 157.

Kobayashi, H., and M. Wada. (1973). Neuroendocrinology in birds. In "Avian Biology," Vol. 3. (D. S. Farner and J. R. King, Eds.). New York: Academic Press, Chapter 4.

Kragt, C. L., and J. Meites. (1965). Stimulation of pigeon pituitary prolactin release by pigeon hypothalamic extracts *in vitro*. *Endocrinology, 78*, 1169.

Legait, H. (1959). Contribution à l'étude morphologique et expérimentale du système hypothalamo-neurohypophysaire de la poule Rhode-Island. Theses, University of Louvain, Nancy, France.

Lehrman, O. S., and P. Brody. (1961). Does prolactin induce incubation behavior in the ring dove. *J. Endocrinol., 22*, 269.

Libby, D. A., J. Meites, and J. Schaible. (1955). Growth hormone effects in chickens. *Poultry Sci., 34*, 1329.

Ma, R. C. S., and A. V. Nalbandov. (1963). Discussion on the transplanted hypophysis. In "Advances in Neuroendocrinology" (A. V. Nalbandov, Ed.). Urbana: University of Illinois Press, p. 306.

McFarland, L. Z., M. K. Yousef, and W. O. Wilson. (1966). The influence of ambient temperature and hypothalamic lesions on the disappearance rates of [131]I in the Japanese quail. *Life Sci., 5*, 309.

Meier, A. H. (1969). Diurnal variations of metabolic responses to prolactin in lower vertebrates. *Gen. Comp. Endocrinol., 2*, (Suppl.), 55.

Meier, A. H., J. I. Burns, and J. W. Dusseau. (1969). Seasonal variations in the diurnal rhythm of pituitary prolactin content in the white throated sparrow. *Gen. Comp. Endocrinol., 12*, 282.

Meites, J., and C. W. Turner. (1950). Lactogenic hormone. In "Hormone Assay" (C. W. Emmens, Ed.). New York: Academic Press, p. 237.

Meites, J., and C. S. Nicoll. (1966). Adenohypophysis: Prolactin: *Ann. Rev. Physiol., 28*, 57.

Mialhe-Voloss, C., and J. Benoit. (1954). L'intermedine dans l'-hypophyse et al 'hypothalamus du canard. *Compt. Rend. Soc. Biol., 148*, 56.

Mikami, S. I. (1958). The cytological significance of regional patterns in the adenohypophysis of the fowl. *J. Fac. Agri., Iwate University, 3(4)*, 473.

Mikami, S., A. Vitums, and D. S. Farner. (1969). Electron microscope studies on the adenohypophysis of white crowned sparrow. *Z. Zellforsch. Mikrosk. Anat., 97*, 1.

Moszkowski, A. (1949). Pouvoir corticotrope et gonadotrope de l'hypophyse de l'embryonde poulet. *Compt. Rend. Soc. Biol., 143*, 1332.

Moudgal, N. R., and C. H. Li. (1961). Immunochemical studies of bovine and ovine pituitary growth hormone. *Arch. Biochem. Biophys., 93*, 122.

Muller, E. E., S. Awano, and A. V. Schally. (1967). Growth hormone releasing activity in the hypothalamus of animals of different species. *Gen. Comp. Endocrinol., 9*, 349.

Munsick, R. A. (1964). Neurohypophyseal hormones of chickens and turkeys. *Endocrinology, 75*, 104.

Munsick, R. A., W. H. Sawyer, and H. B. Van Dyke. (1960). Avian neurohypophyseal hormones: Pharmacological properties and tentative identification. *Endocrinology, 66*, 860.

Nakajo, S., and K. Imai. (1961). Gonadotropin content in the cephalic and the caudal lobes of the anterior pituitary in laying, nonlaying and broody hens. *Poultry Sci., 40*, 739.

Nakajo, S., and K. Tanaka. (1956). Prolactin potency of the cephalic and the caudal lobe of the anterior pituitary in relation to broodiness in the domestic fowl. *Poultry Sci., 35*, 990.

Nalbandov, A. V., and L. E. Card. (1942). Hormonal induction of broodiness in roosters. *Poultry Sci., 21*, 474. (Abstr.)

Nalbandov, A. V., and L. E. Card. (1943). Effect of hypophysectomy of growing chicks. *J. Exp. Zool., 94*, 387.

Nelson, D. M., H. W. Norton, and A. V. Nalbandov. (1965). Changes in hypophyseal and plasma LH levels during the laying cycle. *Endocrinology, 77*, 889.

Newcomer, W. S., and F. S. Huang. (1974). Thyrotropin-releasing hormone in chicks. *Endocrinology, 95*, 318.

Nicholls, J. J., C. G. Scanes, and B. K. Follett. (1973). Plasma and pituitary LH in Japanese quail during photoperiodically induced gonadal growth and regression. *Gen. Comp. Endocrinol., 21*, 84.

Oishi, T., and J. K. Lauber. (1973). Photoreception in the photosexual response of quail. II. Effects of intensity and wavelength. *Am. J. Physiol., 225*, 880.

Oksche, A. (1965). The fine structure of the neurosecretory system of birds in relation to its functional aspects. Proc. 2nd Int. Congr. Endocrinol., London, 1964. *Excerpta Med. Int. Congr. Ser., 83*, 167.

Opel, H. (1966). Release of oviposition inducing factor from the median eminence—pituitary stalk region in neural lobectomized hens. *Anat. Rec., 154*, 396.

Opel, H., and R. M. Fraps. (1961). Blockade of gonadotropin release for ovulation in the hen following stimulation with stainless steel electrodes. *Proc. Soc. Exp. Biol. Med., 108*, 291.

Opel, H., and P. D. Lenore. (1967). Ovulating hormone releasing factor in chicken hypothalamus. *Poultry Sci., 46*, 1302.

Opel, H., and P. D. Lenore. (1972). *In vivo* studies of luteinizing hormone releasing factor in the chicken hypothalamus. *Poultry Sci., 51*, 1004.

Papkoff, H., and T. Hayashida. (1972). Pituitary growth hormone from the turtle and duck. Purification and immunochemical studies. *Proc. Soc. Exp. Biol. Med., 140,* 251.

Péczely, P., and G. Zboray. (1967). CRF and Activity in median eminence of pigeon. *Acta Physiol., 32,* 229.

Péczely, P., J. D. Bayle, J. Boissin, and I. Assenmacher. (1970). Activitiés de corticotrope et CRF dans l'éminence médiane et activité, et activité corticotrope de greffes hypophysaires chez le pigeon. *Compt. Rend. Acad. Sci. ,Paris., 270,* 3274.

Radke, W. J., and R. B. Chiasson. (1974). Thyroid stimulating hormone location in the chicken pars distalis. *J. Endocrinol., 60,* 187.

Rahn, H., and B. T. Painter. (1941). The comparative histology of the bird pituitary. *Anat. Rec., 79,* 297.

Ralph, C. V., and R. M. Fraps. (1959). Long term effects of diencephalic lesions on the ovary of the hen. *Am. J. Physiol., 197,* 269.

Ravoña, H., N. Snapir, and M. Perek. (1973). The effect on the gonadal axis in cockerels of electrolytic lesions in various regions of the basal hypothalamus. *Gen. Comp. Endocrinol., 20,* 112.

Riddle, O., and R. W. Bates. (1939). The preparation, assay, and actions of lactogenic hormones. In "Sex and Internal Secretions" (2d ed.) (E. Allan, Ed). Baltimore: Williams and Wilkins Co., p. 1088.

Riddle, O., R. W. Bates, and E. L. Lahr. (1935). Prolactin induces broodiness in the fowl. *Am. J. Physiol., 111,* 352.

Ringer, R. K. (1965). Thyroids. In "Avian Physiology" (2nd ed.) (P. D. Sturkie, Ed.). Ithaca, N.Y.: Cornell University Press, Chapter 19.

Rothchild, I. (1948). A simplified technique for hypophysectomy of domestic fowl. *Endocrinology, 43,* 293.

Rudolph, H. J., and N. C. Pehrson. (1961). Growth hormone effect on the blood plasma proteins in the parakeet. *Endocrinology, 69,* 661.

Saeki, Y., and Y. Tanabe. (1955). Changes in prolactin content of fowl pituitary during broody periods and some experiments on the induction of broodiness. *Poultry Sci., 34,* 909.

Salem, M. H. M., H. W. Norton, and A. V. Nalbandov. (1970a). A study of ACTH and CRF in chickens. *Gen. Comp. Endocrinol., 14,* 270.

Salem, M. H. M., H. W. Norton, and A. V. Nalbandov. (1970b). The role of vasotocin and CRF and ACTH release in the chicken. *Gen. Comp. Endocrinol., 14,* 281.

Scanes, C. G., and B. K. Follett. (1972). Fractionation and assay of chicken pituitary hormones. *Brit. Poultry Sci., 13,* 603.

Schlumberger, H. G., and H. J. Rudolph. (1959). Growth promoting effect of a transplantable pituitary tumor in parakeets. *Endocrinology, 65,* 902.

Schooley, J. P. (1939). Technique for hypophysectomy in pigeons. *Endocrinology, 25,* 373.

Schooley, J. P., O. Riddle, and R. W. Bates. (1941). Replacement therapy in hypophysectomized juvenile pigeons. *Am. J. Anat., 69,* 123.

Senior, B. E., and F. J. Cunningham. (1974). Estradiol and LH during the ovulatory cycle of the hen. *J. Endocrinol., 60,* 201.

Shirley, H. V., and A. V. Nalbandov. (1956). Effects of neurohypophysectomy in domestic chickens. *Endocrinology, 58,* 477.

Stainer, I. M., and W. N. Holmes. (1969) Some evidence for the presence of a corticotropin releasing factor (CRF) in the duck. *Gen. Comp. Endocrinol., 12,* 350.

Stetson, M. H. (1969). Hypothalamic regulation of FSH and LH secretion in male and female Japanese quail. *Am. Zool., 9,* 1078.

Stetson, M. H. (1973) Recovery of gonadal function following hypothalamic lesions in Japanese quail. *Gen. Comp. Endocrinol., 20,* 76.

Stetson, M. H. (1972). Feedback regulation by estradiol of ovarian function in Japanese quail. *J. Reprod. Fert., 31,* 205.

Stockell-Hartree, A., and F. J. Cunningham. (1969). Purification of chicken pituitary FSH and LH. *J. Endocrinol., 43,* 609.

Stockell-Hartree, A., and F. J. Cunningham. (1971). The pituitary gland. "Physiology and Biochemistry of Domestic Fowl" (Vol. 1, D. J. Bell and B. M. Freeman, Eds.). London: Academic Press, Chapter 16.

Sturkie, P. D. (1965). "Avian Physiology" (2nd ed.) (P. D. Sturkie, Ed.). Ithaca, N.Y.: Cornell University Press, Chapter 17.

Sturkie, P. D., and Y. C. Lin. (1966). Release of vasotocin and oviposition in the hen. *J. Endocrinol., 35,* 325.

Sturkie, P. D., and Y. C. Lin. (1967). Further studies on oviposition and vasotocin release in the hen. *Poultry Sci., 46,* 1591.

Takahara, H., T. Sonoda, and Y. Kato. (1967). Cytological change of the hypophysis and the gonads after hypothalamic lesions in the cockerel. *Jap. J. Zootech. Scil, 38* (Suppl)., 60.

Tanaka, K., and S. Nakajo. (1962). Participation of neurohypophyseal hormones on oviposition with hen. *Endocrinology, 70,* 453.

Tanaka, K. and W. O. Wilson. (1966). Prolactin content in the anterior lobe of pituitary in sexually motive coturnix. *Poultry Sci., 44,* 614.

Tanaka, K., and S. Yoshioka. (1967). LH activity of hens pituitary during the egg laying cycle. *Gen. Comp. Endocrinol., 9,* 374.

Tanaka, K., W. O. Wilson, F. B. Matherson, L. Z. McFarland. (1966a). Diurnal variation in gonadotropic potency of the adenohypophysis of Japanese quail. *Gen. Comp. Endocrinol., 6,* 1.

Tanaka, K., Y. Fujisawa, and S. Yoshioka. (1966b). LH content in the pituitary of laying and non-laying hens. *Poultry Sci., 45,* 970.

Tanaka, K., M. Kamiyoshi, and M. Sakaida. (1974). Changes in gonadotropin-releasing activity of the hypothalamus during an ovulating cycle of hen. *Poultry Sci., 53,* 1555.

Tanaka, K., M. Kamiyoshi, and M. Tagami. (1969). *In vitro* demonstration of LH releasing activity in hypothalamic of the hen. *Poultry Sci. 48,* 1985.

Tixier-Vidal, A., and B. K. Follett. (1973). The adenohypophysis. In "Avian Biology," Vol. 3 (D. S. Farner and J. R. King, Eds.). New York: Academic Press, Chapter 2.

Tixier-Vidal, A., B. K. Follett, and D. S. Farner. (1968). The anterior pituitary of the Japanese quail. The cytological effects of photoperiodic stimulation. *Z. für Zellforsch., 92,* 610.

Tougard, C. (1971). Researchers sur l'origine, cytologique de l'hormone melanophorotrope. Chez les Oiseaux. *Mikrosk. Anat., 116,* 375.

Van Tienhoven, A., and R. J. Planck. (1973). The effect of light on avian reproductive activity. In "Handbook of Physiology," Sect. 7, Vol. 2. Washington, D.C.: American Physiological Society.

Van Tienhoven, A., and A. V. Schally. (1972). Mammalian luteinizing hormone releasing hormone induces ovulation in the domestic fowl. *Gen. Comp. Endocrinol., 19,* 594.

Vitums, A., S. I. Mikami, A. Oksche, and D. S. Farner. (1964). Vascularization of the hypothalamo—hypophyseal complex in the white-crowned sparrow. *Z. für Zellforsch., 64,* 541.

Wilson, F. E. (1967). The tubero—infundibulum system: A component of the photoperiodic control mechanism of the white-crowned sparrow. *Z. Zellforsch Mikrosk. Anat., 82,* 1.

Wilson, S. C., and P. J. Sharp. (1973). Variations in plasma LH levels during the ovulatory cycle of the hen, *Gallus domesticus. J. Reprod. Fert., 35,* 561.

Wingstrand, K. G. (1951). "The Structure and Development of the Avian Pituitary." Lund, Sweden: C. W. K. Gleerup.

# 16

# Reproduction
# in the Female
# and Egg Production

## P. D. Sturkie

with W. J. Mueller

# ANATOMY OF THE FEMALE REPRODUCTIVE SYSTEM

The reproductive organs of the avian female include the left ovary and left oviduct. Although the right ovary and oviduct are formed in the embryonic stages, they usually do not persist in adult life. A persistent right ovary and oviduct have been reported in some avian species (raptors) and in rare instances in ducks and chickens where both ovaries and oviducts were functional (see Sturkie, 1965; Lofts and Murton, 1973).

## Ovary

The left ovary is situated on the left side of the body at the cephalic end of the kidneys and is attached to the body wall by the mesovarian ligament. The ovary consists of an outer cortex, made up of follicles containing ova, and an inner medulla (see Figures 16–1 and 16–2).

The ovary of the immature bird is made up of a mass of small ova, at least 2000 of which are visible to the naked eye in the chicken; there are also about 12,000 ova of microscopic size (see Sturkie, 1965). Only a relatively few of these (200–300) reach maturity and are ovulated in certain domesticated species and considerably fewer do in wild ones.

**Ovarian follicle.** The individual follicles vary in size depending on the species and the size of egg laid, but in the sexually mature chicken they attain a diameter of approximately 40 mm before ovulation. Histologically the structure of the avian ovarian follicle is very much like that of mammals. The follicle encircles the ova, which is made up of an innermost layer, zona radiata, the granulosa layer, the theca interna, and the theca externa (Figure 16–1; see also Gilbert, 1971a).

The ovarian follicle is highly vascular except for the stigma, which to the naked eye appears avascular, although microscopic examination shows that small arteries and veins extend across it, according to Nalbandov and James (1949), (Figure 16–3). The ovary receives its blood supply from the short ovarian artery, which usually arises from the left renolumbar artery but may branch directly from the dorsal aorta (Figure 16–4) (see Nalbandov and James, 1949, for details; also Hodges, 1965; Gilbert, 1971a). The ovarian artery divides into many branches, and usually from two to four separate arterial branches lead to a single follicular stalk. A few arteries immediately surround the ovum; after branching, they pass through the theca, become arterioles, and form a capillary network peripheral to the basement membrane.

The venous system of the follicle is more prominent than the arterial system, and forms three lay-

303

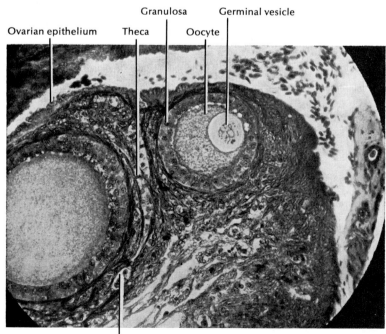

**16–1**

Cross-section of the chicken ovary at 2 months of age. (From Benoit, 1950.)

Ovarian epithelium  Theca  Granulosa  Oocyte  Germinal vesicle

Interstitial cells of medulla

304

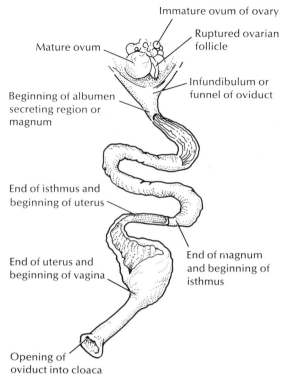

Immature ovum of ovary

Mature ovum

Ruptured ovarian
follicle

Infundibulum or
funnel of oviduct

Beginning of albumen
secreting region or
magnum

End of isthmus and
beginning of uterus

End of magnum
and beginning of
isthmus

End of uterus and
beginning of vagina

Opening of
oviduct into cloaca

16–2   Reproductive tract of the laying hen.

16–3

Mature ovarian follicle of the hen. (From
Nalbandov and James, 1949.)

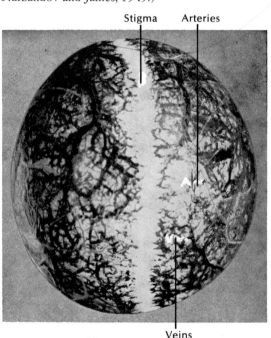

Stigma          Arteries

Veins

ers or beds: (1) the innermost, located in the theca;
(2) a middle layer; and (3) the outer or peripheral
layer, consisting of a few large veins that encircle
the follicle and leave via the stalk. Eventually all of
the veins from the ovary unite into the two main
anterior and posterior veins, which empty into the
posterior vena cava.

The follicle is intensely innervated and contains
both adrenergic (Freedman, 1968; Bennett and
Malmfors, 1970; Gilbert, 1969) and cholinergic
fibers (Gilbert, 1969).

## Structure of Oviduct; Position and Movement of Egg

The oviduct consists of five distinct areas or
parts, which vary in size depending on species and
state of reproduction. The description that follows
applies to the laying *Gallus domesticus* (chicken):
for details on oviduct histology see Aitken (1971);
on the infundibulum and magnum, see Wyburn *et al.*
(1970); and on the uterus, see Nevalainen (1969).
The principal parts are as follows: (1) infundibulum
or funnel (about 9 cm long); (2) the magnum (33
cm); (3) the isthmus (about 10 cm); (4) the shell
gland or uterus (about 10 cm long), a pouchlike portion of the oviduct that is very thick and muscular;
and (5) the vagina, the part extending from the shell
gland to the cloaca (Figure 16–2). Located at the
uterovaginal junction are the tubular glands in
which spermatozoa from the male are stored (Gilbert *et al.* 1968; Lorenz *et al.*, 1967).

**Infundibulum.** The infundibulum (IF) is the
thin fimbrated portion that engulfs the ovum when
it is ovulated into the body cavity. The activity of
the IF is conditioned by the ovum, for it is normally quiescent until the ovum is liberated. There are
glands in the infundibulum where sperm are stored
(sperm nests) (see van Drimmeln and also van Kreg
*et al.* in Chapter 17).

If a foreign body is placed in the abdominal cavity at the time of ovulation and the ovum is removed, the IF will engulf the foreign body. If this
is done at some time before or after ovulation, the
IF remains inactive. Thus, the activity of IF is
conditioned by ovulation. Occasionally the ovum is
not picked up and the hen appears to be laying but
never does so. The cause of the defective IF is not
known but may be related to certain respiratory
diseases. The ovum, when not engulfed by the IF,
can be absorbed in the body cavity in 24 hr or less
(Sturkie, 1955).

**Magnum.** The ovum passes to the magnum, the
largest single portion of the oviduct (hence its

Spiral artery

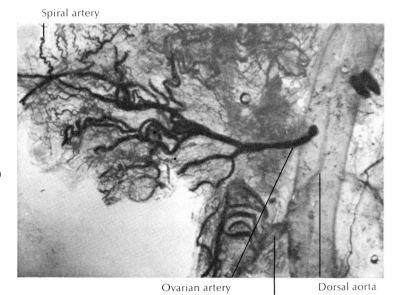

**16–4**
Arterial supply to ovary of the hen.
(From Nalbandov and James, 1949.)

Ovarian artery          Dorsal aorta

Renolumbar artery

name), measuring 33 cm in length. Here most of the protein of the egg (albumen) is formed. Details on the formation of the various layers of albumen are discussed in a later section. Histologic studies by a number of workers reveal that the magnum is highly glandular and contains two types of glands, tubular and unicellular (see Aitken, 1971). The tubular glands are composed of nongoblet cells that are not ciliated, but the unicellular glands are of the goblet type.

**Isthmus.** The peristaltic movements of the magnum force the ovum into the isthmus. The line of demarcation between it and the magnum is distinct; the folds of the glands in the isthmus are not as large and numerous as those in the magnum. The inner and outer shell membranes are formed in the isthmus (for review of earlier workers, see Sturkie, 1965). Some researchers have believed that some albumen is added to the egg here, but the data of other workers (Burmester, 1940) suggest that no albumen and only insignificant amounts of water are added.

**Uterus or shell gland.** The uterus is pouchlike, thick, and muscular. It contains tubular and unicellular glands, the function of which is unknown. It is presumed that they form the watery uterine fluid which is added to the albumen through the shell membranes. Whether or not these glands are concerned in shell formation is unknown.

The ovum receives the shell in the uterus and water and salts are added to the albumen. The pig-

ment of the shell is formed in the uterus during the last 5 hr before the egg is laid (Warren and Conrad, 1942). The brown pigment, porphyrin, is synthesized by the shell gland in chickens from δ-amino levulinic acid (Polin, 1957). The pigment is evenly distributed throughout the shell but is absent from the shell membranes; in quail egg, which is more deeply pigmented, the pigment is more prominent in the cuticle and pigment is deposited 3.5 hr before the egg is laid (Woodward and Mather, 1964).

*Motility of the genital tract* has been studied *in vitro* by Chen and Hawes (1970). Spontaneous activity was observed; a gradient was reported highest in the fimbrial region and lowest in the vaginal region, and particularly so in the uterovaginal junction.

**Duration of egg passage down tract.** The average time of passage of ovum through the various parts of the tract are as follows: Infundibulum, 18 min (¼–½ hr); magnum, 2 hr and 54 min (2–3 hr), isthmus, 1 hr and 14 min (1¼ hr). The time elapsing from the ovum's engulfment by the funnel to its reaching the uterus therefore averages 4 hr and 26 min. The egg remains in the uterus for approximately 20 hr and 46 min. These figures are for chickens (Warren and Scott, 1935) but the figures for turkeys (22–24 hr; Wolford *et al.,* 1964) and *Coturnix coturnix japonica* (19–20 hr; Woodward and Mather, 1964) are approximately the same (except eggs are held longer in the uterus of turkeys; Wolford et al., 1964).

306

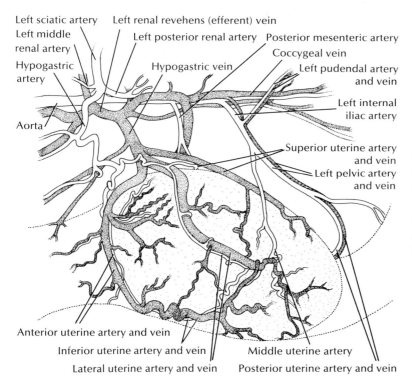

Left sciatic artery   Left renal revehens (efferent) vein
Left middle
renal artery      Left posterior renal artery   Posterior mesenteric artery
Hypogastric                                     Coccygeal vein
artery            Hypogastric vein              Left pudendal artery
                                                     and vein
Aorta                                           Left internal
                                                     iliac artery
                                           Superior uterine artery
                                                     and vein
                                           Left pelvic artery
                                                     and vein

Anterior uterine artery and vein
    Inferior uterine artery and vein       Middle uterine artery
        Lateral uterine artery and vein    Posterior uterine artery and vein

**16–5**
Lateral view of the blood vessels to the uterine portion of the hen's oviduct. The arterial system is in white and the venous system is shaded. Drawn to scale. (After Freedman and Sturkie, 1963a.)

**Vagina.** The vagina is the part of the oviduct leading from the uterus to the cloaca; it takes no part in the formation of the egg but may be involved in the expulsion of the egg. A sphincter is situated at the border of the uterus and vagina and the uterovaginal glands are located here, where spermatozoa are stored (Gilbert *et al.,* 1968; Lorenz *et al.,* 1967; see also Chapter 17).

### Blood and Nerve Supply

The early literature has been reviewed by Freedman and Sturkie (1963a, b) and Sturkie (1965). Early research described nerve plexuses and blood vessels in the oviduct but without sufficient detail as to differentiation of region. Freedman and Sturkie (1963a, b) reported in detail on the blood vessels and nerves (Figure 16–5), particularly to the shell gland, and most of these details have been confirmed by Hodges (1965).

Blood is supplied to the hen's uterus by three arteries, all of which originate from the left side of the body. The hypogastric artery bifurcates into an anterior uterine and superior uterine artery. Lateral and inferior uterine arteries originate from the anterior uterine artery on both surfaces of the uterus. For blood vessels to other parts of the tract see Figure 16–6 from the work of Hodges (1965).

Nerves have been described by Freedman and

Sturkie (1963a, b), Bennett and Malmfors (1970), and Freedman (1968). The parasympathetic pelvic nerves originate from the pelvic visceral rami of spinal nerves 30–33 or lumbosacral nerves (LSN) 8–11, but the principal contribution is from LSN 8 and 9. LSN 8 represents the first pelvic nerve in the chicken (see Figure 16–7). The pudendal nerve, homologous to that in mammals, arises mainly from LSN 8 and 9. Only the left pelvic nerve innervates the uterus of the hen, via branches that accompany the middle and posterior uterine arteries (Freedman and Sturkie, 1963b); this is probably related to the fact that only the left mullerian duct persists in the chicken. Where the oviduct is bilateral, as in mammals, the pelvic plexus is also bilateral.

The sympathetic innervation to the uterus is from the hypogastric nerve, which represents a direct continuation of the aortic plexus. This nerve (present only on the left side) courses along with the hypogastric artery. The uterovaginal junction is abundantly innervated (Gilbert and Lake, 1963).

## OVIPOSITION OR LAYING, AND BROODING HABITS OF BIRDS

In their laying and brooding habits birds vary in (1) the number of eggs laid in a given time, (2) the sequence in which the eggs are laid, (3) the intervals or breaks in the sequence, and (4) whether or not they incubate their eggs.

Wild birds usually lay one or more eggs in sequence and then stop laying and sit on them (clutches). The number of clutches and the number of eggs in the clutch vary with the species and the season. Some birds, such as the auk and penguin, lay only one egg before sitting; the pigeon usually lays two and the partridge as many as 12–20 eggs before sitting (Romanoff and Romanoff, 1949). Removal of eggs from the nests of some birds prolongs the laying time or number of eggs laid (indeterminate species), but is without effect in others (determinate species).

Some birds are continuous breeders and lay and mate at anytime of year (domesticated chickens, ducks, turkeys, quails); some are multibrooding, particularly when kept in equitable environments, and others are seasonal and breed once or twice a year. During these seasonal and multibrooding cycles the ovary undergoes periods of growth and regression.

The weight of the European starling ovary may fluctuate from 8 mg during the regression phase to 1400 mg at the height of breeding season (Lofts and Murton, 1973). In the domesticated species (a continuous breeder) the ovary usually remains well developed most of the year except when the bird is molting or, more rarely, when it is not laying for extended periods of time. After ovulation the ruptured follicles regress and finally degenerate. The

16–6  Blood vessels in the oviduct. Arteries are crosshatched and white, veins are black. (After Hodges, 1965.)

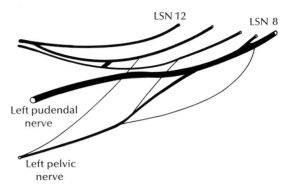

16–7  Diagrammatic representation of the formation of the left pelvic nerve from lumbosacral spinal nerves. (After Freedman and Sturkie, 1963b.)

postovulatory follicles of the chicken are usually resorbed within days or weeks, whereas those of the pheasant and mallard duck may persist for months. There is no corpora lutea in birds.

In some wild species mating or copulation is related to nest building, which begins at about the time the female is sexually receptive. Nest building in some species is also related to the time the first egg is laid, usually beginning a few days beforehand (Lehrman, 1961; Lofts and Murton, 1973).

## Laying Cycle and Rate of Laying

Many of the domesticated species, notably the chicken, quail *(Coturnix)*, and duck, lay a number of eggs on successive days (a sequence); then the sequence is interrupted for one or more days before

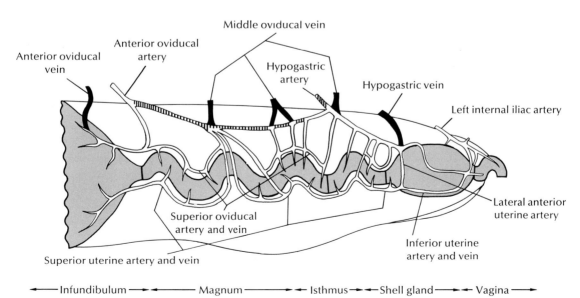

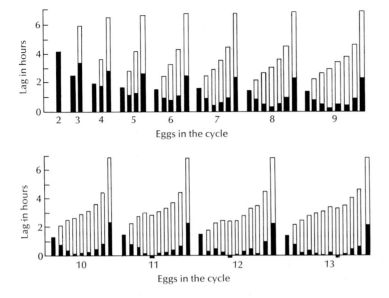

Eggs in the cycle

Eggs in the cycle

**16–8**

The delay or lag in hours between the laying of successive eggs in a cycle. A two-egg cycle is represented by one bar; a three-egg cycle by two bars, etc. A lag of 0 hr means an interval of 24 hr between eggs. A lag of 4.2 hr occurs between the laying of the first and second egg of a two-egg cycle (black bar). For the three-egg cycle, the lag between the first and second eggs is about 2.5 hr, and between the second and third, about 3.4 hr (second black bar). The cumulative lag (white bar) is about 5.9 hr. In a sequence, the lag between the last egg and the preceding one is always greatest. (Courtesy of Dr. R. M. Fraps, based on data of Heywang, 1938.)

laying is resumed; such birds usually do not incubate their eggs. The terms "cycle" and "clutch" have been used to designate such behavior. Neither of these terms, however, adequately describes the rate and rhythm of laying by domesticated birds. Strictly speaking, "cycle" means a regularly recurring succession of events; applied to laying, it involves a sequence and the time intervals interrupting the sequence. Thus, a hen with a three-egg laying cycle would lay three eggs on successive days, before skipping a day or more, and then repeat the performance.

Some of the variations in rhythm or pattern of laying exhibited by chickens or other continuous layers may be illustrated as follows:

| | |
|---|---|
| xx – xx – xx – | Two-egg cycle |
| xxx – xxx – xxx – – – | Regular sequence; irregular skip |
| xx – xxx – x – xxx – | Irregular sequence; regular skip |
| xxxxxxxxxxxxxx – | Long sequence |

The rate of lay, or laying frequency, is the number of eggs laid in a given period of time, without regard to the pattern or rhythm of laying. For example, a hen laying 15 eggs in 30 days lays at a rate of 50%. More details concerning sequences and cycles are reported by Fraps (1955). Selected hens of the better laying laying breeds of chickens lay between 250 and 270 eggs per bird per year. The number of successively laid eggs for most good laying hens ranges from four to six, but some may lay for many days without an interruption in the sequence. Some

breeds of domesticated ducks and Japanese quail also are high rate layers.

Cycle and sequence are terms frequently used interchangeably. $C_1, C_2, \ldots, C_T$ refer to ovulation and oviposition sequences in a cycle, $C_1$ represents first egg or ova of a cycle or sequence and $C_T$, the terminal egg of cycle.

The interval between eggs laid on successive days by most hens ranges from 24 to 28 hr, depending on the length of the laying sequence (Heywang, 1938). This is illustrated in Figure 16–8, which shows the delay or lag in hours between successively laid eggs in a cycle. The lag or the interval between eggs is greater in short than in long sequences, and the intervals between the first two and the last two eggs of the sequence are greater than for intervening eggs, regardless of the length of the cycle. These differences in lag represent mainly differences in time of ovulation. Lag represents not the interval between successive ovipositions but the temporal difference in time of day of one oviposition with respect to its predecessor (Fraps, 1955). Most of the laying sequences of *Coturnix* are two, three, and four eggs, in that order.

Lag bewtween $C_1$ and $C_T$ eggs is much greater in chickens (4–5 to 8 hr, depending on sequence) than in Japanese quail (1.5 – 2 hr; Opel, 1966a). The mean interval between eggs of chickens and *Coturnix* are about the same but there is less variation in *Coturnix* with variable sequences (Opel, 1966a); the interval is slightly longer in turkeys (Woodward and Mather, 1964).

The interval between successively laid eggs of

the pigeon is 40–44 hr, but the number of clutches and the interval between clutches varies with the season. Records from the New Jersey pigeon test (Platt, 1946) show that the number of clutches laid by pigeons averages eight a year, and that the interval between clutches is approximately 45 days in the fall and winter and from 30 to 32 days in the spring and early summer.

Ovulation in chickens usually occurs soon after the onset of light; in *Coturnix* however, it occurs about 8–9 hr after the onset of light (Opel, 1966a). Twelve or more hours of light (either natural or artificial) are required in order to obtain maximum lay in domesticated species.

The actual time of day when eggs are laid depends on the length of the sequence and position of the egg in the sequence, and also on the length of the day (hours of daylight). Although hens may lay eggs during any of the daylight hours, most of them lay in the forenoon, and they tend to lay earlier when the days are longer.

The laying and breeding seasons of some birds are influenced by climatic conditions, such as temperature and rainfall, and by the availability of food. For more details on the relation of behavior and reproduction in wild birds, consult Marshall (1961), Lehrman (1961), and Lofts and Murton (1973). For details on laying behavior of bobwhite quails see Wilson *et al.* (1973).

The differences observed in the laying and brooding habits among different species of birds suggest differences in the release of pituitary hormones concerned in the growth and maturation of the follicles and in ovulation and broodiness. These are discussed later in this chapter and in Chapter 15.

### Control of Oviposition

Little is known concerning the immediate causes of uterine contraction and oviposition, but there is evidence that the time of laying is influenced by the ruptured ovarian follicle from which the egg is ovulated (Rothchild and Fraps, 1944a, b). Although recently ruptured follicles influence laying time, older ruptured ones also influence it, suggesting the release of some inhibitory factor from the ruptured follicle. However, no such factor has been isolated.

**Neurohypophyseal hormones.** There is good evidence that arginine vasotocin, the hormone from the posterior lobe of the pituitary, may initiate the contraction of the uterus that leads to oviposition (see Chapter 15 for greater detail). Work by Munsick *et al.* (1960) demonstrated conclusively that the avian posterior pituitary lobe contains this hormone and that the chicken uterus is considerably more sensitive to it than it is to oxytocin.

Assays of the posterior lobe by Tanaka and Nakajo (1962) revealed the least amount of vasotocin coincident with laying, suggesting that it was released at this time into the blood. Sturkie and Lin (1966; see also Chapter 15) revealed that the posterior lobe releases this hormone. Prior to oviposition the concentration in the blood was low (150–167 $\mu$U/ml) and immediately prior to and during oviposition, the level increased to 7059 $\mu$U. Similar results were reported by Niezgoda *et al.* (1973). Gilbert and Lake (1964) revealed a decrease in a blood amino peptidase that normally deactivates oxytocin and vasotocin, coinciding with the increase in these substances at time of oviposition.

Other agents, such as acetylcholine, nembutal, and uterine distension, which may cause premature oviposition, did not cause the release of vasotocin (Sturkie and Lin, 1967). Stimulation of the preoptic area of the brain caused a release of vasotocin into blood and premature oviposition (Opel, 1966b). Although hens continue to lay after surgical removal of the posterior lobe (Chapter 15), the median eminence is still intact and it contains vasotocin; so does the anterior lobe of the pituitary.

Pure synthetic arginine vasotocin (available from Sandoz), containing 250 pressor units per milligram, is very effective at dosages of 0.1–0.4 $\mu$g/kg in inducing premature oviposition in chickens (Rzasa and Ewy, 1971). Synthetic oxytocin (Sandoz), containing 450 oxytocic units per milligram, was effective also in causing premature oviposition at dosages from 1.0 to 4.0 $\mu$g/kg. Both substances increased intrauterine pressure considerably but vasotocin had the greater effect.

Earlier work on the effects of posterior hormones dealt with mixtures of oxytocic and pressor factors; injections of these were effective, particularly the latter, in inducing oviposition (see Sturkie, 1965; Gilbert, 1971b, for review). Obstetrical pituitrin, containing mainly the oxytocic factor, when injected at a level of 0.1 to 0.2 ml is effective intravenously in most birds within 3–4 min; it causes contraction of the uterus and premature oviposition. The sensitivity of the uterus to oxytocin and vasopressin increases at normal oviposition time (Sturkie, 1965).

**Drugs and other hormones.** Morash and Gibbs (see Sturkie, 1965) demonstrated that histamine, acetylcholine, and ergotoxine produced contraction and that epinephrine produced relaxation of the uterus. Atropine blocks the effects of acetylcholine.

310

Acetylcholine and histamine cause premature oviposition, and ephedrine retards laying from 4 to 24 hr in the intact hen (Weiss and Sturkie, 1952). Sodium pentobarbital at an anesthetic dose (30 mg/kg) caused premature ovipositions in about 33% of birds, if injected a few hours before normal oviposition.

Epinephrine retarded oviposition in the intact chicken, inhibited the motility of uterine strips, and caused the circular muscles of the vagina to contract; however, it had no effect on longitudinal muscles (Sykes, 1955b). Polin and Sturkie (1955) observed a hen that habitually laid soft shelled eggs. After administration of ephedrine sulfate, which relaxes uterine muscle, the hen laid normal shelled eggs. Hypothermia causes hens to expel eggs prematurely (Sturkie, 1946). Premature oviposition was induced in quail *(Coturnix)* by intrauterine injection of prostaglandin, PGE (0.01 $\mu$g dose) by Hertelendy (1974).

**Neural control.** Because the shell gland receives sympathetic and parasympathetic innervations, one might expect the motility of the gland to be influenced by these nerves. However, transection of the pelvic nerves (Sturkie and Freedman, 1962) or of the hypogastric sympathetic nerves (Freedman and Sturkie, 1962) had no effect on oviposition. Studies involving cholinesterase stains indicate that the pelvic nerves are cholinergic. Administration of a cholinergic blocker (atropine) did not influence oviposition time (Sturkie and Freedman, 1962). The results of these studies indicate that the sympathetic and parasympathetic innervation of the uterus has little influence on oviposition.

Sykes (1953a, b; 1955a) reported that the "bearing down" reflex is initiated by cloacal or vaginal stimuli, such as occur when an egg enters the vagina, or it can be evoked by other stimuli; it causes the hen to squat. Evocation of the reflex leads to an increase in respiratory rate and strong contraction of the abdominal muscles. He concluded that the contraction of both uterus and vagina is necessary for laying, and that "bearing down" aids greatly in the expulsion of the egg. Sturkie *et al.* (1962) abolished the activity of abdominal and cloacal skeletal muscle by administering curare, which paralyzes skeletal muscle but not smooth muscle. Their results demonstrated that abolition of the abdominal press did not prevent oviposition, although it delayed it slightly.

Opel (1964) reported that electrical stimulation of certain areas of the brain, particularly the preoptic area, caused premature oviposition in a high percentage of birds, most of the eggs being laid 2– 6 hr before the expected time of oviposition. Even insertion of electrodes without stimulation was effective, and the author presumed that the premature ovipositions were caused by immediate release of neurohypophysial hormone (vasotocin) following the stimulations.

## Orientation of the Egg in the Oviduct

The orientation of the egg in the oviduct and its movement and rotation have been subjects of controversy. Early workers, including Purkinje in 1825, Von Baer in 1828, and some others since, observed that the egg in the uterus of the opened hen lay with its pointed end caudad. Olsen and Byerly (1932) in an extensive study, observed that the pointed end appeared first in from 66 to 82% of the eggs laid. These results have in general been confirmed by Wood-Gush and Gilbert (1969), although in one group of hens 46% of eggs were laid blunt end first. Bradfield (1951), by fluoroscopic examinations of the egg in the uterus of the bird, showed that during most of the 18–20 hr that the egg was in the uterus it remained in the same position, with the pointed end directed caudally, but that just prior to laying the egg was rotated through 180° and most were laid with the blunt end caudad.

## Other Factors and Oviposition

*Foreign bodies.* Sutures (thread) placed in the uterus cause hens to expel eggs prematurely (Sykes, 1953a; Lake and Gilbert, 1964). Insertion of a glass catheter in the shell gland resulted in the premature expulsion of eggs and the cessation of laying (Koga, 1965).

*Shelless eggs.* The mechanism responsible for the laying of shelless eggs is not known. They may be the result of premature contraction of the uterus and expulsion of the egg before calcium deposition has occurred, or there may be some defect in the mechanism of calcium deposition. Most of the shelless eggs are laid by young pullets in the early laying stage and between the hours of 5 and 9 p.m. (Hughes and Parker, 1971).

*Oviposition and body temperature.* At oviposition the body temperature of the laying hen reaches its peak (Winget *et al.*, 1965).

*Fistulation.* A technique of fistulation of hens oviduct through the abdominal wall has been described by Gilbert and Wood-Gush (1963), such that ovulated ova were picked up by the infundibulum and shunted through the fistulated portion through the body wall to the exterior.

## FORMATION AND GROWTH OF OVA

As the female approaches sexual maturity, the immature ova begin growing at a rapid rate; in the chicken they reach maturity within 9–10 days. The weight of the ova and yolk during the 7 days preceding ovulation increases approximately 16-fold and in a regular and straight-line manner. The final weight of the chicken ovary is approximately 16 g (Warren and Conrad, 1939). This rapid growth phase, however, has been reported as variable and ranging from 5 to 11 days, according to most investigators (see Gilbert, 1971a, for review). The rate of growth in wild species is similar to that in the chicken, with the final period of rapid growth ranging from 4 to 11 days preceding ovulation, depending on the species (Lehrman, 1961).

Using Sudan III, a fat dye, Conrad and Warren (1939) found that, during the growth period the yolk material is laid down in concentric rings. However, Bohren et al. (1945) found no such concentric rings in birds fed diets rich in xanthophyll pigments. Shenstone (1968) also doubted the deposition of yolk in concentric layers. For further details on the formation and composition of yolk, consult Gilbert and Wood-Gush (1971) and Gilbert (1971c, d).

There is some controversy about whether yolk deposition continues up to the time of ovulation. Some workers have suggested that no yolk is deposited in the last 24 hr preceding ovulation, and the work of Gilbert (1970), based on fat dye deposits, indicates that in about 20% of the eggs (ova) of the first sequence ($C_1$) there was no yolk deposited in the last 24 hr.

### Follicular Hierarchy

There is a gradation in maturation of developing ovarian follicles (hierarchy). The hierarchy usually involves four to six follicles in the chicken, but the number varies among individuals and the number of graded follicles is usually larger in those with longer laying sequences. The control or regulation of this follicular hierarchy is not understood. It is true that the growth of the follicle is in response to the endogenous elaboration of follicular stimulating hormone (FSH) and luteinizing hormone (LH), and it may be that the ovary itself controls or influences the hierarchy. However, this does not explain the facts that the administration of FSH and LH in chickens prevents the hierarchy and that there are

multiple maturations and even ovulations (Fraps et al., 1942; Opel and Nalbandov, 1958, 1961a, b). Moreover, in ovarian transplants with no intact nerves the follicles respond to endogenous FSH with multiple maturations and no gradations (Gilbert and Wood-Gush, 1970). In some wild birds, however, the follicular hierarchy occurs even after the administration of FSH (van Tienhoven, 1961a).

The administration of FSH does not mimic in kind or quantity the release and action of endogenous FSH. Mitchell (1967a, b), by careful administration of FSH, was able to maintain an almost normal follicular hierarchy in hypophysectomized hens.

Warren and Conrad (1939) reported that the first egg of the sequence had a larger yolk than succeeding ones, but more recent data indicate that this is incorrect. The size of ova in a sequence is purely random (Gilbert and Wood-Gush, 1971). In white-crowned sparrows the ovary develops in the spring, and there is a hierarchy of ova only in laying sparrows (Kern, 1972). Kern describes the ovaries and types of atretic follicles in wild sparrows and those kept in captivity, and there are differences.

## OVARIAN HORMONES

The principal ovarian hormones are estrogens and progesterone. Structural formulas of some of these are shown in Figure 16–9.

### Progesterone

In the mammalian ovary progesterone is produced by the corpora lutea, which is absent in birds; progesterone is produced by the ova of Aves (Furr, 1970). The granulosa cells of mammals produce progesterone and this is probably true also of Aves, although the evidence is conflicting (Lofts and Murton, 1973). These cells probably are also the site of estrogen synthesis (Chieffi, 1967), but other data suggest that the theca cells may also be involved (Lofts and Murton, 1973).

Progesterone is formed in the ovary as follows:

Cholesterol $\rightarrow$ pregnenolone $\rightarrow$ progesterone

The liver is a major site of progesterone metabolism (Wells, 1971).

**Assays and levels.** Progesterone has recently been determined in chicken plasma at different stages before ovulation by a sensitive radioimmunoassay method (Furr et al., 1973). Their results follow:

312

| Hours before ovulation | Progesterone (ng/ml) |
|---|---|
| 27–24 | 2.68 |
| 23–20 | 2.56 |
| 19–16 | 2.69 |
| 15–12 | 2.75 |
| 11–8 | 4.39 |
| 7–4 | 6.47 |
| 3–0 | 4.6 |

Similar results were reported by Kappauf and van Tienhoven (1972; competitive protein-binding method), with the highest levels occurring 4–7 hr before ovulation; there was no peak concentration on days when ovulation did not occur. At comparable stages, however, these absolute levels were lower than those of Furr *et al.* (1973); the latters' figures compare favorably with those of Arcos and Opel (1971), who employed gas liquid chromatog-

raphy. It is presumed that the variable blood levels reflect variable release of progesterone from the ovarian follicle. Apparently the avian ovary does not store appreciable quantities of progesterone, based on the uptake of radioactive progesterone (Adamic *et al.,* 1971).

Plasma progesterone levels in male ring doves determined by radioimmunoassay averaged 1.27 ng/ml and varied little, whereas in females the levels were influenced by sexual behavior. While they were incubating eggs and brooding, the level averaged 1.13 ng/ml; 5 days after courtship began, however, the level rose to 3.01 ng/ml (Silver *et al.,* 1974) and there was a significant correlation between follicle development and progesterone.

**Effects of progesterone.** When administered in large doses, progesterone causes follicular atresia (see van Tienhoven, 1961b), and inhibits ovulation in chickens and quails (Jones, 1969). Molting may

16–9
Structural formulas of certain gonadal hormones.

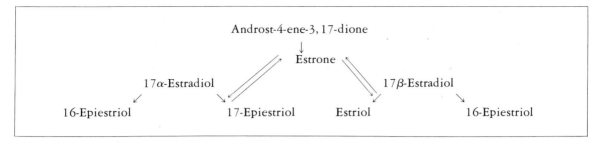

also be induced by large doses of progesterone (Sturkie, 1965). Other effects of progesterone are discussed under ovulation.

### Estrogen

The principal naturally occurring estrogens in the urine, blood, and ovaries of aves are estrone ($E_1$), and $17\beta$-estradiol ($17\beta$-$E_2$), and $17\alpha$-estradiol ($17\alpha$-$E_2$) (Common et al., 1965). Present also in the hen's urine are four estriol epimers of 14-keto-$17\beta$-estradiol (Mathur and Common, 1967). These steroids are probably derived from androgens as in mammals, and are formed in the ovary and liver as shown above (see Gilbert, 1971e).

O'Grady and Heald (1965) reported $E_1$ and $17\beta$-$E_2$ in the plasma of hens, based on an isotope dilution technique, but their values for estrone and those of others (see Peterson and Common, 1972) were higher than those reported by Layne et al. (1958) and by Peterson and Common (1972). The latter workers employed the radioimmunoassay for $E_2$, which measures $17\beta$-estradiol, principally, and estrone. The levels of these in the blood at different times before and after ovulation were as follows:

| | Estrone (pg/ml) | Estradiol (pg/ml) |
|---|---|---|
| Hours before ovulation: | | |
| 26–22 | 77 | 144 |
| 22–18 | 69 | 129 |
| 18–14 | 82 | 124 |
| 14–10 | 47 | 95 |
| 10–6 | 29 | 66 |
| 6–2 | 88 | 180 |
| Hours after ovulation: | | |
| 2–6 | 47 | 117 |

It is apparent that both estrogens increase significantly 6–2 hr before ovulation (see also Chapter 15). Senior (1974) also determined estradiol ($E_2$) by the radioimmunoassay in chickens at different stages before and during sexual maturity as follows:

| | |
|---|---|
| 7 weeks before first egg | 94 pg/ml |
| 2–3 weeks before first egg | 355 pg/ml |

| | |
|---|---|
| After laying | 138 pg/ml |

The very high level 2–3 weeks before laying is probably related to the rapid formation and growth of ova (egg yolk) and the synthesis of Ca and proteins.

Chan and Common (1974) also demonstrated that $17\alpha$-estradiol is a major phenolic steroid of hens blood. $17\beta$-Estradiol levels of plasma of ring doves (by radioimmunoassay) vary according to their sexual stage and behavior (Korenbrot et al., 1974) as follows:

| | |
|---|---|
| Females, isolated | 40 pg/ml or less |
| Female, male introduced | 85 pg/ml |
| Female, nest building | 67 pg/ml |
| Female, incubating eggs | Not detectable |

Estradiol was not detectable in the plasma of males at any of these stages.

A number of synthetic estrogens are available, including diethylstilbesterol, dianisylhexene, and dienestrol.

**Assays.** Most biological assays for estrogen are based on changes in oviduct weight, but the treatments of data vary among investigators (Sturkie, 1965; Lorenz et al., 1962).

**Effects of estrogen.** Apart from the role that estrogens may play in growth and development of the ovarian follicle, and possibly in the release of the ovulating hormone, it has many other functions, many of which are mentioned elsewhere and later in this chapter. Endogenous estrogen is responsible for the increase in plasma lipids (Chapter 13), calcium, and proteins (Chapter 12) that occurs at the time of sexual development (for review, see Sturkie, 1965; Lofts and Murton, 1973) and also for the tremendous increase in size and growth of the oviduct at this time.

*Estrogen and secondary sexual characteristics.* Estrogen influences certain secondary sex changes, particularly color of feather plumage and shape of feathers, in breeds that exhibit plumage dimorphism, such as the Brown Leghorn chicken and many wild species (Lofts and Murton, 1973; Sturkie, 1965). The plumage of the Brown Leghorn female castrate reverts back to the more brilliantly colored male plumage but the plumage of the castrate male is unchanged, so estrogen is responsible for the changes. In African weaver finches the female has the neutral type of plumage. In black breeds of chickens, the intensity of the black pigment in the feathers is usually greater in the female.

*Estrogen and differentation of sex.* When estrogen is injected into incubating eggs and, before sexual differentiation in embryos, into genetically determined (zygotic) females, the right oviduct, which normally is small or degenerated at hatching time, persists and is hypertrophied. Estrogen administered to zygotic male embryos causes the development of an ovotestis on the left side and sometimes on the right side. With large doses, ovarian follicles may be present on the left side. The right testis is much less responsive.

*Effects of estrogen on output of pituitary gonadotropins.* Administration of large doses of estrogen or androgen depresses the output of pituitary gonadotropins (Nalbandov and Baum, 1948; see also other sections and Chapter 15).

The influence of estrogen on the output of other pituitary hormones is less clear (see chapters on other endocrine organs).

*Effects of estrogen on growth, fat deposition, and fat storage in tissues.* Estrogen administration increases the blood lipids and the deposition of fat in tissues, possibly making the bird fatter and more desirable as a meat bird. The feasibility of this practice has been tested by a number of investigators, with varying results. The results have been reviewed in detail by Sturkie (1954, 1965).

*Ovariectomy.* Castration in the female is termed ovariectomy. The effects of sinistral and bilateral ovariectomy are different. Usually two operations are required for bilaterral ovariectomy. In the first operation, the left ovary is removed (sinistral). Then a hypertrophy of the rudimentary right gonad produces an ovotestis and androgen first. Soon after the sinistral operation and following the next molt, the new plumage is like that of the male in color and structure; later, after the right gonad has further developed and begun to secrete estrogen, however, the new plumage following the next molt may revert to the female type. The right gonad is then removed and the plumage reverts to the male type which is retained. Development of the rudi-

mentary right gonad in castrates can be inhibited by the administration of estrogen (see Sturkie, 1965).

## OVULATION

The release of the ovum from the ovarian follicle (ovulation) is caused by the rupture of the follicular membrane at the stigma, a relatively avascular area of the follicle. Ovulation occurs in most domesticated species within 15 to 75 min after oviposition, and within 4 to 5 hr after the first egg is laid in pigeons. The interval between oviposition and ovulation of the next egg in a sequence is similar in those species that lay eggs daily in sequence, such as chicken, duck, turkey, and quail.

### Hormonal Effects

**LH.** Ovulation is caused by the cyclic release of the ovulating hormone (luteinizing hormone in mammals, LH) from the anterior pituitary (see Chapter 15 and Fraps, 1955). This hormone is released 6–8 hr prior to ovulation. When the anterior pituitary was surgically removed (hypophysectomy; Rothchild and Fraps, 1949) 2 hr prior to ovulation, it did not affect ovulation time; when the operation was performed 8 hr prior to normal ovulation time, however, ovulation was inhibited in most cases. Factors affecting the release of LH and its releasing hormone are discussed in Chapter 15.

The LH content of pituitaries and blood have been determined and related to time of ovulation. Later determinations involving more sensitive assay methods indicate that there is at least one peak of LH concentration in the blood occurring 4–8 hr prior to ovulation and coinciding in general with the lowest level of pituitary LH (see Chapter 15). This peak in concentration is probably the one related to ovulation. Others have reported a second peak at 18–20 hr, the significance of which is not known (Chapter 15).

Premature ovulation can be induced by the injection of the ovulating hormone or by progesterone or other substances that cause the release of the hormone (Fraps, 1955). For example, certain adrenocortical hormones may either block or induce ovulation, depending on the amount administered (van Tienhoven, 1961b). Time of ovulation is not influenced by time of oviposition because neither premature oviposition, which can be induced by certain drugs, nor retarded oviposition, which can be produced by administration of epinephrine, influences ovulation. The prematurity of ovulation extends from 17 to 30 hr in some instances, depending on the dose of LH (Fraps *et al.*, 1942b;

Fraps, 1955), but the ovarian follicle is most sensitive to LH 6–8 hr before normal ovulation.

**Progesterone and estrogen.** Neher and Fraps (1950), by injecting progesterone or LH, were able to increase the number of eggs laid in a 12-day period significantly. The yolk of the laid eggs was smaller than normal, however, suggesting that ovulation occurred before all ova were matured. Injection of small amounts of progesterone into the preoptic region of the hypothalamus caused premature ovulation, but not injections into the hypophysis (Ralph and Fraps, 1960).

Progesterone is also ineffective in the hypophysectomized chicken, indicating that it normally stimulates the pituitary to release LH (Rothchild and Fraps, 1949). Does endogenous progesterone play a role in LH release? Determinations of plasma progesterone at different stages of the ovulatory cycle (Kappauf and van Tienhoven, 1972) revealed a peak concentration at from 4 to 6 hr prior to ovulation, or at about the same time as the main LH peak. It then declined but was still above basal levels at ovulation time. There was no peak on days when there was no ovulation.

Similar results were reported by Furr *et al.* (1973), who employed radioimmunoassays for both progesterone and LH (see Chapter 15, and a later section). An increase in the level of progesterone either preceded that of LH or the two increased simultaneously. Never did the increased level of LH occur before the rise in progesterone. The latter results suggest that progesterone causes or influences the LH peak and is somehow involved in the feedback that may be involved in the release of LH.

Fraps (1955) postulated a diurnal variation in the threshold of a neural component (probably the LH-releasing factor) concerned with LH release, which he considered was sensitive to an "excitation" hormone secreted by the ovarian follicle. This might suggest that progesterone is the excitation hormone of Fraps. However, this excitation hormone may also be estrogen, because Senior and Cunningham (1974) have reported that the plasma LH peak occurs about 2 hr after the peak concentration of plasma estrogen (estradiol) is realized, suggesting an LH releasing role for estrogen (Senior and Cunningham, 1974). However, implants of estrogen into the hypothalamus or hypophysis prevented LH release and ovulation in Japanese quail (Stetson, 1972).

**LH-releasing hormone.** Synthetic porcine LH-RH (NIH), injected at a dose of 15–20 µg per chicken (i.v.), caused premature ovulation in a high percentage of cases (van Tienhoven and Schally, 1972; see Reeves *et al.*, 1973, for further data involving injections of a combination of FSH and LH releasing factors).

**LH and FSH preparations.** Most of the data on premature ovulations induced by pituitary preparations involved mixtures of LH and FSH. Recent data on pure synthetic LH and FSH, singly and in combination, have been reported by Kamiyoshi and Tanaka (1972) (Table 16–1). It is apparent that the addition of FSH to LH increased its effectiveness in causing ovulation.

Imai (1973) compared mammalian (ovine) FSH and LH (NIH–FSH–S7; LH–S–15) and other preparations, including bovine pituitary preparation (BAP) and avian preparations (CAP), in inducing ovulation in hens pretreated with pregnant mare serum (PMS) (Table 16–2). The higher doses caused multiple ovulations. Adding FSH to the LH did not increase the effect of LH appreciably. Moreover CAP was more effective in causing multiple ovulations than was NIH–LH.

Opel (1966a) induced ovulations in Japanese quail with mammalian LH (available from Armour) and dried chicken pituitary. Premature ovulations were produced within 5–9 hr in 94% of the cases; in birds that were pretreated with (PMS), which tends to suppress ovulations, however, only 81% ovulated.

### Ovulation *in Vitro*

Olsen and Neher (1948) demonstrated that excised ova can be made to ovulate *in vitro* by

***Table 16–1*** *Effect of LH and FSH (synthetic) on premature ovulation*

| Dosage FSH (µg)[a] | Dosage LH (µg)[a] | Premature (ovulations) (%)[b] |
|---|---|---|
| 0 | 5 | 0 |
| 0 | 10 | 29 |
| 0 | 20 | 30 |
| 0 | 40 | 73 |
| 5 + | 20 | 29 |
| 20 + | 20 | 32 |
| 100 + | 20 | 65 |
| 500 + | 20 | 71 |
| FSH alone | | No effect |

[a]The LH was NIH-S14; FSH was NIH-S6.
[b]Data from Kamiyoshi and Tanaka (1972).

**Table 16–2**  *Effects of ovulating hormones*

| Preparation and dose (mg) | Number of hens | Number ovulating | Percent |
|---|---|---|---|
| 1.25 CAP | 4 | 3 | 75 |
| 2.5 CAP | 3 | 3 | 100 |
| 5.0 CAP | 3 | 3 | 100 |
| 20–160 BAP | 12 | 0 | 0 |
| 25 LH (NIH) | 3 | 0 | 0 |
| 50 LH (NIH) | 6 | 5 | 83 |
| 100 LH (NIH) | 6 | 6 | 100 |
| 200 LH (NIH) | 5 | 5 | 100 |

placing them in Ringer's solution at a temperature of 107° F.

Excised follicles were made to ovulate *in vitro* by applying proteolytic enzymes directly to the follicles (Nakajo *et al.*, 1973). Ogawa and Nishiyama (1969) studied ovulation *in vitro* following removal of ova at different stages before expected ovulation and treating them with (1) saline alone, (2) chorionic gonadotropin (HCG) alone, (3) HCG plus blood plasma, and (4) HCG, blood plasma, and pregnant mare serum (PMS). Treatments (1) and (2) were ineffective, but treatment (3) was very effective in ovulating ova removed 2–3 hr before the expected time of ovulation. Treatment (4) caused ovulation in follicles removed 24 hr or more before the expected time of ovulation. The authors conclude that some substance in the blood other than circulating LH (probably proteins) acting with the other agents was involved.

### Interruption of Ovulation

Ovulation is more easily interrupted or inhibited than induced; this applies to birds more than to mammals. It may be inhibited in a number of ways. Subcutaneous injections of such substances as ovalbumen, casein, peptone, desiccated brain, muscle, and other tissues delay ovulation in the chicken from 6 to 10 hr when small dosages are administered, but large doses produce prompt and extensive follicular atresia (Fraps and Neher, 1945).

Abdominal operations usually cause a temporary cessation of ovulation in the chicken. Rothchild and Fraps (1945) found that the incidence of follicular atresia and the time before resumption of ovulation following operations were inversely proportional to the rate of ovulation preceding the operation.

Progesterone-induced ovulation can be blocked by administration of adrenergic blocking agents, such as SKF 501 and dibenamine, and of atropine, an anticholinergic agent (see van Tienhoven, 1961a).

Electrical stimulation of the hypothalamus of certain mammals causes a release of LH, but such attempts have been unsuccessful in the chicken. Lesions produced in the preoptic region of the hypothalamus prevent progesterone-induced ovulation in the hen (Ralph and Fraps, 1959; Opel and Fraps, 1961). The latter workers showed that stimulation with stainless steel electrodes was effective but that stimulation with platinum electrodes was ineffective, as has been reported in mammals.

Ovulation can also be inhibited by intrauterine insemination involving trauma to the uterovaginal junction (Bobr *et al.*, 1965).

Large doses of prolactin (100 IU) were effective in preventing premature ovulation, normally induced by LH (Tanaka *et al.*, 1971).

### Calcium-Deficient Diets

Many years ago, Titus showed that when hens were fed a diet low in calcium they would lay about one or two normal eggs per month; then they stopped laying and ovulating until enough calcium was mobilized for the shell of another egg. Recent studies by Gilbert and co-workers (see Gilbert and Wood-Gush, 1971; Lake, 1974) have confirmed and further extended the observations by Titus. They conclude that calcium may act to affect the response of the target tissue or influence the gonadotropin output of the pituitary.

### Effects of Light on Ovary and Ovulation

The stimulating effect of light on ovulation, laying, and testes growth is well known and has been reviewed more recently by Farner and Follett (1966; see Chapters 15 and 17), van Tienhoven and Planck (1973; see Chapter 15), Meier and Mac-Gregor (1972), and Oishi and Lauber (1973a). It is also known that light (natural or artificial) causes birds to start laying earlier than usual and to lay more intensely during the fall and winter months if they are continuous layers; however lights do not usually increase average annual egg production. Maximum stimulation is produced in chickens by continuous lighting for 12–14 hr, either daylight or artificial. This amount of continuous light is not necessary, however, if the light is interrupted with periods of darkness. The fact that some hens may continue to lay even if kept in complete darkness (Wilson and Woodward, 1958), indicates that light is not the only factor that affects the release of the ovulating hormone. Intermittent light and flashing light have been used, but these did not increase laying rate significantly (Sturkie, 1965). Darkness appears to influence the time at which ovulation occurs, even though it may not increase the ovulation rate; this was demonstrated by Lanson (1959), who showed that a minimum of 1¼ hr of darkness in 24 hr was sufficient to alter the time of laying and ovulation. For example, when 1¼ hr or more of darkness were imposed beginning at 5 p.m. and extending to midnight, most of the birds laid their eggs during the hours of 5–7 a.m. If the birds were held in darkness from midnight to 7 a.m., however, most of the hens laid their eggs in the afternoon (2–3 p.m.). Similar results were obtained by Wilson et al. (1963). Van Tienhoven and Ostrander (1972) imposed a light–dark regime of 8 hr L:10D:2L:4D, or a total of 12 hr of light interspersed with darkness, and found that egg production was as good if not better than in birds with 14L : 10D.

Morris (1967) revealed that age at sexual maturity in chickens varied inversely with hours of light exposure. The response was roughly linear and inverse after 2–12 hr of light exposure (with decreasing age and with increasing light) but after 12 hr the response was curvilinear, exhibiting a slight increase with increasing light. However, as the bird approaches sexual maturity, the response to light tends to increase. Variations in light cycles at time of ovulation and oviposition have been reported by Rosales et al. (1968) and by Foster (1969). Combinations of 14 hr light, followed by 9, 11, or 13 hr of darkness, yielding cycles of 23, 25, and 27 hr, were tried and it was found that increasing cycle length beyond the normal inherent cycle length tended to increase number of eggs laid. Similar results were obtained by Foster (1969) but the increase in eggs laid was much less.

**Wave lengths and intensity.** Red and orange lights have a greater stimulating effect on the pituitary and gonads, particularly testes, than green and blue lights. For further details see Chapters 15 and 17 and reports by van Tienhoven and Schally (1972), Lake (1974), Oishi and Lauber (1973a, b), and Gilbert (1971a).

## FORMATION OF ALBUMEN AND SHELL MEMBRANES, AND SHELL

The components of the egg are shell, shell membranes, albumen, and yolk. The proportionate part of the total of each of these components is shown in Table 16–3. A number of investigators have studied the formation of the egg components. The subject is reviewed by Romanoff and Romanoff (1949), Warren (1949), Gilbert (1971b, d), and Sturkie (1965).

### Albumen

There are four distinct layers of albumen in the

*Table 16–3*  *Composition of the hen's egg[a]*

|  | | Albumen layers | | | | |
|---|---|---|---|---|---|---|
|  | Yolk | Outer | Middle | Inner | Chalaziferous | Shell |
| Weight (g) | 18.7 | 7.6 | 18.9 | 5.5 | 0.9 | 6.2 |
| Water (%) | 48.7 | 88.8 | 87.6 | 86.4 | 84.3 | 1.6 |
| Solids (%) | 51.3 | 11.2 | 12.4 | 13.6 | 15.7 | 98.4 |

|  | All layers | | |
|---|---|---|---|
|  | Yolk | Albumen | Shell |
| Proteins (%) | 16.6 | 10.6 | 3.3 |
| Carbohydrates (%) | 1.0 | 0.9 | — |
| Fats (%) | 32.6 | Trace | 0.03 |
| Minerals (%) | 1.1 | 0.6 | 95.10 |

[a]From Romanoff and Romanoff (1949).

laid egg: (1) the chalaziferous layer, attached to the yolk; (2) the inner liquid layer; (3) the dense or thick layer; and (4) the outer thin or fluid layer. Approximately one-fourth of the total albumen is found in the outer layer and one-half in the dense, thick layer. The inner layer comprises 16.8% and the chalaziferous layer 2.7% of the total (Table 16–3).

An egg taken from the hen just berfore it enters the isthmus contains only one layer of albumen, thick and jellylike in consistency. At this time the egg contains approximately one-half the amount of albumen of the laid egg and about twice the amount of protein per given volume (Scott *et al.,* 1937). The presence of the different strata of albumen and the relative decrease in the proteins and solids of the laid egg therefore suggest that after the egg leaves the magnum mainly water is added to the albumen and that this change, plus other physical changes resulting from rotation and movement of the egg down the oviduct, is responsible for the stratification of albumen.

About 60% of the total albumen is found in the thick white layer, 25% is in the outer thin layer, and the remainder is in the inner thin white and chalazae (Table 16–3). Shortly after the albumen is secreted in the magnum, water is added to it mainly in the uterus and the albumen is diluted considerably (see also the section on shell formation). Actually, the quantity of albumen in the laid egg is approximately twice what it was when it was first secreted.

**Types and concentrations of proteins in albumen.** This has been studied by a number of workers (see reviews by Gilbert, 1971b; Feeney and Allison, 1969). Egg albumen is made up a number of different proteins (Feeney and Allison, 1969), including (1) ovalbumen, 54%; (2) ovotransferrin (conalbumen), 13%; (3) ovomucoid, 11%; (4) ovoglobulin, 3%; (5) lysozyme, 3.5%; and (6) ovomucin, 2%. The functions of several of these are not known.

The lysozyme of egg albumen is an important enzyme that is well characterized. Its main biologic property is its lytic activity against bacterial cell walls; it also hydrolyzes polysaccharides.

Ovomucoid is a protein enzyme inhibitor (of proteases). Chicken ovomucoid inhibits only trypsin but that from other avian species inhibits trypsin and chymotrypsin (Gilbert, 1971; Feeney and Allison, 1969). Ovomucin is an insoluble, fibrous, acidic glycoprotein and it probably is responsible for the gel-like qualities of egg white, particularly the thick white.

Hughes and Scott (1936) determined the amounts of mucin, globulin, and albumen in the different layers of laid and oviducal eggs and the percentage of the total nitrogen contributed by the different types when the oviducal eggs had been in the uterus about 4–5 hr and most of the albumen had been formed. Ovomucin concentration was highest in the middle thick layer and chalazae and lowest in the inner thin layer of both laid and oviducal eggs, but it was higher in all layers of the oviducal egg than in the laid egg (see also Feeney and Allison, 1969). The amount of mucin is responsible for the higher viscosity of the thick white layer, yet this layer contains slightly more water than the outer thin white layer. Ovoglobulin, however, is higher in all layers of the laid eggs than that in oviducal eggs. Globulin is highest in the inner thin layer and lowest in the outer thin layer. There is little or no difference in the relative amounts of ovoalbumen in the laid and oviducal eggs with respect to a given layer of albumen, but the highest amount is found in the outer thin white layer.

**Formation of albumen layers.** The chalazae are the paired twisted strands of albumen attached at opposite poles of the yolk, and parallel to the long axis of the egg. The chalazae are formed by the mechanical twisting and segregation of the mucin fibers from the inner layer of albumen (Conrad and Phillips, 1938; Scott and Huang, 1941). The chalazae are twisted clockwise and counterclockwise at the large and small ends of the egg, respectively, suggesting that the egg is rotated on its long axis, so as to produce the twisting of the strands. Conrad and Phillips (1938) were able to produce clalazae artificially by placing isthmian eggs in a mechanical rotater.

Sturkie and Polin (1954) removed oviducal eggs from the uterus 2–3 hr after they had left the magnum, where albumen is secreted, and compared the condition of the albumen with that of freshly laid eggs, which varied greatly in albumen quality. It was concluded that albumen deteriorates in quality (becomes thinner) before the egg leaves the magnum and enters the uterus and that poor quality in the albumen (thinness of the white) is caused mainly by changes taking place in the uterus rather than by secretory activity in the magnum.

**Rate of albumen formation.** The weight of the albumen of the egg leaving the magnum and entering the uterus is approximately one-half that of the laid egg. During the first 6–8 hr in the uterus, the increase in weight of albumen is rapid and fairly constant; after this time there is little change in weight (Burmester, 1940), however, and most of the albumen is formed.

The formation of the inner and outer thin layer begins as the egg enters the uterus; this is at the expense of the thick or gel-like layer. After the egg has been in the uterus for 18–20 hr, the volumes of the outer and inner thin albumen approximate 5 and 9 ml, respectively (Sturkie, 1965). The final volume of the thick albumen is now only 58% of what it was when it left the magnum. An increase in the outer thin layer implies a decrease in the volume of the thick layer, but such a decrease does not occur until about the twelfth hour (Burmester, 1940). This suggests that while the egg is in the uterus, water is added at a more rapid rate than its diffusion into and through the thick white.

The great decrease in thick albumen occurring during the first 5–6 hr in the uterus is caused mainly by the addition of water; the slight but progressive decrease thereafter, particularly after shell is formed, is mainly a result of the breakdown of mucin, the constituent that makes albumen thick. With the addition of water through the shell membranes to the thick albumen, there is a corresponding decrease in the percentage of solids, mainly protein, during the first 4–6 hr; there is no change thereafter.

**Stimulation of albumen formation.** The stimulus for the magnum and other parts of the oviduct to elaborate albumen, shell membranes, and shell is believed by many to be a reflex reaction to the passage of a body or object through the oviduct. The pressure of the yolk stimulates the magnum to secrete albumen, and the amount formed is believed to be related to the size of the yolk. There are cases on record, however, of the secretion of albumen by isolated loops of the oviduct while an egg passed through the intact portion of the tract and of yolkless eggs containing albumen (Burmester and Card, 1939, 1941). Stimuli other than mechanical therefore appear also to be concerned in the secretion of albumen.

**Nervous control of and the effects of drugs on albumen formation.** That the ovary and oviduct are innervated by the autonomic system has been noted, but the role of these nerves in albumen secretion has not been determined. Sturkie *et al.* (1954) studied the effects of sympathomimetic and parasympathomimetic drugs on the secretion of albumen. Among the drugs they used were ephedrine sulfate (sympathomimetic) and acetylcholine (parasympathomimetic). The drugs produced minor but insignificant changes in most instances. The

results suggest that sympathetic and parasympathetic nerves play a minor role in albumen formation in the magnum.

**Effects of diseases, environment, and heredity on formation and deterioration of albumen.** High environmental temperature decreases the amount and viscosity of the albumen of laid eggs. Respiratory ailments, such as Newcastle disease and bronchitis, cause deterioration of the thick albumen in laid eggs (Sturkie, 1965). The duration of the effect of bronchitis virus on albumen quality apparently depends on the type and virulence of the strain, because some birds recover fairly soon after an attack of bronchitis, whereas others persist in laying poor eggs indefinitely.

By selective breeding strains of chickens have been developed that differ markedly in the amount of thick and thin white produced in the egg (Sturkie, 1965).

It is well known that the thick albumen of normal freshly laid eggs deteriorates with age, length of storage, temperature, and other factors. This suggests that freshly laid eggs containing albumen of low viscosity (thin, watery albumen) may result also from the breakdown of mucin in the isthmus and uterus. Results obtained by Sturkie and Polin (1954), discussed in the section on albumen layer formation, support this view.

## Shell Membranes

There are two shell membranes, an inner one and an outer one. Each consists mainly of the protein keratin, with minute amounts of carbohydrates of various sorts. Hydroxyproline is in both membranes (Balch and Cook, 1970). For details of ultrastructure of the membrane, see Candlish (1970).

The inner membrane is formed first. An egg partly extending into the isthmus can be observed to have the membrane (inner) formed on that part of the egg. By the time all of the egg is in the isthmus, the outer membrane is believed to have been formed. Data from other sources tend to support this view.

The amount of membrane formed in relation to the time the egg moves into the isthmus and the time it remains there has been studied by a number of workers. The relation of the rate of protein formation in the membranes to the distance that the center of the egg has traversed in the isthmus is a linear one, according to Burmester (1940). The membranes are semipermeable and permit the passage of water and crystalloids.

## EGG SHELL AND SKELETAL METABOLISM

### Introduction

Certain aspects of the material covered in this section have been reviewed by Simkiss (1967), Mongin (1968), Schraer and Schraer (1971), Taylor (1971), Simkiss and Taylor (1971), and Mueller and Leach (1974). Because of the voluminous literature, most of the following references are to reviews and to recent papers wherein a description of earlier work can be found. If a reference is not to the original paper, the word "see" has been placed before the author's name.

### Structure, Composition, and Formation of the Egg Shell

Avian egg shells contain the following layers (see Figure 16–10) from the inside to the outside: (a) two proteinaceous membranes that are rich in cystine and contain hydroxyproline and hydroxylysine (see Draper *et al.,* 1972), (b) the true shell, and (c) a proteinaceous cuticle.

The cuticle varies greatly among species in thickness and chemical composition. In some species, but rarely in the hen, a calcified layer called the "cover" is deposited on top of the cuticle (see Simons, 1971). The true or calcified shell consists of the mammillary and the pallisade or spongy layer. Its dry matter contains 2% organic material. The remainder is mostly crystalline calcium carbonate in the form of calcite but it also contains small

quantities of magnesium, phosphate, and citrate and traces of sodium and potassium. The organic matrix permeates the entire true shell. Chemically it is a glycoprotein with an amino acid composition similar to that of cartilage. In the basal caps and the inner part of the cone-shaped mammillae (Figure 16–10) the organic matrix forms a fine fibrous network, which is most dense in the mammillary core (see Simons, 1971). Toward the outer part of the mammillae, the fibrils break into loosely arranged strands of granules. Short fibrils that run parallel to the shell surface are also a dominant feature of the decalcified pallisade layer.

The deposition of the mammillary cores and their initial calcification, i.e., the beginning of true shell formation, occur in the isthmus. According to Stemberger (1971) the outer shell membrane of eggs removed from the posterior granular isthmus (Draper *et al.,* 1972) is seeded with approximately 20,000 granules per square millimeter that have a diameter of $1-10$ $\mu$m, stain intensely for divalent cations, and seem to be loosely attached. When the egg reaches the next section of the oviduct, which has been called isthmouterine junction by Richardson (1935) and the red isthmus by Draper *et al.* (1972), the number of deposits is only about 4500 per mm² but their diameter has increased to $28-90$ $\mu$m. The decrease in number may be caused by aggregation of the initial granules, but it is also possible that several of them are engulfed by newly deposited material.

When the egg reaches the shell gland, the deposition of the mammillary cores and the nucleation

**Crystalline structure**

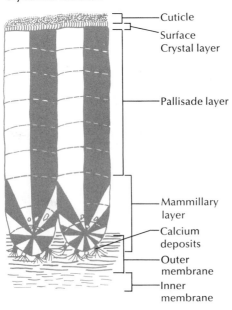

Cuticle

Surface Crystal layer

Pallisade layer

Mammillary layer

Calcium deposits

Outer membrane

Inner membrane

**Organic structure**

Mammillary cores

16–10

Diagram of a radial section through the shell and membranes of a hen's egg, showing crystalline structure and organic material that remains after calcium carbonate has been dissolved (After Simons, 1971.)

of the calcite crystals have already taken place (see also Wyburn *et al.*, 1973). Shell formation in this part of the oviduct therefore consists primarily of crystal growth with concomitant matrix deposition, followed by the formation of the cuticle. When the egg enters the shell gland, the deep folds of the mucosa are stretched and the numerous capillaries are brought into close proximity with the epithelium (Schraer and Schraer, 1971). Blood flow to the shell gland during shell formation is about 360% of the flow to the inactive tissue (Boelkins *et al.*, 1973; see also Chapter 4).

The egg remains in the shell gland for approximately 20 hr. During the first 5 hr, calcium carbonate deposition increases gradually to a rate of approximately 300 mg/hr, which then remains constant until about 2 hr before oviposition (Burmester, 1940; Sauveur and Mongin, 1971). The first 5 hr of slow calcification coincide roughly with the formation of the mammillary knobs. During this period, water containing electrolytes moves across the shell membranes into the albumen at a constant rate of 0.46 ml/g albumen dry matter per hour (Sauveur and Mongin, 1971). About 5–6 hr after the egg has entered the shell gland, water movement into the albumen decreases sharply to a new rate of 0.04 ml/hr/g albumen dry matter and remains constant until shell calcification is complete. There are other changes in shell gland function during the process of calcification the significance of which is still unknown. Most investigators who have studied shell gland fluid have noticed that the amount that can be collected by expelling the egg decreases considerably between early and late shell calcification. This seems to indicate that the fluid space between the shell gland epithelium and the forming shell decreases as calcification progresses. Furthermore, there are large changes in the ion content of the shell gland fluid (El Jack and Lake, 1967; Sauveur and Mongin, 1971). For example, its sodium concentration decreases from 143 meq/liter at the onset of shell formation to 40 meq/liter just before oviposition, whereas potassium increases from 8 to 68 meq/liter (Figure 16–11).

The passage of water into the albumen stretches the shell membranes and increases the distance between the tips of the mammillae. Simulatenously, the calcite crystals that radiate from the mammillary core in all directions become larger (see Simons, 1971). Those directed inward enclose

16–11 Tentative model of the ion transfers during shell formation. Figures in square brackets indicate approximate concentrations in millimoles per liter; the values for $P_{CO_2}$ are in mm Hg. If two concentrations are given, the first refers to early, the second to late shell formation. The values for shell gland fluid and albumen are from Sauveur and Mongin (1971).

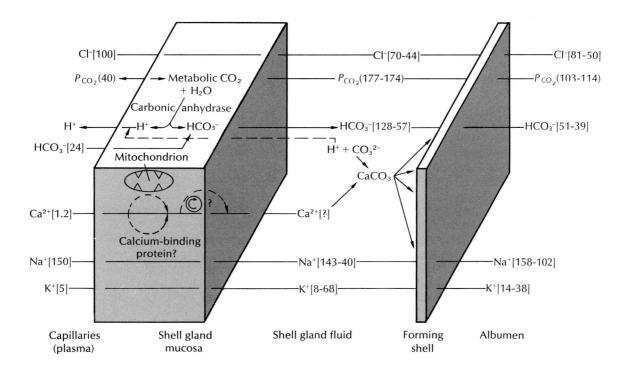

Cl⁻[100] — Cl⁻[70-44] — Cl⁻[81-50]

$P_{CO_2}$(40) ← → Metabolic $CO_2$ + $H_2O$ — $P_{CO_2}$(177-174) — $P_{CO_2}$(103-114)

Carbonic anhydrase

H⁺ ← H⁺ ← HCO₃⁻ — HCO₃⁻[128-57] — HCO₃⁻[51-39]

HCO₃⁻[24] — Mitochondrion — H⁺ + CO₃²⁻ → CaCO₃

Ca²⁺[1.2] — Ca²⁺[?] — CaCO₃

Calcium-binding protein?

Na⁺[150] — Na⁺[143-40] — Na⁺[158-102]

K⁺[5] — K⁺[8-68] — K⁺[14-38]

Capillaries (plasma) | Shell gland mucosa | Shell gland fluid | Forming shell | Albumen

322

some membrane fibers, anchoring the true shell, and are then stopped from growing further by the shell membranes. Crystals that form laterally eventually abut with crystals from other mammillae, whereas those that grow outward may extend to the shell surface or may terminate in a thin layer of small vertical crystals (Figure 16–10). At some points the crystals do not grow completely together, leaving the pores that permit the exchange of gases across the shell. The calcite crystals contain numerous pitlike holes with diameters varying from 0.3 to 9 $\mu$ (see Simons, 1971).

We can only speculate which cells of the shell gland transport calcium and which elaborate the carbonate and organic matrix precursors. Neither do we understand how these precursors aggregate in the lumen to form the shell. Even less is known about the control signals that initiate and terminate discrete events, such as nucleation of the shell membrane, plumping, or formation of the true shell and cuticle. Although much of the early work has dealt with calcium, there is no proof that calcium transport, as opposed to carbonate formation or organic matrix secretion, is the driving force in shell formation. It therefore seems best to assume that each of these three processes may be important in shell formation and to summarize present knowledge in all three areas.

### Calcium Metabolism

The turnover of calcium in female birds during reproduction is many times more rapid than in mammals. A hen that lays 250 eggs a year secretes a quantity of calcium, in the form of shells, corresponding to about 20 times the calcium content of her entire body. It is therefore not surprising that birds are being used increasingly for basic studies of calcium metabolism and transport. Three questions seem particularly important. (1) How are the large quantities of calcium moved across the shell gland mucosa? (2) What are the sources of egg shell calcium? (3) What are the special adaptive mechanisms that facilitate this rapid calcium metabolism?

**Movement of calcium across the shell gland.** During the last 15 hr of shell formation, calcium moves across the shell gland of the hen at a rate of 100–150 mg/hr. It has been suggested that this transport may be active (see Schraer and Schraer, 1971). Shell formation does involve expenditure of metabolic energy, as shown by the increased oxygen consumption when the gland is active (Misra and Kémeny, 1964) and the inhibition of both calcium transport (see Schraer and Schraer, 1971) and

potential gradients (Hurwitz et al., 1970) by anaerobic conditions and metabolic poisons. Furthermore, the calcium-binding protein, which is believed to mediate the active transport of calcium in the intestine, has also been found in the shell gland of hens (Corradino et al., 1968). However, although its concentration in the intestine changes with the physiologic need for calcium, the amount in the shell gland remains relatively constant (Bar and Hurwitz, 1973).

Transport is only considered to be active if an ion moves against an electrochemical gradient, i.e., an electrical potential and/or a concentration gradient. The potential gradient across the shell gland is either zero or negative in the direction of $Ca^{2+}$ flow (Leonard, 1969; Schraer and Schraer, 1971). Hurwitz et al. (1970) measured a negative gradient of 10 mV and calculated that this gradient alone would cause the calcium activity in the shell gland fluid to be twice as large as in blood if the mucosa were permeable to calcium. If one considers the concentration of total calcium, the element appears to move against a gradient, because shell gland fluid contains as much as 26 mmoles/liter (El Jack and Lake, 1967) and serum only 6–7 mmoles/liter. However, much of the calcium in shell gland fluid seems to be bound. The concentration of ionic calcium, which is the form that would be transported actively, is similar to the concentration in blood, based on measurements with a specific ion electrode (Mueller, unpublished data). Therefore, it is still uncertain whether the movement of calcium across the shell gland involves active transport.

**Changes in plasma calcium.** Because the shell gland does not store significant quantities of calcium, the ion must be extracted continuously from the blood. Practically all blood calcium is in the plasma and can be separated into two components: an ultrafiltrable fraction, which is primarily ionic calcium, and a nonultrafiltrable fraction, which is protein bound. The two forms are, with the possible exception of a small fraction (Hurwitz, 1968), in a dynamic equilibrium that can be described as follows:

$$\frac{[Ca^{2+}] \times [Prot^{2-}]}{[CaProt]} = K_{CaProt}$$

The concentration of serum calcium rises from 10 mg% to 16–30 mg% during the 10 days before a pullet starts to lay (see Simkiss, 1967). A similar increase is observed if capons are injected with estrogen, showing that androgen is not involved. In both cases, the increase is limited to the nonultrafiltrable calcium fraction and can be attributed to the appearance of a complex of phospholipoproteins, which bind large quantities of calcium (see McIndoe, 1971). Ultrafiltrable calcium, which is important in homeostasis, remains at 5–6 mg%, a value similar to that found in immature birds, cocks, and mammals. The most important new phosphoprotein is phosvitin. It is synthesized by the avian liver in response to estrogen (see McIndoe, 1971).

Most of the phospholipoprotein, which indirectly causes the increase of plasma calcium in laying hens, is ultimately deposited in the yolk. It has been suggested that the primary function of the increase in plasma calcium is yolk and not shell formation (Urist, 1967). This is supported by the observations that these proteins and plasma calcium also increase in amphibians and reptiles, which form noncalcified shells, and that calcium affects the solubility as well as the aggregation of these proteins (see McIndoe, 1971). However, as mentioned earlier, the protein-bound calcium of blood is in rapid equilibrium with the ionized form, so that any lowering of the ionic calcium concentration during the passage of blood through the shell gland causes an immediate decrease in protein-bound calcium.

The effect of shell formation on plasma calcium has been the subject of numerous studies (for references, see Hodges, 1970). Measurements of calcium concentration in systemic blood yield little quantitative information on the rate of withdrawal by the shell gland because they also reflect alterations in the exchange with bone, in intestinal absorption, and in excretion by the kidney and intestine. However, they seem to indicate that the shell calcium is derived from both the protein-bound and the diffusible calcium of blood (see Simkiss, 1967). The direct effects of shell formation on blood calcium have been studied most recently by Hodges (1970), who measured arteriovenous gradients between the sciatic artery and the inferior oviducal vein, which drains part of the shell gland. The gradients started to increase 2 hr after an egg entered the shell gland, ranged from 2 to 4 mg% between the fifth and the sixteenth hour of shell formation, and then decreased gradually. This seems to indicate that the shell gland withdraws between 10 and 20% of the blood calcium during the rapid phase of calcification.

**Sources of egg shell calcium.** The blood of a laying hen contains about 20–30 mg calcium. Because shell formation involves the withdrawal of 100–150 mg/hr, the concentration of calcium in blood would be zero within 8–18 min if it were not replenished continuously through intestinal absorption and mobilization from bone. The relative importance of these two organs as sources of egg shell calcium seems to depend on the concentration of calcium in the food. If dietary calcium levels are 3.56% or higher, most of the egg shell calcium is derived directly from the intestine (Hurwitz and Bar, 1969). If the concentration is 1.95%, bone supplies 30–40% of the shell calcium (see Mueller et al., 1969), and on calcium-free diets the skeleton is obviously the principal source. However, it is likely that these relationships vary depending on the time of day. Much of the shell is formed during the night, when the calcium content of the digestive tract decreases gradually. Bone may therefore be a particularly important source of shell calcium during the early morning hours (Tyler, 1954).

**Changes in calcium absorption.** The retention of dietary calcium and phosphate rises markedly about 10 days before a pullet starts to lay (see Simkiss, 1967), where retention equals intake minus excretion. The skeletal weight increases by about 20% during the same period (see Taylor, 1970), indicating that most of the additional mineral is incorporated into bone. Experiments with sexually immature pullets (Common et al., 1948) have shown that the improved mineral retention is caused by the synergystic action of estrogen and androgen. However, it is still not certain whether the two hormones act directly on the intestine or whether the response is mediated by their skeletal effects (see section on medullary bone, below). Most of the increased mineral retention is a result of improved intestinal absorption, which in turn is associated with an increase in the duodenal concentration of calcium-binding protein (Bar and Hurwitz, 1972; see also Chapter 10).

There are also marked changes in the intestinal absorption of calcium during the process of egg formation. When the shell gland is inactive, about 40% of the feed calcium are absorbed, whereas during the late stages of shell formation absorption rises to 72% (Hurwitz and Bar, 1969). The greatest increase occurs in the upper jejunum (Hurwitz et al., 1973; see also Chapter 10). This is in contrast to the improvement in calcium utilization during calcium depletion and at the onset of sexual maturity, which is most pronounced in the duodenum, and suggests that different mechanisms may be involved.

**Medullary bone.** Most of the increase in skeletal weight during the 10 days before sexual maturity is caused by the formation of a new type of bone, which occurs only in female birds. Because this new bone is most easily observed in the marrow

324 cavity of the femur and tibia it has been called medullary bone. Simkiss (1967) should be consulted for early references on medullary bone.

*Formation.* In the femur, medullary bone grows from the endosteal surface of the cortex in the form of interlacing spicules, which leave the vascular system of the marrow intact, although they can eventually fill the entire marrow cavity. The resulting large blood supply may facilitate the rapid mobilization of bone mineral during shell formation as well as its subsequent replacement. That the degree of vascularization is an important factor in medullary bone formation has been shown by Taylor *et al.* (1958). They reported that bone fracture, which is associated with increased blood supply, induces medullary bone formation in the metatarsus, from which it is normally absent.

Medullary bone formation is caused by the synergistic action of estrogens and androgens; administration of either hormone alone is ineffective in the capon (see Simkiss, 1967). This is in contrast to the increase in serum calcium, which depends only on estrogen. It is therefore possible to induce and study the two phenomena separately.

*Changes during egg formation.* The changes in medullary bone during egg formation are most easily observed in pigeons, which have clutches consisting of only two eggs separated by an interval of about 46 hr. In this species, shell formation is accompanied by a marked increase in the number of osteoclasts, indicating bone resorption, whereas osteoblasts, which are bone-forming cells, predominate when no shell is deposited (Bloom *et al.,* 1941).

The shifts in medullary bone histology during the egg cycle are considerably less definite in laying hens (Bloom *et al.,* 1958; Taylor and Bélanger, 1969). This may be because of the shorter interval between successive periods of shell calcification, a greater constancy of estrogen levels in blood resulting from the presence of multiple ova, and/or the higher calcium content of laying hen diets, which reduces the dependence on medullary bone. Nevertheless, there is evidence that periods of bone formation and destruction alternate during the egg cycle of hens, even if dietary calcium is relatively high. Morris and Taylor (1970) reported that hens fed 3% calcium excreted twice as much hydroxyproline, a breakdown product of collagen, on days when an egg was laid. Most of the increase occurred during shell formation, when the collagenolytic enzyme activity of both medullary and cortical bone was increased (Bannister and Candlish, 1973). Conversely, the synthesis of matrix proteins, as measured by lysine incorporation into medullary bone, decreases significantly between early and late shell formation (Candlish, 1971).

How the cyclic shifts in bone metabolism during the egg cycle are controlled has been a matter of considerable controversy. One group has claimed that bone resorption during shell formation is caused by a decrease in the estrogen concentration of blood, whereas the other has ascribed it to increased parathyroid hormone levels (see Simkiss, 1967; Taylor, 1970). In laying hens medullary bone resorption does not seem to be accompanied by a decrease in blood estrogen, for the estradiol concentration increases from about 2 hr after the start of rapid shell calcification until it reaches a peak 5–6 hr before oviposition (Senior and Cunningham, 1974). Much of the opposition to a role of parathyroid hormone was based on experiments by Urist and co-workers (see Urist, 1967) showing that large doses of this hormone cause changes in bone which differ from those observed during shell formation. Recent work with more physiologic dosages of the hormone has demonstrated that the changes in histology (Taylor and Bélanger, 1969) and metabolism (Candlish, 1970) are similar.

One set of data that is difficult to explain are the changes which occur in bone during calcium depletion. If laying hens are fed calcium-free diets, they cease laying after producing about six shells of decreasing thickness. Production can be maintained by daily injections with luteinizing hormone or an extract of the hypothalamus, whereas follicle-stimulating hormone is ineffective (Roland *et al.,* 1974). During calcium depletion, hens can mobilize as much as 38% of their bone mineral (see Simkiss, 1967). Surprisingly, most of the resorption occurs in cortical bone, whereas the amount of medullary bone remains constant or increases, although there is some demineralization (Zambonin and Mueller, 1969). This shows clearly that medullary bone is not just a reservoir from which calcium is withdrawn in times of need. Furthermore, the same hormones have opposite effects in different areas of the same bone. This indicates that the response of the target cells in bone to a hormonal stimulus may be modified by local factors, such as the degree of vascularization and differences in the structure and composition of the extracellular phase.

## Carbonate Deposition

The egg shell mineral contains about 60% carbonate. The importance of this ion in shell formation and shell quality problems was largely neglected until the early 1960's and many questions still remain to be solved. It should be emphasized that the following account and Figure 16–11, which stress the role of bicarbonate, are simplifications. The formation and precipitation of the carbonate radical of the shell involve equilibra between seven molecular species related to $H_2O$ and $CO_2$, namely $CO_2$, $H_2CO_3$, $HCO_3^-$, $CO_3^{2-}$, $H^+$, $OH^-$, and $H_2O$. The concentration of any of these substances in blood cell sap, or shell gland fluid does not vary independently, therefore, but involves changes in the concentrations of each of the other six species. Readers who are interested in this topic should consult a text on acid–base balance and the review by Maren (1967).

**Source of carbonate: bicarbonate.** The deposition of calcium carbonate in the forming shell is probably maintained through continuous secretion of $HCO_3^-$ by the shell gland, rather than by secretion of $CO_3^{2-}$ (Gutowska and Mitchell, 1945) or $CO_2$. The salts of $CO_3^{2-}$ with divalent cations are poorly soluble, so that formation of $CO_3^{2-}$ within the cells would probably cause intracellular precipitation of carbonate. If $CO_2$ were secreted, moreover, it would have to be hydrated in the lumen. Shell gland fluid and shell membranes have no measurable activity of carbonic anhydrase, the enzyme that catalyzes this reaction (Bernstein *et al.*, 1968), and the uncatalyzed rate seems too slow to maintain calcification. However, as indicated in Figure 16–11, once bicarbonate has been secreted into the lumen it equilibrates with $H^+$ and $CO_3^{2-}$ as well as the other molecular species mentioned above. Precipitation of $CaCO_3$ in the shell may be facilitated by the affinity of the organic matrix for divalent cations and/or a local decrease of pH on the shell surface (see Mueller and Leach, 1974). The latter could be caused by release of $NH_3$ from the albumen, followed by rapid formation of $NH_4^+$ (Reddy and Campbell, 1972).

Lörcher *et al.* (1970) studied the origin of the secreted bicarbonate by infusing $^{14}C$-bicarbonate continuously into a wing vein and measuring its transfer into the forming shell. The rate of incorporation was only 20% of what would be expected if the shell carbonate were derived from blood bicarbonate. They concluded that a large fraction of the secreted $HCO_3^-$ is formed from metabolic $CO_2$ produced within the cells of the shell gland. A metabolic origin of $HCO_3^-$ is in concert with data for other bicarbonate secreting organs, such as the mammalian pancreas (Maren, 1967).

**Bicarbonate formation: carbonic anhydrase.** The hydration of metabolic $CO_2$ to $HCO_3^-$ within the shell gland mucosa is catalyzed by carbonic anhydrase. Autoradiographic localizations (Gay and Mueller, 1973), which have been confirmed with fluorescent antibody techniques, indicate that the cells of the tubular glands and the epithelium contain about equal amounts of the enzyme.

The first indication that carbonic anhydrase may be important in shell formation came from studies showing that its inhibition with sulfonamides reduced shell thickness. The effect has been confirmed repeatedly and is specific because substitution of the sulfonamide group abolishes both enzyme inhibition and shell thinning (for references see Mueller and Leach, 1974). It should be cautioned, however, that reduced shell thickness by itself does not prove that a substance reduces the rate of shell formation. The same result is obtained if the egg is expelled prematurely. Such an effect has been reported for high dosages of sulfonamides; at lower dosages the egg stays in the shell gland for the normal time and the reduction of shell thickness is proportional to the amount of inhibitor (see Mueller and Leach, 1974). Complete inhibition of carbonic anhydrase with 12–15 mg/kg acetazolamide reduces the rate of calcium carbonate deposition by 80% in the hen. The uncatalyzed reaction therefore seems to account for about 20% of the bicarbonate formation. A peculiarity of carbonic anhydrase is that tissues in which it plays a role contain a large excess of the enzyme, so that over 99% of the active sites must be inhibited before any physiologic effect is seen (Maren, 1967). It is therefore not surprising that studies (see Heald *et al.*, 1968) have failed to show any correlation between shell thickness or the stage of egg formation and the carbonic anhydrase activity of the shell gland.

**Acid production during shell formation.** The formation of $HCO_3^-$ in the mucosa and its precipitation as calcium carbonate in the shell are accompanied by release of hydrogen ions (Figure 16–11) that must be buffered in the shell gland fluid and cells or released into the blood. Egg shell calcification causes a decrease in the intracellular pH of the shell gland mucosa that is abolished if carbonic anhydrase is inhibited (Simkiss, 1970). Furthermore, as shown by Hodges (1970), the arteriovenous pH gradient across the shell gland increases from 0 02 to 0 08 pH units during the first 15 hr of shell formation.

That shell formation causes changes in the acid–base status of blood was first shown by Mongin and Lacassagne (1966a). They found that the pH of systemic venous blood decreases from a maximum of 7.53, when the egg enters the shell gland, to 7.41 about 17 hr later, whereas the serum bicarbonate concentration decreases from 31.5 to

326 20.7 meq/liter. These are the symptoms of a metabolic acidosis, which an animal can counteract by increasing the respiratory rate and urinary acid excretion. Both effects have been observed in laying hens. The respiratory rate increases from 7.2 per minute before shell formation to 11.8 per minute during shell calcification (Mongin and Lacassagne, 1966b). The renal effects of shell formation include an increase in urinary ammonia, phosphate, and titrable acidity as well as practically complete reabsorption of bicarbonate (Anderson, 1967). The increased phosphate excretion probably results from the mobilization of medullary bone, which by itself causes increased acid release into blood (Mueller *et al.*, 1969). However, bone phosphate may also play a role as $H^+$ acceptor because it is mobilized as $PO_4^{3-}$ and excreted as $HPO_4^{2-}$ or $H_2PO_4^-$.

The importance of acid–base balance in shell formation is further supported by numerous experiments on the effects of acidifying and alkalinizing substances or treatments (for references see Mueller and Leach, 1974). Shell thickness is reduced during metabolic acidosis caused by feeding $NH_4Cl$, $HCl$, $(NH_4)_2SO_4$, or $H_2SO_4$; during exposure to high environmental temperature, which causes respiratory alkalosis; and during acute hypercapnia. Attempts to improve shell thickness through modification of the acid-base balance have been less successful. Prolonged exposure to air containing 2–5% $CO_2$, i.e., chronic hypercapnia, increased shell thickness in two experiments, whereas feeding of sodium bicarbonate produced variable results.

## Organic Matrix

Little is known about the synthesis and secretion of the precursors that form the organic matrix of the shell. Nevertheless, there is evidence that the matrix plays an important role in the calcification of the shell. The organic mammillary cores are the sites where the first crystals are formed. Their distribution, microscopic structure, and staining property are abnormal in thin, weak shells (Robinson and King, 1970; El-Boushy *et al.*, 1968), indicating that they may influence the structure and strength of the entire shell. Furthermore, the structural organization of the organic matrix, which permeates the entire true shell, suggests that matrix and mineral deposition occur in a closely linked manner. This hypothesis is supported by the finding that β-amino proprionitrile and manganese deficiency, which inhibit the formation of organic matrix in bone, also interfere with egg shell formation (see Mueller and Leach, 1974).

## REFERENCES

### Reproduction

Adamic, O., M. Fellegi, and J. Kollar. (1971). The metabolism of labelled progesterone in the laying hen. *Brit. Poultry Sci.*, 12, 151.

Aitken, R. N. C. (1971). The oviduct. In "Physiology and Biochemistry of Fowl" (D. J. Bell and B. M. Freeman, Eds.). New York: Academic Press, Chapter 53.

Arcos, M., and H. Opel. (1971). Abstracts, 53rd meeting of the Endocrine Society, p. 243.

Balch, D. A., and R. A. Cooke. (1970). A study of the composition of hens egg shell membranes. *Ann. Biol. Anim. Biochem. Biophys.*, 10, 13.

Bennett, T., and T. Malmfors. (1970). The adrenergic nervous system of the domestic fowl. *Z. Zellforsch.*, 102, 22.

Benoit, . . (1950). In "Traite de Zoologie," Tome XV (P. P. Grasse, Ed.). Paris: Mason & Co., Figure 279.

Bobr, L. W., P. E. Lake, F. W. Lorenz, F. X. Ogasawara, and H. Krzanowska. (1965). Inhibition of ovulation in the domestic hen by intrauterine insemination. *Poultry Sci.*, 44, 659.

Bohren, B. B., C. R. Thompson, and C. W. Garrick. (1945). The transfer of carotenoid pigments to the egg yolk. *Poultry Sci.*, 24, 356.

Bradfield, J. R. G. (1951). Radiographic studies on the formation of the hen's egg shell. *J. Exp. Biol.*, 28, 125.

Burmester, B. R. (1940). A study of the physical and chemical changes of the egg during its passage through the isthmus and uterus of the hen's oviduct. *J. Exp. Zool.*, 84, 445.

Burmester, B. R., and L. E. Card. (1939). The effect of resecting the so-called "chalaziferous region" of the hen's oviduct on the formation of subsequent eggs. *Poultry Sci.*, 18, 138.

Burmester, B. R., and L. E. Card. (1941). Experiments on the physiology of egg white secretion. *Poultry Sci.*, 20, 224.

Candlish, J. K. (1970). The outer membrane of the avian egg shell as a reticular structure. *Brit. Poultry Sci.*, 11, 341.

Chan, A. H. H., and R. H. Commom. (1974). Identification of radioactive estradiol–17-α and estradiol-17-β in the plasma of the laying hen after injection of estrone-4- $^{14}C$. *Comp. Biochem. Physiol.*, 49B, 105.

Chen, T. W., and R. O. Hawes. (1970). Genital tract motility in the domestic hen. *Poultry Sci.*, 49, 640.

Chieffi, G. (1967). Occurrence of steroids in gonads of non-mammalian vertebrates and sites of their biosynthesis. *Proc. Intl. Congr. Horm. Steroids.* 2nd 1966 Intl. Congr., Ser. No. 132, 1047.

Common, R. H., L. Ainsworth, F. Hertelendy, and R. S. Mathur. (1965). The estrone content of hen's urine. *Can. J. Biochem.*, 43, 539.

Conrad, R. M., and R. E. Phillips. (1938). The formation of the chalazae and inner white in the hen's egg. *Poultry Sci.*, 17, 143.

Conrad, R. M., and D. C. Warren. (1939). The alternate white and yellow layers of yolk in the hen's ova. *Poultry Sci.*, 18, 220.

Farner, D. S., and B. K. Follett. (1966). Light and other environmental factors affecting avian reproduction. *J. Anim. Sci.*, 25, 90.

Feeney, R. E., and R. G. Allison. (1969). "Evolutionary Biochemistry of Proteins." New York: J. Wiley & Sons.

Foster, W. H. (1969). Egg production under 24, 26 and 28 hour light dark cycles. *Brit. Poultry Sci.*, 10, 273.

Fraps, R. M. (1955). Egg production and fertility in poultry. In "Progress in Physiology of Farm Animals" (John Hammond, Ed.). London: Butterworth, Chapter 15.

Fraps, R. M., and B. H. Neher. (1945). Interruption of ovulation in the hen by subcutaneously administered non-specific substances. *Endocrinology*, 37, 407.

Fraps, R. M., M. W. Olsen, and B. H. Neher. (1942a). Forced ovulation of normal ovarian follicles in the domestic fowl. *Proc. Soc. Exp. Biol. Med.*, 50, 308.

Fraps, R. M., G. M. Riley, and M. W. Olsen. (1942b). Time required for induction of ovulation following intravenous injection of hormone preparations in the fowl. *Proc. Soc. Exp. Biol. Med.*, 50, 313.

Freedman, S. L. (1968). The innervation of the suprarenal gland of the fowl. *Acta Anat., 69,* 18.

Freedman, S. L., and P. D. Sturkie. (1962). Disruption of the sympathetic innervation of the fowl's uterus. *Poultry Sci., 41,* 1644.

Freedman, S. L., and P. D. Sturkie. (1963a). Blood vessels of the chicken's uterus (shell gland). *Am. J. Anat., 113,* 1.

Freedman, S. L., and P. D. Sturkie. (1963b) Exrinsic nerves of the chicken's uterus. *Anat. Rec., 147,* 431.

Furr, B. J. A. (1970). Identification of cholesterol, 7-oxocholesterol, pregnenolone, progesterone, 20-hydroxybregn-4-en-3-one epimers and 5β-androstane-3, 17-dione in plasma and ovarian tissue of the domestic fowl. *Steroids, 16,* 471.

Furr, B. J. A., R. C. Bonney, R. J. England, and F. J. Cunningham. (1973). LH and progesterone in peripheral blood during the ovulatory cycle of the hen. *J. Endocrinol., 57,* 159.

Gilbert, A. B. (1969). Innervation of the ovary of the domestic hen. *Quart. J. Exp. Physiol., 54,* 404.

Gilbert, A. B. (1970). Yolk deposition in the chicken oocyte and its relationship with ovulation. *J. Reprod. Fert., 23,* 539.

Gilbert, A. B. (1971a, b, c, d, e). The ovary, Chapter 50; Egg albumen and its formation, Chapter 54; Transport of egg through oviduct and oviposition, Chapter 56; The egg: its physical and chemical aspects, Chapter 58; Chapter 61. In "Phsyiology and Biochemistry of the Fowl," Vol. 3 (D. J. Bell and B. M. Freeman, Eds.). London and New York: Academic Press.

Gilbert, A. B., and P. E. Lake. (1963). Terminal innervation of the uterus and vagina of the domestic hen. *J. Reprod. Fert., 5,* 41.

Gilbert, A. B., and P. E. Lake. (1964). *5th Int. Cong. Anim. Reprod.* Trento, *3,* 317.

Gilbert, A. B., and D. G. M. Wood-Gush. (1963). A technique for the fistulation of the hen's oviduct through the abdominal wall with recovery of the ovum. *J. Reprod. Fert., 5,* 451.

Gilbert, A. B., and D. G. M. Wood-Gush. (1970). Observations on ovarian transplants and their bearing on normal ovarian function. *Res. Vet. Sci., 11,* 156.

Gilbert, A. B., and D. G. M. Wood-Gush. (1971). Ovulatory and ovipository cycles. In "Physiology and Biochemistry of the Fowl," Vol. 3 (D. J. Bell and B. M. Freeman, Eds.). New York and London: Academic Press, Chapter 57.

Gilbert, A. B., M. E., Reynolds, and F. W. Lorenz. (1968). Distribution of spermatozoa in the oviduct and fertility in domestic birds. VIII. Innervation and vascular supply of the uterovaginal sperm-host glands of the domestic hen. *J. Reprod. Fert., 17,* 305

Hertelendy, F. (1974). Effect of prostaglandins, cyclic AMP, seminal plasma, indomethacin and other factors on oviposition in Japanese quail. *J. Reprod. Fert., 40,* 87.

Heywang, B. W. (1938). The time factor in egg production. *Poultry Sci., 17,* 240.

Hodges, R. D. (1965). The blood supply to the avian oviduct, with special reference to the shell gland. *J. Anat., 99,* 485

Hughes, B. L., and J. E. Parker. (1971). Time of oviposition of shell-less eggs. *Poultry Sci., 50,* 1509.

Hughes, J. S., and H. M. Scott. (1936). The change in the concentration of ovoglobulin in egg white during egg formation. *Poultry Sci., 15,* 349.

Imai, K. (1973). Effects of avian and mammalian pituitary preparations on induction of ovulation in the domestic fowl. *J. Reprod. Fert., 33,* 91.

Jones, R. E. (1969). Effect of prolactin and progesterone on gonads of breeding California quail. *Proc. Soc. Exp. Biol. Med., 131,* 172.

Kamiyoshi, M., and K. Tanaka (1972). Augmentative effect of FSH on LH induced ovulation in the hen. *J. Reprod. Fert., 29,* 141.

Kappauf, B., and A. van Tienhoven. (1972). Progesterone concentrations in peripheral plasma of laying hens in relation to the time of ovulation. *Endocrinology, 90,* 1350.

Kern, M. D. (1972). Seasonal changes in the reproductive system of the female white crowned sparrow in captivity and in the field. *Z. Zellforsch., 126,* 297.

Koga, O. (1965). Nervous control on egg formation in the hen. *Jap. Poultry Sci., 2,* 20.

Korenbrot, C. C., D. W. Schomberg, and J. Erickson. (1974). Radioimmunoassay of plasma estradiol during the breeding cycle of ring doves. *Endocrinology, 94,* 1126.

Lake, P. E. (1974). The physical environment and reproduction in domesticated birds (abstract). 15th World Poultry Congress. Symposium on Management and Physiology. Monday; pages 2–13.

Lake, P. E., and A. B. Gilbert. (1964). The effect on egg production of a foreign object in the lower oviduct regions of the domestic hen. *Res. Vet. Sci., 5,* 39.

Lanson, R. K. (1959). The influence of light and darkness upon the reproductive performance of the fowl. Ph.D. thesis, Rutgers University, New Brunswick, New Jersey.

Layne, D. S., R. H. Common, W. A. Maw, and R. M. Fraps. (1958). Presence of estrone, estradiol and estriol in extracts of ovaries of laying hens. *Nature* (London), *181,* 351.

Lehrman, D. S. (1961). Hormonal regulation of parental behavior in birds and infrahuman mammals. In "Sex and Internal Secretions" (W. C. Young, Ed.). Baltimore: Williams and Wilkins, Chapter 21.

Lofts, B., and R. K. Murton. (1973). In "Avian Biology," Vol. 3 (D. S. Farner and J. R. King, Eds.). New York: Academic Press, Chapter 1.

Lorenz, F. W., R. E. Burger, E. B. Bennett; and W. Reimann. (1962). Hepatic and renal effects on potency of estrogenic stilbene derivatives. *Endocrinology, 71,* 649.

Lorenz, F. W., Reynolds, M. E., and Gilbert, A. B. (1967). Secretory activity of the sperm-host glands of the domestic fowl. *Physiologist, 10,* 236.

Marshall, A. J. (1961). "Biology and Comparative Physiology of Birds," Vol. II. New York: Academic Press, Chapters 21, 23 and 24.

Mathur, R. S., and R. H. Common. (1967). Chromatographic identification of estriol and 16, 17-epiestrol as constituents of urine of laying hen. *Can. J. Biochem., 45,* 531.

Meier, A. H., and R. MacGregor III. (1972). Temporal organization in avian reproduction. *Am. Zool., 12,* 257.

Mitchell, M. E. (1967a). Stimulation of the ovary in hypophysectomized hens by an avian pituitary preparation. *J. Reprod. Fert., 14,* 249.

Mitchell, M. E. (1967b). The effects of avian gonadotropin precipitate on pituitary-deficient hens. *J. Reprod. Fert., 14,* 257.

Morris, J. R. (1967). In "Environmental Control in Poultry Production" (T. C. Carter, Ed.). Edinburgh: Oliver & Boyd.

Munsick, R. A., W. H. Sawyer, and H. B. Van Dyke. (1960). Avian neurohypophysial hormones: Pharmacological properties and tentative identification. *Endocrinology, 66,* 860.

Nakajo, S., A. H. Zakaria, and K. Imai. (1973). Effect of the local administration of proteolytic enzymes on the rupture of the ovarian follicle in the domestic fowl. *J. Reprod. Fert., 34,* 235.

Nalbandov, A. V., and G. J. Baum. (1948). The use of stilbestrol inhibited males as test animals for gonadotropic hormones. *Endocrinology, 43,* 271.

Nalbandov, A. V., and M. F. James. (1949). The blood-vascular system of the chicken ovary. *Am. J. Anat., 85,* 347.

Neher, B. H., and R. M. Fraps. (1950). The addition of eggs to the hen's clutch by repeated injections of ovulating inducing hormones. *Endocrinology, 46,* 482.

Nevälainen, T. J. (1969). Electron microscope observations on the shell gland mucosa of calcium deficient hens. *Anat. Res., 164,* 127

Niezgoda, J., J. Rzasa, and Z. Ewy. (1973). Changes in blood vasotocin activity during oviposition in the hen. *J. Reprod. Fert., 35,* 505.

Ogawa, K., and H. Nishiyama. (1969). Studies on the mechanism of ovulation in the fowl. *Mem. Fac. Agri., Kagoshima Univ., 7,* 1.

O'Grady, J. E., and P. J. Heald. (1965). Identification of estradiol and estrone in avian plasma. *Nature* (London), *205,* 390.

Oishi, T., and J. K. Lauber. (1973a). Photoreception in the photosexual response of the quail. II. Effects of intensity and wave length. *Am. J. Physiol., 225,* 880.

Olsen, M. W., and T. C. Byerly. (1932). Orientation of the hen's egg in the uterus during laying. *Poultry Sci., 11,* 266.

328    Olsen, M. W., and B. H. Neher. (1948). The site of fertilization in the domestic fowl. *J. Exp. Zool., 109*, 355.

Opel, H. (1964). Premature oviposition following operative interference with the brain of the chicken. *Endocrinology, 74*, 193.

Opel, H. (1966a). The timing of oviposition and ovulation in the quail (*Coturnix*). *Brit. Poultry Sci., 7*, 29.

Opel, H. (1966b). Release of oviposition inducing factor from the median eminence—pituitary stalk region in neural lobectomized hens. *Anat. Rec., 154*, 396.

Opel, H., and R. M. Fraps. (1961) Blockade of gonadotrophin release for ovulation in the hen following stimulation with stainless steel electrodes. *Proc. Soc. Exp. Biol. Med., 108*, 291.

Opel, H., and A. V. Nalbandov. (1958). A study of hormonal control of growth and ovulation of follicles in hypophysectomized hens. *Poultry Sci., 37*, 1230.

Opel, H., and A. V. Nalbandov. (1961a). Ovulability of ovarian follicles in the hypophysectomized hen. *Endocrinology, 69*, 1029.

Opel, H., and A. V. Nalbandov. (1961b). Follicular growth and ovulation in hypophysectomized hens. *Endocrinology, 69*, 1016.

Peterson, A. J., and R. H. Common. (1972). Estrone and estradiol concentrations in peripheral plasma of laying hens as determined by radioimmunoassay. *Can. J. Zool., 50*, 395.

Platt, C. S. (1946). Report of the New Jersey Pigeon Breeding Test, Millville, N.J. New Jersey Agricultural Experiment Station New Brunswick, New Jersey.

Polin, D. (1957). Formation of porphyrin from delta amino-levulinic acid by uterine and liver tissue from laying hens. *Proc. Soc. Exp. Biol. Med., 94*, 276.

Polin, D., and P. D. Sturkie. (1955). Prevention of premature oviposition and shell-less egg with ephedrine. *Poultry Sci., 34*, 1169.

Ralph, C. L., and R. M. Fraps. (1960). Induction of ovulation in the hen by injection of progesterones in the brain. *Endocrinology, 66*, 269.

Ralph, C. V., and R. Fraps. (1959). Long term effects of diencephalic lesions on the ovary of the hen. *Am. J. Physiol., 197*, 1279.

Reeves, J. J., P. C. Harrison, and J. M. Casey. (1973). Ovarian development and ovulation in hens treated with synthetic porcine LH releasing hormone and FSH releasing hormone. *Poultry Sci., 52*, 1883.

Romanoff, A. L., and A. J. Romanoff. (1949). "The Avian Egg." New York: John Wiley & Sons, Inc.

Rosales, A. A., H. V. Bieller, and A. B. Stephenson. (1968). Effect of light cycles on ovipositions and egg production. *Poultry Sci., 47*, 586.

Rothchild, I., and R. M. Fraps. (1944a). Relation between light—dark rhythms and hour of lay of eggs experimentally retained in the hen. *Endocrinology, 35*, 355.

Rothchild, I., and R. M. Fraps. (1944b). On the function of the ruptured ovarian follicle of the domestic fowl. *Proc. Soc. Exp. Biol. Med., 56*, 79.

Rothchild, I., and R. M. Fraps. (1945). The relation between ovulation frequency and the incidence of follicular atresia following surgical operation in the domestic fowl. *Endocrinology, 37*, 415.

Rothchild, I., and R. M. Fraps. (1949). The induction of ovulating hormone release from the pituitary of the domestic fowl by means of progesterone. *Endocrinology, 44*, 141.

Rzasa, J., and Z. Ewy. (1971). Effect of vasotocin and oxytocin on intrauterine pressure in the hen. *J. Reprod. Fert., 25*, 115.

Scott, H. M., J. S. Hughes, and D. C. Warren. (1937). Augmentation of nitrogen to the egg white after the formation of the shell membranes in the fowl. *Poultry Sci., 16*, 53.

Senior, B. E. (1974). Estradiol concentration in the peripheral plasma of domestic hen. *J. Reprod. Fert., 41*, 107.

Senior, B. E., and F. J. Cunningham. (1974). Estradiol and LH during the ovulatory cycle of the hen. *J. Endocrinol., 60*, 201.

Shenstone, F. S. (1968). In "Egg Quality: A Study of the Hen's Egg" (T. C. Carter, Ed.). Edinburgh: Oliver & Boyd.

Silver, R., C. Reboulleau, D. S. Lehrman, and H. H. Fedder. (1974). Radioimmunoassay of plasma progesterone during reproductive cycle of male and female ring doves. *Endocrinology, 984*, 1574.

Stetson, M. H. (1972). Feedback regulation by estradiol of ovarian function in Japanese quail. *J. Reprod. Fert., 31*, 205.

Sturkie, P. D. (1946). The effects of hypothermia upon the reproductive tract of the hen. *Poultry Sci., 25*, 369.

Sturkie, P. D. (Ed.). (1954). "Avian Physiology" (1st ed.). Ithaca, N.Y.: Cornell University Press.

Sturkie, P. D. (1955). Absorption of egg yolk in body cavity of the hen. *Poultry Sci., 34*, 736.

Sturkie, P. D. (Ed.). (1965). "Avian Physiology" (2nd ed.) Ithaca, N.Y.: Cornell University Press, Chapter 15.

Sturkie, P. D. (1966). The effects of sodium pentobarbital on oviposition of the hen. *Poultry Sci., 45*, 851

Sturkie, P. D., and S. L. Freedman. (1962). Effects of transection of pelvic and lumbosacral nerves on ovulation and oviposition in fowl. *J. Reprod. Fert., 4*, 81.

Sturkie, P. D., and Y. C. Lin. (1966). Release of vasotocin and oviposition in the hen. *J. Endocrinol., 35*, 555

Sturkie, P. D., and Y. C. Lin. (1967). Further studies on oviposition and vasotocin release in the hen. *Poultry Sci., 46*, 1591.

Sturkie, P. D., and D. Polin. (1954). Role of magnum and uterus in the determination of albumen quality of laid eggs. *Poultry Sci., 33*, 9.

Sturkie, P. D., and H. S. Weiss. (1950). The effects of sympathomimetic and parasympathomimetic drugs upon egg formation. *Poultry Sci. 29*, 781. (Abstr.)

Sturkie, P. D., P. Joiner, and S. L. Freedman. (1962). Role of the "bearing down" reflex on oviposition in the chicken. *Endocrinology, 70*, 221.

Sturkie, P. D., H. S. Weiss, and R. K. Ringer. (1954). Effects of injections of acetylcholine and ephedrine upon components of the hen's egg. *Poultry Sci., 33*, 18.

Sykes, A. H. (1953a). Premature oviposition in the hen. *Nature* (London), *172*, 1098.

Sykes, A. H. (1953b). Some observations on oviposition in the fowl. *Quart. J. Exp. Physiol., 38*, 61.

Sykes, A. H. (1955a). Further observations on reflex bearing down in the fowl. *J. Physiol., 128*, 249.

Sykes, A. H. (1955b). The effect of adrenaline on oviduct motility and egg production in the fowl. *Poultry Sci., 34*, 622.

Tanaka, K., and S. Nakajo. (1962). Participation of neurohypophyseal hormone on oviposition with hen. *Endocrinology, 70*, 453.

Tanaka, K., M. Kamiyoshi, and Y. Tanabe. (1971). Inhibition of premature ovulation by Prolactin in the hen. *Poultry Sci., 50* 63.

van Tienhoven, A. (1961a). Endocrinology of reproduction in birds. "Sex and Internal Secretions," Vol. II (W. C. Young, Ed.). Baltimore: Williams & Wilkins Company, Chapter 28.

van Tienhoven, A. (1961b). The effect of massive doses of corticotrophin and of corticosterone on ovulation of the chicken. *Acta Endocrinol., 38*, 407.

van Tienhoven, A., and C. E. Ostrander. (1973). The effect of interruption of the dark period at different intervals on egg production and shell breaking strength. *Poultry Sci., 52*, 998.

van Tienhoven, A., and R. J. Planck. (1973). The effect of light on avian reproductive activity. In "Handbook of Physiology" Vol. II, Endocrinology" part 1. Bethesda, Maryland: American Physiological Society, p. 79.

van Tienhoven, A., and A. V. Schally. (1972). Mammalian LH releasing hormone induces ovulation in domestic fowl. *J. Gen. Comp. Endocrinol., 19*, 591.

Warren, D. C. (1949). In "Fertility and Hatchability of Chicken and Turkey Eggs." (J. E. Parker, Ed.). New York: John Wiley & Sons, Chapter 2.

Warren, D. C., and R. M. Conrad. (1939). Growth of the hen's ovum. *J. Agri. Res., 58* 875.

Warren, D. C., and R. M. Conrad. (1942). Time of pigment deposition in brown-shelled hen eggs and in turkey eggs. *Poultry Sci., 21*, 515.

Warren, D. C., and H. M. Scott. (1935). The time factor in egg production. *Poultry Sci., 14*, 195.

Weiss, H. S., and P. D. Sturkie. (1952). Time of oviposition as affected by neuromimetic drugs. *Poultry Sci., 31*, 227.

Walls, J. W. (1971). The metabolism of progesterone in the laying hen. *Comp. Biochem. Physiol., 40A*, 61.

Wilson, H. R., M. W. Holland, and R. L. Renner, Jr. (1973). Egg laying cycle characteristics of the bobwhite (*Colinus virginianus*). *Poultry Sci., 52*, 1571.

Wilson, W. O., and A. E. Woodward. (1958). Egg production of chickens kept in darkness. *Poultry Sci., 37*, 1054.

Wilson, W. O., A. E. Woodward, and H. Abplanalp. (1963). Exogenous regulation of oviposition in chickens. *Poultry Sci., 42*, 1319.

Winget, C. M., E. G. Averkin, and T. B. Fryer. (1965). Quantitative measurement by telemetry of ovulation and oviposition in the fowl. *Am. J. Physiol., 209*, 853.

Wolford, J. H., R. K. Ringer, and I. H. Coleman. (1964). Ovulation and egg formation in the Beltsville Small White turkey. *Poultry Sci., 43*, 187.

Wood-Gush, D. G. N., and A. B. Gilbert. (1969). Observations of the laying behavior of hens in battery cages. *Brit. Poultry Sci., 10*, 29.

Woodward, A. E., and F. B. Mather. (1964). The timing of ovulation and movement of the ovum through the oviduct, pigmentation and shell deposition in Japanese quail. *Poultry Sci., 43*, 1427.

Wyburn, G. M., H. S. Johnston, M. H. Draper, and M. F. Davidson. (1970). The fine structure of the infundibulum and magnum of the oviduct of gallus domesticus. *J. Exp. Physiol., 55*, 213.

## Eggshell Formation

Anderson, R. S. (1967). Acid–base changes in the excreta of the laying hen. *Vet. Rec., 80*, 314.

Ascenzi, A., C. Francois, and D. S. Bocciarelli. (1963). On the bone induced by estrogens in birds. *J. Ultrastruct. Res., 8*, 491.

Bannister, D. W., and J. K. Candlish. (1973). The collagenolytic activity of avian medullary bone: effect of laying status and parathyroid extract. *Brit. Poultry Sci., 14*, 121.

Bar, A., and S. Hurwitz. (1972). Relationship of duodenal calcium-binding protein to calcium absorption in the laying fowl. *Comp. Biochem. Physiol., 41B*, 735.

Bar, A., and S. Hurwitz. (1973). Uterine calcium-binding protein in the laying fowl. *Comp. Biochem. Physiol., 45A*, 579.

Bernstein, R. S., T. Nevalainen, R. Schraer, and H. Schraer. (1968). Intracellular distribution and role of carbonic anhydrase in the avian (*Gallus domesticus*) shell gland mucosa. *Biochim. Biophys. Acta, 159*, 367.

Bloom, W., M. A. Bloom, and F. C. McLean. (1941). Calcification and ossificaion. Medullary bone changes in the reproductive cycle of female pigeons. *Anat. Rec., 81*, 443.

Bloom, M. A., L. V. Domm, A. V. Nalbandov, and W. Bloom. (1958). Medullary bone of laying chickens. *Am. J. Anat., 102*, 411.

Boelkins, J. N., W. J. Mueller, and K. L. Hall. (1973). Cardiac output distribution in the laying hen during shell formation. *Comp. Biochem. Physiol., 46A*, 735.

Burmester, B. R. (1940). A study of the physical and chemical changes of the egg during its passage through the isthmus and uterus of the hen's oviduct. *J. Exp. Zool., 84*, 445.

Candlish, J. K. (1970). The urinary excretion of calcium, hydroxy-proline and uronic acids after the administration of parathyroid extracts. *Comp. Biochem. Physiol., 32*, 703.

Candlish, J. K. (1971). The formation of mineral and organic matrix of fowl cortical and medullary bone during shell calcification. *Brit. Poultry Sci., 12*, 119.

Common, R. H., W. A. Rutledge, and R. W. Hale. (1948). Observations on the mineral metabolism of pullets. VIII. The influence of gonadal hormones on the retention of calcium and phosphorus. *J. Agri. Sci., 38*, 64.

Corradino, R. A., R. H. Wasserman, M. H. Pubols, and S. I. Chang. (1968). Vitamin $D_3$ induction of a calcium-binding protein in the uterus of the laying hen. *Arch. Biochem. Biophys., 125*, 378.

Draper, M. H., M. F. Davidson, G. M. Wyburn, and H. S. Johnston. (1972). The fine structure of the fibrous membrane forming

region of the oviduct of *Gallus domesticus. Quart. J. Exp. Physiol., 57*, 297.

El-Boushy, A. R., P. C. M. Simons, and G. Wiertz. (1968). Structure and ultrastructure of the hen's egg shell as influenced by environmental temperature, humidity and Vitamin C additions. *Poultry Sci., 47*, 456.

El Jack, M. E., and P. E. Lake. (1967). The content of the principal inorganic ions and carbon dioxide in uterine fluids of the domestic hen. *J. Reprod. Fert., 13*, 127.

Gay, C. V., and W. J. Mueller. (1973). Cellular localization of carbonic anhydrase in avian tissues by labeled inhibitor autoradiography. *J. Histochem. Cytochem., 21*, 693.

Gutowska, M. S., and C. A. Mitchell. (1945). Carbonic anhydrase in the calcification of the eggshell. *Poultry Sci., 24*, 159.

Heald, P. J., D. Pohlman, and E. G. Martin. (1968). Shell strength and carbonic anhydrase activity of the shell gland of the domestic fowl. *Poultry Sci., 47*, 858.

Hodges, R. D. (1970). Blood pH and cation levels in relation to egg-shell formation. *Ann. Biol. Anim. Biochim. Biophys., 10 (2)*, 199.

Hurwitz, S. (1968). Calcium exchange in plasma of the fowl. *Biochim. Biophys. Acta, 156*, 389.

Hurwitz, S., and A. Bar. (1969). Intestinal calcium absorption in the laying fowl and its importance in calcium homeostasis. *Am. J. Clin. Nutr., 22*, 391.

Hurwitz, S., A. Bar, and I. Cohen. (1973). Regulation of calcium absorption by fowl intestine. *Am. J. Physiol., 225*, 150.

Hurwitz, S., I. Cohen, and A. Bar. (1970). The transmembrane electrical potential difference in the uterus (shell gland) of birds. *Comp. Biochem. Physiol., 35*, 873.

Leonard, E. M. (1969). The transmural potentials in the functional oviduct of the hen. *J. Physiol. (London), 203*, 83.

Lörcher, K., C. Zscheile, and K. Bronsch. (1970). Transfer of continuously i.v. infused $NaHC^{14}O_3$ and $Ca^{47}Cl_2$ to the hens egg shell. *Ann. Biol. Anim. Biochim. Biophys., 10(2)*, 193.

Maren, T. H. (1967). Carbonic anhydrase: chemistry. physiology and inhibition. *Physiol. Rev., 47*, 595.

McIndoe, W. A. (1971). Yolk synthesis. In "Physiology and Biochemistry of the Domestic Fowl" (D. J. Bell and B. M. Freeman, Eds.). New York: Academic Press, Chapter 51.

Misra, M. S. and A. Kemény. (1964). Studies on the oviduct and serum of fowls. I. Oxygen uptake, alkaline phosphatase activity, concentrations of phosphorus, calcium and magnesium in adult Hungarian yellow hens. *Acta Vet. Hung., 14*, 387.

Mongin, P. (1968). Role of acid–base balance in the physiology of egg shell formation. *World's Poultry Sci. J., 24*, 200.

Mongin, P., and L. Lacassagne. (1966a). Equilibre acido-basique du sang et formation de la coquille de l'oeuf. *Ann. Biol. Anim. Biochim. Biophys., 6*, 93.

Mongin, P., and L. Lacassagne. (1966b). Rythme respiratoire et physiologie de la formation de la coquille de l'oeuf. *Ann. Biol. Anim. Biochim. Biophys., 6*, 101.

Morris, K. M. L., and T. G. Taylor. (1970). Urinary excretion of hydroxyproline and acid phosphatase in relation to egg-shell formation in the domestic fowl. *Ann. Biol. Anim. Biochim. Biophys., 10 (2)*, 185.

Mueller, W. J., and R. M. Leach, Jr. (1974). Effects of chemicals on egg shell formation. *Ann. Rev. Pharmacol., 14*, 289.

Mueller, W. J., R. L. Brubaker, and M. D. Caplan (1969) ) Egg shell formation and bone resorption in laying hens. *Fed. Proc., 28*, 1851.

Mueller, W. J., R. L. Brubaker, C. V. Gay, and J. N. Boelkins. (1973). Mechanisms of bone resorption in laying hens. *Fed. Proc., 32*, 1951.

Reddy, G., and J. W. Campbell. (1972). Correlation of ammonia liberation and calcium deposition by the avian egg and blood ammonia levels in the laying hen. *Experientia, 28*, 530.

Richardson, K. C. (1935). The secretory phenomena in the oviduct of the fowl, including the process of shell formation examined by the microincineration technique. *Trans. Roy. Soc. London, Series B, 225*, 149.

Robinson, D. S., and N. R. King. (1970). The structure of the organic mammillary cores in some weak egg shells. *Brit. Poultry*

330

Sci., 11, 39.

Roland, D. A., Sr., D. R. Sloan, H. R. Wilson, and R. H. Harms. (1974). Relationship of calcium to reproductive abnormalities on the laying hen (*Gallus domesticus*). *J. Nutr., 104,* 1074.

Sauveur, B., and P. Mongin. (1971). Etude comparative du fluide utérin et de l'albumen de l'oeuf in utero chez la poule. *Ann. Biol. Anim. Biochim. Biophys. 11*:213.

Schraer, H., and R. Schraer. (1971). Calcium transfer across the avian shell gland. In "Cellular Mechanisms for Calcium Transfer and Homeostasis" (G. Nichols and R. H. Wasserman, Eds.). New York: Academic Press, p. 351.

Scott, H. M., and Huang. (1941). Histological observations on the formation of the chalaza in the hen's egg. *Poultry Sci., 20*: 402.

Senior, B. E., and F. J. Cunningham. (1974). Oestradiol and luteinizing hormone during the ovulatory cycle of the hen. *J. Endocrinol., 60,* 201.

Simkiss, K. (1967). "Calcium in Reproductive Physiology." New York: Reinhold Publishing Co.

Simkiss, K. (1970). Effect of acetazolamide on intracellular pH of the avian shell gland. *J. Physiol. (London), 207,* 63.

Simkiss, K., and T. G. Taylor. (1971). Shell formation. In "Physiology and Biochemistry of the Domestic Fowl" (D. J. Bell and B. M. Freeman, Eds.). New York: Academic Press, Chapter 55.

Simons, P. C. M. (1971). "Ultrastucture of the Hen Eggshell and its Physiological Interpretation." Wageningen, Netherlands: Centre for Agricultural Publishing and Documentation.

Stemberger, B. (1971). Microscopic examination of the avian egg membrane from the posterior oviduct to study the formation of the mammillae. M. S. thesis, The Pennsylvania State University, University Park, Pa.

Taylor, T. G. (1970). The role of the skeleton in egg-shell formation. *Ann. Biol. Anim. Biochim. Biophys., 10 (2),* 83.

Taylor, T. G. (1971). The skeleton: its structure and metabolism. In "Physiology and Biochemistry of the Domestic Fowl" (D. J. Bell and B. M. Freeman, Eds.). New York: Academic Press, Chapter 26.

Taylor, T. G., and L. F. Bélanger. (1969). The mechanisms of bone resorption in laying hens. *Calcium Tissue Res., 4,* 162.

Taylor, T. G., J. H. Moore, and R. M. Loosmore. (1958). Some effects of bone fracture in hens. *Zentblatt. Vet. Med., 6,* 574.

Tyler, C. (1954). Studies on egg shells. IV. The site of deposition of radioactive calcium and phosphorus. *J. Sci. Food Agri., 5,* 335.

Urist, M. R. (1967). Avian parathyroid physiology: including a special comment on calcitonin. *Am. Zool., 7,* 883.

Wyburn, G. M., H. S. Johnston, M. H. Draper, and M. F. Davison. (1973). The ultrastructure of the shell forming region of the oviduct and the development of the shell of *Gallus domesticus. Quart. J. Exp. Physiol., 58,* 143.

Zambonin, A. A., and W. J. Mueller. (1969). Medullary bone of laying hens during calcium depletion and repletion. *Calcium Tissue Res., 4,* 136.

# 17

# Reproduction in the Male, Fertilization, and Early Embryonic Development

P. D. Sturkie

with H. Opel

## 332  ANATOMY OF THE MALE REPRODUCTIVE SYSTEM: PASSAGE AND STORAGE OF SPERM

**Anatomy.** The reproductive system of the male consists of paired testes, the epididymi, the vasa deferentia (which transport the spermatozoa to the penis), and the penis (Figure 17–1). The testes are near the cephalic end of the kidneys and ventral to them. The weight of the testes in chickens comprises about 1% of the total body weight (Parker, 1949), or about 9–30 g per single testis at sexual maturity, depending on breed, state of nutrition, and other factors. In old cocks testis weight may approach 40–60 g.

In wild species the testes weigh less but are greater in terms of total body weight. The epididymi in birds are small in comparison to those in mammals. The bird, unlike mammals, has no Cow-

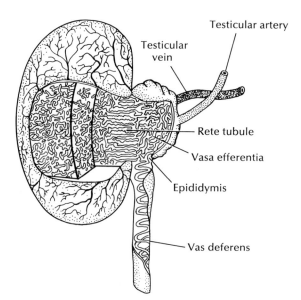

17–2  Internal structure of the chicken testes. (After Marshall, 1961.)

17–1  Urogenital system of the male chicken.

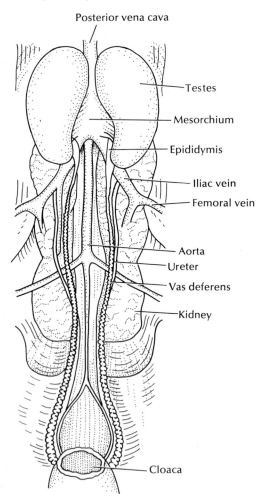

per's gland or seminal vesicle. The avian testis is without septa and lobules, and consists of seminiferous tubules, the rete tubules, and vas efferentia (Figure 17–2).

The penis of chickens is quite small and when erected is engorged with lymph from the lymph folds (Nishiyama, 1955). This lymph fluid is added to the semen in the vas deferens and both are ejected simultaneously along the longitudinal groove of the phallus. (Figure 17–3). The reproductive organs of turkeys are similar to those of the chicken. Ducks and geese have well-developed phalli, which are spirally twisted and which serve as intromittent organs (Sturkie, 1965). Penislike organs have been reported in certain ratite birds (Tinamidae and Cracidae; see Lofts and Murton, 1973).

Nerves to the ductus deferens and penis include pelvic nerves (lumbosacrals 8–11), some of which are involved in erection of the penis (see Chapter 16), and probably sympathetic fibers (hypogastric), which are most probably involved in ejaculation (Lake and Sturkie, unpublished).

**Passage and storage of sperm.** From the seminiferous tubules, the sperm pass to the rete tubules and then to the vas efferentia, epididymis, and vas deferens. Normally, at least in the chicken, sperm are stored not in the epididymis but in the vas deferens (Lake, 1957, 1971).

In passerine birds, the terminal part of the vas deferens is enlarged and is often referred to as the seminal vesicle; however, Marshall (1961) states

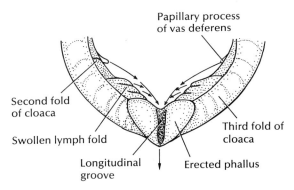

Papillary process
of vas deferens

Second fold
of cloaca

Swollen lymph fold

Third fold of
cloaca

Longitudinal
groove

Erected phallus

17–3 Diagram showing the ejaculation of the
semen of the cock. Shown is the ejection of
vas deferens semen from the papillary
process of the vas deferens, and outflow
of transparent fluid from the swollen
lymphfold, as well as the ejaculation of the
semen (the mixture of vas deferens semen
with transparent fluid) along the longitudinal
groove of the erected phallus to the outside
anus. (After Nishiyama, 1955.)

that structurally this organ has nothing in common
with the seminal vesicle of mammals, and he pre-
fers the designation "seminal sac." Sperm, however,
may be stored here.

# DEVELOPMENT OF THE TESTES, SPERMATOGENESIS, AND SEMEN PRODUCTION

The growth and development of the testes and
spermatogenesis have been studied in detail by a
number of workers (see Sturkie, 1965; Lake, 1971;
Lofts and Murton, 1973). Detailed studies of spermatogenesis in ducks have been made by Clermont
(1958) and more recently by Johnson (1966).

The testes of all species undergo marked
changes during the development of spermatogenesis and these are essentially similar in most species.
Details of these changes have been studied by
Kumaran and Turner (1949a,b) and Blivaiss (1947)
as follows: during the first 5 weeks of age the tubules are organized and multiplication of the basal

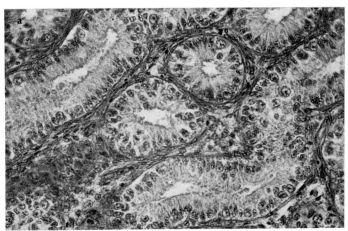

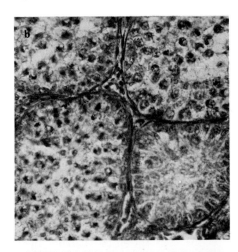

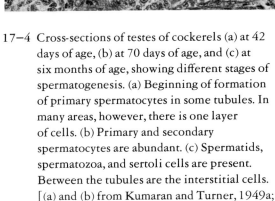

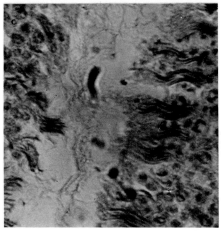

17–4 Cross-sections of testes of cockerels (a) at 42
days of age, (b) at 70 days of age, and (c) at
six months of age, showing different stages of
spermatogenesis. (a) Beginning of formation
of primary spermatocytes in some tubules. In
many areas, however, there is one layer
of cells. (b) Primary and secondary
spermatocytes are abundant. (c) Spermatids,
spermatozoa, and sertoli cells are present.
Between the tubules are the interstitial cells.
[(a) and (b) from Kumaran and Turner, 1949a;
(c) from Blivaiss, 1947.]

334 layer of cells, the spermatogonia, occurs. The primary spermatocytes begin to appear at about the sixth week. During the next 2 or 3 weeks, growth of the primary spermatocytes takes precedence over the further multiplication of the spermatogonial layer.

The secondary spermatocytes begin to appear at about 10 weeks of age as a result of the reduction division of the primary spermatocytes (Figure 17–4b). Spermatids (immature spermatozoa) begin to appear in the seminiferous tubules at about 12 weeks of age and by the twentieth week are usually present in all of the tubules (Figure 17–4c).

The seminiferous tubules of prepuberal males are small and are lined with a single layer of cells (Figure 17–4a). The mature testis has a multilayered epithelium representing the various stages of spermatogenesis. From the wall of the tubule to the lumen may be found spermatogonia, primary spermatocytes, secondary spermatocytes, spermatids, the nutritive cells (cells of Sertoli) to which the spermatids are attached, and the spermatozoa (Figure 17–4).

The time involved in the completion of all stages of spermatogenesis and sperm transit has been estimated in (Japanese quail) to be approximately 25 days (Jones and Jackson, 1972) based on the use of anti spermatogonial chemicals (Myleran and cyclohexane). The time necessary for sperm to pass through the epididymes and vas deferens of cocks (chickens) was 4 days, and the time required for primary spermatocytes to become mature spermatozoa was 12 days (Takeda, 1969).

### Spermatozoa

Mature spermatozoa (SZ) of birds exhibit a great deal of variation in size and shape, depending on the species (Lake, 1971). Romanoff (1960) has described and shown photographs of spermatozoa from many avian species. Electron microscopic studies of fowl spermatozoa have been conducted by Grigg (1951), Lake et al. (1968), and Harris et al. (1973). In the chicken, the spermatozoon has a long headpiece with a pointed acrosome and a short midpiece, to which is attached the long tail (Figure 17–5).

Avian spermatozoa are small compared to those of mammals; their average volume is 9.2 $\mu m^3$ (Lake, 1971). Based on the ultrastructure, the following description is from Lake et al. (1968) and Lake (1971). The acrosome is simple; the midpiece is a cylindrical distal centriole surrounded by a sheath of mitochondria (Lake et al., 1968; Lake, 1971). The chicken acrosome is about 1.75 $\mu m$ in length, the head is about 12.5 $\mu m$ long, the mid-

piece is 4 $\mu m$ long, and the principal tail piece is 80 $\mu m$ long (Lake, 1971).

Rapid freezing and thawing produce pronounced changes in the ultrastructure of SZ (Harris et al., 1973). The fate of SZ retained in the vas deferens after its ligation was studied by electromicroscopy (Tingari and Lake, 1972). The spermatozoa showed signs of disintegration mainly in the head region, and there was an uptake of SZ by the epithelial cells lining the male sperm ducts that was increased after ligation of the vas deferens. These observations (according to the authors) may indicate a route for disposal of unejaculated SZ in male chickens.

### Chemical Composition and Physical Properties of Semen

Lake (1966, 1971) has described in detail chemical and physical properties of semen and it is clear that avian semen is different in important respects from that of mammals. These differences are attributable to the absence of seminal vesicles and prostate glands and the presence of a rudimentary epididymis (Lake, 1971). Fowl seminal plasma is almost completely lacking in fructose, citrate, ergothioneine, inositol, phosphoryl choline, and glyceryl phosphoryl choline. The chloride content of avian semen is low, and potassium and glutamate contents are high. The source of the large glutamate content (see Lake, 1971) may be the seminiferous

17–5 Diagram of the spermatozoon of the chicken. (Modified slightly from Grigg, 1951.)

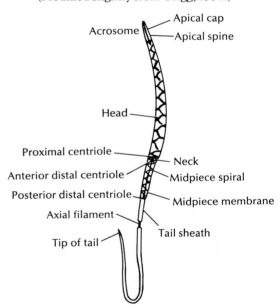

- Apical cap
- Acrosome
- Apical spine
- Head
- Proximal centriole
- Neck
- Anterior distal centriole
- Midpiece spiral
- Posterior distal centriole
- Midpiece membrane
- Axial filament
- Tail sheath
- Tip of tail

*Table* 17–1    *Chemical composition and physical properties of fowl semen*[a]

| Constitutent or property | Whole semen | Spermatozoon | Seminal plasma with little or no transparent fluid |
|---|---|---|---|
| Water content (%) | — | 59.9 | 96.4 |
| Specific gravity | — | 1.1722 | 1.011 |
| Calcium (meq/liter) | 2.46 | 0.72 | 2.55 |
| Magnesium (meq/liter) | 5.8 | 17.09 | 5.11 |
| Sodium (meq/liter) | 152.99 | 53.58 | 158.76 |
| Potassium (meq/liter) | 15.6 | 61.38 | 12.93 |
| Copper (meg/liter) | — | — | 10.0 |
| Zinc (meq/liter) | — | — | 0.275 (0.06–0.52) |
| Chloride (meq/liter) | 41.6 | 37.2 | 37.2 |
| Uric acid (mg/100 ml) | 40.5 (10.1–88.2) | — | — |
| Urea (mg/100 ml) | 9.1 (1.8–22.5) | — | — |
| Protein (mg/100 ml) | 1.8–2.8 | — | — |

[a]Results are average values (range in parentheses) expressed in mg/100 ml fluid or cells unless otherwise stated. Abstracted from detailed table of Lake (1971).

tubules. Some of the physical and chemical characteristics are presented in Table 17–1 from a compilation by Lake (1971).

Semen from the cock is usually white and opaque but may be clear and watery, particularly when the concentration of spermatozoa is low. The pH of cock semen is 7.0–7.6 depending on the amount of transparent fluid present in semen (Lake 1971).

## Number of Spermatozoa and Amount of Semen Produced

The volume of semen of a given ejaculation has been measured by a number of workers; some of the variation reported may be attributable to the methods of collection. Some have collected the semen from the cloaca of the hen after a normal mating, and some have collected it directly from the male, obtaining it artificially by massaging the abdomen after the technique of Burrows and Quinn (1937).

Parker (1949), who reviewed the subject, compiled the results of a number of investigators, including his own. The volumes reported (averages) range from 0.11 ml (collected from the cloaca of the hen) to 1 ml (collected from the male directly). Spermatozoa per cubic millimeter of semen average about 3.5 million. In a given ejaculate (0.5 to 1 ml volume), therefore, the number of spermatozoa ranges from 1.7 to 3.5 billion. Lake (1957) reported averages of 7 billion and a maximum of 8.2 billion in Brown Leghorn cocks.

Marini and Goodman (1969) reported great differences in SZ concentration and volumes of semen of chickens selected and bred for high and

slow growth rates. These numbers ranged from 4.9 million SZ per cubic millimeter in the slow growing strain to 2.3 million in the rapid growth line. There were also differences in the numbers of abnormal SZ between the strains.

Turkeys produce less semen than chickens, but the concentration of spermatozoa (SZ) is much greater. The amounts average about 0.2 ml per collection, and the concentration varies from 6.2 to 7 million per cubic millimeter, depending on breed (McCartney and Brown, 1959). The amount of semen obtained from *Phasianus colchicus* (pheasant) is 0.1 ml or less (Shaklee and Knox, 1954).

## FACTORS AFFECTING FERTILITY IN THE MALE

A minimum of 100 million spermatozoa must be inseminated to obtain optimum fertility according to Parker et al. (1942). However, Weakley and Shaffner (1952) reported little change in fertility when semen was diluted 1:10, and each insemination supplied less than 100 million sperm; optimum fertility was obtained by Nishiyama et al. (1968) with 70 million.

**Maturing of spermatozoa.** Munro (1938) demonstrated that spermatozoa of the chicken must be ripened or matured in the epididymis before they are capable of fertilization. Spermatozoa taken directly from the testes do not fertilize ova, and those taken from the epididymis fertilized only 13% of the females inseminated. When semen was taken from the lower vas deferens, 74% of the inseminat-

336 ed females laid fertile eggs. The duration of the ripening period apparently is not long, because it was shown that spermatozoa could pass from the testes through the vas deferens to the cloaca within 24 hr.

**Number of matings.** The number of matings or ejaculations per day influences the volume of semen produced and the concentration of spermatozoa. Both decrease with the frequency of mating, and after three or four successive ejaculations the concentration of spermatozoa is very low in some males (Parker *et al.,* 1940).

The number of times a male chicken mates may range from 25 to 41 per day according to early workers, but more recent work by Guhl (1951) suggests that males may mate still more frequently than this. Guhl made studies on individual males placed in pens with from 30 to 40 females, where mating behavior was observed for 21 min/day for periods as long as 84 days. The observations were made during the first 21 min that the males were introduced to the females. The actual observation time was 29 hr and 24 min. The number of treadings for three males during this period were 410, 788, and 853, or 13.9, 26.7, and 29.0 matings per hour, respectively. It was shown, however, that when males are first introduced into a pen, they mate most frequently during the first 3–6 min. Guhl *et al.* (1945) and Guhl and Warren (1946) demonstrated that the social order or "peck order" of the hens to which males are introduced affects their mating behavior. Males, regardless of their social standing, tend to mate most frequently not with the highest or lowest ranking hens, but with the "middle-class" hens. When three or more males are introduced together in a pen of females, both the frequency of matings and the fertility are highest for the top-ranking male. The lowest ranking male mates with few females because of interference from the higher ranking males.

The number of White Leghorn females to which one male may mate and still obtain optimum fertility is approximately 15 (Brantas *et al.,* 1972). This ratio is narrower for heavy breeds.

**Light.** Natural daylight or artificial light initiates the production of semen in males by stimulating the release of gonadotropic hormones of the anterior pituitary (FSH and LH) (see also Chapters 15 and 16). FSH stimulates growth of seminiferous tubules and spermatogenesis, and LH stimulates the interstitial cells of testes (Leydig cells) to produce androgens.

Usually 12–14 hr of light are required to stimulate the growth and development of the testes maximally in young cockerels and most wild species. When 14 or more hours of light are combined with high ambient temperature, as is normally experienced in the summertime, fertility may decline because there is usually a decrease in sperm concentration caused mainly by the high temperature (Ingkasuwan and Ogasawara, 1966). Testes size and growth, however, although delayed by less than 12–14 hr of light (8 hr), eventually reach normal size and activity (Ingkasuwan and Ogasawara, 1966).

Similar results were reported by Siegel *et al.* (1969). Clark and Sarakoon (1967) have made a detailed study of the effects of different environmental temperatures on fertility.

*Wavelengths and intensity.* Red and orange lights have a greater stimulating effect on the pituitary and gonads, particularly testes, than do green and blue lights (Chapter 15). Light intensity within wide limits (2–50 lux) is not an important factor in gonad stimulation, but dim light may retard sexual development (Gilbert 1971 see also van Tienhoven and Schally, 1972; Lake, 1974; and Oishi and Lauber, 1973a).

Oishi and Lauber (1973a) studied the stimulating effects of different intensities and wavelengths on gonad size (testes) of Japanese quail under continuous illumination (24-hr light). The threshhold for incandescent light intensity to maintain maximal gonad size was between 1.6 and 15.7 $\mu$W/cm$^2$ for males with intact eyes and for those blinded. In intact birds both red (625 nm) and green (500 nm) were effective at low intensity (4.0 $\mu$W/cm$^2$ for red and 9.6 $\mu$W/cm$^2$ for green), but only red light was effective at much lower intensities. Blue light (450 nm) was not effective at either of the low intensities. In blinded birds only red light was effective at low intensity.

Orange-red radioluminescent paint (15 mg) placed beneath the skull immediately over the pineal body elicited a marked gonadal response, but green paint did not. After pinealectomy there was no response to red paint, suggesting that the pineal may be an auxiliary photoreceptor (see also Chapters 15 and 19) or a director of red light to the hypothalamus. The pineal and eyes may be removed, however, without affecting the main response to light (Oishi and Lauber, 1973b).

*Light and wild species.* In many wild species the reproductive system is alternately photosensitive or photorefractive to long days during the annual cycle (Meier and MacGregor, 1972; van Tienhoven and Planck, 1973). This is true of a number of passerine species, including sparrows, juncos, and starlings. The testes of these species regress spontaneously even when the initial effective stimulatory period is continued (van Tienhoven and Schally, 1972). The sensitive period usually begins in the winter and continues until after the breeding season in late summer or early fall. In birds in the temperate zone photorefractoriness usually lasts until late fall or winter when the photoperiod is not long enough to be stimulatory.

Some species, such as bobwhite quail, Japanese quail, wood pigeon, common pigeon, and weaver bird, are not refractory to light. These species respond when day length is sufficiently long. Many investigators believe that the mechanisms controlling synthesis and release of pituitary gonadotropins are involved in photorefractivity (see Farner and Follett, 1966), but others think gonad sensitivity is also involved (Lofts and Murton, 1973).

It is essential to distinguish between the function of light as a cue for synchronizing endogenous circadian rhythms and the function of light as a stimulus for the production of hormones by the pituitary, according to van Tienhoven and Schally (1972). Long photoperiods may stimulate the production of pituitary hormones. The occurrence and properties of circadian rhythms is another matter, (this has been reviewed by van Tienhoven and Schally, 1972). Evidence has been presented that indicates circadian rhythms in responsiveness to light in certain species.

**Other factors.** Other factors affecting the production of semen and fertility of the male and female are season, age, state of nutrition, and health (see Lorenz, 1959; Lake, 1974).

*Diurnal and seasonal variations.* There is a diurnal variation in the production of spermatozoa by the fowl, with the greatest spermatogenic activity at 3 a.m. according to Riley (1940) and at midnight according to Macartney (1942). However, Lake and Wood-Gush (1956) reported a diurnal rhythm in semen production of Brown Leghorns in Scotland in May and June with the greatest concentration of spermatozoa in the collections in the evenings at 17–18 hr.

Male chickens vary in their production of semen and fertility with season (Sturkie, 1965). The amount of semen and the number of spermatozoa increase from December through April and then decline, to reach a low in July and August in chickens. Fertility also declines in the summer.

*Age.* It is generally conceded that fertility declines in males and females in the second and third years of life.

*Enzymes and hormones.* There is evidence that a trypsin-like enzyme, which acts on the acrosome of avian SZ, is necessary for optimum fertility (Palmer and Howarth, 1973). Poly-α-L-glutamic acid has been isolated from the oviduct of the laying female and it extends the life of SZ *in vitro* (Harrison and Heald, 1966). Oxytocin added to semen decreased the motility of SZ and decreased fertility, and injection of oxytocin also decreased fertility (Hughes and Parker, 1970); injections of oxytocin and arginine vasopressin to laying hens also decreased fertility (Hughes and Parker, 1972).

*Behavior.* Whether or not males are aggressive or not has little effect on semen production and quality (Crawford and Proudfoot, 1967). Males that were housed singly in cages produced the most semen and when two males were housed together semen production was least.

**Storage of semen.** Avian semen retains its fertilizing capacity *in vivo* for as long as 35 days in chickens and longer in turkeys. Attempts to store semen *in vitro* without impairing fertility have generally been unsuccessful. Semen can be quick frozen and then thawed immediately without reducing motility but when stored for longer periods fertility is impaired.

Storage at 0°–5° C for 4 hr reduced motility of fresh sperm considerably, but when the sperm were diluted with hypertonic fructose solution, motility after cold storage was good (Tanaka and Okamoto, 1966). Tanaka and Wilcox (1966) have also studied the effects of different hypertonic solutions on sperm motility. Diluted chicken semen was cooled with liquid nitrogen at cooling rates from 1° to 6.7°C/min, from 30°C until frozen, and was stored for 12 days in liquid nitrogen. Highest fertility (77%) was obtained in semen in a special diluent that was cooled at 6°C/min (Harris, 1968). The reason for the differences in the effects of storage of avian and mammalian semen is not known and is still being sought. One of the major differences in the composition of avian and bull semen is the high concentration of glutamate in avian semen (see earlier section). It has been reported that a diluent containing a high concentration of glutamate increased the fertilizing capacity of chicken semen to some extent (van Tienhoven, 1960). Storage of semen for 48 hr decreased motility and fertility of SZ, but the duration of fertility even more. Storage decreased aminopeptidases, fumarase, aconitase, and glutamic oxaloacetic transaminase activity of SZ. There was an increase in lactic dehydrogenase and in aldolase activity (Buckland, 1971).

## Genetic Differences

There is considerable variation in fertility of

338

different breeds and strains of chickens. The lower than average fertility reported in White Wyandotte chickens is well known (Buckland and Hawes, 1968).

Fertility in natural matings of White Plymouth Rocks was higher than in Cornish chickens and the difference was inherited (Soller *et al.,* 1965a) but it was not attributable to amount of semen produced and motility. The difference disappeared after artificial insemination. Likewise, Parker (1965) reported that fertility from natural matings was not related to amount of semen produced, which averaged 1.43 ml per male for the high semen producers and 0.63 ml for the low producers.

Siegel (1963) reported heritability estimates on semen concentration, semen volume, and motility in an unselected line of chickens as 0.01, 0.14, and 0.29, respectively. Soller *et al.* (1965b), in a line of chickens selected for the semen characteristics shown above, reported heritability values of 0.79, 0.78, and 0.83 for the same three characteristics, respectively.

Marina and Goodman (1969) reported highly significant differences in amount of semen and concentration of SZ between lines of chickens selected for rapid and slow growth rates, and the differences were highly heritable.

### Fertility and Time of Mating or Insemination

A number of workers have studied the relation of time of mating or artificial insemination to fertility (see review by Parker, 1939; Johnson and Parker, 1970). Most investigators reported higher fertility if inseminations occurred in the afternoon, when a soft-shelled egg was usually in the uterus, and lowest when a hard-shelled egg was present; however Parker (1950) and others found little difference in fertility between these groups. Johnson and Parker (1970) again found highest fertility with afternoon inseminations when a soft-shelled egg was present but they reported that factors other than the presence of a hard or soft shell are also involved. Their results indicate that hens inseminated 4 hr before laying (hard shell) or 1 hr after laying showed poor fertility.

Maximum fertility in chickens is usually obtained 2 or 3 days after matings. Good fertility is obtained as long as 5 or 6 days after the last matings, and then declines rapidly, but a few fertile eggs may be obtained as late as 35 days after the last mating. Seventy-two hours after the last mating, however, spermatozoa are found only in the infun-

dibulum, according to Van Drimmelen (1945, 1951). In turkeys high fertility is obtained 20 days after insemination; it then decreases slowly with some fertile eggs obtained 10 weeks after insemination (Lorenz, 1959). Spermatozoa are stored in the infundibulum and uterovaginal glands. Lorenz *et al.* (1967), Van Krey *et al.* (1966), and Lorenz and Ogasawara (1968) have shown that when spermatozoa are introduced into the infundibular region or the magnum of the oviduct (where sperm storage glands are located) fertility is prolonged, but there was a high incidence of early embryonic mortality as compared to results when insemination was in the uterovaginal region. Likewise, Schindler and Hurwitz (1966) demonstrated that when spermatozoa were injected into different sites of oviduct, their motility was maintained in all sites for at least 4 hr. The ultrastructure of the uterovaginal glands of the hen has been studied by Burke *et al.* (1972).

### Artificial Insemination

Burrows and Quinn (1937) and Parker (1939) developed a technique for obtaining semen artificially from the male. By this technique it is possible to dilute semen as much as ten times and inseminate a large number of females. To ensure good fertility, inseminations should be made every fourth or fifth day in the chicken. Turkey hens remain fertile after matings much longer than do chickens (as long as 30 days). The duration of fertility and life of a spermatozoon in the body of the female is influenced by sperm nests in the infundibulum and uterovaginal glands.

In a more recent review of the subject, Lorenz (1959) stated that the most satisfactory results (fertility) had been obtained with freshly collected and undiluted semen at 0.05 ml per insemination at 5- to 7-day intervals for chickens and 0.025 ml at 3-week intervals for turkeys. Difficulty, however, is often experienced in successfully inseminating such small quantities. For further details of insemination of turkeys, see Nestor and Brown (1968) and Ogasawara and Rooney (1966).

### Sterility

Ingestion of mestranol by quails induced irreversible sterility in females and sterilized many males (Wentworth, 1970). Abnormal spermatozoa may cause sterility, but apparently very few males produce sufficient numbers of abnormal spermatozoa to produce this effect.

# FERTILIZATION AND EARLY EMBRYONIC DEVELOPMENT

## Site of Fertilization

It was believed for many years that fertilization occurred in birds in the ovary before ovulation. However, Olsen and Neher (1948) showed conclusively that fertilization occurs after ovulation and before the egg reaches the magnum. They removed mature ovarian follicles from the ovaries of sterile nonmated hens just before ovulation. These follicles then ovulated *in vitro* and then were transferred to the oviducts of fertile mated hens. Eighty-two percent of these eggs laid subsequently were fertile. It was also shown by these workers that ova can be fertilized by placing fresh semen in the infundibulum of the oviduct or in the abdominal cavity.

## Transport of Spermatoza in the Oviduct

The time elapsing between copulation and the time the first fertile egg is obtained in chickens may be as low as 19.5 hr, according to one report. If this figure is correct, it means that the egg may be fertilized while it is in the magnum or isthmus (see Parker, 1949).

Mimura (1939) studied the movement of spermatozoa through the oviduct of the fowl and showed that when spermatozoa were introduced into the uterus, they reached the upper part of the oviduct or ovary within as short a time as 26 min. Similar results were obtained by Allen and Grigg (1957). Spermatozoa that were introduced into the vagina of turkey hens reached the infundibulum within 15 min (Howarth, 1971).

## Maturation, Cleavage, and Gastrulation

The growth and development of the fertilized ovum have been studied in detail in the chicken (Olsen, 1942). The ovum in the chicken is still attached to the ovary when the first maturation division and the formation of the first polar body occur. Even the spindle for the second maturation division is formed before ovulation occurs. After ovulation, the egg is fertilized, usually within 15 min. The sperm then penetrates the ova and the second polar body is extruded, and there is fusion of the male and female pronuclei. Approximately 5 hr after ovulation, as the egg enters the isthmus, the first cleavage division takes place. The second division occurs 20 min later. The egg has cleaved to the 4- or 8-cell stage while the egg is still in the isthmus. Four hours after the egg has entered the uter-

us the blastodisc has grown from the 16-cell stage to approximately the 256-cell stage.

Gastrulation occurs in the pigeon about 5–7 hr before the egg is laid. The stage of development of newly laid eggs has been extensively studied in chickens. It has been previously assumed that the chicken egg has reached the gastrula stage by the time it is laid, but this is not necessarily the case (see Sturkie, 1965). Changes in the incubation temperature in the critical or early cleavage stages of the embryo produce abnormalities of development and the incidence of duplications or twinning is increased (Sturkie, 1946).

## Parthenogenesis

Parthenogenesis occurs in the domestic turkey. Olson (1960) reviewed much of his older work and presented new data on turkeys. His results showed that 32.4% of infertile turkey eggs normally underwent parthenogenesis, but the embryos died very early in most of these eggs. A number of parthenogenetic eggs have been hatched and a few of these have survived to sexual maturity. All offspring have been males with the diploid number of chromosomes and some few have sired offspring. The incidence of the parthenogenesis can be increased by inoculation of the hens with Rous sarcoma virus (Olsen, 1961) and by fowl pox virus (Olsen and Buss, 1967). In later work Olsen (1972) recorded the incidence of parthenogenesis in different strains of turkeys, which reached the highest level at 49%.

# MALE SEX HORMONES

## Testicular Hormones

The chief sex hormones of the testes are androgens (see Figure 16–9). In birds, as in mammals, testosterone appears to be the most important androgen.

**Biosynthesis and sites of production.** Early literature on the biosynthesis of androgens by the avian testes has been reviewed by Lake and Furr (1971). There are two important pathways for the synthesis of testosterone (Figure 17–6). All intermediate steroids in the two pathways have been shown to be produced by the testes of chickens and other birds (Lake and Furr, 1971; Nakamura and Tanabe, 1972; Galli *et al.*, 1973; Guichard *et al.*, 1973a, b). Important steroid-metabolizing enzymes have been identified by chemical or histochemical means (Lake and Furr, 1971; Nakamura and Tan-

340

**17–6** Important pathways of androgen biosynthesis in birds.

abe, 1972; Lofts and Murton, 1973). According to Nakamura and Tanabe (1972), the testes of the adult chicken can utilize pathways 1 and 2 to synthesize testosterone. Enzyme activities related to testosterone formation from pregnenolone (both pathways) were found in the microsomal fraction of the testes homogenates. Other *in vitro* studies in chickens (Guichard *et al.*, 1973a) and *Coturnix coturnix japonica* (Japanese quail; Guichard *et al.*, 1973b) show that the embryonic gonad is able to synthesize testosterone most efficiently by the dehydroepiandrosterone (DHEA) pathway.

The newly differentiated testes of the chicken embryo can synthesize testosterone by the seventh day of life (Guichard *et al.*, 1973a; Galli and Wassermann, 1973). In pre- and postembryonic development of the testes, the ratios of the metabolites formed in testosterone synthesis shift with increasing age. In the mammal, such changes in androgen synthesis are associated with maturation of the enzyme systems (Lindner, 1961).

The testes produce the female sex hormones, progesterone and estrogens, but the evidence that these hormones enter the circulating blood is uncertain. Fraps *et al.* (1949) reported the presence of progesterone in the blood of the male chicken, but the bioassay used in their experiments is now known to detect other steroids. The embryonic testes of the chicken (Guichard *et al.*, 1973a) and quail (Scheib *et al.*, 1974) can synthesize small quantities of estrone and estradiol when incubated *in vitro*. High levels of estrone, estradiol, and estriol were found by Höhn and Cheng (1967) and Hohn (1970) in the testes of adult phalaropes and other birds, but the specificity of the procedures used to isolate and identify the estrogens is open to question (Lake and Furr, 1971).

The interstitial Leydig cell is the most probable site of androgen production (see reviews by Lake and Furr, 1971; Lofts and Murton, 1973). Leydig cells of the avian testes have been shown to contain $\Delta^5$-3$\beta$-hydroxysteroid dehydrogenase, the enzyme that converts pregnenolone to progesterone and DHEA to androstenedione (Woods and Domm, 1966). In the Japanese quail, Nicholls and Graham (1972) have shown that the ultrastructure of the Leydig cell undergoes metamorphosis from the nonsecretory into the secretory state within 3 days after exposure to stimulatory light. The possibility that the secretory activity of the Leydig cells is stimulated by LH, which is known to regulate the secretion of androgen, is suggested by the observation of Follett *et al.* (1972) that plasma LH levels in the quail increase significantly within 4 days after photostimulation. Studies in the Pekin duck (Garnier and Attal, 1970; Garnier, 1971) and starling (Temple, 1974) show that the increase in the size of the Leydig cells at the beginning of the annual reproductive cycle is paralleled by an increase in plasma levels of testosterone.

The sertoli cells and the epithelial lining of the excurrent ducts of the testes also contain androgen-metabolizing enzymes (Lofts and Bern, 1972; Lofts and Murton, 1973; Tingari, 1973). There are two possible explanations for the occurrence of steroid synthesis in these tissues: (1) the cells have endocrine function in that they produce and secrete androgens to be used by some target tissue (such as the spermatozoa); (2) the sertoli cells and excurrent ducts are target tissues in which metabolism is a function of steroid utilization. Steroid conversion by target tissues is well known in vertebrates. The uropygial gland of the chicken, which is androgen dependent, has been shown to convert progesterone to testosterone (Nugara and Edwards, 1970).

**Androgen concentrations in testes and blood.** Limitations in research attempting to correlate androgen levels in the testes or blood with reproductive function have been discussed by Lake and Furr (1971). The available data on androgen levels in the testes have been obtained using techniques of questionable specificity (Lake and Furr, 1971).

Levels of testosterone found in the blood plasma of various male birds are summarized in Table 17-2. Rivarola *et al.* (1968) identified testosterone, androstenedione, and DHEA in the peripheral plasma of mature pigeons at levels of 15-98 ng, 62-378 ng, and 0-338 ng per 100 ml of plasma, respectively. The testosterone levels are within the same range as levels reported by Jallageas and Attal (1968) for the pigeon and quail. Other plasma testosterone values reported in Table 17-2 range from a low of 5 ng per 100 ml for the nonbreeding starling (Temple, 1974) to a high of 942 ng per 100 ml for the mature chicken (Schanbacher *et al.*, 1974). Garnier and Attal (1970) found testosterone levels as high as 1360 ng per 100 ml in the testicular vein plasma of the duck.

Variations in the blood levels of testosterone during the annual reproductive cycle of the male have been studied in several birds. In nonmigratory populations of starlings, Temple (1974) found plasma testosterone levels to reach peak values of 42 ng per 100 ml at the height of the breeding season and to decline to levels as low as 5 ng per 100 ml during the postbreeding period. Changes in the nuclear diameter of the Leydig cells and in seminal sac weight were strongly correlated with testosterone titers. Expressions of courtship and aggressive behavior corresponded with periods of high testosterone levels. In captive adult male red-winged blackbirds, Kerlan and Joffe (1974) observed that testosterone levels reached peak values at a point in the photosensitive stage of the testicular cycle when testes weight was only about one-fourth maximum. In the regressive phase, testosterone levels remained uniformly low over a range of gonadal weights of 7.0-800 mg. Low levels of testosterone continued through the photorefractory phase of the cycle. The results were interpreted to mean that the decline in plasma testosterone precedes testicular regression. This is in agreement with studies in the Pekin duck, in which decreases in testosterone levels of both peripheral plasma (Jallageas and Assenmacher, 1974; Garnier, 1971) and testicular vein plasma (Garnier and Attal, 1970) decline prior to gonadal regression.

*Table* 17–2 *Concentration of testosterone in the blood plasma of male birds*

| Bird | Reproductive state | Concentration of testosterone (ng/100 ml) | Reference |
|---|---|---|---|
| Chicken | Mature | 84–783 | Furr and Thomas (1970) |
| | Puberty | 118 | Schröcksnadel *et al.* (1971) |
| | Mature | 207–340 | Schröcksnadel *et al.* (1971) |
| | Mature | 714–942 | Schanbacher *et al.* (1974) |
| Quail | Photostimulated | 18–45 | Jallageas and Attal (1968) |
| Pigeon | Mature | 26–39 | Jallageas and Attal (1968) |
| | Mature | 15–98 | Rivarola *et al.* (1968) |
| Red-winged blackbird | Photosensitive[a] | 44–274 | Kerlan and Jaffe (1974) |
| | Regressive | 49–110 | Kerlan and Jaffe (1974) |
| | Photorefractory | 73–103 | Kerlan and Jaffe (1974) |
| Starling | SI[b] | 5–12 | Temple (1974) |
| | SA | 32–42 | Temple (1974) |
| Duck | SA | 65–270 | Jallageas and Attal (1968) |
| | SI | 3–54 | Garnier (1971) |
| | SA | 126–201 | Garnier (1971) |
| | SI | 31–46 | Jallageas and Assenmacher (1974) |
| | SA | 201–376 | Jallageas and Assenmacher (1974) |
| | Molt | 6–21 | Jallageas and Assenmacher (1974) |
| | SI | 15–21 | Jallageas *et al.* (1974) |
| | SA | 376 | Jallageas *et al.* (1974) |
| | Photostimulated | 289 | Jallageas *et al.* (1974) |
| | SI | 250[c] | Garnier and Attal (1970) |
| | SA | 1360 | Garnier and Attal (1970) |

[a]Phase of annual cycle.

[b]SI, SA = Seasonally inactive, seasonally active phase of annual cycle.

[c]Level in testicular vein plasma; all other values in table are for peripheral plasma.

Jallageas and Assenmacher (1974) observed that during the refractory period that follows breeding in the duck (May–June) the decline in plasma testosterone levels is concomitant with a marked increase in the metabolic clearance rate of testosterone and a depression in the secretion rate of testosterone. Because the thyroid gland exhibits increased activity during the May–June refractory period, and because thyroxine injection resulted in lowered plasma testosterone in association with enhanced metabolic clearance of the hormone, the authors assumed that seasonal hyperthyroidism may play a role in testosterone secretion and metabolism at the onset of the regressive phase of the sexual cycle. In a subsequent experiment, Jallageas *et al.* (1974) reported that the natural increase in day length led to increased testes size paralleled by increased secretion of LH and testosterone. However, during the May–June period, when maximum LH titers coincided with greatest testicular weight, plasma testosterone concentrations were low. Again, it was suggested that seasonal hyperthyroid-

ism might account for this peculiar endocrine situation.

Schanbacher *et al.* (1974) have shown that serum testosterone levels in the chicken exhibit diurnal fluctuation with testosterone titers significantly higher at night than during the daylight hours of a 14-hr light day. In contrast to reports by others, no diurnal changes were observed in spermatogenic activity of the testes as measured by uptake of radioactive thymidine.

### Secondary Sexual Characteristics

Secondary sexual characteristics that differentiate males and females, include differences in comb size, plumage color, structure of feathers, voice, temperament, and behavior. The gonadal hormones are responsible for most of these. Androgen produces comb growth in males and females. In the female, where the comb is smaller, androgen is produced by the medullary cells of the ovary (Sturkie, 1965; Lofts and Murton, 1973).

The hackle and saddle feathers of the male chicken are elongated and tapering in form, and those of the female are shorter and more blunt. This difference is caused not by androgen but by estrogen. Castrated males (capons) and females (Poulards) develop feathers resembling those of the cock in structure except that the feathers are longer (neutral-type plumage).

The response of hen-feathered breeds to sex hormones is different. Males of this breed have the same type of feather structure as females. Henny feathering is dominant over normal feathering. When hen-feathered males are castrated, their plumage reverts to the neutral type. The plumage of the castrated female of the henny breed also reverts to the male or neutral type, as does that of normal females. It has been demonstrated, by testicular grafts and hormone injections, that the gonads of the hen-feathered male produce androgen as do the gonads of normal males. The gene for henny feathering therefore acts directly on the feather follicle but requires androgen for its expression.

**Color changes in plumage and bill.** Some breeds and species of birds exhibit plumage dimorphism and some do not; the plumage color is controlled by genes and may be independent of gonadal hormones.

In many of the species in which plumage is influenced by gonadal hormones, the male plumage is more brilliantly colored than the female. The plumage of the castrate female Brown Leghorn chicken reverts to that of the male in color, but the plumage color of castrate males is unchanged. The difference in male and female plumage color is therefore a result of the action of estrogen. In the herring gull, the cock type of plumage depends on the action of androgens (Sturkie, 1965).

The species showing plumage dimorphism, such as chicken, duck, and red-winged blackbird, had a higher level of testosterone in the testes than ovaries, but in the phalarope, where the female has the dominant plumage, ovarian testosterone level exceeds that of the testes (Höhn and Cheng, 1967).

The color of the beak of the weaver finch and the sparrow is intensified when androgen is injected. In other species (e.g., the common starling) the bills of both sexes are black during the eclipse and bright orange-yellow during the breeding season. Castration in both sexes produces black bills and administration of androgen produces the yellow color (Witschi, 1961). The bill of the house sparrow turns black during the breeding season, apparently because of the action of androgen; castration in the male results in loss of pigmentation (Witschi, 1961). However, androgen does not in-

duce black pigmentation in sparrows in the winter (nonbreeding season), indicating the involvement of pituitary hormones. Androgen plus FSH produces a black bill (Lofts et al., 1973). For further details on the effects of gonadal hormones on plumage changes, see Lofts and Murton (1973).

**Comb growth and pituitary hormones.** The dramatic effect of androgen on comb growth has been demonstrated by a number of workers. Breneman (1939) injected day-old chicks with testosterone propionate and dihydroandrosterone (0.6–2.5 mg/day) over a period ranging from 5 to 10 days. The increase in comb size was tremendous, and some of the chicks began crowing as early as 7 days of age. Testis size was decreased. Kumaran and Turner (1949c) also demonstrated that treatment of the male with androgen decreased the size of the testes and inhibited spermatogenesis by depressing the output of pituitary FSH.

Zeller (1971) studied the effects of administering testosterone propionate (TP) and dihydrotesterone (DHT) to young cockerels (16 days of age) for 9 days on comb growth, pituitary weight, and pituitary FSH activity. Both stimulated comb growth but only TP depressed testes weight and total pituitary gonadotropin content. Both androgens, however, increased the FSH level in the pituitaries of capons (64 days old). Boris et al. (1970) studied the effects of six antiandrogens on comb growth stimulated by testosterone. Based on maximum inhibitions observed, relative potencies of antiandrogens were as follows: cyproterone acetate > RO 5-25377 methyl; B-nortestosterone > RO 2-72397 > cyproterone (free OH). α-Norprogesterone was inactive.

In wild species the effects of androgen on output of FSH and testicular regression is controversial (Lofts and Murton, 1973). Some have reported suppression of FSH and others have not. Much of the controversy may be attributed to the fact that androgens have been administered without cognizance being taken of the precise reproductive condition at the time of administration. If androgen is administered to birds starting testicular growth, there may be retardation of spermatogenesis but if it is administered after spermatogensis is well advanced, gonad size and development may be accelerated (see also Stetson and Erickson, 1971).

The comb of the White Leghorn is 15 times as sensitive to androgen as are the combs of Rhode Island Reds and Barred Plymouth Rocks. Because of the variation in the response of comb growth in different breeds (Dorfman and Dorfman, 1948a, b) and even in strains within a breed (Campos and Shaffner, 1952) to androgens, the use of the chick

344 comb as an assay technique is subject to considerable error. The route of administration of androgen also influences the response. Munson and Sheps (1958) reviewed much of the earlier work on assays of androgen and reported on an improved method of direct application of androgen to the chick's comb. Their experiments involved 162 assays and 20,000 chicks. They found that log (comb weight/body weight) yielded a linear log dose–response curve and minimized the variance.

The response of comb growth to androgen is influenced by exercise (Wong, et al., 1954), which reduces the response to androgen. It has long been observed that normal males kept confined have larger combs than males allowed to run free. Exercise is a factor here, but light and temperature may also be involved. More recent and better controlled experiments (Wong and Hawthorne, 1954) rules out light as a factor, but increased environmental temperature increased the comb response to androgen.

**Castration in the male.** Castration in the male (caponization) produces capons that grow more slowly and put on more fat than the uncastrated male, particularly after 5 months of age. Androgen tends to increase the amount of hemoglobin and the number of erythrocytes in the blood (see Chapter 3). The rate of metabolism in capons is about 13.5% lower than in cocks, according to Mitchell *et al.* (1927).

The anabolic effects of androgen are discussed in Chapter 12. Castration usually produces increased gonadotrophic potency of the pituitaries (Stetson and Erickson, 1971) of male sparrows. In intact birds and in those with testicular regeneration, administration of testosterone (TP) reduced the levels of pituitary gonadotrophins.

## Androgens and Sexual Behavior

Early evidence that androgen injections induce mating behavior was reviewed by Parkes and Emmens (1944). Beach and Inmou (1965) and Kannanheril and Domm (1968) showed that mating behavior in the male quail is terminated by castration and restored by androgen injection. Implantation of crystalline testosterone into the hypothalamic–preoptic area of the brain initiates copulatory behavior in the immature male chicken (Gardner and Fisher, 1968) and in adult cocks and capons (Barfield, 1969). This area of the brain influenced copulatory behavior, but not courtship or aggressive behavior. The preoptic brain of the chick (Meyer, 1973), adult duck (Gogan, 1968), and adult ring dove (Zigmond *et al.*, 1972) has been shown to

selectively take up and retain radioactive testosterone. These observations support the possibility that rising levels of androgen at the onset of sexual maturity act directly on the brain to induce male sexual behavior.

Other studies indicate that the control of mating behavior is not simply a matter of the right level of testosterone. Andrew (1966) found that 2-day-old chicks maintained in isolation from hatching time exhibited male copulatory behavior when an experimenter's hand, with fingers extended, was thrust toward the bird. Testosterone injection did not enforce the behavior. As in sexually mature males, one performance of complete copulation delayed further copulation for some time. Andrew's findings that tactile stimulation of the ventral body surface tends to reinforce future mountings have been repeated and extended by Horridge (1970). Beer (1973) cites other experiments in which social or psychologic experience is able to partly or fully substitute for sex hormone control of other aspects of male reproductive behavior in birds.

Glick and associates (Glick, 1961; Wilson and Glick, 1970) showed that administration of testosterone to chicken embryos prior to the thirteenth day of incubation markedly interfered with the development of normal male sexual behavior. To determine whether testosterone treatment of the embryos chemically altered hypothalamic centers controlling male sexual behavior, Haynes and Glick (1974) compared the effects of hypothalamic lesions on the mating behavior; however, lesions did not alter mating behavior in males subjected to testosterone treatment as embryos. These findings indicate that exposure of embryos to androgen during a critical period either chemically produces lesions in hypothalamic centers or impairs maturation of the centers.

## REFERENCES

Allen, T. E., and G. W. Grigg. (1957). Sperm transport in the fowl. *Austral. J. Agri. Res., 8,* 788.

Andrew, R. J. (1966). Precocious adult behavior in the young chick. *Anim. Behav., 14,* 485.

Barfield, R. J. (1969). Activation of copulatory behavior by androgen implanted into the preoptic area of the male fowl. *Hormone Behav., 1,* 37.

Beach, F. A., and N. G. Inmou. (1965). Effects of castration and androgen replacement on mating in male quail. *Proc. Natl. Acad. Sci. U.S., 54,* 1426.

Beer, C. G. (1973). Behavioral components in the reproductive biology of birds. In "Breeding Biology of Birds" (D. S. Farner, Ed.). Washington, D.C.: National Academy of Sciences.

Blivaiss, B. B. (1947). Interrelationships of thyroid and gonad in the development of plumage and other sex characters in Brown Leghorn roosters. *Physiol. Zool., 20,* 67.

Boris, A., D. C. Cox, & J. F. Hurley. (1970). Comparison of the effects of six antiandrogens on chick comb stimulation by testosterone. *Proc. Soc. Exp. Biol. Med., 134,* 985.

Brantas, G. C., H. G. Dennert, and A. L. Dennert-Distelbrink. (1972). The influence of the number of cocks on the conception rate among White Leghorns. *Arch. Geflügel K., 36,* 16.

Breneman, W. R. (1939). Effect of androgens on the chick. *Proc. 7th Worlds Poultry Cong.,* 91.

Buckland, R. B. (1971) The activity of six enzymes of chicken seminal plasma and spermatozoa. *Poultry Sci., 50,* 1724.

Buckland, R. B., and R. O. Hawes. (1968). Comb type and reproduction in the male fowl. Semen characteristics and testes structure. *Poultry Sci., 47,* 704.

Burke, W. H., F. X. Ogasawara, and C. L. Fuqua. (1972). A study of the ultrastructure of the utero-vaginal sperm-storage glands of the hen, in relation to a mechanism for the release of spermatozoa. *J. Reprod. Fert., 29,* 29.

Burrows, W. H. and J. P. Quinn. (1937). The collection of spermatozoa from the domestic fowl and turkey. *Poultry Sci., 16,* 19.

Campos, A. C., and C. S. Shaffner. (1952). The genetic control of chick comb and oviduct response. *Poultry Sci., 20,* 387.

Clark, C. E., and Sarakoon, K. (1967). Influence of ambient temperature on reproductive traits of male and female chickens. *Poultry Sci., 46,* 1093.

Clermont, Y. (1958). Structure de l'epithelium seminal et mode de renouvellement des spermatogonies chez le canard. *Arch. Anat. Microscop. Morphol. Exp., 47,* 47.

Crawford, R. D., and F. G. Proudfoot. (1967). The effects of cage housing and aggressiveness of chicken males on semen quality. *Poultry Sci., 66,* 672.

Dorfman, R. I., and A. S. Dorfman. (1948a). Studies on the bioassay of hormones: The assay of testosterone propionate and androsterone by a chick comb inunction method. *Endocrinology, 42,* 1.

Dorfman, R. I., and A. S. Dorfman. (1948b). Studies on the bioassay of hormones: The relative reactivity of the comb of various breeds of chicks to androgen. *Endocrinology, 42,* 7.

Follett, B. K., C. G. Scanes, and T. J. Nicholls. (1972). The chemistry and physiology of the avian gonadotrophins. In "Hormones Glycoproteiques Hypophysaires." Paris: Colloque Inserm. pp. 193.

Farner, D. S., and B. K. Follett. (1966). Light and other environmental factors affecting avian reproduction. *J. Animal Sci., 25,* 90.

Fraps, R. M., C. W. Hooker, and T. R. Forbes. (1949). Progesterone in blood plasma of cocks and nonovulating hens. *Science, 109,* 493.

Furr, B. J. A., and B. S. Thomas. (1970). Estimation of testosterone in plasma of domestic fowl. *J. Endocrinol., 48 (Proc. Soc. Endoc. 42).*

Galli, F. E., and G. F. Wassermann. (1973). Steroid biosynthesis by gonads of 7- and 10-day-old chick embryos. *Gen. Comp. Endocrinol., 21,* 77.

Galli, F. E., O. Irusta, and G. F. Wassermann. (1973). Androgen production by testes of Gallus domesticus during postembryonic development. *Gen. Comp. Endocrinol., 21,* 262.

Gardner, J. E., and A. E. Fisher. (1968). Induction of mating in male chicks following preoptic implantation of androgen. *Physiol. Behav., 3,* 709.

Garnier, D. H. (1971). Variations de la testosterone du plasma peripherique chez le Canard Pekin au cours du cycle annuel. *Compt. Rend., Series D., 272,* 1665.

Garnier, D. H., and J. Attal. (1970). Variations de la testosterone du plasma testiculaire et des cellules interstitielles chez le Canard Pekin au cours du cycle annuel. *Compt. Rend. Acad. Sci. Paris, 270,* 2472.

Gilbert, A. B. (1971). The ovary: In "Physiology and Biochemistry of the Fowl," Vol. 3. (D. J. Bell and B. M. Freeman, Eds.). London and New York: Academic Press, Ch. 50.

Glick, B. (1961). The reproductive performance of birds hatched from eggs dipped in male hormone solutions. *Poultry Sci., 40,* 1408.

Gogan, F. (1968). Hypothalamic sensitivity to testosterone in the duck. *Gen. Comp. Endocrinol., 11,* 316.

Grigg, G. W. (1951). The morphology of fowl spermatozoa. *Proc. 9th World's Poultry Cong., 3,* 142.

Guhl, A. M. (1951). Measurable differences in mating behavior of cocks. *Poultry Sci., 30,* 687.

Guhl, A. M., and D. C. Warren. (1946). Number of offspring sired by cockerels related to social dominance in chickens. *Poultry Sci., 25,* 460.

Guhl, A. M., N. E. Collias, and W. C. Allee. (1945). Mating behavior and the social hierarchy in small flocks of White Leghorns. *Physiol. Zool., 18,* 365.

Guichard, A., L. Cedard, and K. Haffen. (1973a). Aspect comparatif de la synthese de steroides sexuels par les gonades embryonnaires de Poulet a differents stades du development. *Gen. Comp. Endocrinol., 20,* 16.

Guichard, A. L. L. Cedard, K. Haffen, and D. Scheib. (1973b). Metabolisme de la pregnenolone et de la progesterone radioactives par les gonades embryonnaires de caille *(Coturnix coturnix japonica)* en culture organotypiques. *Gen. Comp. Endocrinol., 21,* 478.

Harris, G. C., Jr. (1968). Fertility of chickens inseminated intraperitoneally with semen preserved in liquid nitrogen. *Poultry Sci., 47,* 384.

Harris, G. C., Jr., R. J. Thurston, and J. Cundall. (1973). Changes in the ultrastructure of the fowl spermatozoon due to rapid freeze thaw. *J. Reprod. Fert., 34,* 389.

Harrison, D. G., and P. J. Heald. (1966). The isolation of poly a L glutamic acid from the oviduct of domestic fowl. *Proc. Roy. Soc. London, Series B, 166,* 341.

Haynes, R. L., and B. Glick. (1974). Hypothalamic control of sexual behavior in the chicken. *Poultry Sci., 53,* 27.

Hohn, E. O. (1970). Gonadal hormone concentration in northern phalaropes in relation to nuptial plumage. *Can. J. Zool., 48,* 400.

Hohn, E. O., and S. C. Cheng. (1967). Gonadal hormones in Wilson's phalarope and other birds in relation to plumage and sex behavior. *Gen. Comp. Endocrinol., 8,* 1.

Horridge, P. A. S. (1970). The development of copulatory and fighting behavior in the domestic chick. Ph. D. dissertation, University of Sussex, England.

Howarth, B., Jr. (1971). Transport of spermatozoa in the reproductive tract of turkey hens. *Poultry Sci., 50,* 84.

Hughes, B. L., and J. E. Parker. (1970). The effect of oxytocin on fertility in female chickens and on sperm motility. *Poultry Sci., 49,* 810.

Hughes, B. L., and J. E. Parker. (1972). Fertility in female chickens as affected by injection of oxytocin and arginine vasopressin near the time of insemination. *Poultry Sci., 51,* 808.

Ingkasuwan, P., and Ogasawara, F. X. (1966). The effect of light and temperature and their interaction on the semen production of White Leghorn males. *Poultry Sci., 45,* 1195.

Jallageas, M., and I. Assenmacher. (1974). Thyroid gonadal interactions in the male domestic duck in relationship with sexual cycles. *Gen. Comp. Endocrinol., 22,* 13.

Jallageas, M., and J. Attal. (1968). Dosage par chromatographe en phas gazeuse de la testosterone plasmatique no corjugee chez le canard, la caille, le pigeon. *Compt. Rend. Acad. Sci. Paris, 267,* 341.

Jallageas, M., I. Assenmacher, and B. K. Follett. (1974). Testosterone secretion and plasma luteinizing hormone concentration during sexual cycle in the pekin duck and after thyroxine treatment. *Gen. Comp. Endocrinol., 23,* 472.

Johnson, O. W. (1966). Quantitative features of spermatogenesis in the mallard duck. *Auk, 83,* 233.

Johnston, N. P., and J. E. Parker. (1970). The effect of time of oviposition in relation to insemination of fertility of chicken eggs. *Poultry Sci., 49,* 325.

Jones, P. and H. Jackson. (1973). Estimation of duration of spermatogenesis in Japanese quail using antispermatogonial chemicals. *J. Reprod. Fert., 31,* 319.

Kannanheril, J. V., and L. V. Domm. (1968). The influence of gonadectomy on sexual characters in the Japanese quail. *J. Morphol., 126,* 395.

Kerlan, J. T., and R. B. Jaffe. (1974). Plasma testosterone levels during the testicular cycle of the red-winged blackbird *(Agelaius phoeniceus). Gen. Comp. Endocrinol., 22,* 428.

Kumaran, J. D. S., and C. W. Turner. (1949a). The normal development of the testes in the White Plymouth Rock. *Poultry Sci., 28,* 511.

346

Kumaran, J. D. S., and C. W. Turner. (1949b). The endocrinology of spermatogenesis in birds. II: The effect of androgens. *Poultry Sci.*, 28, 739.

Kumaran, J. D. S., and C. W. Turner. (1949c). The endocrinology of spermatogenesis in birds. I: Effect of estrogen and androgen. *Poultry Sci.*, 28, 593.

Kumaran, J. D. S., and C. W. Turner. (1949d). Endocrine activity of the testes of the White Plymouth Rock. *Poultry Sci.*, 28, 636.

Lake, P. E. (1957). The male reproductive tract of the fowl. *J. Anat.*, 91, 116.

Lake, P. E. (1966). In "Advances in Reproduction Physiology," Vol. 1 (A. McLaren, Ed.). London: Loges Press, pp. 93.

Lake, P. E. (1971). The male in reproduction. In "Physiology and Biochemistry of Domestic Fowl" Vol. III (D. J. Bell and B. M. Freeman, Eds.). New York: Academic Press, Chapter 60.

Lake, P. E. (1974). Proc. 15th World's Poultry Cong., Symposium on Management and Physiology, Monday p.m. pp. 2–11.—held at New Orleans, La.

Lake, P. E., and J. A. Furr. (1971). The endocrine testis in reproduction. In "Physiology and Biochemistry of the Domestic Fowl," Vo. 3. (D. J. Bell and B. M. Freeman, Eds.). New York: Academic Press, Chapter 62.

Lake, P. E., and D. G. M. Wood-Gush. (1956). Diurnal rhythms in semen yields and mating behavior of the domestic cock. *Nature (London)*, 178, 853.

Lake, P. E., W. Smith, and D. Young. (1968). The ultrastructure of the ejaculated fowl spermatozoon. *J. Quart. Exp. Physiol.*, 53, 356.

Linder, H. R. (1961). Androgens and related compound in the spermatic vein blood of domestic animals. I. Neutral steroids secreted in the bull testes. *J. Endocrinol.*, 23, 139.

Lofts, B., and H. A. Bern. (1972). The functional morphology of steroidogenic tissues. In "Steroids in Non-mammalian Vertebrates" (D. R. Idler, Ed.). New York: Academic Press, p. 37.

Lofts, B., and A. J. Marshall. (1959). The post nuptial occurrence of progestins in the seminiferous tubules of birds. *J. Endocrinol.*, 19, 16.

Lofts, B., and R. K. Murton (1973). Reproduction in birds. In "Avian Biology," Vol. 3 (D. S. Farner and J. R. King, Eds.). New York: Academic Press, Chapter 1.

Lofts, B., R. K. Murton, and R. J. P. Thearle. (1973). The effects of testosterone propionate and gonadotropins on the bill pigmentation and testes of house sparrow. *Gen. Comp. Endocrinol.*, 21, 202.

Lorenz, F. W. (1959). Reproduction in domestic fowl: Physiology of the male. In "Reproduction in Domestic Animals" (H. H. Cole and P. T. Cupps, Eds.). New York: Academic Press, Chapter 2.

Lorenz, F. W., and F. X. Ogasawara. (1968). Distribution of spermatozoa in the oviduct and fertility in domestic birds. VI. The relations of sperm and embryo mortality with site of experimental insemination. *J. Reprod. Fert.*, 16, 445.

Lorenz, F. W., M. E. Reynolds, and A. B. Gilbert. (1967). Secretory activity of the sperm-host glands of the domestic fowl. *Physiologist*, 10, 236.

Macartney, E. L. (1942). Diurnal rhythm of mitotic activity in the seminiferous tubules of the domestic fowl. *Poultry Sci.*, 21, 130.

McCartney, M. G., and K. I. Brown. (1959). Spermatozoa concentration in three varieties of turkeys. *Poultry Sci.*, 38, 390.

Marini, P. J., and B. L. Goodman. (1969). Semen characteristics as influenced by selection for divergent growth rate in chickens. *Poultry Sci.*, 48, 859.

Marshall, A. J. (1961). Reproduction. In "Biology and Comparative Physiology of Birds" Vol. II. New York: Academic Press, Chapter 18.

Meier, A. H., and R. MacGregor III. (1972). Temporal organization in avian reproduction. *Am. Zool.*, 12, 257.

Meyer, D. C. (1973). Testosterone concentration in the male chick brain; An autoradiographic survey. *Science*, 180, 1381.

Mimura, H. (1939). On the mechanism of travel of spermatozoa through the oviduct in the domestic fowl, with special reference to artificial insemination (trans. by Moore and Byerly, 1942). Sonderabdruck aus Okajimas Folia Anatomica Japonica, Band. 17, Heft 5.

Mitchell, H. H., L. E. Card, and W. T. Haines. (1927). The effect of age, sex, and castration on the basal heat production of chickens. *J. Agri. Res.*, 34, 945.

Munro, S. S. (1938)) Functional changes in fowl sperm during their passage through the excurrent ducts of the male. *J. Exp. Zool.*, 79, 71.

Munson, P. L., and M. C. Sheps. (1958). An improved procedure for the biological assay of androgens by direct application to the combs of baby chicks. *Endocrinology*, 62, 173.

Nakamura, T., and Y. Tanabe. (1972) In vitro steroidogenesis by testes of the chicken (*Gallus domesticus*). *Gen. Comp. Endocrinol.*, 19, 432.

Nakamura, T., and Y. Tanabe. (1973). Dihydrotestosterone formation *in vitro in the epididymis of the domestic fowl*. *J. Endocrinol.*, 59, 651.

Nestor, K. E., and K. I. Brown. (1968). Method and frequency of artificial insemination and turkey fertility. *Poultry Sci.*, 47, 717.

Nicholls, T. J., and G. P. Graham. (1972). Observations on the ultrastructure and differentiation of Leydig cells in the testis of the Japanese quail (*Corturnix coturnix japonica*). *Biol. Reprod.*, 6, 179.

Nishiyama, H. (1955). Studies on the accessory reproductive organs in the cock. Reprinted from *J. Fac. Agri.*, *Kyushu Univ.*, *Japan*, 10 (3).

Nishiyama, N., K. Ogawa, and Y. Nakanishi. (1968) Studies on the artificial insemination in the domestic fowl. II. Effects of dilution of semen and insemination interval on the fertility of pullets. *Mem. Fac. Agri.*, *Kagoshima Univ.*, 6, 135.

Nugara, D., and H. M. Edwards. (1970). In vitro androgen metabolism by fat-deficient cockerel testis and uropygial gland. *J. Nutr.*, 100, 539.

Ogasawara, F. X., and W. F. Rooney. (1966). Artificial insemination and fertility in turkeys. *Brit. Poultry Sci.*, 7, 77.

Oishi, T., and J. K. Lauber. (1973a). II. Effects of intensity and wave length. *Am. J. Physiol.*, 225, 880.

Oishi, T. and J. K. Lauber. (1973b). Photoreception in the photosexual response of the quail. *Am. J. Physiol.*, 225, 155.

Olsen, M. W. (1942). Maturation, fertilization and early cleavage in the hen's egg. *J. Morphol.*, 70, 513.

Olsen, M. W. (1960). Nine year summary of parthenogenesis in turkeys. *Proc. Soc. Exp. Biol. Med.*, 105, 279.

Olsen, M. W. (1961). Rous sarcoma virus associated with parthenogenesis in turkey eggs. *Nature (London)*, 190, 191.

Olsen, M. W. (1972). Influence of turkey sires and dams on the level of parthenogenesis in eggs of their daughters. *Poultry Sci.*, 51, 2035.

Olsen, M. W., and Buss, E. G. (1967). Role of genetic factors and fowl pox virus in parthenogenesis in turkey eggs. *Genetics*, 56, 727.

Olsen, M. W., and B. H. Neher. (1948). The site of fertilization in the domestic fowl. *J. Exp. Zool.*, 109, 355.

Palmer, M. B., and B. Howarth, Jr. (1973). The requirement of a trypsin-like acrosomal enzyme for fertilization in the domestic fowl. *J. Reprod. Fert.*, 35, 7.

Parker, J. E. (1939). An avian seme collector. *Poultry Sci.*, 18, 455.

Parker, J. E. (1945). Relation of time of day of artificial insemination to fertility and hatchability of hen's eggs. *Poultry Sci.*, 24, 314.

Parker, J. E. (1949). Fertility and hatchability of chicken and turkey eggs. In "Fertility in Chickens and Turkeys" (L. W. Taylor, Ed.). New York: John Wiley & Sons, Inc., Chapter III.

Parker, J. E. (1950). The effect of restricted matings in flocks of New Hampshire chickens on fertility and hatchability of eggs. *Poultry Sci.*, 29, 268.

Parker, J. E. (1965). Semen production of cockerels as related to their subsequent capacity to fertilize hens in flock matings. *Poultry Sci.*, 44, 474.

Parker, J. E., F. F. McKenzie, and H. L. Kempster. (1940). Observations on the sexual behavior of New Hampshire males. *Poultry Sci.*, 19, 191.

Parker, J. E., F. F. McKenzie, and H. L. Kempster. (1942). Fertility in the male and domestic fowl. *Mo. Agri. Exp. Sta. Res. Bull., 347.*

Parkes, A. S. and C. W. Emmens. (1944). Effects of androgens and estrogens on birds. *Vit. Hormones, 2,* 361.

Riley, G. M. (1940). Diurnal variations in spermatogenic activity in the domestic fowl. *Poultry Sci., 19,* 360.

Rivarola, M. A., C. A. Snipes, and C. J. Migeon. (1968). Concentration of androgens in systemic plasma of rats, guinea pigs, salamanders and pigeons. *Endocrinology, 82* 115.

Romanoff, A. L. (1960). "The Avian Embryo." New York: The Macmillan Co.

Schanbacher, B. D., W. R. Gomes, and N. L. Van Demark. (1974). Diurnal rhythm in serum testosterone levels and thymidine uptake by testes in the domestic fowl. *J. Anim. Sci., 38,* 1245.

Schieb, D., K. Haffen, A. Guichard, and L. Cedard. (1974). Transformation de dehydroepiandrosterone-4-$^{14}$C par les gonades embryonnaires de la gaille Japanaise *(Coturnix coturnix japonica)* explanties *in vitro. Gen. Comp. Endocrinol., 21,* 262.

Schindler, H., and S. Hurwitz. (1966). The preservation of sperm motility in different regions of the hen oviduct *in vivo. Poultry Sci., 45,* 369.

Schröcksnadel, H., A. Bator, and J. Frick. (1971). Plasma testosterone level in cocks and hens. *Steroids, 18,* 359.

Shaklee, W. E., and C. W. Knox. (1954). Hybridization of the pheasant and fowl. *J. Hered., 45,* 183.

Siegel, P. B. (1963). Selection for breast angle at 8 weeks of age. *Poultry Sci., 42,* 437.

Siegel, H. S., P. B. Siegel, and W. L. Beane. (1969). Semen characteristics and fertility of meat type chickens given increasing daily photo-periods. *Poultry Sci., 48,* 1009.

Soller, M., H. Schindler, and S. B. Bornstein. (1965a). Semen characteristics, failure of insemination and fertility in Cornish and White Rock males. *Poultry Sci., 44,* 424.

Soller, M., H. Schindler, and S. B. Bornstein. (1965b). Heritability of semen concentration, and motility (quantity) in White Rock roosters and their genetic correlations with rate of gain. *Poultry Sci., 44,* 527.

Stetson, M. H., and J. E. Erickson. (1971). Endocrine effects of castration in white-crowned sparrows. *Gen. Comp. Endocrinol., 17,* 105.

Sturkie, P. D. (1946). The production of twins in *Gallus domesticus. J. Exp. Zool., 101,* 51.

Sturkie, P. D. (1965). Chapters 15, 16, and 18. In "Avian Physiology" (2nd ed.) (P. D. Sturkie, Ed.). Ithaca, N. Y. Cornell University Press.

Takeda, A. (1969). Labelling of cock spermatozoa with radioactive phosphorus. *Jap. J. Zootech. Sci., 40,* 412.

Tanaka, K., and S. Okamoto. (1966). The effect of freezing point depression on chicken spermatozoa. *Jap. Poultry Sci., 3,* 5.

Tanaka, K., and F. H. Wilcox. (1966). Studies on the storage of chicken semen diluted with different hypertonic solutions. *Japan. Poultry Sci., 3,* 192.

Temple. S. A. (1974). Plasma testosterone titers during the annual reproductive cycle of starlings *(Sturnus vulgaris). Gen. Comp. Endocrinol., 22,* 470.

Tingari, M. D. (1973). Histochemical localization of $3\beta$- and $17\beta$-hydroxysteroid dehydrogenases in the male reproductive tract of the domestic fowl *(Gallus domesticus). Histochem. J., 5,* 57.

Tingari, M. D. and P. E. Lake. (1972). Ultrastructural evidence for resorption of spermatozoa and testicular fluid in the excurrent ducts of the testes of the domestic fowl. *J. Reprod. Fert., 31,* 373.

Van Drimmelen, G. C. (1945). The location of spermatozoa in the hen by means of capillary attraction. *J. South African Vet. Med. Assoc., 16,* 97. (Abstr.).

Van Drimmelen, G. C. (1951). Artificial insemination of birds by the intraperitoneal route: A study in sex physiology of pigeons and fowls with reports upon a modified technique of semen collection, a new technique of insemination, and observations on the spermatozoa in the genital organs of the fowl hen. *Onderstepoort J. Vet. Res., 1, (Suppl. N.)* 212.

Van Krey, H. P., F. X. Ogasawara, and F. W. Lorenz. (1966). Distribution of spermatozoa in the oviduct and fertility in domestic birds. IV. Fertility of spermatozoa from infundibular and uterovaginal glands. *J. Reprod. Fert., 11,* 257.

Van Tienhoven, A. (1960). The metabolism of fowl sperm in different diluents. *J. Agri. Sci., 54,* 67.

Van Tienhoven, A., and A. V. Schally. (1972). Mammalian LH releasing hormone induces ovulation in domestic fowl. *J. Gen. Comp. Endocrinol., 19,* 591.

Van Tienhoven, A., and R. J. Planck. (1973). The effect of light on avian reproductive activity. In "Endocrinology," II, Part 1, in "Handbook of Physiology." p. 79.

Weakley, C. E., and C. S. Shaffner. (1952). The fertilizing capacity of diluted chicken semen. *Poultry Sci., 31,* 650.

Wentworth, B. C. (1970). Sterility and reproductive inhibition of Japanese quail induced by Mestranol ingestion. *Poultry Sci., 49,* 1477.

Wilson, J. A., and B. Glick. (1970). Ontogeny of mating behavior in the chicken. *Am. J. Physiol., 218,* 951.

Witschi, E. (1961). Sex and secondary sexual characters. In "Biology and Comparative Physiology of Birds" Vol. II (A. J. Marshall, Ed.). New York: Academic Press, Chapter 17.

Wong, H. Y. C., and E. W. Hawthorne. (1954). Influence of filtered light and no sunlight on weight and comb response in androgen treated cockerels. *Am. J. Physiol., 179,* 419.

Wong, H. Y. C., N. Lavenda, and E. W. Hawthorne. (1954). Effect of exercise on comb response of androgen treated capons. *Am. J. Physiol., 178,* 269.

Woods, J. E., and L. V. Domm. (1966). A histochemical identification of the androgen producing cells in the gonads of the domestic fowl and albino rat. *Gen. Comp. Endocrinol., 7,* 559.

Zeller, F. J. (1971). The effects of testosterone and dihydrotestosterone on the comb, testes and pituitary gland of male chickens. *J. Reprod. Fert., 25,* 125.

Zigmond, R. E., J. M. Stern, and B. S. McEwen. (1972). Retention of radioactivity in cell nuclei in the hypothalamus of the ring dove after injection of $^3$H-testosterone. *Gen. Comp. Endocrinol., 18,* 450.

# 18

## Thyroids

### R. K. Ringer

## ANATOMY

### Location; Blood and Nerve Supply

The thyroid glands in avian species are paired organs, oval in shape and dark red in color, with a glistening appearance. They are located on either side of the trachea on the ventral–lateral aspect of the neck just exterior to the thoracic cavity (Figure 18-1) and can be found adhering to the common carotid artery just above the junction of the common carotid with the subclavian artery. They are situated medial to the jugular vein.

The blood supply to the thyroid is by the cranial and caudal thyroid arteries, which originate from a branch directly off the common carotid artery. Return circulation is through veins emptying into the jugular vein. Nothing is known about the innervation of the thyroid in birds: it may stem from the cervical sympathetic ganglion, as in mammals. In man the nerves accompany the blood vessels in the thyroid and mostly end in the perivascular plexus; occasionally they end on the follicular cells.

### Embryology and Histology

The thyroid appears on the second day of incubation of the chick as a midline outgrowth (median anlage) from the ventral pharyngeal wall at the lev-

18–1 Location of thyroids, parathyroids, and thymus in the chicken. (After Nonidez and Goodale, 1927.)

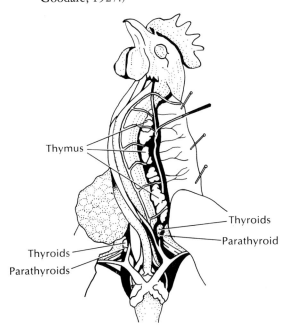

Thymus

Thyroids

Parathyroid

Thyroids

Parathyroids

el of the first and second branchial pouches. The median anlage becomes cuplike and bilobed, with a narrow stalk attached to the pharyngeal wall. The stalk ruptures, and the lobes separate and migrate laterally as crescent-shaped structures, and the glands ultimately develop their definitive shape and position (see Romanoff, 1960).

The cells within the thyroid are arranged in chordlike rows. Colloid secretion commences and displaces the epithelium peripherally, forming spherical vesicles known as follicles. At 7 days of incubation the thyroid of the embryonic chick can concentrate radioactive iodine ($^{131}$I) many times over the amount present in the blood, yet no follicles or colloid are visible. On the ninth day of incubation, droplets of colloid are visible and radioiodine uptake is protein bound. On the thirteenth day the thyroid abruptly increases radioiodine accumulation on injection of $^{131}$I (Waterman, 1959). From the incorporation of radioiodine in the follicular colloid, Hansborough and Khan (1951) and Stoll and Blanquet (1953) concluded that the embryonic chick thyroid becomes functional and secretes thyroxine after 10–11 days of incubation. On the eleventh day the thyroid gland is stimulated by thyrotropin (Mess and Straznicky, 1970). Just prior to hatching the activity of the thyroid increases (Rogler et al., 1959; Kraicziczek, 1956).

Radioiodide administered to hens concentrates in the ovary (yolk) as thyroxine and triiodothyronine (Roche et al., 1956); however, Okonski et al. (1960) reported that only a small fraction of the $^{131}$I was protein bound; the largest segment was in the form of iodide. The iodide is utilized by the developing embryo. At the start of incubation the major portion of radioiodide is concentrated in the yolk, but by the ninth day of incubation, when vascularization has taken place, the first iodide appears concentrated in the embryo thyroid. Concentration continues until at the ninteenth day 40% of the $^{131}$I is in the thyroid, 40% is elsewhere in the embryo, and 20% remains in the egg (Stoll and Blanquet, 1953; also see Wollman and Zwilling, 1953; Okonski et al., 1960).

The thyroid gland can develop both morphologically and functionally in chorioallantoic grafts or in vitro, the gland of the embryo therefore possesses an intrinsic ability to develop autonomously. Both in vitro and in vivo studies of the thyroid show the same schedule of $^{131}$I concentration (Waterman, 1959).

Histologically the thyroid is encapsulated by reticular connective tissue. The follicles are composed of entodermal epithelium of varying height, depending on the state of activity (secretory rate).

350 The epithelial type may vary from squamous to columnar. Depending on the secretory state, the follicles may be filled with or completely devoid of colloid, which is a homogeneous fluid of protein gel composed of an iodinated protein, thyroglobulin. Between the follicles are connective tissue stroma, interfollicular cells, and a rich blood supply (Thommes, 1958).

### Size

The size of the thyroid is influenced by several variables, such as age, sex, climatic conditions, diet, activity, species, and hypophysectomy. In proportion to the total body weight the thyroid in *Gallus domesticus* (domestic fowl) does not vary markedly with increasing age, but its absolute weight increases with age. At 1–2 weeks of age the thyroid weight of the chicken varies from 6.3 to 10.7 mg per 100 g body weight (Snedecor, 1968; van Tienhoven *et al.*, 1966) and at 10–22 weeks from 9.0 to 11.7 mg per 100 g (Rosenberg *et al.*, 1964; Kanematsu and Mikami, 1970). Growth rate of the thyroid is almost constant from hatching until about 50–60 days after hatching. The rate of thyroidal growth is then accelerated until between 100 and 120 days, at which time a pronounced slowing occurs (Breneman, 1954). Female chickens have a greater thyroid weight than males.

That diet has an influence on thyroid size is widely known (see Ringer, 1965). Because iodine is essential in the biosynthesis of the thyroid hormones, a deficiency of iodine produces goiter or enlargement of the thyroid.

Early investigators reported that the thyroid weight of chickens and pigeons was greater in the winter than in the summer. Low environmental temperature increases thyroid activity (see section on control of thyroid activity). Histologic changes indicating follicular stimulation within the thyroid have been reported to coincide with the onset of cold weather (Höhn, 1949). However, two studies on ducks (Rosenberg *et al.*, 1967; Astier *et al.*, 1970) conducted in the Mediterranean region have shown greater thyroid weight and activity in the summer (June) than in the cold months. Astier *et al.* (1970) reported thyroid weights for the adult duck in March and October as 5.82 and 9.28 mg per 100 g body weight, respectively.

An increase in the size of the thyroid may be caused by an increase in cell size (hypertrophy) and/or an increase in the number of cells (hyperplasia), associated with a reduction in colloid content of the follicles. Enlarged thyroids may reflect either a hyper- or a hypofunctioning gland.

TSH stimulates the thyroid and produces both hypertrophy and hyperplasia, together with accelerated formation or secretion of thyroxine. Thiouracil, thiourea, and methimazole (goitrogens) produce the same histologic picture but suppress the formation of thyroxine. The latter occurs through inhibition of thyroid hormone synthesis by interfering with iodide concentration within the thyroid (thiocyanate) or through inhibition of iodination of thyroglobulin (thiourea and thiouracil). Hypophysectomy causes a decrease in thyroid size, because production of thyrotropin (TSH) is abolished.

## THYROID HORMONES
### Synthesis

Synthesis of thyroid hormones in avian species is similar to that which occurs in mammals, where iodide is concentrated within the thyroid, the so-called iodide trap, by the maintenance of a gradient over that of blood. The iodide is converted to $I_2$ and then to $I^+$, which is the iodinating substance. Chickens fed a diet similar in iodine content to that fed to rats had an iodide trapping rate five times that of the rat (Rosenberg *et al.*, 1964). The thyroid proteins are then iodinated. Monoiodotyrosine and diiodotyrosine, shown chromatographically to be present in chicken thyroids (Vlijm, 1958; Frey and Flock, 1958), are thus formed (Figure 18–2). A peroxidase system within the thyroid converts the iodide to iodine and a second enzyme system is responsible for combining the iodinated tyrosines within the protein thyroglobulin to form triiodothyronine ($T_3$) and thyroxine ($T_4$). $T_3$ and $T_4$ have been shown chromatographically in thyroid tissue from chickens (Lague and van Tienhoven, 1969), ducks (Astier *et al.*, 1966), and pigeons (Baylé *et al.*, 1966). Within the thyroid, therefore, thyroglobulin contains monoiodotyrosine, diiodotyrosine, triiodothyronine, and thyroxine. Rosenberg *et al.* (1964) indicated that intrathyroidal iodination and deiodination reactions occur continually and lead to randomization of thyroidal iodine; both of iodotyrosines and of iodothyronines. Thus, within the gland, iodine shifts between the tyrosine and thyronine in a random fashion. The tyrosines must be converted to an iodinated thyronine for release from the thyroid into the bloodstream.

### The Circulating Hormones

Both triiodothyronine and thyroxine have been isolated radiochromatographically from the plasma of chickens, ducks, and turkeys (Wentworth and

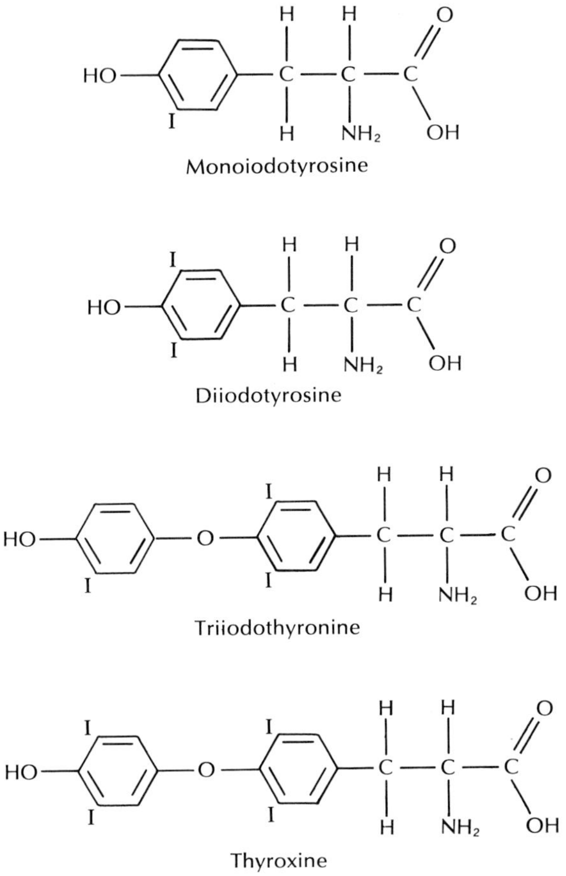

Monoiodotyrosine

Diiodotyrosine

Triiodothyronine

Thyroxine

18–2 Iodinated compounds of the thyroid.

Mellen, 1961). These investigators reported a ratio of 60% thyroxine to 40% triiodothyronine; however, Sadovsky and Bensadoun (1971) reported a diurnal rhythm in plasma iodohormones and a $T_3/T_4$ ratio varying from 1.33 to 2.12.

The thyroid hormones are released from the thyroid as the amino acids thyroxine and triiodothyronine. Once in the blood they are again bound to protein. In man thyroxine-binding globulin is the primary carrier of thyroxine and to a lesser extent triiodothyronine. A second binding protein is prealbumin, whereas serum albumin plays a minor role as a carrier. The absence of a thyroxine-binding globulin in avian species has been shown by many researchers. Both thyroxine and triiodothyronine are bound to serum albumin, and the binding affinity of albumin for $T_3$ and $T_4$ is the same (Tata and Shellabarger, 1959). Heninger and Newcomer (1964) noted that $T_4$ in chicken plasma was bound to the protein-binding sites with greater

affinity than was $T_3$. Farer et al. (1962) found chickens, turkeys, and pigeons to have thyroxine-binding prealbumins as well as albumins. In the pigeon and chicken $T_4$ binds to albumin and a prealbumin zone; $T_3$ binds to prealbumin in the pigeon but not in the chicken or in any other vertebrate studied (Refetoff et al., 1970). Binding of thyroxine to avian albumin is evidently weak compared to that in man; labeled thyroxine binds rapidly with the proteins in human blood when they are mixed together with avian blood. The loose binding to serum proteins results in more free $T_4$ in avian blood than in human (1.4–3.7 ng per 100 ml) or most warmblooded vertebrate's blood (Refetoff et al., 1970). Using a competitive binding assay, Refetoff et al. (1970) reported plasma levels of total $T_4$ for the chicken as 1.4–1.6 $\mu$g per 100 ml with 5.5 ng per 100 ml of free thyroxine. For the pigeon these values were 2.4–3.3 $\mu$g per 100 ml for total $T_4$ and 6.0–6.9 ng per 100 ml as free thyroxine. Etta (1971), using a competitive protein-binding assay for total thyroxine, reported values in chickens of 1.00 $\mu$g $T_4$ per 100 ml serum (layers), 1.75 (nonlayers), 2.10 (males), and, for turkeys, 1.39 (layers), 1.18 (nonlayers), 1.51 (males). Free $T_4$ may be an important index of thyroid status (Refetoff et al., 1970).

In man $T_4$ and $T_3$ have half-lives of 6.7 and 2.7 days, respectively (Sterling et al., 1954), and the half-lives ($t_{1/2}$) of $T_3$ and $T_4$ in birds are almost identical (Tata and Shellabarger, 1959; Heninger and Newcomer, 1964; Singh et al., 1967). The capacity and affinity of avian plasma for triiodothyronine are less than those for thyroxine; therefore factors other than, or in addition to, protein binding must account for their similar disappearance rates from the circulation (Heninger and Newcomer, 1964). The rate of degradation of thyroid hormones is very rapid in birds, as indicated by relatively short biologic half-lives, measured in hours (see Table 18–1). Care must be taken in assessing $t_{1/2}$ for thyroid hormones in birds because values read too soon (< 2 hr) after injection of the radioactive hormone do not allow for complete mixing and those measured 24 hr or more after reflect recycling of metabolized radioiodine (Etta et al., 1972).

In the mammal, triiodothyronine has been shown to be at least six times more potent than an equimolar amount of thyroxine in preventing goiter. Triiodothyronine is a potent thyroid hormone in chicks but is no more potent than thyroxine in preventing goiter (Shellabarger, 1955). The potencies are also equal in stimulating body weight, comb growth, and liver glycogen of propylthioura-

*Table 18–1   Biological half-lives of* [$^{131}$I] *thyroxine in plasma*

| Species | Sampling time after [$^{131}$I] thyroxine injection (hr) | Half-life (hr) | Reference |
|---|---|---|---|
| Chicken | 1–24 | 8.3 | Heninger and Newcomer (1964) |
| | 3–12 | 3.3 | Singh *et al.* (1967) |
| Duck | 2–18 | 4.0 | Assenmacher *et al.* (1968) |
| Japanese quail | 3–12 | 5.4 | Singh *et al.* (1967) |
| Bobwhite quail | 3–12 | 4.6 | Singh *et al.* (1967) |

cil-fed and radiothyroidectomized chicks (Raheja and Snedecor, 1970); in influencing oxygen consumption, heart rate, suffocation time, and feather growth in thiouracil-treated chicks (Newcomer, 1957); or in suppressing the effect of tapazole as indicated by thyroid secretion rate (Singh *et al.,* 1968a). However, thyroxine was reported as more potent than triiodothyronine in preventing goiter in thiouracil-treated chickens (Newcomer, 1957; Mellen and Wentworth, 1959) and in increasing oxygen consumption in cardiac muscle (Newcomer and Barrett, 1960) or metabolic rate (Singh *et al.,* 1968a). $T_3$ was reported as more active than $T_4$ in stimulating intracellular accumulation of certain neutral amino acids by embryonic chick bones (Adamson and Ingbar, 1967).

The principal route of excretion of thyroxine and triiodothyronine is via bile and urine (Hutchins and Newcomer, 1966). Conjugated thyronines, acetic acid derivatives of thyronines, and partially deiodinated thyronines were identified in bile, whereas iodide was the fundamental metabolite in urine.The latter was also reported by Tanabe *et al.* (1965).

## Circadian Rhythm of Thyroid Hormones

The short half-life of thyroxine and triiodothyronine in birds could lead to a measurable diurnal variation in thyroid function whereas in mammals with long half-lives of thyroxine this could not be so. Plasma hormonal iodine levels in chickens show a diurnal rhythm. Total iodohormone curves show two peaks of plasma concentration at 0800 and 1600 hr (Sadovsky and Bensadoun, 1971). At 1600 hr the concentration is two times that at 0400. $T_4$ was fairly stable throughout the day but $T_3$ levels changed.

## Assays

**Protein-bound iodine.** The iodine-containing hormones are precipitated with the serum proteins from the blood. The quantity of protein-bound iodine (PBI) may be chemically analyzed or if $^{131}$I is injected prior to the blood sampling, detection can be made of the labeled protein (PB$^{131}$I).

Representative plasma protein-bound iodine values for chickens, bobwhite quail, and Japanese quail were measured as 1.12, 1.76, and 1.26 µg per 100 ml, respectively (Singh *et al.,* 1967); for the duck, 1.17–1.49 µg per 100 ml (Mellen and Hardy, 1957); and for the pigeon, 1.4–1.8 µg/100 ml (Refetoff *et al.,* 1970). These values are considerably lower than those for mammals and may reflect the lack of a specific thyroxine-binding $\alpha$-globulin in avian blood.

The lack of sensitivity of the PBI test in birds negates its use as an assay of circulating levels of thyroid hormones in the blood. Should any nonhormonal iodoproteins be present they are also precipitated. Avian blood, unlike that of mammals, contains a considerable amount of nonhormonal iodoproteins (Assenmacher, 1973).

By use of a cation-exchange resin to measure hormonal iodine, Sadovsky and Bensadoun (1971) reported values for chicken male plasma ranging from 4.8 to 11.9 µg per 100 ml. These values are seven times those reported for PBI by precipitation. These authors suggest that a large fraction of the iodohormones does not coprecipitate with albumin and is removed from the precipitate during washing. By this method the hen has significantly more iodohormone than does the male.

**Competitive protein binding.** This method is used to measure directly the amount of $T_4$ in plasma or serum. The principle of the method is that thyroxine extracted from plasma competes with tracer $^{125}$I-thyroxine for binding sites in a given quantity of thyroxine-binding globulin. With the assumption that both have equal affinity for the available sites, levels of "cold" endogenous thyroxine compete with labeled $T_4$ for the thyroxine-binding globulin sites. When equilibrium is reached, the addition of a resin-impregnated sponge binds the unbound thyroxine but not the thyroxine-binding, globulin-bound thyroxine. This renders the two components separable (Etta, 1971).

## Thyroxine Secretion Rate (TSR)

In recent years great progress in the accurate determination of individual thyroid secretion rates has come with the use of $^{131}I$ tracer techniques. These methods afford more accurate assessment of thyroid functioning in birds under various physiologic conditions than do measurement of protein-bound iodine (PBI) or the goiter prevention method of TSR (for details see Ringer, 1965). PBI or $PB^{131}I$ do not constitute a sensitive assay technique and, in addition, measure nonhormonal iodoproteins in blood of birds (Astier, 1973). The goiter prevention technique has been questioned because the use of a goitrogen, such as thiouracil or methimazole, decreases peripheral deiodination of thyroxine and gives faulty high TSR values. Singh et al. (1968b) compared four methods of measuring thyroid secretion rate in chickens (1) goiter prevention, (2) thyroid hormone substitution, (3) direct output, and (4) thyroxine degradation. Representative TSR values for chicks to 9 weeks of age by the four methods, expressed as micrograms of $T_4$ per 100 g body weight daily, were 2.32, 2.00, 1.20, and 2.03, respectively (see Table 18–2). These same workers (Singh et al., 1967) reported the TSR of adult bobwhite and Japanese quail as 2.49 and 2.78

$\mu g\ T_4$ per 100 g body weight daily by the thyroxine degradation method.

Earlier workers did not take into account the adequacy of the iodine content of the diet when measuring TSR. Marked lowering of the TSR resulted when chickens were fed an iodine-deficient diet (Singh et al., 1968a).

TSR decreases with advancing age. Tanabe (1965) reported values by the goiter prevention method for cockerels 2–3 weeks, 5–7 weeks, and 13–14 weeks of age as 1.97, 1.57, and 0.63 $\mu g$ per 100 g body weight per day, respectively.

## CONTROL OF THYROID FUNCTION

### Pituitary–Hypothalamus

Within certain limits the function of the thyroid is governed by the concentration of the circulating thyroid hormones and their effects on the pituitary release of TSH. A decrease in the amount of circulating thyroid hormones to a level below metabolic requirements prompts the anterior pituitary to increase the release of thyrotropic hormone. An exogenous injection of thyroxine leads to a decrease in production of the thyrotropic hormone. Therefore, the thyroid–pituitary feedback mechanism is constantly in a state of balance and counterbalance between the hormones.

The secretion of TSH appears to be regulated

*Table 18–2*  *Thyroxine secretion rate (TSR) of various birds*

| Species | Age (weeks) | Body wt (g) | Iodine | TSR/100 g body weight/day ($\mu g\ T_4$) | Method | Reference |
|---|---|---|---|---|---|---|
| Chicken | 5.5 | | Normal | 2.00 | $T_4$ substitution | Singh et al. (1968b) |
| | 4 | | Deficient | 1.66 | $T_4$ substitution | Singh et al. (1968b) |
| | 6 | 645 | Normal | 2.03 | $T_4$ degradation | Singh et al. (1968b) |
| | 5.5 | 405 | Deficient | 0.73 | $T_4$ degradation | Singh et al. (1968b) |
| | 6 | | Normal | 2.32 | Goiter prevention | Singh et al. (1968b) |
| | 4.5 | 425 | Normal | 1.30 | Direct output | Singh et al. (1968b) |
| | 4.5 | 451 | Deficient | 0.46 | Direct output | Singh et al. (1968b) |
| | 56 | 2159 | Normal | 1.02 | $T_4$ degradation | Singh et al. (1968b) |
| | 5.6 | 515 | | 1.8 | Goiter prevention | Tanabe (1964) |
| Duck | | | | 1.90 | Goiter prevention | Hoffman (1950) |
| | | | | 2.05 | $T_4$ degradation | Astier et al. (1972) |
| Pigeon | | | | 1.94 | $T_4$ substitution | Grosvenor and Turner (1960) |
| Turkey | | | | 1.88 | Goiter prevention | Mellen (1964) |
| Japanese quail | 10 | | | 1.62 | Goiter prevention | Lepore and Marks (1967) |
| | | | Normal | 2.78 | $T_4$ degradation | Singh et al. (1968b) |
| Bobwhite quail | 56–68 | | Normal | 2.49 | $T_4$ degradation | Singh et al. (1968b) |

354 by nuclei in the anterior hypothalamus (McFarland *et al.,* 1966; Kanematsu and Mikami, 1970). The central nervous system therefore directly regulates thyrotropin release through a hypothalamic neurosecretion (Chapter 15). This thyrotropin-releasing hormone is transported via the portal vessels of the median eminence to the adenohypophysis. However, sectioning of the median eminence or autotransplanting of the pituitary in ducks (Assenmacher, 1958) and chickens (Ma and Nalbandov, 1963) does not result in thyroid atrophy but does impair thyroid function. Pigeons (Baylé and Assenmacher, 1967) and ducks (Rosenberg *et al.,* 1967) with hypothalamic–pituitary disconnection show a decrease in the rate of iodine metabolism. Twenty-four hours after autografts of the pituitary many indices of thyroid action present a normal picture (Rosenberg *et al.,* 1967; Astier and Baylé, 1970). Basal thyrotropic function has a good degree of autonomy with regard to hypothalamic control in birds (Rosenberg *et al.,* 1967). Mammalian thyrotropin-releasing hormone (TRH) has been shown to be a tripeptide. Avian TRH has not been purified (see Chapter 15). For assays of TSH see Ringer (1965) and Chapter 15.

Hendrich and Turner (1965) estimated TSH secretion rate based on the amount of exogenous TSH that would stimulate thyroidal $^{131}$I release rate equally to that observed with endogenous release. They recorded a mean TSH secretion rate for 48 chickens as 2.5 mu per 100 g body weight per day, varying from a low in September–October (1.7 mu) to a high of 3.5 mu in May–June (1 USP unit = 1000 mu).

## Season and Temperature Influence

As pointed out earlier, the size and histology of the thyroid changes with the season. Reineke and Turner (1945) showed that in young chicks (2 weeks of age) the thyroxine secretion rate in summer was one-half that in winter. Old White Leghorn hens exhibited a similar change with season (Turner, 1948).

In southern France, Astier *et al.* (1970) reported that a definite circannual rhythm of thyroid function was detected in male ducks with a maximum thyroidal $^{131}$I uptake and PB$^{131}$I in June. This time of year corresponds to the period of maximum photoperiod, the seasonal decrease of testicular activity, and the onset of annual molt. The lowest thyroid function was in January and February. In any measure of seasonal effects it is necessary to examine changes in temperature, light, reproductive cycle, and molt, which vary with the season.

Decreases in thyroid secretion with high environmental temperatures have been reported by many (Mueller and Amezcua, 1959; Stahl and Turner, 1961; Huston *et al.* 1962). Conversely, cold temperature has been shown to increase thyroid secretion rate (Mueller and Amezcua, 1959) and also TSH release (Hendrich and Turner, 1965). Iodine uptake and release of thyroidal $^{131}$I increased on short-term exposure to cold of warm-acclimatized chickens and returned to normal after long exposure (Hendrich and Turner, 1963). Continued cold stimulates the hypothalamus and adenohypophysis to a higher level of TSH secretion; long exposure to cold increased TSR for extended periods up to 1 month or more. The TSR change on going from a cold to a warm environment is rapid. Exposure of cold-acclimatized chickens to warm resulted in the thyroxine secretion rate dropping 42% in 7 days (Hahn *et al.,* 1966).

Because uptake and release of iodine by the thyroid do not measure utilization of thyroidal hormones, Hendrich and Turner (1967) measured the half-life of thyroxine and reported no change on short-term exposure to cold. McFarland *et al.* (1966) reported that the calculated half-life of thyroxine for Japanese quail kept at 32°C was 36% lower than for those maintained at 21°C.

## Photoperiod Influence

The interaction of the thyroid with photoperiod is complex. Pituitary thyrotrophs are stimulated in Japanese quail by exposure to long daily photoperiods (Tixier-Vidal *et al.,* 1967). Long daily photoperiods depressed the uptake of $^{131}$I by the thyroid of male ducks (Tixier-Vidal and Assenmacher, 1965), male quail (Baylé and Assenmacher, 1967), and female quail (Follett and Riley, 1967). This action is probably through testicular stimulation and the gonadal steroids that are produced. During photostimulation there is an initial rise in thyroid activity, which is then depressed when the gonads are stimulated and produce steroids (Follett and Riley, 1967). "Long" days seem to exert an inhibitory effect on thyroid function, although they stimulate pituitary thyrotropic activity in birds.

Using castrated ducks, Jallageas and Assenmacher (1972) further demonstrated the relationship of the thyroid, photoperiod, and gonads. Castrated ducks had a thyroxine half-life of 4.14 hr, whereas long photoperiods in castrates resulted in a $t_{1/2}$ of 3.45 hr. Long photoperiods apparently increase peripheral utilization of thyroxine.

## Gonadal Influence

The interaction between the gonads and the thyroid of birds is more pronounced than in mammals, where castration causes only slight effects on thyroid activity. Castration stimulates pituitary thyrotrophs in the duck (Tixier-Vidal and Assenmacher, 1965) and quail (Tixier-Vidal et al., 1967) and increases thyroidal uptake of [131]I (Tixier-Vidal and Assenmacher, 1965). At the peripheral level, castration of ducks increases the half-life of thyroxine (Jallageas and Assenmacher, 1972). Castration plus testosterone administration returned the thyroxine $t_{1/2}$ to normal, indicating that testosterone increases peripheral utilization of thyroidal hormones. In male birds that exhibit annual gonadal cycles, therefore, fluctuations in testosterone production may contribute to variations in thyroid function.

### Molt Influence

Voitkevich (1966) has noted progressive changes in the thyroids of birds in experimentally induced molt. He concluded from his studies that a peak of thyroid activity commonly precedes molt by a few weeks. This relationship is true in many passerine birds but not necessarily in nonpasserines. In domestic species natural molts appear to be independent of increases in thyroid activity (see Ringer, 1965).

## THYROIDECTOMY

Surgical thyroidectomy has been successfully performed on birds, but not without some difficulty. The anatomical location of the thyroids and their proximity to the parathyroid glands in certain species (Figure 18-1 and Chapter 19) make removal of the thyroids without the parathyroids a difficult operation. Radiothyroidectomy, destruction by the injection of large doses of [131]I, is commonly used.

Thyroidectomy (Tx) results in growth retardation, feather structure alteration (fringed and elongated with loss of barbules and color), and reduced gonadal function (see Ringer, 1965). Testes weight and semen quality are decreased following Tx (Hendrich and Turner, 1966; Snedecor and Camyre, 1966).

Pregnant mare serum administration to radiothyroidectomized chicks caused a significant increase in testes weight; therefore, the reduced testes growth in hypothyroidism is probably a lack of gonadotropin and not an absence of thyroid hormone (Snedecor, 1968). In contrast to domestic species, Tx in some passerine birds leads to increased gonad weight and function in both sexes

(Thapliyal and Garg, 1967; Wieselthier and van Tienhoven, 1972).

## GENETIC HYPOTHYROIDISM

A spontaneous case of thyroiditis in an obese strain of chickens (Cole, 1966) has been shown to be the result of the presence of circulating thyroglobulin autoantibodies (Cole et al., 1968). These birds exhibit low $T_4$ levels, obesity, rather silky plumage, delayed sexual development or lack of maturity, and either smaller than normal thyroids or enlarged thyroids (found in those that survive). These observations are characteristic of hypothyroidism.

## FUNCTION OF THYROID HORMONES
### Effect of Hypothyroidism and Hyperthyroidism on Growth

That the thyroid is necessary for normal growth and development is evident in that growth is markedly retarded following thyroidectomy. In mature hens thyroidectomy results in a dwarflike and obese appearance; excessive fat deposits in the neck, back, breast, and viscera; and shortening of the long skeletal bones.

Depressed thyroid activity as a consequence of goitrogen administration is reflected in reduced metabolic rate, increased fat deposition, and in some cases growth depression (see Ringer, 1965). Both thyroidectomy and goitrogen administration reduce comb growth, bursa growth, and the weight of the liver (Raheja and Snedecor, 1970). Marks (1971) and Howarth and Marks (1973) demonstrated depression of growth in Japanese quail from feeding 0.2% thiouracil. The retarded growth brought about by a goitrogen can be restored to normal by thyroid hormone injection. Following methimazole treatment, Singh et al. (1968a) restored the growth of chicks to normal by injecting 2–3 $\mu$g $T_4$ per 100 g body weight per day. Similarly, radiothyroidectomized or propylthiouracil-depressed body weights were restored to near normal levels by daily injections of 0.3 $\mu$g per 100 g body weight of $T_3$ or $T_4$ (Raheja and Snedecor, 1970).

In intact animals low levels of thyroid hormone administration give little (if any) to moderate growth stimulation (see Ringer, 1965). Singh et al. (1968a), using doses ranging from 1 to 6 $\mu$g per 100 g body weight per day, indicated that thyroxine in small doses improved growth of chickens; when administered beyond physiologic doses (6 $\mu$g per

356 100g), however, it depressed growth rate. Thyroxine in toxic doses accelerates catabolic processes and body weight is reduced.

### Effect of Hypothyroidism and Hyperthyroidism on Metabolic Rate (MR)

Thyroid hormones play a major role in regulating oxidative metabolism of birds (see also Chapter 8). Any pronounced alteration in thyroid function, i.e., hyperthyroidism or hypothyroidism, is reflected in an altered metabolic rate. Goitrogens reduce, whereas thyroid hormones stimulate, metabolic rate (see Ringer, 1965).

In contrast to the mammal, in which prolonged MR stimulation follows $T_4$ injection, the chicken exhibits only a transitory rise. A small increase in MR following administration of $T_4$, $T_3$, or a combination of $T_3$ and $T_4$ lasts only for a period of $2-3$ hr. The maximum effect produced by $T_4$ occurred 2 hr after its administration (Singh et al., 1968a). The MR was depressed 24 hr after injection.

Thyroid function parallels the time course of developing thermoregulatory ability in Japanese quail (Spiers et al., 1974). $T_3$ or $T_4$ (300 $\mu$g/kg) injected intraperitoneally was thermogenic in the neonate chicken (Freeman, 1970). Rectal temperature was elevated within 30 min but was significantly higher only in those chicks given $T_3$ at 60 min. Thiouracil impairs thermoregulation in the neonate chicken (Freeman, 1971).

### Effect of Hypothyroidism and Hyperthyroidism on Liver Glycogen

Liver hypertrophy and liver glycogen accumulation are induced by hypothyroidism in the chick (Snedecor and King, 1964; Snedecor and Mellen, 1965; Snedecor and Camyre, 1966; Snedecor, 1968) and are restored to near normal levels by small daily doses of $T_4$ or $T_3$ (Raheja and Snedecor, 1970). Thyroidectomy causes blood glucose levels in the duck to fall below normal (Ensor et al., 1970). It appears that the increased liver glycogen accumulation is largely a result of decreased glycogenolysis, with glucose-6-phosphatase as the limiting enzyme (Raheja et al., 1971).

### Effect of Hypothyroidism and Hyperthyroidism on Reproduction

Hypothyroidism decreases egg production, egg weight, shell thickness, and ovarian weight. In general, males show reduced testes size and semen quality or complete spermatogenic arrest in thyroidectomy. These reproductive changes can be restored by exogenous thyroxine administration.

Feeding thyroprotein on egg production has resulted in little or no stimulation. In the male moderate to heavy dosages depress testicular development (Ringer, 1965).

## REFERENCES

Adamson, L. F., and S. H. Ingbar. (1967). Some properties of the stimulatory effect of thyroid hormones on amino acid transport by embryonic chick bone. Endocrinology, 81, 1372.

Assenmacher, I. (1958). Recherches sur le contrôle hypothalamique de la fonction gonadotrope préhypophysaire chez le canard. Arch. Anat. Microsc. Morphol. Exp., 47, 447.

Assenmacher, I. (1973). The peripheral endocrine glands. In "Avian Biology," Vol. III (D. S. Farner and J. R. King, Eds.). New York: Academic Press, p. 211.

Assenmacher, I., H. Astier, and N. Jougla. (1968). Répercussions thyroidiennes de la sous-alimentation chez le canard domestique. J. Physiol. (Paris), 60, 342.

Astier, H. (1973). Présence d'une fraction importante de protéines iodées "non hormonales" dans le P.B.I. des Oiseaux. Compt. Rend. Acad. Sci., 276, 793.

Astier, H., and J. D. Baylé. (1970). Epuration plasmatique de la $^{125}$I-L-thyroxine après hypophysectomie et autogreffe hypophysaire chez le canard. J. Physiol. (Paris), 62, 237.

Astier, H., F. Halberg, and I. Assenmacher. (1970). Rythmes circanniens de l'activité thyroidienne chez le canard Pekin. J. Physiol. (Paris), 62, 219.

Astier, H., N. Jougla, and I. Assenmacher. (1972). Variation du "taux de sécrétion" (T.S.) de la thyroxine chez le canard mâle soumis à des modifications du niveau alimentaire et de la température ambiante. Compt. Rend. Acad. Sci., 275, 2531.

Astier, H., L. L. Rosenberg, S. Lissitzky, C. Simon, I. Assenmacher, and A. Tixier-Vidal. (1966). Recherches sur la separation chromatographique des iodothyronines intrathyroidiennes chez le canard Pékin. Ann. Endocrinol., 27, 571.

Baylé, J. D., and I. Assenmacher. (1967). Le controle hypothalamo-hypophysaire de la fonction thyroidienne chez les oiseaux. Gen. Comp. Endocrinol. 9, 433.

Baylé, J. D., H. Astier, and I. Assenmacher. (1966). Activite thyroidienne du pigeon après hypophysectomie ou autogreffe hypophysaire. J. Physiol. (Paris), 58, 459.

Breneman, W. R. (1954). The growth of thyroids and adrenals in the chick. Endocrinology, 55, 54.

Cole, R. K. (1966). Hereditary hypothyroidism in the domestic fowl. Genetics, 53, 1021.

Cole, R. K., J. H. Kite, and E. Witebsky. (1968). Hereditary autoimmune thyroiditis in the fowl. Science, 160, 1357.

Ensor, D. M., D. M. Thomas, and J. G. Phillips. (1970). The possible role of thyroid in extrarenal secretion following a hypertonic saline load in the duck (Anas platyrhynchos). Proceedings of Society of Endocrinology, J. Endocrinol., 46, x.

Etta, K. M. (1971). Comparative studies of the relationship between serum thyroxine and thyroxine binding globulin. Ph. D. thesis, Michigan State University.

Etta, K. M., R. K. Ringer, and E. P. Reineke. (1972). Degradation of thyroxine confounded by thyroidal recycling of radioactive iodine. Proc. Soc. Exp. Biol. Med., 140, 462.

Farer, L. S., J. Robbins, B. S. Blumberg, and J. E. Rall. (1962). Thyroxine–serum protein complexes in various animals. Endocrinology, 70, 686.

Follett, B. K., and J. Riley. (1967). Effect of the length of the daily photoperiod on thyroid activity in the female Japanese quail (Coturnix coturnix japonica). J. Endocrinol., 39, 615.

Freeman, B. M. (1970). Thermoregulatory mechanisms of the neonate fowl. Comp. Biochem. Physiol., 33, 219.

Freeman, B. M. (1971). Impaired thermoregulation in the thiouracil treated neonate fowl. *Comp. Biochem. Physiol., 40*, 553.

Frey, H., and E. V. Flock. (1958). The production of thyroid hormone in the day-old chick, with notes on the effect of thyrotrophin on the chick thyroid. *Acta Endocrinol., 29*, 550.

Grosvenor, C. E., and C. W. Turner. (1960). Measurement of thyroid secretion rate of individual pigeons. *Am. J. Physiol., 198*, 1.

Hahn, D. W., T. Ishibashi, and C. W. Turner. (1966). Alteration of thyroid hormone secretion rate in fowls changed from a cold to a warm environment. *Poultry Sci., 45*, 31.

Hansborough, L. A., and M. Khan. (1951). The initial function of the chick thyroid gland with the use of radioiodine $^{131}$I. *J. Exp. Zool., 116*, 447.

Hendrich, C. E., and C. W. Turner. (1963). Time relations in the alteration of thyroid gland function in fowls. *Poultry Sci., 42*, 1190.

Hendrich, C. E. and C. W. Turner. (1964). Estimation of thyroid stimulating hormone (TSH) secretion rates of New Hampshire fowls. *Proc. Soc. Exp. Biol. Med., 117*, 218.

Hendrich, C. E., and C. W. Turner. (1966). Effects of radiothyroidectomy and various replacement levels of thyroxine on growth, organ and gland weight of Cornish-cross chickens. *Gen. Comp. Endocrinol., 7*, 411.

Hendrich, C. E., and C. W. Turner. (1967). A comparison of the effect of environmental temperature changes and 4.4°C cold on the biological half-life $(t_{1/2})$ of thyroxine-$^{131}$I in fowls. *Poultry Sci., 46*, 3.

Heninger, R. W., and W. S. Newcomer. (1964). Plasma protein binding, half-life, uptake of thyroxine and triiodothyronine in chickens. *Proc. Soc. Exp. Biol. Med., 116*, 624.

Hoffman, E. (1950). Thyroxine secretion rate and growth in the white Pekin duck. *Poultry Sci., 29*, 109.

Höhn, E. (1949). Seasonal changes in the thyroid gland and effects of thyroidectomy in the mallard in relation to molt. *Am. J. Physiol., 158*, 337.

Howarth, B., Jr., and H. L. Marks. (1973). Thyroidal $^{131}$I uptake of Japanese quail in response to three different dietary goitrogens. *Poultry Sci., 52*, 326.

Huston, T. M., H. M. Edwards, Jr., and J. J. Williams. (1962). The effects of high environmental temperature on thyroid secretion rate of domestic fowl. *Poultry Sci., 41*, 640.

Hutchins M. O., and W. S. Newcomer. (1966). Metabolism and excretion of thyroxine and triiodothyronine in chickens. *Gen. Comp. Endocrinol., 6*, 239.

Jallageas, M., and I. Assenmacher. (1972). Effets de la photopériode et du taux d'androgène circulant sur la fonction thyroidienne du canard. *Gen. Comp. Endocrinol., 19*, 331.

Kanematsu, S., and S. Mikami. (1970). Effects of hypothalamic lesions on the pituitary—thyroid system in the chicken. *Jap. J. Zootech. Sci., 37*, 28.

Kraicziczek, M. (1956). Histogenese und Funktionszustand der embryonalen Huhnerthyreoiden. *Z. Zellforsch. Mikrosk. Anat., 43*, 421.

Lague, P. C., and A. van Tienhoven. (1969). Comparison between chicken and guinea pig thyroid with respect to the incorporation of $^{131}$I *in vitro. Gen. Comp. Endocrinol., 12*, 305.

Lepore, P. D., and H. L. Marks. (1967). Thyroid status of Japanese quail selected for body weight under different nutritional environments. *Poultry Sci., 46*, 1285.

Ma, R. C. S., and A. V. Nalbandov. (1963). Hormonal activity of the autotransplanted adenohypophysis. *Advan. Neuroendocrinol.,* Proc. Symp., 1961, p. 306.

Marks, H. L. (1971). Selection for four-week body weight in Japanese quail under two nutritional environments. *Poultry Sci., 50*, 931.

McFarland, L. Z., M. R. Yousef, and W. O. Wilson. (1966). The influence of ambient temperature and hypothalamic lesions on the disappearance rate of thyroxine $^{131}$I in the Japanese quail. *Life Sci., 5*, 309.

Mellen, W. J. (1964). Thyroxine secretion rate in chicks and poults. *Poultry Sci., 43*, 776.

Mellen, W. J., and L. B. Hardy, Jr. (1957). Blood protein-bound iodine in the fowl. *Endocrinology, 60*, 547.

Mellen, W. J., and B. C. Wentworth. (1959). Thyroxine vs triiodothyronine in the fowl. *Poultry Sci., 38*, 228.

Mess, B., and K. Straznicky. (1970) Dynamics of ribonucleic acid (RNA) synthesis in the thyroid epithelial cells of normal and decapitated chicken embryos. *Acta Biol. Acad. Sci. Hung., 21*, 115.

Mueller, W. J., and A. A. Amezcua. (1959). The relationship between certain thyroid characteristics of pullets and their egg production, body weight and environment. *Poultry Sci., 38*, 620.

Newcomer, W. S. (1957). Relative potencies of thyroxine and triiodothyronine based on various criteria in thiouracil-treated chickens. *Am. J. Physiol., 190*, 413.

Newcomer, W. S., and P. A. Barrett. (1960). Effects of various analogues of thyroxine on oxygen uptake of cardiac muscle from chicks. *Endocrinology 66*, 409.

Nonidez, J. R., and H. D. Goodale. (1927). Histological studies on the endocrines of chickens deprived of ultraviolet light. *Am. J. Anat., 38*, 319.

Okonski, J., F. W. Lengemann, and C. L. Comar. (1960). The utilization of egg iodine by the chicken embryo. *J. Exp. Zool., 45*, 263.

Raheja, K. L., and J. G. Snedecor. (1970). Comparison of subnormal multiple doses of L-thyroxine and L-triiodothyronine in propylthiouracil-fed and radiothyroidectomized chicks *(Gallus domesticus). Comp. Biochem. Physiol., 37*, 555.

Raheja, K. L., J. G. Snedecor, and R. A. Freedland. (1971). Effect of propylthiouracil feeding on glycogen metabolism and malic enzyme in the liver of the chick *(Gallus domesticus). Comp. Biochem. Physiol., 39*, 833.

Refetoff, S., N. I. Robin, and V. S. Fang. (1970). Parameters of thyroid function in serum of 16 selected vertebrate species: Study of PBI, serum $T_4$, free $T_4$ and the pattern of $T_4$ and $T_3$ binding to serum proteins. *Endocrinology. 86*, 793.

Reineke, E. P., and C. W. Turner. (1945). Seasonal rhythms in the thyroid hormone secretion of the chick. *Poultry Sci., 24*, 499.

Ringer, R. K. (1965). Thyroids. In "Avian Physiology" (2nd ed.) (P. D. Sturkie, Ed.). Ithaca, N. Y.: Cornell University Press, Chapter 19.

Roche, J., R. Michel, and E. Volpert. (1956). Concentration des hormones thyroidennes par les ovocytes de la poule. *Compt. Rend. Soc. Biol., 150*, 2149.

Rogler, J. C., H. E. Parker, F. N. Andrews, and C. W. Carrick. (1959). The effect of an iodine deficiency on embryo development and hatchability. *Poultry Sci., 38*, 398.

Romanoff, A. L. (1960). "The Avian Embryo." New York: The Macmillan Co.

Rosenberg, L. L., H. Astier, G. La Roche, J. D. Bayle, A. Tixier-Vidal, and I. Assenmacher. (1967). The thyroid function of the drake after hypophysectomy or hypopthalamic pituitary disconnection *Neuroendocrinology, 2*, 113.

Rosenberg, L. L., M. Goldman, G. LaRoche, and M. K. Dimick. (1964). Thyroid function in rats and chickens. Equilibration of injected iodide with existing thyroidal iodine in Long-Evans rats and White Leghorn chickens. *Endocrinology 74*, 212.

Sadovsky, R., and A. Bensadoun. (1971). Thyroid iodohormones in the plasma of the rooster *(Gallus domesticus). Gen. Comp. Endocrinol., 17*, 268.

Shellabarger, C. J. (1955). A comparison of triiodothyronine and thyroxine in the chick goiter-prevention tests. *Poultry Sci., 34*, 1437.

Singh, A., E. P. Reineke, and R. K. Ringer. (1967). Thyroxine and triiodothyronine turnover in the chicken and the bobwhite and the Japanese quail. *Gen. Comp. Endocrinol., 9*, 353.

Singh, A., E. P. Reineke, and R. K. Ringer. (1968a). Influence of thyroid status of the chick on growth and metabolism, with observations on several parameters of thyroid function. *Poultry Sci., 47*, 212.

Singh, A., E. P. Reineke, and R. K. Ringer. (1968b). Comparison of thyroid secretion rate in chickens as determined by (1) goiter prevention, (2) thyroid hormone substitution, (3) direct output, (4) thyroxine degradation methods. *Poultry Sci., 47*, 205.

Snedecor, J. G. (1968). Liver hypertrophy, liver glycogen accumula-

358

tion, and organ-weight changes in radiothyroidectomized and goitrogen-treated chicks. *Gen. Comp. Endocrinol., 10,* 277.

Snedecor, J. G., and M. F. Camyre. (1966). Interaction of thyroid hormone and androgens on body weight, comb and liver in cockerels. *Gen. Comp. Endocrinol., 6,* 276.

Snedecor, J. G., and D. B. King. (1964). Effect of radiothyroidectomy in chicks with emphasis on glycogen body and liver. *Gen. Comp. Endocrinol., 4,* 144.

Snedecor, J. G., and W. J. Mellen. (1965). Thyroid deprivation and replacement in chickens. *Poultry Sci., 44,* 452.

Spiers, D. E., R. A. McNabb, and F. M. A. McNabb. (1974). The development of thermoregulatory ability, heat seeking activities, and thyroid function in hatchling Japanese quail *(Coturnix coturnix japonica). J. Comp. Physiol., 89,* 159.

Stahl, P., and C. W. Turner. (1961). Seasonal variation in thyroxine secretion rate in two strains of New Hampshire chickens. *Poultry Sci., 40,* 239.

Sterling, K., J. Lashof, and E. Man. (1954). Disappearance from serum of I¹³¹ labeled L-thyroxine and L-triiodothyronine in euthyroid subjects. *J. Clin. Invest., 33,* 1031.

Stoll, R., and P. Blanquet. (1953). Sur l'activite des thyroides de l'embryon du poulet, provenant d'oeufs "marqués" par l'administration de ¹³¹I à la poule. *Ann. Endocrinol., 14,* 1.

Tanabe, Y. (1964). Comparison of estimates for thyroxine secretion rate determined by the goiter prevention assay and by measuring the activity of serum alkaline phosphate in the chicken. *Endocrinol. Jap., 11,* 260.

Tanabe, Y. (1965). Relation of thyroxine secretion rate to age and growth rate in the cockerel. *Poultry Sci., 44,* 591.

Tanabe, Y., T. Komlyama, D. Kobota, and Y. Tamake. (1965). Comparison of the effects of thiouracil, propylthiouracil and methimazole on I¹³¹ metabolism by the chick thyroid, and measurements of thyroxine secretion rate. *Gen. Comp. Endocrinol., 5,* 60.

Tata, J. R., and C. J. Shellabarger. (1959). An explanation for the difference between the response of mammals and birds to thyroxine and triiodothyronine. *Biochem. J., 72,* 608.

Thapliyal, J. P., and R. K. Garg. (1967). Thyroidectomy in the juveniles of the chestnut-bellied munia *(Munia atricapilla). Endokrinologie, 52,* 75.

Thommes, R. C. (1958). Vasculogenesis in selected endocrine glands of normal and hypophysectomized chick embryos. I: The thyroid. *Growth, 22,* 243.

Tixier-Vidal, A., and I. Assenmacher. (1965). Some aspects of the pituitary-thyroid relationship in birds. *Excerpta Med. Found. Intl. Congr. Ser.,* No. 83, p. 172.

Tixier-Vidal, A., B. K. Follett, and D. S. Farner. (1967). Identification cytologique et fonctionnelle des types cellulaires de l'adénohypophyse chez le Caille mâle, "*Coturnix coturnix japonica*" soumise à différentes conditions expérimentales. *Compt. Rend. Acad., Sci. (Paris), 264,* 1739.

Turner, C. W. (1948). Effects of age and season on the thyroxine secretion rate of White Leghorn hens. *Poultry Sci., 27,* 146.

van Tienhoven, A., J. H. Williamson, M. C. Tomlinson, and K. L. Macinnes. (1966). Possible role of the thyroid and the pituitary glands in sex linked dwarfism in the fowl. *Endocrinology, 78,* 950.

Vlijm, L. (1958). On the production of hormones in the thyroid gland of birds (cockerels). *Arch. Neerl. Zool., 12,* 467.

Voitkevich, A. A. (1966). "The Feathers and Plumage of Birds." New York: October House.

Waterman, A. J. (1959). Development of the thyroid-pituitary system in warm-blooded amniotes. In "Comparative Endocrinology" (A. Gorbman Ed.). New York: John Wiley & Sons, p. 351.

Wentworth, B. C. and W. J. Mellen. (1961). Circulating thyroid hormones in domestic birds. *Poultry Sci., 40,* 1275.

Wieselthier, A. S., and A. van Tienhoven. (1972). The effect of thyroidectomy on testicular size and on the photorefractory period in the starling *(Sturnus vulgaris.* L.). *J. Exp. Zool., 179,* 331.

Wollman, S. H. and E. Zwilling. (1953). Radioiodine metabolism in the chick embryo. *Endocrinology, 52,* 526.

# 19

# Parathyroids, Ultimobranchial Glands, and the Pineal

R. K. Ringer
and D. C. Meyer

## 360 PARATHYROIDS

The major function of the parathyroid glands is calcium homeostasis, which is essential for eggshell formation, muscular contraction, blood clotting, enzyme systems, calcification of tissues, and neuromuscular regulation. Regulation of parathyroid hormone release is mediated by the circulating plasma level of calcium. The principal targets of endogenous parathyroid hormone are (1) bone cells for mobilization of calcium and (2) the renal tubules for tubular excretion of phosphates.

### Anatomy

**Location and blood supply.** Four parathyroid glands develop in avian embryos from the endoderm. In the chicken the pair on each side consists of an anterior larger lobe (parathyroid III) and a posterior smaller lobe (parathyroid IV), which are usually fused and may be attached to or near the posterior pole of the thyroid gland (Figure 18–1). In the pigeon the parathyroids on each side may be separated from the thyroid and remain as four discrete glands. Arterial blood is supplied by branches from the common carotid artery and venous drainage is by the jugular vein (Nonidez and Goodale, 1927).

**Embryology.** The 72-hr chick embryo possesses six pharyngeal pouches (also called branchial pouches). Parathyroids III and IV develop from the third and fourth pouches, respectively (see Romanoff, 1960; Hodges, 1970; Venzke, 1947).

**Histology.** The presence of chief cells without any oxyphil cells characterizes the principal difference between avian and mammalian parathyroids (Benoit, 1950). The chief cells are arranged in elongated and branching cords, separated by a thin connective tissue stroma and capillaries. When actively secreting, chief cell cytoplasm is highly granular with few vacuoles; inactive cells, in contrast, have relatively few granules and some vacuoles. Prosecretory granules and secretory (storage) granules have been observed within the cytoplasm of active chief cells (Nevalainen, 1969). The smaller prosecretory granules are abundant compared to secretory granules. Staining ability of the nucleus, which is approximately 5 $\mu$m in diameter, may change with the degree of secretory activity, the nucleus of the active cell staining darker.

**Size.** The parathyroids of birds have an unusual capacity to exhibit hyperplasia and hypertrophy. If the bird is deprived of ultraviolet light, dietary vi-

*Table 19–1* *Effect of dietary calcium on parathyroid weight of 4-week-old White Leghorn cockerels*[a]

| Dietary calcium | | Body weight (g) | Parathyroid, dry weight (g) |
|---|---|---|---|
| Low | (0.3%) | 212 | 386 |
| Normal | (1.0%) | 231 | 302 |
| High | (3%) | 184 | 196 |

[a]On treatment 2 weeks (Mueller *et al.*, 1970).

tamin D, or calcium, enlargement occurs (see Sturkie, 1965). Dietary calcium (see Table 19–1) has a marked effect on parathyroid size and activity (Mueller *et al.*, 1970). Hypertrophy, resulting from calcium deficiency, occurs more rapidly in birds than in other vertebrates (Urist, 1967). Hypertrophy also results from estrogen administration (Landauer, 1954).

Atrophy of the parathyroids was reported when high calcium (3.0%) and deficient available phosphorus (0.4%) diets were fed to growing pullets (Shane *et al.*, 1969). Suppression of endocrine activity by fasting or hypophysectomy decreases the size of the parathyroids.

### Parathyroidectomy

Ablation of the parathyroids has been performed in the pigeon, by Smith (1945); in the duck, by Benoit *et al.* (1941); and in the chicken, by Polin and Sturkie (1957), Tilgner-Peter (1957), Urist *et al.* (1960), and Hurst and Newcomer (1969). Parathyroidectomy (PTx) in ducks and pigeons caused blood calcium levels to drop precipitously, resulting in severe tetany and death within 48 hr. Administration of vitamin D or injection of calcium enabled most birds to survive.

Polin and Sturkie (1957, 1958) reported that tetany and early deaths in chickens were infrequent and dependent on the presence or absence of accessory parathyroid tissue, food intake, and whether laying hens or cocks were used. Laying hens showed more frequent deaths than cocks (see Urist, 1967).

Blood calcium decreases within 24 hr of surgical removal of the glands in chickens yet returns to normal level in some birds within 48 hr postoperation. If absolutely no parathyroid tissue remains, the majority of the birds die within 48 hr (Urist, 1967). When both parathyroids and ultimobranchial bodies (UBGx) were removed from 6– to 10–week–old cockerels they invariably died within 3–

4 days, whereas birds with either operation alone lived until killed several weeks later (Hurst and Newcomer, 1969). Accessory parathyroid tissue present in the ultimobranchial bodies was sufficient to compensate. When these chickens were PTx only, the blood calcium level returned to normal within 50 hr; however, it remained low in the birds that were both PTx and UBGx. The secretion of parathyroid hormone by the accessory parathyroid tissue is therefore sufficient to restore blood calcium levels to normal within 2 days.

## Parathyroid Hormone

Characterization of the avian parathyroid hormone (PTH) has not been made. In the mammal it is a single-chain polypeptide, composed of 83 amino acids and with a molecular weight of approximately 9000 (Potts and Aurbach, 1965; Potts et al., 1968); it possesses a half-life of 22 min in the rat (Melick et al., 1965) and 5–20 min in the dog (Charbon, 1968). Proteolytic enzymes destroy the hormone, so it must be given parenterally.

**Assay.** An *in vivo* assay for parathyroid hormone using chickens 5–7 weeks of age was reported by Polin et al. (1957). *In vivo* assays are based on the hypercalcemic or the phosphaturic response following parathyroid hormone injection. A simple bioassay using *Coturnix coturnix japonica* (Japanese quail), 2–3 weeks of age, has been reported by Dacke and Kenny (1973). The quail are injected with standard or unknown doses of PTH using at least six birds per group. Sixty minutes after the injection, blood is withdrawn by cardiac puncture for plasma calcium determination. A dose–response curve is plotted, against which unknowns are compared. The quail assay is less sensitive and precise than *in vitro* assays.

*In vitro* assays have been developed using radioimmunoassay (Berson et al., 1963), the release of calcium by bone from mice into tissue culture medium (Zanelli et al., 1969), or the activation of adenyl cyclase from the renal cortex of the rat (Marcus and Aurbach, 1969).

**Physiologic actions.** The primary targets of endogenous parathyroid hormone are the bone cells of the skeleton and the renal tubules. Maintenance of calcium homeostasis is regulated through the process of osteolysis, whereby osteoclasts are differentiated to bring about resorption of metaphyseal and endosteal bone (Urist, 1967) and medullary bone (Taylor and Belanger, 1969). Parathyroid hormone does not produce resorption of intramedullary deposits but causes resorption mainly in the area of bone between the endosteum and

the intramedullary desposits (Urist, 1967). Intramedullary bone is known to be estrogen induced and to fluctuate with egg production (see Chapter 16).

Parathyroid hormone is synergistic with vitamin $D_3$ in the mobilization of bone mineral. Vitamin $D_3$ is converted by hydroxylation in the liver to 25-hydroxycholecalciferol, which is in turn converted in the kidney in various steps to a dihydroxy- and a trihydroxycholecalciferol. The dihydroxy form is known to be an active principle necessary, together with parathormone, for bone mineral mobilization; the role of the trihydroxy form is still questionable. Vitamin D also plays a vital role in increasing the rate of absorption of calcium from the gut.

Parathyroid hormone and estrogen have an additive effect on blood calcium (see Sturkie, 1965). Urist et al. (1960) reported that estrogen injection markedly increased the nonultrafilterable calcium fraction, dependent on an increase in liver synthesis of the phosphoprotein phosvitin, which complexes calcium for blood transport. The ultrafilterable calcium fraction is under parathyroid control. When Urist et al. (1960) parathyroidectomized chickens, estrogen injection afforded no protection against tetany or death, even though it had a marked calcemic effect. The calcemic effect was in the nonultrafilterable fraction and not readily available to the tissues.

Early investigators were able to detect only modest effects of exogenous parathyroid hormone on elevating blood calcium. Polin et al. (1957) clearly demonstrated by serial blood samples that injection of 100 U of parathyroid hormone gave maximal response 3.5 hr subsequent to injection. The response was transient and short lived. Candlish and Taylor (1970) reported that in laying hens 20 USP units per kilogram of bovine parathormone yielded a response time of 8.1 ± 2.1 min to establish a new blood calcium level. Injection of 100 USP units i.v. yielded a 7.2 ± 1.9 min response time. In immature chickens and Japanese quail, maximum response developed in less than 60 minutes (Dacke and Kenny, 1971; see Table 19–2).

*Table 19–2*  *Response time to parathormone*

| Species | Age (weeks) | PTE dose (units/bird) | Plasma calcium rise (mg %) | |
|---------|---------|---------|---------|---------|
| | | | 30 min | 60 min |
| Chicken | 2 | 2.0 (i.v.) | 1.14[a] | 0.07 |
| Quail | 3 | 2.0 (s.c.) | 1.46[a] | 1.35[a] |

[a]Significant change (Dacke and Kenny, 1971).

Two views prevail on the calcemic response of laying hens to parathyroid hormone. One is that the rapid response is a result not of osteoclastic bone resorption but of an extraosseous effect causing a release of calcium from bone (Mueller *et al.*, 1973a, b). These workers have suggested an alteration in bone blood flow initiated by an extraosseous mechanism. These same investigators also suggest that proliferation of osteoclasts, as has been shown in the rat, would not occur until 6–8 hr after parathyroid stimulation. In laying hens the number of osteoclasts in medullary bone does not increase until the later stages of shell calcification (Bloom *et al.*, 1958), whereas plasma calcium, which controls parathyroid activity, decreases at the onset of shell calcification (Hodges, 1969).

This slow osteoclast activation concept is in contrast to the view of Candlish (1970), who has measured calcium, hydroxyproline and uronic acid excretion by the kidney in response to parathyroid extract injection (250 USP units given i.v.) in chickens. Based on the ratios of calcium to hydroxyproline and of calcium to uronic acid in the urine in serial samples, Candlish concluded that calcium was released from the bone during the first hour following injection and that during the second hour the ratios indicated increased end products of bone matrix catabolism. After 2 hr this trend was reversed, with a return to the basal state. Candlish concluded that lysis of the bone by osteoclasts may be sufficiently rapid to play a possible role in egg shell formation.

Brown *et al.* (1970) indicated that hyperphosphatemia occurred in 2 hr following i.m. injection of 500 U of parathyroid extract per kilogram of body weight. In contrast, Levinsky and Davidson (1957) and Urist *et al.* (1960) reported no significant effect of parathyroid hormone on the blood phosphate level.

Mueller *et al.* (1973b) injected 31 U of PTH per kilogram into hens fed either 5.00% or 2.26% calcium in the diet and measured changes in plasma calcium or phosphate from 2.5 to 180 min. PTH caused both a hypercalcemia and hyperphosphatemia, which reached maximum 30 min postinjection. The two ions preceded the elevated state by a decreased concentration level. Both the hypercalcemic and hyperphosphatemic curves were correlated as to time, indicating a possible common mechanism of action. The decay of the plasma calcium and phosphate response was rapid and dependent on the dietary calcium levels. The mechanism by which dietary calcium affects plasma calcium and phosphate response to parathyroid hormone is not known. Some of the variability of the plasma phosphate response to parathyroid hormone reported may reflect variation both in sampling time and in the diet.

**Parathyroid influence on the kidney.** Parathyroid hormone causes a rapid phosphaturia in chickens (Levinsky and Davidson, 1957) that is attributed to an increase in net phosphate excretion by the kidney tubule (Martindale, 1969). In addition to phosphaturia, parathyroid hormone causes calciuria in chickens by acting on the kidney tubule. Buchanan (1961) reported that large doses (100 IU given i.m.) of parathyroid extract to male chickens gave both phosphaturic and calciuric responses within 30 min. At low doses (10 IU) only a phosphaturic response was obtained. Ligation of the renal portal system, which supplies the tubules but does not interfere with glomerular filtration, blocked both the expected calciuria and phosphaturia following parathyroid hormone injection, whereas sham-operated hens showed both effects (Mueller, personal communication). Ligation of the renal–portal system caused significantly greater plasma hypercalcemia and hyperphosphatemia than in the sham-operated controls, indicating that plasma elevation of these ions in response to parathyroid hormone is not medicated by the tubular effects of the hormone. In contrast, the kidney tubules counteract the parathyroid hormone-induced plasma hypercalcemia and hyperphosphatemia.

Candlish (1970) reported that parathyroid extract injection caused an almost instantaneous diuresis.

## ULTIMOBRANCHIAL GLANDS

### Anatomy

**Location: blood and nerve supply.** The ultimobranchial glands (bodies) are paired organs, somewhat elongated or lenticular but often irregular in shape; they are 1–3 mm long, and characteristically pink to red in color. The glands are located posterior to the parathyroid glands on either side the gland lies caudodorsal to the base of the brachiocephalic artery into the common carotid and the subclavian arteries. They are located in the same lateral plane as the jugular vein. On the left side the gland lies caudodorsal to the base of the common carotid, close to the posterior part of parathyroid IV and to the carotid body. The right ultimobranchial body is situated in a position similar to the left but slightly more caudal (see Hodges, 1970, for review). The glands are more readily visible in young birds because adipose tissue in the adult, particularly the female, makes locating the glands difficult.

A branch of the common carotid artery supplies blood to each ultimobranchial gland. Venous drainage is through a small vein that enters the jugular vein just above the junction with the brachial vein.

A branch of the accessory nerve from the nodose ganglion innervates the ultimobranchial gland, and a branch also passes posteriorly to the aortic arch (Nonidez, 1935). The recurrent laryngeal nerve and the sympathetic nervous system also innervate the ultimobranchial gland (Dudley, 1942).

**Embryology and histology.** The sixth pharyngeal pouch in the embryo gives rise to the ultimobranchial glands (Dudley, 1942), which separate from the branchial endoderm on the sixth day of incubation. By the ninth day of incubation the body has become positioned as in the adult (Hodges, 1970). Vesicles, a constant feature of the gland, first appear during the fifteenth day of incubation.

The ultimobranchial glands are uncapsulated; however, the organs have a framework of connective tissue stroma composed of reticular, elastic, and collagen fibers. Adipose connective tissue infiltrates the glands. Vesicles are normally found within the stroma of ultimobranchial glands in birds and they are surrounded by squamous to low columnar epithelium; they contain colloidal, granular and/or cellular material. The size of the vesicles ranges from 20 to 1200 $\mu$m. Secretory granules of the vesicular epithelial cells and the granular secretion are composed of a mixture of glycogen, mucoproteins, neutral mucopolysaccharides, and complex acid mucopolysaccharides (Hodges, 1970).

The vesicles may not be functional: they may be mere vestigial pharyngeal remnants (Hodges, 1970). The role played by this tissue remains to be clarified.

Cells, designated as C cells (calcitonin cells), are usually arranged in cords or strands, or occur as individual cells, in the glands. These cells, which secrete calcitonin, have a well-developed golgi apparatus and are in intimate association with blood capillaries and nerves (Nevalainen, 1969; Stoeckel and Porte, 1969). The C cells vary in diameter from 3.3 to 9.6 $\mu$m, depending on their secretory state, and are virtually negative to stains for glycogen, mucoproteins, and mucopolysaccharides (Hodges, 1970).

Eosinophilic granulocytes are characteristic of the ultimobranchials. Encapsulated parathyroid tissue patches are often found enclosed within the ultimobranchial tissue (see Dudley, 1942).

**Size.** The weights of ultimobranchial glands are shown in Table 19–3. Mueller *et al.* (1970) have suggested that weights of ultimobranchial bodies should be reported as defatted weight because fatty infiltration is considerable and varies widely, causing significant variability in reported weights.

**Ultimobranchialectomy**

The ultimobranchial glands have been removed independently of the thyroids and parathyroids in birds by a number of investigators (see Hurst and Newcomer, 1969; Brown *et al.*, 1969, 1970; Speers *et al.*, 1970; Garlich, 1971).

Ablation of the parathyroids and ultimo-

*Table 19–3*  *Weight of the ultimobranchial glands in relation to the total body weight in the developing chicken*

| Age | Breed[a] | Ultimobranchial bodies | | | References |
|---|---|---|---|---|---|
| | | Body weight (g) | Wet weight (mg) | Wet weight (mg/kg body weight) | |
| 18 day embryo | W. L. | 17 | 0.5 | 30.0 | Dent *et al.* (1969) |
| 3 day | W. L. | 32 | 0.4 | 12.7 | Dent *et al.* (1969) |
| 35 day | W. L. | 297 | 3.4 | 11.4 | Dent *et al.* (1969) |
| 77 day | W. L. | 790 | 5.0 | 6.3 | Dent *et al.* (1969) |
| 105 day | W. L. | 1313 | 6.4 | 4.9 | Dent *et al.* (1969) |
| 490 day | | | | | |
| Male | W.L. | 2680 | 5.6 | 2.1 | Dent *et al.* (1969) |
| Female | W.L. | 1900 | 5.3 | 2.8 | Dent *et al.* (1969) |
| 3 week | W.P.R | | 17.1 | 20.6 | Witterman *et al.* (1969) |
| 3 month | W.P.R. | | 25.2 | 19.3 | Witterman *et al.* (1969) |
| 9 month | W.P.R. | | 31.6 | 16.4 | Witterman *et al.* (1969) |

[a]W.L. = White Leghorn; W.P.R. = White Plymouth Rock.

branchial glands in chicks resulted in death within 3–4 days after the operation. Removal of either gland alone did not affect survival time adversely (Hurst and Newcomer, 1969). Accessory parathyroid tissue in the ultimobranchial bodies apparently compensated for the lack of parathyroids.

## Calcitonin

"Calcitonin" was a name introduced by Copp and co-workers for a hypocalcemic factor in mammals that they attributed to the parathyroid gland (see Copp *et al.*, 1961). It was subsequently shown by Hirsch *et al.* (1963) that the hypocalcemic principle was secreted from the thyroid and they proposed the name "thyrocalcitonin." Copp *et al.* (1967) later demonstrated that the ultimobranchial glands of chickens and turkeys secreted calcitonin. The thyroids of the chicken, however, did not secrete calcitonin (Kraintz and Puil, 1967).

Avian calcitonin probably possesses a polypeptide structure closely resembling that of porcine calcitonin, possessing 32 amino acids in sequence and a molecular weight of approximately 4000 (see Hirsch and Munson, 1969, for review).

Calcitonin in the chicken, turkey, pigeon, and quail is produced by the C cells of the ultimobranchial glands; however, it has been reported that pigeon thyroid extract is about equal in biologic activity to ultimobranchial extract (Moseley *et al.*, 1968). In the pigeon and the turtledove, the ultimobranchial gland and thyroid produce calcitonin (Belanger, 1971). Minute amounts of calcitonin were detected in the thyroid gland of laying and nonlaying geese by Bates *et al.* (1969). It is possible that some C cells of ultimobranchial origin migrate to the thyroid during embryonic development.

The concentration of calcitonin within the ultimobranchial glands of chickens or turkeys is many times that of the content of mammalian thyroids. Plasma calcitonin levels have been determined in pigeon, goose, duck, chicken, and Japanese quail and range between 100 and 1500 MRC units/ml (Kenny, 1971; MRC units defined in Table 19–4). Ultimobranchial cells and C cells have the ability to take up and selectively store amine precursors, such as 5-hydroxytryptophan (5HTP) and dihydroxyphenylalanine (DOPA), and contain decarboxylating enzymes that convert 5HTP and DOPA to 5-hydroxytryptamine (5HT) and dihydroxyphenethylamine (dopamine) (Hirsch and Munson, 1969). Both 5HT and dopamine have been identified in separate cell types of the chicken ultimobranchial gland (Almqvist *et al.*, 1971).

*Table 19–4   Relative calcitonin content in MRC units[a] per milligram fresh gland extracted[b]*

| | |
|---|---|
| Chicken ultimobranchial | 0.43 |
| Turkey ultimobranchial | 0.35 |
| MRC standard thyroid calcitonin (dry weight) | 0.025 |
| Pure calcitonin peptide | 200.0 |

[a]MRC unit = Medical Research Council unit (international unit) defined as the amount of calcitonin in four standard vials of Research Standard for thyroid calcitonin, each vial containing approximately 10 mg of preparation.
[b]From Copp *et al.* (1967).

**Assays for calcitonin.** Assays have failed in avian species because the hypocalcemic response to calcitonin is questionable; they are performed in mammals, where the response is consistent.

In the *in vivo* assay, calcitonin is injected into rats or mice. This is followed by blood withdrawal for calcium determination, at periodic intervals up to 6 hr, measured against a standard preparation response curve. Comparative sensitivity to calcitonin by mice and rats may differ widely (Parsons and Reynolds, 1968).

In the *in vitro* assay, calcitonin is quantitated from the measurement of $^{45}Ca$ released from prelabeled, tissue-cultured, embryonic rat bone.

In the radioimmunoassay, antiserum is produced following several injections of purified calcitonin; then cross-reactivity is measured.

**Secretion and function of calcitonin.** Calcitonin lowers plasma calcium in mammals by inhibiting the bone resorptive activity of the osteocytes (osteolysis) regulated by the parathyroid hormone.

The secretory rate of calcitonin in the bird far exceeds that of the mammal. At normocalcemic levels the goose secretes 25 times more calcitonin per unit of body weight than the normocalcemic pig (Bates *et al.,* 1969). Ziegler *et al.* (1969) perfused the ultimobranchial gland of the hen with calcium, magnesium, potassium, glucagon, cortisone, parathyroid hormone, and thyroid-stimulating hormone. Only hypercalcemic perfusion caused an increased release of calcitonin. Dietary calcium is the principal factor regulating calcitonin secretion in birds. The metabolic activity of the ultimobranchial gland, as measured by the uptake of [$^{14}C$]-labeled $\alpha$-aminoisobutyric acid, is in direct relationship to the dietary calcium level (Mueller *et al.*, 1970). There is a disappearance of secretory granules from the ultimobranchial gland cells of chickens following hypercalcemia (Copp *et al.*, 1968), indicating that calcitonin secretion has been stimulated and is involved in calcium metabolism. Ultimobranchialectomized chicks do not respond to hypercalcemia by secondary lowering of plasma calcium (Brown *et al.*, 1970). In contrast, Gonnerman *et al.* (1972) could not confirm these results and concluded that the control of acute hypercalcemia is probably not the primary role of calcitonin. Hypercalcemia of egg laying does not cause a measurable depletion of calcitonin from the ultimobranchial gland (Witterman *et al.*, 1969), so age is a factor in either calcitonin secretion or target organ response; the latter is probably a more realistic assessment.

In mammals, the primary effect of calcitonin appears to be inhibition of bone resorption. Urist (1967) found no significant lowering of plasma calcium of chicks given chicken thyroid extract, porcine thyroid calcitonin, or avian ultimobranchial calcitonin. He suggests that the bone tissue of birds is highly reactive and that chicks have a rapid hypercalcemic response to exogenous parathyroid hormone, although he obtained no response to calcitonin. Removing one pair of parathyroids of cockerels decreases the response of the other pair, so that rapid adjustments to hypocalcemia produced by avian calcitonin is observed (Kraintz and Intscher, 1969).

That age is important in studies on calcitonin function was demonstrated by Lloyd *et al.* (1970), who administered ultimobranchial extract to laying hens without detectable effect; in 7-day-old and 12-week-old chickens, however, plasma calcium, inorganic phosphate, and plasma magnesium decreased.

Decreased plasma magnesium did not occur until 120 min after calcitonin injection (Lloyd and Collins, 1970). The effect of calcitonin on plasma magnesium in mammals has been variable. Chicken ultimobranchial extract caused depression of plasma calcium and phosphorus, but not magnesium, when injected into dogs (Cramer *et al.*, 1969).

In contrast to these results, Brown *et al.* (1969) ultimobranchialectomized young chicks, thus rendering them calcitonin deficient, without any effect on growth, serum calcium, serum phosphorus, serum alkaline phosphatase, or x-ray appearance of the bones. Gonnerman *et al.* (1972) failed to produce hypocalcemia in intact, 6-week-old cockerels by injection of ultimobranchial extract. Bone calcium, magnesium, phosphorus, hydroxyproline, and hexosamine were unaltered by calcitonin deficiency brought about by ultimobranchialectomy (Brown *et al.*, 1970).

The physiologic function and importance of cal-

citonin in avian species is not yet resolved. Calcitonin appears to have no major role in the conversion of avian medullary bone to calcium for egg shell deposition or bone turnover in normal, young, growing chickens. It may play a role in serum phosphorus homeostasis independent of any action on calcium metabolism.

## THE PINEAL

### Anatomy

**Development, location, size, and structural types.** The pineal gland, or epiphysis cerebri, develops as an evagination of the posterior diencephalic roof and lies between the cerebral hemispheres and the cerebellum, extending dorsally toward the skull. The pineal undergoes structural changes during development and the adult gland is generally a median, compact structure; however, considerable variation exists in its morphology among various species, with no apparent relationship to body size (Quay, 1965a). In the laying hen the gland weighs about 5 mg and its dimensions are $3.5 \times 2.0$ mm (Wight, 1971).

Studnicka (1905) has divided the pineal into three basic structural types: (1) saccular, hollow organs with thick walls (passerine birds); (2) tubules and follicles (domestic pigeon and duck); and (3) solid and lobular (chicken). However, most species would more properly reflect gradations of these basic types and currently it is not feasible to relate morphologic differences to physiology (Ralph, 1970; Menaker and Oksche, 1974).

**Histology.** Nomenclature for the identification of avian pineal cell types varies but in the chicken the following cell types have been identified by Fujie (1968): (1) pinealocytes, the most numerous parenchymal cells; (2) astrocytes, the supporting cells inserted among the pinealocytes and extending microvilli into the lumen; (3) small glial cells containing many filaments; and (4) sympathetic nerve endings near the pinealocytes. Some pineal cells may also have photoreceptor capabilities (Ralph, 1970; Pearson, 1972), but avian pineal sensory cell structure differs in several important aspects from the more familiar photoreceptor organs of fish, amphibians, and reptiles; the gland appears to be predominantly secretory, as in mammals (Wight, 1971; Menaker and Oksche, 1974). This does not exclude the possibility that cells in the nearby ventral diencephalon may be photosensory (Benoit, 1964).

**Innervation and blood supply.** There is evidence for the existence of nerve cells within the pineals of various passerines and pigeons (Quay and Renzoni, 1963; Menaker and Oksche, 1974) but there are no neurons in the various other species, including the chicken (Stammer, 1966). The avian pineal is well innervated via the superior cervical ganglia in the sympathetic autonomic nervous system in *Coturnix coturnix japonica* (Japanese quail; Hedlund, 1970) and White Leghorn cockerels (Hedlund and Nalbandov, 1969). Innervation in the duck and pigeon pineal is sparser but the pineal of the house sparrow is richly innervated (Menaker and Oksche, 1974).

The major blood supply to the pineal is via the posterior meningeal artery, which ascends the anterolateral face of the pineal stalk, where it ramifies near the base of the gland to form a circus vasculosus or rete pinealis (Beatit and Glenny, 1966). Lymphatic vessels are also present in year-old chickens (Quay, 1965); large foci of mature lymphocytes are often observed but their significance is unknown. The avian pineal has no blood–brain barrier (Wight, 1971) and blood flow is probably quite rapid.

## Synthesis of Melatonin and Serotonin

The interrelationships among pineal biochemical rhythms, photoperiod, and reproduction are the key points of pineal physiology. Pinealocytes can actively take up tryptophan from the blood, hydroxylate it to 5-hydroxytryptophan (5HTP), and decarboxylate 5HTP to 5-hydroxytryptamine (5HT or serotonin). Serotonin has a variety of biochemical fates, the most important of which are: (1) degradation to 5-hydroxyindoleacetic acid (5HIAA) and 5-hydroxytryptophol and (2) and conversion to melatonin via N-acetyltransferase and hydroxyindole-O-methyltransferase (HIOMT). These pathways have been delineated for mammals (Wurtman *et al.*, 1968), and there is sufficient evidence in Aves for the presence of biogenic amines (Wight and MacKenzie, 1971), 5-hydroxytryptophol (Wurtman *et al.*, 1968), melatonin (van der Veerdonk, 1965), N-acetyltransferase (Binkley *et al.* 1973), and HIOMT (Axelrod, 1964) to strongly suggest similar pathways in the avian pineal.

The localization of HIOMT is pineal specific in the rat but in some avian species, including the chicken, this enzyme is found in low activity in the retina (Axelrod, 1964; Quay, 1965b). However, melatonin cannot be detected in the serum of pinealectomized chickens (Pelham and Ralph, 1973). The chicken has a large capacity for the synthesis of melatonin (Binkley *et al.*, 1973). In terms of wet pineal weight chickens have seven times the N–acetyltransferase activity, 600 times the HIOMT activity, and 13 times the amount of melatonin found in rats and there are differences in substrate specifics (van der Veerdonk, 1965; Axelrod, 1964)

## Pineal Rhythms.

Quay (1963, 1964) has shown a marked 24-hr rhythm in serotonin, 5HIAA, and melatonin content of the rat pineal and in 5HT and 5HIAA of the pigeon pineal (Quay, 1966). In quail there is a pineal 5HT rhythm that peaks during the light (Hedlund and Ralph, 1967; see Table 19–5). In *Gallus domesticus*, Meyer *et al.* (1973) have shown a 24-hr rhythm in 5HT content of both pineal and blood, with peak levels during darkness; Lynch (1971) has reported a rhythm in pineal and serum melatonin, also with peak values during the same dark portion of the photoperiod (Table 19–5). This is in contrast to the rat indole rhythms, in which 5HT and 5HIAA are closely in phase with a peak during midlight, whereas melatonin peaks during the dark phase. In chickens and possibly other avian species these quantitative biochemical and phase differences suggest a different mode of action of melatonin than occurs in the rat. In Japanese quail and three species of African weaver birds, pineal content of melatonin is highest in the dark phase of their photoperiod and lowest in the light (Ralph *et al.*, 1967).

Changes in HIOMT activity in constant darkness are in opposite direction in diurnally active chickens compared to nocturnally active rats, whereas melatonin content and N-acetyltransferase activity have similar daily rhythms in both animals. The phase of these rhythms is linked to environmental lighting and the corresponding activity state. Binkley *et al.* (1973) show that N-acetyltransferase has a rhythm with maximum activity during the middark period, whereas HIOMT shows no significant relationship to the melatonin rhythm (peak in the middark period). Superior cervical ganglionectomy in the chicken (MacBride *et al.*, 1973) showed that HIOMT variation was abolished, whereas the melatonin and N-acetyltransferase rhythms remained intact. Cyclic changes in pineal melatonin content in chickens therefore appear to be regulated, at least in part, by N-acetyltransferase activity and do not depend on sympathetic innervation from the superior cervical ganglia.

Because 5HT is already at peak levels during the N-acetyltransferase peak, other mechanisms

*Table 19–5*  Maximum and minimum levels of serotonin and melatonin over a 24-hr period in pineals and blood of various avian species

| Species | Age (months) | Sex | Photoperiod | Serotonin | | Melatonin | |
|---|---|---|---|---|---|---|---|
| | | | | Pineal (ng/pin) | Blood (μg/ml) | Pineal (ng/pin) | Blood (ng/ml) |
| *Gallus domesticus* (chicken) | 12 | F | Dark | 90[a] | 6.9 ± 0.7[a] | 38 (3 months)[b] | 0.220 (4 months)[c] |
| | | M | Dark | 70 | 4.4 ± 0.3 | | |
| | 12 | F | Light | 10 | 4.0 ± 0.9 | 5.1 (3 months) | 0 (4 months) |
| | | M | Light | 10 | 3.2 ± 0.1 | | |
| *Columba livia* (pigeon) | Mature | Mixed | Dark | 50[d] | Light{0.7 ± 0.06[e] (male) | | |
| | | | Light | 285 | Light{1.5 ± 0.14 (female) | | |
| *Anas platyrhynchos* (duck) | 6 | F | Light | | 2.1 ± 0.19[e] | | |
| | | M | | | 1.7 ± 0.16 | | |
| *Coturnix coturnix* (Japanese quail) | Mature | Mixed | Dark | 0.45[f] | | 3.2 | |
| | | | Light | 1.5 | | 0.6 | |
| Antarctic penguin | ? | ? | Dark | 63.61[g] | | | |
| | | | Light | 37.4 | | | |

[a]Meyer et al. (1973).
[b]Lynch (1971).
[c]Pelham and Ralph (1973).
[d]Quay (1963).
[e]Sturkie (1972): These are typical values recorded between 9 and 11 a.m. (14 : 10 L : D) 6 a.m. – 8 p.m. light.
[f]Hedlund et al. (1971).
[g]Maria et al. (1973).

368 acting alone or in concert with $N$-acetyltransferase may be regulating the pineal and serum melatonin content. Meyer and Sturkie (1974) have shown that much of the 5HT (30%) in the blood is stored in lymphocytes, although details of uptake, storage, and release have not yet been established. There are large numbers of lymphocytes in the fowl pineal, and the parallel blood and pineal 5HT rhythms suggest that blood-borne lymphocyte 5HT may be contributing to this pineal rhythm.

The control of these circadian rhythms has been linked directly or indirectly to environmental lighting. There is some evidence that light may have a direct effect on photoreceptor elements in the pineal, and a neural pathway for light impulses to reach the pineal in mammals has been revealed (Moore et al., 1968), but evidence for such a pathway in the bird is lacking.

### Pineal and Gonadotropic Hormones

The importance of these diurnal rhythms lies in the gonadotropic and as yet undefined regulatory properties of the various pineal indoles and factors. Melatonin affects sleep, behavior, and brain electrical activity and can induce the formation of pyridoxal kinase to form more pyridoxal phosphate (a coenzyme needed for the decarboxylation of 5HTP to 5HT (Wurtman et al., 1968). There is considerable evidence that various indole derivatives, including melatonin, exert a significant influence over the pituitary gonadotropins in mammals directly or indirectly via the hypothalamus (Reiter, 1973; Quay, 1974). Certain other crude pineal polypeptide fractions modulate pituitary secretion by increasing the content of hypothalamic FSH- and LH-releasing factors in vitro and in vivo (Moszowaska et al., 1973). Pineal extracts from chickens do not induce ovulation but may inhibit (slightly at least) the activity of LH releasing hormone (Harrison et al., 1974).

Melatonin inhibits the growth of the gonads and oviducts of quails (Homma et al., 1967). Singh and Turner (1967) have shown that injected melatonin decreases the weight of testes and ovaries of developing chickens. Melatonin and 5-methoxytryptophol stimulated testes and combs of young cockerels but inhibited growth in these organs in adult males (Balemans, 1972). Because comb growth is dependent on LH activity, the mechanism of action of these indoles is probably manifested through the hypothalamohypophyseal system. Administration of 5-methoxytryptophol in increasing concentrations to adult hens shows an inhibitory effect on ovarian and follicular weight. Because follicular growth is mainly dependent on a FSH/LH ratio, this may reflect the mechanism of action (Balemans, 1973). It is also interesting that sleep and body temperature rhythms are changed by injection of melatonin into sparrows (Gaston and Menaker, 1968) and chicks (Barchas et al., 1967).

### Pinealectomy

Pinealectomy usually produces only slightly accelerated rates of gonadal growth in mammals (Reiter, 1973). Based on pinealectomized chickens (day 1), the pineal appears to have a progonadotropic role up to 20 days of age and an antigonadotropic role between 40 and 60 days of age. Injection of pineal extracts reduced the weight of the testes, and the pineals of capons were hypertrophied (Shellabarger, 1953). Pinealectomy in the chicken had no effect on the rhythm of oviposition in constant light (Harrison and Becker, 1969). Saylor and Wolfson (1967) found that the pineal contributes to the achievement of sexual maturity in the Japanese quail under proper lighting conditions. In pinealectomized birds both maturation and onset of lay are temporarily delayed, suggesting a progonadotropic role. Cardinali et al. (1971) reported that pinealectomy decreased testicular weight and affected the in vitro biosynthesis of steroids in the domestic duck. Pinealectomy of sparrows does not abolish the entrainment response to light cycles and bilaterally enucleated sparrows show entrainment to 24-hr light cycles in a manner similar to normal birds. Neither the eyes nor the pineals are necessary for entrainment, therefore, but the pineal is essential for the continuance of the circadian rhythm in continuous darkness. Binkley et al. (1971) has also shown that pinealectomy abolishes the free-running rhythm of body temperature changes in house sparrows. The function of the pineal in sparrows, therefore, is to serve as a pacemaker for circadian locomotor and temperature rhythms (Gaston and Menaker, 1968).

It appears that the various pineal indoles and factors play a secondary role in the control of reproduction and overall locomotor rhythms in both mammals and birds. The pineal's effect on the gonads is probably mediated via hypothalamic centers containing the releasing factors and tropic hormones that subsequently act on the pituitary. The pineal could also affect the hepatic metabolism of steroids and feedback control or, more importantly, participate in the control of cerebral homeostatic mechanisms (Quay, 1974).

# REFERENCES

## Parathyroids and Ultimobranchial Bodies

Almqvist, S., E. Malmqvist, C. Owman, M. Ritzen, F. Sundler, and G. Swendin. (1971). Dopamine synthesis and storage, calcium-lowering activity, and thyroidal properties of chicken ultimobranchial cells. *Gen. Comp. Endocrinol.,* 17, 512.

Bates, R. F. L., J. Bruce, and A. D. Care. (1969). Measurement of calcitonin secretion rate in the goose. *J. Endocrinol.,* 45, XIV.

Belanger, L. F. (1971). The ultimobranchial gland of birds and the effects of nutritional variations. *J. Exp. Zool.,* 178, 125.

Benoit, J. (1950). Les glandes endocrines. In "Traite' de Zoologie," Vol. 15. (P. P. Grasse, Ed.). Paris: Masson, p. 290.

Benoit, J., G. Fabiani, R. Gangaud, and J. Clavert. (1941). Supression par la parathyroidectomie de l'action hypercalcémiante du dipropionate d'oestradiol chez le canard domestique. *Compt. Rend. Soc. Biol.,* 135, 1606.

Berson, S. A., R. S. Yalow, G. D. Aurbach, and J. T. Potts, Jr. (1963). Immunoassay of bovine and human parathyroid hormone. *Proc. Natl. Acad. Sci. U.S.,* 49, 613.

Bloom, M. A., L. V. Domm, A. V. Nalbandov, and W. Bloom. (1958). Medullary bone of laying chickens. *Am. J. Anat.,* 102, 411.

Brown, D. M., D. Y. E. Perey, P. B. Dent, and R. A. Good. (1969). Effect of chronic calcitonin deficiency on the skeleton of the chicken. *Proc. Soc. Exp. Biol. Med.,* 130, 1001.

Brown, D. M., D. Y. E. Perey, and T. Jowsey. (1970). Effects of ultimobranchialectomy on bone composition and mineral metabolism in the chicken. *Endocrinology,* 87, 1282.

Buchanan, J. D. (1961). Parathyroid influence on renal excretion of calcium. In "The Parathyroids" (R. D. Greep and R. V. Talmage, Eds.). Chapter 6, p. 334.

Campbell, I. L., and C. W. Turner. (1942). The relation of the endocrine system to the regulation of calcium metabolism. *Univ. Mo. Res. Bull.,* 352.

Candlish, J. K. (1970). The urinary excretion of calcium hydroxyproline and uronic acid in the laying fowl after the administration of parathyroid extract. *Comp. Biochem. Physiol.,* 32, 703.

Candlish, J. K., and T. G. Taylor. (1970). The response-time to the parathyroid hormone in the laying fowl. *J. Endocrinol.,* 48, 143.

Charbon, G. A. (1968). Parathormone—a selective vasodilator. In "Parathyroid Hormone and Thyrocalcitonin (Calcitonin)" (R. V. Talmage and L. F. Belanger, Eds.). New York: Excerpta Medica Foundation, p. 475.

Copp, D. H., D. W. Cockcroft, and Y. Kueh. (1967). Ultimobranchial origin of calcitonin, hypocalcemic effect of extracts from chicken glands. *Can. J. Physiol. Pharmacol.,* 45, 1095.

Copp, D. H., A. G. F. Davidson, and B. Cheney. (1961). Evidence for a new parathyroid hormone which lowers blood calcium. *Proc. Can. Fed. Biol. Soc.,* 4, 17.

Copp, D. H., W. A. Webber, B. S. Low, Y. Kueh, and J. Biley. (1968). Effect of dietary calcium on ultimobranchial morphology in chickens. *Proc. Can. Fed. Biol. Soc.,* 11, 34.

Cramer, C. F., C. O. Parkes, and D. H. Copp. (1969). The effect of chicken and hog calcitonin on some parameters of Ca, P and Mg metabolism in dogs. *Can. J. Physiol. Pharmacol.,* 47, 181.

Dacke, C. G., and A. D. Kenny. (1971). Marked rapidity and sensitivity of the hypercalcemic response to parathyroid hormone in birds. *Fed. Proc.,* 30, 417. (Abstr.)

Dacke, C. G., and A. D. Kenny. (1973). Avian bioassay method for parathyroid hormone. *Endocrinology,* 92, 463.

Dent, P. B., D. M. Brown, and R. A. Good. (1969). Ultimobranchial calcitonin in the developing chicken. *Endocrinology,* 85, 582.

Dudley, J. (1942). The development of the ultimobranchial body of the fowl, *Gallus domesticus. Am. J. Anat.,* 71, 65.

Garlich, J. D. (1971). A technique for the surgical removal of the ultimobranchial glands from the domestic fowl. *Poultry Sci.,* 50, 700.

Gonnerman, W. A., R. P. Breitenbach, W. F. Erfling, and C. S. Anast. (1972). An analysis of ultimobranchial gland function in the chicken. *Endocrinology,* 91, 1423.

Hirsch, P. F. and P. L. Munson. (1969). Thyrocalcitonin. *Physiol. Rev.,* 49, 548.

Hirsch, P. F., G. F. Ganthier, and P. L. Munson. (1963). Thyroid hypocalcemic principle and recurrent laryngeal nerve injury as factors affecting the response to parathyroidectomy in rats. *Endocrinology,* 73, 244.

Hodges, R. D. (1969). pH and mineral ion levels in the blood of the laying hen (*Gallus domesticus*) in relation to egg shell formation. *Comp. Biochem. Physiol.,* 28, 1243.

Hodges, R. D. (1970). The structure of the fowl's ultimobranchial gland. *Ann. Biol. Anim. Biochem. Biophys.,* 10, 255.

Hurst, J. G., and W. S. Newcomer. (1969). Functional accessory parathyroid tissue in ultimobranchial bodies of chickens. *Proc. Soc. Exp. Biol. Med.,* 132, 555.

Kenny, A. D. (1971). Determination of calcitonin in plasma by bioassay. *Endocrinology,* 89, 1005.

Kraintz, L., and K. Intscher. (1969). Effect of calcitonin on the domestic fowl. *Can. J. Physiol. Pharmacol.,* 47, 313.

Kraintz, L., and E. A. Puil. (1967). Absence of hypocalcemic activity in chicken thyroid. *Can. J. Physiol. Pharmacol.,* 45, 1099.

Landauer, W. (1954). The effect of estradiol benzoate and corn oil on bone structure of growing cockerels exposed to vitamin D deficiency. *Endocrinology,* 55, 686.

Levinsky, N. G., and D. G. Davidson. (1957). Renal action of parathyroid extract in the chicken. *Am. J. Physiol.,* 191, 530.

Lloyd, J. W., and W. E. Collins. (1970). Hypomagnesemic effect of avian calcitonin. *Poultry Sci.,* 49, 446

Lloyd, J. W., R. A. Peterson, and W. E. Collins. (1970). Effect of an avian ultimobranchial extract in the domestic fowl. *Poultry Sci.,* 49, 1117.

Marcus, R., and G. D. Aurbach. (1969). Bioassay of parathyroid hormone *in vitro* with a stable preparation of adenyl cyclase from rat kidney. *Endocrinology,* 85, 801.

Martindale, L. (1969). Phosphate excretion in the laying hen. *J. Physiol. (London),* 203, 82.

Melick, R. A., G. D. Aurbach, and J. T. Potts, Jr. (1965). Distribution and half-life of $^{131}$I-labeled parathyroid hormone in the rat. *Endocrinology,* 77, 198.

Moseley, J. M., E. W. Matthews, R. H. Breed, L. Galante, A. Tse, and I. MacIntyre. (1968). The ultimobranchial origin of calcitonin. *Lancet,* i(7534), 108.

Mueller, G. L., C. S. Anast, and R. P. Breitenbach. (1970). Dietary calcium and ultimobranchial body and parathyroid gland in the chicken. *Am. J. Physiol.,* 218, 1718.

Mueller, W. J., R. L. Brubaker, C. B. Gay, and J. N. Boelkins. (1973a). Mechanisms of bone resorption in laying hens. *Fed. Proc.,* 32, 1951.

Mueller, W. J., K. L. Hall, C. A. Maurer, Jr., and I. G. Joshua. (1973b). Plasma calcium and inorganic phosphate response of laying hens to parathyroid hormone. *Endocrinology,* 92, 853.

Nevalainen, T. (1969). Fine structure of the parathyroid gland of the laying hen (*Gallus domesticus*). *Gen. Comp. Endocrinol.,* 12, 561.

Nonidez, J. F. (1935). The presence of depressor nerves in the aorta and carotid of birds. *Anat. Rec.,* 62, 47.

Nonidez, F. J., and H. D. Goodale. (1927). Histological studies on the endocrine of chickens deprived of ultraviolet light. I: Parathyroids. *Am. J. Anat.,* 38, 319.

Parsons, J. A., and J. J. Reynolds. (1968). Species discrimination between calcitonins. *Lancet,* i, 1067.

Polin, D., and P. D. Sturkie. (1957). The influence of the parathyroids on blood calcium levels and shell deposition in laying hens. *Endocrinology,* 60, 778.

Polin, D., and P. D. Sturkie. ,(1958). Parathyroid and gonad relationship in regulating blood calcium fractions in chickens. *Endocrinology,* 63, 177.

370

Polin, D., P. D. Sturkie, and W. G. Hunsaker. (1957). The blood calcium response of the chicken to parathyroid extracts. *Endocrinology, 60, 1.*

Potts, J. T., Jr., and G. D. Aurbach. (1965). The chemistry of parathyroid hormone. In "The Parathyroid Glands: Ultrastructure, Secretion and Function" (P. J. Gaillard, R. V. Talmage, and A. M. Budy, Eds.). Chicago: University of Chicago Press, p. 53.

Potts, J. T., H. T. Keutmann, H. Niall, L. Deftos, H. B. Brewer, and G. R. Aurbach. (1968). Covalent structure of bovine parathyroid hormone in relation to biological and immunological activity. In "Parathyroid Hormone and Thyrocalcitonin (Calcitonin)" (R. V. Talmage and L. F. Belanger, Eds.). New York: Excerpta Medica Foundation, p. 44.

Romanoff, A. L. (1960). "The Avian Embryo." New York: The Macmillan Company, p. 878.

Shane, S. M., R. J. Young, and L. Drook. (1969). Renal and parathyroid changes produced by high calcium intake in growing pullets. *Avian Dis., 13,558.*

Smith, G. C. (1945). Technique for parathyroidectomy in pigeons. *Anat. Rec., 92, 81.*

Speers, G. M., D. Y. E. Perey, and D. M. Brown. (1970). Effect of ultimobranchialectomy in the laying hen. *Endocrinology, 87, 1292.*

Stoeckel, M. E., and A. Porte. (1969). Localisation ultimobranchiale et thyroidienne des cellules C (cellules A calcitonine) chez deux columbidae: le pigeon et le tourtereau. Etude au microscope électronique. *Z. Zellforsch., 102, 376.*

Sturkie, P. D. (1965). In "Avian Physiology" (2nd ed.) (P. D. Sturkie, Ed.). Ithaca, N. Y.: Cornell University Press, p. 649.

Taylor, T. G., and L. F. Belanger. (1969). The mechanism of bone resorption in laying hens. *Calcium Tiss. Res., 4, 162.*

Tilgner-Peter, A. (1957). Die Folgen der Parathyreoidektomie bei Huhnern. *Arch. Ges. Physiol. (Pflügers), 265, 187.*

Urist, M. R. (1967). Avian parathyroid physiology: Including a special comment on calcitonin. *Am. Zool., 7, 885.*

Urist, M. R. N. M. Deutsch, G. Pomerantz, and F. C. Mclean. (1960). Interrelations between actions of parathyroid hormone and estrogens on bone and blood in avian species. *Am. J. Physiol., 199, 851.*

Venzke, W. G. (1947). Morphogenesis of the parathyroid glands of chicken embryos. *Am. J. Vet. Res., 8, 421.*

Wittermann, E. R., A. G. Cherian, and I. C. Radde. (1969). Calcitonin content of ultimobranchial body tissue in chicks, pullets and laying hens. *Can. J. Physiol. Pharmacol., 47, 175.*

Zanelli, D. J. Lea, and J. A. Nisbet. (1969). A bioassay method *in vitro* for parathyroid hormone. *J. Endocrinol., 43, 33.*

Ziegler, R., M. Telib, and E. F) Pfeiffer. (1969). The secretion of calcitonin by the perfused ultimobranchial gland of the hen. *Hormone Metab. Res., 1, 39.*

## The Pineal

Axelrod, J., R. J. Wurtman, and C. M. Winget. (1964). Melatonin synthesis in the hen pineal gland and its control by light. *Nature* (London) *201, 1134.*

Balemans, M. (1972). Age-dependent effects of 5-methoxytryptophol and melatonin on testes and comb growth of the White Leghorn (*Gallus domesticus* L.). *J. Neural Trans., 33, 179.*

Balemans, M. (1973). The inhibitory effect of 5-methoxytryptophol on ovarian weight, follicular growth, and egg production of adult White Leghorn hens (*Gallus domesticus* L.). *J. Neural Trans., 34, 159.*

Barchas, J., F. DaCosta, and S. Spector. (1967). Acute pharmacology of melatonin. *Nature* (London), *214, 919.*

Beatit, C. W., and F. Glenny. (1966). Some aspects of the vascularization and chemical histology of the pineal gland in *Gallus. Anat. Anz., 118, 396.*

Benoit, J. (1964). The role of the eye and of the hypothalamus in the photostimulation of gonads in the duck. *Ann. N. Y. Acad. Sci., 117, 204.*

Binkley, S., E. Kluth, and M. Menaker. (1971). Pineal function in sparrows: circadian rhythms and body temperature. *Science, 174, 311.*

Binkley, S., S. MacBride, D. Klein, and C. Ralph. (1973). Pineal enzymes: regulation of avian melatonin synthesis. *Science, 181, 273.*

Cardinali, D. P., A. E. Cuello, J. Tramezzani, and J. M. Rosner. (1971). Effects of pinealectomy on the testicular function of the adult male duck. *Endocrinology, 89, 1082.*

Fujie, E. (1968). Ultrastructure of the pineal body of the domestic chicken, with special reference to the changes induced by altered photoperiods. *Arch. Histol. Jap., 29, 271.*

Gaston, S. and M. Menaker. (1968). Pineal function: The biological clock in the sparrow. *Science, 160, 1125.*

Harrison, P. C., and W. C. Becker. (1969). Extraretinal photocontrol of oviposition in pinealectomized domestic fowl. *Proc. Soc. Exp. Biol. Med., 132, 164.*

Harrison, P. C., C. J. Organek, and L. Cogburn. (1974). Northeastern Regional report (NE-61).

Hedlund, L. (1970). Sympathetic innervation of the avian pineal body. *Anat. Rec., 166, 406.*

Hedlund, L., and A. V. Nalbandov. (1969). Innervation of the avian pineal body. *Am. Zool., 9, 1090.*

Hedlund, L., and C. L. Ralph. (1967). Daily variation of pineal serotonin in Japanese quail and Sprague-Dawley rats. *Am. Zool., 7, 712.*

Hedlund, L., C. L. Ralph, J. D. Chepko, and J. J. Lynch. (1971). A diurnal serotonin cycle in the pineal body of Japanese quail: Photoperiod phasing and the effect of superior cervical ganglionectomy. *Gen. Comp. Endocrinol., 16, 52.*

Homma, K., L. McFarland, and W. O. Wilson. (1967). Response of the reproductive organs of the Japanese Quail to pinealectomy and melatonin injections. *Poultry Sci., 46, 314.*

Lynch, H. J. (1971). Diurnal oscillations in pineal melatonin content. *Life Sci. 10, 791.*

MacBride, S. E., C. L. Ralph, S. Binkley, and D. C. Klein. (1973). Pineal rhythms persist in superior cervical ganglioectomized chickens. *Fed. Proc., 32, 251.* (Abstr.)

Maria, G., P. de Gallardo, and R. S. Piezzi. (1973). Serotonin content in pineal gland of Antartic penguin. *Gen. Comp. Endocrinol., 21, 468.*

Menaker, M., and A. Oksche. (1974). The avian pineal organ. In "Avian Biology," Vol. 4 (D. S. Farner and J. R. King, Eds.). New York: Academic Press, p. 79.

Meyer, D. C., and P. D. Sturkie. (1974). Distribution of 5-HT among the blood cells of the domestic fowl. *Proc. Soc. Exp. Biol. Med., 147, 382.*

Meyer, D. C., P. D. Sturkie, and K. Gross. (1973). Diurnal rhythm in serotonin of blood and pineals of chickens. *Comp. Biochem. Physiol., 46A, 619.*

Moore, Y. S., A. Heller, R. Bhatnager, R. Wurtman, and J. Axelrod. (1968). Central control of the pineal gland: Visual pathways. *Arch. Neurol., 18, 208.*

Moszowska, A., A. Scemama, M. M. Lombard, and M. Hery. (1973). Experimental modulation of hypothalamic content of the gonadotropic releasing factors by pineal factors in the rat. *J. Neural Trans., 34, 11.*

Pearson, R. (1972). "The Avian Brain." New York: Academic Press, p. 431.

Pelham, R. W., and C. L. Ralph. (1973). Diurnal rhythm of serum melatonin in chicken: abolition by pinealectomy. *Physiologist, 16, 236.*

Quay, W. B. (1963). Circadian rhythm in rat pineal serotonin and its modifications by estrous cycle and photoperiod. *Gen. Comp. Endocrinol., 3, 473.*

Quay, W. B. (1964). Circadian and estrus rhythms in pineal melatonin and 5-hydroxyindole-3-acetic acid (5-HIAA). *Proc. Soc. Exp. Biol. Med., 115, 710.*

Quay, W. B. (1965a). Histological structure and cytology of the pineal organ in birds and mammals. In "Structure and Function of the *Epiphysis Cerebri*" (J. A. Kappers and J. P. Schade, Eds.). *Prog. Brain Res.,* Vol. 10.

Quay, W. B. (1965b). Retinal and pineal hydroxyindole O-methyl transferase activity in vertebrates. *Life Sci., 4, 983.*

Quay, W. B. (1966). Rhythmic and light induced changes in levels of pineal 5-hydroxyindoles in the pigeon (*Columba livia*). *Gen. Comp. Endocrinol. 6*, 371.

Quay, W. B. (1974). "Pineal Chemistry." Springfield, Ill.: Charles C Thomas.

Quay, W. B., and A. Renzoni. (1963). Comparative and experimental studies of pineal structure and cytology in passeriform birds. *Rev. Biol., 56*, 363.

Ralph, C. L. (1970). Structure and alleged functions of avian pineals. *Am. Zool., 10*, 217.

Ralph, C. L., L. Hedlund, and W. A. Murphy. (1967). Diurnal cycles of melatonin in bird pineal bodies. *Comp. Biochem. Physiol., 22*, 591.

Reiter, R. J. (1973). Comparative physiology: Pineal gland. *Ann. Rev. Physiol., 35*, 305.

Saylor A., and A. Wolfson. (1967). Avian pineal gland: progonadotrophic response in the Japanese quail. *Science, 158*, 1478.

Saylor A., and A. Wolfson. (1968). Influence of the pineal gland on gonadal maturation in the Japanese quail. *Endocrinology, 83*, 1237.

Shellabarger, C. J. (1953). Observations on the pineal in the White Leghorn capon and cockerel. *Poultry Sci., 32*, 189.

Singh, D. V., and C. W. Turner. (1967). Effect of melatonin upon the thyroid hormone secretion rate and endocrine glands of chicks. *Proc. Soc. Exp. Biol. Med., 125*, 407.

Stammer, A. (1966). Untersuchungen über die Struktur and die Innervation der Epiphyse bei Vögeln. *Acta Biol. (Szeged), 7*, 65.

Studnicka, F. K. (1905). Parietalorgane. In "Lehrbuch der vergleichenden mikroskopischen Anatomie der Werbeltiere," Vol. 5 (A. Oppel, Ed.). Jena: Fischer, p. 1.

Sturkie, P. D., J. J. Woods, and D. Meyer. (1972). Serotonin levels in blood, heart, and spleen of chickens, ducks and pigeons. *Proc. Soc. Exp. Biol. Med. 139*, 364.

Van der Veerdonk, F. C. (1965). Separation method for melatonin in pineal extracts. *Nature* (London), *208*, 1324.

Wight, P. A. L. (1971). The pineal gland. In "Physiology and Biochemistry of the Domestic Fowl" (D. J. Bell and B. M. Freeman, Eds.). New York: Academic Press, p. 549.

Wight, P. A. L., and G. M. MacKenzie. (1971). The histochemistry of the pineal gland of the domestic fowl. *J. Anat., 108*, 261.

Wurtman, R. J., J. Axelrod, and D. Kelly. (1968). "The Pineal," New York: Academic Press.

# 20

## Adrenals

### R. K. Ringer

Mammalia have a distinctly zonated adrenal cortex and central medulla of chromaffin tissue. Diversity in this arrangement is evident along the phylogenetic chain. Cortical (interrenal) and chromaffin tissue are intermingled in Aves; an exception is the brown pelican (Knouff and Hartman, 1951). Phylogenetic diversity also occurs in the secretion of the adrenal steroids.

Those wishing to explore other reviews on adrenal physiology in birds should see deRoos (1963), Frankel (1970), Bell and Freeman (1971), Idler (1972), and Farner and King (1973).

## ANATOMY

The paired adrenal glands are located anterior and medial to the cephalic lobe of the kidneys and immediately posterior to the lungs. They have a light yellow to orange color and are triangular or oval in shape.

**Embryological development.** The interrenal and the chromaffin tissues come from different germinal layers. The first to differentiate, the interrenal tissue, has its origin in cells that bud off from the peritoneal epithelium (mesothelium), ventral and medial to the mesonephros and dorsal to the hind gut, after the first few days of incubation. The origin is therefore mesodermal. These cells migrate dorsally and form paired masses on each side of the aorta on about the fourth day of incubation in the chick. Subsequently these cells form cortical cords.

The first signs of steroid biosynthesis in embryonic adrenals of chickens appear in the fourteenth to fifteenth day of incubation (Bohus *et al.*, 1965).

The chromaffin cells in the chick arise from the primordium of the sympathetic nervous system on each side of the embryonic aorta and migrate into the gland, where they can be recognized histochemically during the sixth day of incubation. The invading sympathetic cells of ectodermal origin enter the gland from all directions and tend to arrange themselves in cords between the cortical cells (see Romanoff, 1960, for details).

The chromaffin tissue of the chick embryo adrenal appears functional on the eighth day.

**Blood and nerve supply.** The blood supply to the fowl adrenal is via the adrenal artery and branches of the renal artery to the left adrenal and only from branches of the renal artery to the right adrenal. Venous drainage is via a single adrenal vein from each adrenal emptying into the posterior vena cava (Figure 20–1).

The extrinsic nerve supply to the adrenal gland originates from sympathetic chain ganglia. These splanchnic nerves form ganglia situated at the cranial and caudal poles of the adrenals (Freedman, 1968). Nonmyelinated fibers from these adrenal ganglia, located on the adrenal pericapsular sheath, penetrate the gland, enter the chromaffin tissue, and innervate the medullary cells. The nerve fibers do not enter the interrenal tissue.

**Histology.** Detailed studies of the anatomy and histology of the avian adrenal are given by Kondics and Kjaerheim (1966), Bhattacharyya *et al.* (1972), and Frankel *et al.* (1967b) for chickens; Sinha and Ghosh (1964) for the pigeon; and Tixier-Vidal and Assenmacher (1963) for the duck; for other avian species see Knouff and Hartman (1951), Péczely (1964), and Bhattacharyya *et al.* (1972). The adrenals of birds are encapsulated with a thin connective tissue containing blood vessels and nerves. In birds there is no defined cortex and medulla, nor is there obvious zonation of cortical tissue into three distinct layers as in mammals (Figure 20–2). The interrenal and chromaffin tissue are intermingled.

20–1

Diagram of arteries (a) and veins (b) of the adrenals of the fowl. (After Hays, 1914.)

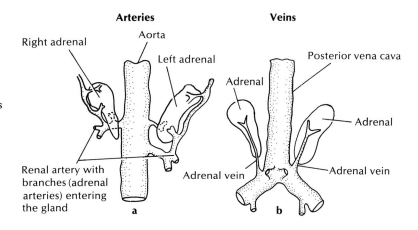

374

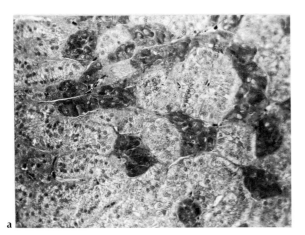 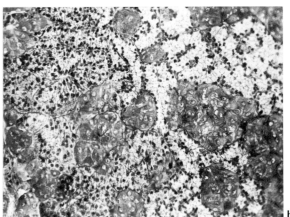

a                                                              b

20–2 Cross-sections of the adrenals of (a) normal and (b) hypophysectomized ducks. In (a) are shown the prominent cortical or interrenal cells (light staining) and the chromaffin cells (darker staining) arranged in islets, as well as blood vessels. In (b), the adrenal of the duck, 47 days after hypophysectomy, shows signs of involution and degeneration of the interrenal cells, which are filled with lipids. (From Benoit, 1950.)

Recent investigations at the ultrastructure level, using experimental conditions that alter adrenal response, indicate that several avian species have zonated interrenal (cortical) tissue. Two of these zones have been described as a thin subcapsular zone and a thicker inner one.

The interrenal cells are arranged in cords or strands of columnar epithelial cells in a double row. These cells stain eosinophilic. The cytoplasm is granular and contains lipid droplets that can be readily depleted by stimulation, mitochondria, a Golgi apparatus, and a smooth endoplasmic reticulum. Carotenoids present in the lipid droplets give rise to the characteristic yellow color of the adrenal.

The medullary cells are not organized into chords or strands but are polygonal in shape, have a central nucleus, and stain basophilic. The cytoplasm contains either small, spherical or large, irregularly shaped granules (Kano, 1959). These granules characterize two cell types and contain catecholamines (Fujita and Manchino, 1962). Associated with the medullary cells are unmyelinated nerve fibers.

**Size.** The size of the adrenals of birds varies considerably both within and between species, ac-

cording to sex, age, state of health, and other factors. Absolute adrenal weight increases with age until about 13 weeks of age in chickens and then plateaus. At 13 weeks of age adrenal weight in chickens is about 9 mg per 100 g body weight and reaches a level of about 6 mg per 100 g body weight as an adult.

The adrenal weight of the adult pigeon is about 5 mg per 100 g body weight (Bhattacharyya et al., 1967) and for the adult duck about 9 mg per 100 g body weight (Boissin, 1967).

Various factors cause adrenal hypertrophy in birds. These include physical stress, thyroxine, insulin, anterior pituitary extract, ACTH injection, vitamin $B_1$ deficiency, such diseases as avian leukosis, exposure to cold, and excessive exercise (see Sturkie, 1965). Perek and Kendler (1969) demonstrated that vitamin A deficiency and riboflavin deficiency increased adrenal weight.

Hypophysectomy did not decrease the size of the adrenal in chickens but weight of this gland was reduced 29% in pheasants (Nagra et al., 1963). Others have shown atrophy of the adrenal in the chicken following hypophysectomy (see Frankel, 1970).

Adrenal cortical hormones, such as cortisone, corticosterone, and hydrocorticosterone, depress adrenal weight of the chickens. Progesterone compounds, $6\alpha$-methyl-$17\alpha$-acetoxyprogesterone or $17\alpha$-acetoxyprogesterone, also cause adrenal atrophy (Nagra et al., 1965).

Considerable early evidence indicated that mammalian ACTH had little or no influence on adrenal weight and lead to the concept of autonomous functioning of the avian adrenal. Present data, however, refute avian adrenal autonomy and support the possibility of an extrahypophyseal source of ACTH (see Frankel, 1970).

## ADRENALECTOMY

Adrenalectomy has been performed in several species (Leroy and Benoit, 1954; Riddle *et al.,* 1944; Brown *et al.,* 1958b). The operation is difficult because the adrenals lie close to the lungs and the kidneys and in close connection with the posterior vena cava. The gonads lie wholly or partially over the adrenals. Surgical removal in the immature male is more readily performed because the enlarged testicles or diffuse ovary makes ablation almost impossible in the adult bird.

Completely adrenalectomized ducks and chickens usually die 6–60 hr after the operation unless given replacement therapy. Adrenalectomized birds can be maintained with 4 mg of deoxycorticosterone acetate (DCA) per kilogram per day or 10 mg cortisone acetate per kilogram per day (Brown *et al.,* 1958a). Untreated birds exhibited decreased excretion of sodium, uric acid, and total nitrogen and decreased water intake. Blood glucose decreased and blood potassium increased prior to death. Pigeons, following adrenal removal, can be maintained for as long as 9 days on DCA or cortical extracts or NaCl and $NaHCO_3$ (Riddle *et al.,* 1944).

## CORTICAL HORMONES

### Synthesis

Early work indicated that corticosterone was the major adrenal steroid in avian plasma (see Sturkie, 1965). Brown (1961) isolated the major peripheral adrenal steroid in turkey plasma and suggested that it was identical with corticosterone. Support of corticosterone as the primary adrenal steroid and information about its biosynthesis have been given by the *in vitro* studies of deRoos (1963), Sandor *et al.* (1963), Donaldson *et al.* (1965), Macchi (1967), Greenman *et al.* (1967), Frankel *et al.* (1967a), and Sandor and Lanthier (1970).

The duck, chicken, and goose adrenal *in vitro* produces relatively large amounts of corticosterone, 18-hydroxycorticosterone, and aldosterone from exogenous progesterone and pregnenolone (Sandor *et al.,* 1963). The high level of 18-hydroxycorticosterone formed under incubation of adrenal slices is apparently from oxygenation of corticosterone accumulation; it does not form to this degree in the intact animal, where corticosterone is released to the bloodstream from the adrenal. Corticosterone and aldosterone are the principal corticosteroid components of adrenal secretion in birds. 18-Hydroxycorticosterone is also present but has not been isolated from the plasma and may repre-

***Table 20–1*** *Corticosteroids in the plasma of Aves in vivo*[a]

| Species | Steroid | Source of plasma | μg/100 ml plasma | Reference |
|---|---|---|---|---|
| Chicken | Corticosterone | Peripheral male | $6.5 \pm 2$ | Urist and Deutch (1960) |
| | | female | $8.0 \pm 3$ | Urist and Deutch (1960) |
| | | Peripheral | $7.3 + 0.3$ | Nagra *et al.* (1960) |
| | | Adrenal vein | $44.3 \pm 5.5$ | Nagra *et al.* (1960) |
| | | Adrenal vein | 15.1 | Nagra *et al.* (1963) |
| | | Adrenal vein | 24.4 | Resko *et al.* (1964) |
| | | Adrenal vein | $7.3 \pm 0.5$[b] | Frankel *et al.* (1967a) |
| | | Adrenal vein | $6.6 \pm 1.5$[b] | Taylor *et al.* (1970) |
| | Aldosterone | Adrenal vein | $0.2 \pm 0.06$[b] | Taylor *et al.* (1970) |
| Turkey | Corticosterone | Peripheral | 12.5 | Nagra *et al.* (1960) |
| | | Peripheral | $7.4 \pm 0.4$ | Brown (1961) |
| | | Adrenal vein | $42.4 \pm 5.3$ | Brown (1961) |
| Pheasant | Corticosterone | Peripheral | $8.6 \pm 0.8$ | Nagra *et al.* (1960) |
| | | Adrenal vein | $34.8 \pm 4.7$ | Nagra *et al.* (1960) |
| | | Adrenal vein | 23.2 | Nagra *et al.* (1963) |
| Duck | Corticosterone | Peripheral | $5.1 \pm 0.5$ | Donaldson and Holmes (1965) |
| | Aldosterone | Peripheral | 0.014 | Sandor (unpublished) |

[a]Modified from Sandor (1972).

[b]Newer technique.

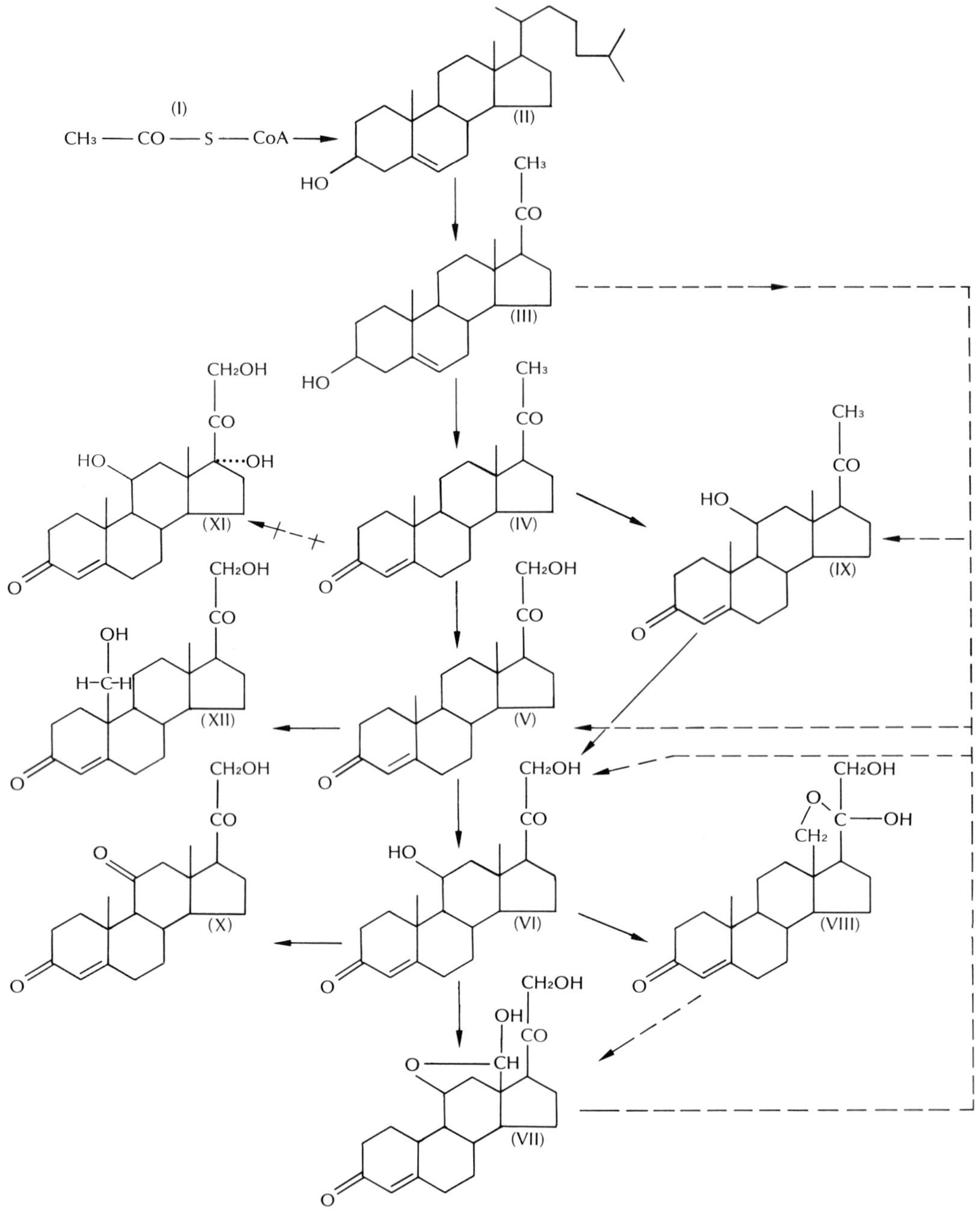

sent an intermediary in the transformation of corticosterone to aldosterone (Sandor, 1972).

The biosynthesis of the adrenal corticosteroids, as determined based on *in vitro* synthesis using exogenous substrates, is shown in Figure 20–3.

## Secretion of Corticosteroids

Some values for the plasma concentration of the corticosteroids in various species of birds are given in Table 20–1.

Plasma corticosterone concentrations show a circadian rhythm in the pigeon under light–dark cycles (Joseph and Meier, 1973), exhibiting a three-fold increase within 4 hr following the onset of darkness (see Figure 20–4). Pigeons maintained on continuous light do not show a circadian rhythm. Boissin and Assenmacher (1968, 1970, 1971) have observed a similar daily rise in the plasma concentration of corticosterone in the Japanese quail and the duck (Assenmacher and Boissin, 1972) and have proposed that darkness triggers the rise.

20–3 *Opposite:* Schematic representation of the biosynthesis of corticosteroids by the adrenals of birds. Validated pathways are shown by heavy arrows, possible or hypothetical ones by broken arrows. Key to compounds: I, acetyl-CoA; II, cholesterol; III, pregnenolone; IV, progesterone; V, 11-deoxycorticosterone; VI, corticosterone; VII, aldosterone; VIII, 18-hydroxycorticosterone 20–18 cyclic hemiketal; IX, 11-hydroxyprogesterone; X, 11-dehydrocorticosterone; XI, cortisol; XII, 19-hydroxy-11-deoxycorticosterone. (After Sandor, 1972.)

The secretion rate of corticosterone in ducks is 2.43 $\mu$g/min/kg of body weight (Donaldson and Holmes, 1965).

## Half-life of Corticosterone and Aldosterone

The biologic half-life of corticosterone in castrated cockerels according to Nagra *et al.* (1965) is 32 min; in the duck it is about 11 min (Donaldson and Holmes, 1965). Thomas and Phillips (1973) injected tritiated corticosterone and aldosterone into domestic ducks and reported a half-life of 8.25 ± 0.19 min and an apparent volume distribution of 780 ± 140 ml/kg body weight for corticosterone. The half-life for aldosterone was 8.34 ± 0.21 min.

Corticosteroids are bound in the plasma to a globulin, transcortin (Seal and Doe, 1963; Steeno and De Moor, 1966).

## Control of Secretion

The neurohumoral control of the avian adrenal is reviewed extensively by Frankel (1970). There is considerable evidence that the administration of mammalian ACTH increases plasma corticosterone levels in chickens, turkeys, ducks, and pheasants.

ACTH stimulates synthesis of corticosterone *in vitro* in the chicken, duck, pigeon, and gull (Sandor 1972), but not synthesis of aldosterone (deRoos, 1961). Subsequent studies on chickens (deRoos and deRoos, 1964) and duck (Donaldson, *et al.,* 1965) adrenal slices, in which ACTH was added to the incubating media, indicated a marked synthesis of aldosterone.

The addition of extracts from chicken (deRoos and deRoos, 1964) and duck (Macchi, 1967) anterior pituitary to adrenal tissue in incubation media support the conclusion that ACTH influences both corticosterone and aldosterone secretion.

ACTH appears to stimulate steroid synthesis in the pathway between cholesterol and progesterone in the adrenal (Frankel, 1970).

"Stresses"—such as cold temperature, water deprivation, surgical procedures, handling, and administration of certain drugs—increase plasma concentrations of corticosterone. Plasma corticosterone levels of cold-stressed hypophysectomized ducks did not change, but the levels of intact ducks increased significantly (Boissin, 1967); ducks in which the hypophyses were transplanted into the kidney exhibited a transient increase in plasma corticosterone. This indicates that stress releases ACTH from the pituitary in the intact birds. Partial control of the adrenal is still exerted by the auto-transplanted birds.

The atrophy of the adrenal of hypophysectomized birds represents mainly a regression of the cortical tissue. Adrenal ascorbic acid level is reduced somewhat, but corticosterone in the blood is reduced to about 50% of the control value (Nagra *et al.,* 1960; Resko, *et al.,* 1964; Boissin, 1967; Baylé *et al.,* 1971). The adenohypophysis, therefore, through ACTH activity, exerts a control over adrenal cortical activity in birds but to a lesser extent than in mammals. Salem *et al.* (1970a, b) reported that the chicken hypothalamus contained an ACTH-like substance based on assay by adrenal ascorbic acid depletion in rats. This ACTH activity

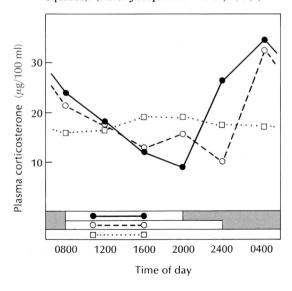

20–4 Concentrations of plasma corticosterone at six times of day in pigeons held on a 12-hr (dark circles) or 16-hr (open circles) daily photoperiod, or on continuous light (open squares). (After Joseph and Meier, 1973.)

378 from the median eminence supports Frankel's concept (1970) that an extrahypophyseal source of ACTH may exist and maintain adrenal cortical activity in the hypophysectomized bird.

In the mammal the renin–angiotensin system is important in the control of aldosterone secretion. The juxtaglomerular cells of the kidney in mammals are thought to be the site of renin production and release (see Chapter 14). Avian species have been reported to have juxtaglomerular cells and to produce a renin-like substance (Taylor *et al.,* 1970). These workers were unable to show any change in either corticosterone or aldosterone levels in adrenal vein plasma following sodium depletion of cockerels or infusion of chicken kidney extracts, techniques used in mammals to demonstrate the renin–angiotensin control of aldosterone.

There is ample reason to assume that a negative-feedback mechanism exists between the adenohypophysis and the adrenal.

## Assays of ACTH, Corticosterone, and Aldosterone

Adrenal ascorbic acid depletion (AAAD) is used in mammalian species as an index of ACTH activity. Hypophysectomized rats are injected with graded doses of ACTH or tissue, such as anterior pituitary, and the adrenal ascorbic acid level is analyzed.

Avian species do not respond to ACTH administration with a depletion of adrenal ascorbic acid unless pretreated with a pituitary blocking agent (Greenman *et al.,* 1967). These investigators point out the care necessary in controlling "stress" when measuring AAAD.

Adrenal venous blood is more sensitive than AAAD in birds as an ACTH assay. Corticosterone is determined by fluorometric analysis from blood withdrawn from the adrenal vein by the method of Nagra *et al.* (1963).

Another corticosterone assay consists of chromatographic purification to remove interfering fluorogens, followed by the addition of a fluorescence reagent (Frankel *et al.,* 1967a).

Both corticosterone and aldosterone can be assayed by the double-isotope dilution derivative method (Stachenko *et al.,* 1964).

## Physiologic Action of Corticosteroids

Much information on the action of the corticosteroids preceded the identification of the adrenal steroids in birds. Data were derived from studies on adrenalectomized birds, replacement therapy, and exogenous administration of adrenal steroids.

The classification of adrenal steroids into glucocorticoids and mineralcorticoids based on their function is an oversimplification because the functional dividing line is not distinct.

**Corticosterone.** *Carbohydrate metabolism.* Corticosterone and hydrocortisone are the most active hyperglycemic steroids when injected into adult White Leghorn chickens (Greenman and Zarrow, 1961). Hydrocortisone (cortisol), however, is not a secretory product of the avian adrenal. Cortisone, which is extremely active in mammals, is virtually inactive in birds on glucose metabolism. The mechanism of action of corticosterone in birds on carbohydrate metabolism is presumably through gluconeogenesis (see Chapter 11).

*Electrolyte metabolism.* Corticosterone appears to be necessary for normal functioning of the nasal gland in ducks (Phillips and Bellamy, 1962). Adrenalectomized ducks fail to secrete salt from the nasal glands (Holmes *et al.,* 1961). This secretion can be restored in hypophysectomized ducks by administering ACTH which releases corticosterone (see also Chapter 14).

*Lipid metabolism.* Hydrocortisone (cortisol) and corticosterone caused an increase in liver, visceral, and carcass fat in the chicken, but cortisone had no effect (Dulin, 1956). The hepatic lipogenesis is characterized by perivascular lipid accumulation. Hyperphagia induced by corticosterone treatment together with altered metabolism causes the increased visceral fat deposition (Nagra and Meyer, 1963). Corticosterone elevates lipids in intact cockerels as well as hypophysectomized birds, which precludes blockage of adipokinetic factor secretion from the adenohypophysis as an explanation of its action (Nagra, 1965). Corticosterone increased depot fat as well as total plasma lipid, cholesterol, and phospholipid. Liver weight was increased but not the concentration of lipid in the liver (Nagra, 1965).

*Body weight.* When injected into chick embryos, corticosteroids cause a marked reduction in growth and development (see Sturkie, 1965). Injections of ACTH or cortisone acetate decreased body weight in 10-week-old cockerels (Brown *et al.,* 1958a). Body weight depression resulted from injection of corticosterone and cortisone, respectively, to White Leghorn chickens (Greenman and Zarrow, 1961; Nagra, 1965) and pigeons (Chaudhuri *et al.,* 1966).

*Blood cells.* The physiologic actions of cortical hormones on blood cells are presented in Chapter 3.

*Gonads.* Egg laying in chickens was depressed by injections of corticosterone (Greenman and Zarrow, 1961). ACTH in graded doses from 10 to 80 IU/day caused ovarian and testicular atrophy in direct proportion to dose (Flickinger, 1966).

*Lymphoid tissue.* Adrenal corticoids, particularly corticosterone, inhibited bursa of Fabricius growth in chicks (Zarrow *et al.,* 1961). Similar results were reported for the thymus (Bellamy and Leonard, 1965).

**18-Hydroxycorticosterone.** No physiologic functions of 18-hydroxycorticosterone have been shown for birds.

**Aldosterone.** Holmes *et al.* (1961) measured total renal excretion of sodium and potassium in the saline-loaded duck. The ducks were treated with 250 $\mu$g (i.m.) of aldosterone at 1.5 and 0 hr prior to saline loading. Aldosterone markedly reduced urine volume and sodium and potassium output. In the water-loaded duck (Holmes and Adams, 1963), injection of 50 or 100 $\mu$g aldosterone at $-1.5$, 1.5, 3.0, and 4.5 hr after loading resulted in highly significant retention of sodium and potassium, with no effect on urine volume (see Chapter 14). Orloff and Burg (1960) stated that aldosterone did not influence electrolyte excretion when administered into the portal system of chickens. No change in the adrenal venous concentration of aldosterone was observed after sodium depletion of the chicken (Taylor *et al.,* 1970).

From these several studies the action of aldosterone in the bird appears to be similar to that of man; that is, increased tubular reabsorption of sodium, with an increased retention of sodium and water, which leads to expansion of the extracellular fluid compartment.

# ADRENAL MEDULLARY HORMONES

In most mammalian species the major catechol hormone is epinephrine. Based on histochemical cytology of avian adrenal medullary tissue, most avian species, except passerformes, contain more norepinephrine-containing cells than epinephrine-containing cells (Table 20–2; Ghosh, 1973).

## Synthesis of Catecholamines

Catecholamines are synthesized within the chromaffin tissue of the adrenal gland, in postganglionic neurons, and in some brain neurons. Synthesis of

catecholamines, based primarily on mammalian studies, is as follows:

Tyrosine
↓
Dihydroxyphenylalanine (dopa)
↓
Dopamine
↓
Norepinephrine
↓
Epinephrine

The conversion of norepinephrine to epinephrine requires methylation of norepinephrine by the enzyme phenylethanolamine-*N*-methyltransferase (see also Chapter 12).

## Control of Catecholamine Synthesis and Release

Ghosh (1973), in his review of the avian adrenal medulla, cites evidence based on previous cytochemical studies that in cortisone-treated pigeons, cortisone stimulates the synthesis of epinephrine presumably through a norepinephrine methylation mechanism. Chaudhuri *et al.* (1966) suggested that increased release of norepinephrine following cortisone treatment might also account for the altered cytochemical picture because cortisone-induced hypertension occurs in the chicken (see Chapter 4).

Release of adrenal catecholamines is undoubtedly evoked by neural stimulation, as in mammals. Chaudhuri and Sadhu (1961) proposed release control through sympathetic innervation in pigeons. Injection of pholedrine, a sympathomimetic drug, caused the secretion of norepinephrine in the chicken and crow, whereas tolazoline, an adrener-

*Table 20–2* *Percentage of norepinephrine (N) to epinephrine (E) cells in the adrenal medullary tissue of some avian species*[a]

| Order/species | N (%) | E (%) |
|---|---|---|
| Galliformes | | |
| *Gallus domesticus* | 80 | 20 |
| *Coturnix coturnix* | 75 | 25 |
| Anseriformes | | |
| *Anas querquedula* | 65 | 35 |
| Columbiformes | | |
| *Columba livia* | 57 | 43 |
| Passerformes | | |
| *Oriolus oriolus* | 21 | 79 |
| *Passer domesticus* | 5 | 95 |

[a]From Ghosh (1973).

*Table 20–3*   *Plasma levels of norepinephrine (N) and epinephrine (E) in pigeons, ducks, turkeys, and chickens*[a]

| Species | Sex | Age (months) | Norephinephrine ($\mu$g/liter) | Epinephrine ($\mu$g/liter) | N/E ratio |
|---------|-----|--------------|--------------------------------|----------------------------|-----------|
| Pigeon  | Mixed | 12        | 0.23 | 5.76 | 0.39 |
| Duck    | Mixed | 2         | 0.83 | 0.32 | 2.60 |
| Turkey  | F     | 7–12      | 0.68 | 1.45 | 0.47 |
| Chicken | M     | 17        | 0.84 | 8.68 | 0.10 |
|         | F     | 17–21     | 1.18 | 8.24 | 0.14 |

[a]From Sturkie *et al.* (1970).

gic blocking agent, did not release catecholamines from the chicken adrenal (Ray, 1970). Pentolinium, a ganglionic blocker, produced an overall depletion of the total catecholamine contents of the adrenal in the fowl (Ray, 1970). Sturkie and co-workers have published a series of papers on catecholamine responses and levels in various tissues (Lin and Sturkie, 1967; 1968; Sturkie and Lin, 1968; Sturkie *et al.*, 1970; Lin *et al.*, 1970; Sturkie and Poorvin, 1972). They have shown that in contrast to the cytochemical picture within the adrenal, circulating levels of epinephrine are greater than norepinephrine in the pigeon, turkey, and chicken. The exception is the duck (Table 20–3). In the pigeon, turkey, and chicken, therefore, the norepinephrine/epinephrine ratio is < 1.0, in contrast to that of the mammal, which is > 1.0 (except the rat). There is a significant sex difference in the norepinephrine level in the fowl, but not in the epinephrine level (Sturkie and Lin, 1968). Sturkie *et al.* (1970) point out that considerable variation occurs in plasma levels caused by handling and excitement; anesthetized birds have lower values.

The discrepancy between the cytochemical findings and circulating blood levels must be accounted for in greater release of epinephrine from the adrenal in the pigeon, turkey, and chicken.

### Assay for Norepinephrine and Epinephrine

Blood plasma is assayed with aluminum oxide–trihydroxyindole and fluorescence is read at 400–500 $\mu$m and 436–520 $\mu$m for norepinephrine and epinephrine, respectively (Anton and Sayer, 1962).

### Physiologic Actions of Epinephrine and Norepinephrine

The physiologic actions of the adrenal medullary catecholamines are discussed in the chapters on carbohydrate metabolism (Chapter 11), blood pressure (Chapter 4), environmental temperature (Chapter 7), and reproduction (Chapters 16 and 17).

### REFERENCES

Anton, A. H., and D. F. Sayer. (1962). A study of the factors affecting the aluminum oxide-trihydroxyindole procedure for the analysis of catecholamines. *J. Pharmacol. Exp. Ther.*, 138, 360.

Assenmacher, I., and J. Boissin. (1972). Circadian endocrine and related rhythms in birds. *Gen. Comp. Endocrinol.*, 3, (Suppl). 489.

Baylé, J. D., J. Boissin, J. Y. Daniel, and I. Assenmacher. (1971). Hypothalamic–hypophysial control of adrenal cortical function in birds. *Neuroendocrinology, 7*, 308.

Bell, D. J., and B. M. Freeman. (Eds.). (1971). "Physiology and Biochemistry of the Domestic Fowl." London and New York: Academic Press.

Bellamy, D., and R. A. Leonard. (1965). Effect of cortisol on the growth of chicks. *Gen. Comp. Endocrinol., 5*, 402.

Benoit, J. (1950). In "Traité de Zoologie," Tome XV (P. P. Grassé, Ed.). Paris: Masson and Co., Figures 249 and 250.

Bhattacharyya, T. K., A. Sarkar, and A. Ghosh. (1967). Effect of hydroxylation blocking agents on corticoids concentration in the pigeon adrenals. *Endocrinol. Jap., 14*, 265.

Bhattacharyya, T. K., D. Sinha, and A. Ghosh. (1972). A comparative histological survey of the avian adrenocortical homologue. *Arch. Histol. Jap., 34*, 419.

Bohus, B., K. Straznicky, and F. Hajos. (1965). The development of 3β-hydroxysteroid-dehydrogenase activity in embryonic adrenal gland of chickens. *Gen Comp. Endocrinol., 5*, 665.

Boissin, J. (1967). Le controle hypothalamo-hypophysaire de la fonction corticosurrenalienne chez le canard. *J. Physiol. (Paris), 59*, 423.

Boissin, J., and I. Assenmacher. (1968). Rhythmes circadiens des taux sanguin et surrenalien de la corticosterone chez la caille. *Compt. Rend. Acad. Sci. (Paris), 267*, 2193.

Boissin, J., and I. Assenmacher. (1970). Circadian rhythms in adrenal cortical activity in the quail. *J. Interdisc. Cycle Res., 1*, 251.

Boissin, J., and I. Assenmacher. (1971). Entrainment of the adrenal cortical ryhthm by ahemeral photoperiods in the quail. *J. Interdisc. Cycle Res., 2*, 437.

Brown, K. I. (1961). Validity of using plasma corticosterone stress in the turkey. *Proc. Soc. Exp. Biol. Med., 107*, 538.

Brown, K. I., D. J. Brown, and R. K. Meyer. (1958a). Effect of surgical trauma, ACTH and adrenal cortical hormones on electrolytes, water balance and gluconeogenesis in male chickens. *Am. J. Physiol., 192*, 43.

Brown, K. I., R. K. Meyer, and D. J. Brown. (1958b). A study of adrenalectomized male chickens with and without adrenal hormone treatment. *Poultry Sci., 37*, 680.

Chaudhuri, D., and D. P. Sadhu. (1961). Histochemical demonstration of adrenaline and noradrenaline in the adrenal medulla of pigeon and baby rabbits exposed to higher ambient temperature. *J. Histochem. Cytochem., 10,* 2.

Chaudhuri, D., I. Ghosh, and A. Ghosh. (1966). Steroidal influence on adrenomedullary catechol hormones of the pigeon. *Acta Morphol. Acad. Sci. Hung., 14,* 245.

deRoos, R. (1961). The corticoids of the avian adrenal gland. *Gen. Comp. Endocrinol., 1,* 494.

deRoos, R. (1963). The physiology of the avian interrenal gland: A review. *Proc. 13th Int. Ornithol. Congr.,* pp. 1041–1058.

deRoos, R., and C. C. deRoos. (1964). Effects of mammalian corticotropin and chicken adenohypophysial extracts on steroidogenesis by chicken adrenal tissue *in vitro. Gen. Comp. Endocrinol., 4,* 602.

Donaldson, E. M.; and W. N. Holmes. (1965). Corticosteroidogenesis in the freshwater and saline-maintained duck *(Anas platyrhynchos). J. Endocrinol., 32,* 329.

Donaldson, E. M., W. N. Holmes, and J. Stachenko. (1965). *In vitro* corticosteroidogenesis by duck *(Anas platyrhynchos)* adrenal. *Gen. Comp. Endocrinol., 5,* 542.

Dulin, W. K. (1956). Effects of corticosterone, cortisone and hydrocortisone on fat metabolism. *Proc. Soc. Exp. Biol. Med., 92,* 253.

Farner, D. S., and J. R. King (Eds.). (1973). "Avian Biology," Vol. III. New York: Academic Press.

Flickinger, D. D. (1966). Effect of prolonged ACTH administration on the gonads of sexually mature chickens. *Poultry Sci., 45,* 753.

Frankel, A. I. (1970). Neurohumoral control of avian adrenal: A review. *Poultry Sci., 49,* 869.

Frankel, A. I., J. W. Graber, and A. V. Nalbandov. (1967b). The effect of hypothalamic lesions on adrenal function in intact and adenohypophysectomized cockerels. *Gen. Comp. Endocrinol., 8,* 387.

Frankel, A. I., B. Cook, J. W. Graber, and A. V. Nalbandov. (1967a). Determination of corticosterone in plasma by fluorometric techniques. *Endocrinology, 80,* 181.

Freedman, S. L. (1968). The innervation of the suprarenal gland of the fowl *(Gallus domesticus). Acta Anat., 69,* 18.

Fujita, H., and M. Manchino, (1962). Election microscopic observations on the secretory granules of the adrenal medulla of domestic fowl. *Arch. Histol. Jap., 23,* 67.

Ghosh, A., (1973). Histophysiology of the avian adrenal medulla, *Proc. 60th Indian Science Congress,* Part II, p. 1.

Greenman, D. L., and M. X. Zarrow. (1961). Steroids and carbohydrate metabolism in the domestic bird. *Proc. Soc. Exp. Biol. Med., 106,* 459.

Greenman, D. L., L. S. Whitley, and M. X. Zarrow. (1967). Ascorbic acid depletion and corticosterone production in the avian adrenal gland. *Gen. Comp. Endocrinol., 9,* 422.

Hays, V. J. (1914). The development of the adrenals in the bird. *Anat. Rec., 8,* 451.

Holmes, W. N., and B. M. Adams. (1963). Effects of adrenocortical and neurohypophysial hormones on the renal excretory pattern in the water-loaded duck *(Anas platyrhynchos). Endocrinology, 73,* 5.

Holmes, W. N., J. G. Phillips, and D. J. Butler. (1961). The effect of adrenocortical steroids on the renal and extrarenal responses of the domestic duck *(Anas platyrhynchos)* after hypertonic saline loading. *Endocrinology, 69,* 483.

Idler, D. R. (1972). "Steroids in Nonmammalian Vertebrates." New York: Academic Press.

Joseph, M. M., and A. H. Meier. (1973). Daily rhythms of plasma corticosterone in the common pigeon, *Columba livia. Gen. Comp. Endocrinol., 20,* 326.

Kano, M. (1959). Electron microscopic study of the adrenal medulla of domestic fowl. *Arch. Histol. Jap., 18,* 25.

Knouff, R. A., and F. A. Hartman. (1951). A microscopic study of the adrenal of the brown pelican. *Anat. Rec., 109,* 161.

Kondics, L., and A. Kjaerheim. (1966). The zonation of interrenal cells in fowls (an electron microscopical study). *Z. Zellsforsch., 70,* 81.

Leroy, P., and J. Benoit. (1954). Surrenalectomie bilaterale chez le canard male adulte: action sur le testicule. *J. Physiol. (Paris), 46,* 422.

Lin, Y. C., and P. D. Sturkie. (1967). Effect of environmental tem-

peratures on the catecholamines of chickens. *Physiologist, 10,* 234.

Lin, Y. C., and P. D. Sturkie. (1968). Effect of environmental temperatures on the catecholamines of chickens. *Am. J. Physiol., 214,* 237.

Lin, Y. C., P. D. Sturkie, and J. Tummons. (1970). Effect of cardiac sympathectomy, reserpine and environmental temperatures on the catecholamine levels in the chicken heart. *Can. J. Physiol. Pharmacol., 48,* 182.

Macchi, I. A. (1967). Regulation of reptilian and avian adrenocortical secretion: Effect of ACTH on the *in vitro* conversion of progesterone to corticoids. *Proc. 2nd Intl. Congr. Horm. Steroids,* in 1966, p. 1094.

Nagra, C. (1965). Effect of corticosterone on lipids in hypophysectomized male chickens. *Endocrinology, 77,* 221.

Nagra, C. L., J. G. Birnie, G. J. Baum, and R. K. Meyer. (1963). The role of the pituitary in regulating steroid secretion by the avian adrenal. *Gen. Comp. Endocrinol., 3,* 274.

Nagra, C. L., and R. K. Meyer. (1963). Influence of corticosterone on the metabolism of palmitate and glucose in cockerels. *Gen. Comp. Endocrinol., 3,* 131.

Nagra, C. L., G. J. Baum, and R. K. Meyer. (1960). Corticosterone levels in adrenal effluent blood of some gallinaceous birds. *Proc. Soc. Exp. Biol. Med., 105,* 68.

Nagra, C. L., A. K. Sauers, and H. W. Wittmaier. (1965). Effect of testosterone, progestagens and metopirone on adrenal activity in cockerels. *Gen. Comp. Endocrinol. 5,* 69.

Orloff, J., and M. Burg. (1960). Effect of strophantihidin on electrolyte excretion in the chicken. *Am. J. Physiol., 199,* 49.

Péczely, P. (1964). The adaptation to salt water conditions of the adrenal structure in various bird species. *Acta Biol. Acad. Sci. Hung., 15,* 171.

Perek, M., and J. Kendler. (1969). The effect of ascorbic acid on adrenal activity during vitamin A and riboflavin deficiencies in chicks (adrenal activity in vitamin deficiency). *Acta Endocrinol., 61,* 203.

Phillips, J. G., and O. Bellamy. (1962). Aspects of the hormonal control of nasal gland secretion in birds. *J. Endocrinol., 24,* 6.

Ray, B. (1970). Action of autonomic effector agents on the catecholamine secretion of the suprarenal medulla of the crow and the fowl. *Z. Biol., 116,* 327.

Resko, J. A., N. W. Norton, and A. V. Nalbandov. (1964). Endocrine control of the adrenal in chickens. *Endocrinology, 75,* 192.

Riddle, O., G. C. Smith, and R. A. Miller. (1944). The effect of adrenalectomy on heat production in young pigeons. *Am. J. Physiol., 141,* 151.

Romanoff, A. L. (1960). "The Avian Embryo." New York: Macmillan and Co.

Salem, M. H. R., H. W. Norton, and A. V. Nalbandov. (1970a). A study of ACTH and CRF in chickens. *Gen. Comp. Endocrinol., 14,* 270.

Salem, M. H. R., H. W. Norton, and A. V. Nalbandov. (1970b). The role of vasotocin of CRF in ACTH release in the chicken. *Gen. Comp. Endocrinol., 14,* 281.

Sandor, T. (1972). Corticosteroids in amphibia, reptilia and aves. In "Steroids in Nonmammalian Vertebrates" (D. R. Idler, Ed.) New York: Academic Press, p. 253.

Sandor, T., and A. Lanthier. (1970). Studies on the sequential hydroxylation of progesterone to corticosteroids by domestic duck *(Anas platyrhynchos)* and the chicken *(Gallus domesticus). Endocrinology, 86,* 552.

Sandor, T., J. Lamoureux, and A. Lanthier. (1963). Adrenocortical function in birds: *In vitro* biosynthesis of radioactive corticosteroids from pregnenolone-7³H and progesterone-4-¹⁴C by adrenal glands of the domestic duck *(Anas platyrhynchos)*, and the chicken *(Gallus domesticus). Endocrinology, 73,* 629.

Seal, U. S., and R. P. Doe. (1963). Corticosteroid-binding globulin: Species distribution and small scale purification. *Endocrinology, 73,* 371.

Sinha, D., and A. Ghosh. (1964). Cytochemical study of the suprarenal cortex of the pigeon under altered electrolyte balance. *Acta Histochem., 17,* 222.

Stachenko, J., C. Laplante, and C. J. P. Giroud. (1964). Double isotope derivative assay of aldosterone, corticosterone, and cortisol. *Can. J. Biochem., 42,* 1275.

382  Steeno, O., and P. DeMoor. (1966). The corticosteroid binding capacity of plasma transcortin in mammals and aves. *Bull. Soc. Roy. Zool. Anvers., 38, 3.*

Sturkie, P. D. (Ed.). (1965). "Avian Physiology" (2nd ed.). Ithaca, N.Y.: Cornell University Press.

Sturkie, P. D., and Y. C. Lin. (1968). Sex difference in blood norepinephrine of chickens. *Comp. Biochem. Physiol., 24,* 1073.

Sturkie, P. D., and D. Poorvin. (1972). Avian cardiac neurotransmitter. *Physiologist, 15,* 279.

Sturkie, P. D., D. Poorvin, and N. Ossorio. (1970). Levels of epinephrine and norepinephrine in blood and tissues of duck, pigeon, turkey, and chicken. *Proc. Soc. Exp. Biol. Med., 135,* 267.

Taylor, A. A., J. D. Davis, R. P. Breitenbach, and P. M. Hartroft. (1970). Adrenal steroid secretion and a renal-pressor system in the chicken *(Gallus domesticus). Gen. Comp. Endocrinol., 14,* 321.

Thomas, D. H., and J. G. Phillips. (1973). The kinetics of exogenous corticosterone and aldosterone in relation to different levels of food and NaCl intake by domestic ducks *(Anas platyrhynchos). Proc. Soc. Endocrinol., 57,* xiv.

Tixier-Vidal, A., and I. Assenmacher. (1963). Action de la metopirone sur la prehypophyse du canard male: essai d' identification des cellules corticotropes. *Compt. Rend. Soc. Biol., 157,* 1350.

Urist, M. R., and N. M. Deutch. (1960). Influence of ACTH upon avian species and osteoporosis. *Proc. Soc. Exp. Biol. Med., 104,* 35.

Zarrow, M. X., D. L. Greenman, and L. E. Peters. (1961). Inhibition of the bursa of Fabricius and the stilboestrol-stimulated oviduct of the domestic chick. *Poultry Sci., 40,* 87.

# 21

## Pancreas

R. L. Hazelwood

## 384   MORPHOLOGY

**Location and size.** Similar to the compact pancreas of the dog, cat, man, and other primates, and dissimilar to the diffuse tissue in rats and rabbits, the avian pancreas is a discrete lobular structure that usually has well-defined clefts or morphologic folds (Figure 21–1). This organ, weighing between 2.5 and 4.0 g in adult chickens, is suspended within the U-shaped duodenal loop of the small intestine and is responsible for two families of secretions, the digestive enzymes (exocrine) and the protein-aceous hormones (endocrine). The exocrine (acinar) tissue synthesizes and releases enzymes into at least three discrete pancreatic ducts, conveying them to the duodenal loop where all semiliquid foodstuffs are subjected to the powerful lipolytic, proteolytic, and amylolytic enzymes (Chapter 10). The avian pancreas also synthesizes and releases directly into the bloodstream peptide hormones which emanate from scattered islet (endocrine) tissue embedded within the sea of acinar tissue. Actually, the exocrine tissue represents at least 99% of the total fresh chicken pancreas, the endocrine portion making up the remainder.

**Embryogenesis.** The singular adult pancreas arises from two separate duodenal outpocketings in the avian embryo: a dorsal evagination arises from the duodenum just anterior to the area that gives rise to the avian liver, and a ventral rudiment also arises from the duodenum but does so ventrally and posteriorly to the liver primordia. The ducts emerging from the ventral lobe(s) appear to be the largest and carry most of the digestive juice to a site in the duodenum near the entrance of the bile duct.

**Ductal, vascular, and neural elements.** Most birds possess three pancreatic ducts; they arise early in embryogenesis and are lined with the usual columnar epithelium interspersed with mucous-type cells. [Ductile (exocrine) tissue has not been observed associated with islet (endocrine) cell groups in Aves, as it has been in many mammals.] The opening of the three ducts on a duodenal papilla common with the opening of the bile duct is considered by most workers to signify the junction site of the duodenum with the jejunem. Whereas the dorsal lobe and the ventral lobe (a part of which is frequently called the "third" lobe) give

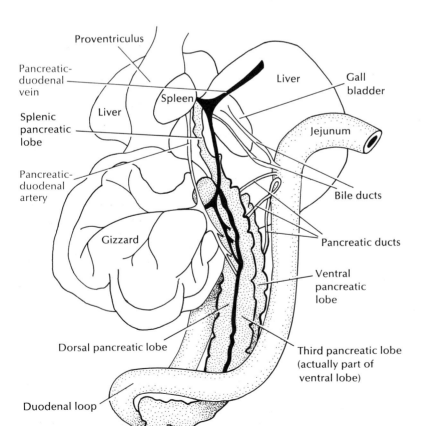

21–1
Anatomical relationships of the avian pancreas.

rise to the exocrine passages, the "tail" of the ventral lobe, which proceeds superiorly to a level near the spleen, apparently does not have an exocrine duct (Figure 21 – 1). However, this splenic lobe is heavily endowed with glucagon-secreting cells (Mikami and Ono, 1962).

Despite the lobular appearance of the compact avian pancreas, very little connective tissue apparently exists (as septa) between or within the parenchymal masses. The pancreatic arteries and vein, which lie centrally within the tissue, course the entire length of the pancreas inferiorly to the "head" region at the apex of the duodenal loop. The pancreas is drained by the pancreaticoduodenal vein, which empties into the gastroduodenal vein; the latter, in turn, joins the hepatic portal vein very near the hilus of the liver. Pancreatic endocrine elaborations, therefore, are subject to immediate alteration and/or destruction by the hepatocyte *before* they enter the general circulation.

**Innervation.** In most mammals autonomic nervous system elements enter the endocrine pancreatic islets (neuroinsular complex) and terminate directly on $\alpha$, $\beta$, and $\delta$ cells. Presence of such nerve elements in the avian pancreas is yet to be established, at least at the islet cell level (King, 1971); however, it is known that branches of both vagi as well as sympathetic branches of the autonomic nervous system innervate the avian pancreas via the pancreatic–duodenal plexus (Hseih, 1951) and are readily identifiable in the acinar tissue (King, 1971). Contrary to findings in mammals (in which vagal stimulation or the direct application of acetylcholine encourage insulin release) there is no evidence to indicate that autonomic nervous control over pancreatic release of insulin is important—or exists—in Aves (King, 1971).

# CYTOLOGY

## Cytodifferentiation

The acinar cell secretes enzymes as early as day 3 – 4 in the duck embryo. It is at this time that zymogenic granules are present within the "stem cells" and are indistinguishable from those granules found in the pancreas of older embryos. These granules are bounded by a single membrane and appear to emanate from the region of the Golgi complex; they stream toward the cell apices simultaneous with lumina formation (Romanoff, 1960; Przybylski, 1967a). As the acinar cell matures, the nucleus becomes peripherally located, the Golgi apparatus characteristically becomes positioned supranuclearly, and the yolk deposits and cyto-

plasmic filaments characteristic of the young cells gradually disappear (Przybylski, 1967a).

Interspersed between cells within both exocrine and islet areas is a nonacinar, noninsular "glycogen cell." The origin and function of these glycogen-laden cells is unknown; however, they are particularly numerous in the first week of life of chick and duck embryos and gradually disappear over the next 14 days. This and other cytodifferentiative processes are markedly different from those reported in the developing mammalian pancreas (Przybylski, 1967a).

Islet (endocrine) tissue in Aves apparently is distributed more sparsely throughout the exocrine tissue than it is in mammals. Derivation of the specific islet cells apparently initiates with the "stem cells," which give rise to ductal and acinar elements and also to the three recognized endocrine cells, $\alpha_1$, $\alpha_2$, and $\beta$ cells. Both $\alpha$ and $\beta$ cells appear simultaneously on the third day of incubation in the chick and granules have been observed on this day with the electron microscope (Przybylski, 1967b). Extensive histologic studies of the embryonic chick (Machino, 1966; Przybylski, 1967b) and the adult chicken, duck, pigeon, sparrow, and thrush pancreas (Mikami and Ono, 1962; Epple, 1968; King, 1971; Machino, 1966; Machino and Sakuma, 1967; and Fujita, 1968) have been made in the last 10 years.

## Distribution of Endocrine Cells

The three endocrine cells appear to be distributed over two types of islets, light islets (mainly $\beta$ cells) and the larger dark islets (mainly $\alpha$ cells); however, these islets are disproportionally distributed among the pancreatic lobes (Oakberg, 1949; Mikami and Ono, 1962). Some workers describe two types of $\beta$ islets (reviewed by King, 1971), which may represent different secretory phases. The distribution of cells within an islet gives rise to the name of that islet; an $\alpha$ islet contains predominantly $\alpha_2$ (glucagon) type cells but also contains some $\alpha_1$ (unknown secretion) cells. Conversely, $\beta$ islets are predominantly composed of $\beta$ cells (insulin) but also contain some $\alpha_1$ cells (Table 21 – 1). Finally, there exists a few mixed islets wherein all three cell types reside in approximately equal numbers. $\alpha_1$ cells are also found in exocrine areas of the avian pancreas.

## Cell Types and Hormones Secreted

**Pancreatic "gastrin."** The $\alpha_1$ cell of the avian pancreas is considered by most workers to be identical with the D cell of the mammalian pancreas, first described by Bloom in the early 1930's. Two

386

**Table 21-1** *Cell population of adult (male) chicken pancreatic islets[a]*

| | $\alpha_1$ (dark) islet | | $\beta$ (light) islet | |
| | $\alpha_1$ cells | $\alpha_2$ cells | $\alpha_1$ cells | $\beta$ cells |
|---|---|---|---|---|
| Total cells | 259 | 1667 | 195 | 1247 |
| Percentage | 28 | 72 | 14 | 86 |

[a]Modified from Mikami and Ono (1962).

distinct $\alpha$ cell populations have been described in Aves, the $\alpha_1$ cell being a metachromatic argyrophilic cell, in contrast to the histochemical properties of the $\alpha_2$ cell. In ducks, pigeons, and chickens, the $\alpha_1$ cells are mainly aggregated near islet capillaries and the cytoplasmic granules are invariably located at the capillary pole of the cell. Evidence indicating that the $\alpha_1$ cell is an active islet component of the avian pancreas comes from histologic and histochemical studies demonstrating typical organization of an active secretory cell, granule shape, size and orientation, and proximity to capillary elements (Hellman, 1961; Epple, 1968; Fujita, 1968; King, 1971). Although the nature of the secretory component of the $\alpha_1$ cell has not been established with certainty, the cell size, structure, and activity are affected in pigeons by hypophysectomy, fasting, and prolactin injections (Miller, 1942). Also, in some migratory avian species (such as the European blackbird), the $\alpha_1$ cell undergoes seasonal alterations from hypertrophy to atrophy within a single season (Epple, 1963).

The possibility that $\alpha_1$ cells normally secrete a "gastrin-like" polypeptide appears quite likely: gastrin has never been isolated from avian intestinal tissue and a non-$\beta$-islet product that markedly stimulates proventricular volume and acid and pepsin

secretion has been isolated from the avian pancreas (only) (Hellman and Lernmark, 1969; Langslow *et al.,* 1973; Hazelwood *et al.,* 1973). This linear polypeptide contains 36 amino acid residues and bears no structural resemblance to insulin, C peptide, or glucagon molecules (Hazelwood, 1973). The effect of this polypeptide on carbohydrate metabolism is discussed in Chapter 11.

**Glucagon.** This hormone is the only secretory product associated with the avian $\alpha_2$ cell of the dark $\alpha$ islets. Glucagon granules can be detected in the 3-day chick embryo, the same day that an insular-capillary network appears. Release of glucagon occurs by day 5 of incubation (Przybylski, 1967b).

In the adult chicken, the location of the $\alpha$ islets appears to be restricted mainly to both the third and splenic lobes of pancreas (Table 21-2). In fact, the islets in the splenic lobe are larger and more numerous than in any other pancreatic area. Most of the zinc found in the avian pancreas is in the $\alpha$ islets; however, in mammals this element is almost exclusively limited to $\beta$ tissue (Falkmer and Patent, 1972).

Whereas the formation of glucagon appears to occur near the Golgi complex of the avian $\alpha_2$ cell, vesicles containing this hormone ultimately migrate to the capillary pole of the cell and fuse with the plasma membrane. As in mammals, avian glucagon is extruded by an emiocytotic process into the extracellular space (Machino and Sakuma, 1967; Machino *et al.,* 1966; Falkmer and Patent, 1972). The influence of glucagon on avian carbohydrate metabolism is discussed in Chapter 11.

**Insulin.** The $\beta$ islets, although containing some $\alpha_1$ cells, secrete the hormone insulin. Of the entire chicken pancreas, the cross-sectional area of $\beta$ islets

**Table 21-2** *Regional distribution of pancreatic islets in adult chickens[a]*

| Region | Type islet | Number of islets[b] | | Islet area |
| | | Range | Total islets | (% of total) |
|---|---|---|---|---|
| Dorsal lobe | $\beta$ | 1020-3780 | 23,520 | 0.365 |
| Ventral lobe | $\beta$ | 600-3060 | 14,820 | 0.292 |
| Splenic and | $\alpha$ | 92-360 | 2,912 | 4.368 |
| third lobes | $\beta$ | 180-960 | 5,650 | 0.527 |

[a]Modified from Mikami and Ono (1962).
[b]Islet counts were made from contiguous (serial) sections. Areas were computed on basis of total tissue, exocrine and endocrine.

is less than that of $\alpha$ islets, 0.35% vs. 0.41%. Cyto-differentiation of $\beta$ islets is clearly evident by day 3 of incubation of the chicken embryo, although insulin granule formation within the $\beta$ cells probably occurs shortly after intestinal evagination (Przybylski, 1967b). Although granules are probably actively secreted by day 5, recognition (by immunologic techniques) of an insulin-like substance in unfertilized chicken eggs that are less than 48 hr old has been reported. Such observations indicate that additions from maternal sources are possible contributing factors in directing growth and differentiation of embryonic tissues during the first week *in ovo* (Trenkle and Hopkins, 1971). The largest $\beta$-cell vesicles containing granules usually contain crystalline (insulin) inclusions (Figure 21-2).

Release of insulin, like that of glucagon, is by emiocytosis. However, chicken insulin is first found in the $\beta$ cell as a "super" molecule, proinsulin; subsequently, the 51-residue structure is cleaved within the cell from its 26 amino acid connecting peptide (Chapter 11). Once released, insulin enters the bloodstream and thence goes to all cells of the body to facilitate, among other anabolic effects, the translocation of glucose to intracellular compartments (see Chapter 11).

# PANCREATECTOMY

Surgical removal of the pancreas of birds is the most direct manner by which one may study the effects of loss of endocrine secretions. Various $\beta$-cytotoxic agents (such as alloxan) are ineffective in causing functional damage of the avian pancreatic cell or islet; this contrasts with their action in mammals (see Chapter 11). The chronology of various attempts to remove the avian pancreas in various species, as well as the degree of success, was thoroughly presented by Sturkie (1965). More recently, attempts have been made to ablate selective portions of the avian pancreas such as by the removal of the third and splenic lobes to produce a glucagon-deficient preparation (Mikami and Ono, 1962). Also, critics of the older work have attempted to produce a "totally depancreatized" bird by

21-2 Electron photomicrographs of chicken pancreas. (a) Acinar (exocrine) tissue from adult female Leghorn chickens ×6250. (b) Endocrine ($\beta$ islet) tissue from same chicken, ×4700. (From King, 1971.)

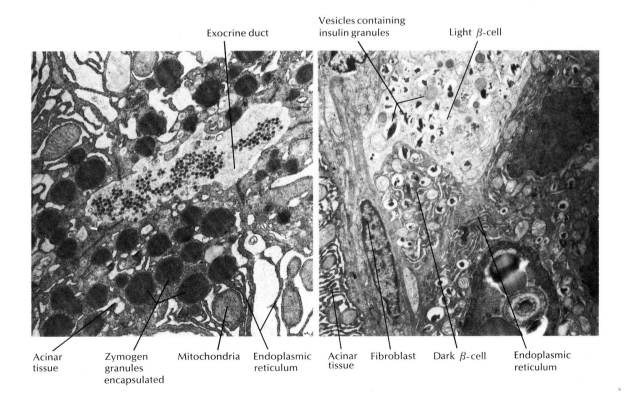

388 taking special care to remove the splenic lobe in ducks (Miahle, 1958), geese (Sitbon, 1967), and chickens (see below). Partial pancreatectomy and its effect on plasma insulin levels was studied by Langslow and Freeman (1972; also see Chapter 11).

Generally speaking, birds do not become permanently diabetic on pancreatectomy; an exception is the goose and maybe the owl. Pigeons appear to fare worse of all operated species examined and most species lose weight, stop egg laying, suffer from anorexia, and "waste away." Digestion and absorption are obviously impaired but can be improved by addition of 10–20% raw pancreas to the daily ration. Such supplementation maintains birds that have 90–95% of the pancreas removed but that still retain the splenic pancreas lobe for several months. Removal of the splenic lobe along with all other pancreas leads to death following a severe hypoglycemic crisis in chickens (Mikami and Ono, 1962). Effects of pancreatectomy on carbohydrate metabolism are discussed in detail in Chapter 11.

# REFERENCES

Epple, A. (1963). Pancreatic islets and annual cycle in some avian species. *Proc. 13th Int. Ornithol. Congr.* Held at Ithaca, New York, 1962. Baton Rouge, La: American Ornithologist Union, p. 974.

Epple, A. (1968). Comparative studies on the pancreatic islets. *Endocrinol. Jap., 15*, 107.

Falkmer, S., and G. J. Patent. (1972). Comparative and embryological aspects of the pancreatic islets. In "Handbook of Physiology, Endocrinology," Vol. I. Washington, D.C.: Amer. Physiological Society, p. 1.

Fujita, T. (1968). D-cell, the third endocrine element of the pancreatic islet. *Arch. Histol. Jap., 29*, 1.

Hazelwood, R. L. (1973). The avian endocrine pancreas. *Am. Zool., 13*, 697.

Hazelwood, R. L., S. D. Turner, J. R. Kimmel, and H. G. Pollock. (1973). Spectrum effects of a new polypeptide (third hormone?) isolated from the chicken pancreas. *Gen. Comp. Endocrinology., 21*, 485.

Hellman, B. (1961). Nuclear differences between the argyophil and non-argyophil pancreatic A cells in the duck. *Acta Endocrinol., 36*, 603.

Hellman, B., and A. Lernmark. (1969). Inhibition of the *in vitro* secretion of insulin by an extract of pancreatic $\alpha_1$-cells. *Endocrinology, 84*, 1434.

Hseih, T. M. (1951). The sympathetic and parasympathetic nervous systems of the fowl. Ph. D. thesis, Royal Veterinary College, Edinburgh.

King, D. L. (1971). Possible parasympathetic control of insulin secretion from the endocrine pancreas of the domestic fowl. M. S. thesis, University of Houston, Houston, Texas.

Langslow, D. R., and B. M. Freeman, (1972). Partial pancreatectomy and the role of insulin in carbohydrate metabolism in *Gallus domesticus. Diabetologia, 8*, 206.

Langslow, D. R., J. R. Kimmel, and H. G. Pollock. (1973). Studies of the distribution of a new avian pancreatic polypeptide and insulin among birds, reptiles, amphibians and mammals. *Endocrinology, 93*, 558.

Machino, M. (1966). Electron microscope observations of pancreatic islet cells of the early chick embryo. *Nature (London), 210*, 853.

Machino, M., and H. Sakuma. (1967). Electron microscopy of islet alpha cells of domestic fowl. *Nature (London), 214*, 808.

Machino, M., T. Onoe, and H. Sakuma. (1966). Electron microscopic observations on the islet alpha cells of the domestic fowl pancreas. *J. Electron Microsc., 15*, 249.

Mialhe, P. (1958). Glucagon, insuline et regulation endocrine de la glycemie chez le canard. *Acta Endocrinol., 36* (Suppl.), 9.

Mikami, S., and K. Ono. (1962). Glucagon deficiency induced by extirpation of alpha islets of the fowl pancreas. *Endocrinology, 71*, 464.

Miller, R. A. (1942). Effects of anterior pituitary preparations and insulin on islet cells of the pigeon pancreas. *Endocrinology, 31*, 535.

Oakberg, E. F. (1949). Quantitative studies of pancreas and islands of Langerhans in relation to age, sex and body weight in White Leghorn chickens. *Am. J. Anat., 84*, 279.

Przybylski, R. J. (1967a). Cytodifferentiation of the chick pancreas. II. Ultrasturcture of the acinar cells. *J. Morphol., 123*, 85.

Przybylski, R. J. (1967b). Cytodifferentiation of the chick pancreas. I. Ultrastructure of the islet cells. *Gen. Comp. Endocrinol., 8*, 115.

Romanoff, A. L. (1960). In "The Avian Embryo." New York. Macmillan Co., Chapter 6.

Sitbon, G. (1967). La pancreatectomie totale chez l'oie. *Diabetologia, 3*, 427.

Sturkie, P. D. (1965). Parathyroids, thymus, pineal, and pancreas. In "Avian Physiology." (2nd ed.) (P. D. Sturkie, Ed.). New York: Cornell University Press, p. 657.

Trenkle, A., and K. Hopkins. (1971). Immunological investigation of an insulin-like substance in the chicken egg. *Gen. Comp. Endocrinol., 16*, 493.

# Index

## A